POMPEII.

ITS HISTORY, BUILDINGS, AND ANTIQUITIES.

AN ACCOUNT OF

THE DESTRUCTION OF THE CITY, WITH A FULL DESCRIPTION
OF THE REMAINS, AND OF THE RECENT EXCAVATIONS,
AND ALSO AN ITINERARY FOR VISITORS.

EDITED BY

THOMAS H. DYER, LL.D.,

OF THE UNIVERSITY OF ST. ANDREWS.

*ILLUSTRATED WITH NEARLY THREE HUNDRED WOOD ENGRAVINGS,
A LARGE MAP, AND A PLAN OF THE FORUM.*

THIRD EDITION.

1871.

Copyright © 2013 Read Books Ltd.
This book is copyright and may not be
reproduced or copied in any way without
the express permission of the publisher in writing

British Library Cataloguing-in-Publication Data
A catalogue record for this book is available from the
British Library

A Short Introduction to the History of Pompeii

Pompeii was an ancient Roman town-city near the modern Italian city of Naples. It is famed for being one of the ill-feted settlements destroyed and buried by the massive eruption of Mount Vesuvius in 79 AD. Along with Herculaneum, Pompeii is of particular interest and historical importance due to its preservation under the several metres of volcanic ash and pumice, protecting it from air and moisture. This created a snapshot of a moment in an ancient civilisation that would otherwise have been eroded by time.

It is believed to have been founded by Osci in the sixth or seventh century BC. By the 4th century it was under the control of the Roman Empire, finally being conquered and becoming a Roman colony in 80 BC following an unsuccessful rebellion against the Republic. At the time of its destruction, Pompeii had a population of around 11,000 and a well developed infrastructure comprising a port, an amphitheatre, a gymnasium, and a complex water system.

The first evidence of the demise of this settlement came in the form of a letter written by Pliny the Younger, the Roman, lawyer, author, and magistrate. In the letter he describes the death of his uncle, Pliny the Elder, an admiral of the Roman fleet, and his demise while trying to rescue the citizens of Pompeii. However, it was not until 1599, when a channel was being dug to divert the river Samo, that the entombed settlement was re-discovered. Domenica Fonatana, a Swiss architect, was called in for his opinion on the finding. He uncovered several frescoes but then decided to cover them over again. Nobody knows exactly why he did this – some see it as a forward-thinking act of preservation, while others contend that the sexual content of many of the works may not have been considered 'good taste' during the counter-reformation period.

If it was an act of censorship then he was certainly not alone in his opinion. When King Francis of Naples visited the Pompeii exhibition at the national Gallery in 1819, he was so embarrassed at being exposed to the artwork, while in the company of his wife and daughter, that he ordered some of it to be locked away in a secret cabinet for the eyes of "people of mature age and respected morals" only. After being opened and closed again several times over the next two hundred years the exhibit reopened in 2000, but it is still not allowed to be viewed by minors unless in the presence of a guardian or with written permission. Aside from the art of the lost city, many other aspects of ancient life were also preserved, such as clothes, coins, furniture, food, and the bodies of the unfortunate residents. Previously it was thought that they had been killed by ash suffocation, but recent testing indicates that they died an instant death from the searing heat of the eruption.

Pompeii is now a hugely popular tourist destination and a UNESCO heritage site. Since the town's excavation however, its exposure to the elements has led to much erosion and many of the buildings are in dire need of restoration. Conservation of such a site is both time consuming and expensive, and an estimated $335 million is needed for the necessary repair work. Pompeii provides us with a fascinating window into the daily lives of an ancient civilisation though, and with one third of the city still to be uncovered, is likely to continue presenting us with yet more insights into a culture frozen in time.

RESTORATION OF POMPEII.

CONTENTS.

PART I.
THE PUBLIC BUILDINGS OF POMPEII.

	PAGE
PREFACE	XV
INTRODUCTION	1

CHAPTER I.
HISTORY OF VESUVIUS 10

CHAPTER II.
HISTORICAL NOTICE OF POMPEII 29

CHAPTER III.
POSITION OF POMPEII—ITS GENERAL APPEARANCE—ROADS, WALLS, GATES, STREETS, &c. 55

CHAPTER IV.
ORIGIN AND USE OF FORUM—ARCHITECTURAL CLASSIFICATION OF BUILDINGS—DESCRIPTION OF FORUM OF POMPEII AND ITS TEMPLES 91

CHAPTER V.
THE REMAINING TEMPLES OF POMPEII 135

CONTENTS.

CHAPTER VI.
BATHS EXCAVATED IN THE YEARS 1824 AND 1858 153

CHAPTER VII.
THE THEATRES 188

CHAPTER VIII.
THE AMPHITHEATRE 215

PART II.
THE PRIVATE HOUSES OF POMPEII.

CHAPTER I.
DOMESTIC ARCHITECTURE OF ITALY 248

CHAPTER II.
POMPEIAN ART 273

CHAPTER III.
PRIVATE HOUSES 301

CHAPTER IV.
HOUSES OF PANSA AND SALLUST 318

CHAPTER V.
THE VIA CONSULARIS, OR DOMITIANA 344

CHAPTER VI.
ART OF BAKING—FULLONICA 353

CHAPTER VII.
HOUSE OF THE TRAGIC POET—OF THE GREAT AND LITTLE FOUNTAINS—OF APOLLO—THE FAUN, &c. 366

CONTENTS. vii

CHAPTER VIII.

PAGE
HOUSES OF CASTOR AND POLLUX—THE CENTAUR—MELEAGER, &c. . 400

CHAPTER IX.

SURVEY OF THE REMAINDER OF THE CITY—INSCRIPTIONS AND GRAFFITI—CASTS OF BODIES 431

CHAPTER X.

SUBURBAN VILLA 480

CHAPTER XI.

TOMBS 499

CHAPTER XII.

DOMESTIC UTENSILS . . . . . , . . 532
ITINERARY 573

ILLUSTRATIONS.

ENGRAVINGS ON STEEL AND WOOD.

	PAGE
Pompeii restored . . . . . *To face the Title*	
Plan of the Forum	96
Mosaic of Battle of Issus	277
Necklace of Amulets	447
View of the Villa of M. Arrius Diomedes . . .	481
Bronze lamps and vases	545
Painting on walls of Pantheon	567
Plan of excavated portion of Pompeii . . .	*End.*

WOODCUTS.

	PAGE
1. Vignette of the Gate of Herculaneum, from Mazois . .	1
2. Plan of the Bay of Naples	30
3. Drawing on a wall in the Street of Mercury . .	35
4. Section of the walls and agger of Pompeii . . .	59
5. Interior battlements restored	60
6. Walls and towers from without.	61
7. Masonry of Pompeii—Isodomon of the Greeks . .	62
8. Greek wall resembling that of Pompeii . . .	*ib.*
9. Gate of Herculaneum restored	64
10. Plan of the pavement of Pompeii	70
11. Plan of a stepping stone in the street, with biga passing	71
12. Window in the house of the Tragic Poet . . .	72
13. View in the Street of Mercury	73
14. Vignette of Mercury with a purse	75
15. A steel-yard	76
16. Steel-yard called Trutina Campana	77
17. Libræ, or Bilances	78
18. Fac-simile of Inscription on the walls of a house . .	79
19. Ditto, on an album	80
20. Ditto	*ib.*
21. View of a sewer	83
22. Manner of carrying the Amphora	84

ILLUSTRATIONS.

	PAGE
23. Bas-relief of a goat over a milk shop	85
24. Section of a public fountain	87
25. Jet d'eau; from an Arabesque painting	88
26. Fountain near the Gate of Herculaneum	89
27. Bronze cock found in Capri	90
28. Plan showing varieties of temples and intercolumniation	93
29. Bronze figures to ornament fountains	101
30. Painting of a galley in the Pantheon	106
31. Ditto, of bread, in same	109
32. Bronze pastry mould	ib.
33. Gold ring with engraved stone	110
34. Painting of Cupids making bread	111
35. Wall paintings in Temple of Augustus	112
36. Ditto, ditto	113
37. View of the Temple of Mercury	114
38. Utensils used in sacrificing	116
39. Sacrificial instruments sculptured on altar	117
40. Urn for warm decoctions	120
41. Section of the same	ib
42. View of Statue of Eumachia and false door	122
43. Plan of columns of the Basilica	125
44. Mosaic border in Temple of Venus	129
45. Terminal figure in same	130
46. Dwarfs, from a painting, ditto	ib.
47. Painting of Bacchus and Silenus in priest's apartment	131
48. Construction of aræostyle portico of Forum	132
49. View of the Forum from the south	133
50. Male Centaur and Bacchante	134
51. Bas-relief of warrior and biga	135
52. View of the Temple of Fortune	136
53. Bronze helmet found at Pompeii	147
54. Greaves worn by the gladiators	148
55. Female Centaur and Bacchante	153
56. Fac-simile of inscription in old Baths	154
57. Plan of the old Baths	157
58. Section of Apodyterium and Frigidarium	159
59. Frieze of the Apodyterium	160
60. Transverse section of the Apodyterium	161
61. Chariot race of Cupids in the Frigidarium	162
62. View of the Tepidarium	163
63. Telamones in the Tepidarium	164
64. Brazier in ditto	165
65. Bronze seat in ditto	166
66. Section of the Caldarium	167

ILLUSTRATIONS.

	PAGE
67. Part of the ceiling of Caldarium	169
68. Ornament of the Tepidarium	170
69. Stucco ornaments in ceiling of ditto	171
70. Ornaments in the Tepidarium	172
71. Plan of Stabian Baths	175
72. Strigiles	179
73. View of west side of Stabian Baths	180
74. Vases for perfumes	187
75. Figure with a mask	188
76. Comic scene from a painting at Pompeii	190
77. Another	ib.
78. Another	191
79. Plan of a Roman theatre	192
80. Masks, dwarf and monkey, from a painting	195
81. Tragic mask, from the Townley Collection	196
82. Another, from the same	197
83. Masks from an ancient MS. of Terence	198
84. Tragic and grotesque masks	ib.
85. Masked figure of Silenus	199
86. Comic scene from a painting at Pompeii	200
87. Tragic scene, ditto	201
88. Mosaic of a Choragus instructing actors	203
89. Plan of the large theatre at Pompeii	204
90. View of the same	206
91. Flute-player, from a painting	207
92. Stone rings for masts of Velarium	208
93. Plan of the small theatre at Pompeii	210
94. Bisellium, or chair of state	211
95. View of the small theatre	213
96. View of the Amphitheatre at Pompeii	216
97. Gladiators, from a painting on wall of arena	227
98. Bestiarius, or combatant of wild beasts	229
99. Bestiarii, or combatants with wild beasts	230
100. Bestiarius, resembling the Spanish matador	231
101. Equestrian gladiators	233
102. Gladiators; a Velès and a Samnite	234
103. Ditto, Thrax, Myrmillo, Retiarii, and Secutores	236
104. Ditto, a Velès and Samnite	237
105. Ditto, Lanista, Myrmillo, and Samnite	238
106. Ditto, Samnite and Myrmillo	ib.
107. Wild boar hunt	239
108. Bestiarius and boar	ib.
109. Bestiarius and bull	ib.
110. Helmets and greaves of Gladiators	240

ILLUSTRATIONS.

		PAGE
111.	Plan of the Amphitheatre at Pompeii	242
112.	Bronze helmet worn by a gladiator	243
113.	Enriched echinus moulding	245
114.	Ionic capital	248
115.	Cabin of the aboriginal Latins	249
116.	Dancing Fauns, from painted walls of Pompeii	258
117.	Fragment of a plan of Rome	263
118.	Ancient bolt	264
119.	Key and hinge	265
120.	Door handles	*ib.*
121.	Door of a private dwelling restored	266
122.	Doric capital	272
123.	Biga, from an Arabesque	273
124.	Mosaic picture by Dioscorides	276
125.	Scipio, Masinissa, and Sophonisba	292
126.	A female painting the bearded Bacchus	294
127.	Studio of an ancient painter	295
128.	Statuette of the dancing Faun	296
129.	Ditto of Silenus	297
130.	Ditto of Narcissus	298
131.	Curule chair, from a Pompeian picture	300
132.	Beehives made of bronze	301
133.	Ground plan of a shop	303
134.	View of a cook's shop restored	304
135.	Street view near the old Baths	305
136.	Ground plan of a shop	306
137.	Ground plan of a small house	308
138.	Bed and table, from a painting	309
139.	Plan of a Triclinium	310
140.	Picture of a domestic supper	311
141.	Ground plan of a small house	312
142.	Painting of Circe and Ulysses	313
143.	Plan of house of Queen Caroline	315
144.	Mercury, from a painting	317
145.	Dancing Faun	318
146.	Plan of Pansa's house	319
147.	View of entrance of ditto	323
148.	Religious painting in kitchen of ditto	325
149.	Kitchen stove in ditto	326
150.	A flat ladle, or trua	*ib.*
151.	Atrium of Pansa's house	327
152.	Ground plan of house of Sallust	329
153.	View of entrance to ditto	331
154.	Summer Triclinium in garden of ditto	336

ILLUSTRATIONS.

	PAGE
155. Venereum in house of Sallust	339
156. Atrium of ditto	341
157. Cornice of the Impluvium in ditto	342
158. Painting of the manner of hanging a picture	343
159. Curule seat	344
160. Female figure with papyri	348
161. Figure playing the harp	349
162. Figure reading a roll of papyrus	ib.
163. Figure from house of female dancers	351
164. A dancing Faun	352
165. Bas-relief of a mule and mill	353
166. Section of a mill	356
167. Painting of serpents in a bakehouse	358
168. Bread discovered in Pompeii	360
169. Painting of fullers at work	361
170. Carding a tunic, from the Fullonica	363
171. Clothes press, from the same	364
172. Small painting in Tragic Poet's house	366
173. Ground plan of island containing Tragic Poet's house, the Fullonica, and Great and Small Fountains	367
174. Mosaic of Cave Canem	368
175. Painting of Achilles delivering up Briseis	372
176. Head of Achilles	373
177. Painted wall in Tragic Poet's house	377
178. Female and Cupid fishing	378
179. The Sacrifice of Iphigenia	379
180. Leda and Tyndareus	380
181. Painting of Centaurs	382
182. Atrium of Poet's house restored	383
183. House of the Great Fountain	386
184. Cupid milking a goat	387
185. Farm yard scene	389
186. House of the Faun	392
187. Acratus on a panther	394
188. Mosaic of doves	395
189. Atrium of house of Ceres	397
190. Painting of Jupiter	398
191. Painting in house of Poet	399
192. Curricle bar, from a Pompeian picture	400
193. Rustic work and cornices, from house of Castor and Pollux	401
194. Plan of house of Castor and Pollux	403
195. Atrium of house of Quæstor	405
196. Thetis dipping Achilles in the Styx	409
197. Piscina in house of Castor and Pollux	411

ILLUSTRATIONS.

		PAGE
198.	Painting of Perseus and Andromeda	412
199.	Ditto of Medea and her children	413
200.	Manner of filling the amphoræ	415
201.	Amphoræ	416
202.	A drinking scene	417
203.	Meleager returned from hunting	420
204.	Plan of house of the Nereids	422
205.	Fountain and table in ditto	424
206.	Capital in ditto	427
207.	Section of house of Nereids	429
208.	Elevation of part of Street of Tombs	ib.
209.	Helmet, sword, &c.	431
210.	Bacchus, from a painting	432
211.	Doorway in Street of Abundance	434
212.	Tools found in house of Sculptor	436
213.	Ground plan of house of Joseph II.	438
214.	Atrium of house of Championnet	441
215.	House of Holconius	445
216.	Painting of Bacchus and Ariadne	452
217.	House of Cornelius Rufus	454
218.	Painting of writing tablet, &c., in ditto	455
219.	House of Lucretius	456
220.	Ground plan of ditto	457
221.	Painting of Hercules drunk	464
222.	View of House of the Balcony	474
223.	Plaster casts of bodies	476
224.	Portico of house of Diomedes	480
225.	Ground plan of ditto	484
226.	Funeral column	509
227.	Ground plan of Street of Tombs	510
228.	Tomb of the marble door	514
229.	Funeral Triclinium	515
230.	Tomb of Nævoleia Tyche	518
231.	Bas-relief of ditto	519
232.	Ditto, ditto	521
233.	Bisellium on tomb of Calventius	522
234.	Tomb of Scaurus, round tomb, and tomb of Calventius	524
235.	Bas-relief on wall of circular tomb	525
236.	Section of round tomb	526
237.	Exedra in Street of Tombs	527
238.	Gold ring	528
239.	Elevation of Mamia's tomb restored	530
240.	Money bag and coins	532
241.	Papyri and tabulæ	533

	PAGE
242. Tabulæ, calamus, and papyrus	534
243. Tubulæ, stylus, and papyrus	535
244. Tabulæ and Calamus	ib.
245. Scrinium and capsa	536
246. Calendar	538
247. A bronze lantern	540
248. Section of ditto	541
249. Upright of ditto	542
250. Extinguisher	ib.
251. Candelabra	544
252. Bronze figure inlaid with embletic work	547
253. Candelabrum	549
254. Moveable tripod	550
255. Brazier	551
256. Kitchen utensils	ib.
257. Brazier	552
258. Bronze vase	553
259. Simpula	554
260. Kitchen utensils of bronze	ib
261. Ditto, ditto	555
262. Terra cotta vase	ib.
263. Rhyton, or drinking cup	556
264. Grotesque vases	557
265. Glass vases	558
266. Clay liquor-basket and glass vessels	559
267. Ornamental drinking glasses	ib.
268. Glass vessels	564
269. Bronze strainer	ib.
270. Draped female statue	566
271. Figure dressed in the Tunico-pallium	567
272. Tunico-pallium displayed	568
273. Harp-player	569
274. Ditto with the plectrum	570
275. Earring	571
276. Ditto, gold pin, and ring	572
277. Combs	ib.

PREFACE.

THE work now offered to the reader is based on one originally published between thirty and forty years ago under the superintendence of the *Society for the Diffusion of Useful Knowledge*, which became deservedly popular, and has been several times reprinted; but it was never re-edited, although, in the long period of time that has elapsed since its first publication, considerable progress has of course been made in the excavations at Pompeii. The present work has therefore been undertaken with the view of supplying some account of these more recent excavations, and thus rendering the book a more full and accurate description of Pompeii in its present state.

For this purpose much new matter has been added, previous descriptions have been altered and enlarged, and new names that have been given to streets, buildings, &c., have been inserted. The method of the book seemed also capable of improvement by transposing some of the descriptions; and indeed the author of the original work has now and then indicated where this might be done with advantage.

The necessary additions would have rendered the volume of inconvenient size had all the original matter been retained.

With a view to avoid this inconvenience, some descriptions which did not appear to be much connected with the subject, such as those of the remains of Greek walls, of the baths at Rome, of the origin of the Greek theatre, &c., have been omitted. The Editor may mention that, with a view to bring down the information to the latest moment, he frequently visited Pompeii during a residence at Naples in the winter of 1865-6, and studied the best and latest authorities on the subject. An Itinerary at the end of the volume may serve to render it a guide for travellers, as well as an index to the principal objects. It may be added that several new illustrations have been given, besides a new map of the excavations, reduced from the Commendatore Fiorelli's plan, with that gentleman's kind permission.

London, March, 1867.

PART I.

THE PUBLIC BUILDINGS OF POMPEII.

Vignette from Mazois' view of the city at the gate of Herculaneum

INTRODUCTION.

THE minute studies of antiquaries have been a very favourite subject of ridicule with those who have not followed them— sometimes with, sometimes without reason. In this, as in every other pursuit, men are apt to forget the value of the object in the pleasure of the chase, and run down some incomprehensible or untenable theory about some matter that never was and never will be of importance, with a zeal and intensity of purpose which might have been better bestowed upon a better end. But notwithstanding the many jokes, good and bad, deserved and undeserved, which have been levelled at this branch of learning, it is one in which all inquiring minds (and no mind that is not inquiring can be worth much), not entirely engrossed by some favourite occupation, will feel more or less of interest. If we could look into the future, the past would probably lose much of its importance in our eyes; and our curiosity would be much more strongly excited to ascertain the state of the world a thousand years hence, than its state a thousand years ago. But this power is denied us; and to form an estimate of the character and capabilities of mankind more comprehensive than the experience of a single generation can afford, we must apply to the retrospect of the past. Not that this curiosity influences none but those who might wish or be expected or draw profit from its gratification; on the contrary, it seems a temper natural, in greater or less degree, to all alike, reflecting or unreflecting. It is that which causes us to look with pleasure on an antiquated town, to grope among ruins, even where there is evidently nothing to repay us for the dirt and trouble of the search; and generally to invest everything entirely out of date with a value which its original possessors would be much puzzled to understand.

But time works constantly, as well as slowly; and therefore, however antiquated the appearance, and however old-fashioned and changeless the habits of any place or people may seem to be, they are sure to present a very imperfect type of what they were even a single century ago. We have often wished, in various parts of England, that we could recall for a moment the ancient aspect of the country; reclothe the downs of Wiltshire with their native sward, and see them studded with tumuli and Druid temples, free and boundless as they extended a thousand years ago, before the devastations of the plough and Inclosure Acts; recall the leafy honours of Nottinghamshire and Yorkshire, and re-people the neighbourhood of Sheffield and the Don with oaks instead of steam-engine and manufactory chimneys; or renew the decayed splendour of those magnificent monasteries whose ruins still strike the beholder with admiration. If the romantic fictions of the middle ages could be realised, which tell of mirrors framed with magic art to represent what had formerly passed, or was passing, in distant parts of the earth, the happy discoverer might soon make his fortune in this age of exhibitions. What exhibition could be found more interesting than a camera-obscura, which should reflect past incidents of historical or private interest, and recall, with the vividness and minuteness of life, at least the external characteristics of long past ages!

INTRODUCTION. 3

Such fancies are but idle speculations. The past can only be recalled by the imagination working upon such details as the pen or the pencil of contemporaries may have preserved; yet, in one single instance, the course of events has done more to preserve a living picture of a former age—one, too, in which the civilized world is deeply interested—than we could reasonably have hoped for. Deserted places are usually too much dilapidated to convey more than a very imperfect idea of the minutiæ of their arrangement, or of the manners of their former occupiers: places which have been preserved by being inhabited, are, of necessity, changed more or less to suit the changing manners of those who tenant them. It was, therefore, matter of no ordinary interest when it was known that a buried Roman city had been discovered; a city overwhelmed and sealed up in the height of its prosperity, and preserved from the ravages of the barbarian conquerors of Italy, and the sacrilegious alterations and pillagings of modern hands. But the hopes which might reasonably have been formed upon the discovery of Herculaneum, at the beginning of the last century, were frustrated in great measure by the depth and hardness of the volcanic products under which that city was buried. The process of clearing it was necessarily one of excavation, not of denudation; and to avoid the labour of raising the quarried matter to the surface, from a depth of 70 or 80 feet, former excavations have been filled up with the rubbish of new excavations, and now, besides a few houses, the theatre is the only building open to inspection, and that an unsatisfactory and imperfect inspection by torch-light. Museums have been profusely enriched with various articles of use or luxury discovered at Herculaneum, which might serve to illustrate the Latin authors, and throw light upon the private life of Italy; but no comprehensive view could be obtained, and consequently no new idea formed of the disposition and appearance of a Roman city. Fortunately, the disappointment was repaired by the discovery of Pompeii, a companion city overwhelmed in the great eruption of Vesuvius, A. D. 79, together with Herculaneum, and destined to be the partner of its disinterment as well as its burial. There was, however, this difference in their fate—that, owing to its greater distance from the volcano, as well as its more elevated situation, Pompeii, was not reached by the streams of lava which have successively flowed over Herculaneum, and elevated the surface of the earth from 70 to 100 feet. Pompeii was buried by a shower of ashes, pumice, and stones, forming a bed of variable depth, but seldom exceeding 20 or 24 feet, loose and friable in texture, and therefore easily removed, so as completely to uncover and expose the subjacent buildings.

The upper stories of the houses, which appear to have consisted chiefly of wood, were either burnt by the red-hot stones ejected from Vesuvius, or broken down by the weight of matter collected on their roofs and floors. With this exception, we see a flourishing city in the very state in which it existed nearly eighteen centuries ago:—the buildings as they were originally designed, not altered and patched to meet the exigencies of newer fashions; the paintings undimmed by the leaden touch of time; household furniture left in the confusion of use; articles, even of intrinsic value, abandoned in the hurry of escape, yet safe from the robber, or scattered about as they fell from the trembling hand, which could not pause or stoop for its most valuable possessions: and, in some instances, the bones of the inhabitants, bearing sad testimony to the suddenness and completeness of the calamity which overwhelmed them. "I noticed," says M. Simond, "a striking memorial of this mighty interruption in the Forum, opposite to the temple of Jupiter. A new altar of white marble, exquisitely beautiful, and apparently just out of the hands of the sculptor, had been erected there; an enclosure was building all round; the mortar, just dashed against the side of the wall, was but half spread out; you saw the long sliding stroke of the trowel about to return and obliterate its own track—but it never did return: the hand of the workman was suddenly arrested, and, after the lapse of 1800 years, the whole looks so fresh and new that you would almost swear that the mason was only gone to his dinner, and about to come back immediately to smooth the roughness."

It is unnecessary to expatiate upon the interest of these discoveries; yet notwithstanding their interest the subject has been hardly accessible to the English reader. The excavations have been prosecuted to a considerable extent since the elegant work of Sir W. Gell was published, which describes only the buildings, leaving untouched one interest-

INTRODUCTION.

ing branch of inquiry connected with the numerous articles which have been found, throwing light upon the private life of the Italians in the first century. There are foreign works of great research and magnificence, but these, from their price, are only accessible to a very small class of readers; and therefore little has been generally known of Pompeii, except what may be gathered from the short and scattered notices of travellers. This work is intended as an attempt to supply the deficiency. It is proposed, first, to give a detailed account of the ruins as they now exist, together with a description of their former state, as far as it can be made out; with occasional digressions upon points connected with the history or antiquities of the place, and notices of the most curious and important articles which have been discovered. The first part will contain the public edifices, so far as they have yet been disinterred: the second will be devoted to the houses and private habits of their tenants.

The chief authorities which have been consulted, are—the great work of M. Mazois on Pompeii; the 'Museo Borbonico,' a periodical work now in course of publication at Naples; Sir W. Gell's 'Pompeiana;' and Donaldson's 'Pompeii.' We have also had the advantage of numerous observations made on the spot by Mr. William Clarke, architect, by whom the materials for this work have been collected and the drawings made, either from the originals or from plates in the above works.

For the use of such readers as may wish to enter upon a deeper study of the subject, we shall here add a list of the principal books that may be consulted.*

Among these, the work of Mazois, already mentioned, is one of the first, both in point of time and of importance. Mazois resided at Naples during the years 1809, 1810, and 1811, and was encouraged and assisted in his researches by Queen Caroline, the wife of Murat, who took a great interest in Pompeii, and to whom he dedicated his book. Mazois died in 1826, before he had finished his work, which was continued by Gau. Its title is *Les Ruines de Pompéi, des-*

* A most extraordinary instance of book-making on this subject was the work of a certain Monsignor Bayardi; in which, at the end of two thick quartos, Hercules had not yet arrived at the Campi Phlegræi, and consequently the foundation of Herculaneum and Pompeii had not been laid.

sinées et mesurées par *Fr. Mazois, architecte, pendant les années* 1809, 1810, et 1811 : 4 vols. large folio, Paris, Didot, 1812—1838. It contains nearly 200 plates, and embraces the results of the excavations from 1757 to 1821.

Sir W. Gell's *Pompeiana* consists of two series, each of two octavo volumes, of which the first series was published at London, in 1824, and the second in 1830. The former contains an account of the excavations down to the year 1819; which is continued in the latter. It has many illustrations, some of them coloured.

Donaldson's *Pompeii, illustrated with Picturesque Views, engraved by W. B. Cooke,* was published in London in 1827. 2 vols. large fol.

The French work of Breton, *Pompeia, décrite et dessinée,* par Ernest Breton, 2nd edition, Paris, 1855, is a handsome book, with many good illustrations, and describes, in one large 8vo. vol., at a moderate price, the progress of the excavations till about the last ten or twelve years.

A more elaborate work than this, and more accurate in point of scholarship, is that of Overbeck, *Pompeji, in seinen Gebäuden, Alterthümern und Kunstwerken, für Kunst- und Alterthums-freunde dargestellt.* Leipsic, Engelmann. Overbeck published his first edition in 1856, without having visited Pompeii, and the book consequently contained many errors and imperfections. These, however, have been remedied in a second edition, the fruits of a visit to Pompeii, to be completed in the present year, and consisting of two volumes, illustrated with numerous cuts. The first volume contains the history and topography of the city, with an account of the buildings; the second is devoted to Pompeian art. Overbeck's book is, for its compass, undoubtedly the fullest and most accurate yet published; though the desire to be original, the besetting sin of most German writers, leads him now and then into some crotchety theories. The volume published contains no account of the tombs; an omission which will probably be supplied in the second volume.

The handsomest work on Pompeii is that of Fausto and Felice Niccolini, now publishing in numbers, entitled, *Le Case ed i Monumenti di Pompei, disegnati e descritti,* fol., Napoli, 1864; but its price will place it beyond the reach of most readers. It contains beautifully coloured plates, besides ground-plans, cuts, &c., with descriptive letter-press. Thirty-two numbers are already published, at 15 francs each.

To those who are studying Pompeii thoroughly and historically, the work of the Commendatore Fiorelli, the present able director of the excavations and of the Museum of Naples, is indispensable. It is entitled *Pompeianarum Antiquitatum Historia*, and contains, in two 8vo. vols., each of three Fasciculi, the records of the excavations, from their commencement in 1748 down to 1860, collected from the journals of the directors. These are printed *verbatim*; not a record of the discovery of a nail, or bolt, or fragment of statuary, or earthenware, is omitted; so that the reader will find the materials for a history rather than the history itself, which the somewhat magnificent title of the book may have led him to expect. To the archæological student of Pompeii, the book, however, is of course invaluable; and it is only to be wished that its perusal had been facilitated by the promised index, or by a commentary. The first part of the journals, down to July, 1764, is in Spanish; after that date in Italian. After the appointment of Signor Fiorelli to the direction of the excavations, he continued to publish the progress of them in a periodical work in numbers, entitled, *Giornale degli Scavi di Pompei*, which, however, appeared irregularly, and has been brought, we fear, to a premature conclusion. The title of it is as much too modest as that of the History is too grand; since it contains, besides the journal of the excavations, elaborate descriptions of the more important houses and works of art discovered, as well as literary disquisitions on matters relating to Pompeii.

Besides the substantive works here enumerated, many interesting and important papers and pamphlets on subjects connected with Pompeii have been published separately, and in various journals, by eminent Italian and other archæologists, as Quaranta, Niccolini, Arditi, Avellino, Bonucci, Fiorelli, Minervini, and others. They will be found in the *Memorie della reale Accademia di Archeologia di Napoli*, the *Annali dell' Instituto di corrispondenza Archeologica* (Rome and Paris, 1829-57), and the *Bulletino Archeologico Napolitano*, of Avellino, afterwards continued by Minervini.

M. Marc Monnier, of Geneva, has also published some good papers on Pompeii in the *Revue des Deux Mondes*, as well as a little book on the subject, which will be useful to those who read as they run, and wish rather to be amused than instructed.

There are also separate works on remarkable Pompeian buildings, as that of Raoul Rochette: *La Maison du Poète Tragique à Pompéi, avec ses Peintures et Mosaiques fidèlement reproduites et un texte explicatif*, fol., Paris : of Bechi, *Del Calcidico e della cripta di Eumachia scavati nel foro di Pompeia, l'anno* 1820, 4to., Napoli : of Millin, *Description des Tombeaux qui ont été découverts à Pompéi dans l'annee* 1812, Naples, 1813; and works by Falkener and Giulio Minervini on the house of Lucretius, &c., &c.

The inscriptions discovered at Pompeii are best given by Mommsen, in his *Inscriptiones Regni Neapolitani*, p. 112 seq. They do not comprehend, however, the *graffiti*, or inscriptions traced with a sharp point on walls and columns. These will be found, up to the date of the respective works, in Dean Wordsworth's *Pompeian Inscriptions, or Specimens and Facsimiles of Ancient Writings on the Walls of Buildings at Pompeii*, London, 1846; and in Garrucci's *Graffi'i di Pompei*, 4to., Paris, 1856; which also contains some ingenious remarks on ancient writing.

Signor Fiorelli has commenced a work entitled, *Monumenta Epigraphica Pompeiana ad fidem archetyporum expressa*, being fac-similes of the existing inscriptions. Only the first part, containing the Oscan inscriptions, has been published.

There are many rich and voluminous publications on the subject of Pompeian art. One of the earliest of them is the *Antichità di Ercolano e Pompei*, large fol., 9 vols., Napoli, 1755—1792. Many of the subjects of this book, as well as others from other sources, were reproduced in a French work published at Paris by Didot, in 8 vols. large 8vo, and entitled 'Herculaneum et Pompei:' *Recveil général de Peintures, Bronzes, Mosaïques, &c., découverts, jusqu'à ce jour et reproduits d'après le Antichità d' Ercolano, Il Museo Borbonico, et tous les ouvrages analogues, augmenté de sujets inédits gravés du trait sur cuivre par M. Roux aîné, et accompagné d'un texte explicatif par M. L. Barre*. The *Real Museo Borbonico*, begun in 1824, forms 14 vols. 4to. in the Italian edition, and, though unequally executed, is the richest collection of Neapolitan antiquities.

The work of Raoul Rochetto may also be mentioned, entitled *Choix de Peintures de Pompei, la plupart de sujet Historique, avec l'explication, et une introduction sur l'histoire de la Peinture chez les Grecs et chez les Romains*, with coloured plates, large fol., Paris, 1844. There are also many other separate publications, which it would be too long to enumerate; and we shall content ourselves with only mentioning the German work of Ternite, *Wandgemälde aus Pompei und Herculanum mit einem erläuternden Texte*, von E. O.Müller, Berlin, 1844; and with reminding the reader that the second volume of Overbeck's new edition is devoted to the subject of Pompeian art.

It remains to mention that the best plan of Pompeii is that of Fiorelli, entitled *Tabula Coloniæ Veneriæ Corneliæ Pompeis*. It is in 42 sheets, which, put together, form a superficies of 140 square palms, being the $333\frac{1}{3}$ part of the true superficies. The small plan, reduced from this, and sold at the gates of Pompeii, is on the scale of 1666 parts of the true superficies. There is also a good plan by Jorio.

CHAPTER I.

HISTORY OF VESUVIUS.

BEFORE commencing the account of Pompeii itself, it will not be out of place to give a short description of the ancient state of the neighbourhood in which it stood, together with a sketch of the history of Vesuvius.

The Bay of Naples, anciently called Crater (the Cup), was known to the ancients at an early period. The remarkable appearance of its shores struck their fancy; and they named them Phlegra, or Phlegræi Campi, Burnt Fields, from the traces of igneous action everywhere visible, and accounted for these natural appearances by the fabled battle between the giants and the gods, assisted by Hercules, in which the giants were cast down and destroyed by Jupiter's thunderbolts. The earth, riven, scorched, and thunderstained, bore enduring witness to the destructive power of these weapons. Here was the celebrated lake Avernus, the mouth of hell, according to the Italian poets, over which no bird could complete its flight, but dropped, overcome by the sulphureous exhalations. This is one, probably, of that numerous tribe of legends which have been framed to fit or to explain a name. Its Greek name is Aornos, literally Birdless; its dreary and terror-striking appearance, when its precipitous sides were thickly clothed with wood, suggested the notion that it was the opening of the nether world; hence the story of the fœtid atmosphere and its deadly effects Yet even here there may be some foundation of truth; for we have the authority of Sir William Hamilton for stating, that while wild fowl abound in other pools and lakes in this quarter, they shun Avernus, or pay it but a passing visit.*
Diodorus derives the name of Phlegra from Vesuvius, which, he says, like Ætna, used to vomit fire, and still retains traces of its former eruptions.† He spoke from observation of the

* Campi Phlegræi. Mr. Lyell is also inclined to admit the story, and adduces instances of similar mephitic exhalations.
† iv. 21.

mountain, not from tradition, for tradition recorded no eruption previous to the Christian era; but he probably erred in the derivation of the name. Traces of volcanic action were as evident round Baiæ and Puteoli as on Vesuvius; and the ancients appear to have had some record of eruptions in this quarter, since they fabled that the giant Typhon, who threw stones to heaven with a loud noise, and from whose eyes and mouth fire proceeded, lay buried under the neighbouring island of Inarime or Pithecusa, now called Ischia.* A similar fable accounted for the eruptions of Ætna.

> By turns a pitchy cloud she rolls on high,
> By turns hot embers from her entrails fly,
> And flakes of mounting flames, that lick the sky.
> Oft from her bowels massy rocks are thrown,
> And, shivered by the force, come piecemeal down.
> Oft liquid lakes of burning sulphur flow,
> Fed from the fiery springs that boil below.
> Enceladus, they say, transfixed by Jove,
> With blasted limbs came trembling from above;
> And where he fell the avenging father drew
> This blasted hill, and on his body threw.
> As often as he turns his weary sides
> He shakes the solid isle, and smoke the heavens hides.
> DRYDEN, Æn. lib. iii. 572.

We need hardly say that the poets vary in these stories: Ovid places Typhon under Ætna.

In the superstitions of the middle ages Vesuvius assumed the character which had before been given to Avernus, and was regarded as the mouth of hell. Cardinal Damiano relates the following stories, in a letter addressed to Pope Nicholas II. "A servant of God dwelt alone, near Naples, on a lofty rock hard by the highway. As this man was singing hymns by night, he opened the window of his cell to observe the hour; when, lo! he saw passing many men, black as Æthiopians, driving a large troop of packhorses laden with hay; and he was anxious to ask who they were, and why they carried with them this fodder for cattle? And they answered, 'We are evil spirits; and this food which we prepare is not for flocks or herds, but to foment those fires which are kindled against men's souls; for we wait, first for Pandulphus, Prince of Capua, who now lies sick; and then for

* Strabo, lib. v. c. 4., § 9.

John, the captain of the garrison of Naples, who as yet is alive and well.' Then went that man of God to John, and related faithfully that which he had seen and heard. At that time the Emperor Otho II., being about to wage war on the Saracens, was journeying toward Calabria. John therefore answered, 'I must first go reverently and meet the Emperor, and take counsel with him concerning the state of this land. But after he is gone I promise to forsake the world, and to assume the monastic habit.' Moreover, to prove whether the priest's story were true, he sent one to Capua, who found Pandulphus dead; and John himself lived scarce fifteen days, dying hefore the Emperor reached those parts; upon whose death the mountain Vesuvius, from which hell often belches forth, broke out into flames, as might clearly be proved, because the hay which those demons got ready was nothing else than the fire of that fell conflagration prepared for these reprobate and wicked men; for as often as a reprobate rich man dies in those parts, the fire is seen to burst from the above-named mountain, and such a mass of sulphureous resin flows from it as makes a torrent which by its downward impulse descends even to the sea. And in verity a former prince of Palermo once saw from a distance sulphureous pitchy flames burst out from Vesuvius, and said that surely some rich man was just about to die, and go down to hell. Alas for the blinded minds of evil men! That very night, as he lay regardless in bed, he breathed his last. There was also a Neapolitan priest, who wished to know more of things not lawful to be known, who, when that infernal pit belched flames more fiercely than usual, with presumptuous boldness resolved to visit it. So having solemnized the mass, he went on his way, armed, as it were, with the sacred vestments; but this rash inquirer, approaching nearer than men use to go, never reappeared, being unable to return. Another priest, who had left his mother sick at Beneventum, as he travelled through the bounds of Naples, and was intent upon the upstreaming flames, heard a voice of one bewailing, which he perceived evidently to be the voice of his mother. He marked the time, and found it to have been the hour of her death."*
This passage is taken from a letter from Cardinal Damiano

* Damiani Epistolæ, lib. i. 9.

to Pope Nicholas II., written about the year 1060. The superstition was natural enough; and similar ones were entertained at a much later date concerning Ætna and the island of Stromboli, in which there is a volcano in almost constant activity.

Strabo, who wrote some part of his work at least in the reign of Tiberius, about the commencement of our era, thus describes the Phlegræan Fields:—"After doubling Misenum, next comes a lake* (now Mare Morto), beyond which the coast falls back in a deep bay, where stands Baiæ and its warm baths, useful both for purposes of pleasure and for the cure of diseases. The Lucrine lake borders upon Baiæ; within it is lake Avernus. Here our ancestors placed the scene of Homer's Nekuia;† and here, they say, was an oracle, where answers were returned by the dead, to which Ulysses came. Avernus is a deep hollow with a narrow entrance, in size and shape well suited for a harbour, but incapacitated for that purpose by the shallow Lucrine lake which lies before it. It is enclosed by steep ridges, which overhang it everywhere, except at the entrance, now highly cultivated, but formerly enclosed by a savage trackless forest of large trees, which threw a superstitious gloom over the hollow. The inhabitants further fabled that the birds which flew over it fell down into the water, destroyed by the rising exhalations, as in other places of this sort, which the Greeks call Plutonia, or places sacred to Pluto; and imagined that Avernus was a Plutonium, and the abode where the Cimmerians were said to dwell. Here is a fountain of fresh water by the sea; but all persons abstain from it, believing it to be the Styx; and somewhere near was the oracle. Here, also, as they thought, was Pyriphlegethon,‡ judging from the hot springs near lake Acherusia. The Lucrine

---

* The text has λιμήν, a *harbour*, though some of the Latin versions have *palus* (λίμνη).

† The title of the XIth book of the Odyssey, the scene of which is laid among the dead.

‡ Pyriphlegethon, burning with fire; one of the three rivers which encompassed hell. Styx was another. It is doubtful whether the Acherusia here meant was Avernus, the Lucrine lake, or the Lago di Fusaro, about two miles from Avernus and between Cumæ and Cape Miseno. There was another lake of the same name in Epirus.

lake in breadth reaches to Baiæ, being separated from the sea by a mound, about a mile long, and wide enough for a broad carriage-road, said to have been made by Hercules as he was driving Geryon's oxen. Being much exposed to the surf, so as not to be easily traversed on foot, Agrippa raised and completed it. The lake admits light ships,* is useless as a naval station, but affords an inexhaustible supply of oysters. Here, according to some, was the lake Acherusia, but Artemidorus makes it the same with Avernus. Next to Baiæ come the shores and city of Dicæarchia, formerly a port of the Cumæans, placed on a hill. During the invasion of Hannibal, the Romans colonized it, and called it Puteoli, from (*putei*) the wells; or, as others say, they so named the whole district, as far as Baiæ and the Cumæan territory, from the stench (*putor*) of its waters, because it is full of sulphur and fire and hot springs. Some think that this is the reason why the country about Cumæ is called Phlegra, and that the thunder-riven wounds of the fallen giants pour out these streams of fire and water. Immediately over it is Vulcan's assembly-room (Hephæsti Agora, now the Solfatara), a level space surrounded by burning heights, with numerous chimney-like spiracles, which rumble loudly; and the bottom is full of ductile sulphur. Next to Dicæarchia, is Neapolis; next to Neapolis, Herculaneum, standing on a promontory remarkably open to the south-west wind (*Libs*), which makes it unusally healthy. This city, and its next neighbour, Pompeii, on the river Sarnus, were originally held by the Osci, then by the Tyrrhenians and Pelasgians, then by the Samnites, who in their turn were expelled by the Romans. Pompeii is the port of Nola, Nuceria, and Acerræ, being situated on the river Sarnus, which is suited for the exportation and importation of cargoes. Above these places rises Vesuvius, well cultivated and inhabited all round, except its top, which is for the most part level, and entirely barren, ashy to the view, displaying cavernous hollows in rocks, which look as if they had been eaten by the fire, so that we

* Strabo has before said that Agrippa cut through this mound, and thus established a communication between Avernus and the sea. What he says here is entirely contrary to the later author, Dion Cassius, who asserts that in the hands of Agrippa Avernus became an excellent port. This whole passage is in many parts very obscure, and may be suspected to be corrupt.

may suppose this spot to have been a volcano formerly, with burning craters, now extinguished for want of fuel."*

It will occur at once to the reader, that this description is totally inapplicable to Vesuvius as it now exists. The general form of the mountain is too well known to need description, and certainly its elevated cone can by no stretch of words be characterised as a level top. It seems probable, from various considerations, that this cone is of comparatively recent origin. It stands within a circular volcanic ridge, called Somma, broken away to the south, where there is still a projection, called the Pedamentina, apparently marking the continuation of Somma. The most experienced observers seem agreed that this ridge is the remains of an ancient volcano, much larger than the existing one, and was once surmounted by a cone like that of Ætna, which, being subject to constant degradation, and requiring constant supplies of fresh materials to maintain its height, sunk down into the earth, in the long period of inactivity which we know to have occurred antecedent to the Christian era. Parallel instances may be found in the lakes of Avernus and Agnano, which are evidently the sites of ancient volcanic cones which have fallen in, not craters of eruption. The reawakened fires of Vesuvius soon blew out the mass of materials which choked their former vent, and have formed around that vent a second cone, concentric with and similar to its predecessor, but of smaller dimensions. Instances exactly similar to this also occur. We may mention Barren Island, in the Bay of Bengal, where an active volcano rises out of the sea, in the centre of what is evidently a sunken cone. The cone of the Peak of Teneriffe also rises in the middle of a circular enclosure, like Somma, and a process analogous to the formation of the cone of Vesuvius may now be frequently observed going on within the crater of that mountain, in which, during its periods of activity, a minor mountain is continually rising.† Finally, some volcanic mountains are known to have fallen in or to have been dispersed, as Papandayang, in the island of Java,

* Strabo, lib. v. c. 4., § 5—8. Such parts of the original as do not bear on our subject have been omitted.

† Campi Phlegræi, pl. 2, where there is a minute representation of the changes thus produced in the form of the mountain.

which, in the year 1772, was reduced in height from 9000 to about 5000 feet. So also, in the province of Quito, a great part of the crater and summit of Carguirazo fell in during an earthquake in 1698.*

Supposing, therefore, that the present cone is based upon the ruins of a larger mountain, it probably did not exist when Strabo wrote the above description, but was thrown up in the first-recorded eruption, in the year 79, or at some later period. This will agree with the negative testimony of other authors, who make no mention of it, or speak cursorily of it; not as we might expect them to mention so prominent a feature as it now is in the much admired scenery of Baiæ and Naples. In Virgil the name occurs only once; and then it is introduced to commend the fertility of the soil. The great battle between the Romans and the Latins, in B.C. 340, in which Decius devoted himself to death, was fought at Vesuvius.† It was on Vesuvius that Spartacus encamped, with his army of insurgent slaves and gladiators. "The Romans besieged them in their fort, situate upon a hill that had a very steep and narrow ascent to it, and kept the passage up to them: all the rest of the ground round about it was nothing but high rocks hanging over, and upon them great store of wild vines. Of these the bondmen cut the strongest strips, and made thereof ladders, like to ship-ladders of ropes, of such a length and so strong that they reached from the top of the hill even to the very bottom: upon those they all came safely down, saving one that tarried above to throw down their armour after them, who afterwards by the same ladder saved himself last of all. The Romans mistrusting no such matter, these bondmen compassed the hill round, assailed them behind, and put them in such a fear, with the sudden onset, as they fled every man, and so was their camp taken."‡ This passage also is totally inconsistent with the present state of Vesuvius. Its lofty summit would be ill suited for an encampment, nor could the wild vine ever have flourished there; but both Plutarch and Strabo will be clear, if we suppose that the even summit of Somma, then probably more perfect than it now is, was the highest part of the mountain, and that it was only accessible by a chasm, such as that

---

* Lyell, Principles of Geology, ch. xxv. p. 436, 445.
† Liv. viii. 8.   ‡ North's Plutarch, Crassus.

which gives admission to Avernus. While the Romans were guarding this spot, they might reasonably feel confident that the enclosed enemy could find no other outlet.

After many centuries of repose, the volcano broke out with great violence, and in its first eruption destroyed Herculaneum, Pompeii, and Stabiæ. This calamity is described by an eye-witness, the younger Pliny, whose narration will form part of the next chapter. It is also mentioned more than a century later by Dion Cassius. The passage seems to indicate, as far as it is intelligible, that the present cone did not exist when he wrote; and is further curious, as proving that the old fables of the Battle of the Gods and Giants, and of the inhumation of the latter, were not forgotten even in the third century.

"During the autumn a great fire broke out in Campania. Vesuvius is a mountain on the coast near Naples, which contains inexhaustible fountains of fire; and formerly it was all of the same height, and fire rose in the middle of it (for the only traces of fire were in the middle), but the outer parts remain fireless to this day. Hence, these continuing uninjured, but the centre being dried up and reduced to ashes, the encircling crags still retain their ancient height: but the burnt part being consumed, in lapse of time has settled down and become hollow, so that to compare small things to great, the whole mountain now resembles an amphitheatre. And the top is clothed with trees and vines, but the circular cavity is abandoned to fire; and by day it sends up smoke and by night flame, so that one would think all sorts of incense vessels were burning there. This continues always with more or less violence, and often, after any considerable subsidence, it casts up ashes and stones, impelled by violent blasts of wind, with a loud noise and roaring, because its vent-holes are not set close together, but are narrow and concealed.*

"Such is Vesuvius, and these things take place in it almost every year. But all eruptions which have happened since, though they may have appeared unusually great to those even who have been accustomed to such sights, would be trifling, even if collected into one, when compared to what occurred at the time of which we speak. Many huge men surpassing human stature, such as the giants are described to have

* This description is not very clear, but neither is the Greek.

been, appeared wandering in the air and upon the earth, at one time frequenting the mountain, at another the fields and cities in its neighbourhood. Afterwards came great droughts and violent earthquakes, so that the whole plain boiled and bubbled, and the hills leapt, and there were noises underground like thunder, and above ground like roaring, and the sea made a noise, and the heavens sounded; and then suddenly a mighty crash was heard as if the mountains were coming together, and first great stones were thrown up to the very summits, then mighty fires and immense smoke, so that the whole air was overshadowed, and the sun entirely hidden, as in an eclipse.

"Thus day was turned into night, and light into darkness, and some thought the giants were rising again (for many phantoms of them were seen in the smoke, and a blast, as if of trumpets, was heard), while others believed that the earth was to return to Chaos, or to be consumed by fire. Therefore men fled, some from the houses out into the ways, others that were without, into their houses; some quitted the land for the sea, some the sea for the land, being confounded in mind, and thinking every place at a distance safer than where they were. Meanwhile, an inexpressible quantity of dust was blown out, and filled land, sea, and air, which did much other mischief to men, fields, and cattle, and destroyed all the birds and fishes, and besides buried two entire cities, Herculaneum and Pompeii, while the population was sitting in the theatre.* For this dust was so abundant that it reached Africa, Syria, and Egypt, and filled the air above Rome, and overclouded the sun; which caused much fear even there for many days, men neither knowing nor being able to conjecture what had happened. But they thought that every thing was to be thrown into confusion, the sun to fall extinguished to the earth, the earth to rise to the sky. At the time, however, these ashes did them no harm, but subsequently they produced a pestilential disease."†

It does not appear that any lava flowed from Vesuvius; the

---

* The wording leaves it doubtful which theatre is meant. The theatres of both cities have been explored, and no remains found. The eruption may have come on while the people were assembled, but they were not destroyed in the theatres.

† Dion Cassius, lib. lxvi. 23.

ejected matter consisted of rocks, pumice, and ashes, which seem, from the operations at Pompeii and Herculaneum, to have been partly changed into liquid mud by torrents of rain. Being reawakened, the volcano continued in pretty constant activity. It is evident from the passage just quoted, that from this year until the commencement of the third century, when Dion wrote, eruptions of more or less violence were continually recurring. Other eruptions are mentioned in the fifth and sixth centuries. Procopius, who died about the middle of the sixth, speaks of the mountain emitting rivers of fire.* He describes it in terms which correspond somewhat with a cone and crater; and, like Dion, conveys the idea of its being constantly at work. " Vesuvius is very precipitous below, encircled with wood above, terribly wild and craggy. In the centre of its summit is a very deep chasm, which we may suppose to reach quite to the bottom of the mountain, and it is possible to see fire in it, if a man dare peep over. Usually, the fire returns upon itself (ἐφ' ἑαυτὴν στρέφεται), without molesting those who live in its neighbourhood; but when the mountain utters a roaring noise, in general it emits soon after a vast body of cinders." He adds, that these ashes were often carried a vast distance, even to the coast of Africa and Byzantium, in which city so much terror was once caused by the phenomenon, that a solemn supplication was established in consequence, and continued yearly.†

The first stream of lava, of which we have authentic account, broke out in the year 1036, during the seventh eruption from the resuscitation of the volcano.‡ Another eruption occurred in 1049, another in 1138 or 9; after which there was a pause of 168 years, till 1306. From this year, to 1631, there was a cessation, except one slight eruption in 1500. During this long pause, a remarkable event occurred in another part of the Phlegræan fields. In little more than

* Bell, Goth. iv. 35.
† Procop. Bell. Goth. ii. 4.
‡ The six previous eruptions were those of 79, 203, 472, 512, 685, and 993. That of 472, recorded in the *Chronicon* of Marcellinus, *ad. ann.*, seems to have been a very violent one. It may be inferred, from Procopius' description of the eruption of 512, that lava was ejected on that occasion:—ῥέει δὲ καὶ ῥύαξ ἐνταῦθα πυρὸς ἐκ τῆς ἀκρωρείας κατατείνων ἄχρι ἐς τοῦ ὄρους τὸι πρόποδα καὶ ἔτι πρόσω.—*Loc. cit.*

twenty-four hours, a new hill, called Monte Nuovo, was thrown up to the height of 440 feet above the level of the sea, its base being nearly a mile and a half in circumference. It stands partly on the site of the Lucrine lake, which has now dwindled into a shallow pool.*

Bracini descended into the crater of Vesuvius shortly before the eruption of 1631. He gives the following account of it: "The crater was five miles in circumference, and about 6000 paces deep; its sides were covered with brushwood, and at the bottom there was a plain, on which cattle grazed. In the woody parts boars frequently harboured. In the midst of the plain, within the crater, was a narrow passage, through which, by a winding path, you could descend about a mile among rocks and stones till you came to another more spacious plain, covered with ashes. In this plain were three little pools, placed in a triangular form; one towards the east, of hot water, corrosive and bitter beyond measure; another towards the west, of water salter than that of the sea; the third of hot water that had no particular taste."†

This account, in spite of its minute enumeration of pools of water and points of the compass, is not very intelligible, and may fairly be presumed not to be very accurate. Judging from the size which he ascribes to the crater, far larger than any which we know to have existed in the present cone, one would suppose that he meant its boundary to be the ridge of Somma, and that the valley between Somma and Vesuvius, now called Atrio de' Cavalli, the hall of horses (because it is here that visitors to the summit of the mountain leave their horses to wait while they ascend the cone on foot), is the plain where cattle grazed. Still this is inconsistent with the further descent in the centre of that plain, unless we suppose that where the cone now stands there was then a chasm; and surely the present cone cannot have grown up within the last two centuries unobserved and undescribed. We have, therefore, but a choice of difficulties in explaining the passage; and a further one occurs in the great depth attributed to the crater, which, according to this statement, must have been accessible at a depth far below the level of the sea. Still, so far as we can form any opinion on it, the

* Lyell, Principles of Geology, chap. xix.
† Campi Phlegræi, page 62.

HISTORY OF VESUVIUS.

mountain, after this long pause, appears to have approximated considerably to the state in which it afforded a safe refuge to Spartacus, as described by Plutarch, and the passage thus furnishes a fresh presumption that the modern cone did not then exist. We may add Sir W. Hamilton's authority to the reasons already given, for supposing Somma to be the ancient Vesuvius. "I have seen ancient lavas in the plain on the other side of Somma, which could never have come from the present Vesuvius."*

A brief period of repose followed the eruption of 1631, but it lasted only till 1666; from which time to the present there has been a series of eruptions, at intervals rarely exceeding ten years, generally recurring much more frequently. Those of 1776 and 1777 are more than commonly celebrated, from having been described at large by an eye-witness, Sir William Hamilton, in his splendid work, entitled 'Campi Phlegræi.' The eruption of 1779 was also described by him, and is remarkable for the beauty and grandeur of its phenomena. During the whole month of July the volcano gave the usual warnings of an approaching paroxysm, by internal rumbling noises, and frequent jets of smoke and red-hot stones. On August the 5th it was in a state of violent agitation: white and sulphureous smoke issued continually from the crater, and lay piled up cloud upon cloud, resembling bales of the whitest cotton, until a mass of them was accumulated above the summit, four times the height and size of the mountain itself. In the midst of this, stones and ashes were continually shot up to a height of 2000 feet or upwards. At this time a quantity of lava was heaved up high enough to clear the mouth of the crater, and took its passage down the side opposite to Somma.

On Friday and Saturday, the 6th and 7th of August, the mountain was less violently disturbed, but at twelve o'clock on the night of the latter day its fermentation increased greatly. "I was watching its motions from the Mole of Naples, which has a full view of the volcano, and had been witness to several picturesque effects produced by the reflection of the deep red fire which issued from the crater of Vesuvius, and mounted up in the midst of the huge clouds,

---
* Campi Phlegræi, page 63.

when a summer storm, called here a Tropea, came on suddenly, and blended its heavy watery clouds with the sulphureous and mineral ones, which were already like so many other mountains piled over the summit of the volcano. At this moment a fountain of fire was shot up to an incredible height, casting so bright a light that the smallest objects could be clearly distinguished at any place within six miles or more of Vesuvius. The black stormy clouds passing over, and at times covering the whole or a part of the bright column of fire, at other times clearing away and giving a full view of it, with the various tints produced by its reverberated light on the white clouds above, in contrast with the pale flashes of forked lightning that attended the Tropea, formed such a scene as no power of art can ever express." One of the king of Sicily's game-keepers, who was out near Ottaiano in this storm, was surprised to find the drops of rain scald his hands and face, a phenomenon occasioned, probably, by the clouds having acquired a great degree of heat in passing by the above-mentioned column of fire.

On Sunday, Vesuvius was quiet till towards six o'clock in the evening, when the smoke began to gather over its crater, and the usual jets of stones and ashes commenced and continued to increase. "At about nine o'clock, there was a loud report which shook the houses at Portici and its neighbourhood, to such a degree as to alarm the inhabitants and drive them out into the streets; and, as I have since seen, many windows were broken, and walls cracked by the concussion of the air from that explosion, though faintly heard at Naples. In an instant, a fountain of liquid transparent fire began to rise, and gradually increasing, arrived at so amazing a height as to strike every one who beheld it with the most awful astonishment. I shall scarcely be credited, when I assert that, to the best of my judgment, the height of this stupendous column of fire could not be less than three times that of Vesuvius itself, which rises 3700 feet perpendicular above the level of the sea.

"Puffs of smoke, as black as can possibly be imagined, succeeded one another hastily, and accompanied the red, transparent, and liquid lava, intercepting its splendid brightness here and there by patches of the darkest hue. Within these puffs of smoke, at the very moment of their emission from the crater, I could perceive a bright, but pale electrical fire, briskly playing about in zig-zag lines. The wind was S.W., and though gentle, sufficient to carry these detached clouds or puffs of smoke out of the column of fire, and a collection of them by degrees formed a black and extensive curtain, if I may be allowed the expression, behind it; in other parts of the sky it was quite clear, and the stars were bright. The fiery fountain of so gigantic a size upon the dark ground above mentioned made the most glorious contrast imaginable, and the blaze of it reflecting strongly upon the surface of the sea, which was at that time perfectly smooth, added greatly to this sublime view. The liquid lava, mixed with stones and scoriæ, after having mounted, I verily believe, at the least 10,000 feet, was partly directed by the wind towards Ottaiano, and partly falling almost perpendicularly, still red-hot and liquid on Vesuvius, covered its whole cone, part of the mountain of Somma, and the valley between them. The falling matter being nearly as vivid and inflamed as that which was continually issuing fresh from the crater, formed with it one complete body of fire, which could not be less than two miles and a half in breadth, and of the extraordinary height abovementioned, casting a heat to the distance of at least six miles around it. The brushwood on the mountain of Somma was soon in a blaze, which flame being of a different tint from the deep red of the matter thrown out by the volcano, and from the silvery blue of the electrical fire, still added to the contrast of this most extraordinary scene."

Another remarkable eruption occurred in 1793, while the late Dr. Clarke was at Naples, and gave him the opportunity of making minute and repeated observations on the mountain. No pen is better calculated to explain these great operations of nature, and to describe their awful magnificence. We shall extract a passage of some length from his journal, illustrative chiefly of those phenomena which we have not yet noticed.

"It was in the month of February that I went with a party to the source of the lava for the first time, to ascertain the real state in which the lava proceeded from the volcano that created it. I found the crater in a very active state, throwing out volleys of immense stones transparent with vitrification, and such showers of ashes involved in thick sulphureous clouds as rendered any approach to it extremely dangerous. We ascended as near as possible, and then crossing over to the lava, attempted to coast it up to its source. This we soon found was impossible, for an unfortunate wind blew all the smoke of the lava hot upon us, attended at the same time with such a thick mist of minute ashes from the crater, and such fumes of sulphur, that we were in danger of being suffocated. In this perplexity I had recourse to an expedient recommended by Sir W. Hamilton, and proposed immediately crossing the current of liquid lava to gain the windward side, but felt some fears, owing to the very liquid appearance the lava there had so near its source. All my companions were against the scheme; and while we stood deliberating, immense fragments of stone and huge volcanic bombs, that had been cast out by the crater, but which the smoke had prevented us from observing, fell thick about us, and rolled by us with a velocity that would have crushed any of us had we been in their way. I found we must either leave our present spot or expect instant death; therefore covering my face with my hat I rushed upon the lava, and crossed safely over to the other side, having my boots only a little burnt, and my hands scorched. Having once more rallied my forces, I proceeded on, and in about half an hour gained the chasm through which the lava had opened itself a passage out of the mountain. To describe this sight is utterly beyond all human ability. My companions shared in the astonishment it produced; and the sensations they felt, in concert with me, were such as can be obliterated only with our lives. All I had seen of volcanic phenomena before did not lead me to expect such a spectacle as I then beheld. I had seen the vast rivers of lava that descended into the plains below, and carried ruin and devastation with them; but they resembled a vast heap of cinders, or the scoriæ of an iron foundry, rolling slowly along, and falling with a rattling noise over one another. Here a vast arched chasm presented itself in the side of the mountain, from which rushed with the velocity of a flood the clear vivid torrent of lava, in perfect fusion, and totally unconnected with any other matter that was not in a state of complete solution, unattended with any scoriæ on its surface, or gross materials of an insolvent nature, but flowing with the translucency of honey, in regular channels cut finer than art can imitate, and glowing with all the splendour of the sun.

"The eruption from the crater increased with so much violence that we proceeded to make our experiments and observations as speedily as possible. A little above the source of the lava I found a chimney of about four feet in height, from which proceeded smoke, and sometimes stones. I approached and gathered some pure sulphur, which had formed itself upon the edges of the mouth of this chimney, the smell of which was so powerful that I was forced to hold my breath all the while I remained there. I seized an opportunity to gain a momentary view down this aperture, and perceived nothing but the glare of the red-hot lava that passed beneath it. We then returned to examine the lava at its source. Sir W. Hamilton had conceived that no stones thrown upon a current of lava would make any impression. We were soon convinced of the contrary. Light bodies of five, ten, and fifteen pounds weight, made little or no impression even at the source; but bodies of sixty, seventy, and eighty pounds were seen to form a kind of bed on the surface of the lava, and float away with it. A stone of three hundredweight, that had been thrown out by the crater, lay near the source of the current of lava. I raised it upon one end, and then let it fall in upon the liquid lava, when it gradually sunk beneath the surface and disappeared. If I wished to describe the manner in which it acted upon the lava, I should say it was like a loaf of bread thrown into a bowl of very thick honey, which gradually involves itself in the heavy liquid which surrounds it, and then slowly sinks to the bottom. The lava itself had a glutinous appearance, and although it resisted the most violent impression, seemed as if it might easily be stirred with a common walking-stick. A small distance from its source, as it flows on, it acquires a darker tint upon its surface, is less easily acted upon, and as the stream gets wider, the surface having lost its state of perfect solution, grows harder and harder, and cracks into innumerable fragments of very porous matter, to which they give the name of scoriæ, and the appearance of which has led many to suppose that it proceeded thus from the mountain; itself being composed of materials less soluble than the rest of the lava, lighter, and of course liable to float continually on the surface. There is, however, no truth in this. All lava at its first exit from its native volcano flows out in a liquid state, and all equally in fusion. The appearance of the scoriæ is to be attributed only to the action of the external air, and not to any difference of the materials which compose it, since any lava whatever, separated from its channel and exposed to the action of the external air, immediately cracks, becomes porous, and alters its form. As we proceeded downward this became more and more evident, and the same lava, which at its original source flowed in perfect solution, undivided, and free from encumbrances of any kind, a little farther down had its surface loaded with scoriæ in such a manner, that upon its arrival at the bottom of the mountain the whole current resembled nothing so much as a heap of unconnected cinders from an iron-foundry.

"Aug. 22, 1793.—There was to-day a most singular appearance in the mountain. On opening the shutters to view it, I perceived the crater to be in great agitation, puff after puff impelling each other with the greatest violence. I could perceive thousands of stones and scoriæ thrown into the air, and falling in all directions. The clouds from the crater were as white as the purest snow; on a sudden, as I was looking at these, a column of smoke rushed impetuously out of another mouth behind the crater, as black as the deepest ink; and rising in curling volumes to a vast magnitude, formed a pillar perfectly unconnected with the smoke from the crater, and presented a striking contrast by opposing its jet black to the snowy whiteness of the other. These appearances continued at intervals the whole day. Sometimes the two columns of different colours rose together, as if emulating each other, and striving which should rise the highest or display the greatest magnitude, but never mixing or interfering with each other. . . .

"Aug. 30.—The lava, which was last night so great, this evening suddenly stopped; hardly a trace of it was visible. But the crater displayed such girandoles of fire, such beautiful columns of light red flame, as I think I never saw before. Millions of red-hot stones were shot into the air, full half the height of the cone itself, and then bending, fell all round in a fine arch. As soon as I got home I fixed the telescope. Sometimes, in the middle of the clear flame, another and another still more bright and glorious displayed itself, breaking on the eye like the full sun, so that the interior was always the most luminous. The interior and bright attendants upon the principal column seemed to be lava in perfect fusion, which boiled and bubbled up above the crater's edge; and sometimes falling over it, I could perceive splash upon the cone, and take its course gently down the side of the mountain. Sometimes, and more usually, it fell again into the crater. I write this with the burning mountain now before my eyes. All the top of the cone is covered with red-hot stones and lava. The flame of the crater continues without intervals of darkness, as usual. It is always in flame, or rather the clouds of smoke, tinged with the boiling matter within, are like burnished gold, and as bright as fire.

"Sept. 5.—Vesuvius continues to throw most superbly; the lava flows again. At sunset he showed that Tyrian hue which he assumes sometimes, and which has a glow beyond description. I had undressed myself and was prepared to get into bed, when a violent shock from the mountain agitated the door of my room, so as to startle me not a little. I went into my sitting-room, and, upon opening the window toward the mountain, I perceived all the top of the cone covered with red-hot matter. At the same time such a roaring was heard as made me expect something more than common. In an instant a column of lucid fire shot up into the air, and after ascending above half the height of the cone itself, fell in a glorious parabolic girandole, and covered near half the cone with fire. This was followed, after an interval of about thirty seconds, by a shock which agitated the doors and windows, and indeed the whole house in a most violent manner. Immediately after this shock the sound of the explosion reached us louder than the greatest cannon, or the most terrible thunder, attended with a noise like the trampling of horses' feet, which, of course, was nothing more than the noise occasioned by the falling of so many enormous stones among the hard lava. The shock of this explosion was so violent that it disturbed many things I had left on my table, such as brushes for painting, &c. I dressed myself again, and remained in the balcony above an hour, during which time I had the pleasure of beholding Vesuvius in his terrific grandeur, and more awfully sublime than I had ever before seen him. The consul, Sir James Douglas, has just been observing to me that he never saw the mountain so agitated since the great eruption of 1779." *

Between the end of the 18th century and the year 1822, the crater of Vesuvius had been gradually filled by the boiling up of lava and the crumbling down of the upper part of the cone. In place, therefore, of a regular cavity, was a rough and rocky surface covered with blocks of lava and scoriæ. But this state of things was totally changed by the eruption of October, 1822, when the whole accumulated mass within the crater, together with a large part of the cone itself, was blown out, so as to leave an irregular gulf about three miles in circumference, when measured along the winding edge of its margin, but somewhat less than three-quarters of a mile in its largest diameter. The depth has been variously estimated, from 2000 feet to less than half that quantity. More than eight hundred feet of the cone was carried away during the eruption, so that the mountain was reduced in height from about 4200 to 3400 feet.†

Vesuvius now consists of a double mountain, upon an extended base, from thirty to forty miles in circumference. Upon this stands the long ridge of Somma, so often mentioned, bending in the form of a crescent, with its convex side presented to the N.E., its points to the S.W. The western horn is separated by a deep valley from a lower mountain, called Cantaroni, which, inclining to the south, meets the lower projection, or terrace, called La Pedamentina. This is again separated by an excavated valley from the eastern horn of Somma. Between Somma and Vesuvius is the deep valley, called Atrio de' Cavalli, the Hall of Horses, and in the centre of the amphitheatre rises the cone

---

* Life of E. D. Clarke.

† There have been several eruptions since that of 1822. The last, and perhaps the most remarkable, of these occurred towards the end of 1861. It was preceded by shocks of earthquake, which overthrew or damaged several houses in Torre del Greco. The editor visited that place a month or two afterwards, and found some of the wells there still boiling; while at a little distance from the shore a sort of fountain was thrown up in the sea by volcanic agency. On this occasion ashes were ejected from several small cones situated less than half a mile from the town.

of Vesuvius itself, dark, sterile, and desolate ; to the eye, a mass of loose scoriæ and ashes, without order or coherence. This however on inspection is proved not to be the case. It consists of alternate layers of sand or ashes, scoriæ, and lava, inclining outwards at an angle of from 45° to 30° with the axis of the cone. The strata of course are partial and irregular in extent and thickness, as circumstances have determined the fall of the ejected matter or the flow of the lava; but the irregularities of these numerous beds compensate for each other, and the general effect, on viewing the interior of the crater, is one of considerable order and regularity. Even the loose substances, falling together half melted, and continually acted on by the hot vapours which steam upwards in all parts of the cone, soon acquire a considerable degree of coherence ; and the solidity of the whole is mainly assisted by dykes of solid lava, injected into the cracks of the mountain when the molten liquid has boiled up to its summit.

CHAPTER II.

HISTORICAL NOTICE OF POMPEII.

POMPEII is situated in that district of Italy named by the ancients Campania, comprised between the mountains of Samnium and the Tyrrhenian sea, and bounded on the north by the river Liris, and on the south by the Silarus. The line of coast included between these points is broken by two far-projecting capes, Misenum and the promontory of Minerva, between which lies a deep recess, called from its shape Crater, the Cup, or the Gulf of Cumæ, and known in modern times as the Bay of Naples. At the bottom of this bay stood Pompeii, about thirteen miles south-east of Naples, and five from Vesuvius. Of its history very little is known. It is related to have been founded by Hercules, as well as its neighbour and fellow-victim, Herculaneum. Solinus says that the name of Pompeii is derived from Pompè, in allusion to the pomp with which Hercules celebrated his victories, while awaiting his fleet at the mouth of the river Sarnus. Being furnished with so respectable and credible an origin, it would be waste of time to inquire any further. An almost impenetrable darkness hangs over these remote ages; and when men are driven to take refuge in mythology, it is plain

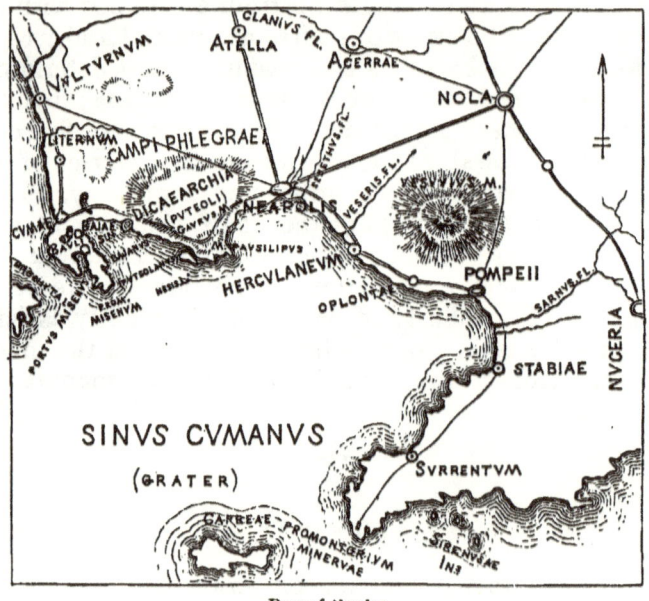

Bay of Naples.

that they can find little satisfaction in history. Strabo, however, asserts that these towns were founded by Pelasgians and Tyrrhenians*: The first inhabitants that we can trace on this coast are the Osci, who appear to have been the same as the Ausones, and of Pelasgian extraction. At an early, but still an unknown period, a colony from Chalcis in Eubœa founded the town of Cumæ. Parthenope, afterwards called Neapolis, now Naples, was an offset from thence, or from a kindred colony of Eretrians. Pompeii and Herculaneum also fell into their power, but their establishments seem to have extended no further in this direction.

Campania, where, in Pliny's words, all imaginable delights were in constant rivalry, has always been celebrated as tempt-

* Lib. v. c. 4, § 8.

ing by its riches the arms of strangers, and punishing the cupidity of its conquerors by enervating, and subjecting them in their turn to some sterner enemy; in consequence, it has experienced a rapid succession of masters.

According to Strabo, in the passage already quoted, Pompeii was first occupied by the Oscans, then by the Tyrrhenians, or Etruscans, and next by the Samnites, who, about the year B.C. 440, or a little after, conquered Campania; and the branch of that nation settled there subsequently assumed the name of Campanians. The cities of Campania appear to have been independent. There is no trace of a central government. Capua was no doubt the chief city, but we hear only of local governments of a republican form, called in Oscan, *meddix*, in which the chief magistrate was entitled *meddix tuticus*.

The first direct notice of Pompeii which we find in history is in B.C. 310, when, during the second Samnite war, a Roman fleet under P. Cornelius entered the mouth of the Sarnus. The crews proceeded up that river as far as Nuceria, and ravaged the country around, but were ultimately driven back with great loss.* How long Pompeii had existed before that date it is impossible to say; but, as Overbeck remarks,† the remains of some parts of its walls, as well as of the Greek temple in the Forum Triangulare, commonly called the Temple of Hercules, seem to denote a period coeval with that of Pæstum, or the seventh century B.C.

When the Romans reduced the Samnites, towards the end of the third century B.C., the cities of the districts occupied by that people, and amongst them those of Campania, appear to have received a municipal constitution. Under this new state of things, Pompeii, as may be inferred from inscriptions, &c., seems to have retained many of its ancient Oscan customs, as well as the Oscan tongue. It was an independent municipium, with a senate and assembly of the people, and magistrates chosen by them, among whom the principal were Quatuorviri. Pompeii no doubt participated in the Campanian revolt, B.C. 216, in the second Punic war, and joined Hannibal, who proposed to make Capua the capital of Italy. His long stay in this delightful climate proved fatal to the discipline even of his victorious troops, and when he was

* Liv. ix. 38. † *Pompeji*, B. i. S. 16.

compelled to abandon Italy the incensed Romans took a terrible revenge on their revolted subjects. Capua, we know, was severely punished; but neither on this occasion, nor on their first occupation of the country, is mention made of Herculaneum or Pompeii.

In the Social, or Marsic war, which broke out in B.C. 91, the Campanian cities raised the standard of revolt. The Pompeians appear to have played a principal part on this occasion, as Appian makes particular mention of them in enumerating the nations which joined the insurrection.* In the second year of the war, L. Sulla having defeated the Samnites under Cluentius, and driven them into Nola, laid siege to Pompeii.† We have no particulars of this siege, but many refer to it the dilapidated state in which the walls of Pompeii have been discovered, whilst others attribute those appearances to the earthquake which preceded the eruption by which the city was destroyed. At the end of the war Capua was severely punished, its inhabitants being dispossessed, and a colony sent from Rome to cultivate their fertile territory. Stabiæ, a town within four or five miles of Pompeii, was entirely destroyed, and scattered villas built where it formerly stood. We know not by what means Pompeii not only escaped this fate, but even obtained the Roman franchise, which was probably granted by virtue of a capitulation. A military colony was however established there by Sulla, which, from the patron goddess of the city, and from Sulla, who had subdued it, obtained the names of COLONIA VENERIA CORNELIA.‡ Subsequently we find this colony under the government of the dictator's nephew, P. Sylla, who, in B.C. 64, was accused of exciting troubles in it, and urging it to revolt from Rome. On this occasion Sylla was defended by Cicero, and ultimately acquitted.§

After the establishment of Sulla's colony, Pompeii, like Baiæ, Puteoli, and other towns in that delightful neighbourhood, became a favourite resort of the wealthy Romans. Among these was Cicero, who mentions his villa at Pompeii.‖ After this period, the Oscan tongue, as well as the Oscan magistrates, were supplanted by Roman. Under the empire

* App. *B.C.*, i. 39. † Vell. Pat. ii. 16, App. *B.C.* i. 50.
‡ Mommsen, *Inscrr. R.N.*, No. 2201. § Cic. *Pro. Sulla.*
‖ Cic. *Epp. ad div.*, vii. 1.

we find two principal classes of citizens: *decurions*, who answered to the Roman senate, and *Augustales*, or priests of Augustus, whose rank was somewhat equivalent to that of the Roman equites. There was besides a popular body, who, in their *comitia*, or assemblies, chose their own magistrates, regulated their own worship and priesthood, made municipal laws, and conferred rewards and distinctions. The heads of the government and supreme administrators of the law were the *Decemviri juri dicundo*, who presided at the assemblies of the *Decurions*, or senate, and resembled, in their way, the Roman consuls. Below these were Ædiles, Quinquennales, or censors, a Quæstor, and other inferior magistrates. The imperial power seems sometimes to have been represented by officers called *Curatores*, whose title is occasionally met with in inscriptions. We should remember that there was always a considerable Greek population in the city.

From this time forward Pompeii shared the common fortune of the empire, and there is little remarkable to be related of it. Tacitus calls it a "populous" town of Campania;* but there is no means of ascertaining the number of its population, which has been variously estimated at from 20,000 to 40,000. Augustus sent thither some Roman colonists in B.C. 7, who established themselves in the northern suburb outside the gate of Herculaneum. This settlement obtained the name of Pagus Augustus Felix. We learn from an anecdote in Suetonius that the emperor Claudius had a villa at Pompeii, whose little son was choked here by throwing up a pear and catching it in his mouth.† In the year 59, Pompeii was made to feel its dependence upon Rome. The senator, Livineius Regulus, who, after having been banished from the Roman capital, appears to have fixed his abode at Pompeii, gave in the amphitheatre of that place some grand gladiatorial shows, which were attended by the inhabitants of the neighbouring towns. During this exhibition, a quarrel, which originated in certain provincial sarcasms, arose between the Pompeians and the people of Nuceria. The dispute terminated in a battle, and the Nucerians were worsted. Not prospering in the *voie du fait*, they went to law, and carried their complaint before the

* "Celebre Campaniæ oppidum." *Ann.* xxv. 2.   † Suet. *Claud.* 27.

D

Emperor Nero, who finally adjudged that, among other things, the Pompeians should be suspended from all theatrical amusements for ten years :* a sentence which, according to modern ideas, we can hardly believe to be serious, but which certainly was both meant and felt to be so, and which bears strong testimony to the importance attached by the Romans to all public amusements.

Upon the external walls of a house in the street of Mercury, as it is called, near the city wall, was found a caricature or rude drawing scratched on the plaster with a sharp-pointed instrument by some patriotic Pompeian, in commemoration of this squabble and the victory of his townspeople. We give a fac-simile of it. It seems to be a joint production; for the armed figure descending the steps is evidently the work of a more skilful hand than that which drew the other two figures, if they deserve that term. The figure on the right seems to be meant for a gladiator, cased in armour, descending the steps of the amphitheatre, bearing in his left hand a shield, and in his right a palm-branch, the token of victory. It is observable that his helmet has a complete visor, and apparently resembles the helmet of the middle ages much more than the usual form of the Roman helmet. The abortive figures on the left probably represent one of the victors on some elevated spot, dragging a prisoner, with his arms bound, after him up the ladder which leads to it. It might not have been very easy to decipher all this; but like the sign-painter who found it necessary to write under his production, "This is a bear!" the artist or artists have thought it prudent to subjoin the following inscription, which, in point of Latin, is much on a par with the drawing:—

<blockquote>Campani victoria una cum Nucerinis peristis;</blockquote>

which may be interpreted, "Campanians, you perished in victory together with the Nucerians."

Four years after this occurrence, an earthquake, which took place on the 5th February, A.D. 63, and has been recorded by Seneca, threw down a great part of Pompeii, and considerably injured Herculaneum and other towns. "A

---

* Tac. *Ann.* xiv. 17.

flock," he says, "of six hundred sheep were swallowed up, statues were split, and many persons lost their reason."*

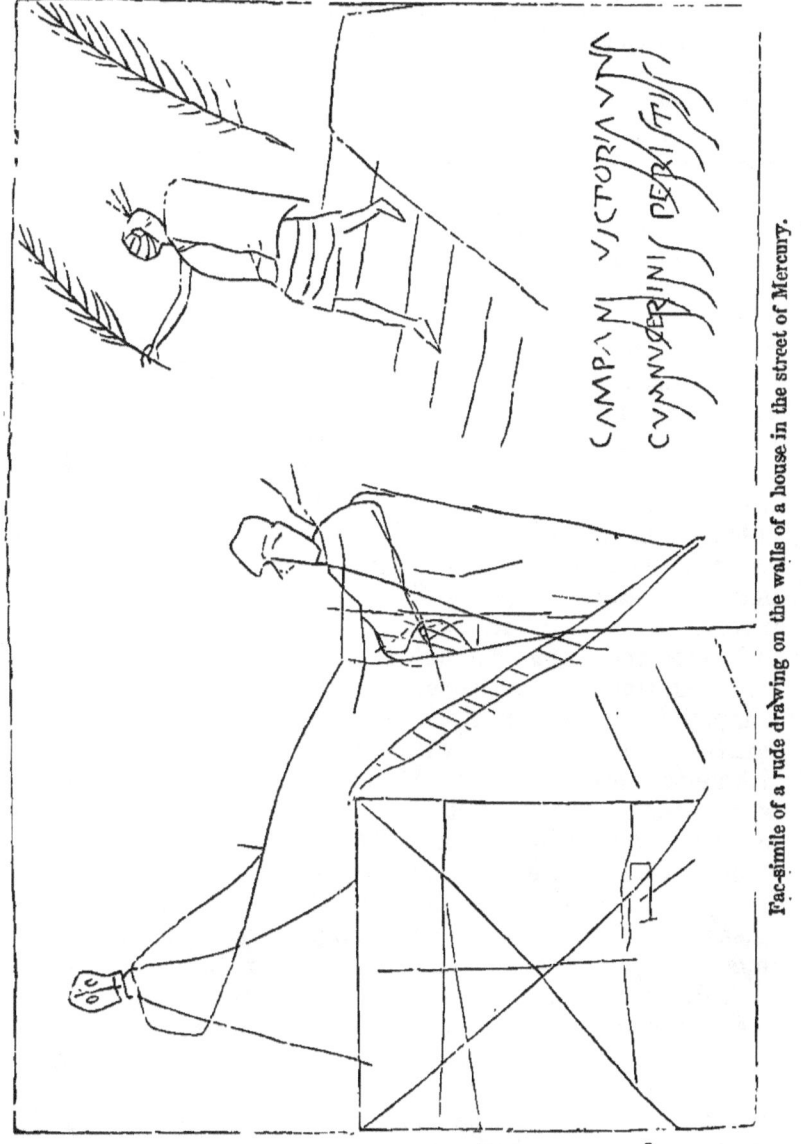

Fac-simile of a rude drawing on the walls of a house in the street of Mercury.

The following year another earthquake took place whilst

* Sen. *Q.N.*, vi. 1, of Tac. *Ann.* xv. 22.

Nero was singing at Naples; the building, unfortunately, fell immediately after the emperor had left it. Vestiges of the injury done by these shocks may even now be seen in the houses which have been excavated at Pompeii, where the mosaic floors are often much out of their level, twisted and broken, and show the repairs which had been made by the inhabitants themselves.

These alarms, the usual presages of a near eruption, were from time to time repeated until the 23rd of August, A.D. 79, the day on which, after a cessation of ages, the first recorded volcanic paroxysm of Vesuvius occurred.

By an unusual good fortune we are in possession of a faithful narrative, furnished by an eye-witness of the catastrophe which overwhelmed Pompeii, and provided a subject for this volume. It is contained in two letters of Pliny the younger to Tacitus, which record the death of his uncle, who fell a victim to his inquiring spirit and humanity.

"Your request that I would send you an account of my uncle's death, in order to transmit a more exact relation of it to posterity, deserves my acknowledgments; for, if this accident shall be celebrated by your pen, the glory of it, I am well assured, will be rendered for ever illustrious. And notwithstanding he perished by a misfortune, which, as it involved at the same time a most beautiful country in ruins, and destroyed so many populous cities, seems to promise him an everlasting remembrance, notwithstanding he has himself composed many and lasting works; yet I am persuaded the mentioning of him in your immortal works will greatly contribute to eternize his name. Happy I esteem those to be whom Providence has distinguished with the abilities either of doing such actions as are worthy of being related, or of relating them in a manner worthy of being read; but doubly happy are they who are blessed with both these uncommon talents—in the number of which my uncle, as his own writings and your history will evidently prove, may justly be ranked. It is with extreme willingness, therefore, I execute your commands; and should indeed have claimed the task if you had not enjoined it. He was at that time with the fleet under his command at Misenum. On the 24th of August, about one in the afternoon, my mother desired him to observe a cloud which appeared of a very unusual size and shape. He had just returned from taking the benefit of the sun,* and after bathing himself in cold water, and taking a slight repast, was retired to his study. He immediately arose and went out upon an eminence, from whence he might more distinctly view this very uncommon appearance. It was not at that distance discernible from what mountain this cloud issued, but it was found afterwards to ascend from Mount Vesuvius.† I cannot give a more exact description of its figure than by resembling it to that of a pine-tree, for it shot up a great height in the form of a trunk, which extended itself at the top into a sort of branches, occasioned, I imagine, either by a sudden gust of air that impelled it, the force of which decreased as it advanced upwards, or the cloud itself, being pressed back again by its own weight, expanded in this manner: it appeared sometimes bright and sometimes dark and spotted, as it was more or less impregnated with earth and cinders. This extraordinary phenomenon excited my uncle's philosophical curiosity to take a nearer view of it. He ordered a light vessel to be got ready, and gave me the liberty, if I thought proper, to attend him. I rather chose to continue my studies; for, as it happened, he had given me an employment of that kind. As he was coming out of the house, he received a note from Rectina, the wife of Bassus, who was in the utmost alarm at the imminent danger which threatened her; for her villa being situated at the foot of Mount Vesuvius, there was no way to escape but by sea: she earnestly entreated him, therefore, to come to her assistance. He accordingly changed his first design, and what he began with a philosophical, he pursued with an heroical turn

---

* The Romans used to lie or walk naked in the sun, after anointing their bodies with oil, which was esteemed as greatly contributing to health, and therefore daily practised by them.

† About six miles distant from Naples. Martial has a pretty epigram, in which he gives us a view of Vesuvius as it appeared before this terrible conflagration broke out:—

> "Here verdant vines o'erspread Vesuvius' sides;
> The generous grape here pour'd her purple tides.
> This Bacchus lov'd beyond his native scene;
> Here dancing satyrs joy'd to trip the green.
> Far more than Sparta this in Venus' grace;
> And great Alcides once renown'd the place:
> Now flaming embers spread dire waste around,
> And gods regret that gods can thus confound."

of mind. He ordered the galleys to put to sea, and went himself on board, with an intention of assisting not only Rectina, but several others, for the villas stand extremely thick upon that beautiful coast. When hastening to the place from which others fled with the utmost terror, he steered his course direct to the point of danger, and with so much calmness and presence of mind, as to be able to make and dictate his observations upon the motion and figure of that dreadful scene. He was now so nigh the mountain, that the cinders, which grew thicker and hotter the nearer he approached, fell into the ships, together with pumice-stones and black pieces of burning rock. They were likewise in danger, not only of being aground by the sudden retreat of the sea, but also from the vast fragments which rolled down from the mountain and obstructed all the shore. Here he stopped to consider whether he should return back again; to which the pilot advising him, 'Fortune,' said he, 'befriends the brave; carry me to Pomponianus.' Pomponianus was then at Stabiæ,* separated by a gulf, which the sea, after several insensible windings, forms upon the shore. He had already sent his baggage on board; for though he was not at that time in actual danger, yet being within the view of it, and, indeed, extremely near, if it should in the least increase, he was determined to put to sea as soon as the wind should change. It was favourable, however, for carrying my uncle to Pomponianus, whom he found in the greatest consternation. He embraced him with tenderness, encouraging and exhorting him to keep up his spirits, and the more to dissipate his fears, he ordered, with an air of unconcern, the baths to be got ready; when, after having bathed, he sat down to supper with great cheerfulness, or at least (what is equally heroic) with all the appearance of it. In the meanwhile, the eruption from Mount Vesuvius flamed out in several places with much violence, which the darkness of the night contributed to render still more visible and dreadful. But my uncle, in order to sooth the apprehensions of his friend, assured him it was only the burning of the villages, which the country people had abandoned to the flames. After this he retired to rest, and it is most certain he was so little discomposed as to fall into a deep sleep; for being pretty fat, and breathing

---

* Now called Castellamare, in the Gulf of Naples.

hard, those who attended without actually heard him snore. The court which led to his apartment being now almost filled with stones and ashes, if he had continued there any time longer, it would have been impossible for him to have made his way out; it was thought proper, therefore, to awaken him. He got up, and went to Pomponianus and the rest of his company, who were not unconcerned enough to think of going to bed. They consulted together whether it would be most prudent to trust to the houses, which now shook from side to side with frequent and violent concussions; or fly to the open fields, where the calcined stones and cinders, though light indeed, yet fell in large showers, and threatened destruction. In this distress they resolved for the fields, as the less dangerous situation of the two; a resolution which, while the rest of the company were hurried into it by their fears, my uncle embraced upon cool and deliberate consideration. They went out then, having pillows tied upon their heads with napkins; and this was their whole defence against the storm of stones that fell around them. It was now day everywhere else, but there a deeper darkness prevailed than in the most obscure night; which, however, was in some degree dissipated by torches and other lights of various kinds. They thought proper to go down further upon the shore, to observe if they might safely put out to sea; but they found the waves still run extremely high and boisterous. There my uncle, having drunk a draught or two of cold water, threw himself down upon a cloth which was spread for him, when immediately the flames, and a strong smell of sulphur, which was the forerunner of them, dispersed the rest of the company, and obliged him to rise. He raised himself up with the assistance of two of his servants, and instantly fell down dead—suffocated, as I conjecture, by some gross and noxious vapour, having always had weak lungs, and being frequently subject to a difficulty of breathing. As soon as it was light again, which was not till the third day after this melancholy accident, his body was found entire, and without any marks of violence upon it, exactly in the same posture that he fell, and looking more like a man asleep than dead. During all this time my mother and I, who were at Misenum *—but as this has no connexion with your history, so your inquiry

---

* See this account continued, in the following letter.

went no farther than concerning my uncle's death; with that, therefore, I will put an end to my letter. Suffer me only to add, that I have faithfully related to you what I was either an eye-witness of myself, or heard immediately after the accident happened, and before there was time to vary the truth. You will choose out of this narrative such circumstances as shall be most suitable to your purpose; for there is a great difference between what is proper for a letter and a history—between writing to a friend and writing for the public. Farewell !" *

"The letter which, in compliance with your request, I wrote to you concerning the death of my uncle, has raised, it seems, your curiosity to know what terrors and dangers attended me while I continued at Misenum; for there, I think, the account in my former broke off.

'Though my shocked soul recoils, my tongue shall tell.'†

"My uncle having left us, I pursued the studies which prevented my going with him, till it was time to bathe. After which I went to supper and from thence to bed, where my sleep was greatly broken and disturbed. There had been, for many days before, some shocks of an earthquake, which the less surprised us as they are extremely frequent in Campania; but they were so particularly violent that night, that they not only shook everything about us, but seemed indeed to threaten total destruction. My mother flew to my chamber, where she found me rising, in order to awaken her. We went out into a small court belonging to the house, which separated the sea from the buildings. As I was at that time but eighteen years of age, I know not whether I should call my behaviour, in this dangerous juncture, courage or rashness; but I took up Livy, and amused myself with turning over that author, and even making extracts from him, as if all about me had been in full security. While we were in this posture, a friend of my uncle, who was just come from Spain to pay him a visit, joined us; and observing me sitting by my mother with a book in my hand, greatly condemned her calmness, at the same time that he reproved me for my careless security. Nevertheless, I still went on with my author. Though it

* Pliny's Letters, Melmoth's translation, vi. 16.
† "Quanquam animus meminisse horret, &c." Virgil, book ii. 12.

was now morning, the light was exceedingly faint and languid; the buildings all around us tottered, and though we stood upon open ground, yet, as the place was narrow and confined, there was no remaining there without certain and great danger: we therefore resolved to quit the town. The people followed us in the utmost consternation; and, as to a mind distracted with terror every suggestion seems more prudent than its own, pressed in great crowds about us in our way out. Being got at a convenient distance from the houses, we stood still, in the midst of a most dangerous and dreadful scene. The chariots which we had ordered to be drawn out, were so agitated backwards and forwards, though upon the most level ground, that we could not keep them steady, even by supporting them with large stones. The sea seemed to roll back upon itself, and to be driven from its banks by the convulsive motion of the earth; it is certain at least the shore was considerably enlarged, and several sea animals were left upon it. On the other side a black and dreadful cloud, bursting with an igneous serpentine vapour, darted out a long train of fire, resembling flashes of lightning, but much larger. Upon this our Spanish friend, whom I mentioned above, addressed himself to my mother and me with great warmth and earnestness: 'If your brother and your uncle,' said he, 'is safe, he certainly wishes you may be so too; but if he perished, it was his desire, no doubt, that you might both survive him: why, therefore, do you delay your escape a moment?' We could never think of our own safety, we said, while we were uncertain of his. Hereupon our friend left us, and withdrew from the danger with the utmost precipitation. Soon afterwards the cloud seemed to descend, and cover the whole ocean; as indeed it entirely hid the island of Capreæ* and the promontory of Misenum. My mother strongly conjured me to make my escape at any rate, which, as I was young, I might easily do: as for herself, she said, her age and corpulency rendered all attempts of that sort impossible. However she would willingly meet death, if she could have the satisfaction of seeing that she was not the occasion of mine. But I absolutely refused to leave her, and taking her by the hand I led her on: she complied with great reluctance, and not without many reproaches to herself for retarding my

* An island twenty miles from Naples, now called Capri.

flight. The ashes now began to fall upon us, though in no great quantity. I turned my head, and observed behind us a thick smoke, which came rolling after us like a torrent. I proposed, while we had yet any light, to turn out of the high road, lest she should be pressed to death in the dark by the crowd that followed us. We had scarce stepped out of the path, when darkness overspread us, not like that of a cloudy night, or when there is no moon, but of a room when it is shut up and all the lights extinct. Nothing then was to be heard but the shrieks of women, the screams of children, and the cries of men; some calling for their children, others for their parents, others for their husbands, and only distinguishing each other by their voices; one lamenting his own fate, another that of his family; some wishing to die from the very fear of dying; some lifting their hands to the gods; but the greater part imagining that the last and eternal night was come, which was to destroy the gods and the world together.* Among these were some who augmented the real terrors by imaginary ones, and made the frighted multitude falsely believe that Misenum was actually in flames. At length a glimmering light appeared, which we imagined to be rather the forerunner of an approaching burst of flames, as in truth it was, than the return of day. However, the fire fell at a distance from us. Then again we were immersed in thick darkness, and a heavy shower of ashes rained upon us, which we were obliged every now and then to shake off, otherwise we should have been crushed and buried in the heap. I might boast that, during all this scene of horror, not a sigh or expression of fear escaped from me, had not my support been founded in that miserable, though strong consolation— that all mankind were involved in the same calamity, and that I imagined I was perishing with the world itself! At last this dreadful darkness was dissipated by degrees, like a cloud of smoke; the real day returned, and even the sun appeared, though very faintly, and as when an eclipse is coming on. Every object that presented itself to our eyes (which were extremely weakened) seemed changed, being

---

* The Stoic and Epicurean philosophers held that the world was to be destroyed by fire, and all things fall again into original chaos; not excepting even the national gods themselves from the destruction of this general conflagration.

covered over with white ashes, as with a deep snow. We returned to Misenum, where we refreshed ourselves as well as we could, and passed an anxious night between hope and fear—though indeed with a much larger share of the latter—for the earthquake still continued, while several enthusiastic people ran up and down, heightening their own and their friends' calamities by terrible predictions. However, my mother and I, notwithstanding the danger we had passed, and that which still threatened us, had no thoughts of leaving the place till we should receive some account from my uncle.

"And now you will read this narrative without any view of inserting it in your history, of which it is by no means worthy; and indeed you must impute it to your own request if it shall deserve the trouble of a letter. Farewell." *

Pompeii was not destroyed by an inundation of lava; its elevated position sheltered it from that fate; it was buried under that shower of stones and cinders of which Pliny speaks. Much of this matter appears to have been deposited in a liquid state, which is easily explained; for the vast volumes of steam sent up by the volcano descended in torrents of rain, which united with the ashes suspended in the air, or washed them, after they had fallen, into places where they could not well have penetrated in a dry state. Among other proofs of this, the skeleton of a woman was found in a cellar, enclosed within a mould of volcanic paste, which received and has retained a perfect impression of her form. Other moulds of a like kind have since been discovered. In the great eruption of 1779, minutely described by Sir William Hamilton, Ottaiano, a small town situated at the foot of Somma, most narrowly escaped similar destruction. The phenomena then observed may be presumed to correspond closely with those which occurred at Pompeii.

"On the night of the 8th of August, when the noise increased, and the fire began to appear above the mountain of Somma, many of the inhabitants of this town flew to the churches, and others were preparing to quit the town, when a sudden violent report was heard, soon after which they found themselves involved in a thick cloud of smoke and

* Pliny's Letters, vi. 20; Melmoth's translation.

minute ashes; a horrid clashing was heard in the air, and presently fell a deluge of stones and large scoriæ, some of which scoriæ were of the diameter of seven or eight feet, and must have weighed more than one hundred pounds before they were broken by their fall, as some of the fragments of them, which I picked up in the streets, still weighed upwards of sixty pounds. When these large vitrified masses either struck against one another in the air, or fell on the ground, they broke into many pieces, and covered a large space around them with vivid sparks of fire, which communicated their heat to everything that was combustible. In an instant the town and country about it was on fire in many parts; for in the vineyards there were several straw huts, which had been erected for the watchmen of the grapes, all of which were burnt. A great magazine of wood in the heart of the town was all in a blaze; and had there been much wind, the flames must have spread universally, and all the inhabitants would infallibly have been burnt in their houses, for it was impossible for them to stir out. Some who attempted it, with pillows, tables, chairs, the tops of wine-casks, &c., on their heads, were either knocked down, or soon driven back to their close quarters, under arches and in the cellars of their houses. Many were wounded, but only two persons have died of the wounds they received from this dreadful volcanic shower. To add to the horror of the scene, incessant volcanic lightning was whisking about the black cloud that surrounded them, and the sulphureous heat and smell would scarcely allow them to draw their breath. In this miserable and alarming situation they remained about twenty-five minutes, when the volcanic storm ceased all at once."* It is evident that if the eruption had continued for a brief space longer, Ottaiano must have perished like Pompeii.

The dreadful effects of the eruption of 79, in changing the external face of nature, are recorded by Roman authors of the period. Tacitus tells us that the view over the bay, from the island of Capri, before so beautiful, had been completely changed by that catastrophe.† And Martial, in the epigram before quoted, gives a glowing picture of the

* Campi Phlegræi, supplement, p. 19.
† Prospectabatque pulcherrimum sinum antequam Vesuvius mons ardescens faciem loci verterat.—*Ann.* iv. 64.

country about Vesuvius before it vanished under heaps of ashes.*

The materials with which Pompeii is buried are from 20 to 24 feet deep. The greater part of this covering is composed of white, or whitish-grey pounded stones or ashes (*lapilli*), which peculiarly characterize the eruption of 79. Pompeii may have subsequently been covered to the depth of a few feet by subsequent eruptions, distinguished by the greyish-black colour of the ashes. Five-sixths of the depth of the materials consist of pumice-stones of an irregular shape, from the size of a pea to two or three inches diameter. Over this is another layer, of an average depth of two feet, which appears to have been attended in its descent with an enormous fall of water, forming what the Italians call a *lava bavosa*. The outer surface has, in process of time, been converted into a fine mould, which now bears lupins and corn, and even mulberry and other trees, as may be seen in the unexcavated parts. It has been pretty generally thought that the ashes descended upon Pompeii in a burning state ; and to this circumstance has been ascribed the carbonization of the wood, bread, and other combustible substances. Overbeck, however, is of opinion † that they were not in that state of excandescence in which they would have set fire to anything, though they were probably hot enough to change any coloured surfaces with which they came in contact, as red into yellow, and to give a green shade to blues, and he refers the process of carbonization to the circumstance of the carbonized articles having been buried so many centuries. Hence, he thinks, that fire was no element in the destruction of Pompeii, though the immense masses of water always thrown up during such eruptions undoubtedly was.

With respect to the number of persons destroyed by the eruption no accurate and authentic calculation has been made, nor in fact can be made till the whole city shall have been uncovered. Even the number of bodies hitherto found in the process of excavation has not been satisfactorily ascertained ; but the frequency with which such discoveries are mentioned in the journals, and sometimes of thirty or forty bodies together, may justify the conclusion thet they amount

---

* *Epp.* iv. 44.   † *Pompeii.* B. i. § 29.

to 600 or 700. This inference is strengthened by the fact that in the small portion of the city uncovered since Fiorelli undertook the direction of the excavations in 1861, more than forty human skeletons have been found, besides those of horses, goats, dogs, and cats.* If, therefore, such discoveries should proceed in the same ratio, we may conclude—since only about one-third of the city has been disinterred—that some 2000 persons must have perished. A sufficiently terrible catastrophe! yet, at the same time, a result which shows that the great bulk of the population had sufficient warning and time to save their lives. The same conclusion may be drawn from the account of Pliny, as well as from the circumstance that though the people were assembled in the amphitheatre when the eruption broke out, but very few bodies have been found there; and even these, as Overbeck remarks, may, perhaps, have been those of gladiators already slain. The skeletons found are probably those of the sick, the infirm, and the irresolute; of those who mistakingly thought that they should find protection against the fatal shower in their houses or their cellars; or of those who, from motives of avarice, and sometimes, perhaps, of affection, lingered in search of their treasures or their beloved ones till there was no longer time to effect their escape.

That the eruption was accompanied with an earthquake may be inferred from the fact that some skeletons have been found of persons killed by the falling of ruins upon them. Thus, on the 14th of June, 1787, eight skeletons were discovered under the débris of a wall,† and on the 5th of May, 1818, were found in the Forum the bones of a man who had been crushed by a marble column falling upon him.‡

This earthquake may have contributed, as well as that of the year 63, to give the town that ruined appearance which is so observable. There can, however, be little doubt that this appearance was also partly caused by searches made after the catastrophe for hidden treasures, statues, marbles, &c. The light nature of the covering under which Pompeii was buried rendered this no difficult task. There are

---

* Overbeck, *Pompeii*, B. i. § 30.
† *Pomp. Ant. Hist.*, T. i. Fasc. ii. p. 37.
‡ *Ibid.* Fasc. iii. p. 203.

evident traces of such searches; and in no other way can we explain the comparative paucity of valuable articles that have been discovered, not only gold and silver, but also sculptures.

Such researches appear to have been carried on during a long period; since it is recorded of the Emperor Alexander Severus that he made Pompeii a sort of quarry, from which he drew a great quantity of marbles, columns, and beautiful statues, which he employed in adorning the edifices which he constructed at Rome.* The Emperor Titus appears to have entertained the idea of rebuilding the ruined cities of Campania;† a plan, however, which was never carried into execution, either on account of the death of that emperor, which shortly after supervened, or more probably, because it was found that the benefit to be derived from such a proceeding would be utterly inadequate to the expense of it.

During a period of 1669 years Pompeii remained buried and seemed entirely forgotten, notwithstanding that its site, probably ever since its destruction, had always borne the name of Cività, or the City. It is singular that it was not discovered sooner, for Dominico Fontana, an eminent architect of the sixteenth century, having been employed in the year 1592 to bring the waters of the Sarno to the town of Torre dell' Annunziata, cut a subterraneous canal under the site of Pompeii, which, entering the city near the Gate of the Sarno, traverses it in a winding direction, passing near the great theatre and under the Forum, till it makes its exit on the western side, a little to the north of the Sea Gate. In the course of this work the basements of buildings were often encountered; yet this circumstance does not seem to have awakened any curiosity, nor to have excited a desire to prosecute further researches. Ruins were also discovered in 1689, and even an inscription with the name of POMPEI; but these indications were disregarded like the former.

* Some buildings now completely excavated bear marks of having been previously searched by the ancients. In such places, all valuable effects and materials have been carried away, as, for instance, the columns of the portico of Eumachia, a building adjoining the Forum, to be described hereafter, and the furniture of the Basilica.

† Suet. *Tit.* 8.

At length, in 1748, in the reign of Charles III., the first Bourbon king of Naples, a Spanish colonel of engineers, named Don Rocco Alcubierre, was employed to examine the subterranean canal before mentioned; and having heard from the inhabitants of Torre Annunziata that the remains of a house, with ancient statues and other objects, had been discovered at a distance of about two miles, he was led to conjecture that some ancient city lay buried there, overwhelmed by the great eruption of Vesuvius in 79. The discovery of Herculaneum early in the 18th century had now drawn the attention of the learned and scientific world to this subject. Colonel Alcubierre obtained permission to undertake some excavations at the spot where the ruined house had been discovered, and early in April, 1748, he commenced his researches, in the street afterwards called the Strada della Fortuna. In a few days his labours were rewarded by the discovery of a picture 11 palms long by 4½ palms high, containing festoons of eggs, fruits, and flowers, the head of a man, large and in a good style, a helmet, an owl, various small birds, and other objects. A regular journal of the discoveries was kept, in Spanish, and was continued in that language down to the 7th of July, 1764, after which the Italian was substituted for it. On the 19th of April, 1748, the first skeleton was found, that of a man lying on the ashes, or *rapillo*, and covered with the lava mud. Near him were eighteen brass, and one silver coin.* Before the end of the year the amphitheatre was excavated, which is declared in the journal capable of holding 12,000 persons—an exaggeration of not more than 2000. It may be remarked that it is called in the journal the amphitheatre of *Stabiæ*.† For several years it was imagined that the remains discovered belonged to that town, which is now known to have occupied the site of the present Castellamare.

The name of *Pompeii* is first used in the journal, November 27th, 1756,‡ but it does not appear how the city came to be identified. Any doubts that might have been entertained upon the subject must however have been removed by the discovery, near the tomb of Mammia (August 20th, 1763), of the following inscription, recording the restoration by Ves-

* Fiorelli, *Pomp. Antiq. Hist.*, t. i. p. 2. † *Ibid.* p. 6.
‡ *Ibid.* p. 46.

pasian to the municipality of the Pompeians of all public ground occupied by private persons :—

> EX AVCTORITATE
> IMP CAESARIS
> VESPASIANI AVG
> LOCA PVBLICA A PRIVATIS
> POSSESSA T SVEDIVS CLEMENS
> TRIBVNVS CAVSIS COGNITIS ET
> MENSVRIS FACTIS REI
> PVBLICAE POMPEIANORVM
> RESTITVIT.*

The following account of the progress of the excavations is taken from an admirable article on Pompeii in the *Quarterly Review* for April, 1864.

"The excavations were carried on for many years on a very limited scale, and with very varying success. The workmen employed were chiefly condemned felons, who worked chained in pairs, and Mohammedan slaves taken from the Barbary pirates. The greatest secrecy was maintained, and no stranger could obtain admission to the ruins. No regular plan seems to have been made of the part of the town uncovered, nor was there any attempt to restore or keep up the buildings. The reports contain accurate descriptions of the discoveries—the statues, paintings on the walls, and the various objects in gold, silver, and other metals. Such things were diligently searched for, and were sent off to the royal collections as soon as discovered. Copies were taken of the most important paintings, which were then detached from the walls and transferred to the Museum, the edifices in which they were found being left to perish, or being again covered up with the rubbish removed from adjoining excavations."

The most important discoveries made during the remainder of the eighteenth century were, that called the Soldier's Quarters, close to the theatres, in December, 1766, and that of the suburban villa of Diomedes. The excavation of the latter was commenced in July, 1771; and such was at that time the dilatoriness of the operation, that it was not till

* Fiorelli, *Pomp. Antiq. Hist.*, t. i. p. 153.

December, 1772, that the corridor, or subterranean passage, containing a group of eighteen skeletons, was discovered. Indeed, during the sway of the Bourbon kings nothing was done in a liberal spirit or from a real love of art. The excavations were a mere source of jobbing and peculation; strangers who visited them were subjected to the most irksome regulations, as well as the demand of exorbitant fees; and it was only with the greatest difficulty and after wearisome delays that permission could be obtained to take a copy of any mosaic, fresco, or other object of interest that might have been discovered. The short period during which the French occupied Naples, beginning in January, 1806, forms an exception to the preceding remarks. During this period the greater portion of the Street of the Tombs, the Forum, and the line of walls were laid open, and the reclearing of the amphitheatre, which appears to have been again filled up, was begun. It was at this time that Mazois commenced his splendid work on Pompeii, under the patronage of Madame Murat, or Queen Caroline. Saliceti, the intelligent minister of Murat, appears to have given an impulse to the work of excavation, and undertook some *scavi* at his own expense.

After the restoration of the Bourbons the works were slowly continued; but it is to this period that several of the most interesting excavations must be referred; as those of several temples round the Forum, of the public baths, the house of the tragic poet, of the Fountain, of the Faun, the Fullonica, and many others which will be specified in the sequel. The revolution which drove the Bourbons from the throne had a great influence on the proceedings of Pompeii. When, in 1859, Garibaldi become dictator of Naples, he appointed the romance writer, M. Alexandre Dumas, director of the Museums and excavations. M. Dumas lived at Naples in princely magnificence; but he was totally unfit for the office assigned to him, and is said to have visited Pompeii only once. After the establishment of Victor Emmanuel's authority in the Neapolitan dominions, as king of Italy, the place of director of the *scavi* was bestowed on the Cavaliere Giuseppe Fiorelli, who had been long distinguished as a scholar and an antiquary, but whose liberal opinions had brought upon him the persecution of the Bourbon government. Respecting the reforms effected by this gentleman in the method of conducting the excavations, we cannot do better than transcribe the following passages from the article before mentioned in the *Quarterly Review*.*

"With the appointment of the Cavaliere Fiorelli a new era commenced at Pompeii. Hitherto the excavations had been carried on without definite or intelligible plan. The aim of those who directed them was to find as many objects of value as possible to add to the already magnificent collection in the Royal Museum. No very careful or accurate observations were consequently made whilst the earth and rubbish were being hastily and carelessly removed. Important and interesting facts were left unrecorded, and the means of restoring many of the architectural details of the buildings discovered were neglected. Signor Fiorelli had perceived how much could be done by removing the volcanic deposits with care, and upon a regular system, taking note of every appearance or fragment which might afford or suggest a restoration of any part of the buried edifices. The plan he pursues is this. The excavations are commenced by clearing away from the surface the vegetable mould, in which there are no remains. The volcanic substances, either *lapillo*, or hardened lava-mud, in which ruins of buildings may exist, are then very gradually removed. Every fragment of brickwork is kept in the place where it is found, and fixed there by props. When charred wood is discovered, it is replaced by fresh timber. By thus carefully retaining in its original position what still exists, and by replacing that which has perished, but has left its trace, Signor Fiorelli has been able to preserve and restore a large part of the upper portion of the buried houses.

"One of the first and most interesting results of the improved system upon which the excavations are thus carried on, has been the discovery and restoration of the second story of a Pompeian house, and especially of the *menianum*, a projecting gallery or balcony overhanging the street. This part of a Roman building, which is frequently represented in the wall-paintings, but the existence of which at Pompeii had been doubted or denied, was built of brick, and supported by strong wooden beams and props. The masonry is still in

* Page 329, seq.

many cases preserved; the carbonized wood had to be restored. Some of these galleries seem to have been entirely open, like a modern balcony, and as they are represented in the frescoes; others formed part of the upper chambers of the house, and were furnished with small windows, from which the inmates could see the passers-by. In the narrow streets of Pompeii, these projecting galleries must have approached so nearly as almost to exclude the rays of even the midsummer sun, and to throw a grateful shade below. The upper stories, which appear to have been sometimes more than one in number, were reached by stairs of brick or wood. Some of those in brick are still partly preserved. Those in wood have perished; but the holes for the beams are there, and the charred beams themselves can be renewed.

"By Signor Fiorelli's careful and ingenious restorations, we can now, for the first time, picture to ourselves the appearance of a Roman town. Previously we only had the bare walls, forming nothing but a collection of shapeless ruins. Had his plan been adopted from the commencement, had the position of every fragment been noted at the time of its discovery, and had the doors, windows, and other woodwork been restored by the process we shall describe, instead of wandering amidst a confused mass of crumbling walls, we should have found ourselves in a Roman town, the houses of which might still have almost harboured its population. As far as we can now judge, Pompeii must have nearly resembled in its principal features a modern eastern city. The outside of the houses gave but little promise of the beauty and richness of the inside. The sudden change from the naked brick walls facing the narrow street to the spacious courtyard, adorned with paintings, statues, and coloured stuccoes, ornamented with flower-beds and fountains, and surrounded by alcoves and porticoes, from which the burning rays of the sun were warded off by rich tapestries and embroidered hangings, will remind the eastern traveller of Damascus or Ispahan. The overhanging galleries, with the small latticed windows; the mean shops—mere recesses in the outer walls of the houses; the brick-built counter, with the earthen jars and pans let into it; the marble slabs, on which the tradesman exposed his wares and received his cash; the awning stretched across the street (the holes by which it was fastened are still visible); the caravanserai or khan, outside the city gate, with its many small rooms opening into a stable behind and a court-yard in front (the skeletons of horses and their metal trappings were found in the ruins of such an hostelry on the Herculean way), are all characteristic of a modern eastern town."

We shall conclude this account of the disinterment of Pompeii with a short general sketch of the progress of the excavations.* The amphitheatre was first partially excavated in 1748. Before the end of the last century, the quarter of the theatres, the Temple of Isis, and the northern portion of the town, from the Gate of Herculaneum to the first fountain, had been disinterred. During the first ten years of the present century the work proceeded very slowly; but the years from 1811 to 1824 were marked by considerable activity. In this period were excavated the Forum and the adjoining temples and houses, the whole of the amphitheatre, the Street of Abundance or of the Merchants, the old baths, the Temple of Fortune, the houses of Pansa, Sallust, &c. In 1825 was uncovered the insula adjoining the house of Pansa on the east, comprising the house of the tragic poet and the Fullonica. During the next five years the excavations were pursued in the Street of Mercury and its vicinity. The principal discoveries in this period were the houses of Meleager, of the Centaur, of Castor and Pollux, of Flora and Zephyrus, of the Anchor, and of the five skeletons.

The Street of Mercury having been cleared, though not all the adjoining buildings, excavations were begun in the autumn of 1830 in the street called the Strada della Fortuna, leading from the Temple of Fortune toward the Gate of Nola. The researches in this direction were rewarded before the end of the year by the discovery of the house of the Faun, one of the finest private houses in Pompeii, without excepting even that of Pansa. Behind it was excavated in 1832 the house of the Labyrinth. Further discoveries in this direction about this period were the houses of the Grand Duke of Tuscany, of the black walls, and of the figured capitals, on the south side of the Street of Fortune. Operations were also pursued in the Street of the Augustals. On

* See Aloe, *Ruines de Pompeii*, p. xlvii.

this side was discovered (1832—33) the House of the Coloured Capitals, better known as the House of Ariadne, adjoining the Vico Storto, and extending from the Street of the Augustals to that of Fortune. The Casa di Apollo, at the bottom of the Street of Mercury, 1835. In 1837 and following years, a good deal was done in the Street of the Tombs; but down to 1843 the excavations were principally continued in the northernmost part of the town, near the house of Apollo. In that and the following year the street which leads from the Porta Marina to the Forum, between the Basilica and Temple of Venus, was cleared. Subsequently, till 1851, the excavations were chiefly continued in the neighbourhood of the Forum and the Vico Storto. In 1847 was discovered the house of M. Lucretius, or of the Suonatrice. The excavations in this direction along the Street of Stabiæ were resumed in 1851, and continued during several subsequent years, as well as in the Street of Holconius, which leads out it to the Street of Abundance. The Porta Stabiana was discovered in 1851, and, soon after, the Stabian, or Great Baths. Since the appointment of the Commendatore to the direction of the works in 1860, operations have been chiefly carried on in the block of buildings formed by the Street of Holconius on the north, that of Isis on the south, that of the theatres on the west, and that of Stabiæ on the east; and the district lying to the north of this, and comprised between the Street of the Augustals, that of Abundance, the eastern side of the Forum, and the Street of Stabiæ. The researches in these two districts have been rewarded by many important discoveries. In the former have been excavated the house of Cornelius Rufus, and that commonly called the house of Holconius; while in the latter have been discovered the house of the Nuova Caccia, of the Balcone Pensile, of the New Fountain, the Lupanar, and other objects which we shall have occasion to mention in the sequel.

CHAPTER III.

POSITION OF POMPEII; ITS GENERAL APPEARANCE, ROADS, WALLS, GATES, STREETS, ETC.

POMPEII is situated on an isolated hill, or plateau, which rises in the plain at the southern foot of Mount Vesuvius. This hill, which is sufficiently marked in form, though of moderate size, must have been produced by a stream of lava thrown up by Vesuvius centuries before the foundation of the city, and in a period too remote for memory or record. On the western side of the town, or that facing the sea, the ascent is so abrupt and sudden as almost to resemble a cliff; whence some writers have been led to conclude that its walls on this side were originally washed by the sea. In support of this opinion it has been said that shells and sea sand have been found by digging on the side adjoining the coast; and it is even asserted that rings have been found close to the ruins, intended, as is supposed, for the mooring of vessels. The authority of Strabo, in a passage before quoted, has been adduced to confirm this view; but his words serve at least equally to prove that the trade of the place was carried on by the river Sarnus, which runs past it a little to the south. If so, however, this stream has shrunk among the other physical changes which have occurred in the country; for it is now nothing more than a rivulet, entirely unsuited to any purposes of trade.

Pompeii at present stands about a mile from the sea, and very strong arguments have been adduced to prove that it must have been at the same distance in ancient times. The writers who hold this opinion consider that the beds of shells and the rings said to have been found prove nothing. The shells may have existed there long before the foundation of Pompeii; and that the rings asserted to have been found, of which there are no longer any traces, served for the mooring of vessels, is a mere conjecture. On the other hand it is affirmed that graves have been found where the harbour must have existed; and Overbeck, one of the latest writers on the subject, says that he has not only found remains of ancient buildings several hundred paces on the other side of the railway to the south of Pompeii, but also that there exist, about half a mile south-west of it, at the mill near the bridge over the Sarno and the mouth of the caual which runs to Torre Annunziata, some very considerable remains of ancient foundations, cisterns, and amphoræ, built into the walls; nay, that these are even buried under *white lapilli*, or pumice stones, such as could have been thrown out only by the eruption of Vesuvius in A.D. 79.* Nor can it be said, that if the ground had the present configuration when Pompeii was founded, the city would have been built by preference closer to the sea. The hill was chosen as a stronger situation, as it would have given the command of the city to any inimical force that might have occupied it. Another argument may be adduced from the circumstance that Herculaneum, to the north of Pompeii, and Stabiæ (Castellamare), to the south, which were overwhelmed by the same eruption, still lie on the margin of the sea, showing that on both sides of Pompeii no alteration in the coast-line was produced by that catastrophe.

The situation of Pompeii appears to have possessed all local advantages that the most refined taste could desire. Upon the verge of the sea, at the entrance of a fertile plain, on the bank of a navigable river, it united the conveniences of a commercial town with the security of a military station and the romantic beauty of a spot celebrated in all ages for its pre-eminent loveliness. Its environs, even to the heights of Vesuvius, were covered with villas, and the coast, all the way to Naples, was so ornamented with gardens and villages, that the shores of the whole gulf appeared as one city; while the prodigious concourse of strangers who came here in search of health and recreation added new charms and life to the scene. But these advantages were dearly purchased. An enemy, at that time unknown, was silently working its destruction—an enemy which, from time to time, still desolates the modern towns which stand upon the buried and long-forgotten cities of antiquity.

* Overbeck, *Pompeii*, &c., B. i., § 13. Winckelmann, in his *Sendschreiben v. d. hercul. Entdeckungen*, § 17, doubted long ago that Pompeii was seated on the sea.

POSITION OF POMPEII.

The chief approach to Pompeii was on the north-west by the Via Domitiana, a branch of the great Appian Way, which, turning off at Sinuossa, ran along the coast from Naples, through Oplontis, Retina, and Herculaneum, entering Pompeii by the gate named after the latter city. A second road, issuing from the Gate of Nola, joined the Popilian Way at that place; while a third, from the Gate of Stabiæ, divided into two branches, one of which ran to the town of the same name, while the other led to Nuceria. These seem to have been the chief approaches, though of course there were roads leading to all the other gates.

The city was anciently surrounded with walls, of which the greater portion has been traced. Its general figure, as defined by them, is something like that of an egg, whose apex is at the amphitheatre. Its circuit is nearly two miles, the greatest length little more than three quarters of a mile, and the breadth less than half a mile. Even Arrius Diomedes, who lived at the extremity of the suburb, would only have had about six hundred yards to walk to the Forum for his business, and less than a mile to the amphitheatre for his pleasure. The area of the city is about one hundred and sixty-one acres; the excavated part, which lies on the western side, is rather more than a third of the whole, and has been one hundred and eighteen years in excavating; so that new discoveries may still await our great-grandsons.

The course of the walls has been traced and ascertained by excavation. From the Gate of Herculaneum they proceeded in an easterly direction to the amphitheatre, and thence along the south side of the city to the quarter of the theatres; but from this point, and along all the western side, they have been pulled down since ancient times, and their place has been occupied on the west by the large three-storied houses built in terrace fashion on the steep declivity of the hill. For the greater part of their circuit the walls are curvilinear, avoiding all sharp angles as much as possible, in accordance with the principle of fortification laid down by Vitruvius, that it is desirable to avoid sharp angles, as offering more protection to the besiegers than to the besieged.* On many

* Directly the reverse is recommended by Vegetius, who further advises that towers should be placed at the salient angles, for the advantage of taking the enemy in flank.

of the stones certain characters have been found, intended, apparently, as directions to the workmen, which are said by M. Mazois to be either Oscan or the most ancient forms of the Greek alphabet; whence some authorities have drawn the conclusion that the walls must be referred to a period antecedent to the Etruscan occupation of this part of Italy, and that they may probably be Pelasgic. Other writers again are of opinion that there are no grounds for referring them to so remote an age. They allow, indeed, that they must be of very considerable antiquity, and built in the times of Oscan independence, though they deny that the marks on the stones before alluded to bear any resemblance to the Oscan alphabet, and consider them to have been mere arbitrary marks of the stone-masons.* It should be observed, however, that the towers and some parts of the walls are of a much later age than the remainder. These, which are probably repairs of the damage inflicted by Sulla in the Social War, consist of what is called *opus incertum;* that is, stones, mostly tufo or lava, broken into small pieces, cemented with mortar, and covered with a coating of stucco, so as to resemble the primitive walls; as may still be observed in some places.

With the exception of these restored parts, the structure of the walls is similar throughout; and consists of large well-hewn pieces of stone—in the lower courses Travertine, in the upper Piperino. They are fitted together without mortar, and join one another vertically in a somewhat oblique direction, so that the surface of each stone is usually a rhomboid or trapezium.

Within this external wall, with towers at intervals, the usual defence of the most ancient Italian cities, there was thrown up an agger, or earthen mound, which Vitruvius considered, when properly combined with masonry, proof against the battering-ram, or mining, or any known method of assault. His directions for constructing it are as follows. A ditch is to be dug as large and deep as possible, the sides perpendicular and walled. The earth is heaped up on the inside, and supported both within and without by walls strong enough to bear its thrust, bonded together, for further

* Overbeck, *Pomp.* B. ii. § 50.

POSITION OF POMPEII.

security, by internal cross walls, between which the excavated material must be firmly rammed down, that it may still offer substantial resistance, even when the external masonry has been ruined. A considerable breadth is to be allowed for this raised platform, so that cohorts may have room to fight along its whole extent, as if ranged for battle.* The walls of Pompeii answer this description; but there is no outer ditch, and it is doubtful whether one ever existed, or whether it was filled up in later times. This construction, however, does not extend to the south side of the city, which was less exposed to the attack of military engines, and therefore required less strength. On the north and north-east, the ramparts of Pompeii, as shown in the annexed cut, consisted of an earthen terrace (B) fourteen feet wide, walled and counter-

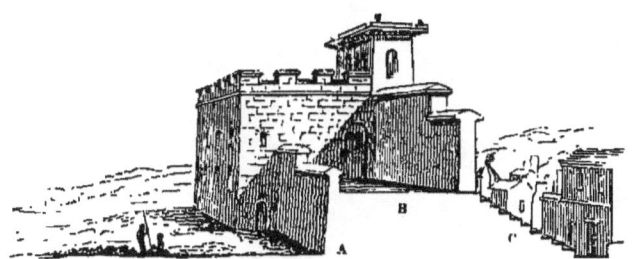

Restored section of the walls and agger of Pompeii.

walled, which was ascended from the city by flights of steps (c), broad enough for several men abreast. The external face (A), including the parapet, was about twenty-five feet high; the inner wall was raised some feet higher. The external wall is inclined slightly towards the city; the lower courses, instead of being inclined, are set slightly back, one behind another. The style of masonry we have already described.

Both walls were capped with battlements, so that from the country there was an appearance of a double line of defence, but the interior was useless except to give a more formidable aspect to the fortifications. These battlements were ingeniously contrived to defend the soldiers, who could throw their missiles through the embrasure in comparative safety,

* Vitruv. i. 5.

being protected by a return or shoulder of the battlement projecting inward. The towers, as we have said, are of less ancient date. They are quadrangular, contrary to the rule laid down by Vitruvius, who says that towers ought to be

Interior of the battlements restored.

circular or polygonal. "Square towers are sooner breached, because the battering-ram breaks their angles; round ones it cannot hurt, but merely drives the stones, which should be cut wedge-like, towards their common centre."* He also

* Vitruv. i. 5.

recommends that they should be placed at no greater intervals than the cast of a javelin, so as to give one another mutual support, and flank the enemy in case of assault. This principle has been adhered to between the Gate of Herculaneum and that of Vesuvius, where they are only eighty paces distant from each other, but towards the east the distance is two, three, and even four hundred and eighty paces. We may suppose, therefore, that the ground in this quarter presented some difficulty to the approach of machines. All of them have archways, allowing a free passage along the agger, and are furnished with a sallyport; all are alike, and each consists of several stories. The walls and towers are much

View of the wall and towers from without.

ruined. It is impossible to attribute this entirely to the earthquakes which preceded and accompanied the eruption of 79. The outer wall of the towers seems invariably to have fallen. Sir W. Gell conjectures that it was demolished by Sulla at the end of the Social War, as the readiest means of rendering the fortifications useless. Probably the place had been dismantled at different periods, as various breaches and repairs seem to indicate. For some time before its catastrophe, defences seem to have been thought unnecessary; for if they ever existed, as most likely they did, on the seaward side, they had been thrown down, and handsome houses, often four or five stories high, erected on their site. The long peace, which Italy enjoyed under Augustus and his immediate successors, rendered fortifications useless, and it is probable that during that period it became convenient to enlarge the city by destroying them. At all events it is certain that, in the later period of its existence, Pompeii was an open town.

The construction of the upper part of the walls, and the battlements of the ramparts, evince an improved knowledge in the science of building, and point out a period much more

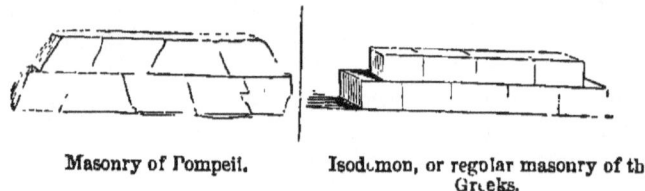

Masonry of Pompeii.   Isodomon, or regular masonry of the Greeks.

modern than that of the lower part; being composed of the isodomon, or regular masonry of the Greeks, above the more ancient basis. Some portions, however, of the upper wall consist, as we have already observed, of masonry of that

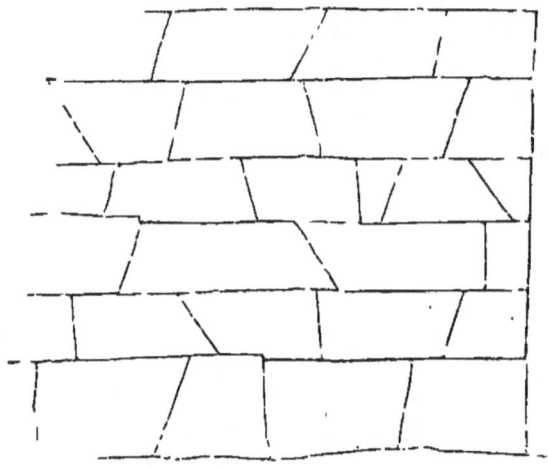

Greek wall, similar in construction to the walls of Pompeii.*

kind called by the ancients *opus incertum*, composed of small rough pieces, placed irregularly, and imbedded in a large quantity of mortar, resembling the flint and rubble masonry

* Dodwell's Travels in Greece.

POSITION OF POMPEII. 63

of our castles and churches. The difference of construction observable in the wall and towers shows that the latter are of much later date. This is what we should expect. The most ancient Greek fortifications, those of Tiryns and Mycenæ, are without towers;[*] in those more recent, as at Orchomenus and Daulis, towers occur, but at considerable distances, and of small elevation. It was not until a much later period that they were built at regular intervals, and of commanding height, as at Platæa, Messene, and other cities.[†]

There are seven gates in the length of wall which now exists, besides what is called the Porta della Marina, or Sea Gate, on the western side, now the principal entrance. They are all, except two, of Roman construction. The first and most important stood at the north-western angle of the city, and led to Herculaneum, whence it has been called the Herculaneum Gate. For about a furlong from the entrance the road is bordered with tombs, as is the Appian Way where it issues from Rome. The gate is double, so that when the first doors had been carried, the assailers could be attacked from a large opening above, and destroyed while attempting to force the second. Strong buttresses of stone sustain the lateral pressure of the earthen rampart, which is ascended from the interior by ten very high and inconvenient steps. This gate in its arrangement resembles Temple Bar: there is a large central and two small side entrances, which, instead of being open to the sky, like the central road, were vaulted through their whole length. The inner gate consisted of folding doors, as the holes in the pavement, in which the pivots turned which served for hinges, evidently show; the outer defence was formed by a portcullis. The archway is constructed in brick and lava, in alternate layers, and covered with a fine white stucco. This, although the principal entrance to the city, is not striking for its beauty, and is small in its dimensions. The stucco is covered with nearly illegible inscriptions of ordinances, &c. The centre archway is in width fourteen feet seven inches, and might, perhaps, have been eighteen or twenty feet in height; but its arch

[*] Except at Tiryns, where the gate is flanked by a solid tower; it is hardly more, however, than a projection in the wall. See the Ground Plan in Gell's 'Argolis.'
[†] Mazois.

Gate of Herculaneum.

does not remain. The smaller openings on each side for foot passengers were four feet six inches wide, and ten feet high; in size, therefore, it scarcely equals Temple Bar. The road rises considerably into the city. On the left, before entering the gate, is a pedestal, which appears to have been placed for the purpose of sustaining a colossal statue of bronze, some fragments of bronze drapery having been found there. We may suppose it to have been the tutelary deity of the city.*

Proceeding from the Gate of Herculaneum in an easterly direction round the walls, the remaining gates occur in the following order: the Gate of Vesuvius, the Gate of Capua, the Gate of Nola, the Gate of the Sarnus, the Gate of Nuceria, and the Gate of Stabiæ, or the Theatres. From this point, as we have said, the wall can no longer be traced; but there is, on the western side, an eighth entrance to the city, which has been called the Porta della Marina, or Sea Gate.

Of these gates, only those of Nola and of the Theatres need arrest our attention, as being evidently older than the rest, and previous to the Roman occupation. The gate of Nola has one or two remarkable peculiarities. It does not begin, like that of Herculaneum, at the outer line of wall, but beyond the inner, at the end of a passage formed by strong masonry, and not much broader than the entry of the door itself. Hence it resembles the Gate of the Lions at Mycenæ. It was double, like that of Herculaneum, but the outer gate has been destroyed, and the second is a reconstruction of the same date as the towers. The mode in which this gate is constructed afforded a great advantage to the garrison over their assailants, who could only approach it in slender columns, and exposed on each side to the arrows and javelins of the defenders. Another peculiarity in this gate is that it does not cut the wall at a right, but at an acute angle; as the wall at this part slants off in a southeasterly direction, whilst the street which leads to the gate runs nearly east.

Viewed from within, this gate displays two different constructions, part of it being of square blocks of hewn stone, and part, of a more recent date, of brick. The key-stone of the arch is adorned, according to Etruscan custom, with a

* Sir W. Gell, p. 93.

head in high relief, much damaged by the weather. If this keystone belonged to the original gate, which there seems no reasonable ground to doubt, it must be one of the oldest in Pompeii. The Oscan inscription beside it appears, however, not to be in its right place, and was probably placed there when the gate was restored. M. de Clarac * and others have translated this inscription as follows: "Caius Popirius, son of Caius, Medixtuticus, restored this gate and consecrated it to Isis;" an interpretation from which the gate has also sometimes obtained the appellation of the "Gate of Isis." But this important and somewhat ludicrous error arose from a mistranslation of the last two words, *isidu pruphatted,* which have no relation to Isis. The whole translation ought to run: "Vibius Popidius, son of Vibius, Medixtuticus, caused this (building) to be erected, and the same approved it."†

The gate near the Theatres, called the Gate of Stabiæ, was discovered in 1851. The walls which flank it are of very ancient construction, being built of large square blocks of hewn stone, put together without mortar. This gate was not closed by a portcullis, but by strong double doors, as is plain from the holes for the bolts. An Oscan inscription, found on a square stone of travertine in this gateway, conveys some important information about Pompeian topography. It has been interpreted as follows by the Commendatore Quaranta:—

> P. SITTIUS M. F. N. PONTIUS P. F.
> ÆDILES HANC VIAM TERMINA
> VERUNT ANTE PORTAM STABIA
> NAM VIÆ TERMINUM STATUERUNT PED
> X. IPSI VIAM POMPEIANAM TERMINA
> VERUNT PEDES III. ANTE CA
> LAM JOVIS MEILICHII HAS VI
> AS ET VIAM JOVIAM ET DECUMANAM VIA
> RUM CURATORES A POMPEIANIS
> SERVIS FIERI FECERUNT IP
> SI ÆDILES PROBAVERUNT.

That is: The Ædiles, Publius Sittius, son of Marcus, and Numerius Pontius, son of Publius, laid down the limits of this street, and fixed the terminus of it ten feet beyond the

* *Pompeii,* 8vo, 1813.   † Overbeck, B. i. S. 57.

Stabian Gate. They also fixed the limits of the Via Pompeiana three feet before the enclosure of Jupiter Meilichius. These streets, as well as the Jovia and Decumana, were constructed by the public slaves of Pompeii, under the direction of the surveyors of the streets, and the same ædiles approved. of them.

From this we learn that the gate we are treating of bore in ancient times the name of Stabiana, and that there were three streets, named respectively, Pompeiana, Jovia, and Decumana, which, or at all events some of them, probably led to gates of the same name. We learn also that Jupiter Meilichius had a temple in Pompeii.

The Porta della Marina, or Sea Gate, consists of a long vaulted passage, through which a steep and narrow ascent leads towards the Forum. For the convenience of foot-passengers, an elevated footway, ascended by steps, ran along the left-hand side of it. On the other side are some ancient buildings, which are being converted into a local museum.

We will now proceed to describe the general aspect of the city, and for this purpose it will be convenient to suppose that we have entered it by the gate of Herculaneum, though in other respects the Porta della Marina is the more usual, and, perhaps, the best entrance.

On entering, the visitor finds himself in a street, running a little east of south, which leads to the Forum. To the right, stands a house formerly owned by a musician; to the left, a thermopolium or shop for hot drinks; beyond is the house of the Vestals; beyond this the custom-house; and a little further on, where another street runs into this one from the north at a very acute angle, stands a public fountain. In the last-named street is a surgeon's house; at least one so named from the quantity of surgical instruments found in it, all made of bronze. On the right or western side of the street, by which we entered, the houses, as we have said, are built on the declivity of a rock, and are several stories high.

The fountain is about one hundred and fifty yards from the city gate. About the same distance, further on, the street divides into two; the right-hand turning seems a by-street, the left-hand turning conducts you to the Forum. The most important feature in this space is a house called the house of Sallust or of Actæon, from a painting in it representing that hunter's death. It stands on an area about forty yards square, and is encompassed on three sides by streets; by that namely which we have been describing, by another nearly parallel to it, and by a third, perpendicular to these two. The whole quarter at present excavated, as far as the Street of the Baths, continued by the Street of Fortune, is divided, by six longitudinal and one transverse street, into what the Romans called islands, or insulated masses of houses. Two of these are entirely occupied by the houses of Pansa and of the Faun, which, with their courts and gardens, are about one hundred yards long by forty wide.

From the Street of the Baths and that of Fortune, which bound these islands on the south, two streets lead to the two corners of the Forum; between them are baths, occupying nearly the whole island. Among other buildings are a milk-shop and gladiatorial school. At the north-east corner of the Forum was a triumphal arch. At the end of the Street of the Baths and beginning of that of Fortune, another triumphal arch is still to be made out, spanning the street of Mercury, so that this was plainly the way of state into the city. The Forum is distant from the gate of Herculaneum about four hundred yards. Of it we shall give a full description in its place. Near the south-eastern corner two streets enter it, one running to the south, the other to the east. We will follow the former for about eighty yards, when it turns eastward for two hundred yards, and conducts us to the quarter of the theatres. The other street, which runs eastward from the Forum, is of more importance, and is called the Street of the Silversmiths;* at the end of which a short street turns southwards, and meets the other route to the theatres. On both these routes the houses immediately bordering on the streets are cleared; but between them is a large rectangular plot of unexplored ground. Two very elegant houses at the south-west corner of the Forum were uncovered by the French general Championnet, while in command at Naples, and are known by his name. On the western side of the Forum two streets led down towards the sea: the excavations here consist almost entirely of public buildings, which will be described hereafter.

* Now the Street of Abundance.

The quarter of the theatres comprises a large temple, called the Temple of Neptune or Hercules, a temple of Isis, a temple of Æsculapius, two theatres, the Triangular Forum, and the quarters of the soldiers or gladiators. On the north and east it is bounded by streets; to the south and west it seems to have been enclosed partly by the town walls, partly by its own. Here the continuous excavation ends, and we must cross vineyards to the amphitheatre, distant from the theatre about five hundred and fifty yards, in the south-east corner of the city, close to the walls, and in an angle formed by them. Close to the amphitheatre are traces of walls supposed to have belonged to a Forum Boarium, or cattle market. Near at hand, a considerable building, called the villa of Julia Felix, has been excavated and filled up again (1756). On the walls of it was discovered the following inscription, which may serve to convey an idea of the wealth of some of the Pompeian proprietors :—

IN PRAEDIS JULIÆ SP. F. FELICIS
LOCANTUR
BALNEUM VENERIUM ET NONGENTUM TABERNÆ PERGULÆ
CŒNACULA EX IDIBUS AUG PRIMIS
IN IDUS AUG. SEXTUS ANNOS CONTINUOS QUINQUE
S. Q. D. L. E. N. C.*

That is: on the estate of Julia Felix, daughter of Spurius, are to be let a bath, a venereum,† nine hundred shops, with booths ‡ and garrets, for a term of five continuous years, from the first to the sixth of the Ides of August. The formula, S. Q. D. L. E. N. C., with which the advertisement concludes, is thought to stand for—si quis domi lenocinium exerceat ne conducito : let no one apply who keeps a brothel.

A little to the south of the smaller theatre was discovered, in 1851, the Gate of Stabiæ, which we have already described. Hence a long straight street, which has been called the Street of Stabiæ, traversed the whole breadth of the city, till it issued out on the northern side at the gate of Vesuvius. It

---

* *Pomp. Ant. Hist.* t. i. p. 38.

† A venereum was that part of a house appropriated to the female members of a family.

‡ The meaning of *pergulæ* is not clearly ascertained. It probably denotes some kind of open workshop.

has been cleared to the point where it intersects the Streets of Fortune and of Nola, which, with the Street of the Baths, traverse the city in its length. The Street of Stabiæ forms the boundary of the excavations; all that part of Pompeii which lies to the east of it, with the exception of the amphitheatre, and the line forming the Street of Nola, being still occupied by vineyards and cultivated fields. On the other hand, that part of the city lying to the west of it has been for the most part disinterred; though there are still some portions lying to the south and west of the Street of Abundance and the Forum, and to the east of the Vico Storto, which remain to be excavated.

The streets of Pompeii are paved with large irregular pieces of lava joined neatly together, in which the chariot wheels have worn ruts, still discernible; in some places they are an inch and a half deep, and in the narrow streets follow one track; where the streets are wider, the ruts are more numerous and irregular, as shown in the annexed illustration, presenting a fac-simile of the pavement. In those places

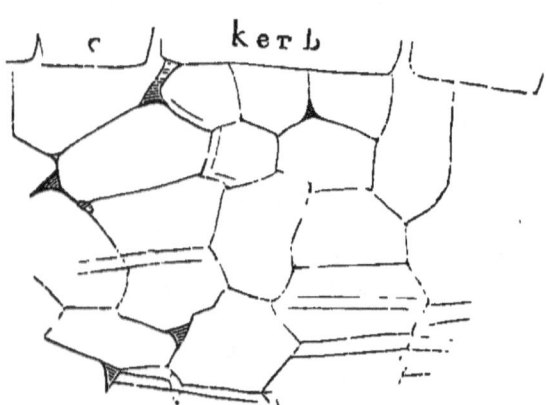

Plan of the pavement, showing the ruts, &c.

where several pieces of lava met in one point, and where, in process of time, a hole was made, the ancients have repaired the injury with pieces of iron, which still remain in the angles. This method has generally been adopted throughout the city. The width of the streets varies from eight or nine feet to about twenty-two, including the footpaths or trottoirs. In many places they are so narrow that they may be crossed at one stride : where they are wider, a raised stepping-stone, and sometimes two or three, have been placed in the centre of the crossing. These stones, though in the middle of the carriage way, did not much inconvenience those who drove about in the biga, or two-horsed chariot, as the wheels passed freely in the spaces left, while the horses, being loosely harnessed, might either have stepped over the stones or passed by the sides. The kerb-stones are elevated from one foot to eighteen

Biga.

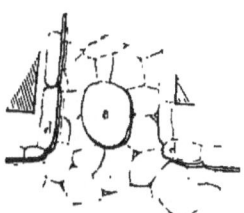

Plan of the stepping-stone in the narrow street.

a, Stepping stone ; *d*, Kerb.

inches, and separate the foot-pavement from the road. Throughout the city there is hardly a street unfurnished with this convenience. Where there is width to admit of a broad foot-path, the interval between the curb and the line of building is filled up with earth, which has then been covered over with stucco, and sometimes with a coarse mosaic of brickwork. Here and there traces of this sort of pavement still remain, especially in those streets which were protected by porticoes.

The area of the Forum or principal square was not paved like the streets, but was covered with large regular slabs of marble. These were joined together and laid with great accuracy; but they appear to have been stripped off in ancient times, and only a little remains of them on the east side, near the temple of Jupiter.

Before describing the Forum, we will add a few notices with respect to the external appearance of the houses and the aspect of the streets. Except in those quarters where the public buildings were collected and grouped together, there can have been nothing striking or magnificent in the appearance of the place. The houses were of small height, and externally gloomy; the lower part being usually a blank wall, plastered over, and often painted with different colours; the upper pierced with small windows to light the apartments on the first floor. Such is the exterior of which we now give a portion: it is taken from the house known by the name of the House of the Tragic Poet, and represents the outer wall, with a small window which lighted a room called the

One of the windows of the House of the Tragic Poet.

library, opening to the peristyle. The windows (for it forms one of a range of windows on the same level) are six feet six inches above the foot-pavement, which is raised one foot seven inches above the centre of the street. They are small, being scarcely three feet high by two. At the side a wooden frame is to be observed, in which the window, if the aperture were glazed, or if not, a shutter might at pleasure be moved backwards and forwards. The lower part of the

POSITION OF POMPEII.

wall is occupied by a range of red panels four feet and a half high. The tiling upon the wall is modern, and merely intended to preserve it from the action of weather. Our view is taken from the alley between this house and the house of Pansa. The alley is only fifteen feet wide, of which space one half is occupied by footpaths, leaving but seven feet six inches for the carriage-way. Expense and ornament were reserved for the interior, on which they were profusely lavished: not a house yet found in Pompeii has any pretension to architectural merit on the score of its elevation; not a house yet found is ornamented with a portico. The villa of Diomedes possesses a porch, formed by one detached column on each side of the doorway, and this is the only approximation to a portico in the place. The annexed view (p. 73), taken in the Street of Mercury, will give a better idea than a long description could of the general appearance of the disinterred city.* This is one of the widest streets in the place, and the scantiness of its proportions, as compared with the streets of modern Europe, may be estimated by comparing the breadth of the opening with the height of the shattered walls on either side. The street is that laid down in the plan as the fourth eastward from the Gate of Herculaneum, and does not exceed thirty feet in width. The view is taken near the city wall, looking southward along the street towards the Forum. In the middle distance is the triumphal arch adjoining the house of Zephyrus and Flora, through which is faintly seen the second triumphal arch at the entrance of the Forum. The first house on the left, a part of which only is included, is that hereafter to be described as the House of the Quæstor, otherwise called the House of the Dioscuri, or sons of Jupiter, Castor and Pollux. Beyond it are the indications of a cross street on each side of the main one. In the distance is Mount Lactarius. The name of the street was derived from a painting on one of the houses of Mercury bearing a purse, as in the annexed cut.

The street running from the Temple of Fortune to the Forum, called the Street of the Forum, and forming a cou-

* This view, together with some others which will occur in the course of the volume, is copied, by permission of the publishers, from the second series of Sir William Gell's Pompeiana. At present, however, the prospect is somewhat altered, owing principally to the disappearance of the trees.

tinuation of that of Mercury, has furnished an unusually rich harvest of various utensils. A long list of these is given by Sir W. Gell, according to which there were found no less

Vignette of Mercury.

than two hundred and fifty small bottles of inferior glass, with numerous other articles of the same material, which it would be tedious to particularise.

A marble statue of a laughing faun, two bronze figures of Mercury, the one three inches and the other four inches high, and a statue of a female nine inches high, were also found, together with many bronze lamps and stands. We may add vases, basins with handles, pateræ, bells, elastic springs, hinges, buckles for harness, a lock, an inkstand, and a strigil; gold earrings and a silver spoon; an oval cauldron, a saucepan, a mould for pastry, and a weight of alabaster used in spinning, with its ivory axis remaining. The catalogue finishes with a leaden weight, forty-nine lamps of common clay ornamented with masks and animals, forty-five lamps for two wicks, three boxes with a slit to keep money in, in one of which were found thirteen coins of Titus, Vespasian, and Domitian. Among the most curious things discovered, were seven glazed plates found packed in straw. There were also seventeen unvarnished vases of terra-cotta and seven clay dishes, and a large pestle and mortar. The scales and steelyard which we have given are said to have been found at the

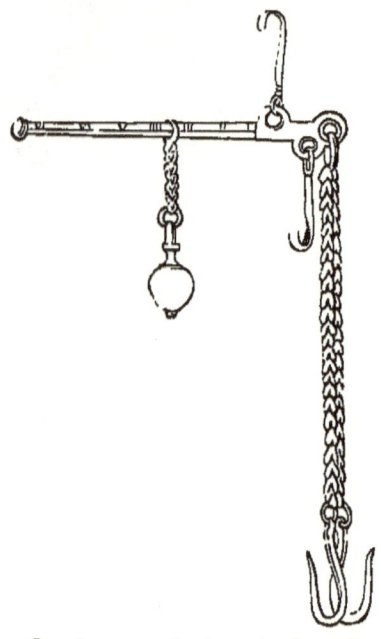

same time. On the beam of the steelyard are Roman numerals from X. to XXXX.; a V was placed for division between each X.; smaller divisions are also marked. The inscription is

IMP. VESP. AVG. IIX.
T. IMP. AVG. F. VI. C.
EXACTA. IN. CAPITO.

which is translated thus :—" In the eighth consulate of Vespasian Emperor Augustus, and in the sixth of Titus, Emperor and son of Augustus. Proved in the Capitol." This shows the great care taken to enforce a strict uniformity in the weights and measures used throughout the empire; the date corresponds with the year 77 of our era, only two years previous to the great eruption. The steelyard found was also furnished with chains and hooks, and with numbers up to

XXX. Another pair of scales (p. 78) had two cups, with a weight on the side opposite to the material weighed, to mark

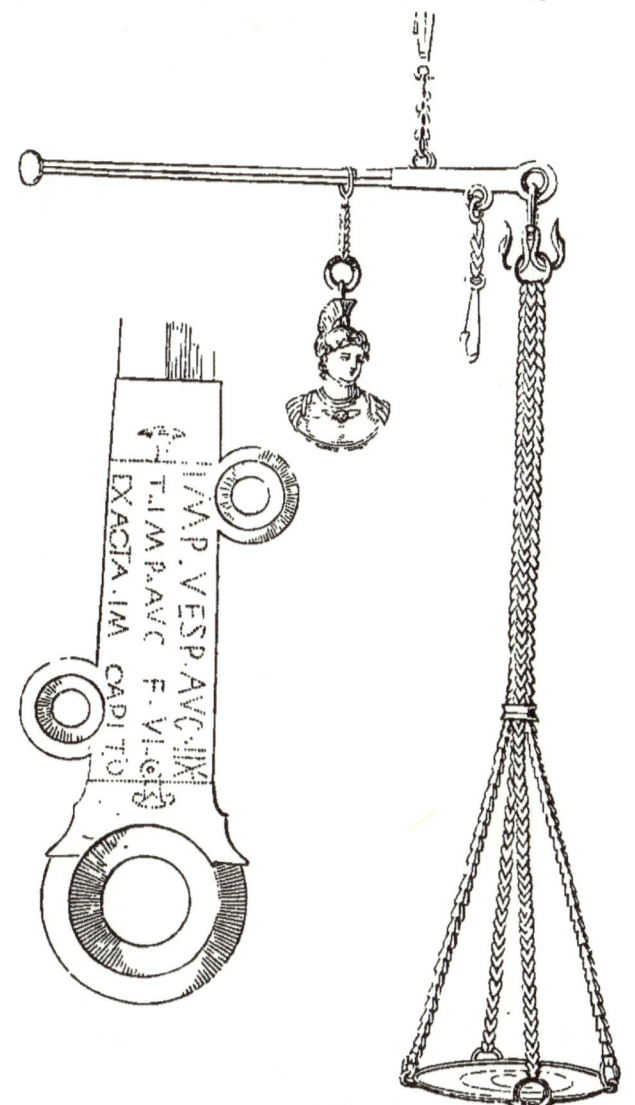

Steelyard, called Trutina Campana, with part of the beam and inscription on a larger scale.

more accurately the fractional weight; this weight was called by the ancients κάνων, ligula, and examen.

78   POMPEII.

Gell tells us that the skeleton of a Pompeian was found here, "who apparently, for the sake of sixty coins, a small plate and a saucepan of silver, had remained in his house till the street was already half filled with volcanic matter." He was found as if in the act of escaping from his window. Two others were found in the same street.

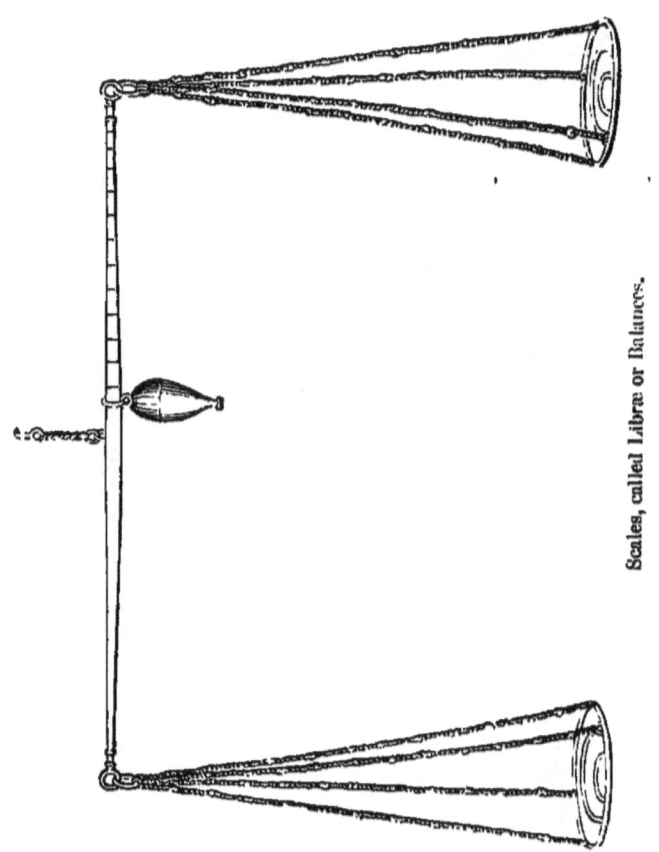

Scales, called Libræ or Balances.

One of the broadest and most regularly built streets in Pompeii is that called the Street of Abundance or of the Silversmiths, from articles of jewellery having been found in some of the shops. These are constructed of masonry, neatly executed, and ornamented with elegant pilasters. Pilasters also flank the doorways. The style of domestic architecture observable in this street is purely Grecian. The entablature is adorned with dentils, or small oblong blocks, placed at intervals on a horizontal line immediately under the cornice: these dentils were formed originally by the projecting beams which supported the roof and floor of any building. The most singular part of the construction of the houses in this street arises from the courses of masonry and the mouldings being inclined with the very gentle slope of the street. This singularity has hitherto escaped the notice of the numerous writers on the antiquities of Pompeii. This method appears to have been adopted to avoid breaking the horizontal lines of the architecture, and thus ruining the uniformity of the street. The inclination of the ground fortunately is very slight, or the expedient, which is we believe unique, could not have been adopted. The carriage-way up to the Forum is interrupted by the platform under the colonnade being raised one step. The street was supplied with water from two fountains, a luxury so common in Pompeii that there is hardly a street without one. They were generally ornamented, and kept constantly supplied from a large reservoir placed near them. One of these fountains, ornamented with the figure of Plenty, with the cornucopia, has caused the street to be called the Street of Abundance. In the passage of one of the houses in this street there was a coarsely executed painting of the twelve principal gods and goddesses, and also a representation of what may be presumed to be Pluto, drawn with black colour on the wall by some indifferent artist; this latter is not unlike the modern vulgar notion of the devil, a fierce black-looking fellow, with horns and cloven feet. The names of the owners are written on their houses. One, belonging to Vettius, has the following inscription,

∧ ⌣ ∨L I J ↳O ·I∨
AEDILIS·FAMILIA·CLADIATORIA·POMPEII
PR·K·IVNIAS·VENATIO·ES·VELA·ERVNT
VETTIVM·AED
Fac-simile inscription on the walls.

painted over another still older and illegible, in the peculiar careless character then in use. The upper line is part of the older inscription. They were usually done in black or red; some were merely scratched on the wall. The album of the Latins (λεύκωμα of the Greeks) is often to be met with on the external walls of the houses of Pompeii, exactly as Suidas describes it; that is to say, a piece of the wall whitened, in order to receive inscriptions. Sometimes the taste of the inscriber led him to enclose this album or whitened wall with a border, in the form of the ancient tabellum or tablet used to write on. One of these inscriptions runs thus:—

MARCUM. CERRINIUM. VATIAM. ÆDILEM. ORAT. UT. FAVEAT. SCRIBA. ISSUS: DIGNUS. EST.

Fac-simile inscription.

Which may be translated—"The scribe Issus beseeches Marcus Cerrinius Vatia, the Ædile, to patronize him: he is deserving."* Faventinus, most probably another scribe patro-

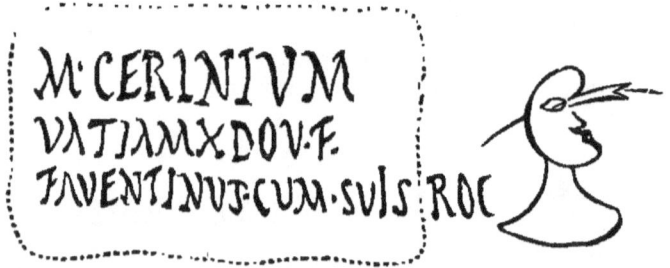

Fac-simile.

* It has lately been discovered, from some specimens written in full, that the letters OF, or OVF, mean *orat vos faciatis*. The translation therefore is: "The scribe Issus beseeches you to make M. C. Vatia ædile; he is deserving." Overbeck, B. ii. S. 94 ff. Ed.

nised by the same Ædile, gives a portrait of himself with his pen behind his ear. At the furthest end of this street was discovered a skeleton, supposed to have been that of a priest of Isis. It was covered with pumice-stones, and other volcanic matter. In the hand * was a bag of coarse linen, not entirely destroyed, containing three hundred and sixty silver coins, forty-two of copper, and six of gold; and near him several figures belonging to the worship of Isis, small silver forks, cups, pateræ in gold and silver, a cameo representing a satyr striking a tambourine, rings set with stones, and vases of copper and bronze.

The general narrowness of the streets, however repugnant to our notions of beauty, comfort, and salubrity, is by no means peculiarly the reproach of Pompeii, but common to the Italian cities of the age in which it perished. Nor, indeed, was that narrowness generally considered a blemish; for when Rome was burnt during the reign of Nero, and the emperor caused it to be rebuilt with more ample streets, persons were not wanting to say that "the ancient form of the city was more healthy, because the narrowness of the streets and height of the houses afforded little access to the sun's rays; henceforward the extent of opening, unprotected by shade, would burn with more distressing heat."† Similar croakers probably were not wanting to complain of the changes in building introduced after the fire of London; though our northern climate does not offer such plausible objections to the free admission of light and air as were to be derived from the torrid sun of Italy. At Pompeii several streets were not broad enough to allow two chariots to pass, small as they were, and not exceeding four feet in width. Wheel carriages indeed we conjecture to have been little used, except for purposes of traffic, from two circumstances: first, that when Mazois published his work in 1824, only two stables had been found,‡ and those, he says, seem meant for mules or asses rather than horses; and we know that the former animals were employed to turn corn-mills: secondly, that the whole arrangement of the pavement seems meant for the accommodation of foot-passengers. This inference is especially supported by the numerous stepping-stones placed

* The hand, with the cloth, is now in the Museum at Naples.
† Tacit. Ann. xv. 43. ‡ Mazois part. ii. p. 36.

in the centre of streets, to facilitate crossing from one raised footpath to the other;* a convenience of no small importance where there were no sunk gutters, and where, during the heavy winter rains, the carriage-way of those streets, which, according to the drainage of the ground, carried off the waters of three or four others, must have flowed like a torrent or a Welsh cross-road. It should be observed that nearly all the streets are straight, and generally intersect one another at right angles. The principal exception is the Vieo Starto, leading from the Street of Fortune to the Street of the Augustals. The southernmost portion of the street leading from the Gate of Herculaneum is also somewhat crooked.

Of the method in which the town was drained, and the numberless impurities of civilized life carried off, little is known, and it will be a curious subject for the investigation of future inquirers. At Rome, as is universally known, there were enormous sewers under-running the whole city—into which, as into our own sewers, there were openings from the streets—works whose grandeur in design and execution, combined with their remote antiquity, has fixed the admiration of all ages. Nothing of this description was to be expected in a provincial town like Pompeii; but for a long time no vestiges of any precautions to prevent the waters from stagnating in all the lowest parts of the city, except where they could find a passage under the gates, were discovered. At last Mazois, having long directed his attention to this point, thought, that in the slope of the streets and in the appearance of the pavement he perceived some reason to suppose that there must have existed sewers to convey rain water without the city; and, after much ineffectual search, at length succeeded in discovering one, of which he has given a drawing. His description is not very precise or satisfactory, and therefore, before attempting to explain the view, we will translate his words as literally as possible: "I have here represented one of the principal sewers (égouts) of the city. The drainage of several streets converging to this point, there were opened for it two passages communicating with an aqueduct, which after traversing the thickness of the city walls and agger, discharged the rain waters from the top of the walls

---

* See the woodcuts, p. 71.

along the rocks, whence they ran into the sea on the side of the port."* In the view here given the covered sewer seems, from the remains of walls, to lead directly under a house; but the locality is not specified, and we cannot tell how far this spot is from the city walls. The term aqueduct is improperly applied, as it is never, we believe, used to signify a channel to carry off waste water. That here described must,

View of a Sewer in the city of Pompeii.

of course, have been below the level of the ground, since the water from the street flowed into it. It seems natural to suppose that it was a real sewer, not such as those of Tarquin, into which a waggon loaded with hay might drive, but constructed rather as we construct our own, and probably communicating with the houses under which it passed. It is inconceivable that there should not have been some such convenience to carry off not merely the grosser dirt, but the fountain waters so profusely supplied. Several similar emissories have been observed in different parts of the town, passing, as this does, beneath the footway, and probably

* Mazois, part ii. p. 99.

under the houses. Mazois mentions having seen, by the side of a fountain at one of the entrances to the Forum, a drain leading to a sewer below, closed by an iron grate in good preservation.* The mouth of a similar sewer was found at the outside of the gate leading to Nola. Mazois seems to imagine that it was merely a channel commencing just within the gate, and meant to draw off the rain waters which ran down the street before they reached the outside, where the descent is very steep, and the ascent difficult, even when not impeded by a violent rush of water.†

Manner of carrying the Amphora.

Throughout the streets numerous signs are to be seen upon the shops, indicative of the trades which were pursued within; a trivial circumstance, yet one which, from its very insignificance, often catches the attention, and seems an earnest to the visitor that he is here in truth to be introduced to the usages of private and humble life, not merely led the round of theatres, temples, and all the costly monuments of public magnificence. The annexed cut, from a terra-cotta bas-relief, representing two men carrying an amphora, probably served as the sign of a wine shop. Another, found upon a shop which belonged to the baths, represents a goat, and is said, we know not with how much propriety, to have denoted that the owner was a milkman. Both these signs were made of baked clay, and coloured; and they were formed in a mould, which seems a proof of their common

* Mazois, part ii. p. 36   † Ibid. part i. p. 53.

recurrence, and therefore furnishes some reason to suppose that they were emblems of some trade, not merely ensigns assumed at the whim of a tradesman. Near the Gate of Herculaneum was a large statue of Priapus, supposed to have indicated the shop of an amulet maker. The protecting care which that deity exercised, not only over gardens but over the human frame, is notorious, and his image was constantly worn as a charm to keep off the evil eye. The establishment of a fencing master, or keeper of gladiators, is

Bas-relief of a Goat over a Milk-shop.

marked by a rude painting of two persons fighting, while the master looks on, holding a laurel crown; this is in the island of the baths, opposite the west end of the Forum. In the recently discovered Street of the Lupanar an inn was denoted by the painted sign of an elephant. The catalogue may be closed with a painting of one boy horsed on another's back, undergoing a flagellation; an ominous indication to truants and idlers that the schoolmaster was at home.

Fountains were numerous both in the streets and houses of Pompeii, but it is not known by what means the city was so profusely supplied with water. Being situated on a rock of lava, no springs of course could be found, and the inhabitants must have been completely dependent upon supplies brought from a distance.* Whence they came is unknown:

* There is a remarkable exception to this observation in a house adjoining the Pantheon, behind the Senaculum, where a well has been sunk through the solid rock to a depth of 116 feet. The water is remarkably cold and slightly brackish.—Gell. Another well, upwards of 80 feet deep, and still furnishing a supply of fresh water, was discovered in 1864, in the house of the dealer in marbles, in the Vico Storto.

the skirts of Vesuvius, the nearest mountain, were not likely to abound in streams, and it seems more likely that they were derived from the distant Mount Lactarius, which overhung Stabiæ.

Traces of aqueducts, however, still remain in the neighbourhood, by which the city may have been supplied from the mountains behind Vesuvius. Nothing certain is yet ascertained on this subject: the probable means have been enumerated by Sir W. Gell. "The calcareous mountains behind Sarno and Palma furnish beautiful and copious sources throughout their whole extent. The modern watercourse, which some say exhibits traces of the ancient opus reticulatum, is certainly too low for any but the parts of the city on the shore (marina), but the great rapidity of its current shows that a much higher level might have been preserved. There can be no doubt, however, that, setting aside the three beautiful springs at the town of Sarno, a third to the north of them exists, and there was an aqueduct which conveyed the water from the neighbourhood of Palma and Sarno, over the plain and by the Ponte Rossi at Naples, to Pausilippo, and that another branch ran to Cumæ and to Baiæ, and all the volcanic parts of the country; and the Cav. Carelli will probably give an account of it. Some of the arches of the aqueduct may be seen not far from Palma, and the place is called Arci, from the ruined arches. This is at a much higher level than Sarno, and hence a branch ran across the plain, towards Vesuvius and Pompeii. which will probably be discovered at a future period, entering the gate called that of Vesuvius, at the highest part of Pompeii. The Canonico Iorio has preserved a remarkable passage, written in the year 1560, by Antonio Lettici, who had passed four years in examining the subject of the sources near Palma and Sarno, for the purpose of forming the modern aqueduct. Speaking of the aqueducts at Arci and Torricelli, he says a branch ran to the ancient town of Pompeii on a height opposite to the town of Torre della Nunziata, " et in detto locho ne appareno multi vestigii." He even says that the ancient aqueducts might be repaired.* It is evident, from its numerous fountains, that Pompeii, in proportion to its size, must have been amply supplied with water, which was

* Gell, Appendix to second series.

POSITION OF POMPEII.   87

distributed to its different quarters by conduits, in masonry, lead, or baked earthen pipes. Leaden pipes, as we must conclude from the number of them found, were almost universally used to fit up the fountains, which have very little of ornament about them, and consist mostly of the head of a man or animal, from whose mouth a stream of water pours into a basin below. The section of one will give a sufficient notion of the construction of all. *a a* is the feeding pipe;

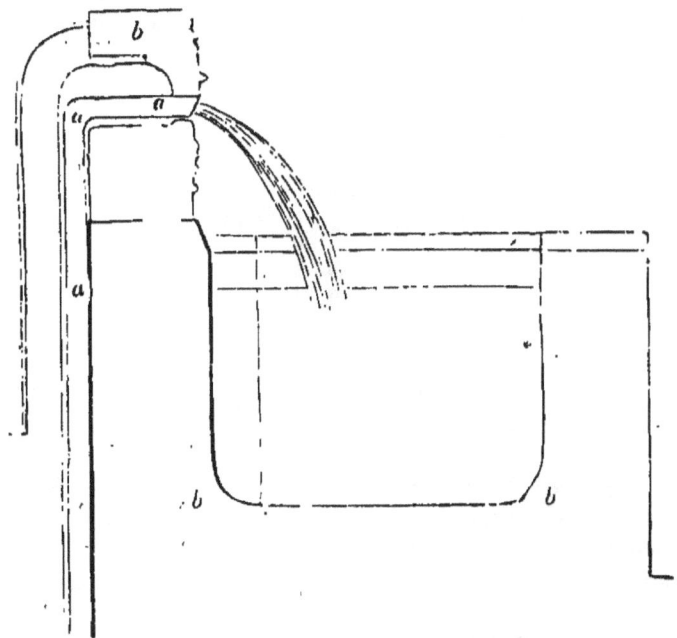

Section of one of the numerous Public Fountains discovered in the Streets of Pompeii.

b, the basin which received the water, made of blocks of travertine cramped together with iron. The projections above and below the orifice of the pipe represent rudely the profile of a faun's head with long flowing moustaches and ass's ears, through whose mouth the water issues. This fountain stands in front of the colonnade or propylæum which gives entrance to the triangular Forum, and the Greek temple.

The ancients were acquainted with that hydrostatical law by which water flowing in a pipe ascends to the level of its source; and it appears further, that they were acquainted with that extension of the law, by which fluids may be made to ascend in a vertical jet to a height proportionate to the pressure which acts upon them. Several fountains, which appear to have been fitted up with jets d'eau, have been found in the houses; and the question, if any doubts were entertained, appears to be decided by a picture found in Pompeii, representing a broad vase with a jet of water rising from the centre. In the original it is surrounded by a railing, which is omitted here. The background is red, the railing and wall beneath it yellow, and the vase and pe-

Jet d'eau; from the arabesque paintings of Pompeii.

destal rise out of a sheet of water. The picture has every appearance of representing the interior of an impluvium, guarded by a low open railing.

Annexed is a view of one of the public fountains which stands *in biviis*, that is, at the point of division between two diverging streets not far from the Gate of Herculaneum. Behind it is a square building, called by Mazois its castellum, or reservoir. There is some difficulty, as it appears to us, in acceding to this, for there is a door in the shaded side of the building (scarcely visible in our engraving), the bottom of which is hardly as high as the orifice of the fountain itself. No head of water, therefore, could have been kept here, unless we suppose that there was an interior cistern, which this outer shell was merely intended to protect. It may have been meant for the reception of the *calices* of private pipes, such as we have above spoken of, which must of course have been accessible to the superintendent; or to protect some large cock for opening or closing the main water-pipes, like that contained in the Museum at Naples, discovered at Capri during the excavations which were made in the palace of Tiberius. Time having firmly cemented the parts together, the water in its cavity has remained hermetically sealed during seventeen or eighteen centuries. Travellers

Fountain in Biviis near the Gate of Herculaneum.

are shown this curious piece of antiquity, which being lifted and shaken by two men, the splashing sound of the contained fluid is distinctly heard. There is nothing at all remarkable in the fountain just described, which consists, as usual, of a pipe spouting into a square trough: the mask, if ever there were any, is gone.

The figures on the castellum are a painting, now entirely effaced, representing a sacrifice to the Lares Compitales, the deities of the highways: beneath it is a small altar dedicated to them. These little gods were the sons of Lara, who was sent down to the infernal regions for having made too free a use of her tongue, and of Mercury, who was appointed her conductor. They loitered on the road, and Lara bore twins, who, as a natural consequence of the circumstances to which they owed their birth, and of their father's vocation, became the guardians of roads. Being only two at first, they multiplied with singular rapidity. Cross roads, ships, public buildings, were all placed under the superintendence of a peculiar tribe; and they obtained the names marini, publici, familiares, compitales, &c., according to the class of objects of which they severally took charge. Augustus re-established their worship after it had fallen into disuse, and ordered that twice a year their images should be crowned with flowers, and adorned with garlands, and fruits offered on their altars. The painting on the castellum represents this ceremony. They were often represented under the form of serpents,* and the paintings which so frequently recur in Pompeii of large serpents, usually in the act of tasting offerings placed on a low altar, and often with a projecting brick or small shelf before them, to receive fruit or a lighted lamp, are in honour of the Lares, and were supposed to sanctify the spot and secure it from pollution.

* Mercury himself presided over roads, whence he was called ὅδιος; and the remarkable statutes terminating in a square trunk, erected as a sort of tutelary gods in the streets, which played so remarkable a part in the Peloponnesian war, were after him named Hermæ.

Bronze cock found in the island of Capri.

CHAPTER IV.

ORIGIN AND USE OF FORUM.—ARCHITECTURAL CLASSIFICATION OF BUILDINGS.—DESCRIPTION OF FORUM OF POMPEII AND ITS TEMPLES.

In describing a Roman city, our attention is first drawn to the Forum, the focus of business, the resort of pleasure, the scene of all political and legal contention. In the early ages of Rome one open space probably served for all the public meetings of the people, whether for the purposes of traffic, for the administration of justice, or for meetings to deliberate upon public affairs. So in Greek, the same word, Agora, derived from *ageiro*, I collect, signifies equally a market, a place of assembly for citizens, and the assembly itself. As wealth and splendour increased, and business became more complicated, it was found inconvenient to have so many different occupations carried on together, and two classes of fora arose—Venalia, mere markets, as the Forum Boarium, or ox-market, Piscarium, fish-market, &c.—and Civilia, those devoted to the other purposes of a place of assembly, of which, however, until the time of Julius Cæsar, there was but one at Rome. He built a second of extraordinary splendour, the area alone of which cost the enormous sum of 800,000*l*.,* from which we may imagine the expense and splendour of the superstructure; and others were afterwards constructed by the Emperors. For the country, however, at all events in small places like Pompeii, a single forum continued to be sufficient.

Some difference existed between the Greek and Roman fora, derived from the difference of the uses to which they were to be applied. The Greek were built square, with columns near each other, to give as much shelter as possible. On these was placed a marble architrave, supporting an upper ambulatory, or gallery for walking. This gallery the Romans

* H. S. millies. Suet.

retained (there appears to have been one at Pompeii), but the area, instead of being square, was oblong, and the pillars set at considerable intervals. These variations seem to have been made to give the greatest possible convenience for viewing shows of gladiators, which, previous to the building of amphitheatres, were exhibited in the Forum. In its simple state it was merely an open area, surrounded by a colonnade, a sort of exchange; but in the period of Roman splendour it was usually encompassed by a series of splendid public buildings, on which all the riches of architecture were lavished. Basilicæ, or courts of justice—curiæ, or places of assembly for the senate or local magistracy—tabularia, where the public records were kept—temples, prisons, public granaries, all things necessary for the public pleasure or convenience, were here collected in immediate neighbourhood to one another. Various trades were exercised under the porticoes; the money-changers had their stalls below; the management of the public revenue was usually carried on in the gallery above. At one end, or in an adjoining basilica, the prætor usually administered justice; within were the rostra from which orators addressed the people. The liveliness and tumult of the scene, where all these employments were carried on, may well be imagined.

It may be convenient, however, and may prevent repetition, if, before we enter upon a particular description of the buildings which usually composed this quarter of the town, a short account be given of the general structure of temples, the most important and interesting, unless we except the baths, of Roman buildings, together with an explanation of the terms employed by Vitruvius in characterizing them. These are universally derived from the disposition of the pillars, the distinguishing feature in all ancient architecture. Technical terms appear hard to those who are ignorant of their meaning; but when once understood, they express much in a small compass, and unless unreasonably multiplied, convey the clearest idea of the object to be described. The body of the temple was usually quadrangular, oblong, and enclosed by walls; this was called cella, the cell. It was adorned on the exterior with columns, varying in their proportions and design, forming porticoes on the front or on the sides, or both; and from the number of columns employed, and the intervals at which they were placed, the building took its architectural denomination. A temple was said to be built in

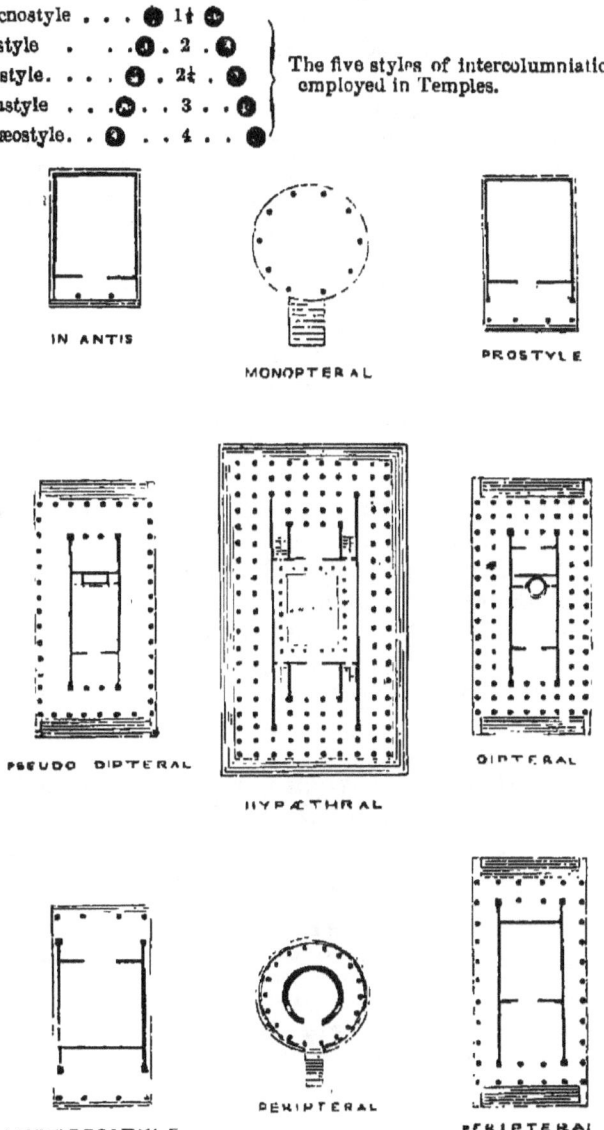

Antis, when square columns (*antæ*) were placed at the angles and along the sides, with two round columns in the front

between the antæ.* If built with a detached portico in front, consisting of any number of columns, it was termed Prostyle;† if both ends were thus ornamented, it was termed Amphiprostyle; if the colonnade extended all round, it became Peripteral;‡ and Dipteral, when built in the most expensive and magnificent shape, when a double range of pillars ran all round. A variety of this style was called Pseudodipteral,§ in which the porticoes projected as far from the cell as in dipteral temples, but the interior range of columns was omitted. This was considered an improvement, both as giving more room under the portico and being less expensive. Another variety consisted merely of a circular colonnade, without a cell, but only an altar in the centre, this was called Monopteral; in another,‖ where the cell was required to be large, the walls were thrown back, so as to fill up the intercolumniations, whence it was called Pseudoperipteral. The two latter were especially devoted to sacrifices. Hypæthral temples were so named because the cell was open to the sky. These were usually of the largest and most magnificent description. The type of them given by Vitruvius consists of a portico of ten columns at either end; it is dipteral, and has within the cell a double range of columns, one supporting the other, detached from the wall. Folding doors opened into it at each end. There was no example of this style at Rome.¶ It originated probably in the difficulty of roofing over so large a space, and of sufficiently lighting the interior, windows not being usually admitted in these buildings. The religious ceremonies performed in these vast temples probably did not require much shelter; and a partial shelter was given by the colonnade within the cell, which was ceiled and roofed, and probably was added with a view

---

* Example, St. Paul's, Covent Garden.
† Prostyle, from πρό, before, and στύλος, a column, with columns in front. Amphiprostyle, from ἀμφί, on either side, prostyle at each end. Peripteral, winged all round, from περί, round, and πτερόν, a wing. Dipteral, double-winged, from δίς, twice. Pseudodipteral, false double-winged, from ψευδής, false. Monopteral, nothing but wing, from μόνος, only. Pseudoperipteral, falsely winged. Hypæthral, open to the sky, from ὑπὸ, under, and αἴθρα, a serene sky.
‡ Examples, the Bourse at Paris, or the circular temple of Vesta at Tivoli.
§ Example, St. Martin in the Fields.
‖ Vitruv. iv. 7. ¶ Vitruv. iii. 2.

to this convenience. The building at Pompeii called the Temple of Jupiter, may be conjectured, from its interior colonnade, to have been hypæthral.

Buildings were further classified with regard to the intercolumniations, or space from one column to another. They were called Pycnostyle * when the columns were placed in the closest order practised, that is, when one and a half diameters apart; Systyle, when two diameters apart; Eustyle, when two and a quarter diameters apart; Diastyle, when three diameters apart; and Aræostyle when the interval was greater than this. Vitruvius objects to the Systyle arrangement as inconvenient, "because, when matrons going with their families to the temple have ascended the steps, they cannot pass arm in arm between the pillars without going sideways." This objection holds good against the temples of Pompeii, which for the most part are on a small scale. In the diastyle he thinks that the pillars are too far apart, and that in consequence the stability of the entablature is endangered. The reader is aware that in Grecian architecture the arch was not used, neither were the ancients acquainted with the means employed by our own architects to cramp together separate stones into one solid body. Blocks therefore were required of sufficient size to stretch from the centre of one column to that of the next; and these, where the interval was large and the material tender, were subject to break even under their own weight, much more with that of the entablature added. In the Aræostyle neither stone nor marble architraves could be used, but beams of timber rested on the columns. Buildings of this description, he says, are low and heavy, and the architraves ornamented with pottery or brazen mouldings. The portico surrounding the Forum at Pompeii was of this description. The Eustyle was, as its name imports, the most perfect, uniting convenience, beauty, and strength. In this the central intercolumniation in front of the temple was of three diameters, displaying to more advantage the door of the cella, with its ornaments, and affording a more ample space for ingress and egress.

* Pycnostyle, close-columned, from πυκνάς, close, and στύλος, a column. Systyle, near-columned, from σύν, together. Eustyle, well-columned, from εὖ, well. Diastyle, open-columned, from δία, apart. Aræostyle, thinly-columned, from ἀραιός, scattered.

"An essential feature in the temples of Pompeii, as distinguished from those of Greece, is to be observed in the podium,* or basement, on which they were elevated. In the religious edifices of an early age no such character appears. They were placed upon two or three steps only, if steps they should be termed, when evidently not proportioned for convenience of access to the interior, but calculated rather with a view to the general effect of the whole structure."† By thus raising the floor to a level with or above the eye, the whole order, from the stylobate, or continuous platform on which the columns rest, to the roof, was brought at once into view. The steps, Vitruvius says, should be of an odd number, that the right foot, being planted on the first step, may also first be placed on the pavement of the temple. To enter with the left foot foremost was considered unlucky. With regard to the proportions of the interior within the porticoes, the breadth is directed to be half the length, and the cell to be a fourth part more in length than in breadth. The building is directed to stand east and west, like our churches, and the statue of the presiding deity to be elevated above the altar, that the suppliants and priests might decently look up to the object of their worship. Thus an hypæthral temple would present a most splendid scene; the worshippers addressing their vows, the image apparently rising to behold them, and the building itself boldly projected on the eastern sky. It will be recollected that these are merely the rules laid down by Vitruvius; it does not follow that they were always observed.

We now proceed to describe the Forum Civile of Pompeii, of which the annexed plate contains a ground-plan, restored from the remains now existing. An examination of this will afford a correct idea of the arrangement of the several edifices.

Upon entering, the spectator finds himself in a large area, about 524 feet long and 140 broad, including the porticoes, surrounded by columns and the ruins of temples, triumphal arches, and other public buildings, the particular uses of which can in general only be conjectured. The red masses of brick divested of their marble casings, the brown and yellow tints of the tufa, the fragments of white stucco

---

* Diminutive of πούς, the foot. † Gell, p. 227.

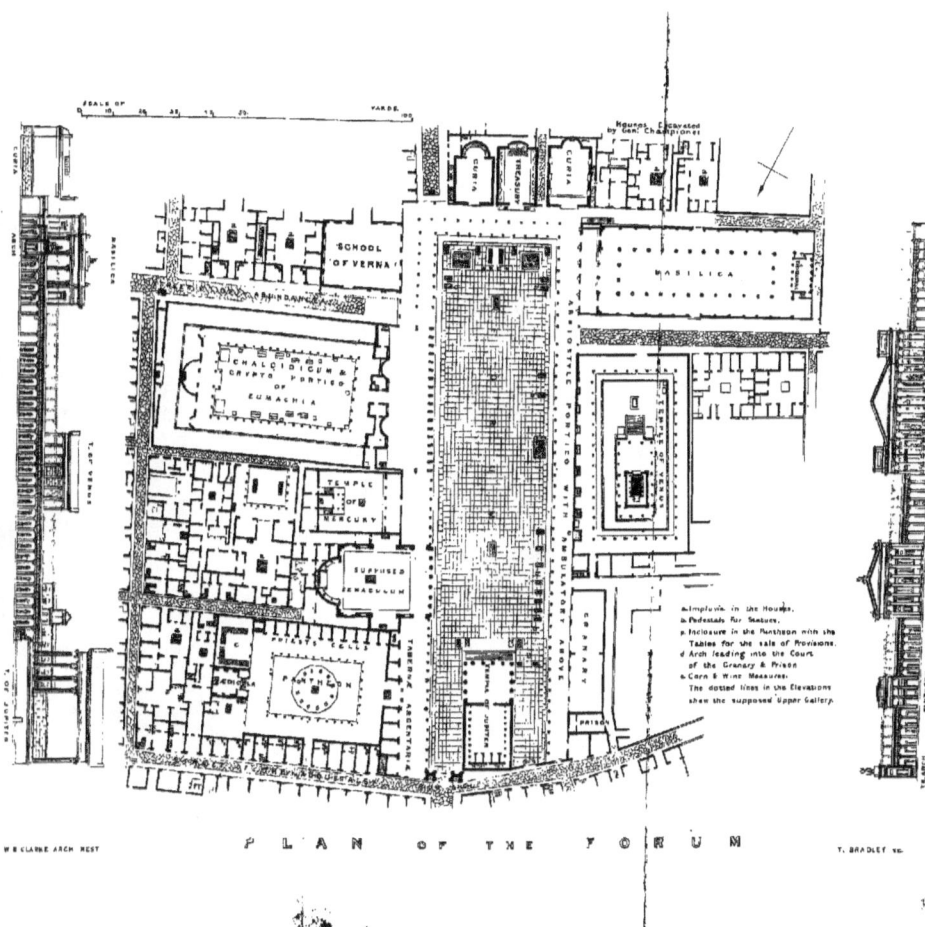

attached to the shattered walls of the different edifices, and the pedestals, which once supported statues commemorating those who had deserved well of their country, are all that now remain to attest its former beauty and magnificence.

Around the west, south, and east sides there runs a Grecian Doric colonnade, uninterrupted, except on the east, where the porticoes of the surrounding buildings in some instances come flush up to the colonnade, and in some places break the line of the upper gallery, preserving an uninterrupted communication below. Where this was the case stairs ran up to the gallery; but probably there was also some communication between these several divisions of it without descending to the ground. True it is, that as no vestige of this upper story remains, it may seem rash to assert its existence so boldly; but the traces of staircases, combined with the authority of Vitruvius, are sufficient to warrant us in doing so. Probably it was built of wood; this would account for its total disappearance. The diameter of the columns was two feet three and a half inches, their height twelve feet, the interval between them six feet ten inches. On the eastern side there still remains a portion of an older arcade, which the inhabitants, at the time of the eruption, were in the course of replacing by the Doric portico. The pillars are of three materials; of fine white caserta stone, resembling marble; of ancient yellowish tufa; and of brick plastered.

An opinion, which seems very probable, is advanced by Overbeck,* that the Forum is of a later date than the rest of the city, and posterior, at all events, to the Roman colonisation, if not to the earthquake in A.D. 63. The grounds for this opinion are, that two small streets on the eastern side of the Forum, namely, that between the Temple of Augustus and the Senaculum, and that between the Temple of Mercury and the Chalcidicum, have been blocked up and converted into *culs de sac* by the encroachment of these buildings; which shows the last to have been of more recent date than the streets. Another reason is, that the whole plan and disposition of the Forum is in conformity with the Roman practice as laid down in the rules of Vitruvius. We may perhaps add that the materials of which the Forum is constructed, such as

* *Pomp.* B. i. S. 68.

the brick pillars and walls covered with coats of stucco or marble, bespeak a much more recent date, than, for instance, the Greek temple in the triangular Forum, with its massive columns of solid stone, of a much earlier and purer style.

Projecting itself on the area of the Forum on the north, stands a building generally called the Temple of Jupiter. It is prostyle, and of the Corinthian order: the columns are pycnostyle, and the portico is pseudo-dipteral and hexastyle, or having six columns in the front. A row of columns runs on each side along the interior of the cella, which, as has been observed, leads us to suppose that it was hypæthral. It is probable that there were two ranges of columns within the cella, one above another, as at Pæstum, the floor of a gallery resting on the lower tier, since the height of the exterior was such as to require two orders in the interior (where the columns were smaller) to reach the roof, the object of the columns being support, and not mere decoration. A narrow staircase at the back of the temple, concealed behind three small chambers at the end of the cella, the walls of which rise to the height of the first order of columns, confirms the belief that there was formerly a gallery. The clear space of the cell, within these chambers and the colonnade, was about forty-two feet by twenty-eight feet six inches. The interior has been painted; red and black are the predominant colours. Diamond-shaped pieces of marble form the centre division of the pavement, which is enclosed within a broad border of black and white mosaic. In the centre of the door-sill there are traces of holes for the bolts of folding doors. Upon the pavement fragments of a colossal statue were discovered. This temple is placed on an elevated basement or podium, which was ascended by many steps. Those nearest the columns are carried along the whole front of the portico, while the steps near the ground are narrow, and sunk in a low parapet forming a basement to the upper flight. Greater breadth of effect and grandeur is communicated to the whole edifice by this mass of solid wall beneath the large columns which it seems to support. A magnificent example of this method of construction is to be seen in the portico of the London University. The dye* of the basement inclines

---

* The dye is that part of the basement which is placed between the under and upper moulding of the whole; it is generally a plain surface.

inwards; it is moulded above and below, and in front formed into pedestals, which are oblong, and adapted to receive equestrian statues. Near one of them a sun-dial was found. Pedestals were also added in front at the angles of the basement of the portico. On the south-east a side door in the basement leads to vaults beneath the temple. The whole of the building, constructed as it is of stone and lava, has been covered with a fine white cement made of marble, still retaining great hardness. The workmanship does not appear to be very good or exact. The columns and the spaces between them vary, none of them being equidistant. The diameters of the columns are three feet seven inches and three feet eight inches, making their height, according to the proportions observed, approach to thirty-six feet, about the size of the lower order of St. Paul's cathedral, so that the whole height of the building was, including the basement, about sixty feet. Without the walls its breadth was forty-three feet, and its length a hundred to the end of the portico. Add twenty feet for the flights of steps, and the total length is one hundred and twenty feet.*

Adjoining the south-western end of the basement stand the ruins of an arch, built of brick, and cased with slabs of white marble, fastened on the brickwork by iron cramps. This arch, which is seen on the left of the Temple of Jupiter given in the view of the Forum, is by some conjectured to have been triumphal; but from its being connected with the temple by a low wall reaching to the height of the adjoining basement, it is more probable that it was only the entrance to a court in front of what may have been the public granaries. This wall evidently proves that the whole was constructed, not for show, but use. Had the arch been

---

* It is the opinion of Overbeck (*Pomp.* B. i. S. 90, 92) that the temple was dedicated to Jupiter, Juno, and Minerva, as a trinity presiding, like the Capitoline deities at Rome, over the safety of the city. But though, from its situation, the temple was no doubt dedicated to a principal deity, yet its narrow oblong form forbids the idea that there would have been room for the statues of three gods. The same author rejects the opinion that the temple was hypæthral. He also questions the discovery of a colossal head of Jupiter; which, however, is recorded in the Journal of the Excavations, January 21st, 1817 (*Pomp. Ant. Hist.* t. i. fasc. iii., p. 190). It should have been stated that the extensive *favissæ*, or cellars, under the temple are lighted by several openings in the floor.

triumphal, it would have been more solidly built, isolated, and not disfigured by a small piece of wall attached to one side only, disfiguring also the basement of the most commanding building in the city. It may be presumed, therefore, to have formed the entrance to a court-yard before the granary and prisons, which are here situated at the north-west corner of the Forum; such a convenience being almost necessary to the former, for the unloading the grain apart from the crowd in the Forum; and to the latter, as an outlet where prisoners, it may be supposed, were allowed to take exercise under the eyes of their guards. That the prison stood here there can be no doubt;* indeed its exact spot is determined by the skeletons of two men, left to perish in the general confusion. Their leg-bones were found still within the shackles. With regard to the other apartment, there certainly is not such convincing evidence to prove that it was the public granary. It is well suited to such a purpose, but the strongest evidence of its destination is to be found in the immediate neighbourhood of the public measures. We may further observe, with regard to the arch, that it is not sufficiently substantial for the purpose which is assigned to it, nor would the plane surface on the top be broad enough either for an equestrian statue or a triumphal car. But attached to the north-east angle of the Temple of Jupiter there is a gateway, having the character of a triumphal arch. The massive piers and part of the columns that adorned them still remain. In each pier were two attached fluted Corinthian white marble columns, of good workmanship. In the centre of each pier, between the columns, are square-headed niches, in one of which there was a fountain, as is evident from the lead pipes which were here discovered. Statues most probably were placed in the four niches, and the fountain formed in one of them may have flowed through a cornucopia, or some other appropriate vessel held in the hands of the figure.† Statues applied to these purposes were commonly placed at the fountains in Pompeii. Among others have been found two boys of beautiful workmanship,

---

* *Vide* Donaldson's Pompeii.

† The niches are deeper on the outer side of the arch, or that facing the Street of Mercury, than on the side facing the Forum, and it is the former that must have contained the fountains. The others could only have held statues.

DESCRIPTION OF FORUM.   101

carrying vases on their shoulders, and two others with masks in their hands, the masks and vases resting on pedestals. Water was conveyed up through the figures, and issued from

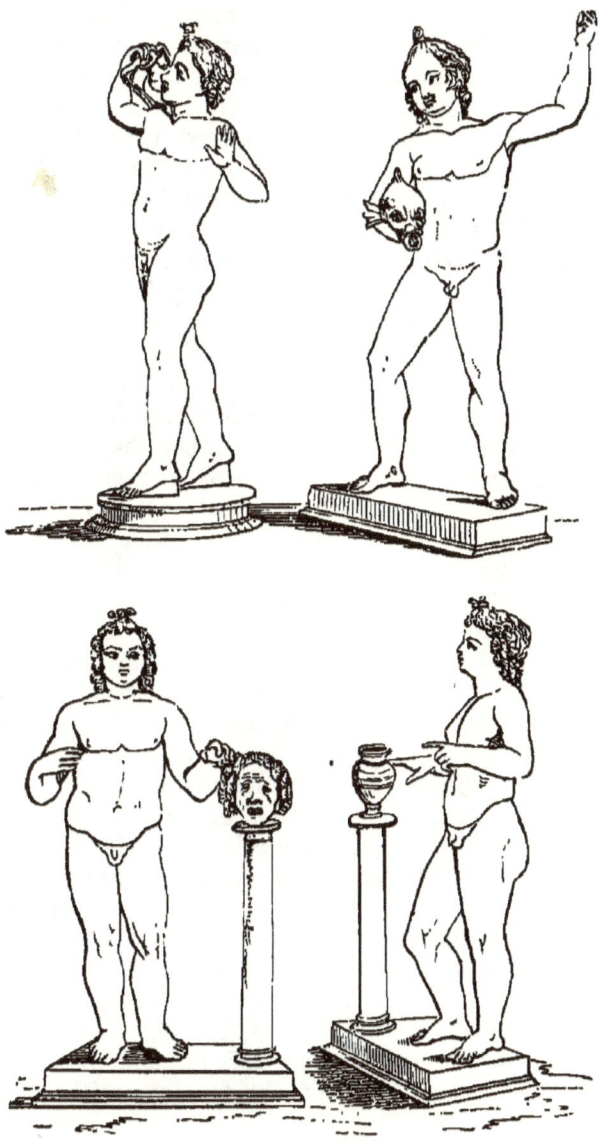

Bronze figures to ornament fountains.

the masks and vases. Conduits of lead were frequently used in Pompeii to conduct the water to the public fountains and private baths. These, however, the late Neapolitan government caused to be torn up, and sold for their value as old metal.

The arch from which this digression has led us, had without doubt an attic or low wall above the cornice, on which was placed either an equestrian statue or a car, the appropriate finish to such a structure. That either one or the other did surmount the attic, may be inferred from the fragments of a bronze statue of a man, and part of the legs of a horse of the same metal, having been found in the immediate vicinity. The arch is built of bricks and lava, and has been covered with thin slabs of marble, a method of construction in use among the ancients; and, from a principle of economy, much practised, not only in Pompeii, but even in Rome, where the brick walls, despoiled of their costly coatings, alone remain. Presuming that the Forum was closed for security, the opening of this arch must have had gates; these, however, no longer exist. Possibly they were of wood, or if of bronze, they may have been carried away by the Pompeians. An additional proof that the Forum was shut up at night is to be found in the small pier attached to the north-west angle of the arch, evidently built to receive the iron or wood-work of a gate closing the foot-entrance by its side. Had it not been necessary to close the Forum, this small pier would have been useless, and the deformity of it would have been avoided. This arch may be considered the principal entrance to the Forum, and, as such, was doubtless chosen for the site of a public monument. It was the only entrance for carriages; the foot entrance is formed by another arch to the right, or east of that already described. This arch is of the same height as the other, but stands on a somewhat higher level. It formed the entrance just mentioned, for foot-passengers only, into the east side of the portico which surrounds the Forum. The top of the arch has fallen in. On the triumphal arch near the baths was placed an equestrian figure of the size of life, the fragments of which were found during the excavations in 1823. The figure of the man is perfect, with the exception of the left leg and foot, but of the horse, only the tail and one of the forelegs without the foot were found. The action of the statue, which is supposed to represent Nero, resembles that of M. Aurelius in the Campidoglio at Rome, but it is of very inferior workmanship. Here was also found a skeleton, with seventy-four small silver coins.*

The buildings hitherto described, with the exception of the granary and prisons, form the north side of the Forum. We will now take those on the east side, and, describing them and their probable uses in the order of their succession, proceed along the south and west sides back to the granary. Adjoining the pedestrian entrance, already mentioned, at the north-eastern angle of the Forum, stands an edifice called the Pantheon,† from twelve pedestals placed in a circle round an altar in the centre of its area, which are supposed to have supported the statues of the Dii Consentes, or Magni, the aristocracy of Italian mythology. The area, one hundred and twenty by ninety feet, is bounded by the back walls of shops on the north and west sides; by the Ædicula (a small temple or shrine), raised to the founder or patron, and two inclosures on the east; and by the eleven cells supposed to belong to the fraternity of priests on the south. Within, perhaps, a rectangular portico or gallery inclosed the twelve pedestals, or they may have been covered with a wooden temple, in the light style of architecture depicted on the walls of Pompeii. No traces however remain of such constructions. In front of this building, under the portico of the Forum, are seven shops, possibly the Tabernæ Argentariæ, or shops of money-changers; the pedestals of some of the tables still remain. In one of these shops 1128 silver and copper coins were found in the remains of a chest. The entrance to the Pantheon is by a small vestibule in the centre of the area. There are four pedestals in front of it, and one at the end of each party wall between the shops. They probably were meant to receive columns. At the end of the shops was a staircase, which may have led to the upper ambulatories.

In the centre of the vestibule stood a small altar, which still remains, with doors opening on each side into the area beyond. Behind the altar was a niche, on which the statue of some one of the gods was placed, so that the devout Roman

* Fiorelli, *Pomp. Antiq. Hist.*, t. ii. p. 86, *et seq.*
† Or, with more probability, the Temple of Augustus.

had an opportunity of leaving his offering as he entered, and propitiating the presiding deity. On the right side, as you enter, are arranged the cells already mentioned; over these were other apartments, as the holes in the side walls for the reception of joists indicate. There are also holes in the piers in front of these cells for the joists and floor of a gallery which gave access to the upper apartments, as in the old inns still existing in London and elsewhere. The staircase has been entirely destroyed, so that its site cannot be ascertained; it is, however, most natural to suppose it near the vestibule. There were other entrances; one in the centre of the north side, and another at the end of the cells, both leading into streets without the Forum. The further end of this building was divided into three compartments. That in the centre was an ædicula, containing niches, in which were statues of Livia, the wife of Augustus, and Drusus. In the side wall opposite to these must have stood the statues of two other members of the imperial family in corresponding niches. The principal statue stood on a large marble base, or pedestal, facing the entrance. The only remains of it found was an arm holding a globe; whence it seems reasonable to conclude that it belonged to a statue of Augustus. The conjecture of Overbeck,* that it might have been part of a statue of Jupiter, is improbable. There would hardly have been two large temples to that deity close together, nor is it likely that he would have been placed in such company. The statues extant were carried to the Neapolitan Museum and replaced by casts. That of Livia is one of the most remarkable found at Pompeii, especially for the execution of the drapery, but unfortunately it wants the right forearm. On the right of the ædicula, a door-way between two columns gave admission, as some have supposed, to a refectory for the use of the priests, or a place for the sale of such provisions as they had reserved from the sacrifice. A low platform or bench surrounds three sides of the room, which may have been meant either for tricliniary couches, or have served as a place on which the provisions for sale were exposed.†

* B. i. S. 116.

† The Romans, it is well known, reclined at their meals, apparently an inconvenient fashion, but not so inconvenient to persons who used no knives and forks as to us, who require two hands to get our food comfortably to our

Round the inside runs a marble gutter, to carry off the water and refuse when the place was cleansed.* On the other side of the ædicula an enclosure has been formed with columns on the exterior, similar to the entrance of the refectory. Within it is a small vaulted ædicula, on a podium ascended by five steps, before which stands an altar. This apartment has been twice stuccoed and painted, the first design having been replaced by a series of arabesques. This style of decoration, common to all the public and private buildings of Pompeii, has been condemned by Vitruvius; yet, even in defiance of his authority, we feel disposed to admire their bold and harmonious colouring, and the lightness, elegance, and variety of their designs. The paintings in this edifice are worthy, for their beauty, of especial notice; the various designs are well composed, and the colours are as brilliant as when first laid on. Among the figures, not the least interesting is one of the paintress herself, holding in one hand an oval white palette, apparently of silver, in the other, brushes tinged with several colours. Her fingers appear to grasp the palette, through as many holes perforated in the metal.

The art of fresco painting is still practised; but the secret of employing a medium so durable as to withstand, first fire, and afterwards the damp of so many ages, is unknown to the moderns. It has been supposed that the medium employed to liquify the pigments used in these paintings was wax mixed with oil. Supposing that wax, than which nothing is more lasting, were used, it may be imagined that the object of a silver or metal palette was to retain so much heat as would liquify the menstruum, without being inconvenient to the artist. The paintings consist of architectural compositions of long aerial columns, vistas through doorways, showing the ornamented ceilings, an abundant variety of figures and borders of flowers, with an almost endless detail of en-

---

mouths. Three couches were usually placed in a dining-room, one at each side of the table, leaving the fourth open to the servants. Hence the word triclinium, τρεῖς κλίναι, three beds, which name is given both to the couches and to the room. The distance between the sides of this podium, and the opening in the east side of it, as represented in the plan, together with the gutter surrounding it, make the second account of it more probable. [The construction of the platform is not adapted to a triclinium.]

* Hence some have conjectured that it was a slaughter-house

richment, painted for the most part with dazzling colours, among which, bright vermilion, jet black, deep crimson, azure blue, and golden yellow, usually form the ground. To these are added a variety of mixed tints, more delicate as the objects are supposed to recede from the eye. The latter consist principally of light greys, pink, purple, and green. It must however be confessed that good taste did not hold exclusive sway in Pompeii; for in that case a proprietor would hardly have painted the exterior of his house with chequers

Painting of a Galley on the walls of the Pantheon.

resembling the sign of a modern alehouse; or have covered the external walls with a decoration similar to the infantine amusement of a child, who, for the first time in possession of a pair of compasses and a colour-box, proceeds to describe circles intersecting each other, and then fills them with a coloured patchwork.* Historical subjects are painted in the centres of the compartments formed by the arabesques; one of these represents Ulysses in disguise meeting Penelope on his return to Ithaca.

Another theory has been adopted by an ingenious Neapolitan architect, Carlo Bonnucci, with regard to this building. The temple at one end he calls the Temple of Augustus, and the remainder he sets apart for the banquets of his priests, the Augustals; and he cites Vitruvius as authority for such a situation as that chosen.† The numerous inscriptions rela-

* It has been imagined that the occupier was a worker in mosaic, and that this patchwork was a sort of sign.

† The Augustals in the provincial towns were of an inferior order to the same priests at Rome, and were commonly *libertini*, or freedmen. They were appointed by the Decurions of the Municipium.

tive to these personages discovered at Pompeii would lead us to infer that they were of some importance, and from one of these they appear to have been six in number. Sir William Gell, following the opinion of Bonnucci, says, " that the Augustals were possessed of funds which supplied them with the means of feasting, and inviting their fellow-citizens to partake in their banquet, for which purpose the building now called Pantheon was so well calculated ; that, whether belonging to a particular order, or the common property of all the inhabitants of Pompeii, it may be safely considered as a place of feasting or carousal under the protection of some deity, who, from his more elevated sacellum, was supposed to overlook and patronise the banquet. That such was the destination of this edifice, and that it differed but little in its uses from that which the Greeks called Lesche, and the modern Italians a trattoria and coffee-house, seems to be rendered more probable by many of its internal decorations ; while its proximity to the Forum, the chief resort of the inhabitants of the city, would point out this situation as the most eligible for a place of conversation and refreshment."

The destination of the building just described has occasioned more perplexity to antiquarians than that of almost any other in Pompeii. The idea that it was a Pantheon is now pretty universally rejected. The twelve stone posts in the centre are said to be not pedestals for statues, but bases, on which rested pillars which supported a circular building; while the apartments on the right, or southern side, are not twelve in number but only eleven. Some have considered it to be a market, some an *hospitium* destined for the reception of ambassadors or other distinguished foreigners—of which, however, there could have been no great quantity in a third rate town like Pompeii—while others have called it a Serapeum. The theory that it was an hospitium is rejected by Overbeck,* who, however, considered it plausible ; and he himself adopts, after Pyl, a very similar one, namely, that it was a Temple of Vesta and Prytaneum, after the Greek fashion. A Greek Prytaneum was to the city what the house was to a private family ; a place of public entertainment, where distinguished and deserving citizens, as well as ambas-

* Book i. S. 118.

sadors and other foreigners of distinction, were entertained at the public expense. For this purpose an ever-burning fire was maintained in it, as in the Temple of Vesta; and Overbeck thinks that the twelve stone bases, placed in a circle in the middle of the area, supported a round building in which was an altar dedicated to that goddess. But of all the conjectures hazarded concerning the building, we consider this to be about one of the most improbable. For, first, Prytaneia were only found in the independent and capital towns of Greece, and would have been misplaced in a third-rate town in Italy like Pompeii, where, as we have already observed, there could have been no great influx of distinguished foreigners. Again, such an establishment does not appear to have been a Roman custom; and Overbeck himself had already remarked that the buildings round the Forum are certainly subsequent to the Roman occupation, and probably belong to a late period of it. Further, if there was any round temple in the middle of the area, it must evidently have consisted of wood; and such a building in so public a place does not seem at all in accordance with the Roman notions of the worship of Vesta.

On the other hand there are many reasons for thinking that the building in question was destined for the worship of Augustus, and for the use of his priests, the collegium of Augustals. Many things show that Augustus was the object of peculiar veneration at Pompeii. His priests, who, as we have said, are frequently mentioned in inscriptions, must have had a place of meeting worthy of him they worshipped, and none can be pointed out more suitable than this building. The statues of the imperial family seem to confirm this destination. The paintings on the wall representing combats of galleys refer probably to the battle of Actium, while those of eatables are in allusion to the feasts given by the Augustals.

The shops in the street on the north side of the Temple of Augustus most probably supplied those who feasted with dainties; and it has been called the Street of Dried Fruits, from the quantity of raisins, figs, plums, and chesnuts, fruit of several sorts preserved in vases of glass, hempseed, and lentils. It is now, however, more generally known as the Street of the Augustals. Scales, money, moulds for pastry

DESCRIPTION OF TEMPLES. 109

and bread, were discovered in the shops; and a bronze statue of Fame, small, and delicately executed, having golden bracelets round the arms.

Bread, from a painting on the walls of the Temple of Augustus.

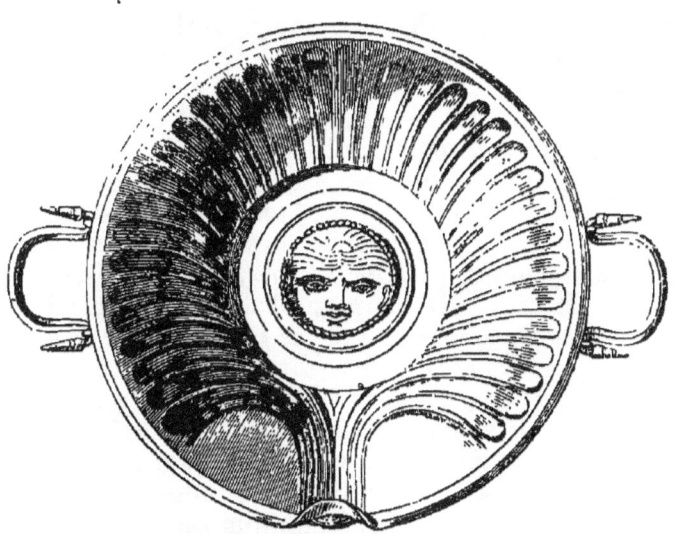

Bronze pastry mould.

In the northern entrance to the building the name CELSVM is written on a pilaster; near it was found in a box a gold ring with an engraved stone set in it, forty-one silver, and a thousand and thirty-six brass coins. Here also on both sides of the walls are representations of Cupids making bread. The mill is placed in the centre of the picture, with an ass on each side, from which it appears that these animals were used in grinding the flour. At the entrance to the south a hatchet is painted, as necessary for cutting up the meat, and the picture

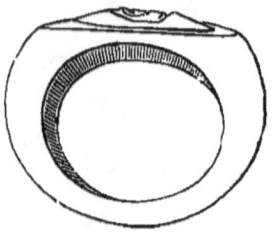

Gold ring with an engraved stone.

is filled up with boars' heads, fish, hams, &c. In other parts of the building, above the elegant paintings already mentioned, are geese, turkeys, vases of eggs, fowls, lobsters, and game ready plucked for cooking, oxen, sheep, fruit in glass dishes, a cornucopia, with various amphoræ for wine, and many other accessories for the banquet.

In the centre of the court, near the twelve pedestals, is a sink, which is said to have been found filled with fish-bones and remains of other articles of food.

The adjoining building has been supposed by some antiquaries to have been the place of meeting of the Augustals; by others, a temple dedicated to three deities, on account of three recesses, apparently for statues, in three sides of the building. It may with more probability be considered the Senaculum, or place of meeting for the senate, or rather decurions; its spacious area, eighty-three feet by sixty, adapts it well to this purpose, and the niches in the wall may have been meant to receive statues of distinguished magistrates. The portico of this edifice was composed of fluted white marble columns of the Ionic order, its front ranging with the portico of the Forum without interrupting the promenade below. There was a staircase at the north end of it, which probably led to the upper gallery, or ambulatory; and a passage may also have been formed over the immediate entrance to the Senaculum, communicating with the ambulatory on the other

DESCRIPTION OF TEMPLES. 111

Cupids making bread.

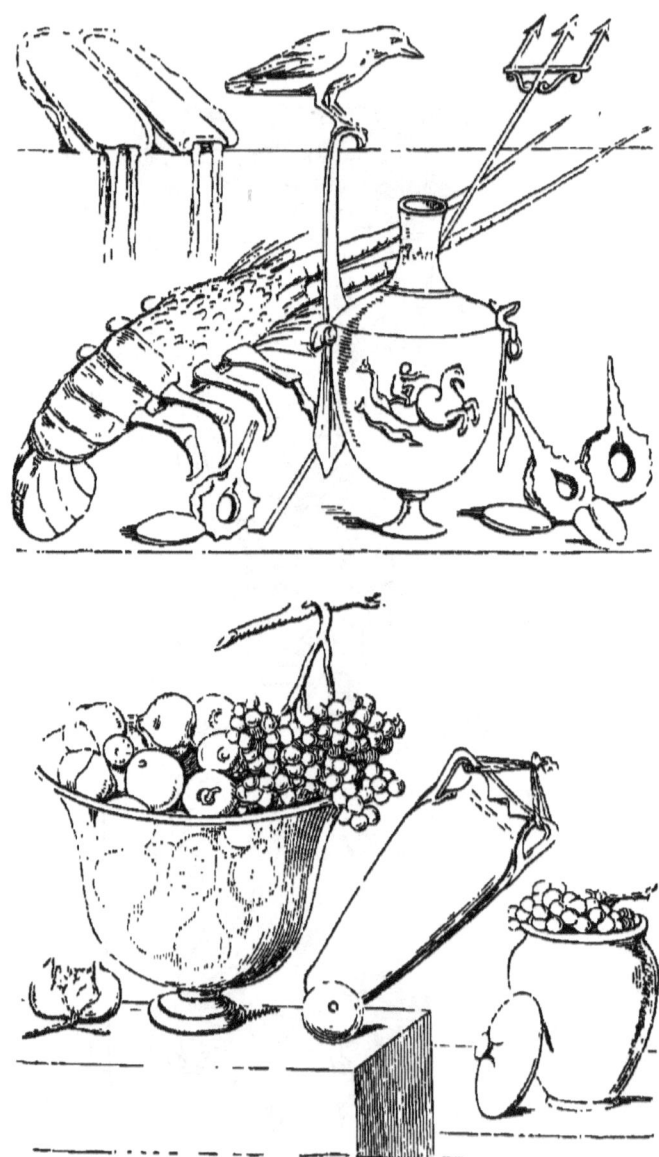

From the paintings on the walls of the Temple of Augustus.

DESCRIPTION OF TEMPLES. 113

side. The columns of this portico were of course larger and loftier than those of the Forum. Within, the pavement of the area is raised above the level of the portico. On each side, upon entering, are two large recesses, with pedestals

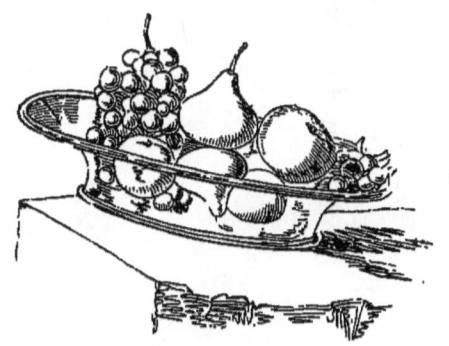

From the paintings in the Temple of Augustus.

attached to the centre of the back wall, possibly destined to support the effigies of the gods to whom the place was sacred. The altar stands in the centre of the area, nearly in front of each statue. The building is terminated at the end by a semicircular recess, where there is a raised seat for the chief magistrates. At the side of one of the recesses is a chamber for records. This building, for convenience, may have been

114   POMPEII.

entirely covered, and the light admitted through the portico. Whether light was also admitted through glass casements in

Temple of Mercury.

the roof or not must remain conjectural; but that the ancients were acquainted with the use of glass windows, is sufficiently proved by the quantity of flat glass discovered during the excavations, and also by its having been found ingeniously fitted (as will be seen in the sequel) to those rare and minute openings which were dignified with the name and office of windows in Pompeii.

Adjoining to the building last described, within an area of fifty-seven feet six inches by fifty feet seven inches, stands a sacellum, or small temple elevated on a basement. It is commonly known as the Temple of Mercury, for which appellation, however, the only grounds that can be assigned are the mention of such a temple in Pompeian inscriptions, and the precept of Vitruvius,* that the Temple of Mercury should be in the Forum. It is also sometimes called the Temple of Quirinus, though this name rests, perhaps, on hardly so good a foundation as the other. It is taken from an inscription found in front of the temple recording the deeds of Romulus, and his deification under the name of Quirinus. This inscription, however, was not found within the precincts of the building, but on the base of a pillar in the colonnade of the Forum; and as there was a precisely similar one on the opposite side relating to Æneas, it is pretty evident that they belonged to two statues erected in honour of those personages.† Nor is the inscription of the kind that would have been placed under the statue of a divinity. The original has been removed to the National Museum, and its place is supplied by a copy. It may be remarked that these inscriptions to the reputed ancestors of the gens Julia are a further proof of the great honour in which Augustus was held at Pompeii. The temple is now shut up with a gate or wicket, and serves as a place of deposit for various objects found in the excavations, but not deemed worthy of a place in the Museum. The temple is approached through a narrow covered vestibule, communicating between the court and the Forum. On each side of the basement are steps leading to the platform

---

* *De Architect* i. 7.

† These inscriptions will be found in Mommsen, Nos. 2188, 2189. The inscription to Romulus, as supplemented by Mommsen, runs as follows:—
"Romulus Martis filius Urbem Romam condidit et regnavit annos duodequadraginta. Isque primus dux duce hostium Acrone rege Cæninensium interfecto, spolia opima Jovi Feretrio consecravit, receptusque in Deorum numerum Quirinus appellatus est."

of the cella; in front of it, in the centre of the court, is an altar of white marble bearing an unfinished bas-relief, which has been imagined to represent Cicero sacrificing, from a supposed resemblance in the principal figure to that great orator. The victim is led by the servant (*popa*), whose office it was to take its life, naked to the waist, bearing his sacrificial axe (*malleus*); he is clothed round the middle with a short cloth, which does not descend to the knees. The sacrificer appears to be a magistrate; he is crowned with a wreath, and his robes partly cover his head. He holds in his hand a patera, as if about to sprinkle the victim, and thereby

Utensils used in sacrificing.

cleanse it from its impurities before offering it to the gods. The popa and an attendant are also crowned with wreaths. A boy follows the principal personage, holding in his hands a vase and patera, or plate, and having the sacred vitta or fillet hanging from his neck; near him is a figure holding a patera filled apparently with bread. Another figure appears to be sounding the tibia, or double flute, followed by lictors, with their fasces. The temple is represented in the background decorated with garlands. On the eastern and opposite side of the altar is a wreath of oak leaves bound with the vitta, having on each side young olive trees sculptured; and

DESCRIPTION OF TEMPLES. 117

on the north and south sides are the various implements and ornaments of sacrifice, as the vase, the patera, vitta, garlands, the incense box, a ladle, and a spiral instrument, the use of which is unknown, unless it belonged to the haruspex, who inspected the bowels of the victims, and prophesied of the future according to the appearances presented to him. Enriched mouldings decorate both the upper and lower part of the altar. The temple, or sacellum, is built of stone, and decorated on the outside with pilasters; its external dimensions are but fifteen feet six inches by thirteen feet eight inches, so as not to admit much more than the statue whose pedestal still remains. The peribolus, or wall surrounding

Ornaments of sacrifice on the sides of the altar.

the whole, is constructed of brick, and, as is shown in the cut, is divided by pilasters into compartments, in which are sunk panels, surmounted at the top by a running ornament consisting of a series of triangles and segments of circles placed alternately. This brickwork having never been covered with stucco, and the altar being unfinished, a conjecture has been formed that the Pompeians were disturbed by the eruption of Vesuvius while they were rebuilding this very temple, which had perhaps been destroyed by the previous earthquake. Here also, as in almost every building destined for religious purposes, were apartments for priests, and in them was found a store of amphoræ, or large earthen vessels in which wine was kept.

The building next in succession partakes of the nature of a basilica, but was probably a sort of exchange. On the architrave over the side-entrance from the Street of Abundance, which runs nearly at right angles to this side of the Forum, is the following inscription, which has been repeated on large blocks of marble found in the Forum:—

EUMACHIA. L.F. SACERD. PUBLIC. NOMINE. SUO. ET.
M. NUMISTRI. FRONTONIS. FILI. CHALCIDICUM.
CRYPTAM. PORTICUS. CONCORDIÆ. AUGUSTÆ.
PIETATI. SUA PEQUNIA. FECIT EADEMQUE
DEDICAVIT.

We learn from hence that a priestess of the name of Eumachia erected at her own expense, and in the name of herself and her son, a chalcidicum, a crypt, or walled gallery,* and a portico, and dedicated them to Pietas and Concordia Augusta. The meaning of the two last words is plain enough, and the situation of the portico and crypt in the building in question can be pointed out with tolerable certainty, the former being the inner colonnade or peristyle surrounding the area of the building, the latter the outer gallery adjoining it. But the exact meaning of the word chalcidicum has never been satisfactorily ascertained. If we adopt the authority of Vitruvius, chalcidica would appear to have been apartments annexed to one end of a basilica, to diminish its area if of too great a length.† Those who accept this interpretation find the chalcidicum in the portico or hall at the entrance of the building, or more probably in the narrow space behind it, in which is the statue of Eumachia, cut off apparently to reduce the building to a regular form. According to another opinion, the name chalcidicum might mean the whole building; and this explanation seems to be favoured by a passage in Arnobius, where he expresses his desire to see the gods in those vast *chalcidica* and palaces of heaven.‡ Nor can we easily explain the chalcidicum, recorded in the Monumentum Ancyranum to have been erected by Augustus next to the Curia at Rome, except on the supposition that it was a sub-

* A crypto-portico (from κρυπτός, hidden) is a gallery, in which the columns on the interior are replaced by walls, merely pierced for windows.

† Sin autem locus erit amplior in longitudine, Chalcidica in extremis constituantur.

‡ Avet animus atque ardet in chalcidicis illis magnis atque in palatiis cœli deos deasque conspicere intectis corporibus. *Arn.* lib. iii.

stantive building.* That the inscription, after mentioning the chalcidicum as a whole, should proceed to enumerate some of its parts, is not unprecedented; since an inscription relating to the theatre, besides naming that building, alludes to its *crypta* and *tribunalia*.†

At the bottom of the building is a large semicircular recess, behind which, in the crypto-portico, was a statue of Eumachia, now replaced by a cast. It is five feet four inches in height, and stands on a pedestal placed in a niche in the centre of the wall, with this inscription :—

EUMACHIÆ. L. F.
SACERD. PUBL.
FULLONES

from which it would appear that the cloth-scourers had, in gratitude to Eumachia, erected this statue to her memory. The whole structure consists of a large area, about one hundred and thirty feet by sixty-five. surrounded by a double gallery, and has in front a pseudo-dipteral portico of eighteen columns, elevated on pedestals. Under its centre was the great public entrance, which was closed with folding doors, turning in sockets of bronze, and secured by bolts shot into the holes still remaining in the marble threshold. This entrance was flanked by two large circular recesses, one on each side; and beyond these again, at the extreme end of the building, by raised platforms, the staircases to which still remain. Hence orators might have harangued an audience sheltered under the portico, and edicts relative to commerce might have been publicly read.

The entrance to the area is through a passage, on each side of which are other passages, with a staircase on the right leading to galleries above. The entrance to the back of the building, where is the statue of Eumachia, is from the Street of Abundance, forming the southern boundary of the building. Here is a small chamber for the doorkeeper, through which is seen a flight of steps ascending to the floor of the chalcidicum and crypto-portico; the walls on each side of the steps are painted in black panels, divided by red pilasters. Under the staircase are the remains of a thermopolium, or

---

* See Dyer's *Rome*, pp. 191 and 198.
† See Overbeck, B. i. S. 122, and the inscription in Mommsen, No. 2229.

120   POMPEII.

Urn for warm decoctions drunk in the Thermopolia

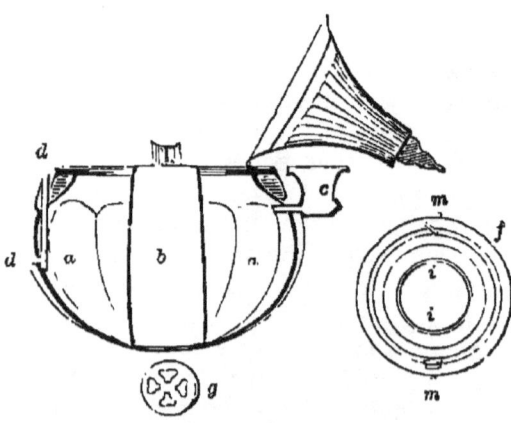

Section of the urn.

shop where warm water and warm decoctions were sold.* A curious vessel for making these preparations has been discovered, something like a modern urn, but much more complicated. The annexed figure shows a section of the urn with its conical cover: $a\,a$ is the body of the urn, b, a small cylindrical furnace in the centre; it has four holes in the bottom, as shown in the plan at g, meant to let the ashes fall through and to create a draught; c, a vase-shaped mouth, by means of which the water was poured in, serving also for the escape of steam; $d\,d$, a tube which, by means of a cock, served to let off the fluid—it is placed thus high to prevent the pipe being stopped up by the ingredient decocted; e, a conical cover, the hollow of which is closed by a thin plate somewhat concave; f, a moveable flat cover, with a hole in the middle, which closes the whole urn except the mouth of the small furnace; $m\,m$, nuts and screws which fasten this moveable cover on the rim of the urn; $i\,i$, rim, convex on the outside and concave within, which, the cover being put on, receives into its concavity the rim of the mouth of the furnace.

The edifice erected by Eumachia had a peristyle or uninterrupted colonnade of white marble Corinthian columns, admirably executed. Unfortunately, only a small portion of one pillar remains; still their plan and disposition are exactly determined by the marble stylobate on which they were placed. Their total disappearance has been accounted for by supposing that the Pompeians themselves, or perhaps Alexander Severus, had dug up and carried off these expensive ornaments subsequently to the demolition of their city. Behind this peristyle the crypto-portico ran round three sides of the building, forming the external boundary on the north, south, and east sides. It was lighted by windows placed at regular intervals, having marble lintels, to which moveable windows were temporarily fixed; but these openings do not always front the spaces between the columns of the area. The east end must have been darker than the north and south sides, from the light being intercepted by the building behind. It appears, however, that this inconvenience was obviated by a borrowed light through that building itself, the back and front of which were pierced with apertures.

* Donaldson's Pompeii.

There were most probably wooden galleries above the colonnade and crypto-portico, and the upper cornice seems to have projected far into the area, thus protecting numerous little tables built of lava and covered with marble, which served for the purpose of displaying the goods which were here exhibited and sold; for it appears probable that this building was for the use of the Pompeian manufacturers of cloth, whose gratitude to Eumachia is expressed by the statue and inscription before mentioned. On one side of the niche where the statue of Eumachia is placed was a false door, six feet wide and ten and a half high, painted on the stucco to correspond with the opening on the other side; it was of a yellow colour, and framed with styles and panels like those

Statue of Eumachia and false door.

now in use. It was divided perpendicularly into three compartments. This door may be presumed to be similar to the door at the entrance from the Street of Abundance. To make the representation more exact, the ring which served for a handle had been imitated. The walls of the crypto-portico are also divided into large panels, painted alternately red and yellow, and decorated in the prevalent fashion; not the least singular part of which, as demonstrative of ancient horticultural taste, are the representations of borders of flowers along the bottom of the walls, representing a plant similar to the iris, except that the colour of the flower is vermilion. In the centre of each panel is a small figure or landscape.

It is probable, as we have already said, that this further

part of the building was the chalcidicum mentioned in the inscription, unless indeed that name should not rather be applied to the whole of it. The situation of this further part corresponds, at all events, with the precept of Vitruvius, that chalcidica should be cut off from one or both ends of a basilica if the area is longer than it ought to be; and in this case such an addition was necessary in order to reduce the form of the main building to a perfect parallelogram. This part is raised above the level of the area, and must have had temporary steps of wood; it is divided into two portions by the recess already mentioned. Near this was found a statue without the head; the robe with which it was draped was edged with a gilded or red stripe. Such an enclosed space was almost necessary (if we are right in considering it as a sort of cloth-market) for the safe custody of goods which remained unsold; as were the tables under the projecting cornice for the display of goods, and the crypto-portico, or inclosed gallery for the transaction of business during the winter. The recess in the centre may also have been occupied by a magistrate, who ratified the sales, received the impost, if any was levied, and settled all disputes arising from the commercial transactions. The building appears to have been repairing at the time of the eruption, as a piece of marble was found on the spot, with a line drawn in charcoal, to guide the chisel of the mason.

On the external wall of the crypt, whose recesses or false windows served as albums, was a notice of a gladiatorial show, as well as an inscription tending to prove the opulence of the city. It is to the effect that "all the goldsmiths invoked Caius Cuspius Pansa the Ædile."

The only other building on the east side of the Forum is that commonly called the School of Verna. It is separated by the Street of Abundance from the Chalcidicum, on the album of which the following inscription was found, which gave rise to the name of the building in question:—

C. CAPELLAM. D. V. I. D. O. V. F. VERNA
CUM DISCENTIBUS.

That is, "Verna with his pupils requests you to make C. Capella Duumvir for administering justice." But as this inscription was not found on the building itself, little can be inferred from it. Some have imagined that they recognized in the building all the characteristics of an eastern school; while others have thought that the podium, or bench, which it contained, marks it out as a place of commerce. The fact is that its destination, like that of many other places in Pompeii, can only be guessed at.

The south end of the Forum is occupied by three buildings, which much resemble one another in their plan, and are nearly of the same size. In the absence of all inscriptions, we have supposed two of these to be curiæ, or places of assembly for the magistrates, and the central one an ærarium, or treasury. Others have thought them to be courts of justice for small causes, or police courts. They have undoubtedly been highly decorated with marble statues and columns, fragments of which, together with pedestals for the latter, still remain on the floors; and it is said that many gold, silver, and copper coins were found in one of them. The floors are elevated above the colonnade, and are reached by steps: they have a circular recess at the end for a tribunal, where a magistrate might preside over the meetings in the curiæ, and a quæstor attend to his duties in the public treasury. These buildings strike the eye of the traveller upon first entering the Forum, from the high dark-red masses of brick contrasting with the verdant mountains at their back, and the low limy buildings around them. We are inclined to think that they were divided into two stories, from traces of stairs which would have led to the upper floor, and also to the wooden gallery above the Forum. There is a narrow passage between the western curia and the ærarium.

On the western side of the Forum are the basilica, a temple supposed to be dedicated to Venus, and the public granaries and prisons, which latter have been already noticed. The basilica,* or court of justice, is the largest building in Pompeii. It is of an oblong form, two hundred and twenty feet in length by eighty, and corresponds in some particulars with

---

* The destination of this building, which is pretty plain from its construction, is accidentally confirmed by a *graffito* of the word "*Bassilica*" (though somewhat misspelt) near one of its side entrances. See Wordsworth, *Inscriptiones Pompeianæ*, p. 14; Garrucci, *Graffiti de Pompei*, p. 81. Another *graffito*, bearing the date of the consulship of Lepidus and Catulus, shows that the building was older than B.C. 79.

DESCRIPTION OF TEMPLES. 125

the usual ancient description of that building. It is placed on the warmest side of the Forum, at its south-west angle, and is entered through a vestibule having five doorways of masonry, in which grooves have been cut for the insertion of wooden door-jambs. From the vestibule the area of the basilica is reached by a flight of four steps, leading through five doorways, as in the vestibule. The roof was supported by a peristyle of twenty-eight large Ionic columns, con-

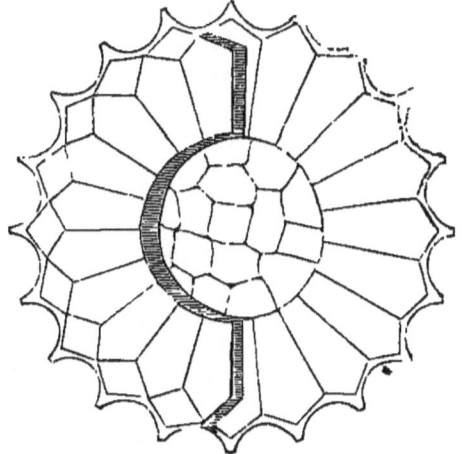

Plan showing the construction of the columns of the Basilica.

structed of brick. Thus the space between the exterior walls and the peristyle was converted into a covered gallery, where the suitors were sheltered from the weather, while the light was admitted hypæthrally from the centre of the peristyle. The tribunal was placed at the furthest end of the building, and on each side of it were two square chalcidica; a smaller order of half columns was attached to the walls, and four whole columns flank and divide the principal entrance; at each corner of the building two columns are joined together, something in the manner of a Gothic pier. This we believe to be a unique example of columns being thus united in Grecian architecture. Upon this smaller order the joists of the upper gallery must have rested at one end: the other most probably was let into the shaft of the larger column, as the smaller is placed immediately behind it. The gallery projected as far as the centre of the large columns. Along the intercolumniations ran a pluteum, or parapet, high enough to prevent persons from falling over: this was most probably repeated all round the back of the gallery, on the face of the lateral walls, upon which, as a basement, a second order was raised. The aggregate height of the two smaller orders was most probably equal to that of the larger order of the peristyle, and the roof was sustained, as has been before mentioned, by the lateral walls and the columns of the peristyle, which rose to the same height.

The second gallery was reached by a staircase, placed without the building; the roof also may have inclined inwards, and the water have been carried away by channels sunk round the marble floors; but there are no remains of these floors, and as the place bears evident marks of having been excavated by the ancients, possibly for records of important trials, it would appear that they had, at the same time, availed themselves of the opportunity afforded them to carry away the pavement of the building, of which only the pozzuolano, in which it was bedded, remains. In the centre of the lateral wall are two entrances, near which are wells. At the furthest end was raised the tribunal for the prætor, or judge, which must have been ascended by wooden steps: it is decorated with small columns, between which, at the back, were small apertures, and at the sides closets, probably for robes of office. Beneath were temporary dungeons for the accused; and there are two holes in the floor, through which orders were transmitted to the person in charge of the prisoners. In front of the tribunal was a pedestal, on which the legs of a bronze statue were found. On each side of the tribunal were two enclosed apartments, intended probably for the use of suitors and their advocates, or the officers, lictors, and necessary attendants of the courts. The external walls are quite plain; but in the interior, courses of masonry are represented in stucco, painted with various colours in imitation of marble. Inscriptions have been faintly scratched on these walls by the loiterers in the courts, by no means remarkable for correctness either in style or sentiment. The large fluted columns which support the roof are singularly constructed with bricks and pieces of tufa, radiating from the centre, as may be seen in the foregoing plan, showing two

DESCRIPTION OF TEMPLES.

alternate layers. All, whether of stone or brick, are covered, as well as the walls, with a fine marble stucco of great hardness. The opinion here expressed, that the lateral walls reached to the height of the larger order, varies from that adopted by Sir W. Gell, who thinks that the peristyle alone supported the principal roof, called testudo, and that it rose above the rest of the building. He also thinks that the roof of the gallery or portico round the testudo inclined inwards, resting against the shaft of the large columns of the peristyle. and thus cutting in two parts the most important feature of the whole building. We dissent from this, because, had the construction been such as Sir W. Gell supposes, the whole would have been covered; and such ingenious architects as the Pompeians employed would hardly have built the roof of the surrounding gallery so as to throw its drippings into the area within the peristyle, which, being covered, would have been the favourite place of assembly.

Next to the basilica, which is an isolated building, is a temple, said to be dedicated to Venus, separated from it by a street leading from the Sea Gate to the Forum. This temple is the largest and finest in Pompeii, and the only peripteral one. Some authorities have called it a Temple of Bacchus, from a painting which it contains of a Bacchic character; while others have considered it to have been dedicated to Mercury and Maia; an inference, however, which rests on a very farfetched interpretation of an inscription.* There are several considerations which lead us to think that the common name is the best. For first, it is natural that Venus, who, as we have seen, was the patron goddess of Pompeii, should have had a magnificent temple set apart for her worship; and if we reject this, it would be difficult to fix upon any other so likely to have been devoted to this purpose. Again, the discovery here of a statue, something in the style of the Medicean Venus, and of a head of the same goddess, serves further to mark the destination of the temple. Further, it is remarked by Breton and Overbeck,† that the altar which stands before the cell is not adapted for bloody or burnt sacrifices, but only for offerings of fruits, cakes, and incense, such as were commonly made to Venus. The following inscription,‡ found in the

* Mommsen, 2199. † Breton, *Pomp.* p. 54; Overbeck, B. i. S. 102.
‡ Mommsen, 2201.

precincts of the temple, has also been thought to confirm its destination:—

> M. HOLCONIVS. RVFVS. D.V.I.D. TERT.
> C. EGNATIVS. POSTVMVS. D.V.I.D. ITER.
> EX. D.D. IVS. LVMINVM.
> OPSTRVENDORVM. H.S. ∞ ∞ ∞
> REDEMERVNT. PARIETEMQVE.
> PRIVATVM. COL. VEN. COR.
> VSQVE. AT. TEGULAS.
> FACIVNDVM. CŒRARVNT.*

Which has been interpreted: "Marcus Holconius Rufus, and Caius Ignatius Posthumus, duumvirs of justice for the third time, by a decree of the Decurions, bought again the right of closing the openings for three thousand sesterces, and took care to erect a private wall to the college of the incorporated Venereans up to the roof." But this interpretation, which was given by Mazois, is inadmissible, inasmuch as the letters COR cannot stand for *corporationis*, a word not used in Latin of the classical age to denote a society or community. On the other hand, if, with Breton † and Mommsen,‡ we render the words "parietemque privatum Col. Ven. Cor.," by "the private wall of the colony *Veneria Cornelia*," it is impossible to understand their meaning.

The temple in question is peripteral and amphiprostyle, and is elevated on a podium, or basement. The portico in front of the cell is tetrastyle and pseudodipteral, and the columns are set aræostyle. Within the cell, which was very small, a beautiful mosaic bordre was found, besides the broken statue already mentioned. The temple stood in an open area, one hundred and fifty feet by seventy-five, surrounded by a wall and portico. At the north end was the priests' apartment, having an outlet into the Forum; the public entrance was at the south. Opposite the latter, bronze ornaments resembling the heads of large nails were found, with which the door might have been decorated, according to a practice common among the ancients. The columns of the temple were Corinthian, fluted, and in part painted blue; those of the colonnade were originally Doric, but afterwards altered to Corinthian, varying in detail, very ill designed, and

---

* Donaldson.　　† *Pompeia*, p. 51.　　‡ *Ad locum.*

badly executed. A perforation has been made in one of the latter to receive a pipe, through which water for the sacrifices

Mosaic border.

flowed into a basin placed upon a circular fluted pedestal. The lower third of them is painted yellow, the rest is white. The details, or characteristic ornaments of the original Doric order, are added with tiles and stucco, and the surface of the architrave is painted with an endless variety of ornament. Both a consular and a terminal figure were found here, but there is no reason for supposing that one of the latter was placed before each column of the colonnade. Channels were formed round the area, under the cornice of this colonnade, to carry off the water from the roof, which inclined inwards like a shed. The ascent to the cell of the temple was by a flight of steps, on each side of which were pedestals; near one of them lay an

Terminal figure in the Temple of Venus.

Dwarfs, from a painting at Pompeii.

Ionic votive column, with a tablet carved in relief upon its shaft, meant to receive the inscription stating by whom and on what occasion it was consecrated. The cell had a pilaster at each of the external angles, and the walls were stuccoed in imitation of masonry. In front of the steps was the great altar. An inscription on the east side of it, which is repeated on the west, records that the Quatuorviri, M. PORCIUS, L. SEXTILIUS, CN. CORNELIUS, and A. CORNELIUS, erected the altar at their own expense. The walls under the colonnade were painted in vivid colours, principally on a black ground, representing landscapes, country-houses, and interiors of rooms with figures, but they are now almost effaced. The groups of figures consisted of dancers, sacrificers to Priapus, battles with crocodiles, &c.; one represented Hector tied to the car of Achilles, another the dispute between Achilles and Agamemnon, and near the ground was a long series of dwarfish figures. In the apartment of the priest was found a very beautiful painting of Bacchus and Silenus. This, which may still be seen, had been removed by the ancients from some other place, and carefully fastened with iron cramps and cement in its present situation. In a recess, at the north-

Painting of Bacchus and Silenus, in the apartment of the priest in the Temple of Venus.

east end of the temple, under the colonnade of the Forum, stood the public measures for wine, oil, and grain. The originals have been carried to the Museum, and those now seen *in situ* are copies. These consist of nine cylindrical holes cut in an oblong block of tufa; there are five large for grain, and four smaller for wine: the former had a sliding bottom, that the grain when measured might be easily removed. The latter are provided with tubes to draw off the liquid. These measures are placed near what we have already supposed to be the horrea, or public granaries.

Having thus completed the circuit of the Forum, it only remains to mention a few less important matters. A portico, as we have often had occasion to mention, surrounds three sides of this space; we will now speak more particularly of its construction. The columns are twelve feet high, and two feet three inches and a half in diameter; they were set aræostyle, about three and a half diameters, or eight feet six inches apart. It has been already mentioned as an objection to this width of intercolumniation, that, except where masses of stone of unusual size could be commanded, the architraves were

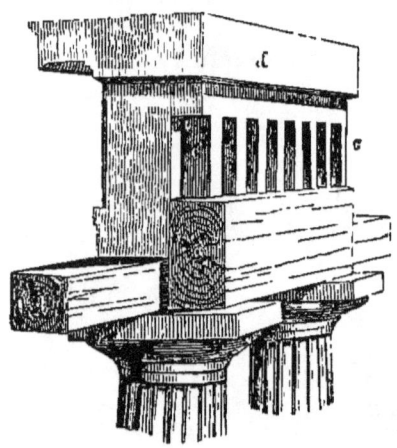

Construction in wood and stone of the aræostyle portico of the Forum.

necessarily either flat arches or beams of wood (*b*). Here the latter material was used, and a stone entablature (*d*) raised upon it, as represented in the annexed engraving. Above this there probably was a gallery;* such at least, we learn from Vitruvius, was the general practice; and this gallery was usually appropriated to the use of those who had the management of the public revenue.

The area of the Forum was adorned with pedestals, for the statues of those who merited or could procure this distinction. Some are of the proportion adapted to equestrian statues. They were all coated with white marble, ornamented with a Doric frieze; and appear to have been still in process of erection,† to replace an older set of pedestals, at the time

* In the holes at *c* the joists of the floor of the upper gallery were most probably fixed.

† It is more probable that the marble was subsequently stripped off them. Five pedestals still retain their marble in whole or in part.

DESCRIPTION OF TEMPLES. 133

when Pompeii was destroyed. Some are inscribed with names, and on one of them may be read that of Pansa. At the south end is a small isolated arch, on which possibly the tutelary genius of the city might have been placed. Such

View of the Forum, looking towards the North.

was the construction of a Roman forum: the reader will not be at a loss to appreciate its combined utility and magnificence. Some surprise may be felt at the expense lavished so prodigally on public buildings in an inconsiderable town.

But the Romans lived in public, and depended on the public for their amusements and pleasure. "A Roman citizen," says M. Simond, "went out early, and did not return home until the evening repast; he spent his day in the forum, at the baths, at the theatre—everywhere, in short, except at his own home, where he slept in a small room, without windows, without a chimney, and almost without furniture." Architectural splendour therefore, both in places of public business and of public pleasure, was far more studied and of far greater importance than it now is; and money, both public and private, was lavished upon such purposes with a profuseness far more than commensurate, according to modern notions, with the objects to which it was directed. We may add, to explain the motives which induced individuals to bestow their money so freely in increasing the splendour of their city, that there was no surer road to power and influence, either in the capital, or in the smaller sphere of a provincial town, than by gratifying the taste of the people for splendour, either in public buildings or in the amusements of the stage or the amphitheatre.

The architecture of Pompeii is not always in the best taste, yet there is much to admire in it, both for the design and the execution. The restoration of the Forum, which forms the frontispiece to this volume, will convey to the reader some idea at once of the artificial and natural beauties of that city.

Male Centaur and Bacchante.

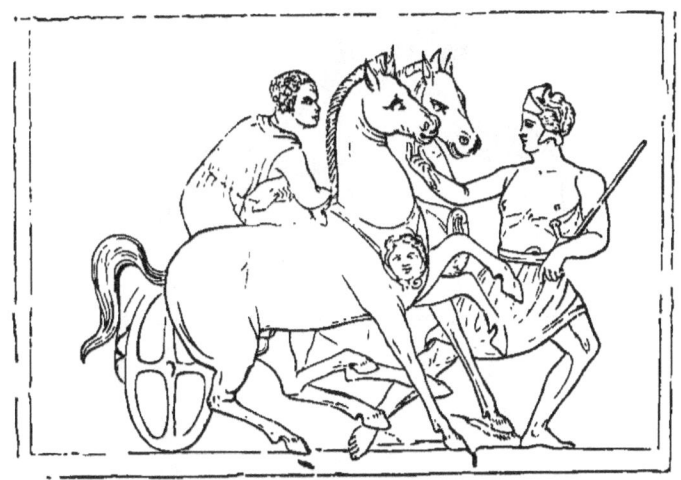

Marble bas-relief found in Pompeii, representing a warrior, and a black slave driving his biga.

CHAPTER V.

THE REMAINING TEMPLES OF POMPEII.

THE present chapter will be devoted to the description of the remaining temples and some other public buildings in various quarters of the city.

At the corner of the main street leading to the Forum and that called the Street of Fortune is a small Corinthian temple, dedicated to Fortune by a private person, one M. Tullius. It has been cased with marble both within and without, and is accessible by two flights, of steps. The lower flight, broken in the middle by a podium or low wall, consists of three, the upper flight of eight steps. There is an altar placed upon the podium, which was protected from wanton intrusion by an iron railing running along the side-margins and in front of the steps. Holes for the reception of the uprights still remain, together with pieces of iron. The portico has four columns in front and two at the sides, and the external walls of the cella are decorated with pilasters. At the end of the building is a semicircular niche, containing a small temple of the Corinthian order, richly finished and designed, under which the statue of the goddess was placed.

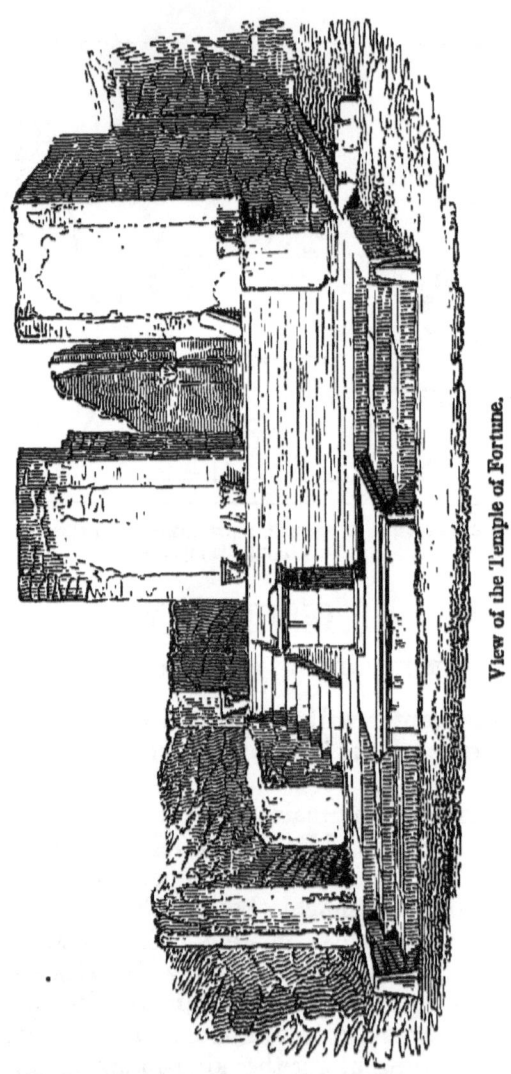

View of the Temple of Fortune.

This Marcus Tullius, who appears from an inscription on the architrave to have erected this temple, has been supposed to be a descendant of the great Cicero. The belief rests on two circumstances: on the finding in the interior of the building a statue of the size of life, said to bear some resemblance to the busts of the distinguished orator; and on an inscription on the architrave of the temple, which may still be seen lying on the floor of the building. It runs as follows:—

M. TULLIUS. M.F.D.V.I.D. TER. QUINQUE. AUGUR. TR. MIL.
A. POP. ÆDEM. FORTUNÆ. AUG. SOLO. ET. PEQ. SUA.

That is: Marcus Tullius, son of Marcus, three times duumvir for the administration of justice, Quinquennalis,* Augur, and Tribune of the soldiers by election of the people, erected this temple of Fortuna Augusta on his own ground and at his own expense." In a small slip of ground on the southeast side of the temple was found another inscription, running as follows:—

M. TULLII. M.F.
AREA PRIVATA.†

The first of these inscriptions, as well as four others, satisfactorily ascertain the temple to have been dedicated to Fortuna Augusta; but whether the builder of it belonged to the family of M. Tullius Cicero, the orator, is a question of some difficulty. Only the father and grandfather of the orator bore the name of Marcus Tullius, and some writers have assumed that the temple was built by one of these.‡ But, as Overbeck remarks,§ the epithet Augusta applied to Fortuna seems to negative this assumption, and to show the building of the temple to have been later than the establishment of the empire.

The statue before mentioned is clothed in the toga prætexta, the robe of office of the Roman magistrates; and what adds value and singularity to the statue, this robe is entirely

---

* The Quinquennalis, as we have said, was a magistrate in coloniæ or municipia, who was elected every five years, and whose functions seem to have resembled those of the censor at Rome.

† For these inscriptions, see Mommsen, Nos. 2219, 2221. Also, for other inscriptions relating to the building, Nos. 2222–6.

‡ Breton, p. 64.

§ *Pompeii*, B. i. S. 95.

painted with a deep purple violet colour. But as in the republican times the prætexta had only a purple hem, and as a toga entirely dyed with that colour was an imperial distinction, first assumed by Julius Cæsar,* there seems reason for believing that the statue must have been intended to represent an emperor, perhaps Augustus. The probability of this inference is increased by the circumstance of a slab of marble having been found in the building, with the following fragmentary inscription :†

STO CÆSARI
PARENTI PATRIÆ.

A female statue, the size of life, was also found within the cella, clothed in a tunic falling to her feet, and above it a toga. The border of the former is gilt; the latter is edged with a red purple bandeau, an inch and a quarter wide; the right arm is pressed upon the bosom, with the hand elevated to the chin, while the left hand holds up the toga. The face of this figure has been sawn off. Some have supposed this a piece of economy of the Pompeians, who, wishing to pay a compliment to some distinguished person, had thought that the cheapest way of doing it was to substitute her face for that originally belonging to the statue.

It is manifest that the ancients have made excavations on this spot, and carried away the columns of the temple and the marble with which it was covered, both within and without. Some of the capitals however remain to show the order of its architecture, and enough is preserved to assure us that it was rich in ornament and highly finished.

Near the theatres, in the Street of Stabiæ, at the angle which it makes with the Street of Isis, is a small temple called the Temple of Æsculapius. The entrance leads into an open court, in which stands an altar, large out of all proportion to the size of the building, peculiar in its character, and bearing a striking resemblance to the sarcophagus of the Scipios in the Vatican; the most remarkable points being the triglyphs with which the frieze is ornamented, which are of rare occurrence in constructions of this size and character, and the volutes at the corners, which are not

---

* Cic. *Philipp.* ii. 34.   † *Hist. Antiq. Pomp.* t. ii. p. 96.

known to occur elsewhere. The court is traversed in its whole width by a flight of nine steps, on the top of which stands the temple itself, comprising a small square cell, with a tetrastyle pseudo-dipteral portico.

In the cell were found two terra-cotta statues as large as life, one male the other female; they are now preserved in the terra-cotta collection in the National Museum. The female statue is taller than the male, its height being 8 palms, while that of the latter is only 7¼ palms.* They are supposed by many authorities to represent Jupiter and Juno, and hence the temple frequently bears the name of those deities. Winkelmann first called them Æsculapius and Hygeia,† and thus gave the temple a new name. The representations of Jupiter and Æsculapius are very similar in ancient works of art, so that, unless they are accompanied by some symbols, it is frequently difficult to distinguish them. It seems however hardly probable, that if these statues represented Jupiter and Juno, the goddess should have been larger than the god; or that the two chief divinities of Olympus should have been crowded into so tiny a temple. There was also found a marble bust of Minerva, which has led Overbeck to talk about a temple of the three Capitoline deities.‡ But the size of it is still more adverse to such a notion. On the other hand, as, by some mythologists, Minerva is represented to have been the child of Æsculapius and Hygeia, this bust might serve to confirm the idea of Winkelmann; and the finding of several *ex voto* offerings of hands, feet, &c., in terra-cotta, affords a further corroboration of it. It is scarcely necessary to mention a third name which has been sometimes given to this temple, namely, that of Neptune, derived from a head sculptured on the capitals of the columns, and thought to represent that deity. We need only add that the robes of the terra-cotta statues bear evident traces of having been coloured red.

Proceeding westward, along the northern side of the same island of building, we come to the Temple of Isis, separated from the Temple of Æsculapius by a narrow passage leading to the great theatre. The destination of this temple is satis-

---
* *Hist. Antiq. Pomp.* t. i. p. 194.
† *Gesch der Kunst*, B. i. 2, 2 ; B. v. 1, 32.
‡ B. i. S. 88.

factorily ascertained by the following inscription above the entrance :—

N. POPIDIVS. N. F. CELSINVS.
ÆDEM. ISIDIS. TERRÆ. MOTV. CONLAPSAM
A. FVNDAMENTO. P. S. RESTITVIT.
HVNC. DECVRIONES. OB. LIBERALITATEM.
CVM. ESSET. ANNORVM. SEXS. ORDINI. SVO.
GRATIS. ADLEGERVNT.*

"Numerius (or Nonnius) Popidius Celsinus, son of Numerius, restored from the foundation, at his own expense, the Temple of Isis, overthrown by an earthquake. The Decurions, on account of his liberality, elected him when sixty years of age to be one of their order free of expense." The earthquake alluded to was probably that in the year 63, sixteen years before the eruption of Vesuvius.

This is one of the most perfect examples now existing of the parts and disposition of an ancient temple. A rude Corinthian portico encompasses the court; the columns are about one foot nine inches in diameter, the shafts painted. To the two nearest the entrance, two lustral marble basins, now in the Museum of Naples, were found attached, and a wooden box, reduced to charcoal, probably a begging-box to receive the contributions of worshippers. The ædes, for the reader will observe that this little building is not in the inscription called a temple, stands insulated in the centre of the court on an elevated podium, and is accessible by a flight of steps occupying only part of its front. On each side of the portico are altars. In front of the cell is a Corinthian tetrastyle portico, comprising six columns. It is flanked by two wings, with niches for the reception of statues: behind that on the left are steps, and a side entrance to the cell. The whole exterior is faced with stucco decorations, capricious in style, and disfigured by a strange mixture of the very commonest species of ornament. Within the temple, at the further end, a strip is parted off, probably for some

* Fiorelli, *Pomp. Ant. Hist.* t. i. p. 174; Mommsen, No. 2243. It should be stated that Mommsen, as well as Overbeck, B. i. S. 107, interprets the word *sexs* by *six*, and explains the difficulty by supposing that Popidius was a rich heir in tutelage, and that the money was laid out in his name by his guardian. Overbeck contends that such a thing might be done in those days.

THE REMAINING TEMPLES OF POMPEII. 141

juggling purposes connected with the worship of the temple.* In the south-east corner of the enclosure is a small building, ornamented with pilasters, with an arched opening in the centre, and over the arch a representation of figures in the act of adoration; a vase is placed between them. This building covered the sacred well, to which there is a descent by steps, and served probably for purification of the worshippers and other uses of the temple. The whole is grotesquely decorated with elegant though capricious stuccos, and whimsically painted. The ground-colour between the pilasters is yellow, that of the frieze red, and the flat space between the arch and the pediment is green, while within the arch it is yellow. The cornice was surmounted by terracotta antefixes, which, from a single fragment remaining, representing a mask, appear to have been executed with great taste and skill.

Before this building stands the chief altar, which seems to have been placed in this situation instead of immediately before the cella, either to save room, or else perhaps because the ceremonies required the priests to visit the small building and the sacred well just described. There were found on this altar the ashes and parts of burnt bones of the victims, and the white stuccoed wall of the adjoining edifice, containing the sacred well, was discoloured with the smoke from the fire. Opposite to it, on the other side of the court, is what appears to be a sort of square fountain, under which Domenico Fontana's canal now flows; but at the time of its discovery it was filled with black ashes, the remains apparently of carbonized fruits.† Before the left wing of the portico of the cell is another smaller altar, probably intended for the worship of the deity whose statue may have stood in the niche already mentioned. On each side of the steps leading up to the cella are two small pedestals which contained the famous basalt Isiac tables. One of them was broken; the other was removed to the National Museum. It is about five feet high and one and a half broad. At the top of it are engraved

---

* This idea is rejected both by Breton and Overbeck, the place in question being open to the gaze of all.

† *Pomp. Ant. Hist.* t. i. p. 172 (June 8th, 1765), and p. 182 (Dec. 14th). Among the fruits were observed dates, chesnuts, nuts, figs, pines, and filberts. *Ibid*, p. 190 (June 21st, 1766).

fourteen figures, thirteen of which are turned towards the first, which is rather larger, and supposed to represent Osiris. Beneath are twenty lines of hieroglyphics, which have been interpreted by the younger Champollion to be an invocation to Osiris and Isis.* By Overbeck, however, it is regarded as a mere sham, and totally unconnected with the worship of Isis, either in general, or at Pompeii in particular.†

On the court wall, in a niche fronting the temple, stood a painted figure of Sigaleon, or Harpocrates, called by the Egyptians Orus, the son of Isis, represented pressing his forefinger to his lip, to impress silence, and intimate that the mysteries of the worship were never to be revealed. Beneath the niche is a shelf, intended perhaps to receive offerings, under which a board was found, supposed to have been meant to facilitate kneeling. In another part of the court a beautiful figure of Isis was found standing on its pedestal, the drapery painted purple, and in part gilt. She held in her right hand the sistrum, an instrument peculiar to her service, made of bronze, in the form of a racket, with three loose bars across it, to serve the purpose of cymbals, or other noisy instruments; in her left, the key of the sluices of the Nile.‡

In the south side of the court, immediately opposite the entrance from the street, there are two chambers and a kitchen, with stoves, on which the bones of fish and other animals were found. A skeleton lay in the outermost room, supposed to be that of one of the priests, who having deferred probably to make his escape until it was too late to do so by the door, was attempting to break through the walls with an axe. He had already forced his way through two, but before he could pass a third was stifled by the vapour. The axe was lying near his remains. Behind the temple is a large chamber, forty-two feet by twenty-five, in which another skeleton was found, who seems, like his companion, to have been at dinner, for chicken bones, egg-shells, and earthen vases were near him. In the sacred precinct lay many other skeletons, supposed those of priests, who reposing a vain hope in the power of their deity, were unwilling to quit

* Breton, *Pompeia*, p. 44.
† B. i. S. 111.
‡ *Pomp. Ant. Hist.*, Mar. 4, 1756 (t. i. p. 185).

her protection, and remained until the accumulation of volcanic matter prevented them from seeking safety in flight.* Pictures were to be seen of the priests of Isis, represented with the head closely shaven, robed in white linen, typical of the introduction of linen among the Egyptians by Isis. They were bound by their vows to celibacy; never ate onions; abstained from salt to their meat, and were forbidden the flesh of sheep or hogs. Fish, we learn from Plutarch, was their chief diet. They were employed day and night in unremitting devotion round the statue of their deity. In several parts of the edifice were termini, or small square columns, surmounted with the heads of various divinities. Statues also were discovered, among which was an image of Venus, with the arms and neck gilt. Paintings of architectural subjects were also discovered detached from the walls; two pictures of the ceremonials then in use among the priests of Isis, as well as a representation of Anubis, with the head of a dog; many priests, with palms and ears of corn, and one holding a lamp in his hand; there was also the representation of a hippopotamus and an ibis, the lotus, various birds, and, on a pilaster, dolphins. All the instruments of sacrifice, made of bronze, were obtained during the excavations.

The modern aqueduct, executed by Dominico Fontana, which conveys the water of the Sarnus to the town of Torre del Annunciata, runs, as we have said, through the court of this temple; and the town having been here first discovered, it diverges, and is arched over, in consequence of the ancient edifices above ground, which would otherwise have been destroyed.

Between the Temple of Isis and the propylæum, or entrance-portico to the triangular Forum, is an oblong building, the purpose of which is not very well defined. It consists of a court, surrounded on three sides by a portico of the Doric order, still pretty perfect, with two rooms at one end, and an elevated pulpitum, for a speaker, at the side. The whole building is seventy-nine feet long by fifty-seven wide; the columns, like almost all found at Pompeii, are very high

* There is no record of these skeletons in the Journals of the Excavations, and we are ignorant of the source from which the author took the account of them.

in proportion to their diameter (1 : 4), being in fact eight and a half diameters, while those of the Parthenon are not quite five and a half. The intercolumniation is seven feet six inches, and the architrave was of course supported by beams. In the centre of the pillar is an elevation, placed to relieve the abacus of the superincumbent weight, which might perhaps have broken it. There are three entrances : one from the street; another, which has been much used and worn, from the portico surrounding the Greek temple; and a third leading directly to the great theatre.

The destination of this building has proved a perfect riddle to antiquarians. Some have given it the name of the Curia Isiaca, and consider it to have been a place for initiating persons into the mysteries of Isis. But it has no communication with the neighbouring temple of Isis, and its whole construction seems too open and public for such a purpose. Some again have taken it to be a school, a court of justice, or a market, and support this opinion by instancing the pulpitum which stands opposite the entrance from the Street of Isis. This pulpitum consists of a sort of pediment between six and seven feet high, and about a yard square at top. It is ascended from behind by a flight of six high but very narrow stone steps, the last of which so much overtops the pulpitum, or pediment, that it might serve for a seat to anybody who had mounted it. Before it stands another smaller pediment, or basis, somewhat resembling an altar, about four feet high. Hence some writers have been led to conclude that the taller pediment was the basis for the statue of some divinity, to whom sacrifice was offered on the smaller one, or altar. Overbeck appears to incline to this view,* and is, at all events, decidedly of opinion that the tall pediment was surmounted by a statue. In support of this view he refers to the Journal of the Excavations, where under date of August 3rd, 1797, we are told that *a pyramid* had been discovered in the building which we are discussing, and on its *soglia* one foot of a marble statue almost entire, and a small part of another.

That the building was immediately connected with the theatre may be inferred from the fact that the third door

* B. i. S. 135.

(not mentioned by Overbeck) leads nowhere else. The following inscription, found in the great theatre, seems also to point the same way:—

M. M. HOLCONII. RUFUS ET. CELER
CRYPTAM. TRIBUNALIA THEATRUM. S. P.*

That is: the two Holconii erected or renovated a crypt, tribunals, and theatre, at their own expense. Hence some writers have been led to call the whole building the Tribunal, but we are not aware that the word is ever so applied. Moreover, the inscription does not say *a tribunal*, but *tribunals*, in the plural; meaning, apparently, some part of the theatre so called, and probably the seats destined for the higher magistrates. It seems to us more probable that the building may have been the crypto-porticus mentioned in the inscription, which would have formed a kind of lobby and retiring room for the spectators in the theatre; but the use of the pediment in question we are unable to explain.

Between this building and the circular back wall of the great theatre there is an open area, where stands a large square mass of building, supposed by some to have been the foundation for a cistern. Its real purpose is doubtful.

Behind the scene of the theatre stands a large rectangular enclosure, one hundred and eighty-three feet long and one hundred and forty-eight wide, surrounded by a Doric colonnade, having twenty-two columns on the longer sides and seventeen on the shorter. The columns are constructed of volcanic tufa, fluted two-thirds of their height, covered with stucco and painted, the lower part red, and the upper alternately red and yellow, except the two centre ones of the east and west sides, the upper parts of which are blue. The surrounding walls were also covered with stucco, painted red below, with yellow above. On the northern side there was a direct communication with both theatres, and the portico of the building must have been of great utility to the spectators, affording additional shelter from the rains when the porticos of the great theatre might have been crowded.

At the time when this building was excavated (1766 and several following years) it was supposed to be a barrack, and obtained the name of the Soldiers' Quarters. After-

---

* Mommsem, *Inscrr. Regni. Neap.*, No. 2299.

wards, however, from its situation near the Forum Triangulare, it came to be considered as a market-place, and was called the Forum Nundinarium, or weekly market. But the arguments on which this view rests are far from being convincing. That it was a sort of barrack hardly admits of a doubt, both from the nature of the place and the objects found in it; but it may be a question whether it was intended for the soldiery or for the gladiators exhibited in the amphitheatre. That a town like Pompeii must have had accommodation for its garrison is evident enough, and the building in question seems excellently adapted for such a purpose. The arms found in it, however, were exclusively of the kind used by gladiators; not a single soldier's weapon was discovered, while the paintings and *graffiti* had also reference to gladiatorial combats. Among these *graffiti*, traced with a hard point on the surface of the ninth column of the east side, was the representation of a fighting gladiator, with these letters, XX Valerius. It has been detached from the wall and carried to the Museum. From these circumstances, Garrucci designated the place as a *ludus gladiatorius*, or school for gladiators, in which view he has been followed by Overbeck.* That, as Breton remarks,† the soldiers' quarters may also have occasionally served for lodgings for the gladiators, and thus have combined both purposes, is not improbable in itself; but the circumstance before mentioned, that no soldiers' weapons were discovered here, seems to negative this view.

Round this colonnade were many small rooms or cells, with an upper story over them, making their number altogether sixty-six. The upper ones were entered from a gallery running round the building, to which there was an ascent by a staircase. These rooms could not well have accommodated more than two men in each, which would give a total of one hundred and thirty-two. To the objection that it would be absurd to suppose that a small town like Pompeii could have supported so large a body of gladiators, Overbeck answers,‡ with much show of reason, that it is evident from its amphitheatre, capable of holding 12,000 or 15,000 spectators, that Pompeii must have been the central place of the whole

---

* *Nuovo Bulletino Napolitano;* Overbeck, B. i. S. 180.
† *Pompeia,* p. 135. ‡ B. i. S. 183 *et seq.*

THE REMAINING TEMPLES OF POMPEII. 147

neighbourhood for the exhibition of gladiatorial shows; and this is also plain from the quarrel before related between the Pompeians and the Nucerians in the amphitheatre of the former. We also learn, from inscriptions found in Pompeii, that thirty or thirty-five pairs of gladiators, or sixty to seventy combatants were sometimes exhibited at one time. We know not how often such shows were given, or whether a larger number of gladiators may not sometimes have been engaged, nearly half of whom may have been killed in the arena, while many more would have died of their wounds.

The upper story of this building has been restored at one of the angles, upon the authority of various indications in

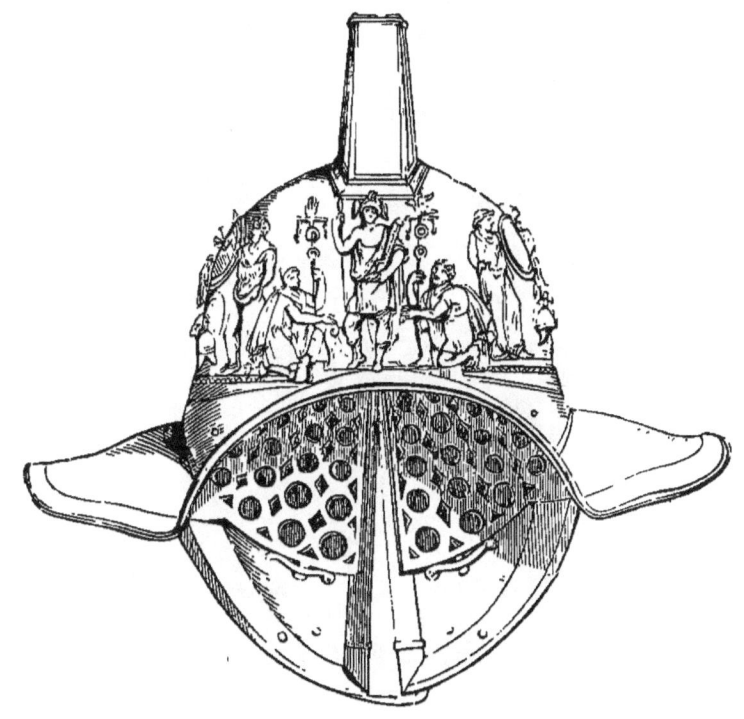

Bronze helmet found at Pompeii.

the construction. Here was found a bronze helmet, highly enriched with bas-reliefs relating to the principal events of the capture of Troy. Another helmet found in Pompeii re-

148   POMPEII.

presents the triumphs of Rome in the midst of her vanquished enemies and captives; this one has a vizor, like those of the lower ages, with square and round holes to see through.

Specimen of the Greaves supposed to have been worn by the Gladiators.

From their size and weight, these pieces of armour have been supposed by some not to have been really worn, but only intended as ornaments for trophies; but Sir W. Hamilton, who was present at their excavation, states distinctly that he saw part of the linings adhering to them, now fallen out, and has no doubt but that they were meant for use, and of their having been worn. Greaves, or coverings for the shins, made of bronze and highly ornamented, were also discovered here; on these were sculptured masks alluding to the dramatic representations. The most remarkable is one with a triple face, representing the tragic, comic, and satiric features.

On the right or eastern side of the colonnade is a small apartment which seems to have served as a prison or place of punishment, since a sort of iron stocks, with holes for the legs, was found in it. In this room were discovered the skeletons of four men, who might probably have been prisoners, but their legs do not appear to have been enclosed in the irons, as some writers have asserted.* Many other skeletons were found in different parts of the building, and in one place thirty-four lay close together.† May not these have been the bodies of killed or badly wounded gladiators? All the cells are much alike. In one of them was found an instrument used apparently as an oil mill; in another was discovered a curious brass trumpet, to which were fitted six ivory flutes mounted with bronze, and a chain for hanging it round the neck.‡

The quarter of the theatres is inferior only to that of the Forum in the variety and beauty of its buildings. As the latter was especially dedicated to business, so was the former to pleasure; and we here find ample provision made for the gratification of the citizens, not only by dramatic entertainments, but by spacious porticos and large areas, which probably were planted and adorned with flowers. It was in such places as these, under the shade of colonnades, or in the open air, as the weather might invite, in each other's company, that the Italians loved to take the mild exercise which suited the climate; for when they engaged in more violent exercise it was in athletic games or similar pursuits: to

---

* *Pomp. Ant. Hist.* t. i. p. 197.   † *Ibid*, pp. 211, 212, 218.
‡ Breton, p. 140.

take a walk, in the English acceptation of the term, was a thing that no one ever thought of doing for pleasure. The theatres themselves, which will be described in a separate chapter, are small and plain compared with those which existed at Rome, yet they bear the remains of considerable magnificence, and the larger at least would be considered of great size in any modern capital. The approach to them must have combined convenience and beauty in no common degree. Just at the point where the two routes from the Forum unite, there stands a propyleum, or vestibule, of eight Ionic columns *in Antis*, raised upon two steps, one foot nine inches in diameter and thirteen feet four inches high, forming one of the best remaining monuments of Pompeii. In the mouldings of the entablature an artifice has been employed by the architect to produce an effect as if black lines had been painted. This is done by cutting deep narrow lines under the projecting mouldings, allowing of no reflection, and consequently producing a sharp and black shadow. In front of one of the columns is a fountain, that never-absent article of Pompeian comfort, supplied with water through a mask sculptured in stone. A marble basin or patera is also attached to one of the columns of the portico, facing you as you enter, which was fed by pipes carried up through the centre of the column. In this vestibule some articles of gold and silver were found, together with an emerald ring. This leads into what is commonly called the Triangular Forum, surrounded by an extentensive colonnade of the Doric order, between the pillars of which were iron bars, to confine the crowd within them. The greater, or eastern side of the triangle is about 450 feet in length, the other being about 300 feet. The third, or southern side, appears to have had no portico, and was perhaps lined with small shops. Within this ample area, which was not properly a forum, but a sacred enclosure, are the remains of an edifice, called, from its style of architecture, the Greek temple, otherwise the Temple of Hercules. This, from its size, arrangement, and style of art, is one of the most important buildings in Pompeii. The Count de Clarac * dates its erection about eight hundred years before the Christian era; and if this remote antiquity can be main-

* See Pompeii, par le Comte de Clarac.

tained, it is one of the most ancient specimens existing of Grecian art, and must have been erected by some of the earliest Grecian colonists. It is in a very dilapidated state; the few indications that can be relied on seem to prove that it had an entire peristyle of columns, three feet ten inches and a half in diameter, diminishing at the top to three feet, and about four and a half diameters, or seventeen feet six inches high, comprising seven columns on the north-west and south-east fronts, and eleven on each of the sides. The intercolumniations are one diameter and two-ninths. This is one of the few instances of an ancient building having an uneven number of columns in front, and consequently an odd one in the centre; another instance occurs in the basilica of Pæstum. The capitals belong to the Grecian Doric; the abacus, or flat stone at the top, is four feet eleven inches square, and the whole capital peculiar, inasmuch as the stone out of which it is worked includes no part of the shaft. Its great depth (one foot ten inches and a quarter) and bold projection indicate a very ancient character.* The masonry has been covered with fine stucco. The cell appears to have been divided into several compartments, paved with mosaic, and there seem to have been two entrances from the portico, one on each side of the centre column. The whole building stands upon a podium or basement, raised five steps above the level of the ground. In front there is a further flight of five steps; these are entire, but much worn. The total length of the building, including the podium, but not the flight of steps, is about 120 feet; its breadth about 70. Before the steps is a square enclosure, supposed to have been a pen to contain victims, and by its side two altars. A little further off stands a small monopteral building, of the Doric order, covering a puteal, or well, from which the water required in the temple was drawn. Otherwise it has been called a bidental, or locus fulminatus, a spot where a thunderbolt has fallen. Such spots were held in especial awe by the ancient Romans, and set apart as sacred to Pluto and infernal deities. The method of its construction will suit either supposition. Eight columns of tufa, one foot four inches in diameter, supported a circular epistyle and roof. Under this

* Gell, p. 241.

is a structure resembling a circular perforated altar, such as was commonly placed for security round the mouth of wells. Exactly the same covering was placed over a bidental, and in either case it was alike called puteal.

It has been supposed that the temple was erected on the site of a still older pottery, from the fragments of vases and tiles which have been discovered under the base. The spot is elevated considerably above the level of the plain, which it overlooks, but is not quite so high as the Forum. Near the south-west corner of the building is an exedra, or seat, placed to afford the worshippers and others the full enjoyment of the magnificent and extensive view. The seat is semicircular, like those in the Street of Tombs. From it a noble prospect presented itself to the eye, embracing Castellamare, Vico, Sorrento, the promontory of Minerva, and the island of Capri, with almost the entire expanse of the dark blue bay of Naples. The city wall appears to have bounded the area upon this, the south side, so that the portico, which would have interrupted the view, was only continued along two sides. Parallel to the eastern portico there runs a long wall, terminated at one end by the altars already mentioned and at the other by a pedestal, inscribed

M. CLAUDIO. M.F. MARCELLO. PATRONO

Female Centaur and Bacchante.

CHAPTER VI.

BATHS EXCAVATED IN THE YEARS 1824 AND 1858.

AFTER the excavations at Pompeii had been carried on to a considerable extent, it was matter of surprise that no public baths were discovered, particularly as they were sure almost to be placed in the most frequented situation, and therefore probably somewhere close to the Forum. The wonder was increased by the small number of baths found in private houses. That public baths existed, was long ago ascertained from an inscription discovered in 1749, purporting that one Januarius, an enfranchised slave, supplied the baths of Marcus Crassus Frugi with water, both fresh and salt. At length an excavation in the vicinity of the Forum brought to light a suite of public baths, admirably arranged, spacious, highly decorated, and superior to any even in the most considerable of our modern cities. They are fortunately in good preservation, and throw much light on what the ancients, and especially Vitruvius, have written on the subject.

Inscription in the Court of the Baths.

DEDICATIONE. THERMARUM. MUNERIS. CNÆI.
ALLEI. NIGIDII. MAII. VENATIO. ATHLETÆ.
SPARSIONES. VELA. ERUNT. MAIO.
PRINCIPI. COLONIÆ. FELICITER.

Fac-simile of the above inscription.

"On occasion of the dedication of the baths, at the expense of Cnæus Alleius Nigidius Maius, there will be the chase of wild beasts, athletic contests, sprinkling of perfumes, and an awning. Prosperity to Maius, chief of the colony."

This announcement of a public entertainment is written on a wall of the court of the baths, to the right hand on entering.*

The provincial towns, imitating the example of Rome, and equally fond of all sorts of theatrical and gladiatorial exhibitions, of which we shall hereafter speak at length in describing the various theatres of Pompeii, usually solemnized the completion of any edifices or monuments erected for the public service by dedicating them. This ceremony was nothing more than opening or exhibiting the building to the people in a solemn manner, gratifying them at the same time with largesses and various spectacles. When a private man had erected the building, he himself was usually the person who dedicated it. When undertaken by the public order and at the public cost, the citizens deputed some magistrate or rich and popular person to perform the ceremony. In the capital vast sums were expended in this manner; and a man who aspired to become a popular leader could scarcely lay out his money to better interest than in courting favour by the prodigality of his expenses on those or similar occasions. It appears, then, that upon the completion of the baths, the Pompeians committed the dedication to Cnæus Alleius Nigidius Maius, who entertained them with a

* Now effaced.

sumptuous spectacle. There were combats (*venatio*) between wild beasts, or between beasts and men, a cruel sport, to which the Romans were passionately addicted; athletic games (*athletæ*), sprinkling of perfumes (*sparsiones*), and it was further engaged that an awning should be raised over the amphitheatre. The convenience of such a covering will be evident, no less as a protection against sun than rain under an Italian sky; the merit of the promise, which may seem but a trifle, will be understood by considering the difficulty of stretching a covering over the immense area of an ancient amphitheatre. We may observe, by the way, that representations of hunting and of combats between wild beasts are common subjects of the paintings of Pompeii. A combat between a lion and a horse, and another, between a bear and a bull, have been found depicted in the amphitheatre. The velarium, or awning, is advertised in all the inscriptions yet found which give notice of public games. Athletæ and sparsiones appear in no other. We learn from Seneca that the perfumes were disseminated by being mixed with boiling water, and then placed in the centre of the amphitheatre, so that the scents rose with the steam, and soon became diffused throughout the building. There is some reason to suppose that the completion and dedication of the baths preceded the destruction of the city but a short time, from the inscription being found perfect on the wall of the baths, for it was the custom to write these notices in the most public places, and after a very short season they were covered over by others, as one billsticker defaces the labours of his predecessors. This is abundantly evident even in the present ruined state of the town, especially at the corners of the principal streets, where it is easy to discover one inscription painted over another. But to return to the Baths. They occupy almost an entire island, forming an irregular quadrangle; the northern front, facing to the Street of the Baths, being about 162 feet in length, the southern front about 93 feet, and the average depth 174 feet. They are divided into three separate and distinct compartments, one of which was appropriated to the fireplaces and to the servants of the establishment; the other two were occupied each by a set of baths, contiguous to each other, similar and adapted to the same purposes, and supplied with heat and water from the same furnace and from the same reservoir. It is conjectured that the most spacious of them was for the use of the men, the lesser for that of the women. The apartments and passages are paved with white marble in mosaic. It appears, from Varro and Vitruvius, that baths for men and women were originally united, as well for convenience as economy of fuel, but were separated afterwards for the preservation of morals, and had no communication except that from the furnaces. We shall call these the *old* Baths by way of distinction, and because they were first discovered; but in reality, the more recently discovered Stabian Baths may probably be the more ancient.

It should be observed here that the old Pompeian *thermæ* are adapted solely to the original purposes of a bath, namely, a place for bathing and washing. They cannot therefore for a moment be compared to the baths constructed at Rome during the period of the empire, of which such magnificent remains may still be seen at the Baths of Diocletian, and especially at those of Caracalla. In these vast establishments the bath formed only a part of the entertainment provided. There were also spacious porticoes for walking and conversing, halls and courts for athletic games and gladiatorial combats, apartments for the lectures and recitations of philosophers, rhetoricians, and poets. In short, they formed a sort of vast public club, in which almost every species of amusement was provided. In the more recently discovered baths, called the Thermæ Stabianæ, which will be described further on, there is indeed a large quadrangular court, or palæstra, which may have served for gymnastic exercises, and among others for the game of ball, as appears from some large balls of stone having been found in it. Yet even this larger establishment makes but a very slight approach to the magnificence and luxury of a Roman bath.

The piscina, or reservoir of the old Pompeian baths, is separated from the baths themselves by the street (W) which opens into the north-western corner of the Forum, now called Vicolo delle Terme. The pipes which communicated between the reservoir and the bath passed over an arch (*w*) thrown across the street. This arch was perfect when the excavation was made; now only the shoulders remain, in which the pipes above mentioned are still visible. There were three entrances to the furnaces which heated the warm and vapour baths. The chief one opened upon a court (*r*) of an irregular figure, fit for containing wood and other necessaries for the use of the establishment, covered in part by a roof, the rafters of which rested at one end on the lateral walls and at the other on two columns constructed with small pieces of stone. From hence a very small staircase

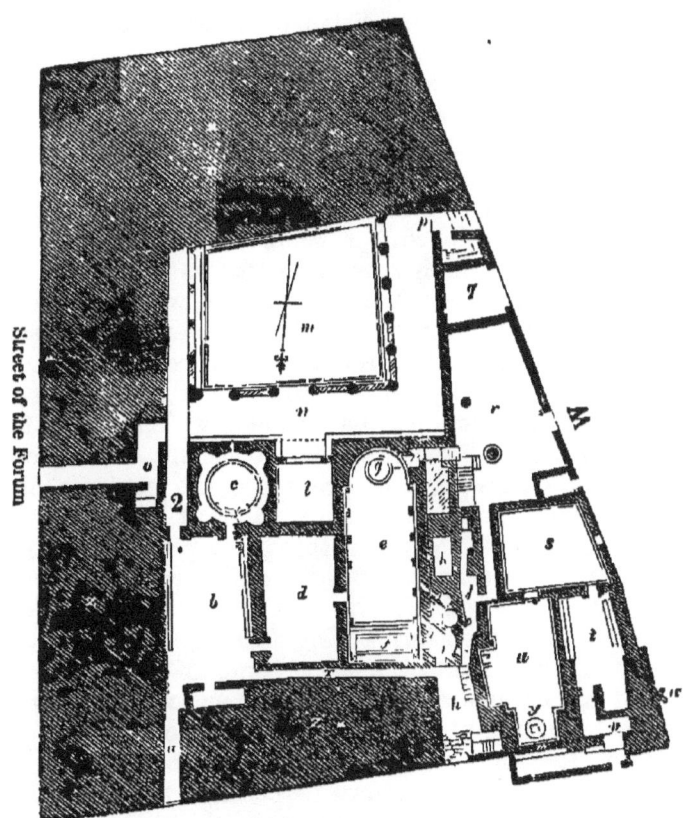

Plan of the Baths.

led to the furnaces and to the upper part of the baths. Another entrance led to a small room (*h*) (*præfurnium*), into which projects the mouth of a furnace (*i*). In this room were the attendants on the furnace, or stokers (*fornacarii*), whose duty it was to keep up the fires. Here was found a quantity of pitch, used by the furnace-men to enliven the fires. The stairs in the room (*h*) led up to the coppers. The third entrance led from the apodyterium of the men's baths by means of a corridor (*x*). It is to be remarked that there is no communication between these furnaces and the bath of the women, which was heated from them. The furnace was round, and had in the lower part of it two pipes, which transmitted hot air under the pavements and between the walls of the vapour-baths, which were built hollow for that purpose. Close to the furnace, at the distance of four inches, a round vacant space still remains, in which was placed the copper (*caldarium*) for boiling water; near which, with the same interval between them, was situated the copper for warm water (*tepidarium*); and at the distance of two feet from this was the receptacle (*k*) for cold water (*frigidarium*), which was square, and plastered round the interior like the piscina or reservoir before mentioned. A constant communication was maintained between these vessels, so that as fast as hot water was drawn off from the caldarium, the void was supplied from the tepidarium, which being already considerably heated, did but slightly reduce the temperature of the hotter boiler. The tepidarium, in its turn, was supplied from the piscina, and that from the aqueduct; so that the heat which was not taken up by the first boiler passed on to the second, and instead of being wasted, did its office in preparing the contents of the second for the higher temperature which it was to obtain in the first. It is but lately that this principle has been introduced into modern furnaces, but its use in reducing the consumption of fuel is well known. It is necessary to apprize the reader that the terms frigidarium, tepidarium, and caldarium, are applied to the apartments in which the cold, tepid, and hot baths are placed, as well as to those vessels in which the operation of heating the water is carried on. The furnace and the coppers were placed between the men's baths and the women's baths, as near as possible to both, to avoid the waste of heat consequent on transmitting the heated fluids through a length of pipe. The coppers and reservoir were elevated considerably above the baths, to cause the water to flow more rapidly into them.

The men's baths had three public entrances (*a*, *o*, and *p*). Entering at the principal one (*p*), which opens to the Vicolo delle Terme, we descend three steps into (*m*) the vestibule, cortile, or portico of the baths, along three sides of which runs a portico (*ambulacrum*). The seats which are to be

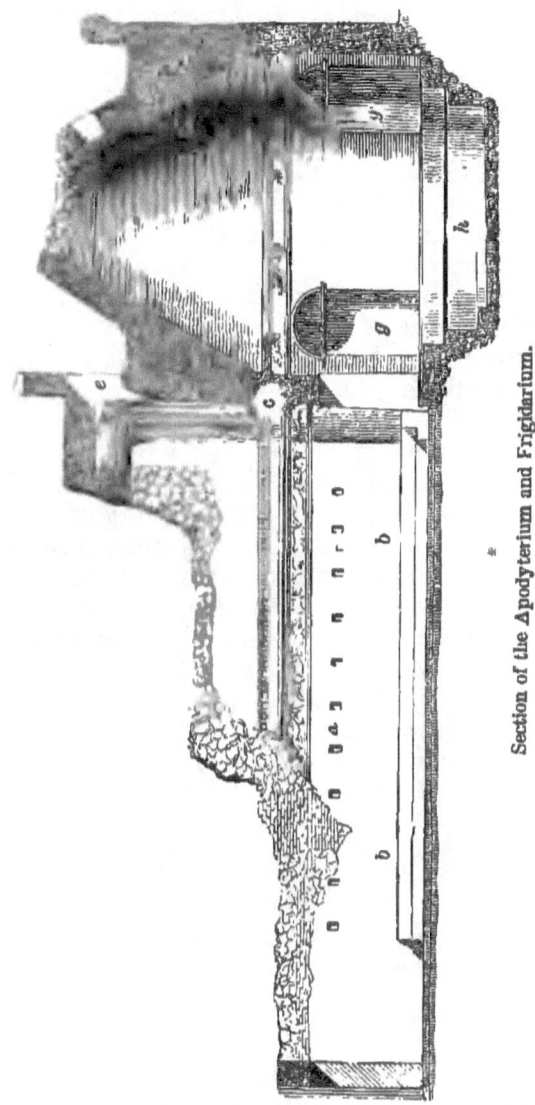

Section of the Apodyterium and Frigidarium.

seen arranged round the walls were for the slaves who accompanied their masters to the baths, and for the servants of the baths themselves, to whom also the apartment (*l*) appears to have been appropriated which opens on the court but extends backward from it. In this court was found a sword with a leather sheath, and the box for the quadrans, or piece of money which was paid by each visitor. It is probable that the sword belonged to the balneator or keeper of the Thermæ. The door (*o*) which opens on the Street of the Forum leads also into the same vestibule. By means of a corridor we proceed through the passage (2) into the apodyterium, or undressing room (*b*), which is also accessible by the corridor (*a*) from the street now called the Strada delle Terme, or Street of the Baths. In this corridor alone were found upwards of five hundred lamps, and upwards of a thousand were discovered in various parts of the baths during the excavations. Of these the best were selected, and the workmen were ordered to destroy the remainder. The greater number were of terra-cotta; some had an impression of the graces on them, and others the figure of Harpocrates —both of inferior execution. The ceiling of this passage is decorated with stars. The apodyterium has three seats, marked *b*, *d* in the two cuts of sections, made of lava, with a step to place the feet on. Holes (*a*) still remain in the wall, in which pegs were fixed, for the bathers to hang up their clothes. This chamber is stuccoed from the cornice to the ground; it is highly finished, and coloured yellow. The cornice is of large dimensions, and, has something of an Egyptian character; below it is carved a frieze, composed of lyres, dolphins, chimæræ and vases in relief, upon a red

Ornamented frieze in the Apodyterium.

ground. In the centre of the end of the room is a very small opening or recess (*c*), once covered with a piece of glass: in this recess, as is plain from its smokiness, a lamp has been placed. In the archivolt, or vaulted roof, immediately over the recess is a window marked *e* in the trans-

verse section, two feet eight inches high and three feet eight
inches broad, closed by a single large pane of cast glass, two-
fifths of an inch thick, fixed into the wall, and ground on one
side, to prevent persons on the roof from looking into the
bath: of this glass many fragments were found in the ruins.
This is an evident proof that glass windows were in use
among the ancients. Underneath the window a large mask
is moulded in stucco, with curling hair and a most venerable
flowing beard. Water is sculptured flowing from the locks of
hair, and on each side two Tritons, with vases on their shoulders, are fighting; there are also dolphins, which encircle with

Transverse section of the Apodyterium.

their tails the figures of children struggling to disengage
themselves. All these are ornaments appropriate to baths,
and of a whimsical invention to symbolize water and bathing.
The floor is paved with white marble worked in mosaic, and
the ceiling appears to have been divided into white panels
within red borders. It has six doors: one leads to the præfurnium, marked *h* in the plan; another into the small room,
perhaps destined for a wardrobe; the third, by a narrow
passage (*a*) to the Street of the Baths; the fourth to the tepidarium (*d*); the fifth to the frigidarium (*c*); and the sixth
along the corridor (2) to the vestibule or portico of the bath.

The frigidarium (*c*), or cold bath, is a round chamber,
incrusted with yellow stucco, with indications here and there
of green, with a ceiling in the form of a truncated cone,
which appears to have been painted blue. Near the top is a
window, marked *f* in the section, by which it was lighted. In

the cornice, which is coloured red, is modelled in stucco a chariot race of Cupids, preceded by Cupids on horseback and on foot.

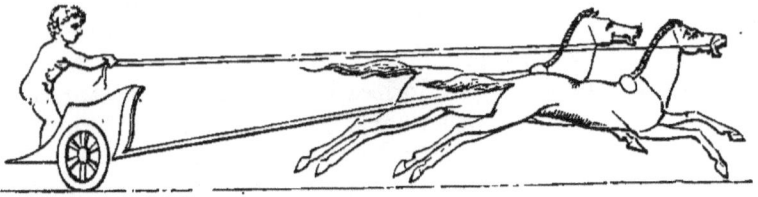

Chariot race of Cupids in the Frigidarium.

The plinth or base of the wall is entirely of marble. The entrance is by the undressing-room. There are four niches (*gg*), disposed at equal distances, painted red above and blue below. In these niches (scholæ) were seats for the convenience of the bathers. The basin (alveus) is twelve feet ten inches in diameter and not much more than a yard deep, and is entirely lined with white marble. Two marble steps facilitate the descent into it, and at the bottom is a sort of cushion (pulvinus), also of marble, to enable those who bathed to sit down. The water ran into this bath in a large stream, through a spout or lip of bronze four inches wide, placed in the wall at the height of three feet seven inches from the edge of the basin. At the bottom is a small outlet for the purpose of emptying and cleansing it, and in the rim there is a waste pipe to carry off the superfluous water. This frigidarium is remarkable for its preservation and beauty.

View of the Tepidarium.

The tepidarium (*d*), or warm chamber, was so called from a warm, but soft and mild temperature, which prepared the bodies of the bathers for the more intense heat which they were to undergo in the vapour and hot baths; and, *vice*

Telamones in the Tepidarium.

versâ, softened the transition from the hot bath to the external air. The wall is divided into a number of niches or compartments by Telamones,* two feet high, in high relief, and supporting a rich cornice. These are male, as Caryatides are female statues placed to perform the office of pillars. By the Greeks they were named Atlantes, from the well-known fable of Atlas supporting the heavens. Here they are made of terra-cotta, or baked clay, incrusted with the finest marble stucco. Their only covering is a girdle round the loins; they have been painted flesh-colour, with black hair and beards : the moulding of the pedestal and the baskets on their heads were in imitation of gold; and the pedestal itself, as well as the wall behind them and the niches for the reception of the clothes of the bathers, were coloured to resemble red porphyry. Six of these niches are closed up without any apparent reason.

The ceiling is worked in stucco, in low relief, with scattered figures and ornaments of little flying genii, delicately relieved on medallions, with foliage carved round them. The ground is painted, sometimes red and sometimes blue. The room was lighted by a window two feet six inches high and three feet wide, in the bronze frame of which were found set four very beautiful panes of glass fastened by small nuts and screws, very ingeniously contrived, with a view to remove the glass at pleasure. In this room was found a brazier, seven feet long and two feet six inches broad, made entirely of bronze, with the exception of an iron lining. The two

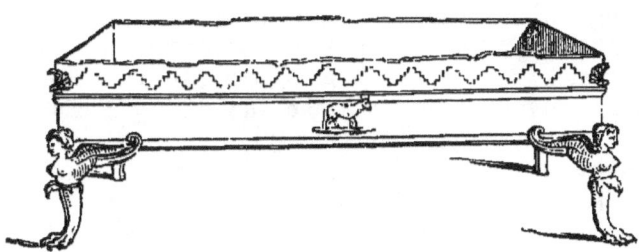

Brazier in the Tepidarium.

front legs are winged sphinxes, terminating in lions' paws; the two other legs are plain, being intended to stand against

* So called from the Greek τλῆναι, to endure. The etymology of Atlas is the same.

the wall. The bottom is formed with bronze bars, on which are laid bricks supporting pumice-stones for the reception of charcoal. There is a sort of false battlement worked on the rim, and in the middle a cow is to be seen in high relief. Three bronze benches also were found, alike in form and pattern. They are one foot four inches high, one foot in width, and about six feet long, supported by four legs, terminating in the cloven hoofs of a cow, and ornamented at the upper ends with the heads of the same animal. Upon the

One of the three bronze seats found in the Tepidarium.

seat is inscribed, M. NIGIDIUS. VACCULA. P. S. Varro, in his book upon rural affairs, tells us that many of the surnames of the Roman families had their origin in pastoral life, and especially are derived from the animals to whose breeding they paid most attention. As, for instance, the Porcii took their name from their occupation as swineherds; the Ovini from their care of sheep; the Caprilli, of goats; the Equarii, of horses; the Tauri, of bulls, &c. We may conclude, therefore, that the family of this Marcus Vaccula were originally cowkeepers, and that the figures of cows so plentifully impressed on all the articles which he presented to the baths are a sort of *canting arms*, to borrow an expression from heraldry, as in Rome the family Toria caused a bull to be stamped on their money.

A doorway led from the tepidarium into the caldarium, or vapour-bath. It had on one side the laconicum, containing the vase (*c*) called labrum. On the opposite side of the room was the hot bath (*q*) called lavacrum. Here it is necessary to refer to the words of Vitruvius as explanatory of the structure of the apartments (cap. xi. lib. v.). "Here should be placed the vaulted sweating-room, twice the length of its width, which should have at each extremity, on one end the *laconicum*, made as described above, on the other end the hot bath." This

DESCRIPTION OF BATHS. 167

apartment is exactly as described, twice the length of its width, exclusively of the laconicum* at one end and the hot bath at the other. The pavement and walls of the whole were hol-

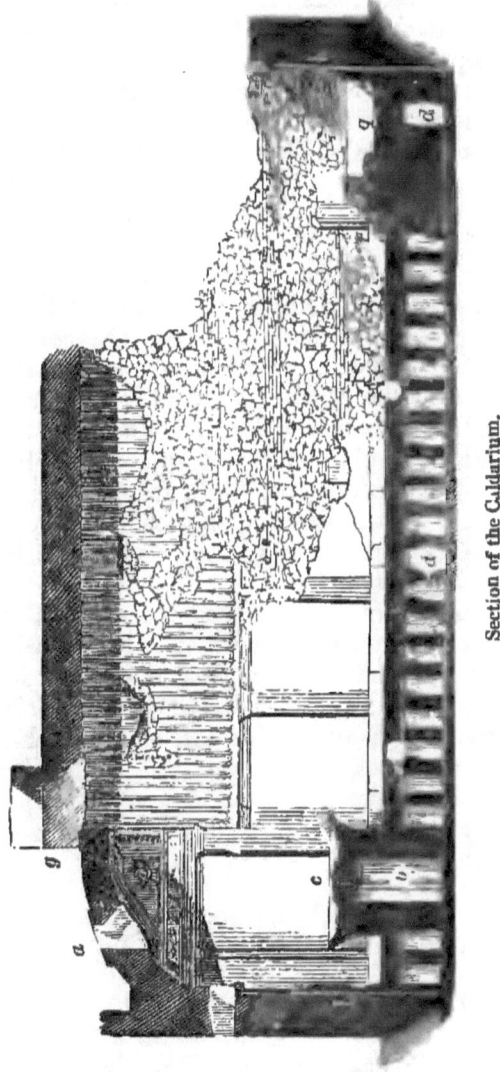

Section of the Caldarium.

* The *Laconicum* was so named after the Lacedæmonians, who, instead of the warm bath, used a dry sweating bath, heated with warm air by means of a stove. Strabo, iii. p. 413; Dion. Cass. liii. p. 515, seq.

lowed to admit the heat. Vitruvius never mentions the laconicum as being separated from the vapour-bath; it may therefore be presumed to have been always connected with it in his time, although in the Thermæ constructed by the later emperors it appears always to have formed a separate apartment. In the baths of Pompeii they are united, and adjoin the tepidarium, exactly agreeing with the descriptions of Vitruvius. The laconicum is a large semicircular niche, seven feet wide and three feet six inches deep, in the middle of which was placed a vase or labrum. The ceiling was formed by a quarter of a sphere; it had on one side a circular opening (*a*), one foot six inches in diameter, over which, according to Vitruvius, a shield of bronze was suspended, which, by means of a chain attached to it, could be drawn over or drawn aside from the aperture, and thus regulated the temperature of the bath. Where the ceiling of the laconicum joined the ceiling of the vapour-bath, there was, immediately over the centre of the vase or labrum, a window (*g*), three feet five inches wide; and there were two square lateral windows in the ceiling of the vapour-bath, one foot four inches wide and one foot high, from which the light fell perpendicularly on the labrum, as recommended by Vitruvius, " that the shadows of those who surrounded it might not be thrown upon the vessel."

The labrum (*c*) was a great basin or round vase of white marble, rather more than five feet in diameter, into which the hot water bubbled up through a pipe (*b*) in its centre, and served for the partial ablutions of those who took the vapour-bath. It was raised about three feet six inches above the level of the pavement, on a round base built of small pieces of stone or lava, stuccoed and coloured red, five feet six inches in diameter, and has within it a bronze inscription, which runs thus :—

GNÆO. MELISSÆO. GNÆI. FILIO. APRO. MARCO. STAIO. MARCI. FILIO. RUFO. DUUMVIRIS. ITERUM. IURE. DICUNDO. LABRUM. EX DECURIONUM DECRETO. EX. PECUNIA. PUBLICA. FACIENDUM. CURARUNT. CONSTAT. SESTERTIUM. D.C.C.L.

Relating that " Cnæus Melissæus Aper, son of Cnæus Aper, Marcus Staius Rufus, son of M. Rufus, duumvirs of justice for the second time, caused the labrum to be made at the public expense, by order of the Decurions. It cost 750 sesterces " (about 6*l*.).* There is in the Vatican a magnificent porphyry labrum found in one of the imperial baths; and Baccius, a great modern authority on baths, speaks of labra made of glass.

This apartment, like the others, is well stuccoed and painted yellow; a cornice, highly enriched with stucco ornaments, is supported by fluted pilasters placed at irregular intervals. These are red, as is also the cornice and ceiling of the laconicum, which is worked in stucco with little figures of boys and animals. The ceiling of the room itself was

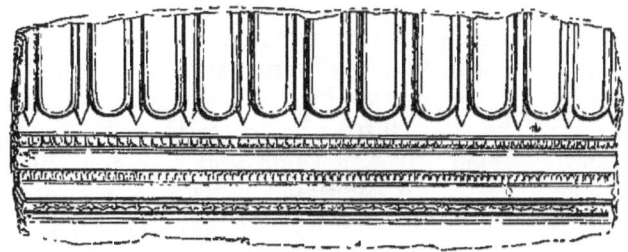

Part of the ceiling of the Caldarium.

entirely carved with transverse fluting, like that of enriched columns, a beautiful ornament, and one but little used for this purpose; no other instance occurring except in certain ruins of villas on the shores of Castellone, the ancient Formiæ. The hot bath (*f* on the plan) occupied the whole end of the room opposite to the laconicum and next to the furnace. It was four feet four inches wide, twelve feet long, and one foot eight inches deep, constructed entirely of marble, with only one pipe to introduce the water, and was elevated two steps above the floor; while a single step led down into the bath itself, forming a continuous bench round it for the convenience of the bathers.

The Romans, who, according to Vitruvius, called their vapour-baths caldaria, or sudationes concameratæ, constructed

* Museum Borbonicum, vol. ii.

them with suspended or hollow floors and with hollow walls* (*d*) communicating with the furnace, that the smoke and hot air might be spread over a large surface and readily raise them to the required warmth. The temperature was regulated by the clypeus or bronze shield already described.

In the Pompeian bath the hollow floors are thus constructed. Upon a floor of cement made of lime and pounded bricks were built small brick pillars (*o*), nine inches square and one foot seven inches high, supporting strong tiles fifteen inches square. The pavement was laid on these and incrusted with mosaic. The hollow walls, the void spaces of which communicated with the vacuum of the suspended pavement, were constructed in the following manner. Upon the walls, solidly stuccoed, large square tiles were fastened by means of iron cramps. They were made in a curious manner. While the clay was moist some circular instrument was pushed through it so as to make a hole, at the same time forcing out the clay and making a projection or pipe about three inches long on the inside of the tile. These being made at the four corners, iron clamps passed through them and fastened them to the wall, the interval being regulated by the length of the projections. The sides of the apartments being thus formed, were afterwards carefully stuccoed and painted. The vacancy in the walls of the Pompeian baths reaches as high as the top of the cornice, but the ceilings are not hollow, as in the baths which Vitruvius described, and which he distinguishes

Ornament of the Tepidarium.

for that reason by the name of concameratæ. The following woodcuts will convey an idea of the style of ornament which

* The Italians call such a floor *vespajo*, from its resemblance to a wasp's nest.

DESCRIPTION OF BATHS. 171

is lavished upon the ceilings of the apartments which we
have just described. The first is a winged child or genius,

Stucco ornaments in the ceiling of the Tepidarium.

riding on one sea-horse and accompanied by another, preceded
by a similar child guiding two dolphins. This occupies the
centre of the ceiling of the tepidarium. Other ornaments

are dispersed around it, from which we have selected some of those that are best preserved. The design is generally better than the workmanship, for they have not been carefully finished, on account, perhaps, of the height at which they were to be placed. A curious piece of economy is visible

Ornaments of the Tepidarium.

in these decorations. Those low down on the walls are executed in relief, but the higher ones are painted as it were in a very liquid stucco; so that the child who sounds a cymbal (see the cut above) in one of the medallions, has one leg, one arm, and the head of stucco, while the wings, the other leg, and the cymbal, which, if also executed in stucco, would have been in lower relief, are either laid on with a brush in this liquid stucco, or left white when the ground was painted. It is so done, that at a certain distance, and to one who does not consider it with nicety, the whole appears to be relieved. The same is to be observed in the bow, which has the two ends formed of goats' heads.

The women's bath resembles very much that of the men, and differs only in being smaller and less ornamented. It is heated, as we have already mentioned, by the same fire, and supplied with water from the same boilers. Near the entrance is an inscription painted in red letters. All the rooms yet retain in perfection their vaulted roofs. In the vestibule (*v*) are seats similar to those which have been described in the men's baths as appropriated to slaves or servants of the establishment. The robing-room (*t*) contains a cold bath; it is painted with red and yellow pilasters alternating with one another on a blue or black ground, and has a light cornice of white stucco and a white mosaic pavement with a narrow black border. There is accommodation for ten persons to undress at the same time. The cold bath is much damaged, the wall only remaining of the alveus, which is square, the whole incrustation of marble being destroyed. From this room we pass into the tepidarium (*s*), about twenty feet square, painted yellow with red pilasters, lighted by a small window far from the ground. This apartment communicates with the warm bath (*u*), which, like the men's, is heated by flues formed in the floors and walls. There are in this room paintings of grotesque design upon a yellow ground, but they are much damaged and scarcely visible. The pavement is of white marble laid in mosaic. The room (*u*) in its general arrangement resembles the hot bath of the men; it has a labrum (*y*) in the laconicum, and a hot bath contiguous to the furnace, as may be seen by the plan. The hollow pavement and the flues in the walls are almost entirely destroyed; and of the labrum, the foot, in the middle of which was a piece of the leaden conduit that introduced the water, alone remains. On the right of the entrance into these women's baths is a wall of stone of great thickness and in a good style of masonry.

These baths are so well arranged, with so prudent an economy of room and convenient distribution of their parts, and are adorned with such appropriate elegance, as to show clearly the intellect and resources of an excellent architect. At the same time some errors of the grossest kind have been committed, such as would be inexcusable in the most ignorant workman; as, for instance, the symmetry of parts has been neglected where the parts correspond; a pilaster is cut off by a door which passes through the middle of it; and other mistakes occur which might have been avoided without difficulty. This strange mixture of good and bad taste, of skill and carelessness, is not very easily accounted for, but it is of constant recurrence in Pompeii.

Vitruvius recommends the selecting a situation for baths defended from the north and north-west winds, and forming windows opposite the south, or if the nature of the ground would not permit this, at least towards the south, because the hours of bathing used by the ancients being from after midday till evening, those who bathed could, by those windows, have the advantage of the rays and of the heat of the declining sun. For this reason the Pompeian baths hitherto described have the greater part of their windows turned to the south, and are constructed in a low part of the city, where the adjoining buildings served as a protection to them from the inconvenience of the north-west winds.

From the smallness of the baths just described, it had long been conjectured that they could not have been the only public establishment of the kind in Pompeii; and this conjecture was confirmed by the discovery, in 1854 and four following years, of other Thermæ on a larger scale than the former ones, and more elegantly decorated. They are situated in the Street of Holconius, marked 1 on the plan, and embrace the whole northern side of it, from the small street called the Via del Lupanare on the west (3), to the Strada Stabiana on the east (2). They are thus completely isolated on their southern, eastern, and western sides, in each of which there are entrances, while on the north they are bounded by private houses. In order to distinguish them from the previously excavated baths, they are sometimes called from their size the Great Thermæ, and sometimes, from one of their sides being in the street leading to the Gate of Stabiæ, the Thermæ Stabianæ.

We learn some particulars about these baths from an inscription on a slab of travertine, found in May, 1857, in a small room on their northern side, and now preserved in the National Museum.* This inscription records, that C. Vulius and P. Aninius, duumvirs for administering justice, caused a Laconicum and Destrictarium to be made, and the Portico and Palæstra to be repaired, in compliance with

---

* *Pomp. Ant. Hist.*, vol. ii. p. 647, seq.

a decree of the Decurions, with the money which they were to lay out according to law, either on some public monument, or in the exhibition of games, and that the same duumvirs inspected and approved the works after their completion. The original runs as follows :—

C. VVLIUS. C. F. P. ANINIVS. C. F. II. V. I. D.
LACONICUM. ET. DESTRICTARIUM.
FACIUND. ET. PORTICUS. ET. PALÆSTR.
REFICIUNDA. LOCARUNT. EX. D. D. EX.
EA. PEQVNIA. QUOD. EOS. E. LEGE.
IN. LUDOS. AVT. IN. MONUMENTO.
CONSUMERE. OPORTUIT. FACIVN.
COERARUNT. EIDEMQUE. PROBARU.

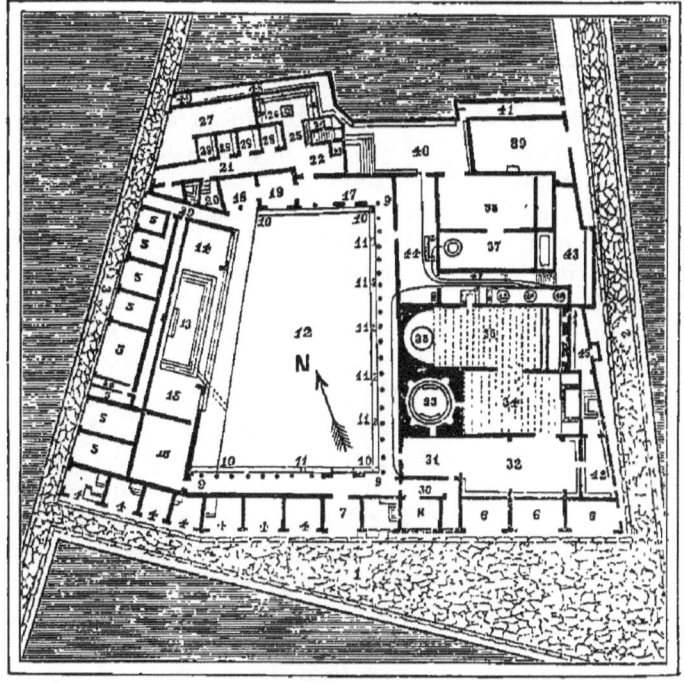

Plan of Stabian Baths.

From this inscription we may learn that these alterations and improvements had been completed before the destruction of Pompeii; and indeed, antiquarians infer from its style and from the character of the letters, that it must be about a century and a half older than that event, and cannot therefore have any reference to the repair of damage occasioned by the earthquake of A.D. 63.* If this be so, and if the inscription is to be referred to about the year B.C. 70, then we must assign a tolerably ancient date to these baths, since the circumstance of the Portico and Palæstra requiring repair, shows that the Thermæ must have been in existence long previously to that date. We are told indeed that Palæstræ did not become common in Italy till the reign of Augustus; but this, as Overbeck remarks, does not exclude their existence absolutely and altogether, and especially in towns of Greek origin. We may rather infer that these Thermæ, like the Temple of Hercules in the Triangular Forum, belonged to the ancient and more Grecian portion of Pompeii; and on the whole it seems probable that they were anterior in date to the baths previously discovered and already described.

The principal entrance to the Thermæ Stabianæ is in the Street of Holconius. After passing the prothyrum, or vestibule (7), which has nothing requiring notice, the visitor finds himself in a large quadrangular court (12, and 10 at the angles), growing however gradually rather narrower towards the further end, from the inward inclination of the western side. On its southern and eastern, and partly on its northern side, this court is surrounded with a portico (9) about nine feet broad, supported by pillars of no regular order, but resembling the Doric more than any other. They are covered with stucco, having their lower third painted red and the rest white. They are not actually fluted, but have stripes resembling channels. Of these columns there are nineteen on the right, or eastern side, seven on the south, besides one let into the wall, and on the north only one. Their capitals, ornamented with leaves, supported a cornice admirably wrought in stucco, a small portion of which, preserved almost in its original state, will convey to the spectator an idea of what it must have been when perfect. The walls within the portico are painted in red compartments surrounded with yellow borders. The figures (11) round the outside of the portico mark depressions

* Overbeck, *Pompeii, &c.*, b. i. s. 205.

and holes in which the dirt was collected, and by which the rainwater from the roof ran off.

The northern side of the portico, towards the left, forms a sort of crypto-porticus, with two rooms or *loggie* looking upon the palæstra. The first of these rooms (19) can be entered only from the portico, but has a large window towards the palæstra and another smaller one looking into the adjoining apartment. In this room was found a handsome bronze brazier, very much resembling that found in the tepidarium of the other Thermæ, and having like it the inscription M. NIGIDIUS, P.S., with the image of a little cow, standing apparently for the surname Vaccula. This brazier, however, affords no clue as to the destination of the room in which it was found. It was evidently not in its proper place, since a small room with two large open windows was quite unfitted to be warmed by such an apparatus.* The next apartment to this is a *loggia* (18) open to the palæstra, from which it is entered by a step. It was probably intended for spectators of the games. The walls are white, and the floor paved with *opus Signinum*.

It cannot be doubted that the large open court formed the palæstra mentioned in the inscription. That it was destined for athletic sports and exercises is evident, as well from the size of its area as from the discovery in it of two large stone spheres or balls. It is about 44 yards long and 27 broad in the middle. It has no pavement, but a floor of hard or beaten earth. Along its west side, a little raised above the level of the ground, runs a strip of tufo pavement, about a yard and a half broad. On this were found the large and heavy stone balls or globes just mentioned, which were probably intended to be rolled along it in some game of strength or skill.

We will now proceed to describe the buildings which surround this court or palæstra. The south side, by which we have entered, has little else behind the portico but shops facing to the Street of Holconius (marked in the plan 4, 5, and 6), and will not require any particular description. The left, or western side, is almost entirely engrossed by a large *natatio*, or swimming bath (13), with its appur-

---

* See Overbeck, B. i. S. 213. Cf. *Pomp. Antiq. Hist.* t. ii. p. 650.

tenances. The oblong basin is about 50 feet long and half that breadth. It has steps to descend into it on all its sides except the further one, where there are only a few, intended apparently for seats. It is about six and a half feet deep, and open to the air. Anciently it was lined with slabs of white marble, of which only a few now remain. At each end of the *piscina* or bath are square apartments (14, 15), exactly similar in arrangement and decoration. Both are entered from the palæstra by a large arched doorway, while similar doorways lead from the rooms to the steps of the bath. The purpose to which these rooms were applied has been the subject of much speculation; but from their situation and arrangement, there can, we think, be little doubt that they were intended for the comfort and convenience of the bathers, and probably served as places where they might undress and dress themselves, sheltered from the weather and the rays of the sun. In the wall that fronts the entrance of each room is a square niche, or recess, probably intended for a statue. On both sides of these recesses are paintings of females holding in their hands large scollop shells or basins, and under each niche is a round hole, from which perhaps issued a pipe with a *jet d'eau*. The walls of these apartments are painted with landscape and architecture, dancing satyrs, pigmies, dolphins, sphinxes, &c. The lower part of the walls to about a yard from the floor is not painted, but seems to have been covered with slabs of marble, which are now missing. The southernmost of these rooms leads into another apartment (16), which has also a door towards the portico. It is a plain apartment, with little decoration, and the purpose of it cannot be satisfactorily ascertained. Some have called it an *apodyterium*, or stripping room, but its situation seems not at all suited for such a purpose. It was much more probably the *destrictarium* mentioned in the inscription before quoted. This was an apartment appropriated to the operation of scraping off the perspiration and the oil and sand with which the body had been anointed and sprinkled as a preparation for the exercises of the palæstra. The situation of the room, close to the place where the game with the balls before mentioned was played, seems to favour this supposition. The iron hooks observed in this apartment may have served to hold the *strigiles* with which this operation was performed.

DESCRIPTION OF BATHS. 179

These implements were of bronze or iron, of various forms, as will be seen from the annexed cuts. They were applied to the

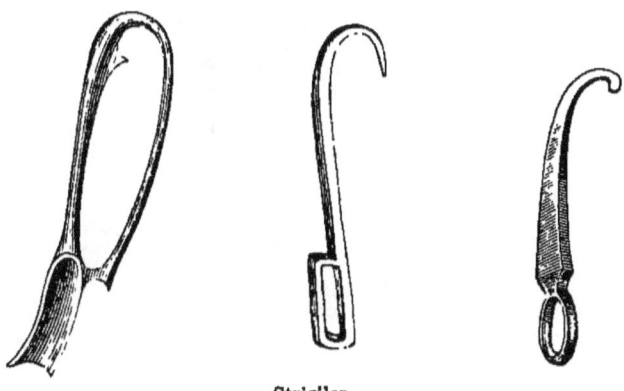

Strigiles.

body much in the same way as we see a piece of hoop applied to a sweating horse. The operation was rather a rough one, and, as we learn from Suetonius, the Emperor Augustus suffered from having been too rudely handled.

The outside walls of these apartments on the left hand side of the palæstra are very richly ornamented with paintings and designs executed in stucco. Fantastic pieces of architecture, consisting of tall slender columns with cornices, appear to divide the walls into two stories and into various compartments, some square, some vaulted. Sometimes are seen doors and steps which seem to lead into inner apartments. There are projecting balconies, draperies hanging from the cornices, garlands suspended from pillar to pillar, and other light and cheerful, but exceedingly fantastic decorations. Over the doorway of the first room adjoining the *natatio* is a well-preserved figure of a Jupiter in stucco. The king of gods and men is sitting on a square stone, on which he rests with his left arm, whilst in his right hand he holds his sceptre. Before him, on a short pillar, sits his eagle. On the northern wall are also the remains of two or three female figures in relief.

To the north of the *Natatio* and its adjoining apartment is a long passage (29) with an entrance into the palæstra from the Vico del Lupanare. It communicates with another entrance on the south (50). On the other side of the Baths.

180 POMPEII.

is an entrance from the Strada Stabiana into the corridor (43), and another into that marked 42 and 45.

West Side of Stabian Baths.

The side of the palæstra opposite to that just described contains the warm baths. They consist, like the baths previously discovered, of two complete suites of apartments, each having an apodyterium, frigidarium, tepidarium, and caldarium, and between them the furnace (47) by which both suites were heated. This arrangement of the furnace seems to show that both these sets of baths were used *simultaneously*; and as it does not appear to have been the Roman custom to have distinct baths for the richer and poorer classes, we are naturally led to the conclusion that one of these sets was intended for men and the other for women. Here, however, we are met by the objection that neither of the sets is completely isolated and private, as is the case with the baths assigned to the women in the previously discovered *Thermæ*, but that both sets have an entrance from the palæstra. Hence some writers, like Michaelis, have been led to conclude that the set which occupies the further or northern part of this side of the building, which is smaller and less decorated than the other, formed at one time the only set, to which were afterwards added the larger and more elegant baths to the south of them. Overbeck has shown* that such a theory is inconsistent with the whole plan of the building. It assumes, for instance, that half the eastern portico must at one time have adjoined buildings which did not belong to the establishment, a thing not at all probable. Again, if we suppose that the area now occupied by the larger set of baths was at one time private property, and therefore to be struck out of the original ground plan of the establishment, the form of the remaining ground plan would be so strange and irregular as to render such a supposition in the highest degree improbable. But though we agree with Overbeck in rejecting this view, we cannot say that we are entirely satisfied with his own. He supposes that both sets of baths were intended for the use of men; and that the plan of double baths, instead of one large and magnificent one, was adopted from motives of economy both in the construction and the heating of them. He further explains the different degree of elegance in the decoration of the two sets by supposing that the baths were in process of restoration, which in the southern set had been completed, but not in the northern.

Upon this we must remark that, if both sets of baths had

* *Pompeii, &c.*, B. i. S. 221, seq.

been intended for men, there would have been a more direct communication between them than at present exists. For though it is true that each of them is accessible from the palæstra, yet, in order to pass from one to the other, such a round-about way must be taken as to show plainly that they were not intended to be used in common. The rules for the separation of the men's and women's baths do not appear to have been always strictly observed, and were not finally established till the time of Hadrian, consequently after the destruction of Pompeii. But in the present instance, though the women's baths are not so strictly isolated as they are in the other Thermæ, yet with some common precautions, such as keeping the doors leading to them shut, or having doorkeepers, they were sufficiently so to insure perfect decency. The arrangement and decoration of the further set of baths are so similar to that of what in the other Thermæ are agreed on all hands to have been the women's baths, as to make it difficult to suppose that they were not applied to the same purpose. It may be further remarked that the wall of the lobby or corridor (44) which forms the entrance to these baths from the palæstra is decorated with a painting of a small temple and serpents, intended probably to warn a profane intruder of the male sex that he had no business to enter those precincts.

We will now proceed to describe the baths, beginning with those near the principal entrance of the palæstra, which we have assumed to be the men's baths. Entering the first door under the portico on the right, we find ourselves in a sort of passage, or prothyrum (30), handsomely painted, and having on the left a stone bench. On the right is a door leading into a plain apartment (8), with two windows, probably used by the attendants. Passing the prothyrum, we enter another long passage which on the right had an exit to the Street of Holconius through a door now walled up, while on the left we enter a vaulted apartment (31) more handsomely ornamented than any other in these baths. The red walls are decorated with various designs, whilst the roof is richly worked in stucco, with round and octagonal cassettes, or sunken panels, in which are variously coloured reliefs, in the former on a blue, in the latter on a black ground. The reliefs represent sea-monsters and Cupids; while in four larger compartments are female figures partly undraped. This apartment, which seems to have been the waiting-room, is paved with marble. It has a door leading into the portico of the palæstra, and another forming the entrance to a handsome circular bath-room (33), lighted by an aperture or lanthorn in the roof. This, which was no doubt the *cella frigidaria,* or cold bath, bears considerable resemblance to the apartment destined for the same use in the other baths. In its circumference are four vaulted recesses, or niches, large enough to hold a chair. Another little niche, opposite to the entrance, was furnished with a *jet d'eau.* All round the basin are steps to descend into it. The walls were adorned with stucco ornaments and paintings, now much effaced. Of the latter, all that can be made out is the figure of a sleeping Venus, with her back turned to the spectator.

From the apartment or waiting-room first described, we descend by one step into the apodyterium (32), a large hall twelve or thirteen yards long by about ten broad. Four strong square pillars projecting from the side walls, and supporting two arches of the vaulted roof, divide the chamber into three compartments, but of very different sizes, the largest being in the middle. A stone bench with a step beneath surrounds the room, with the exception of the left side of it, as far as the second pillar. Over the bench are niches for depositing clothes, or for perfume jars, &c. They rest upon an abacus, like those in the other baths, but the intervals are not ornamented with Telamones. In other respects this apodyterium is more richly ornamented than the same apartment in the baths first excavated. The floor is of marble; the vaulted roof is tastefully adorned with ornaments in stucco, but unfortunately the greater part of it has fallen in. The ornaments consist of square or sexagonal panels, in which are rosettes, Cupids, and Bacchic figures. At the sides of the arches over the pillars are females holding dolphins which terminate in arabesques. The semicircular compartments formed by the vaulted roof in the walls of entry and exit are also richly adorned with reliefs in stucco.

A door in the further wall of the apodyterium leads into a sort of corridor or passage behind (42), whilst another door on the left conducts us into what must have been the tepidarium (34). At the bottom is a large bath, originally lined with marble, which seems to have been heated by a stove underneath. One of the slabs of marble appears to have contained a dedicatory inscription to the Emperor Augustus, bearing the date of his eleventh consulship, which fell in the second year of the Christian era. The slab was placed in the bath with the inscription downwards, which has thus left its impression in high relief in the mortar in which it was fixed. There is no basin like that just described in the tepidarium of the other baths. It was probably intended, as Overbeck remarks, for those who took a luke-warm bath, by way perhaps of preparation for the caldarium. This apartment is also adorned with reliefs in stucco, but not so richly as the tepidarium of the other baths. The floor, like that of the latter, rested on small brick pillars (*suspensura*), thus leaving a hollow for the circulation of the warm air. But the whole room is in a ruinous condition.

From the tepidarium a door communicates with the caldarium (36), which has also a floor like that just described. The hot air from the furnaces beyond, which circulated under this apartment, was communicated, of course in a cooler state, to the floor of the tepidarium by means of an opening under the doorway. The arrangement of the caldarium is the same as that seen in the earlier discovered baths—a labrum at the circular end (35), in the middle the sudatorium, with hollow walls besides the suspended floor, and at the other end a large basin for the hot bath, having over it three niches for statues. Adjoining the northern side of the caldarium, but without any visible communication with it, was the furnace. The caldarium does not appear to have been very richly ornamented, and is now almost in ruins.

We will now proceed to describe the other set of baths, which we have ventured to assign to the women. On the northern side of the palæstra, just opposite the principal entrance from the Street of Holconius (at 17), stands a female terminal figure, with well-executed drapery. It might perhaps seem a rather strained inference to assume that this figure was intended to denote the purpose to which this part of the building was devoted; though in deductions which must in a great degree depend upon conjecture, we have sometimes seen more far-fetched arguments adduced. However this may be, it is certain that this figure stands before one of the principal apartments of this second set of baths, and seems to mark their termination towards the west. The entrance to them is by a door near the top of the eastern side of the portico, which leads into the long corridor (44) already mentioned having a picture of a temple and snakes. A door at the end of this corridor, on the left, leads into a large oblong hall (40), having at its western or left extremity a raised basin, destined apparently for the cold bath, with steps to ascend to it. The apartment has a bench round it and niches in the wall. It was undoubtedly an apodyterium, and bears so striking a resemblance to the apodyterium of the women's baths in the Thermæ first discovered, as to afford no slight confirmation to the opinion that it served the same purpose here. The apartment, which is well preserved, is much more simply decorated than the apodyterium of the men's baths. The walls between the bench and the abacus of the niches are red, and the remainder white. The vaulted roof has two round openings or windows, and there is another over the bath. The floor is paved with *opus Signinum*. There are two other entrances to this apodyterium, on the right and left, from a long and narrow passage or corridor which runs along the whole northern side of the establishment. The passage on the right (41) leads from the Street of Stabiæ, that on the left (48, 48), which is much longer, from the Street of the Lupanar. It may be observed that these passages lead only into that part of the establishment which we have assigned to the women's baths, thus ensuring their privacy on this side. The apartment marked 39 in the plan has no communication whatever with the Baths. It has an opening into the Strada Stabiana, and was probably a shop.

A door in the right-hand corner of the apodyterium, close to that by which it is entered from the corridor, leads into the tepidarium (38). This apartment is very simply decorated. The floor, which rests on *suspensuræ*, is paved with coarse white mosaic; the walls are also hollow in order to circulate the hot vapour; and even its vaulted roof seems to have had a hollow coating of stucco, which, however, has now fallen in. A door in the middle of the right-hand side of the tepidarium leads into the caldarium (37). This apartment, except that it is not so large, corresponds precisely with the caldarium already described in the men's baths and with that of the previously discovered Thermæ. On one of its smaller sides, on the left, is a large oblong bath of white marble, in a perfect state of preservation, having at the bottom of one of its sides a large semicircular aperture for the admission of hot water, and above it a bronze tube, capable of being closed with a cock, to let in cold water. At the opposite end of the hall is the semicircular *laconicum*, with its *labrum*, or large round vase of white marble, having a pipe in the middle to fill it with hot water. The floor and walls of this apartment are also hollow. It is more elegantly decorated than the rooms just described. The walls are red, and are picked out with little stucco pilasters painted yellow, with white capitals, and springing from a narrow marble border. The wall of the laconicum is richly adorned with stucco, and has a window lighted from the corridor leading into the palæstra. The floor is of fine white mosaic. Between this caldarium and that of the other set, or men's baths, is situated the furnace for heating both.

Behind the left or western half of the northern side of the palæstra lies another set of rooms, the destination of some of which is sufficiently obvious, while that of others is difficult to be explained. This suite of apartments is entered by a long passage (21) from the Street of the Lupanar, leading to a room (22) abutting upon the western end of the women's apodyterium, and communicating with the palæstra by a door on the right. At the further end of this room is a staircase (24), which led to an upper story. On the left-hand side of the passage, coming from the street, are four small rooms (28) adjoining one another, fitted up as private baths, or what the ancients called *solia*. Beyond these, a passage on the left (25) leads into a good-sized room (26), having round it a sort of channel or canal. It is supposed to have been a *latrina*. The room beyond, already mentioned as adjoining the apodyterium and having an entrance into the palæstra, has a small compartment, or cabinet (23), the use of which it is not easy to determine. On the left was a steep staircase leading to an upper story. The space marked 27 appears to have been unoccupied.

On the right-hand side of the long passage leading from the Via del Lupanare, and close to the entrance, are three rooms, the destination of which is uncertain. The first may

DESCRIPTION OF BATHS. 187

possibly have been the lodge of the *ostiarius* or porter. The second has steps leading down to what appears to be a sort of cellar, but is thought to have given admission to the canal or drain by which the water of the baths was carried off. The destination of the third room (20) cannot even be conjectured.

Before concluding this account of the Stabian baths, we should mention that under the portico, near the entrance to the men's baths, was found a sun-dial, consisting as usual of a half circle inscribed in a rectangle, and with the gnomon in perfect preservation. It was supported by lion's feet and elegantly ornamented. On its base was an Oscan inscription, which has been interpreted as follows by Minervini: Marius. Atinius, Marii filius, quæstor, ex multatitia pecunia conventus decreto fieri mandavit. That is: the Quæstor M. Atinius, in accordance with a decree of the assembly, caused it to be made out of money levied by fines. The title of "Quæstor" seems to show that this inscription must have been written after the occupation of Pompeii by the Romans, but at the same time at a period when the Oscan tongue continued to be generally spoken.* The fines alluded to were probably levied for breaches of the rules to be observed in the palæstra.

* Breton, *Pompeii*, p. 159. Overbeck however is of opinion that the Pompeians had magistrates called Quæstors before the Roman occupation; but this does not seem very probable.

Vases for Perfumes.

Figure with a mask, from a painting in Pompeii.

CHAPTER VII.

THE THEATRES.

THE regular drama was not of indigenous growth, and never took firm root in Italy. It was unknown until about two centuries and a half before Christ, when Grecian literature began to be cultivated, and never rose to be more than a feeble transcript of the original. The Romans were first led to theatrical amusements as a means of appeasing the anger of the gods, having been before only acquainted with gymnastic exercises and circus races. During a desolating pestilence, which seemed proof against all remedies, they sent for *histriones* from Etruria, B.C. 364. These, however, seem to have been merely dancers, or tumblers rather, such as are represented on the Etruscan monuments. The oldest spoken plays, the Fabulæ Atellanæ, were borrowed from the Osci, of whom we often have had to speak, and appear to have been rude improvisatory attempts at rustic satire. It was more than 500 years after the era usually assigned to the foundation of Rome, that Livius Andronicus first attempted to imitate the Grecian tragedy. He was followed by Ennius and Nævius, and, later, by a number of writers in the Augustan age and under the emperors; but, with the exception of some fragments, and the tragedies ascribed to Seneca, all their works are lost. This is the less to be lamented, because it does not appear that a single Roman tragedy was ever composed upon a Roman subject.

In the comic department the Romans displayed more originality. The Fabulæ Atellanæ were so popular, that youths of noble family engaged in the representation of them; and, in consequence, the professional actors employed in them were exempted from the ignominy which attached to other theatrical artists. Similar to these probably, but more polished, were the Mimi. These were composed in verse, in the Latin language, and sometimes were delivered extempore. Laberius and Syrus are the two most celebrated writers of them. The former was compelled by a request, equivalent to a command, from Julius Cæsar to appear on the stage, although his compliance was attended with the loss of civil rights; and the prologue which he spoke on this occasion is still extant, and expresses nobly and feelingly his sense of the injury. Time has left us no specimens of either of these species of composition; and the scanty notices which remain concerning them do not enable us to form a clear idea of their nature.

The regular comedy of the Romans, which is preserved to us in Plautus and Terence, was for the most part *palliata*, that is, it appeared in a Grecian dress and represented Grecian manners. But they had also a comœdia *togata*, so called from the Roman dress which was worn in it. Afranius was the principal writer in this walk. We have no remains whatever of his writings, nor can we determine whether the *togatæ* were original comedies of new invention, or merely Grecian comedies adapted to Roman manners. The latter case is the more probable, yet it is not easy to conceive how Attic comedies could well be adapted to local circumstances of so different a nature. The way of living of the Romans was in general serious and grave, during the republic. The diversity of ranks was politically marked in a very decided manner, and the wealth of private individuals was frequently not inferior to that of princes; women lived much more in society, and acted a much more independent part with them than among the Greeks; and from this independence they fully shared in the general refinement of manners, and the corruption by which that refinement was accompanied. In

Comic Scene from a Painting in the house of Castor and Pollux at Pompeii.

these points, Athenian habits were the antipodes of Roman; and with such essential differences between them, an original Roman comedy would have been a most valuable production,

Comic Scene from a Painting at Pompeii.

and would have given us that insight into the private feelings and private life of this remarkable people, which is of all knowledge the most curious and important. That this, however, was not accomplished in the *comœdia togata*, the indifferent manner in which it is mentioned by the ancients will hardly allow us to doubt. Quintilian himself informs us that the Latin literature "was lamest in comedy." *

Vitruvius has given some minute directions, strongly illustrative of the importance of the subject, for choosing a proper situation for a theatre. "When the Forum is finished, a healthy situation must be sought for, wherein the theatre may be erected to exhibit sports on the festival days of the immortal gods. For the spectators are detained in their seats by the entertainment of the games, and remaining quiet for a long time, their pores are opened, and imbibe the draughts of air, which, if they come from marshy or otherwise unhealthy places, will pour injurious humours into the body. Neither must it front the south; † for when the sun fills the concavity, the inclosed air, unable to escape or circulate, is heated, and then extracts and dries up the juices of the body. It is also to be carefully observed that the place be not unfitted to transmit sound, but one in which the voice may expand as clearly as possible." ‡

It is probable that the natural sweep of some dell, hollowed out in a hill-side, furnished the original design of a theatre;

Comic Scene from a Painting at Pompeii.

and the Greeks always availed themselves, if possible, of a hill-side, or some locality which lightened the labour of the

* The above sketch of the Roman theatre is compressed from Schlegel's Lectures on Dramatic Literature, sect. viii.
† Which, however, is the case with the theatre of Pompeii.
‡ Vitruv. v. 3.

building. At Nyssa the theatre occupies an angle in a ravine partially filled up; and it is said that the only instances now known of Grecian theatres built in a plain, are those of Mantineia and Megalopolis, and a small one in Asia Minor.* The Roman theatres, on the other hand, were usually elevated upon arches, wherever a suitable situation could be found, without regard to economical considerations. That at Pompeii, however, is hollowed out of a hill; which may lead us to conclude that it was originally founded by a Greek population, though it was evidently reconstructed after the Roman occupation.

In a Roman theatre the orchestra was bounded towards the cavea by a semicircle. Complete the circle, draw the diameters BB, HH, perpendicular to each other, and inscribe four equilateral triangles, whose vertices shall fall severally upon the ends of the diameters; the twelve angles of the

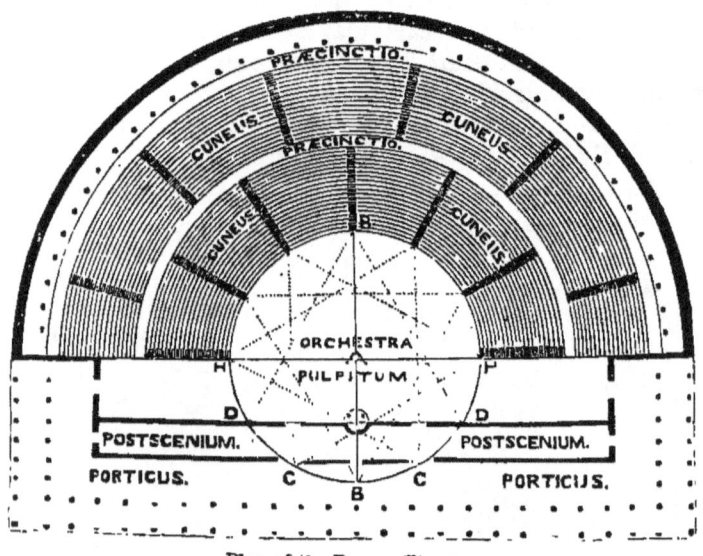

Plan of the Roman Theatre.

triangles will divide the circumference into twelve equal portions. The side of the triangle opposite to the angle at B will be parallel to the diameter HH, and determines the place of the scene, as HH determines the front of the stage,

* Stuart's *Athens*, vol. iv.; On the Greek Theatre. p. 36.

or pulpitum. By this construction the stage is brought nearer to the audience, and made considerably deeper than in a Greek theatre; its depth being determined at a quarter of the diameter of the orchestra, which itself was usually a third or somewhat more of the diameter of the whole building. The length of the stage was twice the diameter of the orchestra. The increased depth of the stage was rendered necessary by the greater number of persons assembled on it, the chorus and musicians being placed here by the Romans. A further consequence of the construction is, that the circumference of the cavea could not exceed one hundred and eighty degrees. Sometimes, however, the capacity of the theatre was increased by throwing the stage further back, and continuing the seats in right lines perpendicular to the diameter of the orchestra. This is the case in the great theatre at Pompeii, and seems also to indicate that it was originally of Greek construction. Within the orchestra were circular ranges of seats for the senate and other distinguished persons, leaving a level platform in the centre. The seven angles which fall within the circumference of the orchestra mark the places at which staircases up to the first præcinctio, or landing, were to be placed; those leading from thence to the second, if there were more than one, were placed intermediately opposite to the centre of each cuneus. The number of staircases, whether seven, five, or three, of course depended on the size of the theatre. In the great theatres of Rome, the space between the orchestra and first præcinctio, usually consisting of fourteen seats, was reserved for the equestrian order, tribunes, &c.: all above these were the seats of the plebeians. Women were appointed by Augustus to sit in the portico, which encompassed the whole. The lowest range of seats was raised above the area of the orchestra one-sixth of its diameter: the height of each seat is directed not to exceed one foot four inches, nor to be less than one foot three. The breadth is not to exceed two feet four inches, nor to be less than one foot ten. The stage, to consult the convenience of those who sit in the orchestra, is only elevated five feet, less than half the height given to the Grecian stage. The ancient scene was not, like that of the modern stage, capable of being shifted. It consisted of a solid building (*scena stabilis*), representing the façade of a royal palace, and adorned with the richest architectural orna-

o

ments. It was built of stone, or brick cased with marble, and had three doors, of which the middle one, called *porta regia*, larger and handsomer than the others, was supposed to form the entrance to the palace. This was used only in the representation of tragedies, and then only by the principal personages of the drama. The door in the right wing was appropriated to inferior personages, and that on the left to foreigners or persons coming from abroad. In our plan, the five angles of the triangles not yet disposed of determine the disposition of the scene. Opposite the centre one are the regal doors; on each side are those by which the secondary characters entered. Behind the scene, as in the Greek theatre, there were apartments for the actors to retire into; and under it were vaults or cellars, which, as in the modern stage, served for the entrance of ghosts, or the appliance of any needful machinery. The *proscenium*, or space between the orchestra and the scene, answering to our stage, though deeper than the Greek, was of no great depth, which was not required for the performance of ancient dramas, in which only a few personages appeared on the stage at once. Besides, in the absence of any roof, the voice of the performers would have been lost if the stage had been too deep. That of Pompeii is only about twenty-one feet broad, though its length is one hundred and nine. Along the front of the stage, and between it and the orchestra, runs a tolerably deep linear opening, the receptacle for the *aulæum*, or curtain, the fashion of which was just the reverse of ours, as it had to be depressed instead of elevated when the play began. This operation, performed by machinery of which we have no clear account, was called *aulæum premere*, as in the well known line of Horace: *—

<blockquote>Quatuor aut plures aulæa premuntur in horas.</blockquote>

It should however be mentioned that the ancients seem also to have had moveable scenery (*scena ductilis*), to alter the appearance of the permanent scene when required. This must have consisted of painted board or canvas.

Another method of illusion was by the use of masks. These were rendered necessary by the vastness of the ancient theatres, and the custom of performing in the open air.

* Epp. ii. 1, 189.

Under these circumstances the more distant spectators could neither have distinguished the features of the actor nor heard his voice. To obviate these inconveniences masks were invented, which not only by their exaggerated features and expression could be discerned in the remotest part of the theatre, but also seem to have been contrived to assist the voice of the actor, and render it audible from afar. These masks were brought to a great degree of beauty and perfection, so that, as may be seen at Pompeii in several instances, they were frequently imitated by architects in cornices and mouldings, and by artists in paintings of festoons and other ornaments. It will not therefore be out of place here to give some account of their origin and nature.

We have not the means, nor would it be to the purpose, to describe the earliest form of the mask, or to trace its progress. Ultimately it was formed of brass or some sonorous material, or the mouth at least lined with metal, so as to collect and reverberate the voice with something like the power of a speaking-trumpet. The Greeks called it προσώπειον,

Masks, Dwarf, and Monkey, from a painting.

the Latins persona, a personando, from resounding, "because the head and mouth being entirely covered by it, and only one passage left for the voice, this cannot be dissipated, but being collected into a body is thus rendered clearer and more sonorous."* Masks were made to contain the whole head, covered with hair of colour suitable to the characters they were meant to represent, and seem to have been coloured, for minute directions are given as to the complexion and smooth or wrinkled character of the face. No doubt can exist as to the minute attention paid to this subject by the Greeks, for Julius Pollux enumerates no less than twenty-six classes of

* Aul. Gell. v. 7.

tragic masks, each distinguished by what apparently is its technical name. He divides them into the ranks of men, young men, slaves, and women, and names six of the first, eight of the second, three of the third, and nine of the last. As a sample of the arrangement we give the first class, which consists of " The shaven man, the white, the dishevelled grey, the black, the brown, the deeper brown."* The other classes are similarly subdivided, and to each is attached a short description of the character of face which it should portray. "The shaven man is the oldest of all, his hair quite white, and collected upon the foretop (ὄγκος). The foretop is the upright projection above the face, in shape like the letter Λ. His beard is close shaven, and his cheeks pendulous. The black man is named from the darkness of his complexion: his hair and beard are curling, his face rough, and his foretop large."† Such is the exact detail continued through the four classes, and these seem merely to have been the regular stock of the theatre or mask-maker; for he afterwards

enumerates extraordinary personages, as Actæon with his horns, or many-eyed Argus, or Tyro with bruised cheeks, as

* τὰ μὲν τραγικά. ξυρίας ἀνήρ, λευκὸς, σπαρτοπόλιος, μέλας ἀνήρ, ἀνὴρ ξανθὸς, ἀνὴρ ξανθότερος. IV.

† Pollux Onomasticon, IV. 19.

introduced by Sophocles, or Gorgon, or Death, or a Fury, and a host more of mythological personages, or Thamyris, with one eye blue and the other black. This last is the most extraordinary. It appears from the marble masks still extant that the white of the eye was imitated, leaving only the aperture of the iris to see through; but the irides themselves of Thamyris's eyes must have been imitated—an extraordinary instance of minute attention to propriety, when two-thirds of the spectators probably could not tell whether he had any irides at all. The same may be observed of Tyro's black and blue face.

There are two very striking tragic masks in the Townley Gallery. The male is remarkable for the great elevation of the hair (ὄγκος), to give increased stature and dignity to the actor; its features are stern and exaggerated. Those of the female are regular and beautiful, and bear a wild, intense,

inspired expression of terror, such as Cassandra may have worn while darkly presaging her own fate, and the evils about to fall on the house of Atreus. But it is very difficult to convey the expression of a mask by an engraving. The comic masks are still more numerous than the tragic. The annexed masks belong to some of Terence's characters: they are given by Mad. Dacier, on the authority of a very ancient manuscript in the Royal Library at Paris, and serve to illustrate the varieties of countenance considered applicable to different characters.

There are others devoted to the satyric drama. This was something of a medium between tragedy and comedy; in spirit and cheerfulness it resembled the latter, but its external form was derived from the former, and its subject was

Tragic and Grotesque Masks.

mythological. Its distinctive mark was a chorus of satyrs, who accompanied such heroic adventures as were of a more cheerful hue with lively songs, gestures, and movements. The immediate cause of this species of drama was derived from the festivals of Bacchus, in which satyr masks were a common disguise. In these representations, therefore, the severe beauty of the tragic mask, softened in its features and

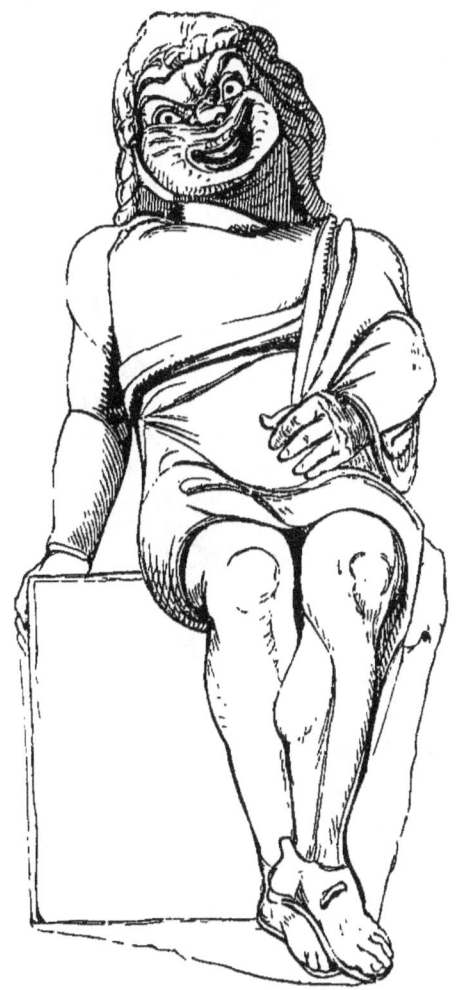

Masked figure of Silenus.

expression, was combined with and opposed to the grotesque character usually given to Fauns and Sileni, and the ancient sculptors seem to have been fond of thus contrasting them. There are some instances of this in the Townley Gallery, from which a drawing is given on p. 198. We also give a masked figure of Silenus from the same collection. The only existing satyric drama is the Cyclops of Euripides.

The tragedians rarely travelled out of the mythic age: indeed there are only three known instances of subjects being taken from a more recent period—the capture of Miletus, and the Phœnissæ by Phrynichus, and the Persæ by Æschylus, the two latter written in commemoration of the overthrow of Xerxes. Hence the same persons, Achilles, Hercules, Orestes, Theseus, were continually reappearing on the stage. We know that a peculiar costume was assigned to them—as Priam was always shaven; Ulysses dressed in a cloak, that being the Ithacan habit; Achilles and Neoptolemus were introduced with diadems. It is not improbable, therefore, that they had a traditionary cast of features assigned them; and if Mr. Flaxman's assertion be correct, that the Grecian artists had for each of their principal deities an ideal model to which they always conformed, we may be sure that when introduced on the stage the orthodox countenance was strictly followed. The nature of their characters therefore created a further inducement to retain and improve the mask, rather than to cast it aside as a rude and mean appendage of the art in its infancy.

Comic Scene from a Painting at Pompeii.

Devoted as the Greeks were to beauty, an ugly or plebeian Prometheus, or Agamemnon, or Achilles, would have been intolerable, but an ugly Apollo would inevitably have been hooted off the stage. Many imitations of masks carved in marble still exist, which display great beauty and excellence of workmanship. We know much less of the minutiæ of the Roman than of the Greek theatre. It appears from a passage in Cicero that the celebrated Roscius sometimes played without his mask, and that this was preferred by his audience.

It is evident that the heads of the actors, when covered with a mask, must have appeared disproportionately large. To remedy this, and to raise their stature to the heroic

Tragic Scene from a Painting at Pompeii.

standard, a thick-soled boot was invented, called ἐμβάς, and κόθορνος, from which the words buskin and cothurnus have become almost convertible with tragedy in the Augustan age of Latin, and that which has been called the Augustan age of English literature. Distinguished from these was the comic shoe, ἐμβάτης, in Latin, soccus, which word is in like manner used to denote comedy. Both the cothurnus and the ὄγκος above-mentioned are represented in the annexed outline of a painting found in the house of Castor and Pollux at Pompeii. The proportion of the figure, thus increased in height, was preserved by lengthening the arms with gloves and by stuffing and padding the body, so as to convey the idea of superhuman size and strength. How all this was consistent with anything like natural speech or action, it is not easy to imagine. Distance certainly at once rendered the increase of bulk more necessary, and softened the awkwardness of such made-up figures; still, in spite of the acknowledged purity of Grecian taste, and of the exquisite art and splendour lavished on their adornment, they must surely have seemed constrained and unnatural to any eye not habituated to such spectacles. It is evident that while this method of representation continued, tragedy could never lose its uniform and measured character. If the author had thought it consistent with the dignity of the occasion and of his subject to introduce those tumultuous scenes, that abrupt and impassioned dialogue, which in the hands of our elder dramatists produce such astonishing effect, they would have been lost in the delivery.

The theatre was usually surrounded with porticoes, which being under cover, served better for the purposes of rehearsal than the open stage. A very beautiful mosaic has been found in the house of the tragic poet at Pompeii, representing the Choragus,* or master of the chorus, instructing his actors in their parts. He is represented as sitting on a chair in the Choragium, or place devoted to these rehearsals, surrounded by performers. At his feet, on a stool, are the various masks which were used; another is behind him, on a pedestal; these he seems about to distribute. One of the actors, assisted by another, is putting his arms through the sleeves of a thick shaggy tunic; while the Choragus appears to be addressing him who has lifted his mask, that he may show by the expression of his countenance his attention to what is being said. In the middle of the picture is a female, crowned with a wreath, playing on the double flute, or perhaps tuning the instrument. Two of the figures are merely covered round the loins with goat-skins. Behind the figures are represented the Ionic columns of the portico, with its entablature; above this is a kind of gallery, decorated with figures and vases, and garlands are also hung in festoons between the columns. This mosaic is composed of very fine

---

* The Romans termed Choragus the person whom the Greeks named Chorodidascalus, the maître du ballet. The Choragus, in the proper sense of the word, was the person at whose expense the chorus and decorations were provided.

THE THEATRES. 203

pieces of glass,* and is esteemed one of the most beautiful that has yet been discovered. The ground is black and the

Mosaic, representing the Choragus instructing the Actors.

* Until lately it was supposed that the small and fine mosaics found at Pompeii were made of stone; but it has since been ascertained that they are made of glass, in a similar manner and with similar materials to the modern Roman mosaics now so celebrated.

figures of the natural colour. The dresses are mostly white, but the robe of the flute-player is bordered with purple; her garland, flutes, and mouth-band (*capistrum*), with most of the ornaments, are gold-coloured. It is to be remarked that the masks are all coloured in imitation of life, and with different complexions and hair, according to the age and character to be represented. The lips in all are of a bright red.

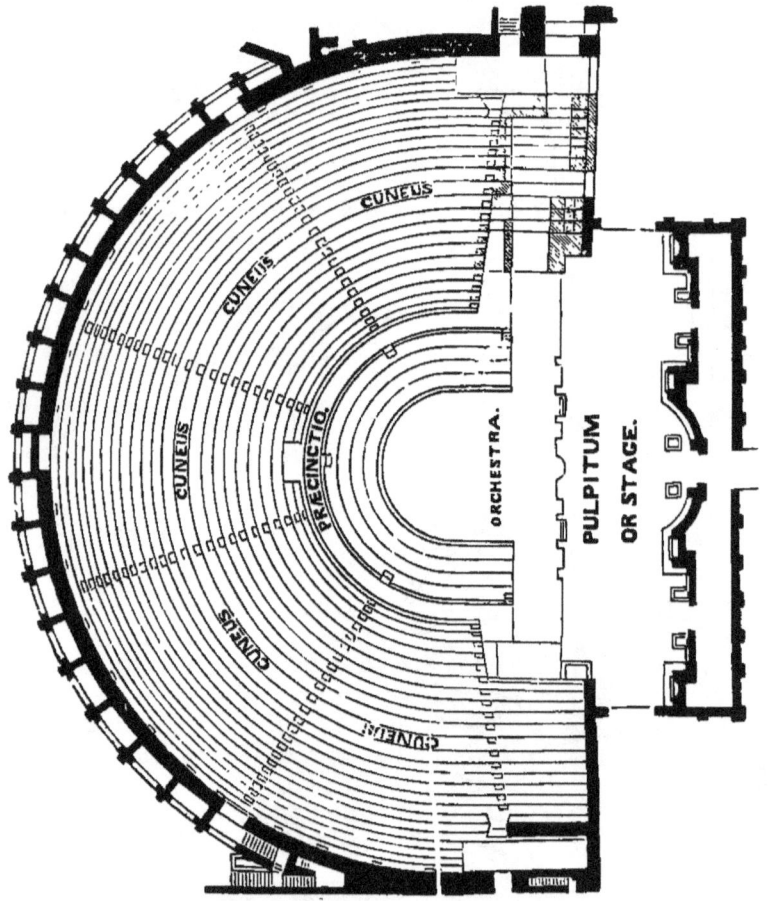

Plan of the large Theatre at Pompeii.

In the eastern portico of the Triangular Forum are four entrances to different parts of the greater theatre. The first two, as you enter, lead into a large circular corridor surrounding the whole cavea; the third opens on an area behind the scene, from which there is a communication with the orchestra and privileged seats; the fourth led down a long flight of steps, at the bottom of which you turn, on the right, into the soldiers' quarter, on the left, into the area already mentioned. The corridor is arched over. It has two other entrances, one by a large passage from the east side, another from a smaller passage on the north. Six inner doors, called vomitoria, opened on an equal number of staircases which ran down to the first præcinctio. The theatre is formed upon the slope of a hill, the corridor being the highest part, so that the audience upon entering descended at once to their seats, and the vast staircases, which conducted to the upper seats of the theatres and amphitheatres at Rome, were saved. By the side of the first entrance is a staircase which led up to the women's gallery above the corridor: here the seats were partitioned into compartments, like our boxes. The benches were about one foot three inches high and two feet four inches wide. One foot three inches and a half was allowed to each spectator, as may be ascertained in one part, where the divisions are marked off and numbered. There is space to contain about five thousand persons.* Here the middle classes sat, usually upon cushions which they brought with them; the men of rank sat in the orchestra below, on chairs of state carried thither by their slaves. Flanking the orchestra, and elevated considerably above it, are observable two divisions, appropriated, one perhaps to the proconsul, or duumvirs and their officers, the other to the vestal virgins, or to the use of the person who gave the entertainments. This is the more likely, because in the smaller theatre, where these boxes, if we may call them so, are also found, they have a communication with the stage.

This theatre appears to have been entirely covered with marble; the benches of the cavea were of marble, the orchestra was of marble, the scene with all its ornaments was also of marble; and yet of this profusion of marble only a few fragments remain. It appears, from an inscription found in it, to have been erected, or much improved, by one

* Donaldson's Pompeii.

Holconius Rufus. Upon the first step of the orchestra was another inscription, composed of bronze letters let into the marble. The metal has been carried away, but the cavities

Flute-player, from a Painting at Pompeii.

in the marble still remain. They were placed so as partly to encompass a statue, and run thus :—

M. HOLCONIO. M. F. RVFO. II. V.I.D. QVINQVIENS. ITER.
QVINQ. TRIB. MIL. A. P. FLAMEN. AVG.
PATR. COLON. D.D.

signifying, that the colony dedicated this to its patron, M. Holconius Rufus, son of Marcus: then follow his titles.

View of the large Theatre.

In the middle of this inscription is a vacant space, where probably stood the statue of Holconius, as the cramps, by which something was fastened, still remain. Or possibly it may have been an altar, as it was the custom among the ancients to sacrifice to Bacchus in the theatre. The view on p. 207 represents the building which we have been describing,

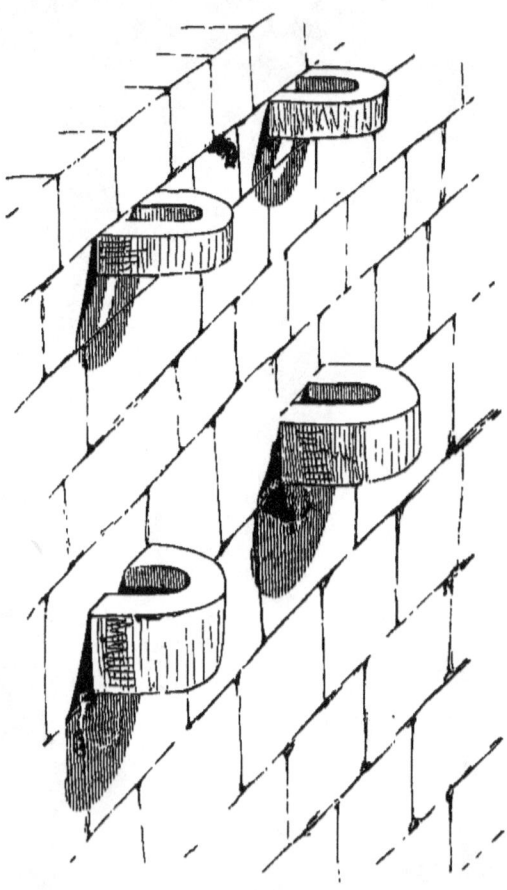

Stone Rings, to receive the Masts of the Velarium, from the Great Theatre at Pompeii.

as seen from one of the entrances leading to the orchestra, having on the right hand the scene. In the wall which supported the front of the stage are seven recesses, similar to those discovered in the theatre at Herculaneum. These are supposed to have been occupied by the musicians.* In front is the entrance to the orchestra; above may be seen the six rows of steps which encircled it; then the cavea, despoiled of its marble, but still showing the lines of benches and stairs dividing them into cunei, and the vomitoria, or doors of entrance. Still higher is the women's gallery, and above that the external wall, which never was entirely buried, and might have pointed out to any curious observer the exact situation of Pompeii. In our general view, the reader will observe one of the masts which supported the velarium, or awning, restored: it passed through two rings of stone projecting from the internal face of the wall. At the Coliseum these masts were supported by consoles on the outside.

Respecting the scene we have little to add to what we have already said. Enough remains to show that the three chief doors were situated in deep recesses; those at the sides rectangular, the central one circular. In front of the latter were two columns. Behind it is the postscenium. From the eastern side of the stage a covered portico led into the orchestra of the small theatre, and seems to have been meant as a communication between the privileged seats of either house, for the convenience of those who were entitled to them. At the end of this portico is another communication with the square called the soldiers' quarters.

The same plan and the same disposition of parts are observable in the small theatre sometimes called the Odeum. In form, however, it is different, the horns of the semicircle being cut off by lines drawn perpendicular to the front of the stage. Another, and a more remarkable difference is, that it appears from the following inscription to have been permanently roofed, though probably only with wood:—

C. QVINCTIVS. C. F. VALG.
M. PORCIVS. M. F.
DVO. VIR. DEC. DECR.
THEATRVM. TECTVM.
FAC. LOCAR. EIDEMQ. PROB.

" Caius Quinctius Valgus, son of Caius, and Marcus Porcius

* The cut on p. 206 represents a musician playing on the double flute. It is kept close to his mouth, and the breath hindered from escaping by a band, called φορβεῖον by the Greeks, capistrum by the Latins.

son of Marcus, Duumvirs, by a decree of the Decurions let out the covered theatre to be erected by contract, and the same approved it." It is supposed to have been erected shortly after the end of the Social War, and is inferior to the other theatre in decoration and construction. It is built of the tufa of Nocera, but the stairs which separate the cunei

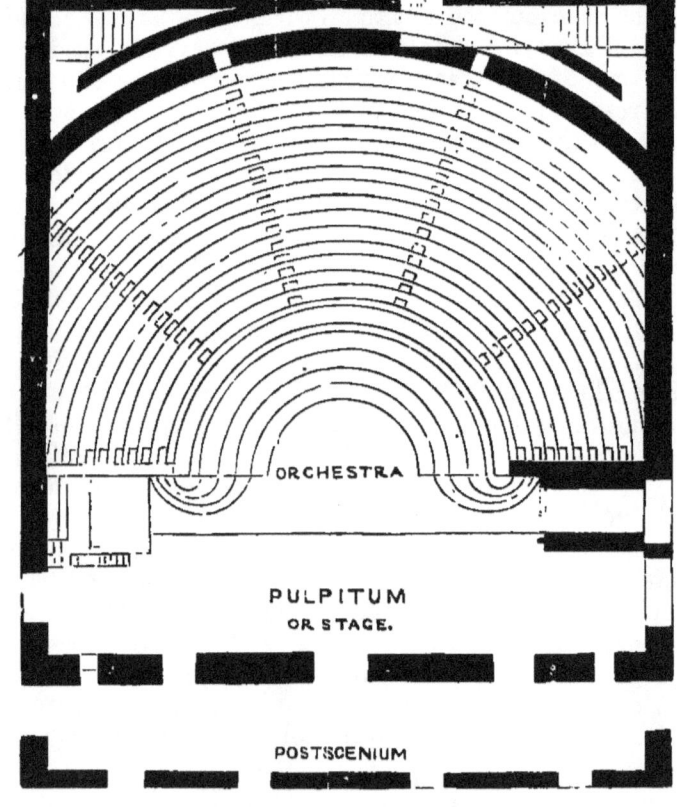

Plan of the small Theatre.

are of a very hard Vesuvian lava, well fitted to withstand the constant action of ascending and descending feet. The front wall of the proscenium, the scene, and the pavement of the orchestra, were entirely of marble of various colours—African breccia, giallo antico, and a purple marble. A band of marble, striped grey and white, runs across the orchestra from end to end of the seats, and in it are inlaid letters of bronze, eight inches and a half long, and level with the surface, forming the following inscription:—

M. OLCONIUS. M.F. VERUS. IIVIR. PRO. LVDIS.

"Marcus Olconius Verus, son of Marcus, Duumvir for the

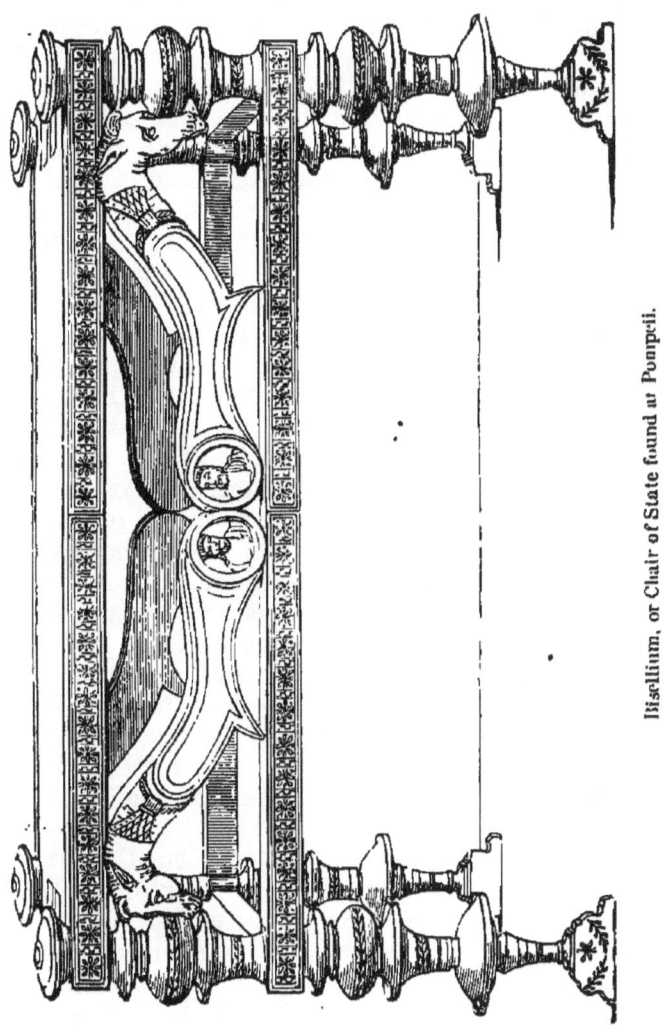

Bisellium, or Chair of State found at Pompeii.

games:" signifying probably that he laid down the pavement. Within the orchestra itself there were four tiers of benches, upon which were placed the bisellia, or chairs of state, upon which the municipal authorities and persons of distinction sat. These were usually made of bronze, handsomely ornamented, and supported by four legs. The Romans always provided conspicuous and distinct seats for their magistrates. The curule chair, composed of ivory, was peculiar to those of the metropolis; the inhabitants of the colonies and municipalities placed their authorities upon a large chair, capable of containing two persons, though only one occupied it, whence this seat of honour was called bisellium. An inscription found at Nocera tells us that the perpetual duumvirate was conferred on one M. Virtius; and beneath is carved the bisellium, with its footstool (scabellum), and two lictors at the side, as the insignia of the duumvirate. Two inscriptions in the Street of Tombs lead us to infer that this distinction was highly prized by the ancients, and only given to persons of eminent services or distinguished merit. Under both of them, bisellia, with their footstools and cushions, are carved. These bisellia were of several forms and different heights, according to the places for which they were intended: the highest, probably, were meant for the highest authorities; but high and low they had footstools, of one, two, three, or even more steps. Two have been found at Pompeii, of one of which we give an engraving. In form and ornament they are much alike, but they are very unequal in height. Both are made of bronze inlaid with silver. In execution and elegance they are equal, if not superior, to anything of the kind in modern art, and in the workmanship an extraordinary finish and accuracy is visible. These were placed, as we have said, on the four ranges of steps within the orchestra, which are not so deep as the steps of the cavea, nor have they places hollowed out for the feet, to defend the backs of the inferior row of spectators, the different arrangement of seats making this unnecessary.

In the view which is given of this small theatre, the reader will plainly see the different parts of the building. Behind the four benches of the orchestra rises a high parapet, which separated the privileged and unprivileged seats. Behind this ran the præcinctio or landing, accessible from below by the four curved steps at each end of the orchestra. Two of the stairs are visible, and a complete cuneus included between them. Above the cavea is the gallery for women. The cavea contained seventeen rows of seats. The only

View of the small Theatre.

direct access to it is by a passage behind, also communicating with the orchestra of the large theatre, which opens into a circular corridor, where are the vomitoria and stairs to ascend to the gallery. It has been computed that there is accommodation for fifteen hundred persons. The ends of the parapet are ornamented with winged griffins' legs. Behind, two sculptured figures, stoutly proportioned, appear to support the side wall of the cavea, upon which ponderous bronze candelabra formerly stood. To the left are the stage, scene, and postscenium. The centre door, or valvæ regiæ, and one of the side ones, are visible, and the wall of the postscenium closes the view behind. The cavity running along the front of the stage was most likely meant to hold the curtain, which, as we have said, was raised, not let down, when it was necessary to conceal the scene. The marble facings of this part of the building seem to have been carried away after the eruption of Vesuvius. In front, there appear two entrances, one to the pulpitum or stage, the other to the orchestra: between them is a flight of steps which led up to the chamber or box above mentioned, as set apart probably for the person who celebrated the games.

CHAPTER VIII.

THE AMPHITHEATRE.

SOME hundred yards from the theatres, in the south-eastern angle of the walls of the town, stands the amphitheatre. Although, perhaps, of Etruscan origin, the exhibitions of the amphitheatre are so peculiarly Roman, and Pompeii contains so many mementos of them, that a detailed account of them will not perhaps be misplaced. At an early period, A. U. 490, the practice of compelling human beings to fight for the amusement of spectators was introduced; and twelve years later the capture of several elephants in the first Punic war proved the means of introducing the chase, or rather the slaughter, of wild beasts into the Roman circus. The taste for these spectacles increased of course with its indulgence, and their magnificence with the wealth of the city and the increasing facility and inducement to practise bribery which was offered by the increased extent of provinces subject to Rome. It was not however until the last period of the republic, or rather until the domination of the emperors had collected into one channel the tributary wealth which previously was divided among a numerous aristocracy, that buildings were erected solely for the accommodation of gladiatorial shows; buildings entirely beyond the compass of a subject's wealth, and in which perhaps the magnificence of imperial Rome is most amply displayed. Numerous examples scattered throughout her empire, in a more or less advanced state of decay, still attest the luxury and solidity of their construction; while at Rome the Coliseum asserts the pre-eminent splendour of the metropolis—a monument surpassed in magnitude by the Pyramids alone, and as superior to them in skill and varied contrivance of design as to other buildings in its gigantic magnitude.

The Greek word, which by a slight alteration of its termination we render amphitheatre, signifies a theatre, or place of spectacles, forming a continuous inclosure, in opposition to the simple theatre, which, as we have said, was semicir-

216 POMPEII.

cular, but with the seats usually continued somewhat in advance of the diameter of the semicircle. The first amphi-

View of the Amphitheatre at Pompeii.

theatre seems to have been that of Curio, consisting of two moveable theatres, which could be placed face to face or back to back, according to the species of amusement for which they were required. Usually, gladiatorial shows were given in the Forum, and the chase and combats of wild beasts exhibited in the Circus, where once, when Pompey was celebrating games, some enraged elephants broke through the barrier which separated them from the spectators. This circumstance, together with the unsuitableness of the Circus for such sports, from its being divided into two compartments by the spina, a low wall surmounted by pillars, obelisks, and other ornamental erections, as well as from its disproportionate length, which rendered it ill adapted to afford a general view to all the spectators, determined Julius Cæsar, in his dictatorship, to construct a wooden theatre in the Campus Martius, built especially for hunting (θέατρον κυνηγετικόν), "which was called amphitheatre [apparently the first use of the word] because it was encompassed by circular seats without a scene."* The first permanent amphitheatre was built partly of stone and partly of wood, by Statilius Taurus, at the instigation of Augustus, who was passionately fond of these sports, especially of the hunting of rare beasts. This was burnt during the reign of Nero, and though restored, fell short of the wishes of Vespasian, who commenced the vast structure—completed by his son Titus—called the Flavian Amphitheatre, and subsequently the Coliseum. The expense of this building it is said would have sufficed to erect a capital city, and, if we may credit Dion, 9000 wild beasts were destroyed in its dedication. Eutropius restricts the number to 5000. When the hunting was over the arena was filled with water, and a sea-fight ensued.

The construction of these buildings so much resembles the construction of theatres, that it will not be necessary to describe them at any great length. Without, they usually presented to the view an oval wall, composed of two or more stories of arcades, supported by piers of different orders of architecture adorned with pilasters or attached pillars. Within, an equal number of stories of galleries gave access to the spectators at different elevations, and the inclined plane of the seats was also supported upon piers and vaults, so that the ground plan presented a number of circular rows

---

* Dion Cassius, xliii.

of piers, arranged in radii converging to the centre of the arena. A suitable number of doors opened upon the ground floor, and passages from thence, intersecting the circular passages between the piers, gave an easy access to every part of the building. Sometimes a gallery encompassed the whole, and served as a common access to all the stairs which led to the upper stories. This was the case in the amphitheatre at Nismes. Sometimes each staircase had its distinct communication from without: this was the case at Verona. The arrangement of the seats was the same as in theatres; they were divided horizontally by præcinctiones, and vertically into cunei by staircases. The scene and apparatus of the stage was of course wanting, and its place occupied by an oval area, called arena, from the sand with which it was sprinkled, to absorb the blood shed, and give a firmer footing than that afforded by a stone pavement. It was sunk twelve or fifteen feet below the lowest range of seats, to secure the spectators from injury, and was besides fenced with round wooden rollers turning in their sockets, placed horizontally against the wall, such as the reader may have observed placed on low gates to prevent dogs from climbing over, and with strong nets. In the time of Nero these nets were knotted with amber,[*] and the Emperor Carinus caused them to be made of golden cord or wire.[†] Sometimes, for more complete security, ditches, called *euripi*, surrounded the arena. This was first done by Cæsar, as a protection to the people against the elephants which he exhibited, that animal being supposed to be particularly afraid of water.[‡] The arena was sometimes spread with pounded stone. Caligula, in a fit of extravagance, used chrysocolla; and Nero, to surpass him, caused the brilliant red of cinnabar to be mixed with it.

In the centre of the arena was an altar dedicated sometimes to Diana or Pluto, more commonly to Jupiter Latiaris, the protector of Latium, in honour of whom human sacrifices were offered. Passages are to be found in ancient writers, from which it is inferred that the games of the amphitheatre were usually opened by sacrificing a *bestiarius*, one of those gladiators whose profession was to combat wild beasts, in honour of this bloodthirsty deity.[§] Beneath the arena dens

---

[*] Pliny, lib. xxxv.   [†] Calpurnius.
[‡] Pliny, lib. viii.   [§] Lipsius, De Amphitheatro, cap. iv.

are supposed to have been constructed to contain wild beasts. At the Coliseum numerous underground buildings are said by Fulvius to have existed, which he supposed to be sewers constructed to drain and cleanse the building.* Others with more probability have supposed them to be the dens of wild beasts. Immense accommodation was requisite to contain the thousands of animals which were slaughtered upon solemn occasions, but no great provision need have been made to carry off the rainwater which fell upon the five or six acres comprised within the walls of the building. Others again have supposed them formed to introduce the vast bodies of water by which the arena was suddenly transformed into a lake when imitations of naval battles were exhibited. In 1813 the arena was excavated, and numerous substructures discovered, which have since been filled up, the ground having become a swamp for want of drainage. Doors pierced in the wall which supported the podium communicated with these, or with other places of confinement beneath the part allotted to the audience, which being thrown open, vast numbers of animals could be introduced at once. Vopiscus tells us that a thousand ostriches, a thousand stags, and a thousand boars were thrown into the arena at once by the Emperor Probus. Sometimes, to astonish, and attract by novelty, the arena was converted into a wood. "Probus," says the same author, "exhibited a splendid hunting match, after the following manner. Large trees torn up by the roots were firmly connected by beams, and fixed upright; then earth was spread over the roots, so that the whole circus was planted to resemble a wood, and offered us the gratification of a green scene."†

The same order of precedence was observed as at the theatre—senators, knights, and commons having each their appropriate place. To the former was set apart the podium, a broad precinction or platform which ran immediately round the arena. Hither they brought the curule seats or bisellia, described in speaking of the theatres of Pompeii; and here was the suggestus, a covered seat appropriated to the emperor. It is supposed that in this part of the building there were also seats of honour for the exhibitor of the games and

* De Mirabilibus Urbis, lib. i.
† In Probo.

the vestal virgins. If the podium was insufficient for the accommodation of the senators, some of the adjoining seats were taken for their use. Next to the senators sat the knights, who seem here, as in the theatre, to have had fourteen rows set apart for them; and with them sat the civil and military tribunes. Behind were the popularia, or seats of the plebeians. Different tribes had particular cunei allotted to them. There were also some further internal arrangements, for Augustus separated married from unmarried men, and assigned a separate cuneus to youths, near whom their tutors were stationed. Women were stationed in a gallery, and attendants and servants in the highest gallery. The general direction of the amphitheatre was under the care of an officer named *villicus amphitheatri*. Officers called *locarii* attended to the distribution of the people, and removed any person from a seat which he was not entitled to hold.

We may notice, as a refinement of luxury, that concealed conduits were carried throughout these buildings, from which scented liquids were scattered over the audience. Sometimes the statues which ornamented them were applied to this purpose, and seemed to sweat perfumes through minute holes, with which the pipes that traversed them were pierced. It is this to which Lucan alludes in the following lines:—

>———As when mighty Rome's spectators meet
>In the full theatre's capacious seat,
>At once, by secret pipes and channels fed,
>Rich tinctures gush from every antique head;
>At once ten thousand saffron currents flow,
>And rain their odours on the crowd below.
>
>Rowe's *Lucan*, book ix.

Saffron was the material usually employed for these refreshing showers. The dried herb was infused in wine, more especially in sweet wine. Balsams and the more costly unguents were sometimes employed for the same purpose.

Another contrivance, too remarkable to be omitted in a general account of amphitheatres, is the awning by which spectators were protected from the overpowering heat of an Italian sun. This was called Volum, or Velarium; and it has afforded matter for a good deal of controversy, how a temporary covering could be extended over the vast areas of these buildings. Something of the kind was absolutely necessary, for the spectacle often lasted for many hours, and when anything extraordinary was expected the people went in crowds before daylight to obtain places, and some even at midnight. The Campanians first invented the means of stretching awnings over their theatres, by means of cords stretched across the cavea and attached to masts which passed through perforated blocks of stone deeply bedded in the wall. Quintus Catulus introduced them at Rome when he celebrated games at the dedication of the Capitol, A. U. 684. Lentulus Spinther, a contemporary of Cicero, first erected fine linen awnings (carbasina vela). Julius Cæsar covered over the whole Forum Romanum, and the Via Sacra, from his own house to the Capitol, which was esteemed even more wonderful than his gladiatorial exhibition.* Dio mentions a report that these awnings were of silk, but he speaks doubtfully; and it is scarcely probable that even Cæsar's extravagance would have carried him so far. Silk at that time was not manufactured at Rome; and we learn from Vopiscus, that even in the time of Aurelian the raw material was worth its weight in gold. Lucretius, speaking of the effect of coloured bodies upon transmitted light, has a fine passage illustrative of the magnificence displayed in this branch of theatrical decoration.

> This the crowd surveys
> Oft in the theatre, whose awnings broad,
> Bedecked with crimson, yellow, or the tint
> Of steel cerulean, from their fluted heights
> Wave tremulous; and o'er the scene beneath,
> Each marble statue, and the rising rows
> Of rank and beauty, fling their tint superb,
> While as the walls with ampler shade repel
> The garish noonbeam, every object round
> Laughs with a deeper dye, and wears profuse
> A lovelier lustre, ravished from the day.†

Wool however was the most common material, and the velaria made in Apulia were most esteemed, on account of the whiteness of the wool.

* Pliny, Hist. Nat. xix. 6.
† Lucretius, iv. 73; Good's translation. In the seventh line, "rank and beauty" is an interpolation of the translator's, taken from the practice of the modern theatre. In the Roman theatre they were as widely separated as are the boxes and one shilling gallery in our own.

Those who are not acquainted by experience with the difficulty of giving stability to tents of large dimensions, and the greater difficulty of erecting awnings, when, on account of the purpose for which they are intended, no support can be applied in the centre, may not fully estimate the difficulty of erecting and managing these velaria. Strength was necessary, both for the cloth itself and for the cords which strained and supported it, or the whole would have been shivered by the first gust of wind, and strength could not be obtained without great weight. Many of our readers probably are not aware, that however short and light a string may be, no amount of tension applied horizontally will stretch it into a line perfectly and mathematically straight. Practically the deviation is imperceptible where the power applied is very large in proportion to the weight and length of the string. Still it exists; and to take a common example, the reader probably never saw a clothes-line stretched out, though neither the weight nor length of the string are considerable, without the middle being visibly lower than the ends. When the line is at once long and heavy, an enormous power is required to suspend it even in a curve between two points; and the amount of tension, and difficulty of finding materials able to withstand it, are the only obstacles to constructing chain bridges which should be thousands, instead of hundreds of feet in length. In these erections the piers are raised to a considerable height, that a sufficient depth may be allowed for the curve of the chains without depressing the roadway. Ten times—a hundred times the power which was applied to strain them into that shape would not suffice to bring them even so near to a horizontal line but that the most inaccurate and unobservant eye should at once detect the inequality in their level; and the chains themselves would probably give way before such a force as this could be applied to them. The least diameter of the Coliseum is nearly equal in length to the Menai bridge; and if the labour of stretching cords over the one seems small in comparison with that of raising the ponderous chains of the other, we may take into consideration the weight of cloth which those cords supported, and the increase of difficulties arising from the action of the wind on so extensive a surface. In boisterous weather, as we learn from Martial and other authors, these difficulties were so great that the velum could not be spread. When this was the case the Romans used broad hats, or a sort of parasol, which was called *umbella* or *umbraculum*, from *umbra*, shade.* We may add, in conclusion, that Suetonius mentions as one of Caligula's tyrannical extravagances, that sometimes at a show of gladiators, when the sun's heat was most intense, he would cause the awning to be drawn back, and at the same time forbid any person to leave the place.

The difficulty of the undertaking has given rise to considerable discussion as to the means by which the Romans contrived to extend the velum at such a height over so great a surface, and to manage it at pleasure. Sailors were employed in the service, for the Emperor Commodus, who piqued himself on his gladiatorial skill, and used to fight in the arena, believing himself mocked by the servile crowd of spectators, when once they hailed him with divine honours, gave order for their slaughter by the sailors who were managing the veils.† Concerning the method of working them no information has been handed down. It is evident however that they were supported by masts which rose above the summit of the walls. A view of one of these, with the method of fastening it, has been given in the chapter on theatres. Near the top of the outer wall of the Coliseum there are 240 consoles, or projecting blocks of stone, in which holes are cut to receive the ends of spars, which ran up through holes cut in the cornice to some height above the greatest elevation of the building. A sufficient number of firm points of support at equal intervals was thus procured; and this difficulty being overcome, the next was to stretch as tight as possible the larger ropes, upon which the whole covering depended for its stability.

The games to which these buildings were especially devoted were, as we have already hinted, twofold—those in which wild beasts were introduced, to combat either with

---

* The following epigrams of Martial will illustrate these points:—

> In Pompeiano tectus spectabo theatro,
> Nam populo ventus vela negare solet.

> Accipe quæ nimios vincant umbracula soles:
> Sit licet et ventus, te tua vela tegent.

† Lampridius.

each other or with men, and those in which men fought with men. Under the general term of gladiators are comprised all who fought in the arena, though those who pitted their skill against the strength and ferocity of savage animals were peculiarly distinguished by the name of *bestiarii*. In general these unhappy persons were slaves or condemned criminals, who by adopting this profession purchased an uncertain prolongation of existence, but freemen sometimes gained a desperate subsistence by thus hazarding their lives; and in the decline of Rome, knights, senators, and even the emperors sometimes appeared in the arena, at the instigation of a vulgar and degrading thirst for popular applause.

The origin of these bloody entertainments may be found in the earliest records of profane history and the earliest stages of society. Among half-civilized or savage nations, both ancient and modern, we find it customary after a battle to sacrifice prisoners of war in honour of those chiefs who have been slain. Thus Achilles offers up twelve young Trojans to the ghost of Patroclus,* and similar examples may be easily found among our northern ancestors and the indigenous American tribes of the present day. In course of time it became usual to sacrifice slaves at the funeral of all persons of condition; and either for the amusement of the spectators, or because it appeared barbarous to massacre defenceless men, arms were placed in their hands, and they were incited to save their own lives by the death of those who were opposed to them. In later times, the furnishing these unhappy men became matter of speculation, and they were carefully trained to the profession of arms, to increase the reputation and popularity of the contractor who provided them. This person was called *lanista* by the Romans. At first these sports were performed about the funeral pile of the deceased, or near his sepulchre, in consonance with the idea of sacrifice in which they originated; but as they became more splendid, and ceased to be peculiarly appropriated to such occasions, they were removed, originally to the Forum, and afterwards to the Circus and amphitheatres.

Gladiators were first exhibited at Rome, A.U. 488, by M. and D. Brutus, on occasion of the death of their father.

* Il. xxiii. 175.

This show consisted only of three pairs. A.U. 537, the three sons of M. Æmilius Lepidus,' the augur, entertained the people in the Forum with eleven pair, and the show lasted three days. A.U. 552, the three sons of M. Valerius Lævinus exhibited twenty-five pairs. And thus these shows increased in number and frequency, and the taste for them strengthened with its gratification, until not only the heir of any rich or eminent person lately deceased, but all the principal magistrates, and the candidates for magistracies, presented the people with shows of this nature to gain their favour and support.

This taste was not without its inconveniences and dangers. Men of rank and political importance kept *families*, as they were called, of gladiators—desperadoes ready to execute any command of their master; and towards the fall of the republic, when party rage scrupled not to have recourse to open violence, questions of the highest import were debated in the streets of the city by the most despised of its slaves. In the conspiracy of Catiline so much danger was apprehended from them, that particular measures were taken to prevent their joining the disaffected party; an event the more to be feared because of the desperate war in which they had engaged the republic a few years before, under the command of the celebrated Spartacus. At a much later period, at the triumph of Probus, A.D. 281, about fourscore gladiators exhibited a similar courage. Disdaining to shed their blood for the amusement of a cruel people, they killed their keepers, broke out from the place of their confinement, and filled the streets of Rome with blood and confusion. After an obstinate resistance they were cut to pieces by the regular troops.

The oath which they took upon entering the service is preserved by Petronius, and is couched in these terms: "We swear, after the dictation of Eumolpus, to suffer death by fire, bonds, stripes, and the sword; and whatever else Eumolpus may command, as true gladiators we bind ourselves body and mind to our master's service."

From slaves and freedmen the inhuman sport at length spread to persons of rank and fortune, insomuch that Augustus was obliged to issue an edict, that none of senatorial rank should become gladiators; and soon after he laid a similar restraint on the knights. Succeeding emperors, according to their characters, encouraged or endeavoured to suppress this degrading taste. Nero is related to have brought upwards of four hundred senators and six hundred knights upon the arena; and in some of his exhibitions even women of quality contended publicly. The excellent Marcus Aurelius not only retrenched the enormous expenses of these amusements, but ordered that gladiators should contend only with blunt weapons. But they were not abolished until some time after the introduction of Christianity. Constantine published the first edict which condemned the shedding of human blood, and ordered that criminals condemned to death should rather be sent to the mines than reserved for the service of the amphitheatre. In the reign of Honorius, when he was celebrating with magnificent games the retreat of the Goths and the deliverance of Rome, an Asiatic monk, by name Telemachus, had the boldness to descend into the arena to part the combatants. "The Romans were provoked by this interruption of their pleasures, and the rash monk was overwhelmed under a shower of stones. But the madness of the people soon subsided; they respected the memory of Telemachus, who had deserved the honours of martyrdom, and they submitted without a murmur to the laws of Honorius, which abolished for ever the human sacrifices of the amphitheatre."* This occurred A.D. 404. It was not however until the year 500 that the practice was finally and completely abolished by Theodoric.

Some time before the day appointed for the spectacle, he who gave it (*editor*) published bills containing the name and ensigns of the gladiators, for each of them had his own distinctive badge, and stating also how many were to fight, and how long the show would last. It appears, that like our itinerant showmen, they sometimes exhibited paintings of what the sports were to contain. On the appointed day the gladiators marched in procession with much ceremony into the amphitheatre. They then separated into pairs, as they had been previously matched. The annexed engraving, taken from a picture on the wall of the amphitheatre at Pompeii, seems to represent the beginning of a combat. In the middle stands the arbiter of the fight, marking out with a long stick the space for the combatants. On his right stands a gladiator

* Gibbon, chap. xxx.

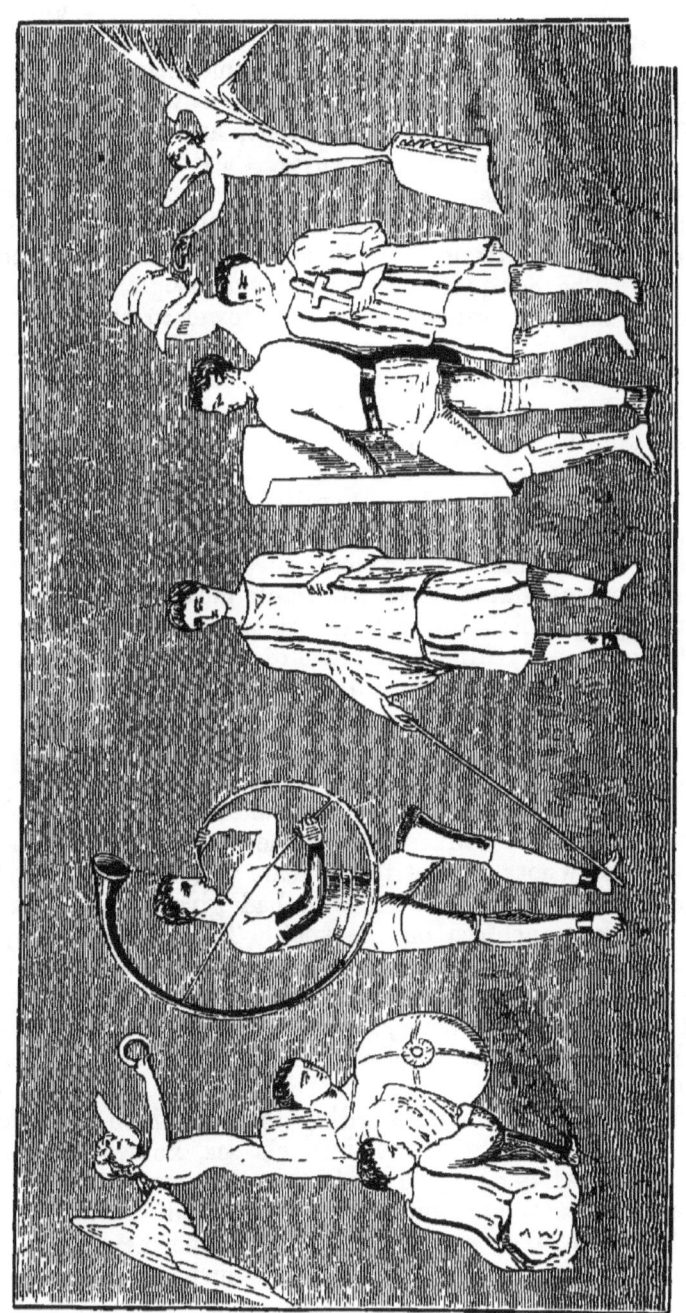

Gladiators, from a painting on the wall of the Arena at Pompeii.

only half armed, to whom two others are bringing a sword and helmet. On the left another gladiator, also only partly armed, sounds the trumpet for the commencement of the fight; whilst behind him two companions, at the foot of one of the Victories which enclose the scene, are preparing his helmet and shield. At first, however, they contended only with staves, called *rudes*, or with blunted weapons; but when warmed and inspirited by the pretence of battle, they changed their weapons, and advanced at the sound of trumpets to the real strife. The conquered looked to the people or to the emperor for life; his antagonist had no power to grant or to refuse it; but if the spectators were dissatisfied and gave the signal of death, he was obliged to become the executioner of their will. This signal was the turning down the thumbs; as is well known. If any showed signs of fear, their death was certain; if on the other hand they waited the fatal stroke with intrepidity, the people generally relented. But fear and want of spirit were of very rare occurrence, insomuch that Cicero more than once proposes the principle of honour which actuated gladiators as an admirable model of constancy and courage, by which he intended to animate himself and others to suffer everything in defence of the commonwealth.

The bodies of the slain were dragged with a hook through a gate called Libitinensis, the Gate of Death, to the *spoliarium*. The victor was rewarded with a sum of money, contributed by the spectators or bestowed from the treasury, or a palm-branch, or a garland of palm ornamented with coloured ribbons—ensigns of frequent occurrence in ancient monuments. Those who survived three years were released from this service, and sometimes one who had given great satisfaction was enfranchised on the spot. This was done by presenting the staff (*rudis*) which was used in preluding to the combat; on receiving which, the gladiator, if a freeman, recovered his liberty; if a slave, he was not made free, but was released from the obligation of venturing his life any further in the arena.

Gladiators were divided, according to the fashion of their armour and offensive weapons, into classes, known by the names of Thrax, Samnis, Myrmillo, and many others, of which a mere catalogue would be tedious, and it would be the work of a treatise to ascertain and describe their distinctive marks. The reader who has any curiosity upon the subject may consult the Saturnalia of Lipsius, in which a vast body of minute information is collected. It falls however strictly within our province to describe a tomb at Pompeii, ornamented with bas-reliefs in good preservation when copied by Mazois and Millin, which represent the two branches of amusement practised in the amphitheatre—hunting and gladiatorial fights, and throw a light upon many parts of our subject.

It is situated in the Street of Tombs, as it is called, without the gate leading to Herculaneum, and consists of a square chamber serving as a basement, surmounted by three steps, upon which and on the uppermost part of the basement are placed the sculptures, of which we proceed to speak. The whole is terminated by a square cippus, or funeral pillar, which bore the following inscription :—

<pre>
          RICIO. A.F. MEN
             SCAVRO
           II VIR. I. D.
       - - - ECVRIONES. LOCVM. MONVM.
    - - ∞ ∞ IN. FVNERE. ET. STATVAM. EQVEST.
       - - - ORO. PONENDAM. CENSVERVNT.
           SCAVRVS. PATER. FILIO.*
</pre>

"To Aricius Scaurus, son of Aulus, of the tribe Menenia, Duumvir of Justice, the decurions decreed the site of the monument, two thousand sesterces for funeral expenses, and an equestrian statue in the Forum. Scaurus the father to his son."

We give drawings of the most interesting of these sculptures, from Mazois, to whose researches we are also indebted for the following account of them. The earlier ones relate

* The marble is broken, so that the first name (*prænomen*) and the first letters of the name are lost. The latter has been differently read, Aricius Castricius, Patricius. Which is right is of little importance. The beginnings of all the longer lines are wanting, and the symmetry of the inscription would lead us to suppose that the cipher which stands for a thousand should be prefixed once oftener in the fifth line: which will make three thousand sesterces, about £24.

to the chase (*venatio*), and are taken from the steps which support the cippus. The first represents a man, naked and

unarmed, between a lion and a panther; the second, a wild boar apparently running at a man, also naked and defenceless, and in a half-recumbent posture. Mazois conjectures that these figures were of that class of combatants who, trusting in their activity alone, entered the arena merely to provoke the wild beasts after they were let loose; and he adds that this dangerous exercise was still practised in the bull-fights at Rome. Defenceless as these figures are, they show no signs of alarm, and in particular, he who is opposed to the boar seems collecting himself for a spring to baffle his enemy. In the continuation of the same relief is a wolf at full speed, gnawing a javelin deeply fixed in his chest, and further on a stag, with a rope attached to his horns, pulled down by two dogs or wolves. The next group is the most curious of this series, for it seems to represent the process by which the *bestiarii* were trained in their profession. It exhibits a youth— his legs and thighs protected by a sort of armour, a javelin in each hand—attacking a panther. The freedom of the beast's movements is hampered by a cord attached at one end to a collar round its neck, and at the other to a broad girth which passes round the body of a bull. By this arrangement the novice is in part protected, while at the same time far more activity and wariness is required than if the animal were attached to a fixed point. Behind the bull is another figure with a lance, who seems to goad the bull forwards, and thus offer more scope for movement to the panther.

Another bas-relief represents a man fighting a bear—a sword in one hand and a veil in the other, the very equip-

ment of the matador in the Spanish bull-fights to the present day. This circumstance, of little importance in itself, deserves remark, because it serves to fix the period of the construction of the tomb. We learn from Pliny * that

* N. H., viii. 16.

the veil was not employed in the arena against wild beasts before the reign of Claudius. Claudius became Emperor A.D. 41. In the year 59 all theatrical exhibitions were interdicted for ten years. Four years afterwards occurred the earthquake, to which we have had occasion to make frequent reference; and as the building bears evident marks of injury from this cause, and repair, we must conclude that it was erected at some time between the dates already given, probably during the ten or twelve years antecedent to the year 59.

The sculptures on the basement are divided into two lines of figures, forming a sort of double frieze. Here, as in the upper series, they are made of stucco; indeed there is no marble about the tomb except the slab on which the inscription was engraved. The figures appear to have been moulded separately, and attached to the plaster ground by brass or iron pins, more frequently the latter. These in many instances have been destroyed by rust, and have suffered the figures to drop. It is worthy of observation that the sculpture has been in part restored, and that under the present figures others have been found, of better workmanship, and, in some instances, differently armed.

In various portions of the frieze are written the name of the person to whom the gladiators belonged—one Ampliatus —the names of the combatants, and the number of their victories. Ampliatus probably was the *lanista* of the city; for an inscription found on the outer wall of the basilica, states that the family of N. Festus Ampliatus will contend a second time on the 17th May. These names are written in black, the letters narrow and ill shaped.

The upper frieze contains eight pairs of gladiators. The first pair, on the left, represents an equestrian combat. The first figure is called Bebrix, a barbarous name, which denotes a foreign origin. The numerals added to his name denote the number of contests in which he has been victorious; they are much effaced, but have been read XII.* His

* The letters IVI occur over most of the figures. In conjunction with the numerals, Mazois seems to interpret them, "conquered so many times;" but he does not tell of what word he supposes them to be the abbreviation, nor are we prepared to suggest any. [The letters seem rather to be TVL. standing for *tulit*, i.e., victorias, which last word is understood. See Breton, p. 92.]

adversary is called Nobilior, and reckons XI victories. Both are armed alike with a light lance, a round buckler (*parma*) elegantly ornamented, and helmets, with vizors which cover the whole face, and more resemble the helmets of the Middle Ages than the Roman helmet as it is usually represented. The right arms of both and the thigh of Nobilior are protected by a sort of armour resembling successive bands of iron. These two gladiators are clothed in the *inducula*, a short and light cloak which formed part of the dress of the Roman knights; the legs are naked. Bebrix has shoes resembling those now in use, but Nobilior wears the *semiplotia*, a kind of hunting shoe bound with thongs,

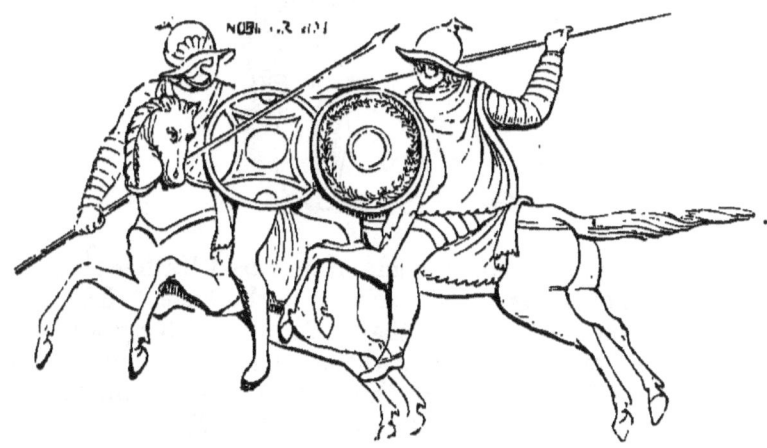

round the leg.* The horse is covered with the *sagma*, a square saddle-cloth in use among the Roman cavalry; the crupper is painted red. The action of the figures is good. Bebrix appears to have aimed at Nobilior a blow with his lance, who having received it on the buckler, attacks in his turn Bebrix, who now places himself on the defensive.

The group next in succession represents two gladiators whose names are defaced. The first wears a helmet having a vizor, much ornamented, with the long buckler (*scutum*).

---

* Similar to the moccasins of the Indians or the Scotch brogue. A similar article of home manufacture, made of raw hide, is still in use among the peasants of southern Italy.—See *Pinelli's Costumes*.

It is presumed that he should have for offensive weapon a
sword, but the sculptor has neglected to represent it. Like
all the other gladiators, he wears the *subligaculum*, a short
apron of red or white stuff fixed above the hips by a girdle
of bronze or embroidered leather. On the right leg is a

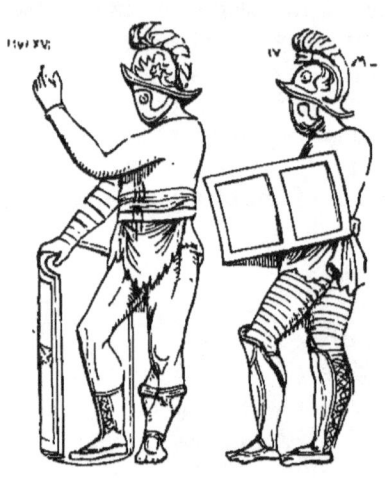

kind of buskin, commonly made of coloured leather ; on the
left an ocrea or greave, not reaching to the knee. The left
leg is thus armed, because that side of the body was the
most exposed by the ancients, whose guard on account of the
buckler was the reverse of the modern guard; the rest of
the body is entirely naked. The other figure is armed
with a helmet ornamented with wings, a smaller buckler,
thigh-pieces formed of plates of iron, and on each leg the
high greave, called by the Greeks κνημὶς. These figures
appear to represent one of the light-armed class, called *Veles*,
and a Samnite (*Samnis*), so called because they were armed
after the old Samnite fashion. The former, who has been
sixteen times a conqueror in various games, has at last encountered a more fortunate, or a more skilful adversary.
He is wounded in the breast, and has let fall his buckler,
avowing himself conquered ; at the same time he implores
the pity of the people by raising his finger towards them,
for it was thus that gladiators begged their life. Behind
him the Samnite awaits the answering sign from the spectators,

that he may spare his antagonist or strike the death-blow, as they decree. The third couple represents (*Thrax*) a Thracian, so called from the fashion of his armour, especially the round Thracian shield (*parma*), and one called Myrmillo, a name of doubtful origin. It appears, however, that the Myrmillones were for the most part Gauls, and armed somewhat in the Gallic style, and that the Thrax and the Myrmillo were usually opposed to each other. The Thrax wears a helmet, with greaves and thigh-pieces like those of the Samnite; and we may here observe that the right arm of every figure is protected by a banded armour which we have already described. The upper part of the body is naked. The dress of the Myrmillo is nearly the same, except that he has not the thigh-pieces. A conqueror XV times, he is now worsted, and his adversary gains the XXXVth victory; and the letter Θ over his head, the initial of θανών indicates that he was put to death. The M which precedes it is interpreted to be the initial of Myrmillo.*

The next group consists of four figures. *Two are *secutores*, followers, the other two, *retiarii*, net men, armed only with a trident and net, with which they endeavoured to entangle their adversary, and then despatch him. These classes, like the Thrax and Myrmillo, were usual antagonists, and had their name from the secutor following the retiarius, who eluded the pursuit until he found an opportunity to throw his net to advantage. Nepimus, one of the latter, five times victorious, has fought against one of the former, whose name is lost, but who had triumphed six times in different combats. He has been less fortunate in this battle. Nepimus has struck him in the leg, the thigh, and the left arm; his blood runs, and in vain he implores mercy from the spectators. As the trident with which Nepimus is armed is not a weapon calculated to inflict speedy and certain death, the secutor Hyppolitus performs this last office to his comrade. The condemned wretch bends the knee, presents his throat to the sword, and throws himself forward to meet the blow, while Nepimus his conqueror pushes him, and seems to insult the last moments of his victim. In the distance is the retiarius, who must fight Hyppolitus in his turn. The

---

* Overbeck interprets the M by *mors*, and the Θ by θάνατος.

secutores have a very plain helmet, that their adversary may have little or no opportunity of pulling it off with the net or

trident; the right arm is clothed in armour, the left bore a *clypeus*, or large round shield; a sandal tied with narrow bands forms the covering for their feet. They wear no body armour, no covering but a cloth round the waist, for by their lightness and activity alone could they hope to avoid death and gain the victory. The retiarii have the head bare, except a fillet bound round the hair; they have no shield, but the left side is covered with a demi-cuirass, and the left arm protected in the usual manner, except that the shoulder-piece is very high. They wear the caliga, or low boot common to the Roman soldiery, and bear the trident; but the net with which they endeavoured to envelope their

adversaries is nowhere visible. This bas-relief is terminated by the combat between a light-armed gladiator and a Samnite. This last beseeches the spectators to save him, but it appears from the action of the principal figure that this is not granted. The conqueror looks towards the steps of the amphitheatre; he has seen the fatal signal, and in reply prepares himself to strike.

Between the pilasters of the door the frieze is continued. Two combats are represented. In the first a Samnite has been conquered by a Myrmillo. This last wishes to become his comrade's executioner without waiting the answer from the people, to whom the vanquished has appealed; but the *lanista* checks his arm, from which it would seem that the Samnite obtained pardon. The following pair exhibits a similar combat, in which the Myrmillo falls, stabbed to death. The wounds, the blood, and the inside of the bucklers are painted of a very bright red colour. The

swords, with the exception of that of Hyppolitus, are omitted; it is possible that it was intended to make them of metal.

The bas-reliefs constituting the lower frieze are devoted to the chace and to combats between men and animals. In the upper part are hares pursued by a dog; beyond is a wounded stag pursued by dogs, to whom he is about to become the prey; below, a wild boar is seized by an enormous dog, who has already caused his blood to flow. In the middle of the composition a *bestiarius* has transfixed a bear

with a stroke of his lance. This person wears a kind of short hunting boot, and is clothed as well as his comrade in

a light tunic without sleeves, bound round the hips, and called *subucula*. It was the dress of the common people,

as we learn from the sculptures on Trajan's column. The companion of this man has transfixed a bull, which flies, carrying with him the heavy lance with which he is wounded. He turns his head towards his assailant, and seems to wish to return to the attack; the man by his gestures appears astonished, beholding himself disarmed and at the mercy of the animal, whom he thought mortally stricken. Pliny (lib. viii. cap. 45) speaks of the ferocity shown by bulls in these combats, and of having seen them, when stretched for dead on the arena, lift themselves up and renew the combat. The following cuts represent the helmets of two of the figures at large, and the greaves, or boots.

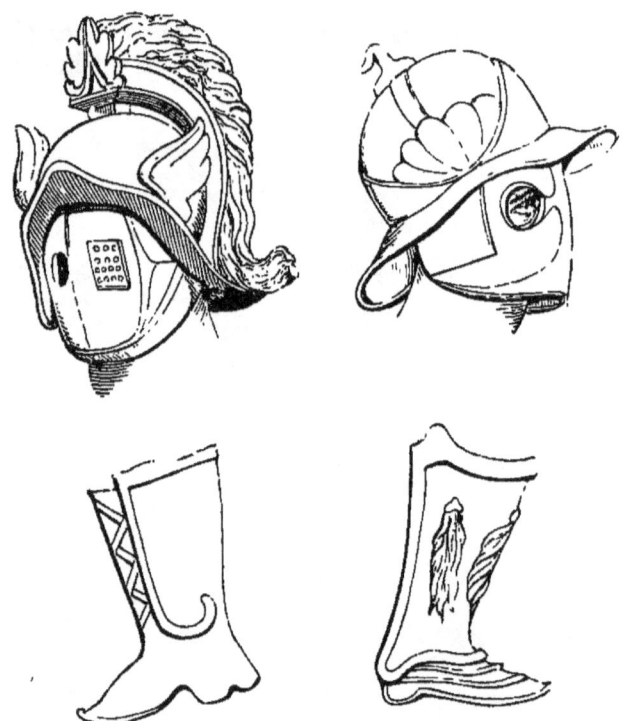

Another sort of amphitheatrical amusements consisted in witnessing the death of persons under sentence of the law, either by the hands of the executioner, or by being exposed to the fury of savage animals. The early Christians were especially subjected to this species of cruelty. Nero availed himself of the prejudice against them to turn aside popular indignation after the great conflagration of Rome, which is commonly ascribed to his own wanton love of mischief; and we learn from Tertullian, that, after great public misfortunes, the cry of the populace was, "To the lions with the Christians."* The Coliseum now owes its preservation to the Christian blood so profusely shed within its walls. After serving during ages as a quarry of hewn stone for the use of all whose station and power entitled them to a share in public plunder, it was at last secured from further injury by Pope Benedict XIV., who consecrated the building about the middle of the last century, and placed it under the protection of the martyrs, who had there borne testimony with their blood to the sincerity of their belief.

There is nothing in the amphitheatre of Pompeii at variance with the general description of this class of buildings, and our notice of it will therefore necessarily be short. Its form, as usual, is oval: the extreme length, from outside to outside of the exterior arcade, is 430 feet, its greatest breadth is 335 feet. The spectators gained admission by tickets, which had numbers or marks on them, corresponding with similar signs on the arches through which they entered. Those who were entitled to occupy the lower ranges of seats passed through the perforated arcades of the lower order; those whose place was in the upper portion of the cavea ascended by staircases between the seats and the outer wall of the building. From hence the women again ascended to the upper tier, which was divided into boxes, and appropriated to them. The construction consists for the most part of the rough masonry called *opus incertum*, with quoins of squared stone, and some trifling restorations of rubble. This rude mass was probably once covered with a more sumptuous facing of hewn stone; but there are now no other traces of it than a few of the key-stones, on one of which a chariot and two horses is sculptured, on another a head; besides which there are a few stars on the wedge-stones.

At each end of the ellipse were entrances into the arena for the combatants, through which the dead bodies were dragged out into the spoliarium. These were also the principal approaches to the lower ranges of seats, occupied by

---

* Tertullian, Apol. 40.

the senators, magistrates, and knights, by means of corridors to the right and left which ran round the arena. The ends of these passages were secured by metal gratings against the intrusion of wild beasts. In the northern one are nine

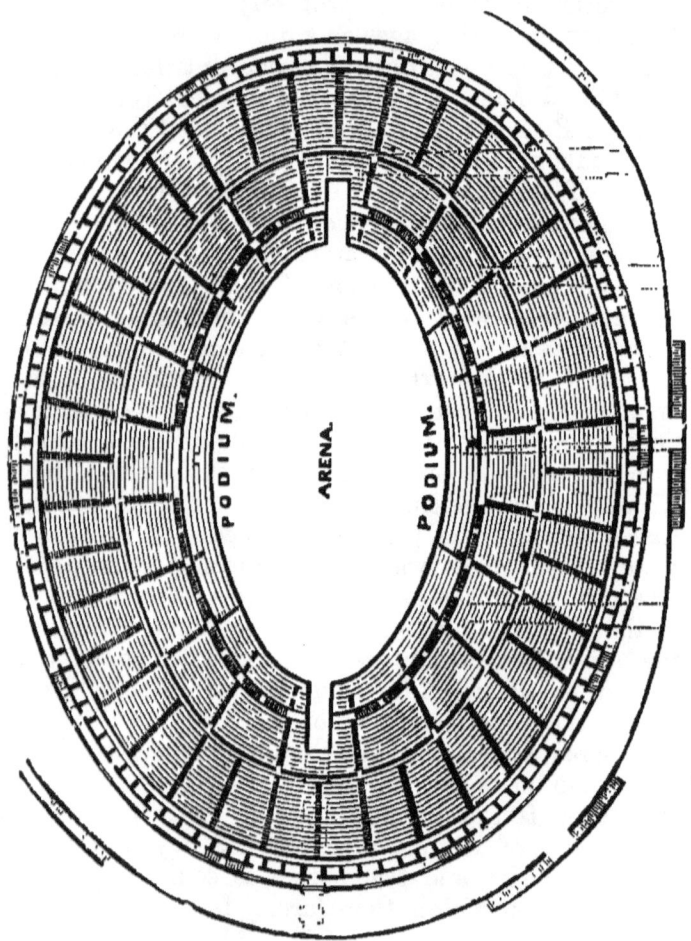

Plan of the Amphitheatre at Pompeii.

places for pedestals to form a line of separation, dividing the entrance into two parts of unequal breadth. The seats are elevated above the arena upon a high podium or parapet, upon which, when the building was first opened, there remained several inscriptions, containing the names of duumvirs who had presided upon different occasions. There were also paintings in fresco, one representing a tigress fighting with a wild boar; another, a stag chased by a lioness; another, a battle between a bull and bear. Other subjects comprised candelabra, a distribution of palms among the gladiators, winged genii, minstrels, and musicians; but all disappeared soon after their exposure to the atmosphere. The amphitheatre comprises twenty-four rows of seats, and about 20,000 feet of sitting-room: it would consequently afford accommodation for something more than ten thousand people, exclusive of those who were obliged to take up with standing room.

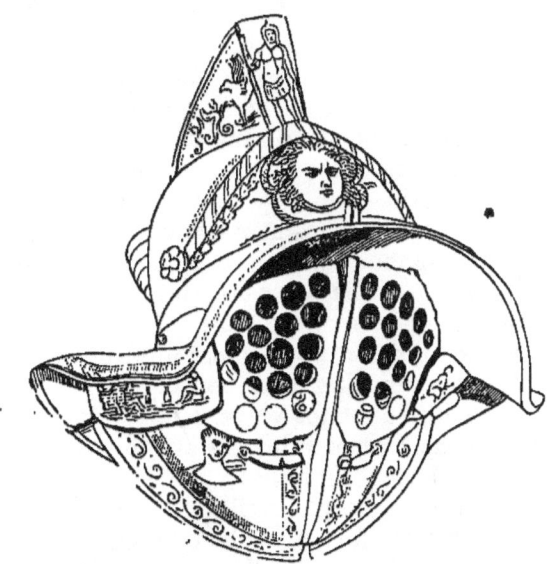

Bronze Helmet, supposed to have been worn by a gladiator.

It may be observed that the arena of the amphitheatre of Pompeii appears to be formed of the natural surface of the earth, and has none of those vast substructions observable at Pozzuoli and Capua. It does not therefore appear capable of being turned into a Naumachia, nor indeed would it have been easy to find there water enough for such a purpose.

Having now described all the public buildings of Pompeii, it will not be out of place to say a few words on their architectural character. The city, as might be expected from its antiquity and from its change of masters, having been a Greek colony long before its subjugation by the Romans, presents us with examples both of Greek and Roman architecture, domestic as well as public. The Romans borrowed their knowledge of building from the Greeks, but they borrowed it as imitators, not as copyists. They aimed at variety by altering the details and proportions of the several orders, and what they gained in novelty they lost in beauty. Hence the Doric and Ionic of the one are immediately distinguishable from the Doric and Ionic of the other: the difference between the Corinthian orders is less perceptible, consisting chiefly in the foliage of the capital. In Greece the Doric gradually changed its character, being most robust in the most ancient examples. But the standard examples of it, built in the age of Pericles, are still robust in character, with twenty flutings, or longitudinal channels cut in the pillars. The Romans made the column more slender, and at the same time increased the number of flutings. The original was placed upon the temple floor, without even a plinth—the copy was raised upon a pedestal; the capital of the former was grave and simple—that of the latter was more elaborate, and enriched with mouldings. At Pompeii the most characteristic parts of the buildings, the entablatures and capitals, are almost all destroyed. Still enough remains for us in most instances to ascertain the style of what remains, and consequently to ascribe to them something like a comparative date. Thus the columns which surround the Forum fulfil the above-named conditions of the Grecian Doric; they have no base, contain twenty flutings, and have a simple capital. Similar in style are those of the triangular forum in the quarter of the theatres; and the schools or tribunal, and the square called the soldiers' quarters are also evidently of Greek design and construction, though repaired by their last possessors. It is to be observed, however, that the Doric of Pompeii, though it preserves the Greek taste in the detail of its mouldings, is exceedingly slender, and in this respect varies materially from the most esteemed models of the order.

Another characteristic of Greek architecture, which points out its originality in a striking manner, is that the profiles of all its mouldings are drawn by hand, and cannot be mechanically described, whereas the Roman mouldings are all formed on some geometrical construction. Hence the latter are always similar, while the former admit of indefinite variety, according to circumstances which might influence the architect, though they escape our notice. The reader may see an instance of this in a capital from the Parthenon, now in the British Museum. Upon cursory examination the projecting moulding of the capital under the abacus would be taken for the frustum of a cone, whereas it is really a very delicate curve. What the object of the architect was in tracing this line, which viewed from below must have appeared a straight line, it may not be easy to determine; but without doubt in taking this trouble he was influenced by some delicate perception of beauty. It is from this peculiarity in the mouldings that we conclude the small portico, propylæum, or entrance to tho triangular forum, was designed by a Greek architect. It is of the Ionic order; the mouldings and the volutes or spiral horns are more elegant than in the Roman style. In addition to this the deep sinking under some of the mouldings, which the strictness of Roman rules did not allow, stamp it as a Greek work, where variety and thought were permitted.

The capital of the Ionic order found in this city differs in one respect from all the examples, both Greek and Roman, with which we are acquainted. We allude to the ornamented echinus moulding which runs under the volutes, which usually is carved to represent eggs within a shell. thus :—

But in the Pompeian examples the egg is very small, and the shell or husk is of a different form, more like the section

of a horse-chesnut, showing a small portion of the nut where the rind is partially split, from which indeed the idea may possibly have been taken.

The Basilica is similar in the details of its architecture to the celebrated Temple of Vesta at Tivoli, supposed to have been erected by a Greek architect, and displays marks of Grecian taste.

The oldest building in Pompeii is the Temple of Hercules, perhaps erected by the first Greek colonists, or at least raised on the site of a more ancient temple. It is Doric, and of course Grecian; and the style observable in its scanty remains leads the learned to refer it to the most remote antiquity. The most remarkable feature is the swelling of the flat part of the echinus moulding, which, when the order became perfected in the Parthenon and Temple of Theseus at Athens, was made flat or insensibly curved, as may be seen in the capital above referred to. The basements also of some of the temples may be considered as more ancient than the columns reared upon them, and it is very possible that both the basement of the Temple of Jupiter and that of the Temple of Venus may be of Greek construction. The Romans either repaired or rebuilt many of the public buildings of the city. The ruins of brick at the end of the Forum, opposite the Temple of Jupiter, were built by them; the baths, with their vaulted ceiling, they also constructed. The Temple of Fortune was erected by a Roman individual, as the inscription sets forth; and the Pantheon, Temple of Mercury, with the building placed between them, as well as the crypto-portico of Eumachia, which is partly built of brick, bear evident marks of a Roman origin. The Temple of Venus may be considered as Roman, its original Greek design having been changed by a coat of plaster, as we have already observed. The theatres and amphitheatre are evidently Roman. That the former were so is ascertained from inscriptions,* while the latter was, as we well know, of

---

* The inscriptions do not necessarily mean that the theatres *were built* by those whose names they record. At all events, if they are originally of Roman construction, their situation on the side of a hill is after the Greek fashion; while their vicinity to the Greek temple shows that they were in the oldest part of the city. The inscriptions will be found in Mommsen's *Inscrr. Regni Neapolitani*, p. 115.

their own invention. The triumphal arches are of course Roman, such buildings having been unknown to the Greeks. In private dwellings, as well as in public edifices, the same mixed character is evident, and adds to their interest. But this branch of the subject belongs to the next part

END OF PART I.

PART II.

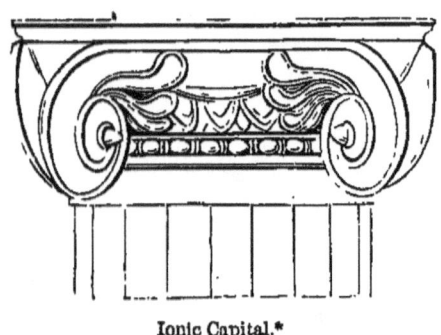

Ionic Capital.*

CHAPTER I.

DOMESTIC ARCHITECTURE OF ITALY.

THE first part having been employed in describing the public buildings which are preserved in Pompeii, the second will contain an account of the most remarkable houses which have been disinterred; of the paintings, domestic utensils, and other articles found in them; and such information upon the domestic manners of the ancient Italians as may seem requisite to the illustration of these remains. This branch of our subject is not less interesting, nor less extensive than the other. Temples and theatres, in equal preservation, and of greater splendour than those at Pompeii, may be seen in many places; but towards acquainting us with the habitations, the private luxuries and elegancies of ancient life, not all the scattered fragments of domestic architecture which exist elsewhere have done so much as this city, with its

---

* Ionic capital, from Pompeii, with angular volutes. The order partakes much of the Doric; being without a base, and having the shaft sharply terminated. Four similar capitals are to be seen at the four angles of the Greco-Siculan sepulchral monument at Girgenti, commonly called the Sepulchre of the Horse.

DOMESTIC ARCHITECTURE OF ITALY.   249

fellow-sufferer, Herculaneum. But as these ancient houses differ very much from any now in use, and as we shall have continual occasion to use the terms by which Vitruvius, and, after him, modern architects, have named their several apartments, it will be useful to preface our descriptions by a short account of the steps by which the Romans advanced from huts to palaces, as the residences of the more wealthy individuals among them may be termed, and of the distribution and purposes of the rooms, for a general resemblance is to be found in the ground-plan of all of them. We shall also give an explanation of those architectural terms which we shall have occasion most frequently to employ.

If we ascend to the earliest period of Roman story, and mention the thatched cottage of Romulus, religiously preserved in the Capitol, and repaired from time to time with the same rude materials of which it was originally built, it is not with the purpose of drawing any inference with respect to the domestic architecture of that remote and fabulous time, or of fatiguing the reader by tracing the progress of this art from the cottage of Romulus to the golden house of Nero. But there is a singularly interesting relic of antiquity preserved by Mazois, which this mention of the founder of Rome may serve to introduce to our notice. Some time since, a quantity of cinerary vases were discovered in the

Cabin of the Aboriginal Latians.

neighbourhood of Alba, which, on that eminent architect's authority,* "belong unquestionably to the first inhabitants

* Part ii. p. 5.

of Latium, and ascend beyond the earliest known epochs of Italian history, since the spot in which they were found is entirely covered with thick beds of lava which have flowed from Monte Albano, a volcano of whose eruptions all memory is lost in the night of antiquity." That which makes these urns most curious, is, that they represent the rude habitations of the time; and granting that they are genuine, of which Mazois expresses no doubt, the nature of these representations is sufficient warranty of their high antiquity. Here, probably, we see the cabins of the aboriginal Latians; and such, we may conjecture, was the cottage so long preserved with religious veneration in the Capitol.

To the reign of the first Tarquin is ascribed the introduction of the Etruscan style of architecture, as well in the arrangement of houses, as in the magnificent public works, the walls, sewers, and Forum, which are said to have been built by him. But, to pass hastily over this doubtful ground, it is enough to state that we have authority for giving an Etruscan origin to the principal divisions of the Roman houses.* These in the early ages were poor and mean. For the first five hundred years of the city, the use of tiles was unknown, thatch or shingles forming the materials of roofs; and a story is told that the consul Publicola, having built a house of such splendour, according to the notions of the age, as to excite the jealousy of the people, demolished it in a single night in hope of regaining his popularity; conclusive proof against the solidity, at least, of the building. Excessive expense was guarded against by sumptuary laws; and it was forbidden to build walls exceeding about a foot and a half in thickness. This restriction, with the weak nature of the materials employed in early times, at first unbaked bricks, then wooden frame-work filled up with masonry, limited the height of houses to one story, as we are told by Vitruvius: and even after baked bricks were known, their size, which exceeded the size of those now in use,† rendered it difficult to break the joints, and bond the walls sufficiently for lofty

---

* Varro and Festus, quoted by Mazois, part ii. p. 7.

† They were a foot and a half long, and a foot broad. This being the case the wall would only have been one brick thick, and liable to open at any of the joints. We give solidity to walls which are no thicker, by interweaving the bricks so that no joint may run through.—Vitruv. ii. 3, 8.

erections. As population increased, and with it the value of ground in the city, economy of room was sought in added height, and the increased skill of the architect found means to raise houses of several stories. They were then surmounted by a terrace named *solarium*, from *sol*, the sun, whose genial warmth the inhabitants enjoyed there in the winter: while in the summer they frequented it for the sake of the cool evening breeze, and the magnificent prospects of the city and its environs. Here the Romans loved to take their evening repast, and hence the upper story received the name of *cœnaculum*, the supper-room. At last houses reached such an extreme height, that Augustus forbad a greater elevation than seventy feet to be given them.

Towards the last years of the republic, the Romans naturalized the arts of Greece among themselves; and Grecian architecture came into fashion at Rome, as we may learn, among other sources, from the letters of Cicero to Atticus, which bear constant testimony to the strong interest which he took in ornamenting his several houses, and mention Cyrus, his Greek architect. At this time immense fortunes were easily made from the spoils of new conquests, or by peculation and maladministration of subject provinces, and the money thus ill and easily acquired was squandered in the most lavish luxury. One favourite mode of indulgence was in splendour of building. Lucius Cassius was the first who ornamented his house with columns of foreign marble: they were only six in number, and twelve feet high. He was soon surpassed by Scaurus, who placed in his house columns of the black marble called Lucullian, thirty-eight feet high, and of such vast and unusual weight that the superintendent of sewers, as we are told by Pliny,* took security for any injury which might happen to the works under his charge, before they were suffered to be conveyed along the streets. Another prodigal, by name Mamurra, set the example of lining his rooms with slabs of marble. The best estimate, however, of the growth of architectural luxury about this time may be found in what we are told by Pliny, that, in the year of Rome 676, the house of Lepidus was the finest in the city, and thirty-five years later it was not the hundredth.† We may mention, as an example of the lavish

* Nat. Hist. xxxvi. 2. † Ib. xxxvi. 15.

expenditure of the Romans, that Domitius Ahenobarbus offered for the house of Crassus a sum amounting to near £48,500, which was refused by the owner.* Nor were they less extravagant in their country houses. We may again quote Cicero, whose attachment to his Tusculan and Formian villas, and interest in ornamenting them, even in the most perilous times, is well known. Still more celebrated are the villas of Lucullus and Pollio; of the latter some remains are still to be seen near Pausilipo.

Augustus endeavoured by his example to check this extravagant passion, but he produced little effect. And in the palaces of the emperors, and especially the Aurea Domus, the Golden House of Nero, the domestic architecture of Rome, or, we might probably say, of the world, reached its extreme point of magnificence. But these wonders do not belong to our pages; and to dwell on them would but discredit the edifices which it is our province to describe, spacious in themselves and sumptuous, yet mean in comparison with those of which we have just spoken. We therefore proceed to offer to the reader a sketch of the arrangement of a Roman house of the better class.

This arrangement, though varied, of course, by local circumstances, and according to the rank and circumstances of the master, was pretty generally the same in all. The principal rooms, differing only in size and ornament, recur everywhere; those supplemental ones, which were invented only for convenience or luxury, vary according to the tastes and circumstances of the master.

Vitruvius directs our attention to one principle of distribution, strange to modern habits, but of importance towards understanding the construction of a Roman house; that every considerable mansion might be divided into two parts, one intended for public resort, the other destined for the private service of the family. The origin of this may be found in the constitution of Rome, by which every plebeian might choose from among the patricians a *patron*, whose *client* he became, and to whose house he resorted freely for advice or assistance. To have a large body of clients was esteemed both honourable and advantageous, as the patron might of course reckon on their votes and support in all civil matters.

* Sexagies sestertium. Plin. Hist. Nat. xvii. 1.

With this view, lawyers of eminence gave free access to all who wished to consult them; and generally by day-break, or before it, the vestibules and ante-rooms of persons of any eminence, but especially of those who were distinguished by wealth or political power, were filled with a crowd, each coming with some particular object, one to recommend himself by the regularity of his attendance, another to request some favour, another from a wish to display his intimacy with the rich and powerful owner, others to receive the dole of meat or money which was distributed to needy retainers.* This crowd was of course received in the outer rooms, so as to disturb as little as possible the privacy of the mansion. These rooms, which constituted what Vitruvius calls the public part, were the portico, vestibule, cavædium or atrium, tablinum, alæ, fauces, and others less important, added at the will of the owner or architect.

The private part comprised the peristyle, bed-chambers, triclinium, œci, picture-gallery, library, baths, exedra, xystus, &c. We proceed to explain the meaning of these terms.

Before great mansions, but not in that class of houses which we find at Pompeii, there was generally a court or area, upon which the portico opened, either surrounding three sides of the area, or merely running along the front of the house. In smaller houses the portico ranged even with the street. Within the portico, or if there was no portico, opening directly to the street, was the vestibule, consisting of one or more spacious apartments. It was considered to be without the house, and was always open for the reception of those who came to wait there until the doors should be opened. The prothyrum, in Greek architecture, was the same as the vestibule. In Roman architecture, it was a passage-room, between the outer or house-door which opened to the vestibule, and an inner door which closed the entrance of the atrium. In the vestibule, or in an apartment opening upon it, the porter, *ostiarius*, usually had his seat.

The atrium, or cavædium, for they appear to have signified the same thing,† was the most important, and usually the

---
* ——————— Sportula primo
Limine parva sedet, turbæ rapienda togatæ.—Juv. i. 95.
See also Cic. ad Att. v. 2, and the Satirists, passim.

† Some commentators on Vitruvius, and among them Mr. Wilkins, deny this. The term cavædium is certainly equally applicable to any other open

most splendid apartment of the house. Here the owner received his crowd of morning visitors, who were not admitted to the inner apartments. The term is thus explained by Varro: "The hollow of the house (cavum ædium) is a covered place within the walls, left open to the common use of all. It is called Tuscan, from the Tuscans, after the Romans began to imitate their cavædium. The word atrium is derived from the Atriates, a people of Tuscany, from whom the pattern of it was taken."* Originally, then, the atrium was the common room of resort for the whole family, the place of their domestic occupations; and such it probably continued in the humbler ranks of life. A general description of it may easily be given. It was a large apartment, roofed over, but with an opening in the centre, called *compluvium*,† towards which the roof sloped, so as to throw the rain-water into a cistern in the floor called *impluvium*. Vitruvius, however, distinguishes five species of atria.

1. The Tuscanicum, or Tuscan atrium, the oldest and simplest of all. It was merely an apartment, the roof of which was supported by four beams meeting one other at right angles, the included quadrangular space forming the compluvium. Many of these remain at Pompeii.

2. The tetrastyle, or four-pillared atrium, resembled the Tuscan, except that the girders, or main beams of the roof, were supported by pillars, placed at the four angles of the impluvium. This furnished means of increasing the size of the apartment.

3. The Corinthian atrium differed from the tetrastyle only in the number of pillars and size of the impluvium. A greater proportion of the roof seems to have been left open.

court, as, for instance, to the peristyle; and Pliny, in the account of his Laurentine villa, makes mention of both atrium and cavædium, and speaks also of the peristyle. No wonder that much obscurity and difference of opinion prevail on these subjects, since almost all our knowledge is derived from the scanty account of Vitruvius; and it is obvious that whatever general rules might be recognised by architects, they must have been modified in innumerable instances by the caprice or convenience of individuals. It is dangerous, therefore, to attempt to wrest the text of an author, to make it square with some specimen which has been preserved or described; for we can never be sure that the two were even meant to coincide.

* De Ling. Lat. lib. iv.

† From *con* and *pluvia*, because the rain-water was brought together there. The derivation of impluvium is equally obvious.

The name is entirely unconnected with the order of architecture to which the columns belonged.

4. The atrium displuviatum had its roof inclined the contrary way, so as to throw the water off to the outside of the house, instead of carrying it into the impluvium.

5. The atrium testudinatum was roofed all over, without any vacancy or compluvium.

The roof around the compluvium was edged with a row of highly ornamented tiles, called antefixes, on which a mask or some other figure was moulded. At the corners there were usually spouts, in the form of lions' or dogs' heads, or any fantastical device which the architect might fancy, which carried the rain-water clear out into the impluvium, whence it passed into cisterns; from which again it was drawn for household purposes. For drinking, river-water, and still more, well-water, was preferred. Often the atrium was adorned with fountains, supplied through leaden or earthenware pipes, from aqueducts or other raised heads of water; for the Romans knew the property of fluids, which causes them to stand at the same height in communicating vessels. This is distinctly recognised by Pliny,* though their common use of aqueducts, in preference to pipes, has led to a supposition that this great hydrostatical principle was unknown to them. The breadth of the impluvium, according to Vitruvius, was not less than a quarter, nor greater than a third, of the whole breadth of the atrium; its length was regulated by the same standard. The opening above it was often shaded by a coloured veil, which diffused a softened light, and moderated the intense heat of an Italian sun†. The splendid columns of the house of Scaurus at Rome, were placed, as we learn from Pliny,‡ in the atrium of his house. The walls were painted with landscapes or arabesques—a practice introduced about the time of Augustus,—or lined with slabs of foreign and costly marbles, of which the Romans were passionately fond. The pavement was composed of the same precious material, or of still more valuable mosaics.

* Nat. Hist. xxxi. 6, S. 31: Aqua in plumbo subit altitudinem exortus sui.
† Rubent (vela scil.) in cavis ædium, et muscum a sole defendunt. We may conclude, then, that the impluvium was sometimes ornamented with moss or flowers, unless the words cavis ædium may be extended to the court of the peristyle, which was commonly laid out as a garden. [The latter seems more likely.]
‡ xxxvi. 1.

The tablinum was an appendage of the atrium, and usually entirely open to it. It contained, as its name imports,* the family archives, the statues, pictures, genealogical tables, and other relics of a long line of ancestors.

Alæ, wings, were similar but smaller apartments, or rather recesses, on each side of the further part of the atrium. Fauces, jaws, were passages, more especially those which passed to the interior of the house from the atrium. Thus Virgil uses the word, not merely in a metaphorical sense:—

"Vestibulum ante ipsum, primisq: in faucibus Orci."
Æn. vi. 273.

In houses of small extent, strangers were lodged in chambers which surrounded and opened into the atrium. The great, whose connections spread into the provinces, and who were visited by numbers who, on coming to Rome, expected to profit by their hospitality, had usually a *hospitium*, or place of reception for strangers, either separate, or among the dependencies of their palaces.

Of the private apartments the first to be mentioned is the peristyle, which usually lay behind the atrium, and communicated with it both through the tablinum and by fauces. In its general plan it resembled the atrium, being in fact a court, open to the sky in the middle, and surrounded by a colonnade, but it was larger in its dimensions, and the centre court was often decorated with shrubs and flowers and fountains, and was then called *xystus*. It should be greater in extent when measured transversely than in length,† and the intercolumniations should not exceed four, nor fall short of three diameters of the columns.

Of the arrangement of the bed-chambers we know little. They seem to have been small and inconvenient. When there was room they had usually a procœton, or ante-chamber. Vitruvius recommends that they should face the east, for the benefit of the early sun. One of the most important apartments in the whole house was the triclinium, or dining-room, so named from the three beds, τρεῖς κλίναι, which encompassed the table on three sides, leaving the fourth open to

* From tabula, or tabella, a picture. Another derivation is, "quasi e tabulis compactum," because the large openings into it might be closed by shutters.

† This rule, however, is seldom observed in the Pompeian houses.

the attendants. The prodigality of the Romans in matters of eating is well known, and it extended to all matters connected with the pleasures of the table. In their rooms, their couches, and all the furniture of their entertainments, magnificence and extravagance were carried to their highest point. The rich had several of these apartments, to be used at different seasons, or on various occasions. Lucullus, celebrated for his wealth and profuse expenditure, had a certain standard of expenditure for each triclinium, so that when his servants were told which hall he was to sup in, they knew exactly the style of entertainment to be prepared; and there is a well-known story of the way in which he deceived Pompey and Cicero, when they insisted on going home with him to see his family supper, by merely sending word home that he would sup in the Apollo, one of the most splendid of his halls, in which he never gave an entertainment for less than 50,000 denarii, about £1600. Sometimes the ceiling was contrived to open and let down a second course of meats, with showers of flowers and perfumed waters, while rope-dancers performed their evolutions over the heads of the company. The performances of these *funambuli* are frequently represented in paintings at Pompeii. Those in the cut in p. 258 have the characteristics of Fauns, or, according to Lord Monboddo's theory, have not yet rubbed off their tails. Mazois, in his work entitled "Le Palais de Scaurus," has given a fancy picture of the habitation of a Roman noble of the highest class, in which he has embodied all the scattered notices of domestic life, which a diligent perusal of the Latin writers has enabled him to collect. His description of the triclinium of Scaurus will give the reader the best notion of the style in which such an apartment was furnished and ornamented. For each particular in the description he quotes some authority. We shall not, however, encumber our pages with references to a long list of books not likely to be in the possession of most readers.

"The triclinium is twice as long as it is broad, and divided, as it were, into two parts—the upper occupied by the table and the couches, the lower left empty for the convenience of the attendants and spectators. Around the former the walls, up to a certain height, are ornamented with valuable hangings.* The decorations of the rest of the room are noble, and yet appropriate to its destination; garlands, entwined

Dancing Fauns. From the decorated walls of Pompeii.

with ivy and vine-branches, divide the walls into compartments, bordered with fanciful ornaments; in the centre of

* It was the fall of such hangings that created such confusion at Nasidienus' supper.

"Interea suspensa graves aulæa ruians
In patinam fecere; trahentia pulveris atri
Quantum non Aquilo Campanis excitat agris."
                                        Hor. Sat. ii. 8. 54.

each of which are painted with admirable elegance young Fauns, or half-naked Bacchantes, carrying thyrsi, vases, and all the furniture of festive meetings. Above the columns is a large frieze, divided into' twelve compartments; each of these is surmounted by one of the signs of the Zodiac, and contains paintings of the meats which are in highest season in each month; so that under Sagittary (December), we see shrimps, shell-fish, and birds of passage; under Capricorn (January), lobsters, sea-fish, wild-boar, and game; under Aquarius (February), ducks, plovers, pigeons, water-rails, &c.

"Bronze lamps,* dependent from chains of the same metal, or raised on richly-wrought candelabra, threw around the room a brilliant light. Slaves, set apart for this service, watched them, trimmed the wicks, and from time to time supplied them with oil.

"The table, made of citron wood † from the extremity of Mauritania, more precious than gold, rested upon ivory feet, and was covered by a plateau of massive silver, chased and carved, weighing five hundred pounds. The couches, which would contain thirty persons, were made of bronze overlaid with ornaments in silver, gold, and tortoise-shell; the mattresses of Gallic wool, dyed purple; the valuable cushions, stuffed with feathers, were covered with stuffs woven and embroidered with silk mixed with threads of gold. Chrysippus told us that they were made at Babylon, and had cost four millions of sesterces.‡

"The mosaic pavement, by a singular caprice of the architect, represented all the fragments of a feast, as if they had fallen in common course on the floor; so that at the first glance the room seemed not to have been swept since the last meal, and it was called from hence, ἀσάρωτος δἶκος, the unswept saloon. At the bottom of the hall were set out vases

---

* The best of these were made at Ægina. The more common ones cost from £20 to £25; some fetched as much as £400.—Plin. Hist. Nat. xxxiv. 3.

† These citreæ mensæ have given rise to considerable discussion. Pliny says that they were made of the roots or knots of the wood, and esteemed on account of their veins and markings, which were like a tiger's skin, or peacock's tail (l. 13, xiv.). Some copies read *cedri* for citri; and it has been suggested that the cypress is really meant, the roots and knots of which are large and veined; whereas the citron is never used for cabinet work, and is neither veined nor knotted.

‡ About £32,200.

of Corinthian brass. This triclinium, the largest of four in the palace of Scaurus, would easily contain a table of sixty covers;* but he seldom brings together so large a number of guests, and when on great occasions he entertains four or five hundred persons, it is usually in the atrium. This eating-room is reserved for summer; he has others for spring, autumn, and winter, for the Romans turn the change of season into a source of luxury. His establishment is so appointed that for each triclinium he has a great number of tables of different sorts, and each table has its own service and its particular attendants.

"While waiting for their masters, young slaves strewed over the pavement saw-dust dyed with saffron and vermilion, mixed with a brilliant powder made from the lapis specularis, or talc." †

The reader must not expect to find this magnificent picture realized in the comparatively humble houses of Pompeii; though the triclinia which still exist bear witness to the elegance of the taste which adorned them. In speaking of these remains, we shall find opportunity to introduce some further account of the Roman banquets. We must now pass on to those apartments which are yet undescribed.

Œci, from δικος, a house, were spacious halls or saloons, borrowed from the Greeks. Œci, like atria, were divided into tetrastyle and Corinthian; another sort was termed Egyptian. They are directed to have the same proportions as triclinia, but to be made larger, inasmuch as they are ornamented with columns, which triclinia are not. In the Corinthian œci there was but one row of pillars in height, supporting the architrave, cornice, and a vaulted roof. The Egyptian were more splendid, and more like basilicæ, it is said, than Corinthian triclinia. In them the pillars supported a gallery with paved floor, open to the sky, forming a walk round the apartment; and above this lower range a second range of pillars was placed, a fourth part less in height, which

* The common furniture of a triclinium was three couches, placed on three sides of a square table, each containing three persons, in accordance with the favourite maxim, that a party should not consist of more than the Muses nor of fewer than the Graces, not more than nine nor less than three. Where such numbers were entertained, couches must have been placed along the sides of long tables.
† Palais de Scaurus, chap. ix. p. 210.

supported the roof. The interstices between the pillars were closed by walls, for windows are directed to be made between them. Another sort of œcus, called by the Greeks cyzicene, is said not to have been generally used in Italy; but some rooms answering to the description have been found at Pompeii. They were meant for summer use, looking to the north, and if possible facing gardens, to which they opened by folding doors. Their length and width should be such, that two triclinia, or tables, with their couches, facing each other, may be placed in them, with ample room for the servants to pass round.

Pinacotheca, the picture-gallery, and Bibliotheca, the library, need no explanation. The latter was usually small, as a large number of rolls (*volumina*) could be contained within a narrow space.

Exedra bore a double signification. It is either a seat, intended to contain a number of persons, like those before the Gate of Herculaneum, or a spacious hall for conversation and the general purposes of society. In the public baths, the word is especially applied to those apartments which were frequented by the philosophers.

Of baths, a frequent adjunct to private houses, there is no occasion to say anything more than has been already stated.

Such was the arrangement, such the chief apartments of a Roman house; they were on the ground-floor, the upper stories being for the most part left to the occupation of slaves, freedmen, and the lower branches of the family. We must except, however, the terrace upon the top of all (solarium), a favourite place of resort, often adorned with rare flowers and shrubs, planted in huge cases of earth, and with fountains and trellises, under which the evening meal might at pleasure be taken.

The reader will not, of course, suppose that in all houses all these apartments were to be found, and in the same order. From the confined dwelling of the tradesman to the palace of the patrician, all degrees of accommodation and elegance were to be found. The only object of this long catalogue is to familiarize the reader with the general type of those objects which we are about to present to him, and to explain at once, and collectively, those terms of art which will be of most frequent occurrence.

The reader will gain a clear idea of a Roman house from

the ground-plan of that of Pansa, given in a subsequent chapter, which is one of the largest and most regularly constructed at Pompeii.

It may not be uninteresting to subjoin the principles laid down by Vitruvius for giving to each apartment an aspect appropriate to its use, and his observations on the quality of accommodation which was requisite for the several classes of Roman citizens.

"The winter eating-rooms and winter baths ought," he says, "to face the winter west,* for they are to be used in the afternoon, and require both light and heat at that time of the day. Bedchambers and libraries should front the east, an aspect suited for the better preservation of books, for the southern and westerly winds are most laden with moisture, and tend to generate damp and moths. The spring and autumn triclinia should also look to the east, the summer triclinium to the north, that the former may enjoy a temperate, the latter as cool an atmosphere as can be gained. Picture-galleries and rooms for painting and embroidery should also look to the north, because the colours used in this work retain their brilliancy longer when exposed only to a regular and constant light.

"The next thing to be considered is by what rules we are to be directed in laying out the private parts of houses, and how they should be connected with the public part. For those parts are private into which strangers enter not except by invitation, as the chambers, triclinia, baths, and the like. Other parts are common, and any one may enter them uninvited, as the vestibule, cavædium, peristyle, &c.† To men of ordinary fortune, therefore, magnificent vestibules, and tablina, and atria, are needless, for they attend on others instead of being attended at home. Those who sell their rural produce require shops and stables at the entrances of their houses,‡ granaries and storehouses below, and other

---

* "Hyberna triclinia et balnearia occidentem hybernum spectent."—Vit. lib. vi. cap. 7.

† This mention of the peristyle seems at variance with the distribution of Mazois, in accordance with whose authority we have above ranked the peristyle among the private apartments.

‡ Several instances of this arrangement are observable at Pompeii. The shops for disposing of the master's produce always communicate with the interior of the house.

DOMESTIC ARCHITECTURE OF ITALY. 263

arrangements which tend more to use than to beauty. The houses of money-lenders and of those who farm the revenue, should be handsomer and secured from attacks. Lawyers and public speakers require more elegant accommodation, and rooms that may receive a large assembly. For nobles who hold the offices and honours of the state, and consequently are exposed to a crowd of suitors, regal vestibules, high halls, and spacious peristyles are necessary, with plantations and extensive walks, laid out with every attention to magnificence. They should also have libraries, picture-galleries, and basilicæ laid out upon the scale of public buildings, for in their mansions both public business and private suits are often decided." *

There are preserved in the Capitoline Museum at Rome some curious fragments of a plan of Rome engraved on

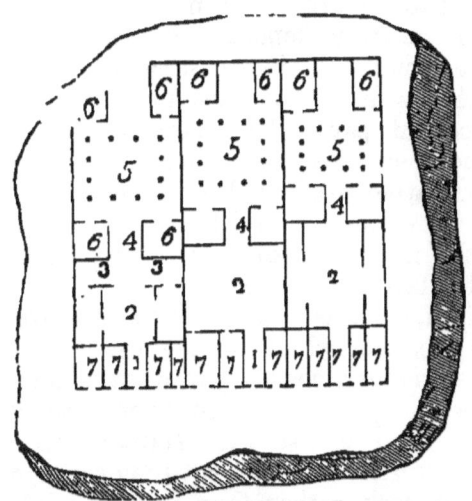

Fragment of a Plan of Rome, engraved on marble.
1. Prothyra, or vestibules; 2. Tuscan atria; 3. Alæa, or wings; 4. Fauces; 5. Peristyles; 6. Inner apartments; 7. Shops.

marble, about the time of Septimius Severus. Mazois refers to them, in proof that the houses at Pompeii are in their origin and disposition Roman houses, and not Grecian, as has been generally supposed from the Grecian taste which prevails in the architecture and decorations. The constant recurrence

* Vitruv. vi. 7, 8.

of the atrium, which was not found in the Greek houses, leaves in his opinion no doubt upon this subject. We copy one of these fragments, both as a curious relic, and that the reader may have the opportunity of judging for himself of the resemblance in general arrangement between the three ground-plans contained in it, and those which we shall give hereafter from Pompeii.

We may here add a few observations, derived, as well as much of the preceding matter, from the valuable work of Mazois, relative to the materials and method of construction of the Pompeian houses. Every species of masonry described by Vitruvius, it is said, may here be met with; but the cheapest and least durable sorts have been generally preferred, and by far the greater part of the private, and many of the public edifices are built of bricks, or of the rough masonry called *opus incertum*. Hence arises their rapid decay on being exposed to the air. The mortar also, upon which such edifices must entirely depend for their stability, does not possess that remarkable hardness which is so often seen in ancient works; a fault attributed by some to the bad quality of its component parts: by others to the baking which it received when enveloped in the heated cinders. But as the exterior decorative stuccos have received no damage from this cause, it seems more likely that carelessness in the choice of the materials, or in working them together, has produced this badness of quality.

Copper, iron, lead, have been found employed for the same purposes as those for which we now use them. Iron is more plentiful than copper, contrary to what is generally observed in ancient works. It is evident from articles of furniture, &c., found in the ruins, that the Italians were highly skilled in the art of working metals, yet they seem to have excelled in ornamental work, rather than in the solid and neat construction of useful articles. For instance, their lock-work is coarse, hardly equal to that which is now executed in the same country; while the external ornaments of doors, bolts, handles, &c., are elegantly wrought. We give specimens of

Ancient Bolt.

DOMESTIC ARCHITECTURE OF ITALY. 265

some of these. The key was found in Pompeii, and from its size seems to have been a door-key. The bolt is preserved

Key and Hinge.

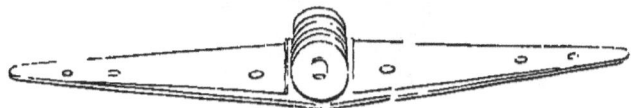

in the Museum at Naples. The hinge and door-handles, one of which is remarkably rich, are from various authorities.

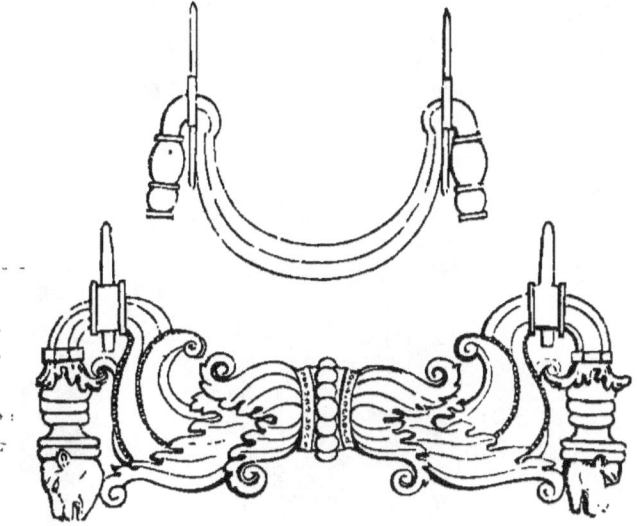

Door-handles.

Not a single wooden door has been preserved in Pompeii. The panelling of that which we give, as restored by Mazois, is taken from a marble door in the Street of Tombs, together with the ring which served as a handle. Almost all the doorways in Pompeii are nearly of the same size and form, a little more or less care in the execution of capitals and entablatures

Door of a private dwelling restored.

making all the difference between them. They seem usually to have been bivalve, to have turned on pivots, not on hinges, and to have been closed by one or two large bolts, such as that above represented, received into the threshold. We may infer from a number of false doors painted on walls, that their colour was generally dark. Their carpentry seems to have been very simple; often beams were not even squared. The carbonized timbers discovered seem to intimate that firwood was in most general use. Doors were sometimes adorned with large nails having gilt heads. They had knockers, or perhaps more generally bells, as may be inferred from a passage of Suetonius, in which he alludes to an idea of Augustus, to make Jupiter Tonans, whose temple was on the ascent to the Capitol, appear as the porter of the Capitoline Jove, by affixing bells to it.* Roman doors always opened inside, or into the house; to have a door that opened outwards, or into the street, was a peculiar privilege accorded to Valerius Publicola. The door was a peculiar object of Roman superstition; it was under the protection of four divinities: Janus, who presided over the whole gateway; Forculus, the protector of the *fores*, or two doors; Limentinus, who watched over the limen, or threshold; and Cardea, the special patroness of the *cardines* or hinges. To enter a doorway with the left foot was considered a bad omen; on which account a boy seems to have been sometimes specially appointed to admonish visitors to put the right foot forwards.†

Very little costly decoration is to be found in the houses, with the exception of mosaic pavements, which are numerous and beautiful; even in the public buildings marble is of rare occurrence. Its place, however, was not inadequately filled by a stucco of great beauty, equally adapted to receive paintings, or to be modelled into bas-reliefs. No marble wainscotings or columns hewn from single blocks are seen in the atria of Pompeii; but in their place there is a gaiety and capricious elegance, of which but a very inadequate idea can be conveyed by description, aided by the wood engravings which we are able to present. The walls are carefully prepared for the reception of this stucco by several coats of a coarser plaster,

* Sueton. Aug. 91.
† Exclamavit puer qui super hoc officium erat positus, Dextro pede. Petron. Sat. 30.

made of lime, and the sand called pozzolana. The stucco itself was called *albarium*, from its whiteness, or *opus marmoratum*, from its resemblance to marble. It seems to have been made of calcined gypsum, or plaster of Paris, mixed with pulverized, but not calcined stone, and, in the more expensive sort, with powdered marble. Traces left on some unfinished work intimate that it was spread with an instrument resembling that which our plasterers use. A difference in quality, and an economy in the use of it, is observable, which make it probable that the expense varied greatly according to the fineness of the material. Not only is the stucco coarser in mean habitations, but where the quality is good in general, it is found coarser in those places which are least exposed to view. Vitruvius recommends that it should be of considerable thickness; not less, he says, than three coats.* Yet on the columns of the oldest temple in Pompeii, the Greek temple, we see a stucco of extreme beauty, harder than stone, and not more than a line in thickness. The temples at Pæstum have received a coat still thinner, and Mazois has expressed an opinion founded on his personal observation, that the stucco will be found thinner in proportion to the age of the building, and that thick stuccos intimate a late date, and the decline of the art.

Ornamental work in relief was formed either by modelling or by stamping with a mould. The latter method was used for cornices, borders, and other works where the same pattern was repeated. The joinings of the moulds are often visible, as in a printed muslin where the ends of the blocks have not been accurately fitted. We may conjecture that the stucco was dashed in a mass on the wet plaster, the mould forcibly applied, and form and adhesion thus given by a single operation. A bas-relief, or a pattern of uncertain form, was modelled by hand. The workman traced the outline of his design upon the plaster, and proceeded to fill it up with stucco worked to proper consistency, as our sculptors model a design in clay. But as the plastic matter soon set, and when set was incapable of alteration or addition, no small skill was requisite to execute the varied designs, of which a number of examples have already been given. The difficulties of this

* vii. 3.

art are nearly the same as those of fresco painting, in which it is well known none but the greatest masters have succeeded.

For the common floors a sort of composition was used, resembling probably the compost floors to be seen in Welsh farm-houses and in the north of England. A superior sort was called *opus Signinum*, from Signia, a town celebrated for its tiles. In this case, the plaster basis was thoroughly mixed with pounded tile, which increased its solidity, and gave it something the appearance of red granite. Sometimes floors were inlaid, while soft, with pieces of white marble, set in Grecian frets, and intricate patterns: sometimes the ground is white, and the pattern is made of lozenge-shaped pieces of tile. Grounds of other colours also occur, of which yellow is the most common. Sometimes pieces of marble of all shapes and colours were imbedded in a composition ground, and in these floors the chief aim was to collect the greatest possible variety of marbles.* Such floors, which Pliny calls *barbarica* or *subtegulanea*, appear to have been antecedent to, and to have given the first idea of, mosaics, and from the method of their construction is derived their name, *pavimentum*, from *pavire*, to ram down. An intermediate step between these pavements and mosaics occurs in what Pliny calls *scalpturatum*, which seems to have resembled inlaid work; a pattern being chiselled out in the solid ground, and filled up with thin leaves of coloured marble. Mosaic floors, as we have said, are frequent in the better class of houses, and will be fully spoken of in the next chapter. Marble floors are of rare occurrence, and mostly destroyed, even where we can ascertain their former existence.

Of the style and mechanical execution of the paintings which have been found in such numbers, we shall here say nothing. The subject is so interesting and extensive, that a separate chapter will be necessary even to a brief sketch of it.

Numerous preparations of glass, in vases, drinking-cups, and other utensils, have been found; but the most curious discovery connected with this subject is, that in the first century the Romans were incontestably acquainted with the use of glass for windows. The first distinct testimony to this

* This has been imitated in the new hall of the bronzes, in the Museum at Naples.

effect is that of Lactantius, about the end of the third century, who speaks of windows fitted with shining glass, or talc:* and as neither Pliny nor Seneca, who both speak of windows, mention their being composed of the former material, a natural conclusion has been drawn that as yet it had not been applied to that purpose. Pliny's omission is the more remarkable, because he speaks at length of the qualities of glass and of the construction of windows. The invention of transparent windows, of whatever materials, is inferred, from a passage of Seneca, not to have been earlier than the Christian era.† Before this time thin hides, prepared perhaps like parchment, are mentioned as having been employed, and probably plates of horn, of which Pliny speaks as though they were made into lanterns. Such imperfect contrivances probably were only brought into use when inclement weather rendered some protection necessary: and the poor must have been contented with curtains or shutters. The transparency of talc, and the readiness with which it splits into the thinnest laminæ, naturally suggested to some ingenious person the idea of framing it, and thus at pleasure entirely excluding the air; and hence its name of *lapis specularis*: for it seems much more reasonable to conclude that *specularis* is derived from the general term *specular*, a window, than that whenever the word *specular* is used, it is to be understood as glazed with the lapis specularis, as some authors have thought. Another stone employed for the same purpose was called *phengites*, from φέγγος, light. Pliny's account of these two substances runs as follows:—

"As touching talc, it is by nature easy to be cloven into as thin flakes as a man will. This kind of glass stone the hither part of Spain only in old time did afford us, and the same not all throughout, but within the compass of a hundred miles, namely, about the city Segobrica; but in these we have it from Cyprus, Cappadocia, and Sicily, and of late it has been found in Barbary: howbeit the best glass stone cometh from Spain and Cappadocia, for it is the tenderest, and carrieth the largest panels, although they be not altogether the clearest, but somewhat duskish. There be also of

* De Opificio Dei, cap. v.
† Quædam nostra demum prodiisse memoria scimus, ut speculariorum usum, perlucente testa, clarum transmittentium lumen.—Ep. 90.

them in Italy, about Bologna: but the same be short and small, full of spots also, and joined to pieces of flint; and yet, it seemeth that in nature they be much like unto those that in Spain be digged out of pits, which they sink to a great depth. Moreover, there is found of this talc, enclosed in a rock, and lying under the ground, which must be hewed out if a man would have them. But for the most part it lieth in manner of a vein in the mine by itself, as if it were perfectly cut already by nature; and yet was there never any piece known to be above five foot long. Some are of opinion that it is a liquid humour of the earth congealed to an ice, after the manner of crystal. Certes, that it groweth hard into the nature of a stone, may appear evidently by this: that when any wild beasts are chanced to fall into such pits where this glass stone is gotten, the very marrow of their bones (after one winter) will be converted and turned into a stony substance like to the talc itself. Otherwhiles there is found of this kind which is black; but the white is of a strange and wonderful nature, for being (as it is well known) tender and brittle, nothing more, yet it will endure extreme heats and frozen cold, and never crack; nay, you shall never see it decay for age, keep it so long as you will, so that it may escape outward injuries: notwithstanding we do see many stones in building laid with strong mortar and cement, yet subject to age. There hath been devised also another use of talc, namely, to strew with powder of it the floor of the great circus in Rome during the running of chariots and other feats of activity there performed, to the end that their whiteness might give a more lovely gloss to commend the place. In the days of Nero, late emperor, there was found in Cappadocia a stone as hard as marble, white and transparent, even where it is marked with certain tawny streaks or spots: in which regard, for that it is so resplendent, it hath found a name to be called phengites. Of this stone the said emperor caused the Temple of Fortune to be built, called Seia (which King Servius had first dedicated), comprised within the compass of Nero's golden house: and therefore when the doors were shut it was in the interior as light as day; yet so as if all the light were enclosed within it, and not let in from the air through the windows. Moreover, King Juba writeth, that in Arabia there is a certain stone found, transparent like glass, whereof the inhabitants of those parts do make their mirrors or looking-glasses." *

Pliny speaks of *vitreæ cameræ,* glassy chambers, an expression the exact meaning of which is doubtful; but is in general understood to mean rooms lined or wainscoted with glass. We have met with a passage, which, if the facts contained in it were more certainly related, would go far to decide the question; and vague as the information is, it is still worth extracting. "I received a letter from my learned correspondent at Rome, Abate Venuti, dated Dec. 30th, 1759, wherein he informs me that he had lately read in some anecdotes of Cardinal Maximin, 'that as they were digging on the ruins on Mount Cœlius in the last century, they found a room belonging to an antique dwelling-house, that had all its sides within ornamented with plates of glass, some of them tinged with various colours, others of their own natural hue, which was dusky, occasioned by the thickness of the mass of which they consisted. There were likewise in the same apartment window-frames composed of marble, and glazed with laminæ of glass.' But as the Abate did not take upon himself to ascertain the real age of this building, I shall not pretend to lay any greater stress on this discovery than I did on the observation for the sake of which I produced it, for proving the point I had then in view, viz., that the usage of glass for windows was probably nearly of the same antiquity with that of adorning houses with it." †

* Pliny, translated by Holland, xxxvi. 22 (45, 46).
† The curious reader will find this passage, with a more detailed consideration of the subject, in two papers relative to the antiquity of glass windows, by Mr. Nixon.—Phil. Transact. vol. l. p. 601; lii. 123.

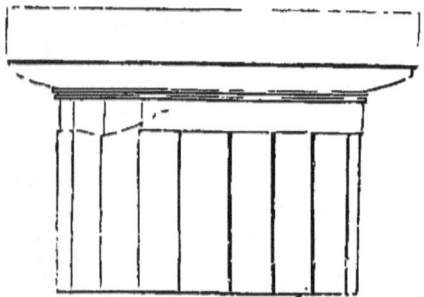

Doric Capital, cut in tufa and covered with coloured stucco. The stucco having partially fallen, the carving beneath it is shown.

Biga; from the arabesques.

CHAPTER II.

POMPEIAN ART.

The most remarkable objects with which the interiors of Pompeii reward the labour of excavation are paintings and mosaics. Frequent mention of these branches of art will be made in the course of this work, and it seems expedient therefore to collect in a prefatory chapter such information respecting them as has been gathered by the diligence of learned men either from personal observation, or from the scattered notices of ancient writers. The subject of working in mosaic will not occupy us long. The art is still exercised with success at least equal to that of the Roman workmen, as is proved by the magnificent copies of some of the best pictures of Italian masters recently executed in the Vatican. The most remarkable circumstance connected with the practice of it in ancient times is the profusion with which mosaics were produced, insomuch that the dwellings of a second-rate town abound in specimens rich enough to be transferred to the palaces of Naples, and to be enumerated among their most precious ornaments. The expense of such works is now so great that they are rarely to be seen even in palaces.

The mosaics of Pompeii are chiefly composed of black frets, or meandering patterns, on a white ground, or white ones on a black ground: some of them, however, are executed in coloured marbles. We may refer to Mr. Donaldson's work on Pompeii, which contains coloured drawings of several, for a better notion of these beautiful floors than our means enable us to give. In the same work are contained the plans of eight others, all elegant, and most of them intricate, taken from the suburban villa; one of which is remarkable for being surrounded by a city wall with gates and towers; probably taken from that which then existed at Pompeii. The materials of which they are chiefly composed, are small pieces of black and white marble, and red tile, some larger than others ( ), so as to take deeper hold in the mortar than the rest, and thus form a sort of bonding course, which gave stability to the whole. These were set in a very fine cement, laid upon a deep bed of mortar, which served as a base. The history of their introduction, and the method of preparing the foundation on which they were laid, are thus told by Pliny:—

"Painted floors* were first used by the Greeks, who made and coloured them with much care, until they were driven out by the mosaic floors called *lithostrota*. The most famous workman in this kind was Sosus, who wrought at Pergamus the pavement which is called *asarotus oikos*, the unswept hall, made of quarrels or square tesserae of different colours, in such a way as to resemble the crumbs and scraps that fell from the table, and such-like things as usually are swept away, as if they were still left by negligence upon the pavement. There also is admirably represented a dove drinking, in such a way that the shadow of her head is cast on the water. Other doves are seen sitting on the brim of the vessel preening themselves and basking in the sun. The first paved floors which came into use were those called barbarica and subtegulanea, which were beaten down with rammers, as may be known by the name pavimentum, from pavire, to ram. The pavements called scalpturata were first introduced into Italy in the Temple of Jupiter Capitolinus, after the beginning of the third Punic war. But ere the Cimbric wars began, such pavements were in common use at Rome, and men took great delight and pleasure therein.

---

* These seem to have been merely floors made of stucco, and painted, like the sides of walls, of a similar colour. It is not impossible, however, but that they may have been painted in patterns, and with various colours, and that the idea of mosaics was derived from thence.

"For galleries and terraces open to the sky, they were devised by the Greeks, who, enjoying a warm climate, used to cover their houses with them; but where the rain waters freeze, pavements of this sort are not to be trusted. To make a terrace of this sort, it is necessary to lay two courses of boards, one athwart the other, the ends of which ought to be nailed, that they should not twist nor warp; which done take two parts of new rubbish, and one of tiles stamped to powder; then with other three parts of old rubbish mix two parts of lime, and herewith lay a bed of a foot thickness, taking care to ram it hard together. Over this must be laid a bed of mortar, six fingers thick, and upon this middle couch, large paving-tiles, at least two fingers deep. This sort of pavement is to be made to rise to the centre in the proportion of one inch and a half to ten feet. Being thus laid, it is to be planed and polished diligently with some hard stone; but, above all, regard is to be had that the boarded floor be made of oak. As for such as do start or warp any way, they be thought naught. Moreover, it were better to lay a course of flint or chaff between it and the lime, to the end that the lime may not have so much force to hurt the board underneath it. It were also well to put at the bottom a bed of round pebbles.

"And here I must not forget another kind of those pavements which are called Græcanica, the manner of which is this:—Upon a floor well-beaten with rammers, is laid a bed of rubbish, or else broken tile-shards, and then upon it a couch of charcoal, well beaten, and driven close together, with sand, and lime, and small cinders, well mixed together, to the thickness of half a foot, well levelled; and this has the appearance of an earthen floor; but, if it be polished with a hard smooth stone, the whole pavement will seem all black. As for those pavements called lithostrota, which are made of divers coloured squares or dice, they came into use in Sylla's time, who made one at Præneste, in the temple of Fortune, which pavement remaineth to be seen at this day."*

It may be remarked here, that the Roman villa at Northleigh, in Oxfordshire, examined and described by Mr. Hakewill, abounded with beautiful pavements. The substratum

* Plin. xxxvi.

of one of these, which had been broken, was investigated, when it was found that the natural soil had been removed to a depth of near seven feet, and the space filled up with materials which bear a near resemblance to those which Pliny recommends. The section is thus given by Mr. Hakewill:—

	ft.	in.
Plaster in which the tesseræ are set.	0	9
Stone pitching	0	9
Ashes and residue of burnt matter	1	3
Soil, &c.	1	0
Rough stone rubble	1	0
Dirt, ashes, oyster-shells, broken pots, &c.	1	9

Below this is the natural soil.

A specimen of the coarser sort of mosaic pavement is to be seen in the Townley Gallery, in the British Museum.

Some very remarkable mosaic pavements have been found

Mosaic Picture by Dioscorides of Samos.

in Pompeii, which may truly be called pictures in mosaic, and surpass in beauty any specimens which have been found

MOSAIC OF BATTLE OF ISSUS.

elsewhere. One of these has been drawn and described in p. 203, Part I.: it occupied the central compartment in the tablinum of the House of the Tragic Poet. Another was found in the house called the Villa of Cicero, without the walls, in April, 1762;* which, the first and only picture of the kind which had then been brought to light, became a wonder to all who understood ancient art, and could appreciate its merits; and was esteemed one of the most precious ornaments of the royal collection. The picture represents a scene containing four masked figures, playing upon various instruments; a tambourine, cymbals, the double pipe, and the Pandean pipe; a selection not unlike the equipment of a Pandean band in modern times. The drapery is elegant and well folded, and the whole composition is excellently grouped and drawn with precision. It is formed of very small pieces of glass, of the most beautiful colours, and of various shades. The hair, the small leaves which ornament the masks, and the eyebrows, are expressed so delicately as almost to escape observation. An additional curiosity is given to this valuable relic by the name of the painter, which is worked in it at the top in black letters—ΔΙΟΣΚΟΥΡΙΔΗΣ. ΣΑΜΙΟΣ. ΕΠΟΙΗΣΕ (Dioscorides of Samos wrought this). Winckelmann says that a good copy of this was found at Stabiæ, in the year 1759.†

Another and a still more remarkable mosaic was discovered in the House of the Faun, and is perhaps the most beautiful and magnificent specimen of the art that has yet been found. This mosaic, which is now preserved in the museum at Naples, is about eighteen feet long by nine broad. The subject represents a battle between Greeks and barbarians, the latter apparently of eastern race; but a variety of conjectures have been hazarded as to what battle is actually depicted. Some have seen in it the combat between Patroclus and Sarpedon, and the death of the latter; others have recognized in it the battles of the Granicus, of Arbela, of Platæa, of Marathon, &c. But the opinion most commonly adopted is that of Professor Quaranta, who refers the picture to the battle of Issus. The Grecian leader, supposed to represent Alexander the Great, is drawn with great beauty and vigour. Charging, bareheaded, in the midst of the fight,

* Pomp. Ant. Hist. t. i. p. 150; and Fasc. ii. p. 105.
† Mus. Borb. vol. iv. pl. 34.

he has transfixed with his lance one of the Persian leaders, whose horse, wounded in the shoulder, had already fallen. The expression of physical agony in the countenance of the wounded man is admirably depicted. Another horse, which an attendant had brought for him, has arrived too late. The death of the Persian general has evidently decided the fortune of the day. In the background, the Persian spears are still directed against the advancing Greeks. But at the sight of the fallen general, another Persian leader in a quadriga, who, from the richness of his dress and accoutrements, the height of his tiara, and his red chlamys, is probably Darius himself, stretches forth his right hand in an attitude of alarm and despair, while the charioteer urges his horses to precipitate flight. Nothing can exceed the vigour with which both men and animals are depicted in this unequalled mosaic. If the Grecian hero really represents Alexander the Great, the mosaic may probably be a copy of a picture by Apelles, the only artist privileged to paint the Macedonian conqueror. It is unfortunate that the work has suffered much damage on the left side, or that which contains the Grecian host. It was, however, in this mutilated state when discovered, and seems to have been under a process of reparation. The border represents a river, apparently the Nile, with a crocodile, hippopotamus, ichneumon, ibises, &c.; whence some have been led to think that the mosaic is a copy of a picture on the same subject known to have been painted by a female Egyptian artist named Helena, and brought to Rome by Vespasian.

Although the designs of many of the ancient mosaics remain unrivalled, yet the execution of them by no means equals the best efforts of modern art.*

The subject of ancient painting will occupy a greater share of our attention. We shall not enter into any antiquarian discussions concerning the first exercise of a faculty which seems almost as natural to man as the use of words; nor attempt to give a history of ancient art, which would lead to a long digression little connected with Italian history, and not very edifying: for though Pliny has collected a vast quantity of amusing gossip relative to the Grecian painters and their

* The editor states this on the authority of an eminent professor of the art, the Commendatore Barberi of Rome.

most celebrated works, this, in losing its diffuseness, would lose the best part of its merits. Italy had no school of her own, except the Etruscan, which is entirely foreign to Pompeii, until she became the rendezvous of Grecian talent. The following account is chiefly taken from our constant guide, Mazois, verified, and in some instances corrected and enlarged, by reference to his originals, and to the researches of Sir Humphry Davy concerning the colours employed by the ancients in painting.*

The custom of decorating walls with paintings may be traced to a most remote antiquity, without conceding all the claims of the Egyptians, who pretend to have discovered it six thousand years before the Greeks. Without the parade of quoting authorities, recent discoveries, more especially those of Belzoni among the royal tombs, prove the existence of both drawing and colouring among that remarkable nation many centuries before the birth of Christ. The art of portraiture was not unknown to the Jews, as we may infer from a passage in Ezekiel, xxiii. 14. Homer was acquainted with the effects produced by contrast of colours, both in the working of metals and in the labour of the loom or needle; but we believe he makes no mention of painting, except with respect to ships, which he calls "vermilion-cheeked."† The art of design is said to have been first introduced to Greece in Corinth, and to have been transported from Greece to Italy. This, however, to say the least, is by no means certain. The Etruscan tombs and vases, found in such profusion, testify that at a very remote period the art of painting was cultivated among the Italian nations with zeal, and not without success. Pliny speaks of paintings in a temple at Ardea older than the foundation of Rome, and others of equal antiquity at Lanuvium and Cære; a date which, whether true or false, will at all events hardly command belief in the absence of all proof except the historian's assertion. The first Grecian painters who came to Italy are said to have been brought over by Demaratus, the father of Tarquinius Priscus, king of Rome. At all events the influence which Etruria exercised over the arts at Rome during the reign of the Tar-

---

* Phil. Transactions, 1815.
† οὐ γὰρ Κυκλώπεσσι νέες πάρα μιλτοπάρηοι
'Οὐδ' ἄνδρες νηῶν ἔνι τέκτονες.—Odyss. ix. 125.

quins can hardly be questioned; and it is about this time therefore at which we may fix the application of painting to purposes of internal and external decoration in that city. But the first recorded specimen of Roman art was not executed until near two hundred years later, when one of the noble tribe of Fabii painted the Temple of the Goddess of Health, and obtained from his performance the surname, Pictor, A. U. 450. His performance commanded admiration in its day, and was to be seen until the temple was burnt in the reign of Claudius. The next artist mentioned by Pliny is Pacuvius, the poet, who, one hundred and fifty years later, amused his old age by painting the Temple of Hercules in the Forum Boarium. Until the time of Augustus, however, it seems to have been usual only to paint the walls of houses one single colour, relieved with capricious ornaments. That sovereign is said by Pliny to have been the first who thought of covering whole walls with pictures and landscapes. In his time a painter named Ludius invented that style of decoration which we now call arabesque, or grotesque. It spread rapidly, insomuch that the baths of Titus and Livia, the remains discovered at Cumæ, Pozzuoli, Herculaneum, Stabiæ, Pompeii, in short, whatever buildings about that date have been found in good preservation, afford numerous and beautiful examples of it. Vitruvius was entirely out of conceit with this sort of ornament, and declares that such fanciful paintings as are not founded in truth cannot be beautiful; but the general voice, both in ancient and modern times, has pronounced a very different opinion. It was from the paintings found in the baths of Rome that Raphael derived the plan of those beautiful frescoes which have made celebrated the gallery of the Vatican; and other distinguished artists of the same era, the golden period of Italian art, followed in the path which he had struck out, until the public and private edifices of Italy were filled with these elegant and varied designs. This style derived its modern name of grotesque from the subterranean rooms (grotte) in which the originals were usually found; rooms not built below the surface of the ground, but buried by the gradual accumulation of soil, and by the ruin of the lofty thermæ of which they had formed a part. Herculaneum and Pompeii present as rich a mine for modern artists to draw from as was possessed by the great masters of the Italian school; and it is to be regretted that this method of decoration should not supersede the perishable, and therefore not less expensive, hangings of silk and paper in modern palaces.

We may here mention a strange, and, as far as we know, unique method of painting, of which a few examples are observable at Pompeii, which is described as follows by Sir W. Gell. "It is singular that in many cases, though a picture be not ill preserved, and may be seen from the most convenient distance, a style of painting has been adopted, which, though calculated to decorate the wall, is by no means intelligible on a nearer approach. In a chamber near the entrance of the Chalcidicum, by the statue of Eumachia, is a picture, in which, from a certain distance, a town, a tent, and something like a marriage ceremony might be perceived, but which vanished into an assemblage of apparently unmeaning blots, so as to entirely elude the skill of an artist who was endeavouring to copy it at the distance of three or four feet. Another picture of the same kind is or was visible in the chamber of the Perseus and Andromeda. An entire farm-yard, with animals, a fountain, and a beggar, seemed to invite the antiquary to a closer inspection, which only produced confusion and disappointment, and proved that the picture could not be copied, except by a painter possessing the skill and touch of the original artist. It is probable that those who were in the habit of painting these unreal pictures had the art of producing them with great ease and expedition, and that they served to fill a compartment where greater detail was judged unnecessary."*

* "This art of representing the effect of a picture upon a wall, instead of imitating nature itself, is applied with considerable success in the decoration of certain modern Italian habitations. The author has seen in the Palazzo Sannizzi, at Rieti, a room of magnificent dimensions, on entering which a visitor imagines himself in an apartment hung with green damask, and decorated with a profusion of splendid pictures. There are Madonnas and Holy Families, landscapes, animals, and battle pieces, which recall at the moment the names and works of the most distinguished artists. A further examination, on a nearer approach, shows that no one of the objects has any decided form or outline, or intelligible sign. Not only does the whole collection consist in the representation of pictures, but their seemingly gold frames are merely wooden mouldings, roughly painted with ochre, most scantily touched here and there, in the prominent parts, with gilding, to represent the effects of catching lights. Behind each sham picture was nothing but the white wall, and the apparently rich silk hangings consist in a few narrow stripes of the stuffs between the frames—yet the whole has a good effect."—(Pompeiana, second series, vol. i. p. 165-6.)

Landscapes are of frequent occurrence, the perspective of which is not very accurate, though the ancients were by no means ignorant of that science. Vitruvius, in the preface to his eighth book, speaks of three Athenians—Agatharcus, Democritus, and Anaxagoras—who had left treatises on linear perspective, and he himself speaks of the radical principles of the science; that is, of the point of sight, which he calls *acies oculorum*, and the point of distance, which he calls *oculorum extensio*. In the landscapes at Pompeii, buildings usually form a prominent feature. They often partake of that indefinite character which we have just described. One of these is given further on, in the description of the House of the Smaller Fountain.

The ancients painted on wood, cloth, parchment, ivory, and plaster, by means of different processes. The most esteemed of all was the encaustic method, which was itself divided into three. The first was executed in coloured waxes, so prepared as to be liquid enough to be laid on cold. Naphtha, or spirit of turpentine, or any volatile ethereal oil, would be proper menstrua to liquify the wax, as they would entirely evaporate, leaving the colours solid and firmly fixed behind. The second sort was done with a graver upon ivory. It was confined to very small pictures, and probably held the same station in ancient as miniature in modern art. The process consisted in first sketching the subject with a graver and then introducing colours into the lines.* In the third sort, coloured wax was melted by heat and laid on warm with a brush. The Punic

* This is Mazois' explanation. It is not clear how either of these methods deserved the name of *encaustic*, *burnt in*, unless indeed the wax used for the second of them was liquified by fire: but Pliny's account is so concise, that every commentator may put a fresh construction upon it. " Encausto pingendi duo fuisse antiquitus genera constat, cera et in ebore, cestro, id est viriculo, donec classes pingi cœperunt" (xxxv. 41). In an anonymous French history of painting we find the following explanation: " In the first method wax was employed, tinged with various colours, and applied to wood, following a sketch traced with a hot iron. In the second, which was done on ivory, not merely the outline, but the contours of the figures and a general notion of the whole subject was given, by means of a sharp heated tool, after which colours were laid on for the shade, leaving the ivory itself for the lights, and completing the whole by means of fire."—(Histoire de la Peinture Ancienne, fol. Lond. 1725, Bowyer.) The meaning of the last clause is ambiguous: perhaps that process of melting the wax is meant which is described in the third method of encaustic painting. It is to be observed that Pliny makes no mention of a hot tool, or of the use of fire in any way, in speaking of the first two methods. Encaustic painting has recently been tried in Germany, and it is said with success.

or Carthaginian wax was considered the best. It was prepared by bleaching yellow wax for some time in the open air, then seething it in the purest sea-water, taken up at a distance from shore, mixed with nitre, and skimming off the pure particles as they rose to the surface. This was again boiled in sea-water, and then exposed to the sun and moon to bleach again. If the highest degree of purity was required it was boiled a third time. For encaustic painting it was mixed with oil, to render it more liquid. Colours thus prepared were found to be perfectly uninjured by the action of the weather or sea-water, and were therefore much used in painting vessels and for all sorts of out-of-door wood-work. When it was meant to apply one uniform coat of colour to a wall, the stucco was first suffered to dry completely; then an even coat of wax and boiling oil, which served as a vehicle for the colouring material, was laid on with brushes. The wax was then sweated (to use the only word which conveys our meaning) by bringing a chafing-dish of hot coals as near as possible to the walls, which were then well rubbed with pieces of wax taper, and finally received the last polish from a fine linen cloth.

Besides this method, the ancients painted in fresco, as is indisputably proved by examination of the paintings found at Pompeii, Herculaneum, and the thermæ at Rome. That they did so, is also a necessary induction from a passage in which Pliny names those colours which were unfit to be applied upon moist plaster. In some places at Pompeii, where detached figures have been painted upon a coloured ground, the partial destruction of the colours has exposed to view the outline, traced upon the wall apparently while wet, by means of a graver. None of the ancient authors have given reason to suppose that lime-water was used in this process; it is possible that the colours were embodied in a thin glue or gum. We never find two layers of paint one over the other, except in the case of figures or ornaments painted on a coloured ground; and it is to be remarked that the designs so painted are those which have suffered most from the action of damp and air.

This is very plainly to be observed in a painting of the Three Graces, in a private house in the Street of Abundance. The entire colour laid subsequently upon the coloured ground has peeled off in consequence of damp and recent exposure to the air, while the outline remains, cut deep into the background with some sharp instrument. The vigour of the touches by which some of these figures are expressed is really astonishing. The ancients appear to have painted the lighter parts with great body of colour, and rather exaggerated the dark touches of the eyes and mouths of their heads, which gives to them almost a speaking expression. Besides animal glue, the ancients made use of several sorts of gums for painting; of these the most esteemed was called sarcocolla. They also employed milk, although this application of it is regarded as of modern invention.

The historical paintings of the Romans were chiefly confined to poetical and mythological subjects, the only ones which seem to have obtained popularity in the hands of either poets or painters. We give a few observations on this subject from the author whom we have above quoted, premising that the observations which he thinks it necessary to make on the imperfection of his beautiful engravings will apply with double force to our rough outlines. "In attempting to preserve a memorial and record of these paintings, the author does not imagine that anything more than a faint idea of them can be furnished to the reader. An artist of the first skill would find it a difficult task to preserve in scanty outlines the traces of the force or expression of the original, where there is often no outline at all, it being shaded off till the forms become indistinct. Indeed, where it can be done, nothing is so difficult as to trace an outline from the originals, even upon the most transparent paper. At an immense expense only, and on a large scale, could any idea be furnished of the touch and style of the painters of antiquity. Many also are incorrect as to drawing, yet the additions of shade and colour diminish the defect, which in outline becomes glaring. Those, however, who wish to study the grouping and composition of the ancients, will here find great assistance, and history and poetry may be illustrated from authority, instead of from fancy. There is no doubt a certain degree of sameness even in the coloured originals—a defect which must be more visible in outline. The Romans only copied themselves and the Greeks, therefore they had not that range over all ages and all situations which is open to modern art. The Greeks, who only depicted themselves, and an occasional Persian or Amazon, were still more confined as to models. The shading of a modern picture is generally artificially contrived by a light let in by a small window, or even a small hole in a shutter, purposely closed, and which produces an effect rarely observed in nature. The ancients, on the contrary, seem to have preferred the light of day for their works, and one curious advantage is gained by it. The pictures of the ancients produce a pleasing effect when only surrounded by a simple line of red; while the very best of modern paintings is very much indebted to the carver and gilder for its gorgeous and burnished frame, without which its beauties are so much diminished, that it almost ceases to be a decoration to an apartment."*

The earlier Grecian masters used only four colours: the earth of Melos for white; Attic ochre for yellow; sinopis, an earth from Pontus, for red; and lamp-black: and it was with these simple elements that Zeuxis, Polygnotus, and others of that age, executed their celebrated works. By degrees new colouring substances were found, so that at a later period, when Apelles and Protogenes flourished, "the art was perfected," to use the language of Cicero, from whom the preceding statement is also derived. So great indeed is the number of pigments mentioned by ancient authors, and such the beauty of them, that it is very doubtful, whether with all the help of modern science, modern artists possess any advantage in this respect over their predecessors.

The Romans divided colours into two classes, florid and grave (floridi et austeri). The former, on account of their high price, were usually provided for the artist by his employer. These were again divided into natural and artificial, or factitious. The florid colours appear to have been six: minium, red; chrysocolla, green; armenium, purpurissum, indicum, ostrum, various shades of blue.

Minium was that colour which we now call vermilion, or cinnabar. This was at first got from the environs of Ephesus, afterwards from Spain, where there was a mine which yielded a large revenue. It produced yearly about ten thousand pounds weight of ore, which was brought crude to Rome

* Pompeiana, second series, vol i. pp. 106–7

under the seal of the sworn superintendents of the mine, and prepared there for use. The article being thus monopolized, an act was passed that the price should not exceed seventy denarii, about £2 5s. the pound. Minium, besides its beauty, was in high estimation as a sacred colour. "Verrius allegeth and rehearseth many authors, whose credit ought not to be disproved, who affirm, that the manner was in times past to paint the very face of Jupiter's image, upon high and festival days, with vermilion : as also that the valiant captaines who rode triumphant into Rome, had in former times their bodies coloured all over therewith; after which manner noble Camillus, they say, entered the city in triumph. And even at this day, according to that ancient and religious custom, ordinary it is to colour all the unguents that are used at festival suppers at a high and solemn triumph with vermilion. And no one thing do the censors give charge and order to be done at their entrance into office before the painting of Jupiter's visage with minium. The cause and motive that should induce our ancestors to this ceremony, I marvel much at, and cannot tell what it should be."*

Chrysocolla was a native substance, found in mines of gold, silver, copper, and lead: the best quality was found in copper mines, the second in silver mines, the worst in lead mines. An artificial sort was made from the sediment of water left standing in metallic veins. Pliny says that it was rendered green by the herb *lutum*, woad. There is every reason to believe that the native chrysocolla was carbonate of copper (malachite), and that the artificial was clay impregnated with sulphate of copper (blue vitriol), rendered green by a yellow dye.† The name of chrysocolla (gold glue) was probably derived from the green powder used by goldsmiths as solder, into which copper entered. All the ancient greens examined by Davy proved to be combinations of copper. The best quality of this dye cost seven denarii the pound ; the second, five ; the third, three. These sums will be, respectively, 4s. 6d., 3s. 2d., 1s. 11d.

Armenium took its name from the country whence it came. Like the two already described, it was a metallic

* Pliny, Hist. Nat. xxxiii. 7.

† Davy on the colours employed by the ancients in painting.—Phil. Trans. 1815.

colour, and was prepared by being ground to an impalpable powder. It was of a light blue colour, and cost thirty sesterces a pound, about 4s. 10d. A spurious sort, nearly equal to it in quality, was made of a particular sand, brought from Spain, and dyed. The price of this was only six denarii, about 3s. 10d.

Purpurissum, purple, was made from creta argentaria, a fine chalk or clay (for the ancients seem to have been ignorant of the difference between calcareous and aluminous earths), steeped in a purple dye. In colour it ranged between minium and blue, and included every degree in the scale of purple shades. The best sort came from Pozzuoli. It varied in price from one to thirty denarii, from $7\frac{3}{4}d.$ to near a pound sterling. Purpurissum Indicum was brought from India. It was of a deep blue, and probably was the same as indigo. It sold for twenty denarii the pound, about 12s. Several lumps of a deep blue substance, found in the baths of Titus, were analyzed by Davy, and found to consist of a frit made by means of soda, coloured with oxide of copper. Powdered and mixed with chalk, they produced tints exactly corresponding with the blues still preserved on the wall of the same baths.*

Ostrum was a liquid colour, to which the proper consistence was given by adding honey. It was produced by the juice of a fish called murex, and differed in tint according to the country from which it came; being deeper and more violet when brought from the northern, redder when from the southern coasts of the Mediterranean.† A pot, containing a rose-coloured substance, also found in the baths of Titus, was submitted to Davy. The outside had turned to a pale cream colour, the interior had a lustre approaching to that of carmine. He made many experiments without being able to determine whether the colouring substance were animal or vegetable; but the impression made on his mind seems to have been that this was a specimen of the best Tyrian purple.

The austere colours were more numerous. Parætonium, or Ammonia, was brought from a place of the same name in Egypt, on the Mediterranean shore. It was a very thick white colour, and was also used to make those stuccos which

---

* Phil. Trans. 1815. † Vitruv. vii. 13.

required an exceeding hardness. Six pounds were sold for one denarius. Among the colours analyzed by Davy was a fine white aluminous clay, which may be the same. Another sort of white, used especially for the carnations of female figures, was called annulare. It was made of chalk and that kind of glass of which rings (annuli) were made for the common people of Rome. Cerussa, or white lead, was also used, especially in the article of ladies' complexions.

Of reds, the ancients had red lead (cerussa usta), which is said to have been discovered in consequence of a fire in the Piræus, which caught some of the toilet furniture of the Athenian ladies. The best sort was of a purplish hue, came from Asia Minor, and cost sixteen denarii, about 10s. 4d. Of this colour much use was made in shades.* The reader must not confuse this colour, which we call minium, with the ancient minium or cinnabar, the sulphuret of mercury. A spurious sort of burnt cerussa was made at Rome by calcining a stony sort of ochre, sil marmorosum, and then quenching it in vinegar. Sinopis was an earth of a beautiful red, brought from the city of Sinope in Pontus; with it are made most of those beautiful red grounds so much admired at Pompeii and elsewhere. It was of three shades, the red, the middle, and the less red. The best quality came from Lemnos, stamped, to show that it was genuine (thence called terra Lemnica, terra sigillata), from the Balearic Islands, and from Cappadocia. It was also furnished from Egypt. The best quality cost three denarii, near 2s. a pound. An inferior sort from Africa was called cicerculum, and cost only eight asses, about 6d. There was also a colour, called cinnabar by the Indians, said to be produced by the mixed blood shed by the elephant and dragon in their deadly fights, which of all colours most aptly represented blood. This is conjectured by Mazois to be cochineal. It is more likely to be the substance still called dragon's blood, and much used in the arts, which is of a deep red colour; nor do we believe that cochineal was known before the discovery of America.†

Sandaracha was a colour found in gold and silver mines,

---

* Sine usta non fiunt umbræ.—Plin. xxxv. 6.

† During the residence of a friend of the author near Pompeii, a pot of red colour (crimson) was found, and used with great success as a body colour, by a French artist, who bought it of the workmen.

varying in shade between red and yellow. The redder was the most esteemed. Roasted with an equal proportion of red lead, it made the colour called sandyx, of a dull hue, which, when mixed with sinopis, was called syricum. This was chiefly used as a ground colour. When finished with a coat of purpurissum, laid on with white of egg, it counterfeited minium, or cinnabar; when ostrum was laid on with it, it made a purple.*

For yellows there were used a paler sort of sandaracha, which is used by Nævius to describe the colour of a blackbird's beak; orpiment, or sulphuret of arsenic (auri pigmentum); and several sorts of ochre, of which the Attic was most highly esteemed. This cost two denarii, or 1s. $3\frac{1}{2}d$. The ochre of Achaia was used in shades, and cost about $4d$, The Gallic, or shining ochre, was used for lights, and was still cheaper.

Atramentum, or black, was of two sorts, natural or artificial. The natural was made from a black earth, or from the blood of the cuttle-fish, sepia. The artificial was made of the dregs of wine carbonized, calcined ivory, or lamp-black. The Indian atramentum was esteemed the best: its composition was unknown, but it was best imitated with the dregs of wine. Kalcanthon, or vitriolic black, was only used for staining wood. The black powder, in whatever way prepared, was used for writing-ink when mixed with gum: when used for painting walls it was mixed with glue.

Cæruleum, or azure, was a sand brought from Egypt, Scythia, and Cyprus. It was afterwards manufactured in Spain and at Pozzuoli. This imitation was called cælon. The price of the cæruleum was eight denarii. This colour was dyed with the juice of herbs, like the chrysocolla. From the cæruleum, washed and pounded, was made a paler blue, called lomentum. This cost ten denarii. Cæruleum was forged with the white earth of Eretria, coloured with dried violets macerated in water.

The green called appianum was a very ordinary colour, used to imitate the chrysocolla lutea. It was a chalk, or clay, and sold for one sesterce the pound.

Of these colours, purpurissum, purpurissum indicum cæruleum, melinum, auri pigmentum, appianum, and cerussa,

* See Histoire de la Peinture Ancienne.

could not be used in painting on a wet surface; consequently not for frescoes. They were mixed with wax, and employed in encaustic painting.

The following table presents a general view of all the colours of which we have spoken :—

Colour	Type	Pigments
Red	Florid	Minium, or cinnabar.
	Austere	Cerussa usta, or red lead. Sinopis, of three shades. Cicerculum. Indian cinnabar, or dragon's blood. Sandaracha. Sandix. Syricum.
Yellow	Austere	Sandaracha. Orpiment. Ochre, of several shades.
Blue	Florid	Armenium. Purpurissum. Purpurissum indicum, or indigo. Ostrum, or Tyrian purple.
	Austere	Cæruleum. Cælon, or vestorianum. Lomentum.
Green	Florid	Chrysocolla, native. ————, artificial.
	Austere	Viride appianum.
White	Austere	Parætonium. Cerussa, or white lead. Annulare.
Black	Austere	Atramentum. ———— Indicum. Kalcanthon.

We will quote, in conclusion, a few general observations of Sir Humphry Davy upon this subject. "It appears from the facts which have been stated, and the authorities quoted, that the Greek and Roman painters had almost all the same colours as those employed by the great Italian masters at the period of the revival of the arts in Italy. They had indeed the advantage over them in two colours, the Vestorian or Egyptian azure, and the Tyrian or marine purple.

"The azure, of which the excellence is proved by its duration for 1700 years, may be easily and cheaply made. I find that fifteen parts by weight of carbonate of soda, twenty parts of powdered opaque flint, and three parts of copper filings, strongly heated together for two hours, gave a substance of exactly the same tint and nearly the same degree of fusibility, and which, when powdered, produced a fine deep blue.

"The azure, the red and yellow ochres, and the blacks, are the colours which seem not to have changed at all in the ancient fresco paintings. The vermilion is darker than recently-made Dutch cinnabar, and the red lead is inferior in tint to that sold in the shops. The greens in general are dull.

"Massicot and orpiment were probably among the least durable of the ancient colours.

"If red and yellow ochres, blacks and whites, were the colours most employed by Protogenes and Apelles, so are they likewise the colours most employed by Raphael and Titian in their best style. The St. John and Venus, in the tribune of the gallery at Florence, offer striking examples of pictures, in which all the deeper tints are evidently produced by red and yellow ochres and carbonaceous substances."*

The annexed picture appears to represent either the marriage of Masinissa and Sophonisba, or the death of Sophonisba, but it is chiefly remarkable for containing a portrait of Scipio. What business the Roman general had to be present on either of those occasions, it is hard to say. The picture is much mutilated, and the back part of Scipio's head and most of his figure are destroyed; but the face remains perfect, and is recognized by Visconti as coinciding with the most authentic busts, and especially with a fine bronze head in the Museum at Naples. This we believe is the only known portrait which has been found. It shows that artists did introduce the likenesses of great men into their historical compositions, and gives some slight ground to hope that other likenesses may hereafter be discovered and identified. The figures are placed under a portico, projecting upon a garden. A green curtain is stretched from column to column, so as to form a back-ground to the principal figures. The couch on which the two principal figures recline is also green, but it is covered in part with a

---

* Davy on the colours used in painting by the ancients.—Phil. Trans. 1815.

large violet-coloured cloth, which passes over the shoulders of Masinissa, and down to the feet of Sophonisba. Both

Scipio, Masinissa, and Sophonisba.

have their heads encircled with a regal diadem. The flesh of Masinissa is painted of a clear olive-brown. Sophonisba is dressed in a yellow pallium and green tunic. Scipio wears his warrior's dress, with a red mantle. The candelabrum behind Masinissa seems meant to represent ivory.

We cannot close this account better than with two pictures of rather different character, both representing artists at work. The first is a female employed in painting a picture of the bearded Bacchus. She is dressed in a light-green tunic, without sleeves, over which she wears a dark-red mantle. Beside her is a small box, such as, we are told by Varro, painters used, divided into compartments, into which she dips her brush. She mixes her tints on the palette, which she holds in her left hand.

The other exhibits a gentleman painter of antiquity in his studio, pencil in hand, with a sitter before him, and surrounded by the apparatus of his art. This subject is represented in the engraving on page 295, copied by Mazois from a painting found in the Casa Carolina, which fell in pieces upon the first rain. It is of grotesque character, like one or two which we have already given copies of, representing deformed pigmies; but these grotesque paintings are for the most part worthy of our attention, for they generally represent domestic scenes, and consequently furnish us with many hints relative to domestic life and every-day business. The picture of which we now speak is one instance of this. It represents a pigmy painter, whose only covering is a tunic, very remarkably scant in longitude behind. He is at work upon the portrait of another pigmy, clothed in a manner to indicate a person of distinction: the sinus, or gathering of the bosom of the toga, is very observable. The artist is seated opposite to his sitter, at an awful distance from the picture, in an attitude which makes no common share of steadiness of hand requisite to apply the pencil with any pretence to accuracy. The picture, already pretty far advanced, is placed upon an easel, similar in construction to ours. By the side of the artist stands his palette, which is a little table with four feet, and by it is a pot to wash his pencils in. He therefore was working with gum, or some sort of water-colours. But he did not confine himself to this branch of the art, for to the right we see his colour-grinder, who prepares, in a vessel placed on some hot coals, colours mixed with punic wax and oil. Two amateurs, or parasites perhaps of the person who is sitting, enter the studio, and

A female painting a picture of the bearded Bacchus.

POMPEIAN ART. 295

Studio of a Painter of antiquity.

appear to be conversing with respect to the picture. On the noise occasioned by their entrance, a scholar seated in the distance turns round to look at them. The bird is supposed by Mazois to typify some singer, or musician, such as it might be customary to introduce to amuse the guests: we have no more plausible conjecture to offer. The picture is not complete: a second bird, and on the opposite side a child playing with a dog, had perished before Mazois copied it.

But though the paintings and mosaics are the most characteristic remains of ancient art discovered in Pompeii, yet the sculptures found there, and especially the bronzes, though

The Dancing Faun.

in general not equal to those from Herculaneum, deserve a passing word of notice. Some of the smaller bronzes from Pompeii especially are unsurpassed for character and vigour of execution. Such, particularly, is the statuette of the Dancing Faun, found in the house to which it gave name. Nothing can exceed the vigour and animation with which the

POMPEIAN ART. 297

figure is executed, as will be seen from the annexed engraving. It is bearded, and has the horns and tail of a goat. An oaken garland with acorns, some of which seem to have fallen from their shells, encircles his head, and proclaims his sylvan character. His attitudes display all the animated gestures of a drunken dance. His wide-spread arms seem to accompany the movements of his feet, and he snaps his fingers for joy.

Silenus.

Another little bronze statuette about the same size, representing Silenus bearing a sort of tray, on which stood a vase, discovered in 1864 in a house of no importance, is not inferior to the preceding one in character, though the nature of the subject does not admit the same spirited execution. Silenus seems to stagger under the weight which he is supporting.

The left arm and shoulder are elevated to bear the tray, his head sinks upon his chest, his right arm and right leg are extended, to enable him to keep his balance. His bald head is crowned with a garland of leaves and berries, his loins are encircled with a cloth, and on his feet he wears sandals. A snake that begins to coil round his arm helps to support the tray. The whole figure has so much nature and character that we have transferred it to our pages.

Narcissus.

Other small and graceful statues in the same material are the Narcissus, the Hermaphrodite Apollo, Fortune on a globe, the group of Bacchus and Ampelus, &c. The attitude of Narcissus, and the earnest expression of his face, as he listens for the voice of Echo, are admirably rendered. It is considered one of the finest works yet discovered at Pompeii. The annexed plate will convey an idea of it.

Pompeii has yielded but few marble statues of any note; but some of those discovered confirm the opinion that the ancients sometimes coloured their statues. Thus a statue of Venus leaving the bath, naked from the waist upwards, and wringing her dishevelled locks, discovered February 16th, 1765, has the hair painted yellow, round her neck is a gilt necklace, the breasts and upper part of the stomach are also gilt, whilst the drapery which covers the lower members is painted blue.* On the same day was discovered close to this statue the bronze head of an old man on a marble hermes, the eyes of which were formed of some white substance, while the pupil was of black glass or some transparent stone.† A small marble statue of Bacchus, found behind the cell of the temple of Isis, February 8th, 1766, had the hair, eyebrows, and eyes partly painted, partly gilt; the grapes which formed a garland round his head were also coloured. On his neck was a gilt necklace, round his arms and wrists gilt bracelets. The goat-skin which hung from his shoulders was covered with gilt spots; his buskins were partly coloured, partly gilt; the tree against which he leant, and the tiger which stood near him, were also tinted.‡ Another larger marble statue of a woman, also found in the Temple of Isis, had the flowers on her head, her bracelets, and the upper part of her vest, gilt; whilst her girdle and the lower part of her dress were painted red, with gold ornaments.§ A colossal statue of an emperor, in Greek marble, discovered June 22nd, 1853, had the hair painted red, the mantle purple, and the buskins black.‖ There were also traces of colour on the statue of Holconius found on the pedestal at the bottom of the street which bears his name, and on that of Eumachia discovered in the Chalcidicum.

It may be inferred from the parts of another marble statue, nearly the size of life, also discovered in the Temple of Isis, March 4th, 1766, that the ancients used sometimes to dress their statues. The parts found were the head, having earrings in the ears, the left hand, the right arm and hand, holding a bronze sistrum, and the fore parts of the feet. From the appearance and position of these fragments,

---

* Fiorelli, *Pomp. Antiq. Hist.*, t. i. p. 165. Cf. *Quart. Rev.* No. 230, p. 319.
† *Hist. &c.*, ib.   ‡ Ib. p. 184.   § Ib. p. 185.   ‖ Ib. t. ii. p. 563.

300   POMPEII.

it was evident that they had never formed integral parts of a marble statue, and as no remains of the body were found, it is conjectured that it must have been of wood.* In this case the statue must have been so draped as to conceal all but the marble portions of it.

* *Hist. &c.*, t. i. p. 186.

Curule Chair; from a picture in Pompeii.

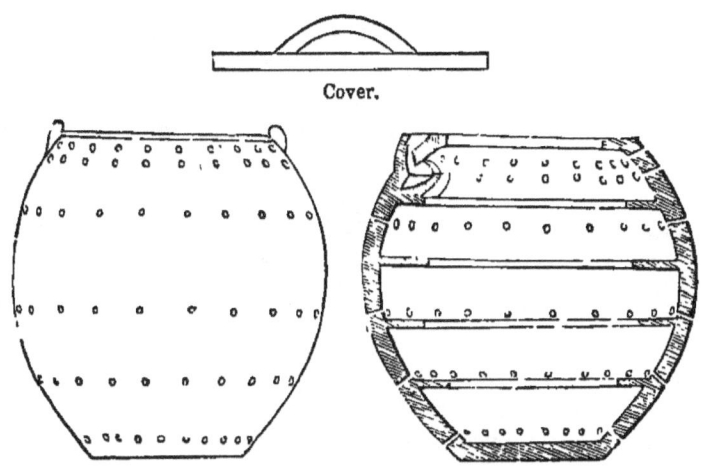

Bee-hives made of Bronze.

CHAPTER III.

PRIVATE HOUSES.

To notice all the houses excavated at Pompeii, even if there were materials for it, would be wearisome in the extreme. We intend therefore merely to select some of the most important, to be described at length, the arrangement of which may serve, with variations according to place and circumstances, as a type of the whole. Some, which offer no particularity in their construction, are remarkable for the beauty of their paintings or other decorations; and, indeed, it is from the paintings on the walls that many of the houses have derived their names. Some again are designated from mosaics or inscriptions on the threshold, from the trade or profession evidently exercised by the proprietors, or from some accident, as the presence of distinguished persons at their excavation—as, for instance, those called the House of the Emperor Joseph II., del Gran Duca, degli Scienziati, &c. As it is the object of this work to convey a general notion of the remains of Pompeii, and to exhibit, as far as our materials will permit, the private life of the first century in all its degrees, we shall begin with one or two of the shops. These present great similarity in their arrangements, and indicate that the tribe of shopkeepers was very inferior in wealth and comfort to that of our own time and country. They are for the most part very small, and sometimes without any interior apartment on the ground floor. The upper floor must have comprised one or two sleeping-rooms; but there is, as we believe, only one house in which the upper floor is in existence.

It is rare at Pompeii to see a whole house set apart for purposes of trade, a part being occupied by the shop itself, the rest furnishing a comfortable dwelling for the owner. The houses of the richer classes, instead of presenting a handsome elevation to the street, were usually surrounded with shops, let out to hire, of that mean, or at least uncomfortable sort, which we have already described. They furnished a very considerable source of revenue. Cicero, in a letter to Atticus, speaks of the ruinous state into which some of his shops had fallen, "insomuch that not only the men, but the mice had quitted them," and hints at the gain which he hoped to derive from this seemingly untoward circumstance.* One Julia Felix possessed nine hundred shops, as we learn from an inscription in Pompeii, to which we have already adverted. We give here the ground-plan of a shop, together with a view of the interior, as it has been restored, somewhat fancifully, or at least without very sure data, by Mazois. 1. Curb-stone, which is pierced with several holes, perhaps to attach beasts of burden.† 2. The footpath. 3. The shop. The whole front was entirely open, excepting in so far as it is occupied by a broad counter of masonry, into which are built four large jars of baked earth, their tops being even with the surface of the counter. Behind are two small rooms (5, 5), containing nothing of importance. The traces of a staircase (4) indicate that there was an upper floor. At night the whole front was closed with shutters, sliding in grooves cut in the lintel and basement wall before the counter, and by the door, which in the restored view annexed is thrown far back, so as to be hardly visible.

* Lib. xiv. 9.
† More probably to fasten an awning projecting over the pavement.

There is an oven at the end of the counter furthest from the street, and three steps on the left side, which in the view have been presumed to support different sorts of vessels or measures for liquids. From these indications it is supposed to have been a cook's shop; for the sale, perhaps, both of undressed and dressed provisions, as is indicated in the view. The oven probably served to prepare, and keep constantly hot, some popular dishes for the service of any chance customer:

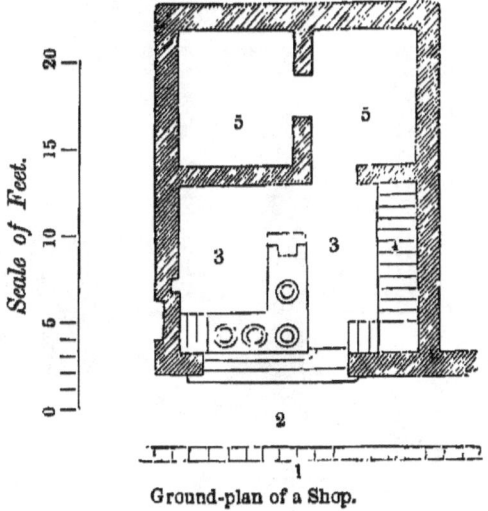

Ground-plan of a Shop.

the jars might hold oil, olives, or the fish-pickle called *garum*, an article of the highest importance in a Roman kitchen, for the manufacture of which Pompeii was celebrated.* Fixed vessels appear inconvenient for such uses on account of the difficulty of cleaning them out; but the practice, it is said, continues to this day at Rome, where the small shopkeepers

---

* It was made of the entrails of fish macerated in brine. That made from the fish called scomber was the best. This word is sometimes translated a herring, but the best authorities render it a mackerel. It was caught, according to Pliny, in the Straits of Gibraltar, entering from the ocean, and was used for no purpose but to make garum. The best was called garum sociorum, a term of which we have seen no satisfactory explanation, and sold for 1000 sesterces for two congii, about £4 a gallon. An inferior kind, made from the anchovy (aphya), was called alec, a name also given to the dregs of garum. "No liquid, except unguents," Pliny says, "fetched a higher price."—Hist. Nat. xxxi. 43.

keep their oil in similar jars, fixed in a counter of masonry.*
All the ornaments in the view are copied from Pompeii. In
front of the shop, which stands opposite the passage leading
behind the small theatre to the Soldiers' Quarters, are three
stepping-stones, to enable persons to cross the road without
wetting their feet in bad weather.

In conjunction with a street view, we give the view of
another shop, which has also a counter containing jars for

View of a Cook's Shop restored.

the reception of some liquid commodity. By some it is
called a Thermopolium, or shop for the sale of hot drinks,
while others call it an oil-shop. In front is a fountain. It
is situated at the angle of the street immediately adjoining
the House of Pansa, and, as may be seen by referring to the
map, appears to be of greater extent, and to contain more
conveniences than is usual in establishments of this sort.
The left-hand street leads to the Gate of Herculaneum; the
right, skirting Pansa's house, is terminated by the city walls.
Tracks of wheels are very visible on the pavement. The

* Mazois, p. 44.

PRIVATE HOUSES. 305

interior was gaily painted in blue panels and red borders, as we learn from the coloured view in Mr. Donaldson's Pompeii, from which this is taken. The counter is faced and covered

Street view near the Baths.

with marble. Numerous thermopolia have been discovered in Pompeii, many of them identified, or supposed to be identified, by the stains left upon the counters by wet glasses.

The following engraving is the ground-plan of another shop, affording much more accommodation, and, therefore, probably occupied by a more wealthy tradesman. 1. Entrance. 2. Shop. 3. Covered court, which, in a house of more pretension, would be called an atrium. It is pseudotetrastyle,

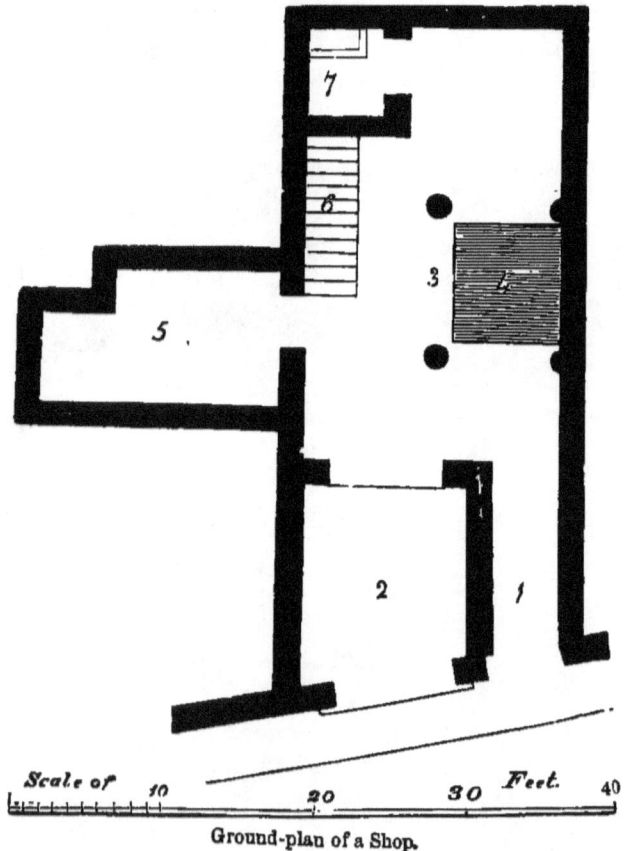

Ground-plan of a Shop.

the roof being supported by four pillars, two of which are engaged in the wall. 4. Impluvium. 5. This room probably was the owner's bedchamber. 6. Staircase leading to one small room over the kitchen, 7. Part of the wall of the small upper chamber still remains. The columns are perfect, and are painted red for the lower third of their height: the rest is white. It would be easy to multiply examples, but those already given are enough to convey a general notion of this class of houses, and there is little or nothing interesting in their details.

We regret very much that the nature of the remains furnishes so little information with respect to the course of trade. Two remarkable buildings have been found, which will be described by themselves, and at length: one a bakehouse; the other an establishment for fulling and dying cloth, of which we may conjecture that a considerable manufacture was here carried on, from the ample accommodation provided for the dealers in that article in the building called the Chalcidicum of Eumachia. With these exceptions, and with one or two brief notices of articles found in different quarters, we can give no further information connected with the trade of the place.

Our next plan is that of a small house, yet one superior to the last, both in accommodation and in the rank of its possessor. It was not inhabited by a shopkeeper, for there is no shop; but its limited extent shows that the occupier was a person of narrow income, probably either exercising some profession, or living on a small independent property. Small as it is, it approaches more nearly in character to the superior class of houses than any yet described. 1. Entrance. 2. Passage. 3. Staircase leading to a small room, probably the master's bedchamber, and to a terrace extending over the length of the passage. 4. Small room for a servant. 5. Large room, perhaps serving at once for a kitchen and winter eating-room. Or the kitchen may be supposed to have been placed in the space 10, since the humble suppers of persons in this rank of life required no extensive preparation. 6. Court, or garden, half covered with a trellis, as is evident from the holes which received the ends of the beams. It was meant to shade a stone triclinium, 9 (for the couches themselves, as well as the room which contained them were so named), which still exists. 7. Canal to receive the rain water, and conduct it into a cistern, from which it was drawn for household uses through a well-hole, 8. Cisterns of this sort were very carefully made. The walls were lined with a strong cement, made of five parts of sharp sand and two of quick-lime, mixed with flints, the bottom being paved with the same, and the whole well beaten with an iron rammer. If it was wished

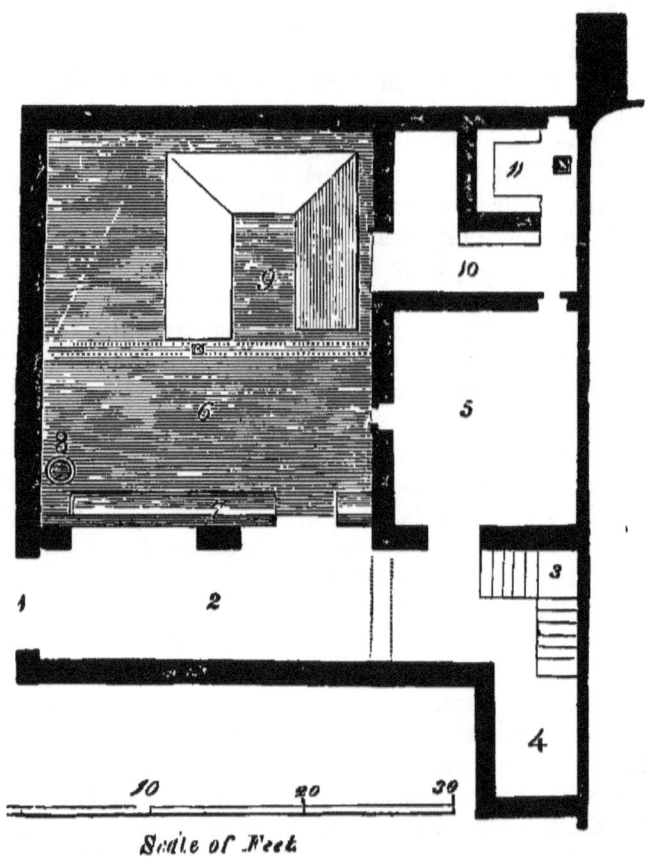

Ground-plan of a small House.

to have the water perfectly pure they did not content themselves with a single cistern, but made two or three at different levels, so that the water successively deposited the grosser and the lighter impurities with which it might be charged. Cistern water, when drunk, was usually boiled, to free it from any impure matters or smell which it might have contracted in the reservoir. It was not in high esteem, and was considered to make the voice of those who drank it hoarse and disagreeable. Such is the abundance of fountains in Pompeii, that it probably was little used except for household purposes. 11 is a *lararium*, or domestic chapel, of very small dimensions, with a bench running round two sides of it. In the centre is a small altar, placed before a niche, ornamented with the painting of some goddess holding a cornucopia. She is reposing on a couch, closely resembling a modern French

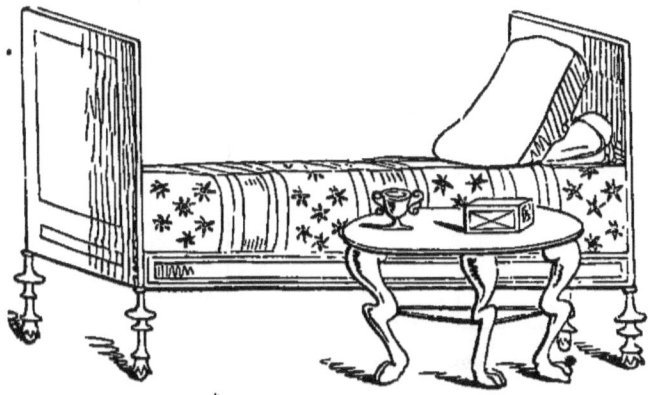

Bed and Table; from a painting.

bed. The mattress is white, striped with violet, and spotted with gold: the cushion is violet. The tunic of the goddess is blue, the bed, the table, and the cornucopia, gold. This house stands just by the Gate of Herculaneum, adjoining the broad flight of steps which leads up to the ramparts. Bonucci supposes that it belonged to the officer appointed to take charge of the gate and walls.

We may take this opportunity to describe the nature and arrangement of the triclinium, of which such frequent mention has been made. In the earlier times of Rome men sat at table—the habit of reclining was introduced from Carthage after the Punic wars. At first these beds were clumsy in form, and covered with mattresses stuffed with rushes or straw. Hair and wool mattresses were introduced from Gaul at a later period, and were soon followed by cushions stuffed with feathers. At first these tricliniary beds were small, low, and round, and made of wood: afterwards, in the time of Augustus, square and highly ornamented couches came into fashion. In the reign of Tiberius they began to be veneered with costly woods or tortoiseshell, and were covered with valuable embroideries, the richest of which came from Babylon, and cost incredible sums.

Each couch contained three persons, and, properly, the whole arrangement consisted of three couches, so that the number at table did not exceed the number of the Muses, and each person had his seat according to his rank and

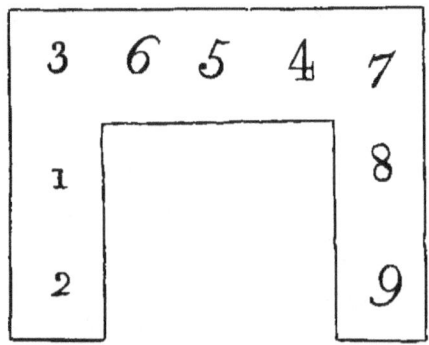

Plan of a Triclinium, showing the disposition of the guests.

dignity. The places were thus appropriated :—1. The host. 2. His wife. 3. Guest. 4. Consular place, or place of honour. This was the most convenient situation at table, because he who occupied it, resting on his left arm, could easily with his right reach any part of the table without inconvenience to his neighbours. It was therefore set apart for the person of highest rank. 5, 6, 7, 8, 9. Other guests. We may here introduce a picture of a domestic supper-party. The young man reclining on the couch is drinking from a horn pierced at the smaller end, so as to allow the wine to flow in a thin stream into his mouth. The female seated beside him stretches out her hand to a servant, to receive what appears to be her *myrotheca*, or box of perfumes. The table and the ground are strewed with flowers.

The entertainment itself usually comprised three services; the first consisting of fresh eggs, olives, oysters, salad, and other light delicacies; the second of made dishes, fish, and roast meats; the third of pastry, confectionary, and fruits. A remarkable painting, discovered at Pompeii, giv a curious idea of a complete feast. It represents a table set out with every requisite for a grand dinner. In the centre is a large dish, in which four peacocks are placed, one at each corner, forming a magnificent dome with their tails. All round are

Picture representing a domestic Supper-party.

lobsters—one holding in his claws a blue egg, a second an oyster, a third a stuffed rat, a fourth a little basket full of grasshoppers. Four dishes of fish decorate the bottom, above which are several partridges, and hares, and squirrels, each holding its head between its paws. The whole is surrounded by something resembling a German sausage; then comes a row of yolks of eggs; then a row of peaches, small melons, and cherries; and lastly, a row of vegetables of different sorts. The whole is covered with a sort of green-coloured sauce.*

Another house, also of the minor class, yet superior to any hitherto described, is recommended to our notice by the beauty of the paintings found. That the proprietor was not rich is evident from its limited extent and accommodation ;

* Donaldson.

yet he had some small property, as we may infer from the shop communicating with the house, in which were sold such articles of agricultural produce as were not required for the

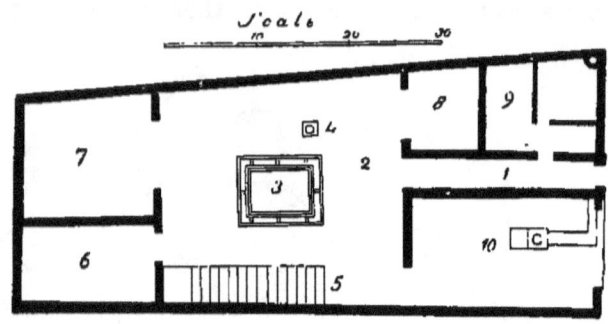

Ground-plan of a small House.

use of the family. 1. Prothyrum. 2. Atrium *displuviatum*, a rare instance of this method of building. That the apartment in question belonged to this class of atria is proved by holes in the outer wall, in which struts to support the projecting eaves were fixed; and also by the impluvium, 3, which has no issue to carry off the water, being merely intended to receive the small quantity of rain which fell through the aperture of the compluvium. And, not being exposed to the heavy drippings of the roof, the low wall round the impluvium is hollowed into little compartments, to be filled with earth and planted with flowers. 4. Wellhole communicating with a cistern under ground. 5. Stair. 6, 7. Apartments carefully decorated, but with nothing to fix their destination to any particular purpose. Probably the larger served as a triclinium. 8. Room, probably of the *atriensis*, the slave who had charge of the house. 9. Kitchen. 10. Shop.

This house was formerly decorated with paintings taken from the Odyssey, and from the elegant fictions of Grecian mythology. When Mazois visited it in 1812, two paintings in the atrium were still in existence, though in a very perishing state. Shortly after he had copied them they fell, owing to the plaster detaching itself from the wall. One of them is taken from the Odyssey, and represents Ulysses and Circe, at the moment when the hero, having drank the charmed cup with impunity, by virtue of the antidote given him by Mercury, draws his sword and advances to avenge his companions.* The goddess, terrified, makes her submission at once, as described by Homer, while her two attendants fly in alarm; yet one of them, with a natural curiosity, cannot resist the temptation to look back, and observe the termination of

Painting representing Circe and Ulysses.

so unexpected a scene. Circe uses the very gesture of supplication so constantly described by Homer and the tragedians, as she sinks on her knees, extending one hand to clasp the knees of Ulysses, with the other endeavouring to touch his beard.† This picture is remarkable, as teaching us the origin of that ugly and unmeaning glory with which the heads of saints are often surrounded. The Italians borrowed it from the Greek artists of the lower empire, in whose paintings it

* " Hence, seek the sty—there wallow with thy friends."
    She spake. I drawing from beside my thigh
    My faulchion keen, with death-denouncing looks
    Rushed on her; she with a shrill scream of fear
    Ran under my raised arm, seized fast my knees,
    And in winged accents plaintive thus began:
        " Say, who art thou," &c.—Cowper's Odyss. A. 320.

† She sat before him, clasped with her left hand
    His knees; her right beneath his chin she placed,
    And thus the king, Saturnian Jove, implored.—Il. i. 500.

generally has the appearance, as we believe, of a solid plate of gold. The glory round Circe's head has the same character, the outer limb or circle being strongly defined, not shaded off and dividing into rays, as we usually see it in the Italian school. This glory was called nimbus,* or aureola, and is defined by Servius to be "the luminous fluid which encircles the heads of the gods." It belongs with peculiar propriety to Circe, as the daughter of the sun. The emperors, with their usual modesty, assumed it as the mark of their divinity; and, under this respectable patronage, it passed, like many other Pagan superstitions and customs, into the use of the church.

The other picture represents Achilles at Scyros, where Thetis had hidden him among the daughters of Lycomedes, to prevent his engaging in the Trojan war. Ulysses discovered him by bringing for sale arms mixed with female trinkets, in the character of a merchant. The story is well known. The painting represents the moment when the young hero is seizing the arms. Deidamia seems not to know what to make of the matter, and tries to hold him back, while Ulysses is seen behind with his finger on his lips, closely observing all that passes.

We will now take a house of a better class, yet still intermediate between those which we have been describing and the houses of the first class in Pompeii; and there is none which will suit our purpose better than the Casa Carolina,

---

* Hence we may collect the true meaning of nimbus in the line—
—————Summas arces Tritonia Pallas
Insedit, *nimbo* effulgens, et Gorgone sæva.—Æn. xi. 615.

Mazois continues, that sculptors, not having the resources of colour, and of light and shade, placed a solid disc about the heads of their statues to represent the nimbus, and that this was the μηνίσκος spoken of by Aristophanes, Aves, v. 1114, ed Dind.

ἢν δὲ μὴ κρίνητε, χαλκεύεσθε μηνίσκους φορεῖν,
ὥσπερ ἀνδριάντες· ὡς ὑμῶν ὃς ἂν μὴ μῆν' ἔχῃ,
ὅταν ἔχητε χλανίδα λευκὴν τότε μάλισθ' οὕτω δίκην
δώσεθ' ἡμῖν, πᾶσι τοῖς ὄρνισι κατατιλώμενοι.

The explanation is plausible, and it seems more probable that the μηνίσκος was used for this purpose, than that it was merely to protect the statue against the ill manners alluded to in the text, as the Scholiast says. But we are not aware that there is any positive evidence in its favour, or that any statues with the μηνίσκος have been found, though the aureola has frequently been observed on bas-reliefs representing Apollo or Diana.—See Antiquités d'Herculaneum, vol. ii. p. 35.

PRIVATE HOUSES. 315

as it is called, the House of Queen Caroline,"* so named because it was excavated in her presence. 1. Vestibule. 2. Corinthian atrium, a species of atrium of rare occurrence in Pompeii. The roof is supported by square pillars, painted with foliage, as if in imitation of climbing-plants, placed upon a pluteum or dwarf wall which surrounds the impluvium, or court rather, for there was a small basin in the centre for the

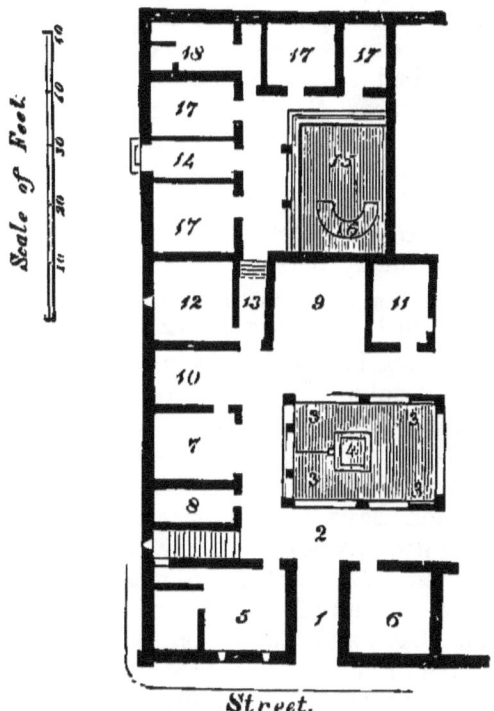

Plan of the House of Queen Caroline.

reception of rain water, which was further supplied by a fountain. 5. Kitchen, lighted by windows to the street. 6, 7, 8, 12. Rooms for various purposes surrounding the atrium. Opposite to the prothyrum is the tablinum, 9, entirely open to the atrium as Vitruvius describes, but closed at the other end, which is not usual. 10. Ala, richly decorated with tasteful paintings, which, when Mazois wrote, were in perfect preservation. 11. Lararium, decorated as richly as

* The wife of Murat.

the ala, and in the same taste. 13. Passage to another division of the house, which contains all the parts necessary for a small but separate establishment, and could have been made such by merely closing up the door of communication. It has, 14, its own entry; a court, 15; a kitchen, 18; and four rooms marked 17, for the various uses of the family. In the centre of the court, where we see the places of two pillars, destined apparently to support a trellis, like that described in the former part of this chapter, there is a circular triclinium, if the expression is allowable, of masonry. This was properly called *stibadium*,* as we learn from Servius's definition of that word, that it is " a semicircular bed suitable to a round table, which the Romans used instead of three beds, after tables made of citron wood came into general use."† This sort of table was also called sigma, from its likeness to the Greek letter, as we learn from Martial, who also tells us how many persons it was meant to hold.

> Accipe lunata scriptum testudine sigma.
> Octo capit; veniat quisquis amicus erit.—xiv. 87.

In another epigram he speaks of seven, as the number which his sigma would hold. In the centre stood a round table on one foot, called thence *monopodium*. Several marble tables of this sort have been found during the course of the excavations.

The paintings found here, described by Mazois as being in good preservation, have been so often wetted to refresh the colours for the gratification of visitors, that very few traces of them now remain. Two of them are engraved in Sir W. Gell's Pompeii. The subject of one is doubtful; it has been explained to be Diana and Endymion, or Venus and Adonis: the latter seems to be the most probable. It contains only three figures: a youth sitting down, whose head is encircled with rays of light, holding two spears; a female figure of great beauty approaching him; and between them Hymen, with his torch and a palm-branch. The female is rather scantily dressed, but richly ornamented with earrings, necklace, armlets, and bracelets. The other picture represents Perseus and Andromeda, after the hero has slain the monster. He holds behind him something like a skull, which is pro-

---

* The diminutive of στιβάς, a bed, from στείβω, to tread; properly a bed of leaves and herbs.

† Serv. ap. Æn. i. 702.

PRIVATE HOUSES. 317

bably intended for Medusa's head, and his double-pointed sword, a very inconvenient-looking weapon, lies beside him on the ground. Andromeda is in full costume, and wears a white tunic with a blue peplum, or large wrapper. The ancient painters seem to have had no very wide choice of subjects. Almost all their serious compositions are mythological, and the desertion of Ariadne and the deliverance of Andromeda recur so frequently at Pompeii, that we may conclude these stories enjoyed a very extensive popularity. They were indeed well suited to that display of the human figure, in which the ancients took so much delight. In a neighbouring house is a beautiful painting of Venus and Adonis. His dogs lie at his feet, and a Cupid armed with two spears stands beside him, bewailing the untimely fate of the young hunter. In the same house are several tasteful decorations, and among them marine horses engaged in a variety of gambols.*

* Gell.

Mercury, from a painting.

Dancing Faun.

CHAPTER IV.

HOUSES OF PANSA AND SALLUST.

The house which we are now about to describe is, in respect of regularity of plan and extent, the most remarkable contained within the walls. It was evidently the residence of one of the chief men of Pompeii, and from the words PANSAM. ÆD. painted in red near the principal entrance, but now obliterated, has been usually denominated the House of Pansa.* It is well observed, however, by Mazois, that the name being in the accusative, this is evidently one of the laudatory inscriptions in honour of an ædile, or some other high officer, common in Pompeii; and that though the ædile Pansa is as likely to have lived here as any other person, there is no dependence on the correctness of the name thus given. We shall continue, however, for the sake of clearness, to use the name under which it is generally known. Several inscriptions bearing the name of Cuspius Pansa, ædile, have been found.

By reference to the map, in which it is marked, the reader will see it occupies an entire insula, that is, it is completely

---

* The whole inscription was :—
PANSAM ÆD.
PARATVS ROG.
whence it is as likely to have been the house of Paratus as of Pansa. See *Pomp. Ant. Hist.*, t. i. fasc. iii. p. 157. The iuscription was not laudatory, but proposed Pansa as ædile. On such inscriptions see below, Chap. ix.—E

HOUSES OF PANSA AND SALLUST. 319

surrounded by streets, in the centre of the town, in one of the best situations, close to the baths, and near the Forum.

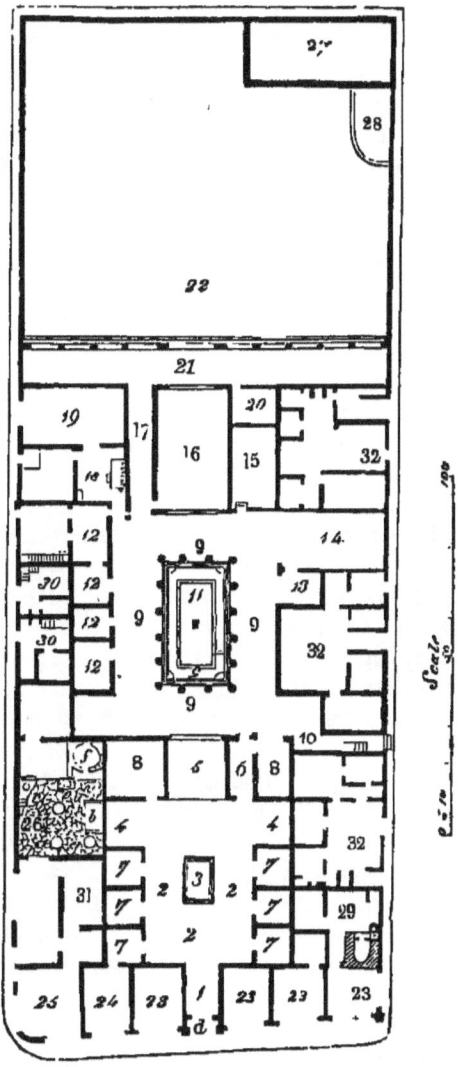

Plan of the House of Pansa.

Including the garden, which occupies a third of the whole length, the area on which it stands is about three hundred feet by one hundred: part of this, however, as is usual, is occupied by shops belonging to the owner, and let out by him.

a, the Vestibulum, the inner threshold of which had a mosaic with the inscription SALVE. 1. Prothyrum paved with mosaic. 2. Tuscan atrium. 3. Impluvium. 4. Alæ. 5. Open tablinum, paved with mosaic, serving as a passage to the peristyle, 8. There is also however a passage (fauces), 6, beside it; and though the tablinum was left open for the sake of the effect produced by thus making the whole length of the house visible at once, it was probably closed by a bronze or wooden railing, so as only to allow the master of the house or the family to pass through it. The apartments, 7, on each side of the atrium were probably meant for the reception of guests entitled to claim hospitality, who came to the House of Pansa when pleasure or business brought them to Pompeii. We have already stated, that when there was no hospitium, or separate building for the reception of such persons, it was customary to lodge them in the atrium, or public part of the house. The larger rooms, beside the tablinum, marked 7, might serve for winter reception-rooms for clients, winter triclinia, or many other purposes, all equally probable and equally uncertain. 9. The peristyle. 10. Private passage* and *posticum*. On the pier, between the two doors, was a painting representing one of the guardian serpents, of which we shall speak fully in describing the House of Sallust, by the side of which is a projecting brick, to receive a lamp lighted in honour of the Dii Custodes. This painting, from its situation, could only be seen by persons within the house; but on the opposite wall there was a cross worked in bas-relief upon a panel of white stucco, in such a way as to be visible to all passers. On this symbol Mazois has founded a conjecture that the owner of the shop may have been a Christian. His words are to the following purport: "Though the first Christians have represented this symbol of Christianity under the form of a Greek, or equibrachial cross, and the limbs of this cross are of unequal length, I cannot bring myself to see merely some unknown instrument in it, as

---

* The use of such a passage to a great man is obvious:—
———— Rebus omissis
Atria servantem postico falle clientem.—Hor. Ep. i. v. 30.

many persons have done, to whom I have shown this drawing of it. In truth, it is difficult not to recognize in it the Latin cross, which would be nothing extraordinary, since Pompeii was not destroyed till the first year of the reign of Titus. But if it be a cross, how can we explain the juxtaposition, the mixture of this symbol of a new and pure religion with the images and practices of one of the most absurd superstitions of antiquity? It is hard to conceive that the same man could at once bow before the cross of Christ, and pay homage to Janus, Ferculus, Limentinus, Cardia, the deities of the thresholds and the hinges of doors; still more that he should adore it in combination with that emblem of an incomprehensible worship which is close at hand.* Perhaps at this time the cross was a mysterious hieroglyphic of meaning unknown, except to those who had embraced the Christian faith; which, placed here among the symbols of paganism, as if in testimony of gratitude, informed the faithful that the truth had here found an asylum with a poor man, under the safeguard of all the popular superstitions."† On the probability of this conjecture we shall offer no opinion, leaving it to the decision of those who are best acquainted with the minutiæ of religious history. If admitted, it would carry the use of the cross to an earlier period than any we believe to which it has yet been traced.‡ But to return from this digression. 11. Basin. 12. Bedchambers. The centre one seems to have been a procæton, or anteroom, since it com-

* Above the aperture of the oven in bas-relief; below are the words, "Hic habitat felicitas."
† Mazois, part ii. p. 84.
‡ This very unsatisfactory story contains the only indication of Christianity, if such it can be called, hitherto discovered at Pompeii. That Christians may have existed there is quite possible, but that they should have ventured to exhibit any public sign of their religion is in the highest degree improbable, as well as that they should have exhibited them in company with pagan emblems. No vestiges remain of the objects so vaguely described by Mazois; and the editor has been assured by the Commendatore Fiorelli, the present learned director of the excavations, that no Christian symbols have ever been discovered at Pompeii. It is said indeed, that in a house in the *Vico dei Lupanari* may be traced, written in charcoal, the letters . . . NI GAVDII . . . HRISTIANI!; which have with probability been supplemented, *igni gaude Christiane* (rejoice in the fire, Christian). But these words may have reference to the burning of the Christians *at Rome*, in the time of Nero (see Overbeck, B. ii. S. 115), and they proceeded at all events from a pagan.—ED.

municates with the one beyond it. 13. Is called by Donaldson the library; by Mazois, a pantry, or room to arrange the dishes before they were introduced into 14, the triclinium. 15. Probably winter triclinium. Donaldson calls this room the lararium. 16. Large œcus. We may call this a cyzicene œcus, or hall, since it exactly corresponds with the definition of this sort of apartment given before, in its spaciousness, its northern aspect, and its large opening to the garden. 17. Fauces leading from the peristyle to the garden, to avoid making a passage-room of the œcus. 18. Kitchen. 19. Servants' hall, with a back door to the street, or it may be a stable. 20. Cabinet looking to the garden. 21. Portico of two stories; a clear indication that this house had at least one upper floor. The staircase however has so entirely perished that its site is unknown, although there is some indication of one in the passage (10). 22. Garden: in one corner, 27, is a reservoir supplying a tank, 28.

Hitherto we have been exclusively concerned with the private house of Pansa, but the insula contains a good deal which was not in his own occupation, and which indeed we may conjecture produced him a handsome rental. 23. Four shops, let out to tenants. 24. Shop belonging to the house, probably intended for the sale of the spare agricultural produce of the owner's estates. A slave named *dispensator* had the charge of it, and seems to have occupied the room behind, which has an entrance both into the shop and atrium. The produce of the farms of the modern Italian nobles is still vended in the same way, in a small room on the ground-floor of their palaces. 25, 29. Two baking establishments, the latter having one of the shops numbered 23.

The ground plan will indicate the disposition of the other bakery. In the centre of the large apartment, 26, are three mills, *a, a, a,* and near them a large table, *b*. Flanking the entrance to the oven, *f*, are three large vases, and in the left-hand corner is a kneading-trough, *c*, with two coppers placed over furnaces. The apartment, 31, from its communication both with the shop and the bakery, was probably used as a storeroom.

The two compartments marked 30 are houses of a very mean class, having formerly an upper story. Behind the last of them is a court, which gives light to one of the chambers of Pansa's house. On the other side of the island are three houses (32), small but of much more respectable extent and accommodation, which probably were also meant to be let. In that nearest the garden were found the skeletons of four women, with gold ear and finger rings having engraved stones, besides other valuables; showing that such *inquilini*, or lodgers, were not always of the lowest class.

View of the Entrance to the House of Pansa.

Our view of this house is taken from the front of the doorway It offers to the eye, successively, the doorway, the prothyrum, the atrium, with its impluvium, the Ionic peristyle, and the garden wall, with Vesuvius in the distance. The entrance is decorated with two pilasters of the Corinthian order. Besides the outer door, there was another at the end of the prothyrum, to secure the atrium against too early intrusion. The latter apartment was paved with marble, with a gentle inclination towards the impluvium. Through the tablinum the peristyle is seen, with two of its Ionic capitals still remaining. The columns are sixteen in number, fluted, except for about one-third of their height from the bottom. They are made of a volcanic stone, and, with their capitals, are of good execution. But at some period subsequent to the erection of the house, probably after the earthquake, A.D. 63, they have been covered with hard stucco, and large leaves of the same material set under the volutes, so as to transform them into a sort of pseudo-Corinthian, or Composite order. It is not impossible that the exclusively Italian order, which we call Composite, may have originated in a similar caprice. Of the disposition of the garden, which occupied the open part of the peristyle, we have little to say. Probably it was planted with choice flowers. Slabs of marble were placed at the angles to receive the drippings of the roof, which were conducted by metal conduits into the central basin, which is about six feet in depth, and was painted green. In the centre of it there stood a jet d'eau, as there are indications enough to prove.* This apartment, if such it may be called, was unusually spacious, measuring about sixty-five feet by fifty. The height of the columns was equal to the width of the colonnade, about sixteen feet. Their unfluted part is painted yellow, the rest is coated with white stucco. The floor is elevated two steps above the level of the tablinum.

A curious religious painting, now almost effaced, was found in the kitchen, representing the worship offered to the Lares, under whose protection and custody the provisions and all the cooking utensils were placed. In the centre is a sacrifice in honour of those deities, who are represented below in the usual form of two huge serpents brooding over an altar. There is something remarkable in the upper

* Donaldson.

figures, of which Mazois, from whom our engraving is copied, has given no explanation. The female figure in the centre holds a cornucopia, and each of the male figures holds a small vase in the hand nearer to the altar, and a horn in the other. All the faces in his engraving are quite black, and the heads of the male figures are surrounded with something resembling a glory. Their dress in general, and especially their boots, which are just like the Hungarian

A religious Painting in the Kitchen of the House of Pansa.

boots now worn on the stage, appear different from anything which is to be met with elsewhere. Are these figures meant for the Lares themselves? On each side are represented different sorts of eatables. On the left a bunch of small birds, a string of fish, a boar with a girth about his body, and a magnificently curling tail, and a few loaves, or rather cakes, of the precise pattern of some which have been found in Pompeii: on the right, an eel spitted on a wire, a ham, a boar's head, and a joint of meat, which, as pig-meat seems to have been in request here, we may conjecture to be a loin of pork; at least it is as like that as anything else. It is suspended by a reed, as is still done at Rome. The execution of this painting is coarse and careless in the extreme, yet there is a spirit and freedom of touch which has hit off the character of the objects represented, and forbids us to impute the negligence which is displayed to incapacity. Another object of interest in the kitchen is a stove for stews and similar preparations, very much like those charcoal stoves which are seen in extensive kitchens at the present day. Before it lie a knife, a strainer, and a strange-looking sort

Stove in the Kitchen of the House of Pansa.

of a frying-pan, with four spherical cavities, as if it were meant to cook eggs. A similar one, containing twenty-nine egg-holes, has been found, which is circular, about fifteen inches in diameter, and without a handle. Another article of kitchen furniture is a sort of flat ladle pierced with holes,

A flat Ladle called Trua.

said to belong to the class called *trua*. It was meant apparently to stir up vegetables, &c., while boiling, and to strain the water from them.

This house has been long excavated, and perhaps that is the reason that, considering its extent and splendour, the notices of it are particularly meagre. Of the decorations we have been able to procure no detailed accounts, though several paintings are said to have been found in it, and among them, one of Danäe amid the golden shower, deserving of notice. Of the garden little can be said, for little is known. According to the best indications which Mazois

Atrium of the House of Pansa.

could observe, it consisted of a number of straight parallel beds, divided by narrow paths, which gave access to them for horticultural purposes, but with no walk for air and exercise except the portico which adjoins the house.

To give a better notion of the appearance and splendour of a Roman house we conclude our account with a view of the interior, as it has been restored by the taste and learning of Mr. Gandy Dering in the first volume of 'Pompeiana,' by whose permission a copy of the plate is here inserted. The view is taken from the atrium, looking through the tablinum and peristyle to the garden. The decorations are taken from indications still existing which point out what had formerly been here, or from specimens preserved in other parts of Pompeii. The figures of the Muses are taken from paintings found on the walls of a house; the candelabra, tripods, &c., from articles preserved in the Neapolitan Museum. The doors on each side of the atrium gave access to the apartments marked 7. Beyond them on each side are the alæ, and in the centre the tablinum, all closed or capable of being closed by *parapetasmata*, or curtains, for the use of doors for these large openings does not appear to have been general.

Inferior to the House of Pansa, and to some others in size, but second to none in elegance of decoration and in the interest which it excites, is a house in the street leading from the Gate of Herculaneum to the Forum, called by some the House of Actæon, from a painting found in it; by others the House of Caius Sallustius. It occupies the southernmost portion of an insula extending backwards to the city walls. It is remarkable that the architects of Pompeii seem to have been careless for the most part whether they built on a regular or an irregular area. The practice of surrounding the owner's abode with shops, enabled them to turn to advantage the sides and corners of any piece of ground, however misshapen. Thus in the plan before us the apartments of the dwelling-house are almost all well shaped and rectangular, though not one of the four angles of the area is a right angle.

1. Prothyrum. 2. Large hall, serving as a vestibule, as is pretty obvious from its arrangement. In the comparatively humble edifices of Pompeii, the reader will not of course expect to find that splendid provision for the convenient

reception of a crowd of importunate suitors which we have described in speaking of the palaces of Rome; still it is interesting to trace the same disposition of apartments on a smaller scale, especially as this throws some light upon the contested question of the Greek or Roman origin of the private houses. There are four doors. One opens to the prothyrum, another to the street—a large opening, closed, according to Mazois, with *quadrivalve* doors, or doors folding back upon themselves, like window-shutters. Of the other two, both communicate with the atrium, one directly, the

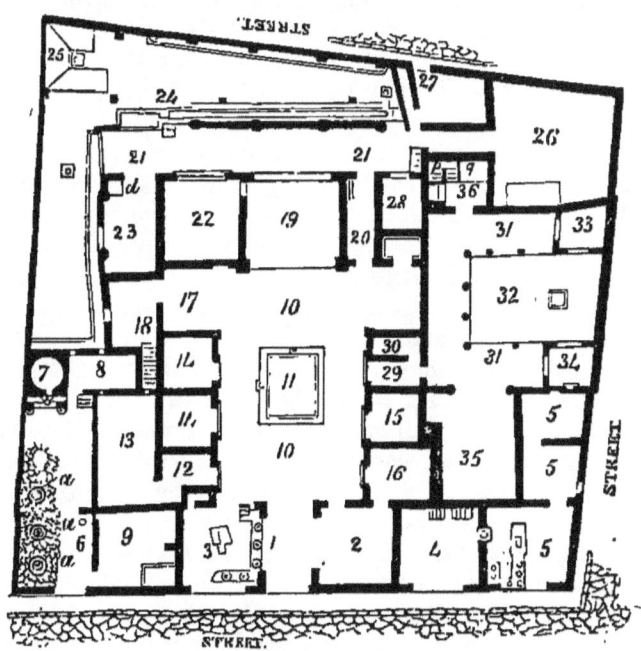

Ground-plan of the House of Sallust.

other through an intermediate room, 16, probably the *cella ostiarii*, the porter's closet, so that at night, when the doors of the atrium were closed, no one could enter without his knowledge. 3. Shop communicating with the house for the sale of the produce of the proprietor's estates. Jars, like those before described, are seen set in the counter, probably to receive his oil or olives. 4. Shop. 5. Shop called a thermopolium, with two rooms backwards. Between 4 and 5, in the party-wall, is the opening of a cistern, common to both. 6. Bakehouse. There were rooms over it, as is proved by a staircase. The four first steps, steep and inconvenient, were of stone, and consequently still remain. The sites of three mills, *a, a, a*, are laid down. 7. Oven. 8, 9. Rooms belonging to the bakehouse. 10. Tuscan atrium. 11. Marble impluvium. 12. Antechamber of a large œcus, or hall, 13, which perhaps was the winter triclinium. This conjecture is founded partly on its neighbourhood to the oven, which would keep it warm and dry, and in a comfortable state for winter use, partly from its size and shape. The length is about twenty-four feet, the breadth twelve, which exactly agrees with the directions of Vitruvius, that the length of a triclinium should be double its breadth. A further reason for thus appropriating it may be found in its central situation, which is such that it must have been very ill lighted, if lighted at all. It was probably therefore intended chiefly for evening use. 14, 15. Rooms probably for the reception of strangers, which, where there was no hospitium, generally were placed round the atrium. The walls of 15 are preserved up to the cornice, and are elegantly stuccoed and painted. 17. Alæ. That on the right opens into a cabinet, probably that of the *atriensis*. To correspond with the doorway, there was in the other ala a false doorway, which served as a lararium, as the paintings which were found in it prove. 18. Open room and staircase leading to a winter apartment placed above the oven. 19. Tablinum, having at its back a low parapet wall. 20. Fauces. 21. Portico. 22. Summer triclinium. 23. Cabinet. 24. Garden or xystus. 25. Triclinium in the open air, covered by a trellis. 26. Kitchen. 27. Back entrance. 28. Chamber. 29. Entrance to venereum. 30. Lodge for a slave whose duty was to keep the door and prevent intrusion. 31, 32. Portico and court of the venereum. 33, 34. Cabinets opening from the portico. 35. Triclinium. 36. Open space containing a stove, and staircase to the terrace above the portico.

Our general view of this house is taken from the street in front, and runs completely through to the garden wall. One of the pilasters which flank the doorway has its capital still in good preservation. It is cut out of grey lava, and represents a Silenus and Faun side by side, each holding one end

View of the Entrance to the House of Sallust, in 1830.

of an empty leather bottle, thrown over their shoulders. Ornaments of this character, which can be comprehended under none of the orders of architecture, are common in Pompeii, and far from unpleasing in their effect, however contrary to established principles. On the right is the large opening into the vestibule. In the centre of the view is the atrium, easily recognized by the impluvium, and beyond it through the tablinum are seen the pillars of the portico. Beyond the impluvium is the place of a small altar for the worship of the Lares. A bronze hind, through the mouth of which a stream of water flowed, formerly stood in the centre of the basin. It bore a figure of Hercules upon its back. The walls of the atrium and tablinum are curiously stuccoed in large raised panels, with deep channels between them, the panels being painted of different colours, strongly contrasted with each other. We find among them different shades of the same colour, several reds for instance, as sinopis, cinnabar, and others. This sort of decoration has caused some persons to call this the house of a colour-seller—a conjecture entirely at variance with the luxury and elegance which reign in it. The floor was of red cement, with bits of white marble imbedded in it.

The altar in the atrium and the little oratory in the left-hand ala belong to the worship of the Lares *domestici* or *familiares*, as is indicated by the paintings found in the false doorway, but now removed. They consisted of a serpent below and a group of four figures above, employed in celebrating a sacrifice to these gods. In the centre is a tripod, into which a priest, his head covered, is pouring the contents of a patera. On each side are two young men, dressed alike, apparently in the prætexta; at least their robes are white, and there is a double red stripe down the front of their tunics, and a red drapery is thrown over the shoulders of each. In one hand each holds a patera; in the other each holds aloft a cow's horn perforated at the small end, through which a stream is spouting into the patera at a considerable distance. This, though an inconvenient, seems to have been a common drinking-vessel. The method of using it has already been described. In the background is a man playing on the double flute.

The worship of the Lares was thus publicly represented,

and their images were exposed to view, that all persons might have an opportunity of saluting them and invoking prosperity on the house. Noble families had also a place of domestic worship (*adytum* or *penetrale*) in the most retired part of their mansions, where their most valuable records and hereditary memorials were preserved. The worship of these little deities (*Dii minuti*, or *patellarii*)* was universally popular, partly perhaps on account of its economical nature,† for they seem to have been satisfied with anything that came to hand, partly perhaps from a sort of feeling of good fellowship in them and towards them, like that connected with the Brownies and Cluricaunes, and other household goblins of northern extraction. Like those goblins they were represented sometimes under very grotesque forms. There is a bronze figure of one found at Herculaneum, and figured in the Antiquités d'Herculanum, plate xvii. vol. viii., which represents a little old man sitting on the ground with his knees up to his chin, a huge head, ass's ears, a long beard, and a roguish face, which would not agree ill with our notion of a Brownie. Their statues were often placed behind the door, as having power to keep out all things hurtful, especially evil genii. Respected as they were, they sometimes met with rough treatment, and were kicked or cuffed, or thrown out of window without ceremony, if any unlucky accident had chanced through their neglect. Sometimes they were imaged under the form of dogs, the emblems of fidelity and watchfulness, sometimes, like their brethren of the highways (Lares compitales), in the shape of serpents. The tutelary genii of men or places, a class of beings closely allied to Lares, were supposed to manifest themselves in the same shape: as, for example, a sacred serpent was believed at Athens to keep watch in the temple of Athene in the Acropolis. Hence paintings of these animals became in some sort the guardians of the spot in which they were set up, like images of saints in Roman Catholic countries, and

* Dii patellarii, idem ac Lares; sic vocati, quia non a potu modo in focum, qui Larium sedes, aliquid iis veteres defunderent, sed ex cibis quoque in patella aliquid ad focum deferrent.—Schol. in Pers. iii. 26.
Oportet bonum civem legibus parere et deos colere, in patella dare μικρὸν κρέας, i.e. parum carnis.—Varr. apud Non. 15, 6, Facciolati.

† O parvi, nostrique Lares, quos thure minuto
Aut farre, et tenui soleo exorare corona.—Juv. ix. 137.

not unfrequently were employed when it was wished to secure any place from irreverent treatment.* From these associations the presence of serpents came to be considered of good omen, and by a natural consequence they were kept (a harmless sort of course) in the houses, where they nestled about the altars, and came out like dogs or cats to be patted by the visitors, and beg for something to eat.† Nay, at table, if we may build upon insulated passages, they crept about the cups of the guests; and in hot weather ladies would use them as live boas, and twist them round their necks for the sake of coolness.‡ Martial, however, our authority for this, seems to consider it as an odd taste.§ Virgil, therefore, in a fine passage, in which he has availed himself of the divine nature attributed to serpents, is only describing a scene which he may often have witnessed:—

> Scarce had he finished, when with speckled pride,
> A serpent from the tomb began to glide;
> His hugy bulk on seven high volumes rolled;
> Blue was his breadth of back, but streaked with scaly gold:
> Thus, riding on his curls, he seemed to pass
> A rolling fire along, and singe the grass.
> More various colours through his body run,
> Than Iris, when her bow imbibes the sun.
> Betwixt the rising altars, and around,
> The rolling monster shot along the ground.
> With harmless play amidst the bowls he passed,
> And with his lolling tongue assayed the taste:
> Thus fed with holy food, the wondrous guest
> Within the hollow tomb retired to rest.
> The pious prince, surprised at what he viewed,
> The funeral honours with more zeal renewed;
> Doubtful if this the place's genius were,
> Or guardian of his father's sepulchre.‖

We may conjecture from the paintings, which bear a marked resemblance to one another, that these snakes were of considerable size, and of the same species, probably that

* Pinge duos angues: pueri, sacer est locus—extra Meiite.—Pers. i. 113.

† Erat ei (Tiberio) in oblectamentis serpens draco, quem e consuetudine manu sua cibaturus, cum consumptum a formicis invenisset, monitus est ut vim multitudinis timeret.—Suet. Tib. x. 72.

‡ Repentes inter pocula siousque iunoxio lapsu dracones.—Seneca de Ira. ii. 31.

§ Si gelidum nectit collo Glacilla draconem.—Mart. vii. 87.

‖ Dryden.—Æn. v. 84, 95.

called Æsculapius, which was brought from Epidaurus to Rome with the worship of the god, and, as we are told by Pliny, was commonly fed in the houses of Rome. These sacred animals made war on the rats and mice, and thus kept down one species of vermin; but as they bore a charmed life, and no one laid violent hands on them, they multiplied so fast, that, like the monkeys of Benares, they became an intolerable nuisance. The frequent fires at Rome were the only things that kept them under.*

Passing through the tablinum, we enter the portico of the xystus, or garden, a spot small in extent, but full of ornament and of beauty, though not that sort of beauty which the notion of a garden suggests to us. It is not larger than a London garden, the object of our continual ridicule; yet while the latter is ornamented only with one or two scraggy poplars, and a few gooseberry-bushes with many more thorns than leaves, the former is elegantly decorated by the hand of art, and set apart as the favourite retreat of festive pleasure. True it is that the climate of Italy suits out-of-door amusements better than our own, and that Pompeii was not exposed to that plague of soot which soon turns marble goddesses into chimney-sweepers. The portico is composed of columns, fluted and corded, the lower portion of them painted blue, without pedestals, yet approaching to the Roman rather than to the Grecian Doric. The entablature is gone. From the portico we ascend by three steps to the xystus. Its small extent, not exceeding in its greatest dimensions seventy feet by twenty, did not permit trees, hardly even shrubs, to be planted in it. The centre, therefore, was occupied by a pavement, and on each side boxes filled with earth were ranged for flowers; while, to make amends for the want of real verdure, the whole wall opposite the portico is painted with trellises and fountains, and birds drinking from them; and above, with thickets enriched and ornamented wit numerous tribes of their winged inhabitants.

The most interesting discoveries at Pompeii are those which throw light on, or confirm passages of ancient authors.

* Anguis Æsculapius Epidauro Romam advectus est, vulgoq. pascitur et in domibus. Ac nisi incendiis semina exurerentur, non esset fœcunditati eorum resistere.—Plin. Hist. Nat. xxix. 22. [Pliny seems to allude to fires purposely kindled to destroy their eggs.]

Exactly the same style of ornament is described by Pliny the Younger as existing in his Tuscan villa. "Another cubiculum is adorned with sculptured marble for the height of the podium; above which is a painting of trees, and birds sitting on them, not inferior in elegance to the marble itself. Under it is a small fountain, and in the fountain a cup, round which the playing of several small water-pipes makes a most agreeable murmur."* At the end of this branch of the garden, which is shaped like an L, we see an interesting monument of the customs of private life. It is a summer triclinium, in

Summer Triclinium in the small Garden of the House of Sallust.

plan like that which has been mentioned in the preceding chapter, but much more elegantly decorated. The couches are of masonry, intended to be covered with mattresses and rich tapestry when the feast was to be held here: the round table in the centre was of marble. Above it was a trellis, as is shown by the square pillars in front and the holes in the

* Plin. Ep. lib. v. 6.

walls which enclose two sides of the triclinium. These walls are elegantly painted in panels, in the prevailing taste; but above the panelling there is a whimsical frieze, appropriate to the purpose of this little pavilion, consisting of all sorts of eatables which can be introduced at a feast. When Mazois first saw it the colours were fresh and beautiful; but when he wrote, after a lapse of ten years, it was already in decay, and ere now it has probably disappeared; so perishable are all those beauties which cannot be protected from the inclemency of the weather by removal. In front a stream of water pours into a basin from the wall, on which, half painted, half raised in relief, is a mimic fountain surmounted by a stag. Between the fountain and triclinium, in a line between the two pilasters which supported the trellis, was a small altar, on which the due libations might be poured by the festive party. In the other limb of the garden is a small furnace, probably intended to keep water constantly hot for the use of those who preferred warm potations. Usually the Romans drank their wine mixed with snow, and clarified through a strainer, of which there are many in the Museum of Naples, curiously pierced in intricate patterns; but those who were under medical care were not always suffered to enjoy this luxury. Martial laments his being condemned by his physician to drink no cold wine, and concludes with wishing that his enviers may have nothing but warm water.* At the other end of the garden, opposite the front of the triclinium, was a cistern which collected the rain waters, whence they were drawn for the use of the garden and of the house. There was also a cistern at the end of the portico next the triclinium.

The several rooms to the left of the atrium offer nothing remarkable. On the right, however, as will be evident upon inspecting the plan, a suite of apartments existed, carefully detached from the remainder of the house, and communicating only with the atrium by a single passage. The disposition and the ornaments of this portion of the house prove that it was a private *venereum*,† a place, if not consecrated to the

---

* vi. 86.

† The author here considers that all this left side of the house was devoted to venereal orgies. But, as Overbeck remarks (B. i. S. 280), these apartments seem only to be destined for the private use of the family, which, from the

goddess from whom it derives its name, at least especially devoted to her service. The strictest privacy has been studied in its arrangements; no building overlooks it; the only entrance is closed by two doors, both of which, we may conjecture, were never suffered to be open at once; and beside them was the apartment of a slave, whose duty was to act as porter and prevent intrusion. Passing the second door, the visitor found himself under a portico supported by octagonal columns, with a court or open area in the centre, and in the middle of it a small basin. At each end of the portico is a small cabinet, with appropriate paintings: in one of them a painting of Venus, Mars, and Cupid is conspicuous. The apartments were paved with marble, and the walls lined breast-high with the same material. A niche in the cabinet nearest the triclinium contained a small image, a gold vase, a gold coin, and twelve bronze medals of the reign of Vespasian; and near this spot were found eight small bronze columns, which appear to have formed part of a bed. In the adjoining lane four skeletons were found, apparently a female attended by three slaves; the tenant perhaps of this elegant apartment. Beside her was a round plate of silver, which probably was a mirror, together with several golden rings set with engraved stones, two earrings, and five bracelets of the same metal. Both cabinets had glazed windows,* which commanded a view of the court and of each other: it is conjectured that they were provided with curtains. The court itself presents no trace of pavement, and therefore probably served as a garden. The opposite page contains a view of the interior,

---

nature of the area on which the house was built, as shown by the ground plan, could not be constructed in their usual situation round the peristyle, which is here altogether wanting. The argument from the pictures be justly regards as futile, since these are not a whit more indecent than many which may be seen in parts of Pompeian houses that certainly were not *Veneria*. We cannot however agree with Overbeck in altogether banishing *Veneria* from Pompeii, to whatever purpose such apartments may have been applied, since they are mentioned in the advertisement of Julia Felix already mentioned. (In prædis Juliæ Felicis locantur Balneum, Venerium, et Nongentum Tabernæ.—*Pomp. Ant. Hist.* t. i. fasc. ii. p. 95.) But as the same advertisement, according to the generally received interpretation, forbids any brothel-keeper to apply, it seems fair to presume that they were not used for profligate purposes.—ED.

* Mazois, part ii. p. 77.

Venereum of the House of Sallust.

as restored by Mazois. The ground of the walls is black, a colour well calculated to set off doubtful complexions to the best advantage, while its sombre aspect is redeemed by a profusion of gold-coloured ornament, in the most elegant taste. The columns were painted with the colour called *sinopis Ponticum*, a species of red ochre of brilliant tint. Nearly all the wall of the court between the cabinets is occupied by a large painting of Actæon, from which the house derives one of its names: on either side it is flanked by the representation of a statue on a high pedestal. The centre piece comprises a double action. In one part we see a rocky grotto, in which Diana was bathing when the unwary hunter made his appearance above: in the other he is torn by his own dogs, a severe punishment for an unintentional intrusion. The background represents a wild aud mountainous landscape. A painted frieze, and other paintings on the walls, complete the decorations of the portico.

The large apartment, 35, was a triclinium for the use of this portion of the house, where the place of the table, and of the beds which surrounded it on three sides, was marked by a mosaic pavement. Over the left-hand portico there was a terrace. The space marked 36 contained the stair which gave access to it, a stove connected probably with the service of the triclinium and other conveniences.

This house also has been restored by Mr. Dering, by whose permission the accompanying plate has been inserted.[*] In the centre of the view is seen the opening into the tablinum, which probably was only separated from the atrium by curtains (*parapetasmata*), which might be drawn or undrawn at pleasure. Through the tablinum the pillars of the peristyle and the fountain painted on the garden wall are seen. To the right of the tablinum is the fauces, and on each side of the atrium the alæ are seen, partly shut off, like the tablinum, by handsome draperies. The nearer doors belong to chambers which open into the atrium. Above the coloured courses of stucco blocks the walls are painted in the light, almost Chinese style of architecture, which is so common, and a row of scenic masks fills the place of a cornice. The

[*] The view, however, hardly conveys an adequate idea of the atrium, being taken from a point too near the impluvium. There are three doors on each side, while in the view only one is shown, besides the ala.—ED.

Atrium of the House of Sallust.

ceiling is richly fretted. The compluvium also was ornamented with a row of triangular tiles called antefixes, on which a mask or some other object was moulded in relief. Below, lions' heads are placed along the cornice at intervals, forming spouts through which the water was discharged into the impluvium beneath. Part of this cornice, found in the house of which we speak, is well deserving our notice, because it contains, within itself, specimens of three different epochs of art, at which we must suppose the house was first built, and subsequently repaired. It is made of a fine clay, with a

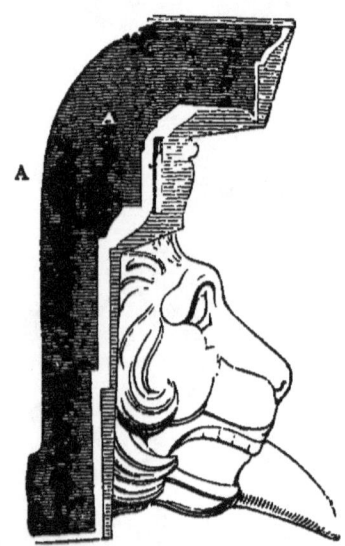

Part of the cornice of the Impluvium of the Atrium of the House of Sallust.

lion's head moulded upon it, well designed, and carefully finished. It is plain, therefore, that it was not meant to be stuccoed, or the labour bestowed in its execution would have been in great part wasted. At a later period it has been coated over with the finest stucco, and additional enrichments and mouldings have been introduced, yet without injury to the design or inferiority in the workmanship; indicating that at the time of its execution the original simplicity of art had given way to a more enriched and elaborate style of ornament, yet without any perceptible decay, either in the taste of the designer or the skill of the workman. Still later

HOUSES OF PANSA AND SALLUST. 343

this elegant stucco cornice had been covered with a third coating of the coarsest materials, and of design and execution most barbarous, when it is considered how fine a model the artists had before their eyes. In the annexed section the three periods are distinguished by different shades. The original cornice is the darker, marked A; the second coating is left white; the third and last is faintly shaded. This was painted, which neither of the two earlier cornices appear to have been. In the restoration, the impluvium is surrounded with a mosaic border. This has disappeared, if ever there was one; but mosaics are frequently found in this situation, and it is therefore at all events an allowable liberty to place one here, in a house so distinguished for the richness and elegance of its decorations. Beside the impluvium stood a machine, now in the National Museum, for heating water, and at the same time warming the room if requisite. The high circular part, with the lid open, is a reservoir, communicating with the semicircular piece, which is hollow, and had a spout to discharge the heated water. The three eagles placed on it are meant to support a kettle. The charcoal was contained in the square base.

Painting representing the manner of hanging a Picture against the wall.

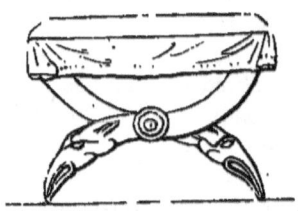

Curule Seat

CHAPTER V.

THE VIA CONSULARIS, OR DOMITIANA.

IN the preceding chapters we have taken indiscriminately, from all quarters of the town, houses of all classes, from the smallest to the most splendid, in the belief that such would be the best way of showing the gradations of wealth and comfort, the different styles of dwelling adopted by different classes of citizens, in proportion to their means. It would however be manifestly impossible so to classify all the houses which contain something worthy of description; and we shall therefore adopt a topographical arrangement as the simplest one, commencing at the Gate of Herculaneum, and proceeding in as regular order as circumstances will permit through the excavated part of the town, concluding at the quarter of the Theatres, beyond which there is nothing excavated except the amphitheatre.

Most of the houses immediately about the gate appear to have been small inns or eating-houses, probably used chiefly by country people, who came in to market, or by the lower order of travellers. Immediately to the right of it, however, at the beginning of the street called the Via Consularis, or Domitiana, there is a dwelling of a better class, called the House of the Musician,* from paintings of musical instruments which ornamented the walls. Among these were the sistrum, trumpet, double flute, and others. Upon the right

---

* Now known as the shop or inn of Albino.

side of the street, however, the buildings soon improve, and in that quarter are situated some of the most remarkable mansions, in respect of extent and construction, which Pompeii affords. They stand in part upon the site of the walls which have been demolished upon this, the side next the port, for what purpose it is not very easy to say: not to make room for the growth of the city, for these houses stand at the very limit of the available ground, being partly built upon a steep rock. Hence, besides the upper floors, which have perished, they consist each of two or three stories, one below another, so that the apartments next the street are always on the highest level. Those who are familiar with the metropolis of Scotland will readily call to mind a similar mode of construction very observable on the north side of the High Street, where the ground-floor is sometimes situated about the middle of the house.

One of the most remarkable of these houses contains three stories; the first, level with the street, contains the public part of the house, the vestibule, atrium, and tablinum, which opens upon a spacious terrace. Beside these is the peristyle and other private apartments, at the back of which the terrace of which we have just spoken offers an agreeable walk for the whole breadth of the house, and forms the roof of a spacious set of apartments at a lower level, which are accessible either by a sloping passage from the street, running under the atrium, or by a staircase communicating with the peristyle. This floor contains baths, a triclinium, a spacious saloon, and other rooms necessary for the private use of a family. Behind these rooms is another terrace, which overlooks a spacious court surrounded by porticoes, and containing a piscina or reservoir in the centre. The pillars on the side next the house are somewhat higher than on the other three sides, so as to give the terrace there a greater elevation. Below this second story there is yet a third, in part under ground, which contains another set of baths, and, besides apartments for other purposes, the lodging of the slaves. This was divided into little cells, scarcely the length of a man, dark and damp; and we cannot enter it without a lively feeling of the wretched state to which these beings were reduced.

A few steps further, on the same side, is another house

somewhat of the same description, which evidently belonged to some man of importance, probably to Julius Polybius, whose name has been found in several inscriptions. Fragments of richly-gilt stucco-work enable us to estimate the richness of its decoration and the probable wealth of its owner. It will be readily distinguished by its immense Corinthian atrium, or rather peristyle. It has the further peculiarity of having two vestibules, each communicating with the street and with the atrium. The portico of the atrium is formed by arcades and piers, ornamented with attached columns, the centre being occupied by a court and fountain. These arcades appear to have been enclosed by windows. Square holes, worked in the marble coping of a dwarf wall which surrounds the little court, were perfectly distinguishable,* and it is concluded that they were meant to receive the window-frames. Pliny the Younger describes a similar glazed portico at his Laurentine villa; and an antique painting, representing the baths of Faustina, gives the view of a portico, the apertures of which are entirely glazed, as we suppose them to have been here. The portico, and three apartments which communicate with it, were paved in mosaic. Attached to one of the corner piers there is a fountain. The kitchen and other apartments were below this floor. There was also an upper story, as is clear from the remains of staircases. This house extends to the point at which a by-street turns away from the main road to the Forum. We will now return to the gate, to describe the triangular island of houses which bounds the main street on the eastern side.

That close to the gate, called the House of the Triclinium, derives its name from a large triclinium in the centre of the peristyle, which is spacious and handsome, and bounded by the city walls. The House of the Vestals is a little further on. What claim it has to this title, except by the rule of contraries, we are at a loss to guess; seeing that the style of its decorations is very far from corresponding with that purity of thought and manners which we are accustomed to associate with the title of vestal. The paintings are numerous and beautiful, and the mosaics remarkably fine. Upon the threshold here, as in several other houses, we find the

* Mazois, part ii. p. 52.

word "Salve" (Welcome), worked in mosaic. We enter by a vestibule, divided into three compartments, and ornamented with four attached columns, which introduces us to an atrium, fitted up in the usual manner, and surrounded by the usual apartments. The most remarkable of these is a triclinium, which formerly was richly paved with glass mosaics. Hence we pass into the private apartments, which are thus described by Bonucci:—" This house seems to have been originally two separate houses, afterwards, probably, bought by some rich man, and thrown into one. After traversing a little court, around which are the sleeping chambers, and that destined to business, we hastened to render our visit to the Penates. We entered the pantry, and rendered back to the proprietors the greeting that, from the threshold of this mansion, they still direct to strangers. We next passed through the kitchen and its dependencies. The corn-mills seemed waiting for the accustomed hands to grind with them, after so many years of repose. Oil standing in glass vessels, chesnuts, dates, raisins, and figs, in the next chamber, announce the provision for the approaching winter, and large amphoræ of wine recall to us the consulates of Cæsar and of Cicero.

" We entered the private apartment. Magnificent porticoes are to be seen around it. Numerous beautiful columns covered with stucco, and with very fresh colours, surrounded a very agreeable garden, a pond, and a bath. Elegant paintings, delicate ornaments, stags, sphinxes, wild and fanciful flowers everywhere cover the walls. The cabinets of young girls, and their toilets, with appropriate paintings, are disposed along the sides. In this last were found a great quantity of female ornaments, and the skeleton of a little dog. At the extremity is seen a semicircular room adorned with niches, and formerly with statues, mosaics, and marbles. An altar, on which the sacred fire burned perpetually, rose in the centre. This is the *sacrarium*. In this secret and sacred place the most solemn and memorable days of the family were spent in rejoicing; and here, on birthdays, sacrifices were offered to Juno, or the Genius, the protector of the new-born child."*

* Not having been able to procure Bonucci's work, we quote from the notes to a little American story, entitled "The Vestal, a tale of Pompeii."

The next house is called the House of a Surgeon, because a variety of surgical instruments were found in it. In number they amounted to forty: some resembled instruments still in use, others are different from anything employed by modern surgeons. In many the description of Celsus is realised, as, for instance, in the specillum, or probe, which is concave on one side and flat on the other; the scalper excisorius, in the shape of a lancet-point on one side and of a mallet on the other; a hook and forceps, used in obstetrical practice. The latter are said to equal in the convenience and ingenuity of their construction the best efforts of modern cutlers. Needles, cutting compasses (circini excisorii), and other instruments were found, all of the purest brass with bronze handles, and usually enclosed in brass or boxwood cases. There is nothing remarkable in the house itself, which contains the usual apartments, atrium, peristyle, &c., except the paintings. These consist chiefly of architectural designs, combinations of golden and bronze-coloured columns placed in perspective, surmounted by rich architraves, elaborate friezes, and decorated cornices, one order above another. Intermixed are arabesque ornaments, grotesque paintings, and compartments with figures, all apparently employed in domestic occupations. Three of these we have selected for insertion. One of them represents a female figure carrying

Female Figure with Papyri.

rolls of papyrus to a man who is seated and intently reading. The method of reading these rolls or volumes, which were written in transverse columns across the breadth of the

THE VIA CONSULARIS, OR DOMITIANA. 349

papyrus, is clearly shown here. Behind him a young woman is seated, playing on the harp. All these figures are placed under the light architectural designs above described, which seem intended to surmount a terrace. It is a common practice at the present day in Italy, especially near Naples, to

Figure playing on the Harp.   Figure reading a roll of Papyrus.

construct light treillages on the tops of the houses, where the inhabitants enjoy the evening breeze, *al fresco*, in the same way as is represented in these paintings. The peristyle is small, but in good preservation. Its intercolumniations are filled up by a dwarf wall painted red, the lower part of the columns being painted blue. This house runs through the island from one street to the other. Adjoining it, on the south, is the custom-house, *telonium*. Here a wide entrance admits us into an ample chamber, where many scales were found, and among them a steelyard, *statera*, much resembling those now in use, but more richly and tastefully ornamented. A description of similar implements has been given in the first part, pp. 76, 77. Many weights of lead and marble were found here; one with the inscription, "Eme et habebis" (Buy and you shall have).* Near the custom-house is a

* There is no trace of these weights and scales in the journals of the excavations, though weights like those described have been found elsewhere. It should have been added that, behind the apartment described, is another quite as large, having its principal entrance from the little street or lane at the back, called *Vicolo di Narcisso*. This has all the appearance of a stable; and the discovery in it of the skeletons of two horses, and some remains of a two-

soap manufactory. In the first room were heaps of lime, the admirable quality of which has excited the wonder of modern plasterers. In an inner room are the soap-vats, placed on a level with the ground. The island is terminated by the fountain, of which there is a view in Part I.

We now come to the House of Sallust, or Actæon, which we have already described. Besides it, the island contains three houses which have been distinguished by names, the House of Isis and Osiris, the House of Narcissus, and the House of the Female Dancers. Of these the latter is remarkable for the beauty of the paintings which adorn its Tuscan atrium. Among them are four very elegant figures of female dancers, from which the name given to the house is taken. Another represents a figure reposing on the border of a clear lake, surrounded by villas and palaces, on the bosom of which a flock of ducks and wild-fowl are swimming. The house of Narcissus is distinguished by the elegance of its peristyle; the intercolumniations are filled up by a dwarf wall, which is hollowed at the top, probably to receive earth for the cultivation of select flowers. Our materials do not admit of a fuller description of the houses in this quarter.

Passing onwards from the House of Sallust, the next island to the south, separated from it by a narrow lane, affords nothing remarkable, except the shop of a baker, to the details of which, in conjunction with the art of dyeing, we purpose to devote a separate chapter. It is terminated in a sharp point by the fountain before mentioned. The disposition of the streets and houses everywhere is most unsymmetrical, but here it is remarkably so, even for Pompeii. Just by the house with the double vestibule the main street divides into two, inclined to each other at a very acute angle, which form, together with a third cross street of more importance, called the Strada delle Terme, or Street of the Baths, another small triangular island. The house at the apex was an apothecary's shop. A great many drugs, glasses, and phials of the most singular forms, were found here: in some of the latter fluids were yet remaining. In par-

---

wheeled cart, tends to confirm this view. Such an adjunct seems hardly to agree with the idea that the front building was a custom-house. See Overbeck, B. i. S. 137.—ED.

Figure from the House of the Female Dancers.

ticular one large glass vase is to be mentioned, capable of holding two gallons, in which was a gallon and a half of a reddish liquid, said to be balsam. On being opened, the contents began to evaporate very fast, and it was therefore closed hermetically. About an inch in depth of the contents has been thus lost, leaving on the sides of the vessel a sediment, reaching up to the level to which it was formerly filled. The right-hand street leads to buildings entirely in ruins, the left-hand one, which is a continuation of the Via Consularis, or Domitiana, conducts us towards the Forum.

Immediately to the eastward of the district just described is the House of Pansa, which occupies a whole island. The island between it and the city walls, on the north, offers nothing remarkable. Beyond, still to the east, is an island separated from it by a narrow street, called the Via della Fullonica, and bounded on the other side by the Street of Mercury, which runs in a straight line from the walls nearly to the Forum. This island contains, besides several private houses of great beauty, the Fullonica, or establishment for the fulling and dyeing of woollen cloths. This, together with the bakehouse above-mentioned, will afford materials for a separate chapter.

Dancing Faun.

Antique Bas-relief in terra-cotta, representing a Mule attached to a Mill.

CHAPTER VI.

ART OF BAKING.—FULLONICA.

THE fame of an actor has been justly said to be of all fame the most perishable, because he leaves no memorial of his powers, except in the fading memories of the generation which has beheld him. An analogous proposition might be made with respect to the mechanical arts: of all sorts of knowledge they are the most perishable, because the knowledge of them cannot be transmitted by mere description. Let any great convulsion of nature put an end to their practice for a generation or two, and though the scientific part of them may be preserved in books, the skill in manipulation, acquired by a long series of improvements, is lost. If Britain be destined to relapse into such a state of barbarism as Italy passed through in the period which divides ancient and modern history, its inhabitants a thousand years hence will know little more of the manual processes of printing, dyeing, and the other arts which minister to our daily comfort, in spite of all the books which have been and shall be

2 A

written, than we know of the manual processes of ancient Italy. We reckon, therefore, among the most interesting discoveries of Pompeii, those which relate to the manner of conducting handicrafts, of which it is not too much to say that we know nothing except through this medium. It is to be regretted, that as far as our information goes, there are but two trades on which any light has yet been thrown, those, namely, of the baker and the dyer. We shall devote this chapter to collecting what is known upon these subjects.

Several bakers' shops have been found, all in a tolerable state of preservation. The mills, the oven, the kneading-troughs, the vessels for containing water, flour, leaven, have all been discovered, and seem to leave nothing wanting to our knowledge; in some of the vessels the very flour remained, still capable of being identified, though reduced almost to a cinder. But in the centre some lumps of whitish matter resembling chalk remained, which, when wetted and placed on a red-hot iron, gave out the peculiar odour which flour thus treated emits. Even the very bread, in a perfect though carbonized form, has in some instances been found in the oven. One of these bakers' shops was attached to the House of Sallust, another to the House of Pansa: probably they were worth a handsome rent. A third, which we select for description, for one will serve perfectly as a type of the whole, seems to have belonged to a man of higher class, a sort of capitalist; for instead of renting a mere dependency of another man's house, he lived in a tolerably good house of his own, of which the bakery forms a part. It stands next to the House of Sallust, on the south side, being divided from it only by a narrow street. Its front is in the main street or Via Consularis, leading from the Gate of Herculaneum to the Forum. Entering by a small vestibule, the visitor finds himself in a tetrastyle atrium (a thing not common at Pompeii), of ample dimensions considering the character of the house, being about thirty-six feet by thirty. The pillars which supported the ceiling are square and solid, and their size, combined with indications observed in a fragment of the entablature, led Mazois to suppose that, instead of a roof, they had been surmounted by a terrace. The impluvium is marble. At the end of the atrium is what would be called a tablinum in the house of a man of family, through which we enter the bakehouse, which is at the back of the house, and opens into the smaller street, which, diverging from the main street at the fountain by Pansa's house, runs up straight to the city walls. The atrium is surrounded by different apartments, offering abundant accommodation, but such as we need not stop to describe.

The workroom is about thirty-three feet long by twenty-six. The centre is occupied by four stone mills, exactly like those found in the other two shops, for all the bakers ground their own flour. To give more room they are placed diagonally, so as to form, not a square, but a lozenge. Mazois was present at the excavation of this house, and saw the mills at the moment of their discovery, when the iron-work, though entirely rust-eaten, was yet perfect enough to explain satisfactorily the method of construction. This will be best understood from the following representation, one half of which is an elevation, the other half a section.

The base is a cylindrical stone, about five feet in diameter and two feet high. Upon this, forming part of the same block, or else firmly fixed into it, is a conical projection about two feet high, the sides slightly curving inwards. Upon this there rests another block, externally resembling a dice-box, internally an hour-glass, being shaped into two hollow cones with their vertices towards each other, the lower one fitting the conical surface on which it rests, though not with any degree of accuracy. To diminish friction, however, a strong iron pivot was inserted in the top of the solid cone, and a corresponding socket let into the narrow part of the hour-glass. Four holes were cut through the stone parallel to this pivot. The narrow part was hooped on the outside with iron, into which wooden bars were inserted, by means of which the upper stone was turned upon its pivot, by the labour of men or asses. The upper hollow cone served as a hopper, and was filled with corn, which fell by degrees through the four holes upon the solid cone, and was reduced to powder by friction between the two rough surfaces. Of course it worked its way to the bottom by degrees, and fell out on the cylindrical base, round which a channel was cut to facilitate the collection. These machines are about six feet high in the whole, made of a rough grey volcanic stone, full of large crystals of leucite. Thus rude, in a period of high refinement and luxury, was one of the commonest and most necessary machines—thus careless were the Romans of the amount of labour wasted in preparing an article of daily and universal consumption. This, probably, arose in chief from the employment of slaves, the hardness of whose task was little cared for; while the profit and encouragement to enterprise on the part of the professional

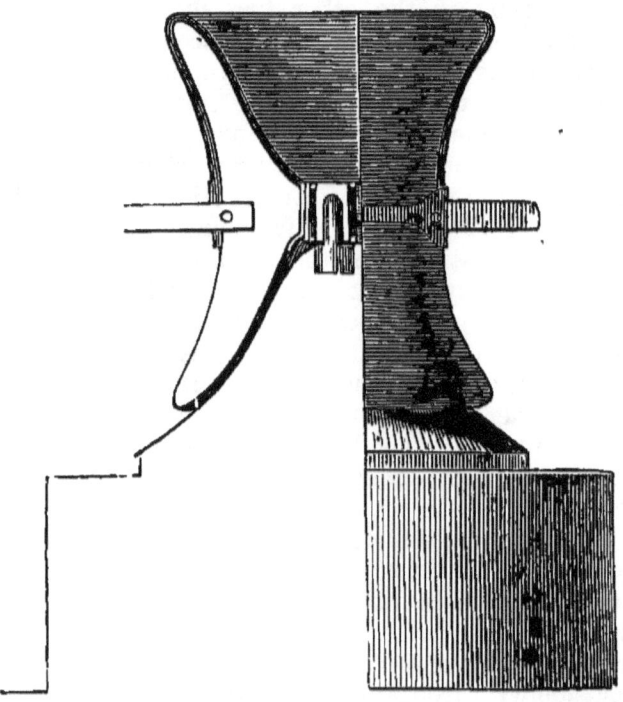

Section of the Mill.

baker was proportionately diminished, since every family of wealth probably prepared its bread at home. But the same inattention to the useful arts runs through everything that they did. Their skill in working metals was equal to ours; nothing can be more beautiful than the execution of tripods, lamps, and vases, nothing coarser than their locks; while at the same time the door-handles, bolts, &c., which were seen, are often exquisitely wrought. To what cause can this sluggishness be referred? In England we see that a material improvement in any article, though so trifling as a corkscrew or pencil-case, is pretty sure to make the fortune of some man, though unfortunately that man is very often not the inventor. Had the encouragement to industry been the same, the result would have been the same. Articles of luxury were in high request, and of them the supply was first-rate. But the demands of a luxurious nobility would never have repaid any man for devoting his attention to the improvement of mills or perfecting smith's work, and there was little general commerce to set ingenuity at work. Italy imported largely both agricultural produce and manufactures in the shape of tribute from a conquered world, and probably exported part of her peculiar productions; but we are not aware that there is any ground for supposing that she manufactured goods for exportation to any extent.

Originally mills were turned by hand,* and this severe labour seems, in all half-savage times, to have been conducted by women. It was so in Egypt;† it was so in Greece in the time of Homer, who employs fifty females in the house of Alcinous upon this service. It was so in Palestine in the time of the Evangelists, and in England in the fourteenth and sixteenth centuries. We find a passage of St. Matthew thus rendered by Wicliffe: "Two wymmen schulen (shall) be grinding in one querne," or hand-mill; and Harrison the historian, two centuries later, says that his wife ground her malt at home upon her quern. Among the Romans poor freemen used sometimes to hire themselves out to the service of the mill when all other resources failed; and Plautus is said to have done so, being reduced to the extreme of poverty, and to have composed his comedies while thus employed. This labour, however, fell chiefly upon slaves, and is represented as being the severest drudgery which they had to undergo. Those who had been guilty of any offence were sent to the mill as a punishment, and sometimes forced to

---

* Many establishments may still be seen in the streets of Naples for grinding corn by means of a hand-mill, turned by a man. Such flour-shops have always a picture of the Madonna inside.—Ed.

† And all the first-born of the land of Egypt shall die, from the first-born of Pharaoh that sitteth upon his throne, even unto the first-born of the maid-servant that is behind the mill, and all the first-born of beasts.—Exod. xi. 5.

work in chains. Asses, however, were used by those who could afford it. The bas-relief at the head of this chapter represents an ass in a mill, and he seems to be blindfolded, to prevent his taking fright. That useful animal seems to have been employed in the establishment we are describing, for the fragment of a jaw-bone, with several teeth in it, was found in a room which seems to have been the stable; and the floor about the mills is paved with rough pieces of stone, while in the rest of the rooms it is made of stucco or compost. The use of water-mills, however, was not unknown to the Romans. Vitruvius describes their construction in terms not inapplicable to the mechanism of a common mill of the present day,* and other ancient authors refer to them. "Set not your hands to the mill, O women that turn the millstone! sleep sound though the cock's crow announce the dawn, for Ceres has charged the nymphs with the labours which employed your arms. These, dashing from the summit of a wheel, make its axle revolve, which, by the help of moving radii, sets in action the weight of four hollow mills. We taste anew the life of the first men, since we have learnt to enjoy, without fatigue, the produce of Ceres."†

In the centre of the pier, at the back, is the aperture to the cistern by which the water used in making bread was supplied. On each side are vessels to hold the water. On the pier above is a painting, ‡ divided horizontally into two

Painting in the Bakehouse.

compartments. The figures in the upper one are said to represent the worship of the goddess Fornax, the goddess of the oven, which seems to have been deified solely for the

* Vitruv. x. 10.
† Antipater of Thessalonica, ap. Brunck. Analecta Græca, tom. ii. p. 119.
‡ Now obliterated.

ART OF BAKING. 359

advantages which it possessed over the old method of baking on the hearth. Below, two guardian serpents roll towards an altar crowned with a fruit very much like a pine-apple; while above, two little birds are in chase of large flies. These birds, thus placed in a symbolical picture, may be considered, in perfect accordance with the spirit of ancient mythology, as emblems of the genii of the place, employed in driving those troublesome insects from the bread.

The oven is on the left. It is made with considerable attention to economy of heat. The real oven is enclosed in a sort of ante-oven, which had an aperture in the top for the smoke to escape. The hole in the side is for the introduction of dough, which was prepared in the adjoining room, and deposited through that hole upon the shovel with which the man in front placed it in the oven. The bread, when baked, was conveyed to cool in a room on the other side the oven, by a similar aperture. Beneath the oven is an ash-pit. To the right is a large room which is conjectured to have been a stable. The jaw-bone above mentioned and some other fragments of a skeleton were found in it. There is a reservoir for water at the further end, which passes through the wall, and is common both to this room and the next, so that it could be filled without going into the stable. The further room is fitted up with stone basins, which seem to have been the kneading-troughs. It contains also a narrow and inconvenient staircase.

Though bread-corn formed the principle article of nourishment among the Italians, the use of bread itself was not of early date. For a long time the Romans used their corn sodden into pap, and there were no bakers in Rome antecedent to the war against Perseus, king of Macedonia,* about A. U. 580. Before this every house made its own bread, and this was the task of the women, except in great houses, where there were men-cooks. And even after the invention of bread it was long before the use of mills was known, but the grain was bruised in mortars. Hence the names *pistor* and *pistrinum*, a baker and baker's shop, which are derived from *pinsere*, to pound. The oven also was of late introduction, as we have hinted in speaking of the goddess Fornax, nor did it ever

* Pliny, xviii.

come into exclusive use. We hear of *panis subcineritius*, bread baked under the ashes; *artopticius*, baked in the *artopta*, or bread-pan, which was probably of the nature of a Dutch oven; and other sorts, named either from the method of their preparation or the purpose to which they were to be applied. The finest sort was called *siligineus*, and was prepared from *siligo*, the best and whitest sort of wheaten flour. A bushel of the best wheat of Campania, which was of the first quality, containing sixteen sextarii, yielded four sextarii of siligo, here seemingly used for the finest flour; half a bushel of *flos*, bolted flour; four sextarii of *cibarium*, seconds; and four sextarii of bran; thus giving an excess of four sextarii.

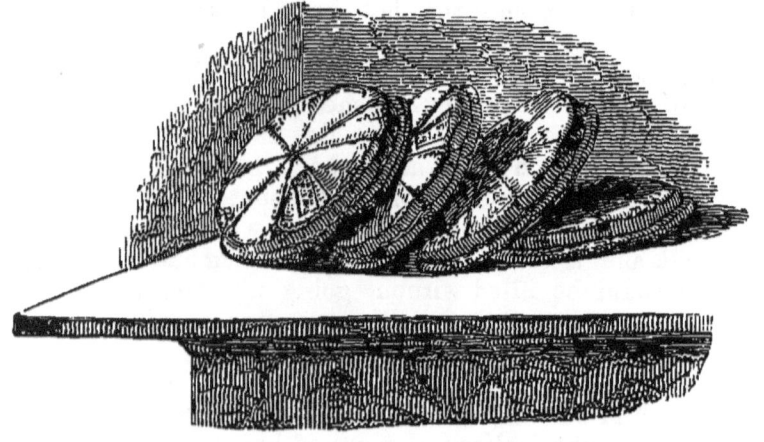

Bread discovered in Pompeii.

Their loaves appear to have been very often baked in moulds, several of which have been found: these may possibly be artoptæ, and the loaves thus baked, artopticii. Several of these loaves have been found entire. They are flat, and about eight inches in diameter. One in the Neapolitan Museum has a stamp on the top:—

SILIGO . CRANII
E . CICER

This has been interpreted to mean that cicer (vetch) was mixed with the flour. We know from Pliny that the Romans used several sorts of grain.

FULLONICA. 361

Fullers at work; from a painting in the Fullonica.

In front of the house, one on each side the doorway, there are two shops. Neither of these has any communication with the house: it is inferred, therefore, that they were let out to others, like the shops belonging to more distinguished persons. This supposition is the more probable, because none of the bakeries found have had shops attached to them; and there is a painting in the grand work on Herculaneum, Le Pitture d'Ercolano, which represents a bread-seller established in the Forum, with his goods on a little table in the open air.*

There is only one other trade, so far as we are aware, with respect to the practices of which any knowledge has been gained from the excavations at Pompeii—that of fulling and scouring cloth. This art, owing to the difference of ancient and modern habits, was of much greater importance formerly than it now is. Wool was almost the only material used for dresses in the earlier times of Rome, silk being unknown till a late period, and linen garments being very little used. Woollen dresses, however, especially in the hot climate of Italy, must often have required a thorough purification, and on the manner in which this was done of course their beauty very much depended. And since the toga, the chief article of Roman costume, was woven in one piece, and was of course expensive, to make it look and wear as well as possible was very necessary to persons of small fortune. The method pursued has been described by Pliny and others, and is well illustrated in some paintings found upon the walls of a building, which evidently was a *fullonica*, or scouring-house. The building in question is entered from the Street of Mercury, and is situated in the same island as the House of the Tragic Poet. A plan of the whole island, including the Fullonica, is given on p. 367.

The first operation was that of washing, which was done with water mixed with some detergent clay, or fuller's earth: soap does not appear to have been used. This was done in vats, where the cloths were trodden and well worked by the feet of the scourer. The preceding cut, taken from the walls of the Fullonica, represents four persons thus employed. Their dress is tucked up, leaving the legs bare: it consists of

* One of the bakeries in the House of Pansa seems to have had a shop attached to it.—Ed.

two tunics, the under one being yellow and the upper green. Three of them seem to have done their work, and to be wringing the articles on which they have been employed; the other, his hands resting on the wall on each side, is jumping, and busily working about the contents of his vat. When dry, the cloth was brushed and carded, to raise the nap —at first with metal cards, afterwards with thistles. A plant called teazle is now largely cultivated in England for the. same purpose. The cloth was then fumigated with sulphur,

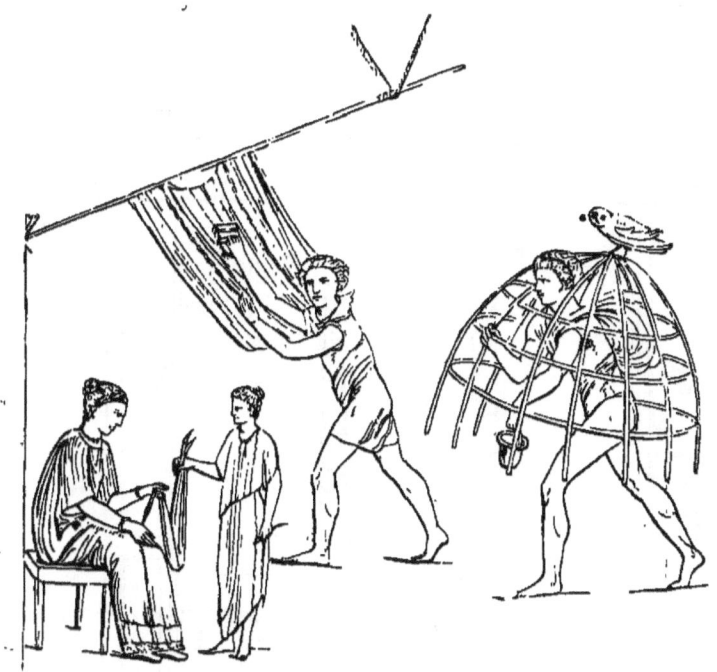

Carding a Tunic; from a painting in the Fullonica.

and bleached in the sun by throwing water repeatedly upon it while spread out on gratings. In the preceding cut the workman is represented as brushing or carding a tunic suspended over a rope. Another man carries a frame and pot, meant probably for fumigation and bleaching; the pot containing live coals and sulphur, and being placed under the frame, so that the cloths spread upon the latter would be fully exposed to the action of the pent-up vapour. The person who carries these things wears something on his head, which is said to be an olive garland. If so, that, and the owl sitting upon the frame, probably indicate that the establishment was under the patronage of Minerva, the tutelary goddess of the loom. Below is a female examining the work which a younger girl has done upon a piece of yellow cloth. A golden net upon her head, a necklace and bracelets, denote a person of higher rank than one of the mere workpeople of the establishment: it probably is either the mistress herself, or a customer inquiring into the quality of the work which has been done for her.

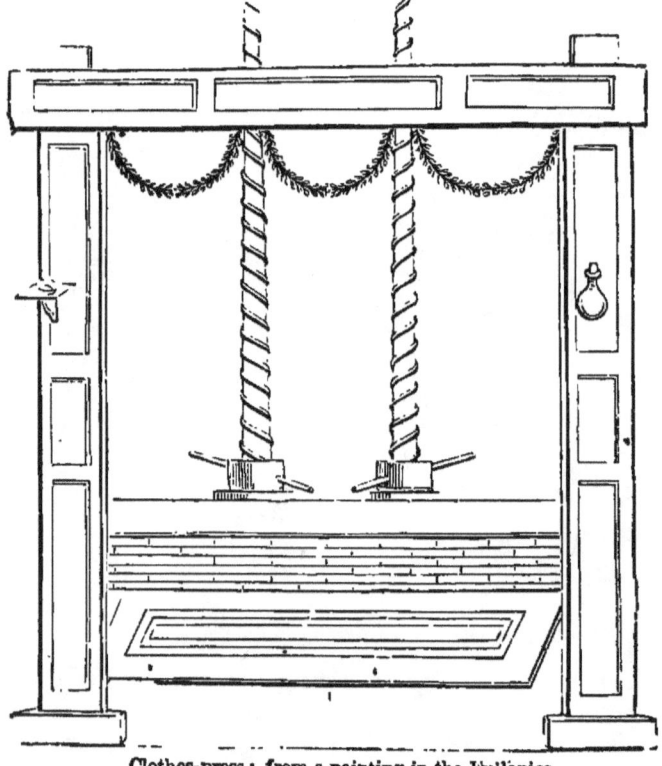

Clothes-press; from a painting in the Fullonica.

These pictures, with others illustrative of the various processes of the art, were found upon a pier in the peristyle of the Fullonica. Among them we may mention one that represents a press, similar in construction to those now in use, except that there is an unusual distance between the threads of the screw. The ancients, therefore, were acquainted with the practical application of this mechanical power. In another is to be seen a youth delivering some pieces of cloth to a female, to whom, perhaps, the task of ticketing, and preserving distinct the different property of different persons, was allotted. It is rather a curious proof of the importance attached to this trade, that the due regulation of it was a subject thought not unworthy of legislative enactments. A. U. 354, the censors laid down rules for regulating the manner of washing dresses; and we learn from the digests of the Roman law, that scourers were compelled to use the greatest care not to lose or to confound property. Another female, seated on a stool, seems occupied in cleaning one of the cards. Both of the figures last described wear green tunics: the first of them has a yellow under-tunic, the latter a white one. The resemblance in colours between these dresses and those of the male fullers above described may perhaps warrant a conjecture that there was some kind of livery or prescribed dress belonging to the establishment, or else the contents of the painter's colour-box must have been very limited.

The whole pier on which these paintings were found has been removed to the museum at Naples. In the peristyle was a large earthenware jar, which had been broken across the middle, and the pieces then sewn carefully and laboriously together with wire. The value of these vessels, therefore, cannot have been very small, though they were made of the most common clay. At the eastern end of the peristyle there was a pretty fountain, with a jet d'eau. The western end is occupied by four large vats in masonry, lined with stucco, about seven feet deep, which seem to have received the water in succession, one from another

Small Painting in the Tragic Poet's House.

CHAPTER VII.

HOUSE OF THE TRAGIC POET—OF THE GREAT AND LITTLE FOUNTAINS—OF APOLLO—THE FAUN, ETC.

THE island which lies eastward of the House of Pansa contains, besides the Fullonica, three houses, the discovery of which excited a great sensation, not so much for their extent, which is small compared with that of several others, but on account of the richness and beauty, or singularity of their decorations. These have respectively received the names of the House of the Tragic Poet, and the Houses of the Great and Little Fountains. We give a larger plan of this island.

The House of the Tragic Poet was excavated towards the end of the year 1824, and excited universal admiration from the number and beauty of its paintings. Of these some have been removed to the Museum at Naples; the rest have

HOUSE OF THE TRAGIC POET. 367

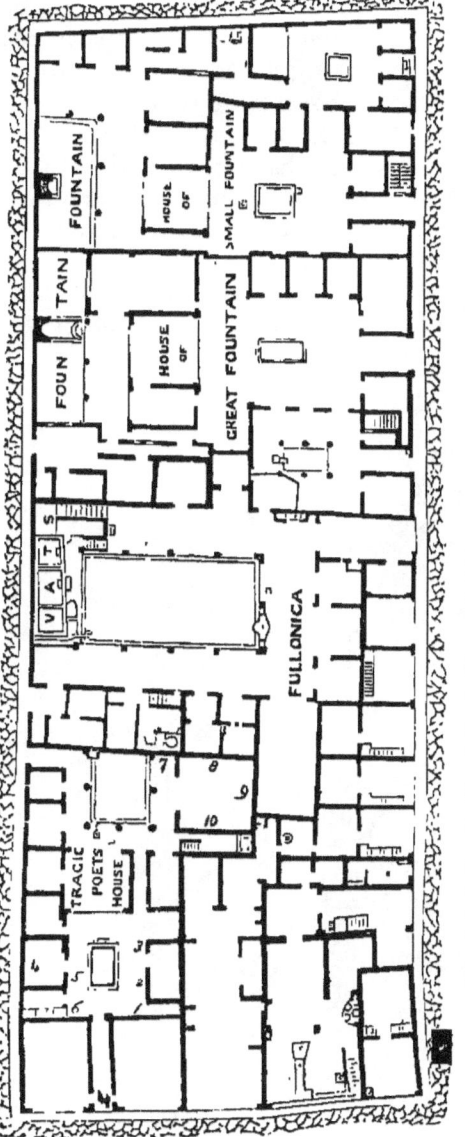

Island, including the Tragic Poet's House, the Fullonica, and the Great and Small Fountains.

368   POMPEII.

perished, or are perishing. This is the more to be regretted, because, at a small expense, the whole house might have been covered in, and preserved for many years in nearly the same state of beauty as when it was first discovered. Fortunately, the art of detaching frescoes from walls, in order to rescue them from the certain ruin consequent on exposure to weather, has been brought to such perfection, that of the numerous experiments which have been, and continue to be made (for every fresco of importance is removed), not one has failed. This process is not one of modern invention, but was known to the ancients.

The doors turned upon pivots, received in two bronze sockets let into the marble threshold, the outer part of which

Mosaic at the entrance of the Prothyrum of the Tragic Poet's House.

rises about an inch higher than the bottom of the door. Upon entering the visitor may be startled, for the first object which meets his eye is a large fierce dog, apparently in the act of springing upon him. This device is worked in mosaic on the pavement, and is well executed: the dog is black, spotted with white, and he has a red collar. Beneath is written, in large legible characters, " Cave Canem " ('Ware Dog).* It appears from ancient authorities that it was not uncommon to place pictures of dogs in the vestibule with this inscription; and, indeed, we may suppose that live dogs were sometimes kept there, since it seems hardly possible to have dispensed with the protection of those watchful animals, where the whole house, as was the ancient custom, stood so invitingly open to every visitor. Below the inscription is a hole in the pavement, to give passage to the rain water which might force its way in ; a clumsy contrivance, indicative of bad workmanship.

The reader will be at no loss to comprehend the disposition of the house after the many examples which have been fully explained, and to recognize the vestibule, atrium, alæ, tablinum, fauces, and peristyle. The large room on the right of the peristyle is the triclinium; beside it is the kitchen; the smaller apartments which surround it and the atrium are chambers for the use of the family. The one next to the private entrance into the peristyle is called the library, and is lighted by the window, of which a view has been already given from without. These rooms are all about twelve feet in height. They were generally closed by folding-doors, as is evident from the sockets let into the thresholds to receive the pivots upon which they turned, and from the two holes in the centre for bolts. The two large apartments on each side of the vestibule appear, from the ample openings in front of them, to have been shops; but they communicate with the corridor, which is not usual, except where the shops were occupied by the master of the house. It has been supposed, from the number of valuable articles found in them, that the occupier was a jeweller or goldsmith, and the arrangement of these shops gives some countenance to this opinion.† Nor is there any strong

* This mosaic is now removed to the floor of the room containing the collections from Pompeii and Herculaneum in the National Museum at Naples.

† This idea was started by Gell. But these valuable articles were found at a height of about six palms from the floor, and seem to have fallen in, together with some pieces of mosaic pavement, from an upper story.—See *Pomp. Ant. Hist.*, Oct. 16, 1824 (t. ii. p. 126).—ED.

evidence to support the belief that it belonged to a poet; for excepting the mosaic representing the distribution of masks, and the picture of a poet reading, there is nothing in the house particularly connected either with tragedy or poetry. The owner, however, was evidently a man of taste and cultivation.

The vestibule is about six feet wide, and nearly thirty long: a curtain or door was probably placed at the entrance of the atrium, which is about twenty-eight feet by twenty. It is provided as usual with impluvium and puteal. The floor is paved with white tesseræ, spotted with black, and round the impluvium there is a well-executed interlaced pattern, also in black. The walls were richly ornamented with paintings, most of which, however, have been carried to the museum. We have inserted figures in the plan, with a view of showing their distribution.

1. Marriage of Peleus and Thetis, otherwise called the interview of Thetis and Jupiter.
2. Parting of Achilles and Briseis.
3. Painting much decayed, supposed to represent the departure of Chryseis.
4. Battle of Amazons.
5. Fall of Icarus.
6. Venus Anadyomene.
7. Sacrifice of Iphigenia.
8. Leda and Tyndareus.
9. Theseus and Ariadne.
10. Cupid.

The subject of the first picture is at best doubtful. It consists of three principal figures—a man of middle age seated, who is in the act of taking the left arm of a female, who seems to extend it reluctantly, with an expression by no means good-tempered. A winged figure, which stands behind her, seems to urge her on, and to induce her to present the right hand. At Peleus' feet are three children, which may be, it is said, the offspring of a former marriage to Antigone. These children, however, if such they are, are men in miniature, though, judging by their size, they should be little better than infants. A similar fault is found by critics in the celebrated group of Laocoon. The countenance of the goddess is, as we have said, by no means amiable. Some perceive in this the reluctance with which she consented to a mortal alliance, especially to a widower with three children; others have imagined that the picture represents the return of Helen to Menelaus, when the lady certainly had good cause to look rather sulky; others believe it to represent the moment when Thetis complains to Jupiter of the injustice done to Achilles. In neither of the two latter interpretations are the children and the winged figure accounted for; and of three unsatisfactory solutions, the first appears the best, especially as a pillar in the back-ground supports instruments of music, which seem more in character with a wedding than with either of the other two occasions. The story is well known. Jupiter was enamoured of Thetis, but was prevented from prosecuting his suit by an oracle which declared that she would bear a son who would prove greater than his father. In consequence of this it was determined to marry her to a mortal, and Peleus was the person fixed upon. The heads and drapery are said to be fine, but, as a whole, the picture is far inferior in beauty to that which we have next to describe; which represents Achilles delivering Briseis to the heralds, who were to conduct her to Agamemnon. Rather than attempt to describe, at second-hand, this, perhaps the most beautiful specimen of ancient painting which has been preserved to modern times, we will avail ourselves of Sir W. Gell's description, from whom indeed nearly the whole of the information contained in this chapter is drawn. The size of the painting is four feet wide by four feet two inches high.

"The scene seems to take place in the tent of Achilles, who sits in the centre. Patroclus, with his back towards the spectator, and with a skin of deeper red, leads in from the left the lovely Briseis, arrayed in a long and floating veil of apple green. Her face is beautiful, and, not to dwell upon the archness of her eye, it is evident that the voluptuous pouting of her ruby lip was imagined by the painter as one of her most bewitching attributes. Achilles presents the fair one to the heralds on his right, and his attitude, his manly beauty, and the magnificent expression of his countenance are inimitable.

"The tent seems to be divided by a drapery about breast-high, and of a sort of dark-bluish green, like the tent itself. Behind this stand several warriors, the golden shield of one of whom, whether intentionally or not on the part of the painter, forms a sort of glory round the head of the principal hero.

"It is probably the copy of one of the most celebrated pictures of antiquity.

"When first discovered the colours were fresh, and the flesh particularly had the transparency of Titian. It suffered much and unavoidably during the excavation, and something from the means taken to preserve it, when a committee of persons qualified to judge had decided that the wall on which it was painted was not in a state to admit of its removal with safety. At length, after an exposure of more than two years,

Achilles delivering Briseis to the Heralds.

it was thought better to attempt to transport it to the Studii at Naples than to suffer it entirely to disappear from the wall. It was accordingly removed with success in the summer of the year 1826, and it is hoped that some remains of it may exist for posterity.

"The painter has chosen the moment when the heralds Talthybius and Eurybates are put in possession of Briseis, to escort her to the tent of Agamemnon, as described in the first book of the Iliad,* and thus translated by Pope :—

> Patroclus now the unwilling beauty brought ·
> She in soft sorrow and in pensive thought
> Passed silent, as the heralds held her hand,
> And oft looked back, slow moving o'er the sand.

"The head of Achilles is so full of fire and animation, that an attempt has been made to introduce a facsimile of it.

Head of Achilles.

Though a facsimile, as far as being traced with transparent paper from the original can make it so, it gives but a very imperfect idea of the divinity which seems to animate the hero of the painting.† The extreme vivacity, dignity and beauty of the head are but faintly expressed, and all those faults seem exaggerated which the skill of the artist and

* A. 345.
† This is very finely engraved in the second series of Sir William Gell's Pompeiana. [The original drawing was made by Ternites.]

the colouring of the original concealed. One of the eyes in particular is larger than the other, and there may be other defects, which totally disappear when observed with the entire painting, leaving the impression of the finest youthful head in existence."* Patroclus stands by Achilles, his face half turned to the spectator with a lowering expression, as if he sympathized in the injury done to his friend, and waited but his signal to resent it, while groups of myrmidons in the background seem to share in his feelings.

Corresponding with this, on the left of the door of the cubiculum, is another picture, which unfortunately is so much defaced that the very subject remains doubtful. The subject of Briseis, however, naturally suggested for its companion the restoration of Chryseis, with which the remains of the picture agree tolerably well; though they have also been taken to represent Andromache with the young Astyanax going into slavery after the capture of Troy. All that can be made out is a female in long robes, under a blue sky, whose hands are kissed by children, while an elderly person looks on from the right; and on the left, under a red portal, an armed man with helmet and plume is seen behind the principal figure. The chief personage seems to be stepping on board a galley.

To the left of this picture is the ala, or wing, of which in this house there is but one. It presents nothing remarkable. Opposite to the picture of Achilles and Briseis is a sea-piece, now almost undistinguishable, though at first it might be recognized as commemorating the fall of Icarus. A winged sea-god on a dolphin seems to be assisting the unfortunate adventurer. The other picture in this atrium, on the left side of the entrance, is a Venus, at whose feet a dove is lying with a myrtle branch in her beak. The figure resembles in attitude the Medicean Venus, and the colouring is complimented by being compared to that of Titian. Still to the left of this is a small chamber painted yellow, with black pilasters, in which there was a staircase which led to the upper floor. During the excavations, the fragments of a mosaic pavement, containing a head of Bacchus which had fallen from above, were found, together with a considerable

---

* Gell, second series, vol. i. p. 155-7; vol. ii. p. 105.

number and variety of female ornaments. Among these were two gold necklaces, a twisted gold cord, four bracelets formed into serpents with many convolutions, one weighing seven ounces, four earrings, each of two pearls, suspended as it were from a balance, and a ring of onyx, with a youthful head engraved on it. These jewels seemed to have fallen from the upper story, and lay not more than five feet below the surface of the soil. Fragments of skeletons were found on the same spot, which bore marks of having been previously searched, though without finding the valuables which probably were known to be contained about this place. In other parts of the house a number of coins, and various articles in bronze, iron, and earthenware were found; among them hatchets, a hammer, kitchen utensils, two heels for boots, with holes for nails, lamps, bottles, &c.

The paintings of one side of the central chamber on this side of the atrium are also remarkable. It is divided into rectangular compartments by three perpendicular and three horizontal lines. Upon a basement stand columns supporting an entablature, on each side of which are represented in perspective other columns, forming galleries, decorated with festoons, vases, and griffins : at the base of the larger columns is a balustrade, which species of ornament appears so frequently in these architectural paintings, that we are led to conclude it was in common use as a protection to the terraces which surmounted the Pompeian houses. In the centre is a painting of Phrixus and Helle, and on each side of the columns are Cupids, carrying different articles of female dress. Above the whole is a broad frieze, upon which is represented, on a white ground, the combat between the Greeks and Amazons. Some of the female warriors are in chariots, some on horses, and they are armed with bows as well as with their usual shields and battle-axes. They are clothed in blue, green, and purple draperies, and are represented in violent action, often pursuing the Greeks, at times falling before them. The men are distinguished by wearing helmets, while the women have the head bare. These figures are more remarkable for their spirited composition than for accuracy of drawing, nor can they be esteemed equal, in respect of finish, to several of the paintings found in this house. One figure of a wounded Amazon, whose horse is falling, and who yet retains her seat, is mentioned as a masterpiece of attitude. In this chamber there is also a painting of Europa and the Bull.

We now come to the tablinum. The most remarkable thing in it is the mosaic representing the distribution of masks to a chorus, which has been figured, and described in Part. I., p. 203. This room also contains the picture of a poet reading, which has been chiefly instrumental in procuring for the house the name which it now bears. In the foreground is a male figure, reading from a roll to two others, one male the other female, all seated. In the background, leaning on a sort of partition which separates them from the others, are Apollo and a female figure, supposed to be a Muse, and on the other side of the painting a woman and an old man. The skin of the reader is considerably darker than that of the others, which has made some persons suppose that he was a slave, and that it represents Plautus, or some of the Athenians taken prisoners at Syracuse, who are reported by Thucydides to have softened the hardships of their fate in consequence of the delight which their masters took in hearing them repeat the verses of Euripides. Others think that it is the celebrated scene which occurred when Virgil was reciting the Æneid to Augustus and Octavia, when he came to the elegiac passage upon the death of Marcellus, but the very scanty drapery of both the male figures rather militates against this conclusion. The walls are adorned with a variety of fantastical ornaments, such as pillars with human heads for capitals, sustaining capricious entablatures, swans, goats, lions, &c., among which we may particularly mention a border of harpies in the form in which they are usually given, as this is said to be perhaps the only ancient authority for the form of those beings yet found.

The peristyle consists of seven Doric columns, enclosing a small court, probably planted with flowers, which stand upon a sort of podium, painted red, as well as the lower part of the pillars. A tortoise was kept in the garden, as we may infer from the shell of the animal being found on the spot. The further wall is painted blue, to imitate the sky, while below it the tops of trees are visible over a parapet, forming another specimen of that sort of painting known by the name of *opera topiaria*, which we have described in speaking

Side of a wall of a small apartment in the Tragic Poet's House.

of the House of Actæon. At the left angle of the colonnade is a small ædicula, or shrine, in which probably stood a statue found near the spot, representing a faun carrying flowers and fruits. A railing ran between the pillars to prevent wanton intrusion upon the flowers, as the holes made for its reception still show. Several frogs in terra-cotta were found here, which served as spouts to the roof of the portico. On this side the tablinum was evidently closed with doors or shutters, of the kind called *volubiles*, in many compartments: to the atrium it was probably closed only by curtains, at least no signs of the existence of shutters on that side are to be seen.

On the left side of the peristyle are two small chambers, one of which is called the library, from a painting of books

Female and Cupid fishing.

and implements of writing; the other contains two pictures, one of Venus and Cupid fishing, the other of Ariadne. Both of these are graceful and well executed. At the end of the right branch of the colonnade is the sacrifice of Iphigenia. The moment is taken at which Chalcas is about to strike the fatal blow. Iphigenia, borne in the arms of two men, is appealing to her father, who stands in the front of the picture, turned away from her, with his head veiled, which we may suppose to have been the received way of treating the subject ever after the first painter received so much

The Sacrifice of Iphigenia.

applause for thus escaping the necessity of expressing passions which his art was unable to portray. The figure of the maiden is beautiful, but, by a strange oversight, she has no legs, or if she has, they are hidden behind one of her supporters in a way which it is not very easy to understand. The draperies are for the most part shades of blue and purple, and the effect of the whole picture is too red. Above,

Diana appears in the clouds, with the hind which was to supply Iphigenia's place as a victim. To the left is seen a golden statue of the goddess, bearing a lighted torch in each hand, and with two dogs at her feet.

At the side of this picture we enter a room near twenty feet square, and of considerable height. It is called the Triclinium, or the Chamber of Leda, from a painting which

Leda and Tyndareus.

occupies the centre of one of the walls. It is painted with the brightest shades of red and yellow, in the fantastic architectural style of which we have so often spoken. In this we have a view of the roof and impluvium of an atrium, which, if there were any doubt as to the internal appearance of that member of the building, would be sufficient to remove it. It is decorated, as we have described in various instances, with ornamental antefixes. The lower part of the wall is decorated with garlands, sea-horses, and other ornaments, on black panels. We give an outline of the painting, which gives its name to the chamber. This is considered to be one of the most beautiful productions of ancient art, not only for elegance of design, but for chastity and harmony of colouring. The mythological fable of the birth of Castor and Pollux, and Helen, is so well known that it need not be repeated. Leda holds her three children in a boat-shaped vessel, that looks almost like an egg-shell, and presents them to her husband Tyndareus, who looks at them with a pleased expression. It is remarkable, if the fact be correctly stated, as an instance of the change which takes place in the colours of these pictures after they have been exposed to the air, that an artist who copied this painting a few days after its discovery, states that the drapery of the princess was green, lined with blue, and the robe of Tyndareus black, lined with green. Yet about a month afterwards the robe of Leda was red and that of Tyndareus purple, and so they have remained to the present day. Reds usually change to black. The landscape in the background is much faded.

The other two numbers in this room refer to pictures, one of which contains a beautiful Cupid, leaning on the knees of Venus, to whom Adonis seems to be addressing himself; the other is the constantly-recurring Ariadne, the most favourite, except perhaps Perseus and Andromeda, of all subjects. It represents her sleeping on a mattress, her head surrounded by an azure glory (the usual colour), while Theseus, who has just quitted her, is in the act of stepping on board his galley, in defiance of distance and perspective. Above, Minerva appears in the air, and seems to direct him. Both of these paintings are much defaced, so that it is not easy to judge of their merit, but the composition of the last has nothing to recommend it.

On the plinth is painted a combat between two centaurs and a lion. The fierce animal is about to spring upon one of them, who seems to call to his companion for help, and the latter, bearing a lance in his hand, turns to defend him. The truth with which the lion is painted is remarkable, and may be attributed to the frequent opportunities which painters

Centaurs painted on a black ground in the Triclinium of the Tragic Poet's House. Now almost effaced.

House of the Tragic Poet, as restored by Sir W. Gell.

had of observing wild animals in the sports of the amphitheatre.

This chamber is prettily paved in mosaic, and is conjectured to have been lighted by a row of small windows elevated above the roof of the peristyle. Even in its present state it is sufficiently lofty.

The plate on p. 383, which represents the interior of this house restored, is one of those which we are permitted to extract from the second series of 'Pompeiana.' Very little of this restoration is the work of fancy, owing to the perfect state in which the building was found. The roof has been added, together with the uppermost part of the walls; the ornaments are given, either from indications which remain, or are copied from similar situations in different houses. The view comprehends the atrium, tablinum, and peristyle, being bounded by the painted wall above described. On the pier on the right hand is the picture of Chryseis. Probably the entrance to the tablinum was closed, either by curtains or by folding doors; but in the uncertainty of the exact nature of the partition, the restorer has judged it better to omit it altogether. This view therefore may be depended upon for conveying a tolerably correct notion of one of the most elegant houses, upon a small scale, contained in Pompeii. The total want of privacy is repugnant to our notions of comfort; but it can hardly be denied that there is an air of splendour in the extensive and richly-decorated suite of rooms, which is scarcely equalled in modern houses of a similar class.

Between the House of the Poet and the triumphal arch are several rooms which bear the appearance of having been used as places of refreshment for those who frequented the baths. In one of these was discovered a skeleton under a stone staircase. He had with him a treasure of considerable value, consisting of rings and earrings of gold, together with about one hundred and forty coins of brass and silver. Somewhere in this neighbourhood there were found, in 1826, vases with olives still swimming in oil. The fruit retained its flavour, and the oil burnt well.

In Herculaneum also olives have been found in a vessel, the upper part of which was full of volcanic ashes, the lower containing the olives imbedded in a sediment of the consistence of butter. In form and size they resemble Spanish olives. Some of them still retain the stalk. The stones are shorter and thicker than in the varieties now cultivated, and the longitudinal channelling is more determined. Their colour is black, mixed with small particles of green, which are recognized by a strong magnifier to belong to the lichens which are generally produced on organic substances during putrefaction. These were not apparent when first discovered, but the action of the air in a very few hours produced an alteration on their surface. They are still soft, and have a strong rancid odour and a greasy taste, which leaves a pricking and astringent sensation on the tongue; and they are so light as to swim in water, which is a mark of a bad olive.

The whole of the island northward of the poet's house is occupied, first by the Fullonica, then by the Houses of the Great and Little Fountains. Of these two houses, the first is of considerable size and pretensions, but part of its area is occupied by a small separate habitation, which communicates with, and appears to belong to, the Fullonica. A handsome entrance in the Street of Mercury leads into a spacious atrium of fifty feet by forty, with the usual distribution of alæ and tablinum. The peristyle contains only three columns of a debased Corinthian order; but to make amends, it has that which gave its name to the house, and the discovery of which excited an unusual sensation at Naples—a fountain of much more magnitude and attempt at decoration than any other which had been discovered. Not that it possesses any great beauty, as will be seen by the annexed view, in which it forms the principal feature. It was novel, however, and at that time indeed almost unique, the only thing resembling it being in the adjoining house; and in addition to this the materials are curious, the whole being incrusted with a sort of mosaic, consisting of vitrified tesseræ of different colours, in which blue predominates. The grand divisions of the patterns and the borders are formed by real shells, which remain perfect and unchanged. Almost all the ornaments bear some reference to water, consisting principally of aquatic plants and birds. On each side of the alcove is a marble mask, hollowed out, and intended, it is conjectured, o receive lights, which at night would have a whimsical and

House of Great Fountain; from 'Pompeiana.'

HOUSE OF THE GREAT FOUNTAIN. 387

rather ghastly effect. The water trickled down a little flight of steps into a sort of raised piscina, in the front of which is a round column, pierced for a pipe, and probably intended for a jet d'eau. It is a remarkable instance of the general negligence of arrangement, that in this house, which was evidently one of considerable pretensions, nothing is symmetrical. The pillars of the peristyle are not equidistant from their antæ, and the fountain is opposite neither to an intercolumniation, nor to the centre of the opening of the tablinum.

The high wall behind the alcove has lost the paintings observable in the plate on p. 386, which is copied from the second series of 'Pompeiana.' The plaster fell soon after Sir W. Gell had taken his view. They presented another specimen of the *opus topiarium*. In the panels are birds killing reptiles, &c., executed with considerable spirit, and below them is painted a variety of garden railings. An upper line of pictures, one of which represents a boar-hunt, forms a sort of frieze.

The House of the Smaller Fountain is in no respect inferior in point of interest to that which we have just described. The impluvium has two mouths for cisterns, one of which communicated by means of leaden pipes, still visible, with

Cupid milking a Goat.

the fountain in the peristyle. Between the atrium and tablinum is a step, faced with a pretty sculpture of leaves and flowers. In the latter apartment there is a painting of Cupid milking a goat, remarkable for the lively expression of the figures. The ala and other apartments offer nothing remarkable till we reach the little peristyle, which is surrounded by a broad colonnade of only four columns. Here again we find a fountain, very like that which we have above described, both in design and material. It presents the same sort of alcove, surmounted by a pediment, the height of which is seven feet seven inches, and the breadth seven feet. The face projects five feet from the wall. In front of it there was a little sedent bronze fisherman, now in the Museum at Naples, which seems, by the position of the hand, to have been meant to hold a rod, as if fishing in the piscina, which had in the centre a little column bearing a bird which spouted water; but whether the said bird was a dove or a goose, is a matter on which authorities disagree. On the right side was a caryatis and a sleeping fisherman, both in marble, but these have been removed. It should seem that there was a mask in the centre of the alcove which spouted water. Besides the loaden pipes which communicated with the cistern of the atrium, the brass cocks still remain, by which the water could be turned on and off at pleasure, as in modern fountains. On the walls of this court there are three landscapes, differing in character from anything yet found in Pompeii. We give one of them as a specimen: it represents a farmhouse, with domestic animals: on the left, leaning against the wall, is the yoke for oxen. At the bottom is a group of figures, one of whom seems to have just brought in a naked infant: it is conjectured that the discovery and adoption of Œdipus by the shepherd of Polybus, or some similar event is here depicted. One of the other pictures represents a seaport, with its moles, boats, villas, and other buildings. It is to be observed that the mole is built upon arches, a method of construction often represented upon ancient medals, and intended to prevent the accumulation of mud, by leaving apertures for the current to scour out the interior. It was found that by suspending floodgates vertically from the piers, the agitation of the waves was checked enough to secure vessels riding in the interior. The horizon is very high in the picture, as is usual, and the blue of the sea and sky is nearly the same. It is not improbable that this may be a view of some place on the coast.

Two rooms, one called a triclinium, the other an exedra,

or hall for company, open into the portico. The former is painted in imitation of brickwork the latter contains pictures of game and hunting. Around the peristyle and atrium the usual allotment of sleeping-rooms is observable. This house has two staircases, and therefore must have had an upper floor; and it is rather remarkable that it possesses a second entrance, which gave access to the peristyle and

Farmyard Scene.

private apartments without passing through the atrium. At the corner of this house, in the Street of Mercury, is the fountain of Mercury, on which the head and caduceus of the god are rudely sculptured. On an opposite wall is painted a figure of the same knavish deity, running away with a stolen purse. About this spot five skeletons were found, with various coins, bracelets, and rings about them.

The island lying to the north of that just described, and between it and the city wall, contains two noticeable houses, the House of Adonis and that of Apollo. The House of Adonis, which lies in the middle of the insula, and has its entrance in the Street of Mercury, derives its name from a picture, with figures of a colossal size, representing Adonis wounded and expiring in the arms of Venus. Other pictures are the toilet of Hermaphroditus, a sleeping Bacchus, &c.

Still more remarkable is the House of Apollo, lying northwards of the House of Adonis, close to the city walls, and also entered from the Street of Mercury. The name was derived from some paintings of Apollo, and especially from a little bronze statue of the hermaphrodite Apollo, found in a niche of the tablinum, and now in the Museum. In an opposite niche was the hind of Diana followed by a young fawn. On the two lateral walls of the same apartment are small pictures, the subject of one of which is Adonis reposing with a little Cupid, and of the other the toilet of Venus. There are also some medallion heads. On the wall of the atrium is a picture representing the course of the sun through the zodiac; a figure of Apollo with rays round his head, holding a whip in the right hand, and in the left a globe. The walls of some of the apartments are adorned with arabesque paintings and ornaments in stucco. In the second court, or peristyle, which, however, has no columns, is a fountain of a somewhat bizarre kind. In the middle is a pyramid, on the top of which stood a little statue, now in the Museum, holding under its arm a goose, from the mouth of which the water issued, falling down four little marble staircases on each of the sides of the pyramid. The wall under which the fountain lies has a large painting representing Diana standing on a pedestal in the middle of a little basin or fountain, in which ducks are swimming. The basin is surrounded with a grove of orange and other trees, filled with birds of splendid plumage.

On the right of this court is a kind of *ala*, communicating with the adjoining *xystus*, and having four small chambers, one of which has a handsome marble pavement. There is a vestibule containing a staircase, and also a kitchen with an oven, and a small *lararium*, with the usual painting of serpents and a priest making a libation. Before it is the little stone altar consecrated to Fornax.* At the bottom of the court is an exedra, with a threshold of oriental alabaster, and a pavement formed by an assemblage of the most precious marbles.

On the right of the court some steps descend to the xystus. It is three or four feet below the level of the court, but a terrace runs round three sides of it of the same height as the court. The walls of the terrace are covered with some not very well executed paintings of trees, birds, and several large female figures resembling Caryatides. At the bottom of this terrace on the left is a handsomely-decorated bedchamber, considered however by some authorities to be a bath. The outward wall has a somewhat rude painting of a landscape, with Bacchanalian figures, and on the left a man driving an ass. The other wall, in which is the entrance, has a rather brilliant mosaic, representing Ulysses discovering Achilles at the court of Lycomedes. On the ground, between the two heroes, is a shield, with the device of Chiron instructing Achilles. The interior of the apartment is richly decorated with paintings, on a blue ground, representing various deities, with columns and other scraps of architecture. Above is an undecorated frieze, which, from some remains, seems to have been covered with a drapery, over which was a stucco cornice.

Three steps lead from this apartment to the lower level of the xystus, in the middle of which is a round marble basin inclosed in a square compartment. At the bottom of the xystus are the remains of a room or saloon 12 or 14 feet square, paved with mosaic, and supported by six columns. In the wall are three niches for statues, the middle one of which has a vaulted summit, in which remains of mosaic and shells may still be seen. It would be difficult to say to what purpose this building was applied. Some call it a triclinium, but it has not the usual shape of that apartment, and it must have been at a considerable distance from the kitchen.

To the east of the Street of Mercury, two narrow streets running parrallel with it from the walls of the town to the Street of Fortune are intersected in the middle by another narrow street running from west to east, thus forming four

---

* Breton, *Pompeia*, p. 272.

insulæ resembling those already described. One of the southernmost of these insulæ is wholly occupied by the House of the Faun, remarkable for its size and beauty. We

House of the Faun.

insert an engraving of it. It was discovered about the time when the first edition of this work was preparing for the press, in October, 1830, and excavated in that and the two

HOUSE OF THE FAUN. 393

following years.* It abuts on the north side of the Street of Fortune, just beyond the Temple of Fortune, on the other side of the way. On the pavement in front of the entrance is inscribed the word *Have* (ave), in letters of coloured marble incrusted in *opus Signinum*. The prothyrum is divided into two unequal portions by a doorway and two steps, the smaller portion being towards the street. The second portion ascends towards the atrium, and is paved with small triangular pieces of variously-coloured marbles. At the top of the walls on either side are miniature representations in stucco of the colonnade of a temple. The walls of the atrium were also covered with stucco painted to resemble marble. The impluvium, lined with marble, occupies the middle of the area. On a little base on one of its sides was found the bronze statuette of the Dancing Faun, now in the Museum at Naples, from which the house derives its name. We have already given a description of this figure in a preceding page, accompanied with an engraving.†

The Tuscan atrium, which is about 36 feet broad and 39 deep, is as usual surrounded with bedchambers and alæ; but, what is seldom or never found elsewhere, a door on the right opens into another, but somewhat smaller atrium, having also an entrance from the Street of Fortune. At the sides of, and between these two atria are four shops, of which that at the western corner communicates with another smaller room behind. These shops, as well as that on the right of the principal entrance, have, or had, doors communicating with the atrium, a circumstance which seems to show that the master of the house must have been concerned in the trade carried on in them. From the number of amphoræ found on his premises, as well as several Bacchic emblems, he was probably a wine merchant. At the bottom of the first atrium is the tablinum, having an apartment on each side of it, and a corridor or *fauces* leading into the peristyle. This is of larger dimensions than usual, occupying nearly the whole breadth of the two atria, and being thus, contrary to what is commonly found, longer in its breadth—if such an expression may be allowed—than in its depth. At the back and in the right side of this peristyle are other apartments. The furthest of these on the right has two or three windows, and

* *Pomp. Antiq. Hist.*, t. ii. p. 240, *seq.*
† ee p. 352.

at a considerable height in the wall, a little niche, or ædicula, containing an altar. This part of the building may also be entered from the second atrium, or that on the right.

At the extremity of the whole ground-plan is a large quadrangular garden, surrounded with columns forming a

Acratus on a Panther.

portico. On the left-hand side of this portico may be seen about a hundred amphoræ for wine, still partially covered with *lapillo*. They are now filled with the same substance, the heat of the ashes having burnt away the corks or stoppers.

But what rendered this house remarkable, even more than its size and beauty, was the richness of its furniture and

HOUSE OF THE FAUN.

decorations, and especially of its mosaics. In an apartment in the middle of the peristyle was found the famous mosaic of the battle of Issus, now in the Museum at Naples, which we have already described. The threshold of one of the doors leading into the atrium had also a mosaic, unique both for its execution and for its state of preservation. It is about nine and a half feet long by nearly two broad, and displays a grand festoon of flowers and fruits, with tragic masks and tympana. In another apartment was the beautiful mosaic of Acratus, mounted on a panther, of which we annex a plate. These have been removed to the Neapolitan Museum but two or three mosaics still remain *in situ*. One of these in a room in the peristyle, representing a large lion, is very much damaged. A smaller mosaic in one of the alæ is in a better state of preservation. It represents three doves and a casket, from which one of the doves is stealing a pearl necklace.

In the tablinum of this house was found the skeleton of a woman, whose attitude vividly recalls one of those agonizing scenes which characterized the last days of Pompeii. She appears to have attempted to escape, but driven back by the overwhelming shower of ashes, to have taken refuge in the tablinum, after throwing on the pavement all her ornaments, her *mundus muliebris*. The apartment, however, afforded no secure shelter. The flooring of the room above began to fall in, and her uplifted arms betray an attempt to support the superincumbent mass which crushed her. In an adjoining room were other skeletons, among them that of an old man. Among the jewellery found, which had probably belonged to the woman, were two gold bracelets of a serpentine form, each weighing a pound; several gold rings with engraved stones, one of which represented Hercules lifting his club against a serpent wound round a tree, and figures of the three flying Hesperides. On one with a cornelian was engraved a very fine head of Atalanta.*

In the insula to the north of the House of the Faun is that of the Labyrinth, which derives its name from a mosaic, in one of the rooms of the gynecæum, representing Theseus slaying the Minotaur in the Cretan labryinth. The Athenian virgins, the destined prey of the monster, are seen in attitudes of fear and despair, while on the ground are the skeletons of those whom the Minotaur has devoured. This house is among the finest in Pompeii. It has two atria, one Tuscan, the other tetrastyle, with handsome Corinthian columns. On the right-hand side of the latter were found the remains of a strong box, ornamented with heads in bronze and a meander pattern, and bronze nails round the lid. A corridor leads into a peristyle having thirty stuccoed columns. In one of the angles of the peristyle was a bronze bath, the only one of the kind yet discovered in Pompeii. The skeleton of a woman, with her jewels, was also found in this garden, at a height of six or seven feet from the ground. After surmounting many obstacles in her attempt to escape, her strength seems to have failed her, and she fell, smothered by the still descending volcanic shower.

In the island opposite to that just described, on the eastern side of the Street of Mercury and close to the triumphal arch, is a house known by the various names of Ceres, of the Bacchante, of the Ship, and more commonly of Zephyrus and Flora. The last name was derived from a large picture, now removed to the Museum, containing a number of figures, which is called the marriage of Zephyrus and Flora, the Dream of Rhea, and several other names. It represents a

---

* Fiorelli, *Pomp. Antiq. Hist.*, vol. ii. p. 248.

Atrium of the House of Ceres; from "Pompeiana."

winged figure, conducted by Cupids or genii, approaching a female sleeping on the ground. Several other allegorical figures are introduced. The composition and drawing are

Painting of Jupiter, from the House of Zephyrus and Flora.

not good, and hardly merit a more particular description. The atrium is sufficiently preserved to show that this dwelling was at least two stories high. Indeed the walls are among the loftiest in Pompeii, and are decorated in such a way as to give the room the appearance of being two stories in height. The general effect of this atrium is very unlike that of other houses in the town. It is represented in the plate on p. 397, which is one of those copied from the second series of 'Pompeiana.' In one of the rooms were found the remains of wheels, of exactly the same construction as those now in use. In the front of the view, which is taken looking towards the vestibule, is a slab of marble covering the mouth of a cistern. In this atrium several beautiful paintings have been found. Among them a figure of Jupiter, in a contemplative attitude, the eagle at his feet, and his golden sceptre in his hand. His head is surrounded with the nimbus, or glory. The throne and footstool are gold, ornamented with precious stones; the former is partly covered by the green cloth. The god's mantle is violet-coloured, lined with azure.

Behind the house of Zephyrus and Flora is the Casa dell' Ancora, or House of the Anchor, so called from a black and white mosaic in the prothyrum representing an anchor. It is also sometimes called the House of Amymone and Neptune, from a mediocre picture in an apartment on the right. There is nothing in this house requiring a particular description.

Painting in the House of the Tragic Poet.

Curricle Bar; from a picture in Pompeii.

CHAPTER VIII.

HOUSES OF CASTOR AND POLLUX, THE CENTAUR, AND MELEAGER, ETC.

On the eastern side of the Street of Mercury, and to the northward of that island which we have just described, are three remarkable houses, lying contiguous to one another. These have been named the House of Castor and Pollux, the House of the Centaur, and the House of Meleager.

The House of Castor and Pollux, also called the House of the Quæstor, is the most southern of the three, and was the earliest discovered, that is, between April 1828 and May 1829. The name given to it by the ciceroni of Pompeii must not be regarded as any certain evidence of the owner's rank. It is derived merely from the circumstance of two large chests of considerable beauty and richness of ornament having been found in the public part of the house, which are supposed to have been meant to receive the moneys paid in on account of the revenue. There must of course have been some superior officer of the revenue in Pompeii to receive the port dues, which in a place of such traffic must have been considerable, as well as other taxes, on the land, the transfer of property, and the various other miscellaneous

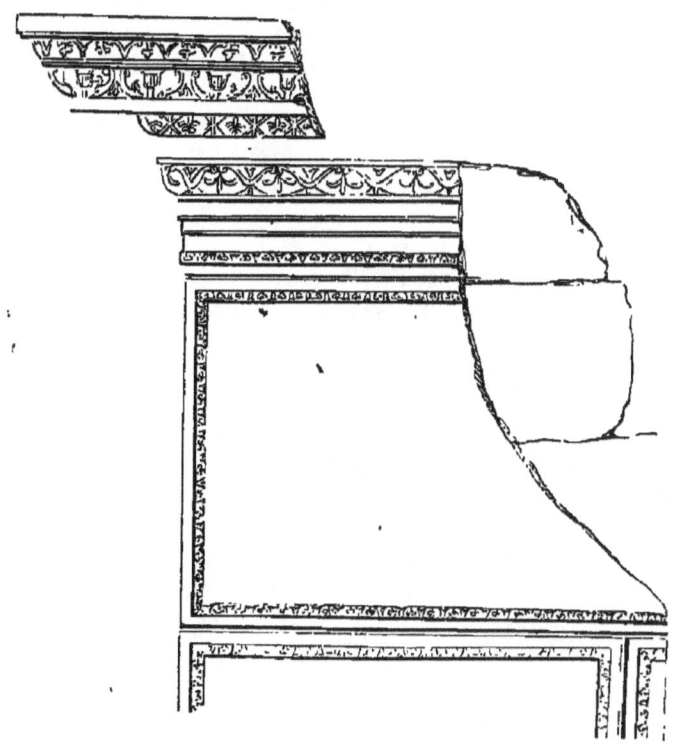

Rustic work and cornices, from the House of Castor and Pollux.

branches of the Roman revenue. Such an officer, whether a quæstor or not, must have been a person of wealth and trust. When, therefore, we find in an extensive and elegant house, and in the public part of it, where clients and others were accustomed to assemble for the despatch of business, two chests, in strength, magnificence of construction, and size, much beyond that required for the traffic of a private

2 D

individual, the conjecture is not improbable that they were intended for the receipt of the public revenue, and that the principal officer in that branch of the public service resided here. The house is otherwise named the House of the Dioscuri, or sons of Jupiter, from two pictures of Castor and Pollux in the vestibule. It is, perhaps, one of the richest and most remarkable yet discovered. The front projects upon the Street of Mercury, and forms one of the corners of a quadrivium, or place where four streets meet. It is composed of two parts communicating with each other, each of which has its separate entrance from the above-named street. That to the right is the largest and the most ornamented, and seems to have been meant for the use of the family; the other part being appropriated to servants and offices.

The ground-plan is delineated in the annexed cut. The façade is rich and ornamented with more than usual care, the walls being worked in rustic with fine white marble stucco, and each block edged with an embossed border formed by stamping the wet plaster with a mould—a cheap and rapid way of producing a rich effect. The narrow channels which divide the blocks are painted blue. The cornice also which surmounted the principal door, being first ro·ghly carved in the tufa of Nocera, was stuccoed, and the stucco moulded in a similar manner. No high relief could be produced thus; and to give more effect, the intermediate spaces between them have been coloured red, black, and blue, so as, by the apparent depth of shadow, to produce an appearance of greater elevation than the projections possess.

1. Street of Mercury. 2. Principal entrance. Upon one of the jambs of the doorway was painted a Mercury with a large purse in his hand, in the act of running. Here we may pause to consider the rich and varied perspective of the interior,—where the Corinthian peristyle with its twelve columns, and fountain in the centre of the impluvium, beyond it the tablinum, rich with paintings, and in the further distance the ædicula, or shrine of the tutelary deity of the house, combined to furnish a coup-d'œil of more than ordinary magnificence. 3. Vestibule, paved with *opus Signinum*. The walls are divided into compartments principally coloured red and yellow, and painted very beautifully with

grotesque designs. Upon either side were spirited paintings of Castor and Pollux—the Dioscuri, from whom the house

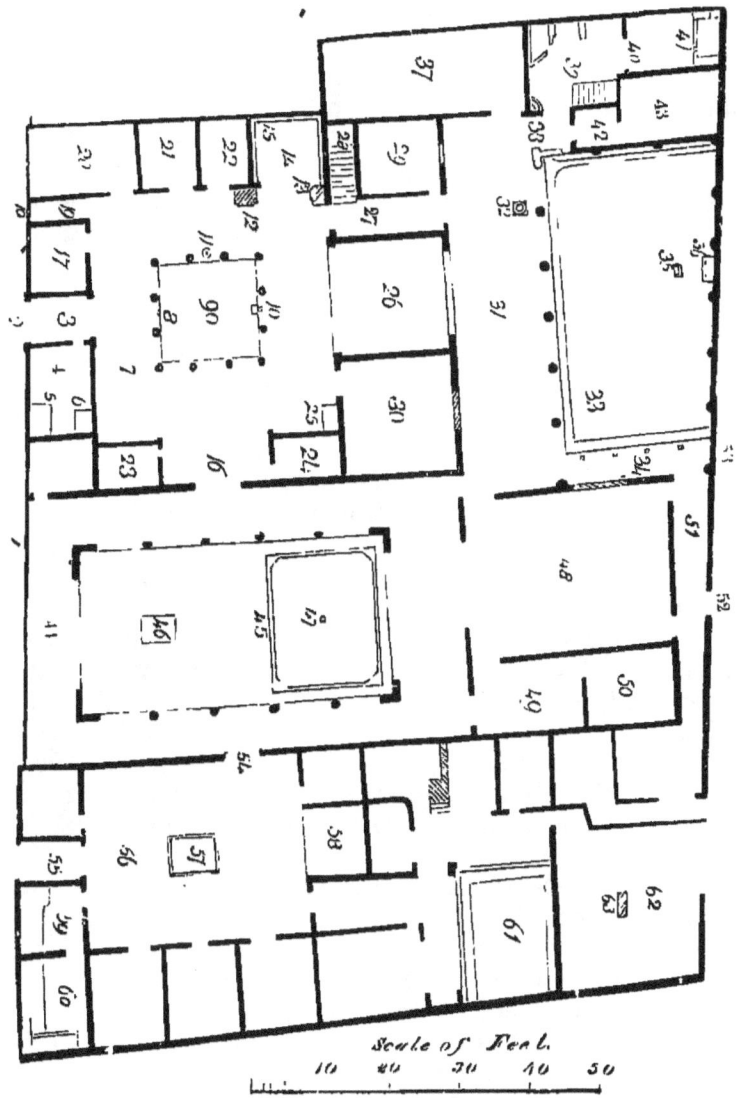

Ground-plan of the House of Castor and Pollux.

derives one of its names—reining in their horses. The door on the right-hand side leads into a small room, 4, probably occupied by the porter, where there are traces of a staircase, 5. 6. Sewer. 7. Atrium. It corresponds with the Corinthian atrium of Vitruvius, and is one of the few examples which remain of that magnificent style of building. The roof was supported by twelve columns placed around the impluvium, formed of the tufa of Nocera, and coated with stucco. They are about twelve feet high and one foot eight inches in diameter. The lower half of the shaft is coloured red, and the flutings are filled up; the upper part is white. The cornice of the atrium is remarkable for containing the dentils of the Ionic order, while the capitals are formed by plain rectangular plinths—a singular and unpleasing novelty, for which it is not easy to account in a house distinguished in general for the richness of its decorations. Like that of the entrance, the pavement is of *opus Signinum*. The impluvium, 8, was ornamented by a small marble fountain, 9, prettily designed, representing a water-plant, upon which reptiles, such as frogs and lizards, are carved. The flow of water was regulated by a bronze key. The basin itself is but a few inches deep, so that when the water was not turned on, persons might walk across it without difficulty. In the central intercolumniation, fronting the tablinum, there is what seems to be the base of an altar, 10, probably appropriated to the worship of the Lares,* and on the left-hand side, 11, the customary puteal, or well-cover. This is made of a white calcareous stone, in which the constant friction of the cords used in raising water has worn deep channels. The walls of the atrium remain perfect nearly to their original elevation, as is proved by the existence of the capitals of the Corinthian pilasters.

On the left-hand side of the atrium in the corner next the tablinum, the two large chests, marked 12 and 13, were found, which have given a name to the house.† Each of them was raised upon a solid plinth, encrusted with marble. They were made of wood, lined with plates of brass, and on the exterior bound with iron, and decorated with handles, bosses, and a variety of other ornaments, many of which had fallen

* More probably, as Overbeck remarks, the base of a statue.
† But without much reason, as similar chests have been found in other houses, while the figure of Mercury seems to denote the house of a merchant.—ED.

Atrium of the House of the Quæstor; from 'Pompeiana.'

off by rust and the decay of the wood, and were found lying beneath. The locks, handles, and other ornaments were made of bronze. When found, the bottom of these chests was formed merely of several parallel bars of iron, which of course supported a planking, now decayed. Through the interstices of one of them, marked 12, forty-five gold and five silver coins had fallen, and were found at the time of excavation. so as to afford a clue to the use of these remarkable chests.* The greater part of the contents however had been extracted in old times; evidently by some person who knew their value, and was at the labour of digging in search of their buried treasure. Owing, however, to some slight error in his measurements, he got into the adjoining room, 22, and greatly increased the difficulty of his task, by thus rendering it necessary to cut through the wall of the atrium, and to extract the money through a small hole in the chest.

The atrium is beautifully painted in the same style as the vestibule, with arabesque designs upon red and yellow grounds. Upon the plinth are flowers, reptiles, and birds pecking at fruit. Above it are painted many excellent figures. We may notice among them Jupiter, seated on his throne, and crowned by Victory; Fortune holding a rudder, her usual emblem; Bacchus with the thyrsus, and beside him a little Faun standing on tip-toe, and endeavouring to catch some drops which fall from a bowl that the God of Wine holds reversed, while a panther, fawning like a dog, pulls at the end of his cloak.† The apartment has but one ala or wing, 14, round which there runs a dwarf wall or plinth, 15, which served as a seat. It is probable, from the position of the chests, that those who received or paid the public money were stationed here. 16. A large recess containing a door which leads into the great court of the piscina. Among the pictures in this part of the atrium were Ceres, Apollo sounding the lyre, Saturn with his scythe, and here and there landscapes containing small figures, not altogether dissimilar in style to those of Nicholas Poussin. Two of them represent scenes near the sea-shore, with hilly undulating ground,

---

* See *Pomp. Ant. Hist.*, t. ii. p. 214 (July 8th, 1828).

† We may here say, once for all, that the visitor will now look in vain for many of these and other paintings described in the accounts of early excavations.—ED.

verdant to the margin of the sea, with incidents appropriate to the scenery. In one is told the story of Perseus contending with the kinsmen of Andromeda, who opposed his marriage with the princess after he had delivered her from the sea-monster. In the other, Jupiter is represented carrying off Europa, and several beautiful Cupids appear in different parts of the picture. The whole atrium, exclusive of the recess, is about forty feet square, and the open space in the centre is about seventeen feet in each of its dimensions.

Various rooms of various uses surround the atrium, some lighted from the street by a window, as 17, 19, 20, others entirely dependent upon the atrium, and lighted imperfectly by a window or lattice placed above the door. 17 is conjectured to have been the apartment of the *atriensis*. It is decorated in the same style and with the same elegance as the atrium. The closet, 19, was probably a storeroom. In 20 there are two small, but remarkably fine pictures; one of Diana descending from heaven, attracted by the beauty of Endymion, with two nymphs in the background; the other of Narcissus. There are other pictures of Bacchantes, flying figures, &c. The pavement is of *opus Signinum*. 21 and 22 contain nothing worth notice except that in the latter there is a mosaic pavement. 23 is merely plastered with white stucco, in which there are two rows of small holes, apparently meant for brackets to support two tiers of shelves. This therefore is supposed to have been a storeroom, especially as bronze and glass vases were found in it. In 24 the same traces of shelves were found as in 23, and a quantity of provisions, such as nuts, lentils, grains, and figs : it was therefore another storeroom. The thresholds of both these apartments are of white marble, and in one of them the iron pivot upon which the door turned still remains. 25 appears to be a plinth, or basement, intended to receive something, but of what nature is uncertain.

The tablinum, 26, is an apartment of remarkable splendour. The pavement is of white mosaic, edged with a black border. The walls are of uncommon beauty. Each of them has in its centre a picture : that on the left-hand, as the visitor enters, represents the quarrel between Agamemnon and Achilles, and Minerva interfering to restrain the latter : that on the right, Ulysses discovering Achilles among the females of the court of Lycomedes. This picture has the appearance of being executed originally in shades of red, covered afterwards with transparent tints, through which the red ground is generally visible. Upon the walls are painted hangings of blue cloth embroidered with gold, with four groups of Fauns and Bacchantes worked upon them. The plinth is black, and ornamented with the usual variety of arabesque patterns, such as lions and centaurs fighting, and Cupids riding in chariots drawn by stags and goats. In another part figures are represented coming out of doors in a colonnade enriched with festoons of fruit and flowers. Not less worthy of notice is the frieze, along which is painted a narrow line of landscapes with figures, one of which is supposed to represent the return of Ulysses to Ithaca. It contains a sedent figure, with a peaked, Chinese-looking hat upon his head, who is offering a cup to another man in tattered garments, stretched on the ground and playing with a dog. This right-hand wall, which presents a surface about twenty feet square, adorned with almost every variety of painting known at Pompeii, is unmatched for beauty and brilliancy of effect.

27. Fauces, or passage giving access to the garden when the tablinum was closed. 28. Narrow staircase, probably leading only to the roof, for the house, judging from the slightness of its walls, can have had no upper story. 29. Probably a bed chamber. It is painted with arabesques, and paved with *opus Signinum* as usual, and contains three pictures worth notice; one of Cephalus and Procris, another of Narcissus, and a third representing a nymph leading a child to Bacchus and Silenus, who initiate him in the use of wine. The room on the other side of the tablinum, 30, may probably have served for a winter triclinium. It is lighted by a large window opening on the garden portico, and is paved in black-and-white mosaic. The disposition of the paintings is remarkable. The plinth is black, relieved by flying Cupids, admirably executed. Above it are architectural arabesques, containing figures of priests, with pateræ and implements of sacrifice, between which there are alternately red and azure panels. The red panels rest upon a blue band and the blue panels on a red band, and the paintings on these bands are varied according to their colour. Upon the red are ferocious animals chasing their prey, or themselves pursued by dogs,

HOUSE OF CASTOR AND POLLUX. 409

or throwing themselves into the water to quench their thirst; on the blue are whimsical aquatic monsters, such as a Triton, with the body of a man and the tail of a lobster, who is driving a sea-horse surrounded by dolphins. Three pictures occupied the centres of the three red compartments, two of which are almost obliterated; the third represents Thetis dipping Achilles in the river Styx. In the blue compartments there still remain a beautiful female playing on the lyre, and a Nereid seated on a Triton's back. She bears a shield, and may be meant for Thetis carrying the armour to Achilles. The upper parts of the walls are more lightly ornamented, and painted on white grounds.

Thetis dipping Achilles in the Styx.

Through the tablinum we enter the peristyle, 31, if the term may be applied to a court like this, which has a colonnade on one side only. The roof was supported by five Doric columns. We spare the reader the details of the paintings here, which are in the same style as those already described; but two dramatic scenes are worthy of notice, which have been represented in Part I., pp. 191, 201. There is also a Phædra and Hippolytus of very good execution. 32. Puteal. 33. Garden, formerly enclosed by a wooden railing, as is proved by vertical channels cut in the pillars to the height of three feet six inches, to receive the uprights. It seems to have been laid out in long straight flower-beds. The wall opposite the tablinum is divided by engaged pillars, and the intermediate spaces filled with paintings representing trees, grass-plots, fishponds, and other accessories of a garden. Immediately opposite the vestibule is an altar, 35, raised before an ædicula, 36, which, from the style of its ornaments, must have been dedicated to the worship of Bacchus. On the right of the garden is a walk, 34, covered by creeping plants trained over a trellis supported on stone blocks, which are still to be seen.

At the other end of the portico is the entrance to a large chamber, 37, which from its size, situation, and elegance, may be supposed to have been occupied by the master of the house. Most of the subjects represented here bear some relation to the chase: there is one in better preservation than the rest, which may represent Meleager or Adonis returned from hunting. 38. Passage leading to 39, a kitchen, intended probably for the private service of the family, to judge from its unusual position in the most elegant and retired part of the house. On the right-hand is a sink, on the left a stair, opposite to which is the fireplace. Fragments of a picture exist, which seem to have represented the goddess Fortune; and there are also two tails of snakes, emblems of the tutelary genii, which, as we have stated in a former chapter, were commonly set up in kitchens as a protection against robbery or wanton insult. 40, 41. Offices. 42, 43. Anteroom and bedchamber, probably meant for the use of some upper servant.

Returning through the tablinum and atrium, we enter the most splendid apartment of the house, called the court of the piscina, from a reservoir of more than common dimensions. The colonnade, 44, is formed by eight columns, four on each side, with angular antæ, and engaged columns at the corners. They are stuccoed and fluted, the lower part of the fluting filled up and painted red, as usual, to the height of four feet eight inches. The diameter at the base is one foot eight inches; at the capital, one foot four inches; the height of the shaft, nine feet eleven inches: the capitals are of stucco, and approximate to the Corinthian order. The whole portico is raised upon a step above the interior court, 45, and the step is painted red. The area of this court was probably partly occupied by flowers, as earth was found here, having a small reservoir, 46, in the centre. The eastern end was

HOUSE OF CASTOR AND POLLUX.

Court of the Piscina of the House of Castor and Pollux; from 'Pompeiana.'

entirely occupied by a large piscina, 47, having in its centre a column, through which the pipe of a fountain still passes. Of this court we give a view, taken, like the view of the atrium, from the second series of Sir W. Gell's Pompeii. It is taken from within the exedra, or triclinium. On the antæ in front were paintings of Perseus and Andromeda, and of

Perseus and Andromeda.

Medea meditating the murder of her children, of which we have given engravings. On the other fronts of these antæ are also paintings; one of a dwarf leading a monkey, engraved in Part I., p. 195; the other a picture of Hygeia. In different parts of the room are other paintings; one is a noble figure

HOUSE OF CASTOR AND POLLUX. 413

of Jupiter. The rest of the walls is occupied, as usual, with a variety of arabesque and capricious ornaments, upon red, white, yellow, and green grounds. This, and the Corinthian atrium, and the peristyle of the house of Meleager, to be described presently, are the most beautiful apartments yet found in Pompeii.

Medea meditating the Murder of her Children.

A noble exedra, or summer triclinium, 48, opens on the upper end of the colonnade. Formerly the pavement was incrusted with precious marbles, as appears from the fragments which have been found, of those scarce and beautiful kinds called rosso and giallo antico, African marble with red spots, and oriental alabaster; but this high-prized ornament has been removed, as is almost invariably the case, by the ancients themselves. Nearly the whole front was open to the court, and might be closed at pleasure by large folding doors, as the marble sockets in which they turned still show. A large window opens on the covered walk beside the garden. The contiguous rooms, 49 and 50, appear to be a bedchamber and anteroom. Two doors open from the triclinium upon a passage, 51, leading from the garden to the servants' apartments at the other end of the house, in which there is a back-door, 52, leading into the lane, 53. 54. Communication with the offices. 55. Entrance to the offices from the Street of Mercury. 56. Tuscan atrium. The inferior finish of this portion of the house shows plainly that it was intended merely for domestic uses. Some persons have supposed it a *hospitium* for the reception of guests. In this case six strangers might have been lodged in the apartments surrounding the atrium, which, with the exedra, would have been common to all. The walls are plainly stuccoed white without any painting; the floor, as usual, is of *opus Signinum*. 57. Impluvium, executed in stone roughly chiselled. 58. Exedra, or hall, painted roughly with landscapes on a black ground. The pavement is *opus Signinum* bordered with a mosaic meander. 59. Kitchen, in which the hearth is distinguishable, and the usual domestic gods are painted above it. 60. Adjoining offices. Above these and the adjoining rooms traces are to be seen of the floor of an upper story, and the doors of communication are still preserved in the walls. The larger apartments, peristyles, atria, &c., were of course much loftier than was necessary for the rooms of servants and offices, so that there might be two stories without the roof of this portion being higher than that of the other. The other rooms on this side of the house appear to have been appropriated to servants, or to have been used as storerooms, &c. Even here the universal taste for paintings is shown by patterns coarsely executed on red and yellow grounds. 61. Court from which the adjoining rooms were lighted. 62. Large room, the ceiling of which appears to have been supported by a central pier, 63. It communicates with the back lane by a broad doorway, large enough to admit a cart, and is conjectured to have been set apart for purposes of household traffic,

HOUSE OF CASTOR AND POLLUX.

Manner of filling the Amphora.

as the laying in of provisions, &c., for which its size and situation seem to adapt it. The other numerous apartments in this quarter of the house are not worth a minute description, being mean and small, and apparently suited only to the occupation of slaves.

Separated from the House of Castor and Pollux by a narrow street, is a house chiefly remarkable for containing pictures of no very decent description. In front it has a thermopolium, or wine-shop; in an inner chamber, full of pictures totally unfit for representation or description, there are two of inoffensive character, which contain some curious details relative to domestic life. One of these represents a winecart, and shows the way of filling the amphoræ, or large earthen vessels in which wine was kept. The clumsy transverse yoke by which the horses are fastened to the pole is worth attention. Another method of yoking them, resembling the modern curricle-bar, is represented in the

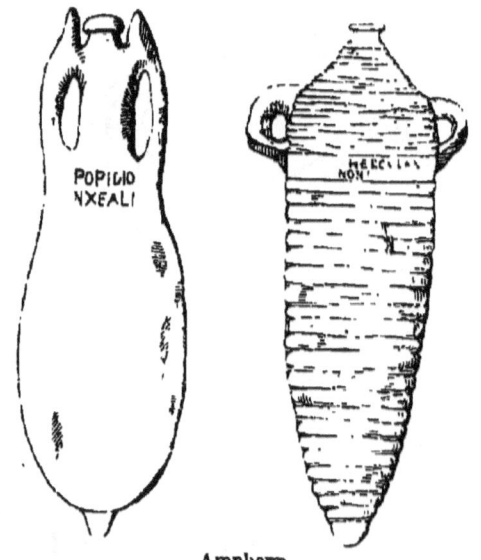

Amphoræ.

head-piece to this chapter. We have also to point out the large skin, occupying the whole of the waggon, and supported by a framework of three hoops. These minutiæ may of course be depended on as copied from the implements in use. The neck of the skin is closed by a ligature, and the wine

HOUSE OF CASTOR AND POLLUX.

is drawn off through the leg, which forms a convenient spout. Two amphoræ may be observed. They are pointed at the bottom, so that they might be stuck into the ground and preserved in an upright position without difficulty. Amphoræ have been found several times thus arranged in the

Drinking Scene.

Pompeian cellars, especially in the suburban villa, and in the House of the Faun, where they may still be seen standing upright, in their original posture.

The other picture represents a drinking scene. Four

figures are seated round a tripod table, hardly higher than the benches. The dress of two of the figures is remarkable for the hoods, which resemble the capotes worn by the Italian sailors and fishermen of the present day. They use horns instead of glasses. Above are different sorts of eatables hung upon a row of pegs. We may conclude, from the style of the figures and of the accommodations represented, that the company which usually frequented this house of entertainment was of a very low class. It is said, however, that excavations of later date have disclosed some interior apartments very superior in elegance and purity to those of which we have already spoken. Nearly opposite to this house several skeletons and articles in gold and silver, brass and earthenware, were found twelve feet above the ancient pavements. These must probably be the remains of some persons who were suffocated by mephitic vapours while searching for valuables among the ruins.

Adjoining to the House of Castor and Pollux, and on the northern side of it, is the House of the Centaur, as it is commonly called upon the spot. This evidently consists of two houses thrown into one. There is only one door of communication between them. The consequence is that there are duplicates, as it were, of all the apartments; and the mansion contains no less than two atria and three peristyles, of considerable size and splendour.

This house, in appearance, character, and general plan, bears so strong a resemblance to the House of the Quæstor that it is unnecessary, and might be tedious, to give a plan of it, and go through a minute examination of the several rooms. Of the two divisions, the northern is the plainer and less handsome, containing the usual suite of vestibule, atrium, tablinum, and peristyle. The Tuscan atrium contains nothing remarkable. Two of the apartments which surround it have evidently been destined for bedchambers, and contain alcoves raised a few inches above the level of the floor, where the beds were placed. In one of them traces are still visible on the ground where heavy furniture has been drawn backwards and forwards. The walls are rusticated, and painted to resemble slabs of different marbles—a gaudy and tasteless practice, which we have elsewhere found occasion to mention. The tablinum was once painted, but little now remains of its ancient decorations. Within it is a peristyle supported by eight columns. One of the angles has been strengthened by a substantial brick pier, erected probably after the earthquake, A.D. 63, which has left everywhere its traces, in the ruin which it produced and in the subsequent restorations. Beyond is a triclinium, the most ornamented room in the house, but the pictures are of inferior quality.

From this, which appears to have been devoted to the inferior members of the family, we descend, by three steps through a doorway broken in the party wall, to the adjoining division, which evidently was at one time a separate house, and is as plainly proved, by its architectural superiority and the number of pictures and mosaics found in it, to have been occupied by a family of wealth and consideration. Upon entering by the above-mentioned doorway, the visitor finds himself in a Corinthian atrium, supported by sixteen columns of somewhat grotesque character, not clearly referable to any order, but bearing some resemblance to the Doric. The apartment is much damaged: it was once richly painted with grotesques upon grounds of various colours. It communicates with the street by a vestibule, which forms a distinct entrance to this portion of the mansion. Communicating with this atrium there is another smaller peristyle on the right, which, in situation and disposition of the adjoining apartments, resembles that excavated many years before in the House of Sallust, and described under the title of the Gynæceum. One of the chambers which open upon the atrium is remarkable for the beauty of its black-and-white mosaic pavement. Beside it there is a small chamber or closet, which has no other opening than a large window to the atrium, above a dwarf wall sixteen inches high, covered with a marble coping, in which the traces of an iron grating are clearly to be seen. There are also, on both sides of the aperture, the marks of locks or latches, from which we may infer that two portions of the grating might be opened or closed at pleasure. The only explanation which we can give of this strange apartment is to suppose that it was the cage of some wild beast; though the chief room of the house seems an odd place for such an inmate.*

---

* Overbeck considers it to have been a sort of storeroom. B. i. S. 305.

420   POMPEII.

Communicating with this atrium is a tablinum, on the walls of which were painted two stories, one of Hercules, the other of Meleager, the one from which the former name of the house was derived. These have been removed to the National Museum. The latter represents the moment at which Meleager presents to Atalanta the boar's head, and his uncles

Meleager returned from Hunting.

are about to take it from her. Meleager sits in the middle of the picture, clothed in a short purple mantle; his sword is suspended by a sash, and in his left hand are two javelins. His head is turned, as if listening to Atalanta, who is leaning on the back of the stone seat on which the hero reposes. At his feet is the head of an immense wild boar and his dogs.

Beside him are his uncles. There is also in this apartment a black frieze, in which are Fauns and Bacchantes in various attitudes, the beauty of which excites a regret that they are not in a higher state of preservation. The floor was mosaic, with pieces of different coloured marbles let into it. The two pilasters which flank the entrance to this apartment are remarkable for containing two little niches painted azure, and intended apparently to receive small statues or some other movable ornament. But the largest and richest apartment of this house is the triclinium, which lies beside the tablinum on the left, and is lighted by a large window opening upon the garden beyond. In the centre of the mosaic pavement is a circle three feet four inches in diameter, containing a noble lion surrounded by Cupids, who are binding him with garlands, while at one side nymphs or Bacchantes look on. It is now in a ruinous condition. The peristyle is small. One circumstance relating to it is worth preserving, because it proves that these small courts were used as gardens : it is said that the remains of shrubs which had been planted here were found during the course of the excavation. This part of the house is completely ruined, for a range of subterranean chambers, used probably as cellars, extends beneath it, and the vaults having fallen in, great part of the garden and peristyle has gone along with them. The wall of the garden had been painted in the style called in a former chapter *opus topiarium*, that is to say, with views of gardens ornamented with railings, fountains, birds, statues, &c. Above these are sea views, containing Nereids as large as life. One of the adjoining rooms is remarkable for a Doric cornice, supported by pilasters with Grecian capitals. Another, and a more beautiful example, has been discovered lately at the entrance of a house opposite to that which we are now describing. These confirm the theory which has been advanced, that the Pompeian architecture is originally of Grecian character, however varied by Roman alterations, and especially by the restorations and improvements consequent upon the great earthquake, sixteen years before the inhumation of the city.

The third house which we have mentioned, that of Meleager, or the Nereids, was uncovered between October, 1830, and May, 1831, and has not, as we believe, been before described, except in the Neapolitan government publication, called the

Museo Borbonico, from which the plan and details here given are extracted. It adjoins the House of the Centaur, and is separated by one dwelling from the city walls, from which its vestibule is only some sixty paces distant. Although not one of the largest, it is one of the handsomest and most

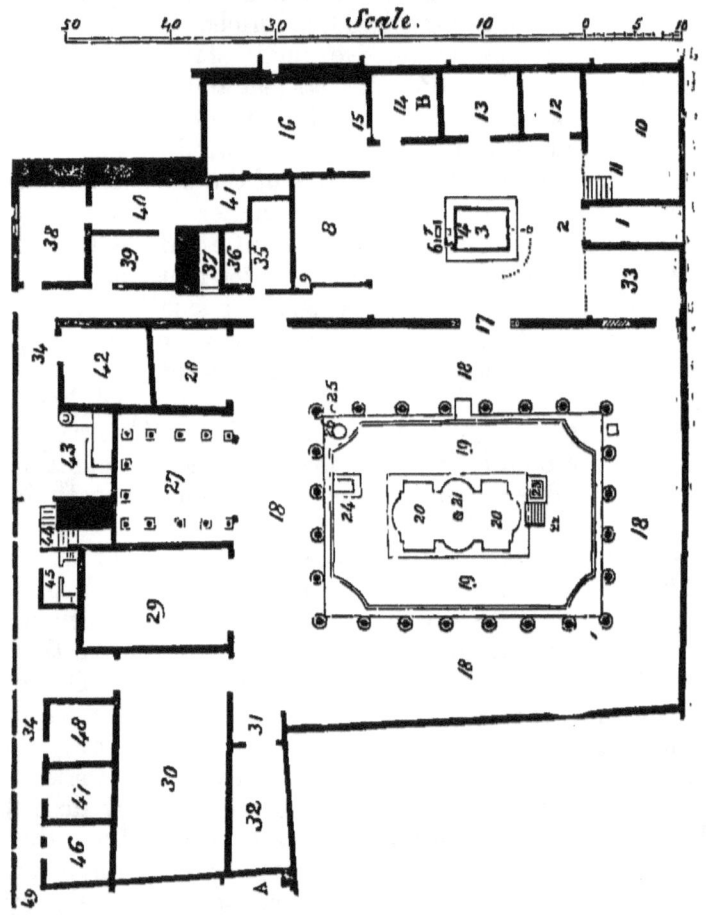

Ground-plan of the House of the Nereids, or Meleager.

charming in Pompeii. The front is covered with a plain white stucco, imitating stone, and resting on a plinth coloured to resemble grey marble, and surmounted by a red fillet. Even in the vestibule we see promise of the abundance of ornament which the mansion contains. The walls are divided into three compartments: the lower, forming the plinth, is black; the centre, red; the upper, white. We may take this opportunity to point out a circumstance which probably has already caught the reader's attention, that in the Pompeian houses the walls are very frequently divided into two or more horizontal bands or compartments of different colours; and that then the darkest colours are almost always placed lowest, the shades becoming lighter as they approach the ceiling. This difference of colour might perhaps be intended to give the effect of greater height and airiness, and the painter further took advantage of it to produce greater variety in his designs. Often the several tiers of colour are charged with arabesques in distinct styles, as indeed in this vestibule, where the black plinth is ornamented with Caryatides bearing javelins, from which depend festoons of fruit and flowers; the red compartment is relieved with architectural arabesques, intermixed with Bacchantes; and in the white the painter has again introduced Caryatides, together with priestesses and architectural designs.

1. Vestibule. 2. Tuscan atrium, paved with *opus Signinum*, intermixed with a more than usual quantity of broken marble. 3. Impluvium. 4. Marble trough. 5, 6. Fountain and marble table, with two hollows, 7, under it, lined with marble, and with marble covers. These probably were meant for wine coolers, and were continually supplied with fresh water from the adjoining fountain, which consists of a rectangular plinth, inlaid with various marbles, among which are dark green serpentine, with lighter spots, and rosso and giallo antico. A small bronze mask was let into the upper part, through which a streamlet spouted into the trough, 4, and thence trickled over into the impluvium. The style of painting is similar to that of the vestibule. A dark red plinth surrounds the room, on which Nereids are painted, reposing on sea-lions and other marine monsters; and from this style of ornament, which is prevalent throughout the whole, the house has received one of its names. Above are architectural arabesques on a black ground—a rare exception to the rule above laid down as to the order in which colours succeed each other. There were several pictures in different parts of the room—Venus, standing by Vulcan, while he

forges armour for Æneas; Dædalus and Pasiphae; Paris and Helen, and some other figures.

Marble Vase, Fountain, and Marble Table in the Atrium of the House of the Nereids.

The tablinum, 8, is paved with *opus Signinum*, enriched with mosaic bands of different patterns. The walls are almost covered with pictures, above which there is a rich frieze, in which are intermingled stucco bas-reliefs and pictures, as in the celebrated baths of Titus at Rome. This is the only example of this kind of decoration yet found in Pompeii; and a conjecture has been made that the decoration of this room was not much anterior to the destruction of the city, since it much resembles that style of ornament which prevailed among the Romans about the time of Vespasian and Titus. Here we find a red plinth, with Nereids, like those in the atrium; above the plinth, a yellow ground with flying figures, and a picture in the centre of each wall.* The subject of one is Isis, of another, Mars and Venus, the third is entirely obliterated. Above this yellow ground is the stuccoed frieze. A small recess, 9, may perhaps have been the lararium. The plan of this house exhibits a deviation from the ordinary practice, inasmuch as the tablinum does

* Now vanished.

not communicate with the peristyle, nor indeed with any apartment except the atrium.

10. Large room, which seems to have been a storeroom, containing a staircase, 11. The small chamber, 12, is remarkable for the beauty of its arabesques, and contained a very pretty picture of Cupid leading Jupiter, in the form of an eagle, to Ganymede, who sleeps profoundly, in an elegant attitude of repose. 13 and 14 are ornamented in the same style, and with the same elegance. These three rooms were probably bedchambers; they were lighted from the atrium by windows placed above the doors. The room, 14, had also a window, 15, looking into the spacious triclinium, 16. This room is chiefly remarkable for three vertical stripes in the wall, roughly plastered over, corresponding with three holes in the pavement; from which appearances it is inferred that the house had been severely shaken in the great earthquake, and that beams, now perished, had been erected in these places to support the superincumbent weight, and relieve the wall.

The atrium communicates with the peristyle, 18, by the door, 17. This arrangement is remarkable as having the peristyle at the side, instead of the back of the atrium, as usual. Owing to the breadth of the aperture, and for the convenience of being able to open or close a part of it, the door was divided into four leaves, which folded back like a window-shutter. This is plain from the holes sunk in the marble threshold. This peristyle is one of the most magnificent and largest apartments yet found in Pompeii. The portico is formed of twenty-four columns, built of bricks and small stones, and coated with stucco. The lower portion of them, as usual, is left unfluted, and is painted red; the upper portion is white. In point of architecture they are irregular, but approximate to the Doric order. Below the abacus is an oval moulding, and under the latter, leaves, on a blue ground. Iron rings are let into the base of each column. To these were attached cords, by means of which an awning could be spread over the impluvium, and the bright glare of day softened at pleasure. We are led to this conclusion by the knowledge that such veils were in common use, as has been formerly mentioned, and by a discovery made in a house recently excavated at Herculaneum, where rings like these were found, together with bars of iron extended along the architrave, between the intercolumniations, which could scarcely have been put to any other purpose than to support a covering. The impluvium, 19, is surrounded by a channel of stone, to collect the rain-water and throw it into the reservoir, 24. It was planted with shrubs and flowers, the roots of which were found. Between the columns were remains of a wooden fence.

The reservoir, 20, is edged with a white marble coping and lined within with stucco, painted with a deep azure, in vivid preservation, resembling cobalt blue. It was fed with a two-fold supply, from a column, 21, in the centre, perforated for a pipe and bronze cock, by which the water could be stopped at pleasure; and from another fountain, 22, which ran down six little steps, forming a diminutive cascade before it reached the reservoir, and gratifying the senses with the sight and sound of falling water, so especially delightful in a sultry climate. The square basin, 23, contiguous to the reservoir, and communicating with it, may have served to preserve the fish, which were probably kept here when it became necessary to empty the larger cistern; or else for the more convenient supply of water to the garden, without damaging the marble border. The mouth of a third cistern, to receive the rain-water, is seen at 24. 25. Puteal, with some remains of a wooden cover. 26. Large earthen pot, containing lime, the presence of which furnishes another reason for supposing that the house was in course of repair at the time of the eruption.

The walls are painted in the same style with those already described. It is remarkable that we again find upon a red plinth the same Nereids accompanied by sea monsters: the owner must surely have had some special reason for his devotion to these marine deities. Of the numerous pictures which once decorated this peristyle some are still visible.

The large apartment, 27, is unique. It will be recollected that according to the descriptions of Vitruvius, the Egyptian oecus differs from the Corinthian, inasmuch as the roof of the latter is supported by one tier of pillars, and all the room is of the same height; while the former has a smaller range of pillars placed above and upon the main range, and is surrounded with a gallery level with the capitals of the lower tier, something like a Gothic church, where the arcades of the nave may represent the lower, the clerestory the upper tier of pillars. We seem to have an example of this method of construction here; but the building does not accurately agree with any of the three kinds of œci described by Vitruvius. The front of the apartment, to the peristyle, is ornamented by four columns of considerably larger diameter than those in the interior, which evidently reached, in a single order, to the height of the two orders which we suppose to have existed within. There is a staircase, 44, at the back of the room, which may have led to the gallery of which we have spoken. The capitals bear some resemblance

Capital from House of the Nereids.

to the Corinthian order. The architraves are not straight, as in pure Greek and Roman architecture, but are formed by a small segment of a circle, upon which the floor of the supposed gallery must have rested. This innovation was a natural consequence of adopting aræostyle intercolumniations. From it, it was a natural step to support arches avowedly on pillars, and abandon straight entablatures—an architectural abuse, as it is termed by critics, which arose among the Romans about the time of Titus, and was much followed by the Byzantines and Goths. The columns and walls of this hall are tinted yellow, and even the pictures are *monochrome*, as it is termed, or painted in one colour, that colour being yellow. This probably was an imitation of that extravagance which made the wealthier Romans cover their walls entirely with gilding. Two of the pictures remain: Theseus conversing with Ariadne after having killed the Minotaur; and, as it should seem, Tiresias, after his transformation into a woman. The floor is mosaic, white bordered with black patterns. Of the two exedræ which flank this noble apartment, 28 is much more plainly decorated than the rest of the house. The cornice is richly wrought in stucco, the rest is a plain white ground; and as it cannot be supposed that this arrangement was intended to be permanent, in the midst of so much splendour, we have a fresh reason for supposing that the eruption of Vesuvius interrupted the restoration of this house. We may also infer, that as the plaster was all laid on at once, it was intended to receive encaustic, or, at all events, not fresco paintings. The exedra, 29, is noble in its proportions, and richly ornamented in the prevailing style.

The great triclinium, 30, is of magnificent dimensions. It has two doors, one to the peristyle, the other to a passage, 34, which traverses the whole breadth of the house. Here again the paintings and the pavement are in the same style which we have described so often in this house, except that there are no Nereids. There is no visible provision for lighting this room, and the day must have been admitted through the roof, or through windows in the upper part of the walls, which, to correspond with the usual lofty proportions of Pompeian rooms, must have been of extraordinary height. There is one well-preserved picture of the Judgment of Paris. 31. Antechamber. 32. Sleeping-room, elegantly painted. 33. Probably the porter's lodge, having two doors, one to the atrium, the other to the peristyle, and two windows, one high and narrow, to the street, the other low and spacious, to the peristyle; so that this room commanded a view of both the chief apartments of resort.

The rest of the house is devoted to humbler purposes and meaner occupiers. The passage, 34, leads from the offices, and communicates with the atrium, the peristyle, and the triclinium. It terminates in a back-door, 49. 35, 36.

HOUSE OF MELEAGER.

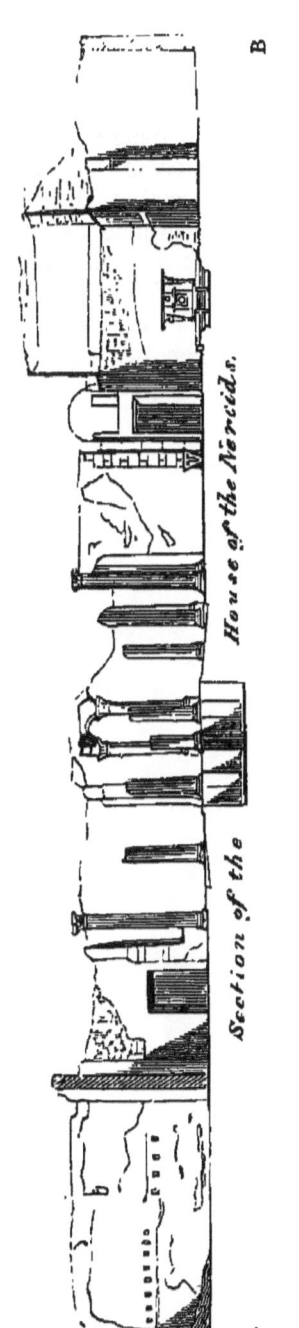

Section of the House of the Nereids.

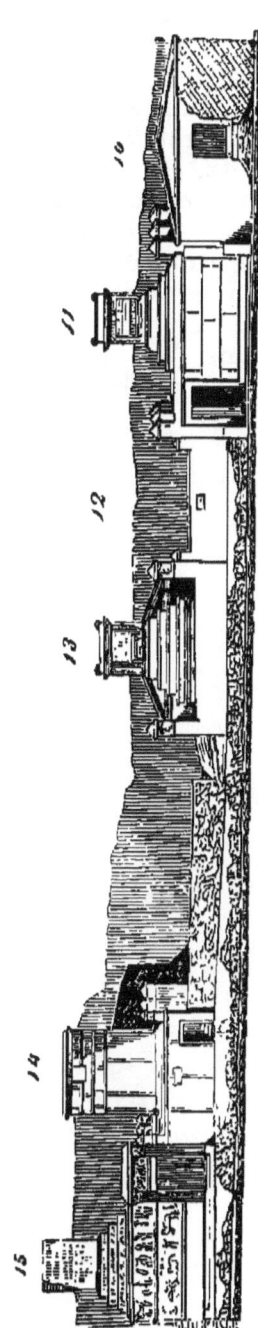

Elevation of part of the Street of Tombs.—See p. 513 to p. 524.

Chamber, and recess for the bed. 37. Inclined plane, terminating in three steps—a very common substitute for a staircase, as in the crypto-portico of Eumachia. 38, 39, 40, 41. Ergastulum, or lodging of the slaves, as is conjectured from the retired situation, the total absence of ornament, and the little light which could have been received by those rooms. 42. A chamber of a better order, which from its neighbourhood to the kitchen was probably occupied by some head servant. 43. Kitchen, open to the passage. Above the hearth is painted a serpent, twined round a tripod, and two *camilli*, or servants of the priest, about to assist at a sacrifice. 45. Sink, &c. 46, 47, 48. Mean rooms, probably occupied by servants. We give a section of the house on p. 429, drawn from A to B on the plan.*

* The section below refers to the tombs.

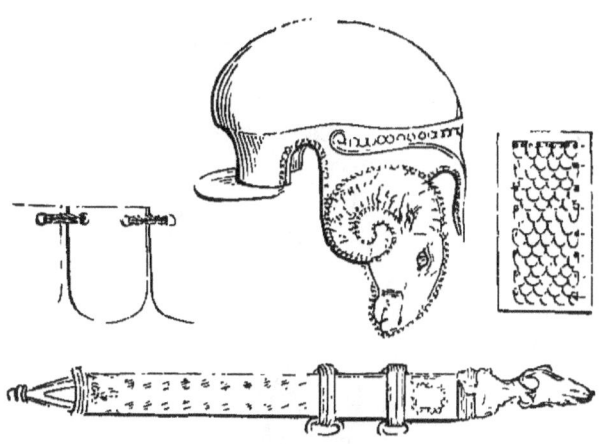

CHAPTER IX.

SURVEY OF THE REMAINDER OF THE CITY.—INSCRIPTIONS AND GRAFFITI.—CASTS OF BODIES.

PROCEEDING southward along the Street of Mercury, we pass under the triumphal arch of Nero, and crossing the transverse street which leads towards the Gate of Nola, enter the Street of the Forum, a continuation of the Street of Mercury, leading straight to the triumphal arch at the north end of the Forum, and bounding the island of the baths on the eastern side. This street is one of the most spacious in Pompeii, being twenty-two feet wide and about two hundred feet long. We have given, in the first part of this work, a long catalogue of articles found here in the course of excavation. One of the houses about the centre of the street, nearly opposite the entrance to the Thermæ, is of more consequence than the rest, and has been named the House of Bacchus, from a large painting of that god on a door opposite to the entry. Channels for the introduction of water were found in the atrium, which has been surrounded by a small trough, formed to contain flowers, the outer side of which is painted blue, to imitate water, with boats floating upon it. The wall behind this is painted with pillars, between which are balustrades of various forms. Cranes and other birds perch upon these, and there is a background of reeds and other vegetables, above which

Bacchus, from a painting.

the sky is visible. The greater portion of the eastern side of the street is occupied by a row of shops with a portico in front of them. It is flanked on either side by footpaths, and must have presented a noble appearance when terminated by triumphal arches at either end, and overlooked by the splendid

Temple of Jupiter and that of Fortune elevated on its lofty basis. It is to be noticed that the last-named edifice does not stand symmetrically either with the Street of the Forum or with the Street of the Baths running past the House of Pansa. "The portico," we quote again from Gell, "is turned a little towards the Forum, and the front of the temple is so contrived that a part of it might be seen also from the other street. It is highly probable that these circumstances are the result of design rather than of chance. The Greeks seem to have preferred the view of a magnificent building from a corner, and there is scarcely a right-angled plan to be found either in ancient or modern Italy."* In the Street of the Forum has been established a temporary museum of articles found in Pompeii. Adjoining it is a library containing all the best works that have been written on the city.

The street running westward between the baths and the Forum presents nothing remarkable, except that in it are the signs of the milk-shop and school of gladiators above described. There is also an altar, probably dedicated to Jupiter, placed against the wall of a house; above it is a bas-relief in stucco, with an eagle in the tympanum. Eastward of the Forum this street assumes the name of the Street of Dried Fruits, from an inscription showing that dried fruits were sold in it; and, indeed, a considerable quantity of figs, raisins, chesnuts, plums, hempseed, and similar articles were found. It is now however usually called the Street of the Augustals. Near the point at which this street is intersected by that of Eumachia, running at the back of the east side of the Forum, there is a remarkably graceful painting of a youthful Bacchus pressing the juice of the grape into a vase placed upon a pillar, at the foot of which is a rampant animal expecting the liquor, apparently meant for a tiger or panther, but of very diminutive size. This picture is one foot five inches high and one foot two inches wide. It probably served for the sign of a wine-merchant. Corresponding with it, on the other side of the shop, is a painting of Mercury, to render that knavish god propitious to the owner's trade.

We will now proceed to the Street of Abundance, or of the

---

* Pompeiana, Second Series, vol. i. p. 70.

Stone Doorway in the Street of the Silversmiths.

Merchants, formerly called the Street of the Silversmiths. This is about twenty-eight feet wide, and bordered on each side by footpaths about six feet wide, which are described as made in several places of a hard plaster, probably analogous to *opus Signinum*. At the end next the Forum it is blocked up by two steps, which deny access to wheel carriages, and is in other parts so much encumbered by large stepping-stones that the passage of such vehicles, if not prohibited, must have been difficult and inconvenient.

We may here take notice of a peculiarity in this street. It slopes with a very gentle descent away from the Forum, and the courses of masonry, instead of being laid horizontally, run parallel to the slope of the ground, a unique instance, as we believe, of such a construction. We give a view of a handsome and (which is rare in Pompeii) a perfect doorway of stone, copied from the second series of Sir W. Gell's Pompeii.* Above it part of a window still remains. In front the reader will observe the stepping-stones of which we have spoken. On the right-hand of the vestibule a monkey is painted playing on the double pipe, as if he were the guardian of the entry. The doors of several shops in this street have left perfect impressions on the volcanic deposit, by which it appears that the planks of which they were made lapped one over the other, like the planks of a boat.

Although the houses that line this street have now been cleared, there still remains a large unexcavated space on its southern side. The only house requiring notice is that called the Casa del Cinghiale, or House of the Wild Boar, a little way down on the right-hand side in going from the Forum. Its name is derived from the mosaic pavement of the prothyrum, representing a boar attacked by two dogs. The house is remarkable for its well-preserved peristyle of fourteen Ionic columns, with their capitals. On the right is a brick staircase leading to a large garden. The atrium is bordered with a mosaic representing the walls of a city with towers and battlements, supposed by some to be the walls of Pompeii.

Just beyond this house is a small street or lane, turning down to the right, called the *Vicolo dei Dodici Dei*, from a

---

* The visitor will now look for it in vain.

painting on the outside wall of the corner house, in the manner of a frieze, representing the twelve greater divinities. Below is the usual painting of serpents. At the corner of the quadrivium is the apothecary's shop, in which was a large collection of surgical instruments, mortars, drugs, and pills. The house is not otherwise remarkable.

Of the early excavations at the southern extremity of the town few records are preserved. In the Quarter of the Theatres, besides the public buildings, which have been fully

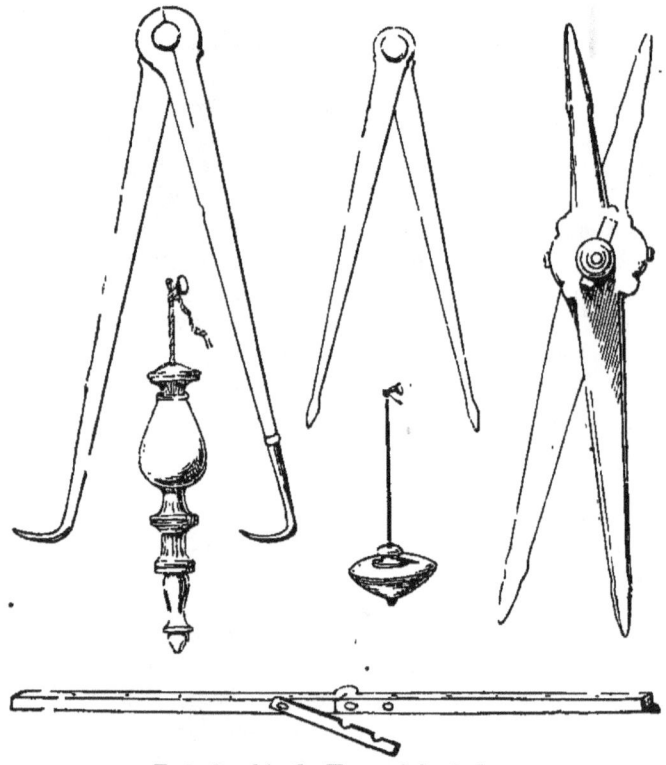

Tools found in the House of the Sculptor.

described, there are but two houses of any interest. These occupy the space between the Temple of Æsculapius and the small theatre. The easternmost of them is one of the most interesting yet discovered in Pompeii, not for the beauty or curiosity of the building itself, but for its contents, which prove it to have been the abode of a sculptor. Here were found statues, some half finished, others just begun, with blocks of marble, and all the tools required by the artist. Among these were thirty-two mallets, many compasses, curved and straight, a great quantity of chisels, three or four levers, jacks for raising blocks, saws, &c., &c. The house has the usual arrangement of atrium, tablinum, and peristyle, but, owing to the inclination of the ground, the peristyle is on a higher level than the public part of the house, and communicates with it by a flight of steps. A large reservoir for water extended under the peristyle, which was in good preservation when first found, but has been much injured by the failure of the vault beneath.

Returning by the southernmost of the two roads which lead to the Forum, we find, beside the wall of the triangular Forum as it is called, one of the most remarkable houses in Pompeii, if not for its size, at least for its construction. The excavations here made were begun in April, 1769, in the presence of the Emperor Joseph II., after whom this house has been named; but after curiosity was satisfied, they were filled up again with rubbish, as was then usual, and vines and poplars covered them almost entirely at the time when Mazois examined the place, insomuch that the underground stories were all that he could personally observe. The emperor was accompanied in his visit by his celebrated minister, Count Kaunitz, the king and queen of Naples, Sir William Hamilton, the English ambassador at Naples, and one or two distinguished antiquaries. This was one of the first private dwellings excavated at Pompeii. It appears to have been a mansion of considerable magnificence, and, from its elevated position, must have commanded a fine view over the Bay of Naples towards Sorrento. The "find" was so good on the occasion of the emperor's visit, as to excite his suspicion of some deceit. The numerous articles turned up afforded Sir W. Hamilton an opportunity to display his antiquarian knowledge. Joseph appears to have been rather disgusted on hearing that only thirty men were employed on the excavations, and insisted that three thousand were necessary.* We give a plan of the three stories in one.

* *Hist. Pomp. Antiq.*, t. i. p. 228, *seq.*

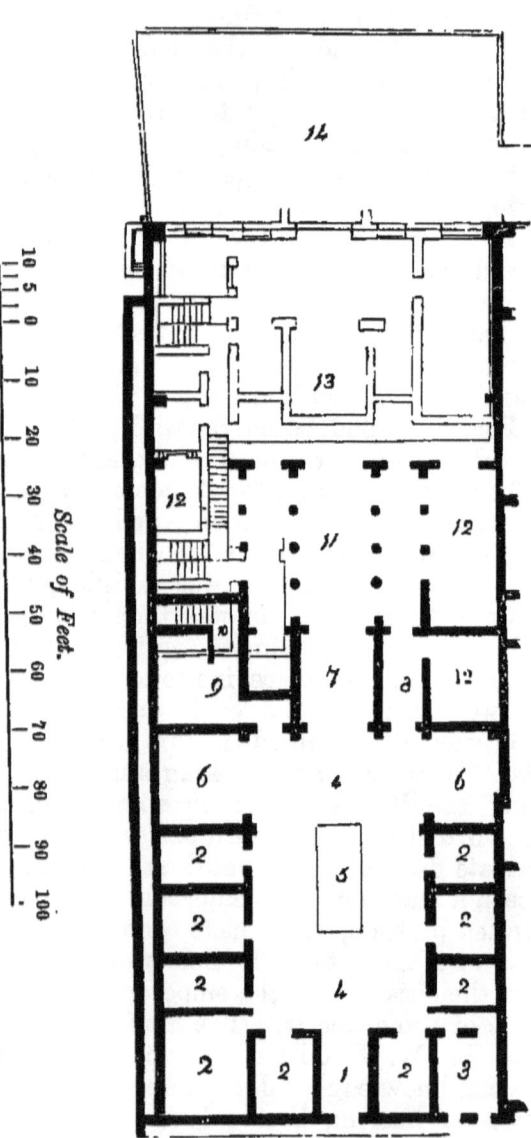

Ground-plan of the House of Joseph II.

HOUSE OF JOSEPH II.

1. Prothyrum. 2. Several rooms surrounding the atrium.
3. Probably a shop. 4. Tuscan atrium. 5. Impluvium.
6. Alæ. 7. Tablinum. 8. Fauces. 9. Antechamber to 10, the staircase which communicates with the lower stories situated under the terrace. 11. This portion of the house had the arrangement and the magnificence of a private basilica. It may probably be considered as a specimen of the Corinthian œcus, which Vitruvius describes as containing a single order of columns supporting an entablature and vaulted roof. 12. Rooms for different uses. All this suite of apartments was on a level with the street, and seems to have been the public part of the house. The effect produced upon the visitor of this princely mansion must have been very striking, when, at first entrance, he saw through the long perspective of the atrium and this noble hall one of the most beautiful landscapes which the world can afford; for the back part of this house is situated on a declivity which anciently sloped down towards the sea, and commanded an uninterrupted view over the bay, towards Stabiæ. 13, 14. Terraces at different elevations. Beneath the terrace attached to the upper floor there was a lower story containing several rooms, which probably were those chiefly devoted to domestic use. One of these was a triclinium, as is indicated by a little oven or stove in one corner, evidently intended for the service of the table. There was also a handsome suite of three rooms, well adapted for the assembling the family or the reception of friends, commanding that delightful view which marks out the brow of this hill as the most enviable situation in the whole town. A second terrace, 14, extends in front of these rooms, below which terrace there is yet a suite of baths. The approach to them is by a staircase, terminated by an inclined plane. We find the usual apparatus of a furnace-room, apodyterium, tepidarium, and caldarium, or sudatorium, but little remains which can illustrate the subject of private baths. The most remarkable part of them is the sudatorium, which in its plan resembles the frigidarium of the Thermæ, being a circular room with four niches, serving as seats, hollowed out in the wall. The vault is conical, terminating in a long tube which is carried up to the terrace floor, and there terminated by a movable stone plug, serving as a ventilator, to give free exit at pleasure to the heated air and vapour. These

curious baths were covered in again in part by the rubbish thrown out from the excavations of the triangular Forum. It was then remarked that the subterranean apartments, in which there was formerly no trace whatever of mephitic vapour, became foul after they were encumbered with *lapilli*, as the small volcanic substances are called with which Pompeii is covered. The subterranean vaults of the amphitheatre were also so impregnated with unwholesome gas before they were cleared, that Mazois, while examining them, encountered a heavy whitish vapour, which rose slowly, and affected his respiration so much that he was compelled to make a hasty retreat before it reached the level of his mouth. It would seem from these observations, that the mephitic air so common in the volcanic district of Naples resides principally in the beds of ashes and scoriæ, and is disengaged by the action of heat and moisture. A skeleton was discovered in the furnace-room of these baths.

Returning westward towards the Forum, we pass by other houses of the same character, consisting of two or three stories, half built, half excavated, on the side of the hill; but they have not been described with minuteness enough to furnish us with anything worth narrating. On the right hand is the house already described under the name of Casa Carolina. We enter the Forum at its south-eastern angle. The south-western corner of the town, between the Forum and the declivity of the hill, has been but partially excavated; and the only houses worthy of notice are two which were excavated by General Championet, while in command of the French troops in occupation of Naples. They lie contiguous to one another, and close to the basilica. Without being large, they impress us, by the elegance of their decoration, with the idea that they belonged to wealthy and cultivated persons. One of them consists of a prothyrum, Tuscan atrium, peristyle, and the usual apartments upon a small scale, and is scarcely worth a minute description: the other is more remarkable, though not larger.

A prothyrum leads from the narrow street which runs beside the basilica into a tetrastyle atrium. The columns have evidently been composed of old materials worked up again, and stuccoed over to make a fair show. At the foot of one where this coating is broken away, part of the fluted shaft of a former column is to be seen surmounted by brickwork, and the upper parts of the others are composed of alternate courses of brick and stone. In the centre is a marble impluvium with a well-hole; the edges of the impluvium are surrounded by mosaic of different patterns. The lower part of the columns has been painted, as usual, of some dark colour. Around this apartment a triclinium, hall, and other rooms are disposed. An open tablinum intervened between the atrium and the peristyle, which enclosed a diminutive xystus, or garden. The most remarkable thing in it is, that apertures

Tetrastyle Atrium of a House excavated by Gen. Championet.

are cut in the basement or pluteum which supported the pillars of the peristyle, to give light to a subterranean set of apartments, accessible either from the peristyle by a staircase, or from the street by a long sloping passage. A chamber which looks upon the peristyle is remarkable for the elegance of its decorations. Around the lower parts of the walls there runs a broad skirting of a deep red, relieved by paintings of flowers, and minute borders and ornaments. The upper part is of a brilliant celestial blue, divided into compartments by broad borders and arabesques, in the centre of which compartments are medallions containing figures of elegant design and execution. Flying Cupids, with peacocks, doves, and other animals, appear to be the favourite subjects.

We have now surveyed, besides the temples and public buildings, all that part of the city lying between the Gate of Herculaneum and adjacent wall on the north, the Street of the Baths and Street of Fortune on the south, the boundary of the city on the west, and the islands containing the House of the Faun and the House of the Labyrinth on the east. We have also taken a view of the Street of the Forum and that of Abundance, together with the houses lying to the southward and westward of the latter. Before proceeding to describe the rest of the city, so far as it has been excavated, it may be as well to lay down a few general landmarks, which will serve to make the description more readily understood.

In continuation of the Street of the Baths and that of Fortune, a long street, called the Street of Nola, runs in an easterly direction to the gate of the same name. The houses that line this street have been partially excavated, but as they did not promise much that would reward research, the excavation of them was abandoned.

The line of streets just described, intersecting the city from west to east, is cut near its centre by another long street running from the Gate of Vesuvius on the north to the Gate of Stabiæ on the south, a little beyond the theatres and the barracks of the gladiators. This street, which, so far as it is cleared, is called the Street of Stabiæ, bounds the excavations to the east, though some of the houses lining its eastern side, and among them one or two remarkable ones, have been cleared. But on its western side are some of the most recent excavations, which we will now proceed to describe.

The Street of Fortune on the north, that of the Augustals on the south, that of the Forum on the west, and that of Stabiæ on the east, form a large isolated district, or insula, intersected, however, by one or two minor streets, as the Vico Storto, a narrow crooked lane running north and south, and another small street leading from the middle of the Vico Storto to the Street of Stabiæ.

On the northern side of the island just defined, and eastward of the Temple of Fortune, lie three noticeable houses, namely, the House of the Black Walls, the House of the Figured Capitals, and the House of the Grand Duke; but they do not offer such striking peculiarities as to require any detailed description here. The next house to the east of these, known as the House of the Coloured Capitals, or of Ariadne, is of considerable size and elegance. It derives its first name from the columns of the peristyle, the capitals of which were painted in bright colours; the other name is taken from a picture in a room next to the tablinum, representing the abandonment of Ariadne. The arrangement of this house is singular. It has two entrances, one in the Street of Fortune, the other in the Street of the Augustals; so that on whichever side the visitor enters, he has before him the usual suite of rooms of a Pompeian house, namely, an atrium terminated by a tablinum, and a peristyle beyond.

The entrance from the Street of Fortune leads into a magnificent Corinthian atrium, with twenty-four columns of the Tuscan order on two of which may still be seen a vestige of the entablature. The atrium is upwards of eighty feet long and forty-three broad. The intercolumniations could be closed with curtains, as was also the case in the House of the Faun. The area, besides a small compluvium, has in the corner a curious design, intended perhaps for a flower-bed, consisting of bricks disposed so as to form four concentric circles within three rectangles. The apartments surrounding the atrium are small and undecorated, except the wing (there is only one), the lintel of which is supported by two columns. Before it is a marble *puteal*, the sides much worn with the cord. In a room on the left of the tablinum is the picture of Ariadne abandoned.

The peristyle was supported by sixteen Ionic columns, the lower third of which is painted yellow. The capitals, as we have said, were brilliantly coloured. In the centre is a large quadrangular basin, sixteen feet long by about six broad, and three feet three inches deep. In the middle of it is a hollow column which threw up a *jet d'eau*. The peristyle had two puteals. The chief paintings with which its walls were adorned have been carried to the Museum. The second chamber on the right, after entering from the tablinum, has paintings of the Battles of the Storks and Pigmies. In a sort of wing on the same side were depicted Venus and Adonis, and a love merchant, or man selling little Cupids. On the floor of the room next to it is a fine and well preserved mosaic of fish. At the bottom of the peristyle, instead of the usual exedra, is another tablinum, belonging to the second atrium beyond. An apartment on the left, entered from the corridor, or fauces, has pictures of Ganymede feeding the eagle of Jove, the Triumph of Galatea, the Dioscuri, and Perseus shewing to Andromeda the head of Medusa, with several female figures, architecture, &c., above. Only the second and third of these pictures now remain *in situ*, and are in a tolerable state of preservation. In the middle of the left side of the peristyle is a large apartment, intended apparently to supply the place of the missing exedra. The bottom of it forms a hemicycle, with a niche for a statue. Among the pictures which decorated it may be discerned a Sacrifice, Leda and the Swan, a priestess receiving an offering, Apollo playing on the lyre before a woman and a young man armed with a sword.

Passing the tablinum, we enter the second, or Tuscan, atrium. It is in a ruinous state. One of its wings has a lararium, and a well-preserved picture of Apollo and Daphne. The prothyrum, forming the entrance to the Street of the Augustals, has a shop on either side, one of which forms the angle of the Vico Storto.

The house at the angle of the Vico Storto and Street of Fortune has obtained the name of *Casa della Caccia*, from a great painting on the wall of the peristyle representing a combat with wild beasts in the amphitheatre. The space between the Vico Storto and the Street of Stabiæ remains for the most part unexcavated.

Passing on to the insula bounded on the north by the Street of Holconius, on the south by the Street of Isis, on the west by the Street of the Theatres, and on the east by that of Stabiæ, we find two remarkable houses excavated within the last few years. That at the northern corner of the Street of the Theatres, numbered 4 on the entrance, is sometimes called the House of Holconius. It was excavated in 1861. The interior is represented in the annexed engraving. The two shops which precede it, numbered 2 and 3, seem to have been the property of the master of the house, and communicate with each other. A third shop, numbered 1, at the angle of the street, appears to have been occupied by a dyer, and is called Taberna Offectoris.* On

House of Holconius.

the front of the house were some inscriptions for electioneering purposes.

* Fiorelli, *Giornale degli Scavi*, No. 1, p. 11.

The pilasters on either side of the main entrance are painted red to about the height of a man, beyond which they are of white plaster. On entering the prothyrum may be observed a large hole in the wall, destined for the reception of the *repagulum*, or strong wooden bar with which the door was secured. The door appears, from the places for bolts on the threshold, to have been composed of two pieces (bifora). The walls of the prothyrum are painted black, with a red podium, divided into three compartments by green and yellow lines, in the middle of which are an aquatic bird, perhaps an *ibis*, a swan with spread wings, and an ornament that cannot be made out. Towards the top the walls are painted with fantastic pieces of architecture on a white ground; amidst which, on one side, is a nymph descending apparently from heaven. She has a golden-coloured vest, on her shoulders is a veil agitated by the breeze, and she bears in her hand a large dish filled with fruits and herbs. On the other side was a similar figure, playing on the lyre, with a sky-blue vest and rose-coloured veil that fluttered about her. The remaining architectural paintings contained little winged Cupids, one holding a cornucopia, another a drum, and two with baskets of fruit and flowers. These were the good geniuses, which, by being depicted at the entrance of a house, repelled all evil influences and rendered it a joyful abode.*

The pavement of the Tuscan atrium is variegated with small pieces of white marble placed in rows. The impluvium in the middle appears to have been under repair, as it is stripped of its marble lining. The walls of the atrium are painted red, with vertical black zones like pilasters, or *antæ*, besides lines and ornaments of various colours. On the wall to the left of the entrance is painted a recumbent Silenus, crowned with ivy, and pressing in his arms the little Bacchus, who in alarm is endeavouring to escape from his embraces. Near it, on a yellow ground, is the bearded head of a man, with two claws projecting from his temples like horns, and a beard floating as if it was in the water. It may probably be a mask of Oceanus, who is represented on coins of Agrigentum in a somewhat similar manner. Under the head is the figure of a hippocampus.

* Fiorelli, *Giornale degli Scavi*, p. 15.

Necklace of Amulets found on a Female Skeleton at Pompeii.
Now in the National Museum, Naples.

A . Canopic Vases
B . Isis, terminal Figure.
C . Hands, symbol of Isis
D . Jackal, attribute of Anubis
E . Hand, making an obscene gesture a potent charm against the Evil Eye
F . Grape-bunch of Bacchus
G . Silenus, terminal Figure, or Osiris
H . An Astragalus
I . Bell
J . Dice
K . Phallus (quiescent)
L . Trochus
M . Bucchio Panther
N . Cigala, a talisman, worn in their hair by the primitive Athenians
P . Pine-cone

Many objects were found in this atrium, some at the height of four or five yards from the floor, which must consequently have fallen in from the upper stories; and others on the pavement itself. But one of the most important discoveries was the skeleton of a woman, near the entrance of the tablinum. She appears to have been in the act of flight, and had with her a small box containing her valuables and nicknacks. Among the most curious of these was a necklace composed of amulets, or charms, which, it will be observed, are all attributes of Isis and her attendant, Anubis, or of her husband Osiris, here considered as Bacchus. The mystic articles kept in the Isiac coffer were, says Eusebius, a ball, dice, (*turbo*) wheel, mirror, lock of wool.* The annexed cut will convey a better idea of this necklace than any description of it.

The first bedchamber on the right of the atrium communicated with the shop No. 3, and was probably occupied by the slave who conducted the business of it. The first bedchamber on the left had a similar communication with the shop outside.

There are few houses in Pompeii in which the paintings are more numerous or better preserved than in that which we are examining. The second bedchamber on the right has several. In this room may be observed a space hollowed in the wall to receive the foot of a bed or couch. The walls are white, with a red podium, and are surmounted by a cornice from which springs the vault. The upper part is painted with lines, between which are depicted griffins in repose, baskets with thyrsi, branches of herbs, and other objects. The lower part of the walls is divided into larger compartments by candelabra supporting little globes. In each compartment are eight small pictures, representing the heads and busts of Bacchic personages, in a very good state of preservation. On the left is Bacchus crowned with ivy, his head covered with the *mitra*, a sort of veil of fine texture which descends upon his left shoulder. This ornament, as well as the cast of his features, reveals the half feminine nature of the deity. Opposite to him is the picture of Ariadne, also crowned with ivy, clothed in a green *chiton* and a violet

* For the explanation of the necklace, the editor is indebted to the kindness of the Rev. C. W. King, of Trinity College, Cambridge.

himation. She presses to her bosom the infant Iacchus, crowned with the eternal ivy, and bearing in his hand the thyrsus. Then follow Bacchic or Panic figures, some conversing, some drinking together, some moving apparently in the mazes of the dance. Paris, with the Phrygian cap and crook, seems to preside over this voluptuous scene, and to listen to a little Cupid seated on his shoulder.

In the chamber on the opposite side of the atrium, fronting that just described, were also four pictures, two of which are destroyed, the walls having apparently been broken through, not long after the destruction of Pompeii, by persons in search of their buried property. Of the other two, which are almost effaced, one represents an aged Faun, holding in his hands a thyrsus and a vase; the other a young woman conversing with an African slave. A wooden chest seems to have stood close to the left-hand wall.

The left *ala*, or wing, has its walls painted in yellow and red compartments, with a black podium. In the middle of each was a valuable painting, but these, with the exception of the greater part of one fronting the entrance, have been almost destroyed. The one saved represents Apollo, who has overtaken Daphne, and is clasping her in his arms, while the nymph, who has fallen on her knees, repels the embraces of the deity. A malicious little Cupid, standing on tiptoes, draws aside the golden-tissued veil which covered the nymph, and displays her naked form. On the left of the same apartment is a picture, almost effaced, of Perseus and Andromeda; and on the right another with three male figures, of which only the lower part remains.

The right *ala*, which, however, from its capability of being closed with a door, does not properly come under that denomination, seems, from various culinary utensils of metal and earthenware found in it, to have served as a kitchen, or rather perhaps as a store-closet.

The tablinum, opposite the entrance, and, as usual, without any enclosure on the side of the atrium, has a small marble threshold, and on its floor little squares of coloured marbles surrounded with a mosaic border. The yellow walls, divided into compartments by vertical stripes of red, white, and black, were beautifully ornamented with the usual architectural designs and flying figures. On each side

HOUSE OF HOLCONIUS.

were two larger pictures, of which only that on the left of the spectator remains. It represents Leda showing to Tyndareus a nest containing the two boys produced from the egg. A stucco cornice runs round the wall, above which a flying nymph is painted on a white ground, between two balconies,.from which a man and woman are looking down. There are also figures of sphinxes, goats, &c.

A wooden staircase on the left of the tablinum, the first step being of stone, led to the floor above. On the right is the passage called *fauces*, leading to the peristyle. On its left-hand side, near the ground, was a rudely traced figure of a gladiator, with an inscription above, of which only the first letters, PRIMI, remain. On the left wall of the fauces, near the extremity, and level with the eye, is another inscription, or *graffito*, in small characters, difficult to be deciphered from the unusual *nexus* of the letters, but which the learned have supposed to express the design of an invalid to get rid of the pains in his limbs by bathing them in water.

At the extremity of the *fauces*, on the right, there is an entrance to a room which has also another door leading into the portico of the peristyle. The walls are painted black and red, and in the compartments are depicted birds, animals, fruits, &c. Two skeletons were found in this room. In the apartment to the left, or east of the tablinum, of which the destination cannot be certainly determined, the walls are also painted black, with architectural designs in the middle, and figures of winged Cupids variously employed. On the larger walls are two paintings, of which that on the right represents the often repeated subject of Ariadne, who, just awakened from sleep, and supported by a female figure with wings, supposed to be Nemesis, views with an attitude of grief and stupor the departing ship of Theseus, already far from Naxos. On the left side is a picture of Phryxus, crossing the sea on the ram and stretching out his arms to Helle, who has fallen over and appears on the point of drowning. The form of this chamber, twice as long as it is broad (Vitruv. vii. 3), its vicinity to the kitchen, and the window, through which the slaves might easily convey the viands, appear to show that it was a triclinium, or dining-room. The floor, which is lower by a step than the peristyle, is paved with *opus Signinum* and ornamented only at one end with a mosaic. On one of the walls, about ten feet from the floor, is the *graffito*, *Sodales Avete* (Welcome Comrades), which could have been inscribed there only by a person, probably a slave, mounted on a bench or a ladder.

The viridarium, or xystus, surrounded with spacious porticoes, was once filled with the choicest flowers, and refreshed by the grateful murmur of two fountains. One of these in the middle of the peristyle is square, having in its centre a sort of round table from which the water gushed forth. The other fountain, which faces the tablinum, is composed of a little marble staircase, surmounted by the statue of a boy having in his right hand a vase from which the water spirted, and under his left arm a goose. The statue is rather damaged. Many objects were found in the peristyle, mostly of the kind usually discovered in Pompeian houses. Among them was an amphora, having the following epigraph in black paint:—

COUM. GRAN.
OF.
ROMÆ. ATERIO. FELICI.

which has been interpreted to mean that it contained Coan wine flavoured with pomegranate, and that it came from Rome, from the stores of Aterius Felix.*

The portico is surrounded by strong columns, and seems to have had a second order resting on the first, as may be inferred from some indications to the right of him who enters from the *fauces*. The walls are painted red and black, with architectural designs, candelabra, meanders, birds, winged Cupids, &c. There are also fourteen small pictures enclosed in red lines, eight of which represent landscapes and sea-shores, with fishermen, and the other six fruits and eatables. On the wall on the right side is the following *graffito*, or inscription, scratched with some sharp instrument:

IIX. ID. IVL. AXVNGIA. PCC.
ALIV. MANVPLOS. CCL.

That is: "On the 7th July, hog's lard, two hundred pounds, Garlic, two hundred bunches." It seems therefore to be a domestic memorandum of articles either bought or sold. Around the portico are several rooms, all having marble

---

* Fiorelli, *Giornale*, No. 2, p. 48.

thresholds, and closed by doors turning on bronze hinges. On the right hand of the peristyle, near the entrance, is a private door, or *posticum*, leading into the Street of the Theatres, by which the master of the house might escape his importunate clients.

The rooms at the sides of the peristyle offer nothing remarkable, but the three chambers opposite to the tablinum are of considerable size, and contain some good pictures. The first on the right has two figures of Nereids traversing the sea, one on a sea-bull the other on a hippocampus. Both the monsters are guided by a Cupid with reins and whip, and followed by dolphins. Another painting opposite the entrance is too much effaced to be made out. The same wall has a feature not observed in any other Pompeian house, namely, a square aperture of rather more than a foot reaching down to the floor, and opening upon an enclosed place with a canal or drain for carrying off the water of the adjoining houses. It seems also to have been a receptacle for lamps, several of which were found there.

Adjoining this room is a large *exedra* with a little *impluvium* in the middle, which seems to indicate an aperture in the roof, a construction hitherto found only in *atria*. The absence of any channels in the floor for conducting water seems to show that it could not have been a fountain. This exedra is remarkable for its paintings. In the wall in front is depicted Narcissus with a javelin in his hand, leaning over a rock and admiring himself in the water, in which his image is reflected; but great part of the painting is destroyed. A little Cupid is extinguishing his torch in the stream. In the background is a building with an image of the bearded Bacchus; and near it a terminal figure of Priapus Ithyphallicus, with grapes and other fruits. This picture was much damaged in the process of excavation.

On the left wall is a painting of a naked Hermaphroditus. In his right hand is a little torch reversed; his left arm rests on the shoulders of Silenus, who appears to accompany his songs on the lyre, whilst a winged Cupid sounds the double flute. On the other side is a Bacchante with a thyrsus and tambourine, and near her a little Satyr, who also holds a torch reversed.

But the best picture in this apartment is that representing

Ariadne discovered by Bacchus. A youthful figure with wings, supposed to represent Sleep, stands at Ariadne's head, and seems to indicate that she is under his influence. Meanwhile a little Faun lifts the veil that covers her, and with an attitude indicating surprise at her beauty, turns to Bacchus and seems to invite him to contemplate her charms. The deity himself, crowned with ivy and berries, clothed in a short

Bacchus discovering Ariadne.

tunic and a pallium agitated by the breeze, holds in his right hand the thyrsus, and lifts his left in token of admiration. In the background a Bacchante sounds her tympanum, and invites the followers of the god to descend from the mountains. These, preceded by Silenus, obey the summons; one is playing the double flute, another sounding the cymbals, a third bears on her head a basket of fruit. A Faun and a Bacchante, planted on a mountain on the left, survey the scene from a distance. The execution of this picture is so spirited that we have transferred the annexed engraving of it to our pages.

The adjoining triclinium, entered by a door from the exedra, had also three paintings, one of which however is almost destroyed. Of the remaining two, that on the left represents Achilles discovered by Ulysses among the damsels of Lycomedes. The subject of that on the right is the Judgment of Paris. It is more remarkable for its spirit and colouring than for the accuracy of its drawing. This apartment has also six medallions with heads of Bacchic personages.

In the same insula as the house just described, and having its entrance in the same street, stands the house of Cornelius Rufus. It is a handsome dwelling, but as its plan and decorations have nothing to distinguish them from other Pompeian houses, we forbear to describe them. The only remarkable feature in this excavation was the discovery of a Hermes at the bottom of the atrium on the left, on which was a marble bust of the owner, as large as life and well executed, having his name inscribed beneath. As this feature does not occur elsewhere, we have given a cut of the interior of the house on the next page.

Not far from the houses just described, in the Street of Stabiæ, at the angle formed by the street leading to the amphitheatre, stands the house of Apollo Citharœdus, excavated in 1864. It derives its name from a fine bronze statue, as large as life, of Apollo sounding the lyre, which was found there, but has now been placed in the Museum at Naples. In this house the tablinum and a peristyle beyond are on a higher level than the atrium; consequently the *fauces*, or passage leading to the latter, ascends. In the peristyle is a semicircular fountain, on the margin of which were disposed several animals in bronze, representing a hunting scene. In the centre was a wild boar in flight attacked by two dogs; at the sides were placed a lion, a stag, and a serpent. These animals, arranged in the same way in which they were found, are now preserved in the Museum.

An unusual arrangement in this house is a second peristyle at the side of the first, and divided from it by a wall having six windows, and a door at each end. At the bottom of this

House of Cornelius Rufus.

second peristyle are some apartments, of which the furthest on the right-hand side is of considerable size.

At the bottom of the first peristyle, on the right-hand side, is a large door or archway, which forms the entry to a small atrium, having rooms at its sides. On the wall is a picture of the Judgment of Paris, but much inferior in execution to that in the House of Holconius. Some of the adjacent chambers have also paintings. On the left side of the same peristyle is a flight of steps leading to another peristyle on a higher level, and belonging to another house, which has its principal entrance in the street that leads to the amphitheatre.

In the same Street of Stabiæ, and on the same side of the way, but at a considerable distance towards the north, stands another house, numbered 33 on the door, remarkable both for its plan and its decorations. It was excavated in 1847. In

a room of the peristyle was discovered a painting, now removed to the Museum, in which was depicted a writing-tablet, style, inkstand, reed, and seal, with the following words: *M. Lucretio Flam. Martis Decurioni Pompei;* whence it has been inferred that the house belonged to one Marcus Lucretius, a Flamen of Mars and Decurio of Pompeii.

A striking architectural arrangement of this dwelling is, that the peristyle is on a considerably higher level than the atrium and tablinum, so that the spectator immediately on entering is struck with a perspective view of the fountain at the bottom of the peristyle. This house, for its size and decorations, is among the most important in Pompeii, but its

House of Lucretius.

arrangement is irregular and capricious, as will be seen from the annexed ground plan. The front is almost entirely occupied by shops, 1, 2, 3. The prothyrum 5, succeeding the vestibule, 4, is adorned with paintings: that on the right side representing a woman crowned with ivy and playing on the double flute, whilst a drunken man leans on her shoulder; whence the house has sometimes been called the *Casa delle Suonatrici*, or House of the Female Musicians. Opposite this

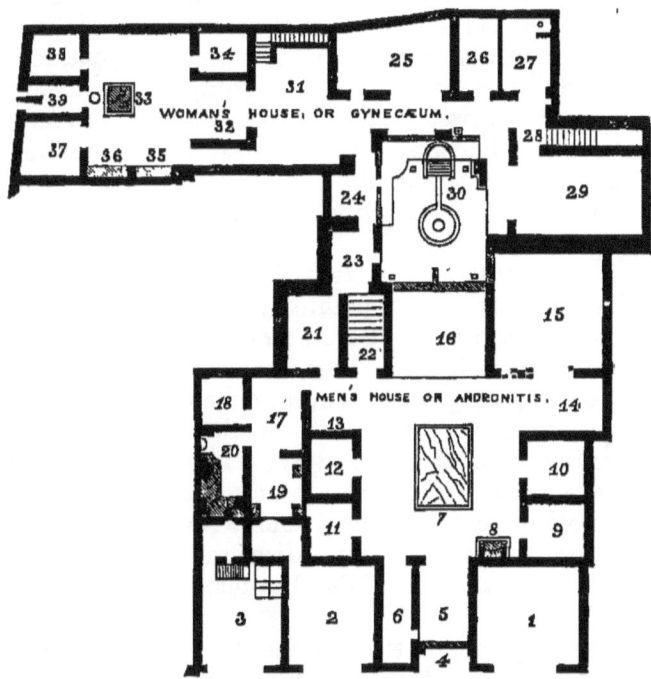

Plan of House of Lucretius.

painting may be observed the lower part of another, representing Ceres with two torches. On the same walls are also three Bacchantes. The floor, which ascends rapidly from the street to the atrium, 7, has a pavement of white and black mosaic. On the left of the prothyrum is the porter's lodge, 6, having a communication with it as well as with the atrium.

The Tuscan atrium is decorated with fantastic architectural views, with tritons, hippocampi, and centaurs. It is surrounded with four bedchambers, 9, 10, 11, 12, two *alœ*, or wings, 13, 14, and the tablinum at the bottom, 16. The impluvium, in rough masonry, appears to have been repairing at the time of the destruction of Pompeii. On the right, after passing the prothyrum, may be observed a lararium, 8, the niche of which, elevated on a base between three and four feet in height, had two columns, and was richly ornamented with coloured stuccos. In it were found three little bronze figures, among them a Hercules. The bedchambers are adorned with paintings. In those on the right are depicted Chiron and Achilles; Thalia and Melpomene; a nymph; Psyche in a long robe, stretching forth her arms towards a lion; Cyparissa seated by her hind, which regards her with affection; Bacchus, with radiated head, and clothed in a woman's robe, placing his foot on an elephant's head, with other figures. Also Cupids and arabesques elegantly executed.

Beyond these chambers the right ala, 14, is entered. The panels of the walls, originally painted yellow, have turned red from the effects of the heat. Seven pictures which originally adorned this apartment have been removed to the Museum. Among those remaining may be observed a Cupid, gracefully holding a crown above his head. A thyrsus and a small fillet are leaning against a large vase, whilst on the ground are cymbals, a tambourine, and a scenic mask. Above this picture is another representing a man with a crown, seated, his legs covered with a chlamys, discoursing with another masked figure. By the side of the first man is a scrinium for books.

A large opening in this wing leads into a magnificent triclinium, 15, which was adorned with three fine paintings, two of which have been removed to the Museum. One of these, with figures as large as life, represented Bacchus in a car drawn by oxen, supported by Silenus, and surrounded by Satyrs and other Bacchic figures. The subject of another picture was Hercules and Omphale; the third, which still remains, represents a Bacchanalian procession: it is near a large window opening on the xystus. It is easy to see that these three pictures, as well as others in the same house, were not painted on the walls but inserted into them.

The two bedchambers on the left of the atrium, 11, 12,

also contained paintings, two of which, representing Narcissus admiring himself in the water, and Phryxus and Helle, have been removed to the Museum. Among those still remaining may be observed two pictures of Venus, a Satyr lifting the robe of a sleeping nymph, Cupid delivering a letter to Polyphemus, medallion heads of Jupiter, Juno, Mars, and Venus, &c. The left wing beyond these chambers, 13, had also paintings, which are now almost effaced. This ala communicated with a kitchen and bakehouse, and other offices, 17, 18, 19, 20. In the kitchen, 20, were found divers culinary utensils, a pastry mould, and a cylindrical iron oven.

The tablinum has a pavement of black and white mosaic, with a centre-piece of coloured marbles, in the middle of which is a round piece of *giallo antico* surrounded with a garland of coloured mosaics. The walls were painted with architectural subjects, and have spaces for two great paintings, which have either been carried away, or had not yet been fixed in their places, at the time when Pompeii was overwhelmed—a proof that the houses were sometimes adorned with moveable pictures.*

To the left of the tablinum are the *fauces*, or corridor, 22, with a flight of eight steps to ascend to the level of the peristyle. On these steps was found a skeleton. The walls are adorned with paintings of birds and masks. On the red part of a pillar at one of the angles of the peristyle was a labyrinth, and the following *graffito* rudely traced with a style : *Labyrinthus. Hic habitat Minotaurus.* The *graffito* is now removed. On the left of this corridor is a sort of store-closet, 21.

The *viridarium*, or garden, in the middle of the peristyle, is adorned with two fountains. That at the end, 30, resembling a little chapel, is ornamented with mosaics and shells, and is surmounted by a small white marble statue of Silenus, which still retains traces of having been painted. The wine-skin on which he leans was coloured black. From it issued a jet of water, which, falling in a cascade down five marble steps, ran down a channel to the circular basin in the middle of the xystus. In the centre of this basin is a column, which also

* Breton, *Pompeia*, p. 321.

threw up a *jet d'eau*. On each side of the upper fountain are marble cippi surmounted by *hermes* with two faces. One of these represents Bacchus and Ariadne; the other a Faun and a Bacchante. Similar *hermes* are likewise placed in the opposite corners of the peristyle, having heads of the bearded Bacchus, and a Bacchante. Around the central basin are arranged small sculptures, in which no proportion of relative size is observed, and which vary much in execution. The best among them are two Fauns, one of which lifts his hand to his head; the other, which terminates like a *hermes*, has under his left arm a kid, and in his right hand a syrinx, or pan-pipe. A she-goat, erect at his feet, seems entreating for her young one. In the centre of the group, facing the tablinum, is Cupid extracting a thorn from the foot of Pan. Round the basin are other figures of Cupid on a dolphin, stags, cows, water-fowl, &c. All these figures seem to have been connected with the fountain and to have thrown jets of water.

The left side of the portico of the peristyle is divided into two little cabinets, 23, 24, which may probably have formed a library. The first cabinet has a picture, almost effaced, of Venus and Cupid. In the second was found the picture of writing materials already described, from which was inferred the name of the master of the house.

At the bottom of this left side of the portico is an open space, 31, probably a sort of court, with a staircase leading to an upper floor. To the left of this is, as it were, another small house, but communicating through its tabliuum, 32, as well as with a corridor or *fauces*, with the house we are describing. Its entrance, 39, opened upon a little street running at right angles to the Street of Stabiæ. We have already had examples of this kind of double house. On each side of the prothyrum was a bedchamber, 37, 38, and another, 34, next to the tablinum. The atrium, paved with *opus Signinum*, had a small compluvium in the centre, 33. On its right side, from the prothyrum, are two small recesses, or closets, 35, 36; on the wall opposite to them was a large painting, now almost effaced.

Returning to the first portion of the house, we find at the bottom of the peristyle two apartments, 25, 26, which probably served as bedchambers. They are paved with *opus Signinum*, intermixed with little pieces of marble. The pictures with which they were ornamented have either been removed or are very much damaged. The last room on the right, 27, was perhaps a wardrobe, with a *latrina* at the bottom of it. Next to this, at the further right-hand corner of the peristyle, is a staircase, 28, which seems to have led to the cellar. The large apartment, 29, which occupies the greater portion of the right-hand side of the peristyle, is thought by some to have been an *œcus* or *exedra*, while others have taken it for a summer triclinium. The latter opinion is favoured by the circumstance that in this apartment were found three little one-handled amphoræ, on one of which was painted in black letters, TVSCOLA (. . . ON) OFFICINA SCAV; and on the others, LIQVAMEN.* Several other articles were found on the occasion of this *scavo*, made in the presence of Queen Christina of Spain, May 22nd, 1847.

Adjoining the house of Lucretius are several shops. That next door but one appears to have belonged to a chemist or colour-maker. On the right of the atrium is a triple furnace, constructed for the reception of three large cauldrons at different levels, which were reached by steps. The house contained a great quantity of carbonised drugs. At the sides of the entrance were two shops for the sale of the manufactured articles. In one of these shops was discovered, some yards below the old level of the soil, the skeleton of a woman with two bracelets of gold, two of silver, four earrings, five rings, forty-seven gold, and one hundred and ninety-seven silver coins, in a purse of netted gold.

The space bounded on the north by the Street of the Augustals, on the south by the Vicoletto del Calcidico, on the east by the Street of Stabiæ, and on the west by the Street of Eumachia, running at the back of the buildings on the east side of the Forum, contains some of the most recent excavations. Of these however we shall select for description only a few of the more important. It is not the main object of this work to serve as a guide, but to give a general idea of Pompeii; and it would be tedious for the general reader to repeat details which necessarily have much sameness.

At the back of the new, or Stabiæn Baths, already described,

---

* *Pomp. Antiq. Hist.*, vol. ii. p. 465.

a small street has been cleared out running parallel with that of Stabiæ, and extending from the Street of the Augustals to that of Abundance, which it enters just opposite to the Street of the Theatres. This new street, or rather lane, for it is very narrow, has obtained the name of Via del Lupanare, from a *Lupanar*, or brothel, situated in about the middle of it. Passing down this street from the Street of Abundance, the visitor finds on the right, just beyond the back wall of the Thermæ Stabianæ, the entrance of a handsome dwelling. An inscription in red letters on the outside wall containing the name of Siricus has occasioned the conjecture that this was the name of the owner of the house; while a mosaic inscription on the floor of the prothyrum, having the words SALVE LUCRU, has given rise to a second appellation for the dwelling. The name of Siricus was also found on a pilaster at the principal entrance of the house in the Via Stabiana. It has also been called the House of the Russian Princes, from some excavations made here in 1851 in presence of the sons of the Emperor of Russia.* By some authorities however the House of the Russian Princes is described as a separate one; but at all events they communicate with each other.

A door on the right of the prothyrum leads into a room having towards the street a window protected by an iron grating, and at too great a height from the floor to allow any one to look through it. The walls are white, divided into compartments by red lines and candelabra. In the middle of them are griffins, swans, discs, among fantastical pieces of architecture, &c.

The walls of the atrium are covered merely with a coarse white plaster, which forms a striking contrast with the elegant paintings of the adjacent apartments. The white marble impluvium is very handsome. In the middle, probably, was a *jet d'eau;* at top stand two marble tables and a plinth, designed apparently to support a small statue, through which also rose a *jet d'eau.* On the right of the impluvium is a puteal of Tiburtine stone. At the wall on the same side was a sort of wooden press or cupboard, to hold domestic utensils, of which many were found here.

* *Giornale degli Scavi*, No. 13, p. 4.

Opposite the entrance, in the place of the tablinum, was an undecorated apartment, which seems to have served for a counting-house or office. The bones of a dog and many objects were found in this room; among them a bronze seal, with the letters SIRICI in relief, and a large and handsome gold ring, having a cornelian engraved with the head of a man.

On the left of the prothyrum is an apartment with two doors, one opening on a wooden staircase leading to an upper floor, the other forming the entry to a room next the street, with a window like that described in the other room next the prothyrum. The walls of this chamber are white, divided by red and yellow zones into compartments, in which are depicted the symbols of the principal deities—as the eagle and globe of Jove, the peacock of Juno, the lance, helmet, and shield of Minerva, the panther of Bacchus, a Sphinx, having near it the mystical chest and sistrum of Isis, who was the Venus Physica of the Pompeians, the caduceus and other emblems of Mercury, &c. There are also two small landscapes.

Next to this is a large and handsome exedra, decorated with good pictures, a third of the size of life. That on the left represents Neptune and Apollo presiding at the building of Troy: the former, armed with his trident, is seated; the latter, crowned with laurel, is on foot, and leans with his right arm on a lyre.

On the wall opposite to this is a picture of Vulcan presenting the arms of Achilles to Thetis. The celebrated shield is supported by Vulcan on the anvil, and displayed to Thetis, who is seated, whilst a winged female figure standing at her side points out to her with a rod the marvels of its workmanship. Agreeably to the Homeric description, the shield is encircled with the signs of the zodiac, and in the middle are the bear, the dragon, &c. On the ground are the breast-plate, the greaves, and the helmet.

In the third picture is seen Hercules crowned with ivy, inebriated, and lying on the ground at the foot of a cypress tree. He is clothed in a *sandyx*, or short transparent tunic, and has on his feet a sort of shoes, one of which he has kicked off. He supports himself on his left arm, while the right is raised in drunken ecstacy. A little Cupid plucks at his garland of ivy, another tries to drag away his ample goblet. In the middle of the picture is an altar with festoons. On the top of it three Cupids, assisted by another who has climbed up the tree, endeavour to bear on their shoulders the hero's quiver; while on the ground, to the left of the altar, four other Cupids are sporting with his club. A votive tablet with an image of Bacchus rests at the foot of the altar, and indicates the god to whom Hercules has been sacrificing.

Hercules Drunk.

On the left of the picture, on a little eminence, is a group of three females round a column having on its top a vase. The chief and central figure, which is naked to the waist, has in her hand a fan; she seems to look with interest on the drunken hero, but whom she represents it is difficult to say. On the right, half way up a mountain, sits Bacchus, looking on the scene with a complacency not unmixed with surprise. He is surrounded by his usual rout of attendants, one of whom bears a thyrsus. The annexed engraving will convey a clearer idea of the picture, which for grace, grandeur of composition, and delicacy and freshness of colouring, is among the best discovered at Pompeii. The exedra is also adorned with many other paintings and ornaments, which it would be too long to describe.

On the same side of the atrium, beyond a passage leading to a kitchen with an oven, is an elegant *triclinium fenestratum* looking upon an adjacent garden. The walls are black, divided by red and yellow zones, with candelabra and architectural members intermixed with quadrupeds, birds, dolphins, Tritons, masks, &c., and in the middle of each compartment is a Bacchante. In each wall are three small paintings executed with greater care. The first, which has been removed, represented Æneas in his tent, who, accompanied by Mnestheus, Achates, and young Ascanius, presents his thigh to the surgeon, Iapis, in order to extract from it the barb of an arrow. Æneas supports himself with the lance in his right hand, and leans with the other on the shoulder of his son, who, overcome by his father's misfortune, wipes the tears from his eyes with the hem of his robe; while Iapis, kneeling on one leg before the hero, is intent on extracting the barb with his forceps. But the wound is not to be healed without divine interposition. In the background of the picture Venus is hastening to her son's relief, bearing in her hand the branch of dictamnus which is to restore him to his pristine vigour.

The subject of the second picture, which is much damaged, is not easy to be explained. It represents a naked hero, armed with sword and spear, to whom a woman crowned with laurel and clothed in an ample *peplum* is pointing out another female figure. The latter expresses by her gestures her grief and indignation at the warrior's departure, the imminence of which is signified by the chariot that awaits him. Signor Fiorelli thinks he recognizes in this picture Turnus, Lavinia, and Amata, when the queen supplicates Turnus not to fight with the Trojans.

The third painting represents Hermaphroditus surrounded by six nymphs, variously employed.

2 H

From the atrium a narrow *fauces* or corridor led into the garden. Three steps on the left connected this part of the house with the other and more magnificent portion having its entrance from the Strada Stabiana. The garden was surrounded on two sides with a portico, on the right of which are some apartments which do not require particular notice.

The house entered, at a higher level, by the three steps just mentioned, was at first considered as a separate house, and as we have said, has been called the House of the Russian Priuces, from some excavations made here in 1851 in presence of the sons of the Emperor of Russia. The peculiarities observable in this house are that the atrium and peristyle are broader than they are deep, and that they are not separated by a tablinum and other rooms, but simply by a wall. In the centre of the Tuscan atrium, entered from the Street of Stabiæ, is a handsome marble impluvium. At the top of it is a square cippus, coated with marble, and having a leaden pipe which flung the water into a square vase or basin supported by a little base of white marble, ornamented with acanthus leaves. Beside the fountain is a table of the same material, supported by two legs beautifully sculptured, of a chimæra and a griffin. On this table was a little bronze group of Hercules armed with his club, and a young Phrygian kneeling before him.

From the atrium the peristyle is entered by a large door. It is about forty-six feet broad and thirty-six deep, and has ten columns, one of which still sustains a fragment of the entablature. The walls were painted in red and yellow panels alternately, with figures of Latona, Diana, Bacchantes, &c. At the bottom of the peristyle, on the right, is a triclinium. In the middle is a small *œcus*, with two pillars richly ornamented with arabesques. A little apartment on the left has several pictures.

In this house, at a height of seventeen Neapolitan palms (nearly fifteen feet) from the level of the ground, were discovered four skeletons together in an almost vertical position. Twelve palms lower was another skeleton, with a hatchet near it. This man appears to have pierced the wall of one of the small chambers of the prothyrum, and was about to enter it, when he was smothered, either by the falling in of the earth or by the mephitic exhalations. It has been thought that those persons perished while engaged in searching for valuables after the catastrophe.*

In the back room of a thermopolium not far from this spot was discovered a *graffito* of part of the first line of the Æneid, in which the *r*s were turned into *l*s :

Alma vilumque cano Tlo.†

We will now return to the house of Siricus. Contiguous to it in the Via del Lupanare is a building having two doors separated with pilasters. By way of sign, an elephant was painted on the wall, enveloped by a large serpent and tended by a pigmy. Above was the inscription : Sittius restituit elephantum ; and beneath the following :—

Hospitium hic locatur
Triclinium cum tribus lectis
Et comm.

Both the painting and the inscription have now disappeared. The discovery is curious, as proving that the ancients used signs for their taverns. Orelli has given in his *Inscriptions*‡ in Gaul, one of a Cock (a Gallo Gallinacio). In that at Pompeii the last word stands for "commodis." "Here is a triclinium with three beds and other conveniences."

Just opposite the gate of Siricus was another house also supposed to be a *caupona*, or tavern, from some chequers painted on the door-posts. On the wall are depicted two large serpents, the emblem so frequently met with. They were the symbols of the Lares viales, or compitales, and, as we have said, rendered the place sacred against the commission of any nuisance. The cross, which is sometimes seen on the walls of houses in a modern Italian city, serves the same purpose. Above the serpents is the following inscription, in tolerably large white characters : Otiosis locus hic non est, discede morator. "Lingerer, depart; this is no place for idlers." An injunction by the way which seems rather to militate against the idea of the house having been a tavern.

---

* Aloe, *Ruines*, &c., p. 137.

† It should be mentioned, however, that the Journal of the superintendent of the *scavi* gives them written in the usual way:—
Arma virumque cano Tro.
See *Pomp. Ant. Hist.*, t. ii. p. 543.

‡ t. ii. p. 270, No. 4329-30. Cf. Fiorelli.

The inscription just mentioned suggests an opportunity for giving a short account of similar ones; we speak not of inscriptions cut in stone, and affixed to temples and other public buildings, but such as were either painted, scrawled in charcoal and other substances, or scratched with a sharp point, such as a nail or knife, on the stucco of walls and pillars. Such inscriptions afford us a peep both into the public and the domestic life of the Pompeians. Advertisements of a political character were commonly painted on the exterior walls in large letters in black and red paint; poetical effusions or pasquinades, &c., with coal or chalk (Martial, *Epig.* xii. 61, 9); while notices of a domestic kind are more usually found in the interior of the houses, scratched, as we have said, on the stucco, whence they have been called *graffiti*.

The numerous political inscriptions bear testimony to the activity of public life in Pompeii. These advertisements, which for the most part turn on the election of ædiles, duumvirs, and other magistrates, show that the Pompeians, at the time when their city was destroyed, were in all the excitement of the approaching comitia for the election of such magistrates. We shall here select a few of the more interesting inscriptions, both relating to public and domestic matters, from those collected by Overbeck in the second volume of his valuable work on Pompeii (ch. 6).

It seems to have been customary to paint over old advertisements with a coat of white, and so to obtain a fresh surface for new ones, just as the London bill-sticker remorselessly pastes his bill over that of some brother of the brush. In some cases this new coating has been detached, or has fallen off, thus revealing an older notice, belonging sometimes to a period antecedent to the Social War. Inscriptions of this kind are found only on the solid stone pillars of the more ancient buildings, and not on the stucco, with which at a later period almost everything was plastered. Their antiquity is further certified by some of them being in the Oscan dialect; while those in Latin are distinguished from more recent ones in the same language by the forms of the letters, by the names which appear in them, and by archaisms in grammar and orthography. Inscriptions in the Greek tongue are rare, though the letters of the Greek alphabet, scratched on walls at a little height from the ground, and thus evidently the work of schoolboys, show that Greek must have been extensively taught at Pompeii.

The normal form of electioneering advertisements contains the name of the person recommended, the office for which he is a candidate, and the name of the person, or persons, who recommended him, accompanied in general with the formula O.V.F. From examples written in full, recently discovered, it appears that these letters mean *orat* (or *orant*) *vos faciatis*: "beseech you to create" (ædile and so forth). The letters in question were, before this discovery, very often thought to stand for *orat ut faveat*, "begs him to favour;" and thus the meaning of the inscription was entirely reversed, and the person recommending converted into the person recommended.* In the following example for instance—*M. Holconium Priscum duumvirum juri dicundo O.V.F. Philippus*; the meaning, according to the older interpretation, will be: "Philippus beseeches M. Holconius Priscus. duumvir of justice, to favour or patronize him;" whereas the true sense is: "Philippus beseeches you to create M. Holconius Priscus a duumvir of justice." From this misinterpretation wrong names have frequently been given to houses; as is probably the case, for instance, with the house of Pansa,† which, from the tenour of the inscription, more probably belonged to Paratus, who posted on his own walls a request to passers-by to make his friend Pansa ædile. Had it been the house of Pansa, when a candidate for the ædileship, and if it was the custom for such candidates to post recommendatory notices on their doors, it may be supposed that Pansa would have exhibited more than this single one from a solitary friend. This is a more probable meaning than that Paratus solicited in this way the patronage of Pansa; for it would have been a bad method to gain it by disfiguring his walls in so impertinent a manner. We do not indeed mean to deny that adulatory inscriptions were sometimes written on the houses or doors of powerful or popular men or pretty women. A verse of Plautus bears testimony to such a custom (Impleantur meæ foreis elogiorum carbonibus. *Mercator*, act. ii. sc. 3). But first, the inscription on the so-called house of Pansa was evidently not of an adulatory, but of a recommendatory

---

* Compare the editor's note at p. 80, Part I.
† See above, p. 318.

character; and secondly, those of the former kind, as we learn from this same verse, seem to have been written by passing admirers, with some material ready to the hand, such as charcoal or the like, and not painted on the walls with care, and time, and expense; a proceeding which we can hardly think the owner of the house, if he was a modest and sensible man, would have tolerated.

Recommendations of candidates were often accompanied with a word or two in their praise; as *dignus*, or *dignissimus est*, *probissimus*, *juvenis integer*, *frugi*, *omni bono meritus*, and the like. Such recommendations are sometimes subscribed by guilds or corporations, as well as by private persons, and show that there were a great many such trade unions at Pompeii. Thus we find mentioned the *offectores* (dyers), *pistores* (bakers), *aurifices* (goldsmiths), *pomarii* (fruiterers), *cœparii* (greengrocers), *lignarii* (wood merchants), *plostrarii* (cart-wrights), *piscicapi* (fishermen), *agricolæ* (husbandmen), *muliones* (muletcers), *culinarii* (cooks), *fullones* (fullers), and others. Advertisements of this sort appear to have been laid hold of as a vehicle for street wit, just as electioneering squibs are perpetrated among ourselves. Thus we find mentioned, as if among the companies, the *pilicrepi* (ball-players), the *seribibi* (late topers), the *dormientes universi* (all the worshipful company of sleepers), and as a climax, *Pompeiani universi* (all the Pompeians, to a man, vote for so and so). One of these recommendations, purporting to emanate from a "teacher" or "professor," runs, *Valentius cum discentes suos* (Valentius with his disciples); the bad grammar being probably intended as a gibe upon one of the poor man's weak points.

The inscriptions in chalk and coal, the *graffiti*, and occasionally painted inscriptions, contain sometimes well-known verses from poets still extant. Some of these exhibit variations from the modern text, but being written by not very highly educated persons, they seldom or never present any various readings that it would be desirable to adopt, and indeed contain now and then prosodical errors. Other verses, some of them by no means contemptible, are either taken from pieces now lost, or are the invention of the writer himself. Many of these inscriptions are of course of an amatory character; some convey intelligence of not much importance to anybody but the writer—as, that he is troubled with a cold—or was seventeen centuries ago—or that he considers somebody who does not invite him to supper as no better than a brute and barbarian, or invokes blessings on the man that does. Some are capped by another hand with a biting sarcasm on the first writer, and many, as might be expected, are scurrilous and indecent. Some of the *graffiti* on the interior walls and pillars of houses are memorandums of domestic transactions; as, how much lard was bought, how many tunics sent to the wash, when a child or a donkey was born, and the like. One of this kind, scratched on the wall of the peristyle of the corner house in the *Strada della Fortuna* and *Vicolo degli Scienziati*, appears to be an account of the *dispensator* or overseer of the tasks in spinning allotted to the female slaves of the establishment, and is interesting as furnishing us with their names, which are Vitalis, Florentina, Amarullis, Januaria, Heracla, Maria (Mária, feminine of Marius, not María), Lalagia (reminding us of Horace's Lalage), Damalis, and Doris. The *pensum*, or weight of wool delivered to each to be spun, is spelt *pesu*, the *n* and final *m* being omitted, just as we find *salve lucru*, for *lucrum*, written on the threshold of the house of Siricus. In this form, *pesu* is very close to the Italian word *peso*.

We have already alluded now and then to the rude etchings and caricatures of these wall-artists, but to enter fully into the subject of the Pompeian inscriptions and *graffiti* would almost demand a separate volume, and we must therefore resume the thread of our description.

A little beyond the house of Siricus, a small street, running down at right angles from the direction of the Forum, enters the Via del Lupanare. Just at their junction, and having an entrance into both, stands the Lupanar, from which the latter street derives its name. We cannot venture upon a description of this resort of Pagan immorality. It is kept locked up, but the guide will procure the key for those who may wish to see it.* Next to it is the House of the Fuller, in which was found the elegant little bronze statuette of Narcissus, now in the Museum. The house contained nothing else of interest.

The Via del Lupanare terminates in the Street of the

* There is an account of its arrangement and inscriptions in Fiorelli's *Giornale*, No. 14., p. 48, *seq*.

Augustals, or of the Dried Fruits. In this latter street, nearly opposite the end of the Via del Lupanare, but a little to the left, is the House of Narcissus, or of the Mosaic Fountain. This house is one of the most recent excavations in Pompeii, having been cleared out in 1865. At the threshold is a mosaic of a bear, with the word *Have*. The prothyrum is painted with figures on a yellow ground. On the left is a medallion of a satyr and nymph; the opposite medallion is destroyed.

The atrium is paved with mosaic. The first room on the right-hand side of it has a picture of Narcissus admiring himself in the water. The opposite picture has a female figure seated, with a child in her arms, and a large chest open before her. The tablinum is handsomely paved with mosaic and marble. Behind this, in place of a peristyle, is a court or garden, the wall of which is painted with a figure bearing a basin. At the bottom is a handsome mosaic fountain, from which the house derives one of its names, with a figure of Neptune surrounded by fishes and sea-fowl; above are depicted large wild boars.

On the opposite side of the way, at the eastern angle of the Street of the Lupanar, is the House of the Rudder and Trident, also called the House of Mars and Venus. The first of these names is derived from the mosaic pavement in the prothyrum, in which the objects mentioned are represented; while a medallion picture in the atrium, with heads of Mars and Venus, gave rise to the second appellation. The colours of this picture are still quite fresh, a result which Signor Fiorelli attributes to his having caused a varnish of wax to be laid over the painting at the time of its discovery.* Without some such protection the colours of these pictures soon decay; the cinnabar, or vermilion, especially, turns black after a few days' exposure to the light.

The atrium, as usual, is surrounded with bedchambers. A peculiarity not yet found in any other house is a niche or closet on the left of the atrium, having on one side an opening only large enough to introduce the hand, whence it has been conjectured that it served as a receptacle for some valuable objects. It is painted inside with a wall of quadrangular

* *Giornale*, No. 15, p. 89.

pieces of marble of various colours, terminated at top with a cornice. In each of the squares is a fish, bird, or quadruped.

This closet or niche stands at the door of a room in which is an entrance to a subterranean passage, having its exit in the Via del Lupanare. There is nothing very remarkable in the other apartments of this house. Behind is a peristyle with twelve columns, in the garden of which shrubs are said to have been discovered in a carbonized state.

Further down the same Street of the Augustals, at the angle which it forms with the Street of Stabiæ, is the house of a baker, having on the external wall the name Modestum in red letters. For a tradesman it seems to have been a comfortable house, having an atrium and fountain, and some painted chambers. Beyond the atrium is a spacious court with mills and an oven. The oven was charged with more than eighty loaves, the forms of which are still perfect, though they are reduced to a carbonaceous state. They are preserved in the Museum.

The narrow street to which we have alluded, as entering the Via del Lupanare nearly opposite to the house of Siricus, has been called the Via del Balcone, from a small house with a projecting balcony, or mænianum. Indications of balconies have been found elsewhere, and indeed there were evidently some in the Via del Lupanare; but this is the only instance of one restored to its pristine state, through the care of Signor Fiorelli in substituting fresh timbers for those which had become carbonized. The visitor may ascend to the first floor of this house, from which the balcony projects several feet into the narrow lane. In the atrium of this house, of which we annex an engraving on p. 474, is a very pretty fountain.

The house next to that of the Balcony, facing the entrance of a small street leading from the Via dell Abbondanza, and numbered 7 on the door-post, has a few pictures in a tolerable state of preservation. In a painting in the furthest room on the left of the atrium Theseus is seen departing in his ship; Ariadne, roused from sleep, gazes on him with despair, while a little weeping Cupid stands by her side. In the same apartment are two other well-preserved pictures, the subjects of which it is not easy to explain. In one is a female displaying to a man two little Cupids in a nest, while four other figures are looking on. The other is sometimes called the

House of the Balcony.

Rape of Helen. There are also several medallion heads around.

In the small street which runs parallel with the eastern side of the Forum, called the Vico di Eumachia, is a house named the *Casa nuova della Caccia*, to distinguish it from one of the same name previously discovered. As in the former instance, its appellation is derived from a large painting on the wall of the peristyle, of bears, lions, and other animals. On the right-hand wall of the tablinum is a picture of Bacchus discovering Ariadne. A satyr lifts her vest, while Silenus and other figures look on in admiration. The painting on the left-hand wall is destroyed. On entering the peristyle a door on the right leads down some steps into a garden, on one side of which is a small altar before a wall, on which is a painting of shrubs.

Proceeding from this street into the Vico Storto, which forms a continuation of it on the north, we find on the right a recently excavated house, which, from several slabs of variously coloured marbles found in it, has been called the House of the Dealer in Marbles. Under a large court in the interior, surrounded with Doric columns, are some subterranean apartments, in one of which was discovered a well more than eighty feet deep, and still supplied with fresh water; almost the only instance of the kind at Pompeii. The beautiful statuette of Silenus, already described, was found in this house. Here also was made the rare discovery of the skeletons of two horses, with the remains of a *biga*.

This description might be extended, but it would be tedious to repeat details of smaller and less interesting houses, the features of which present in general much uniformity; and we shall therefore conclude this account of the more recent discoveries with a notice of a group of bodies found in this neighbourhood, the forms of which have been preserved to us through the ingenuity of Signor Fiorelli.

It has been already remarked that the showers of *lapillo*, or pumice-stone, by which Pompeii was overwhelmed and buried, were followed by streams of a thick, tenacious mud, which flowing over the deposit of *lapillo*, and filling up all the crannies and interstices into which that substance had not been able to penetrate, completed the destruction of the city. The objects over which this mud flowed were enveloped in it

476   POMPEII.

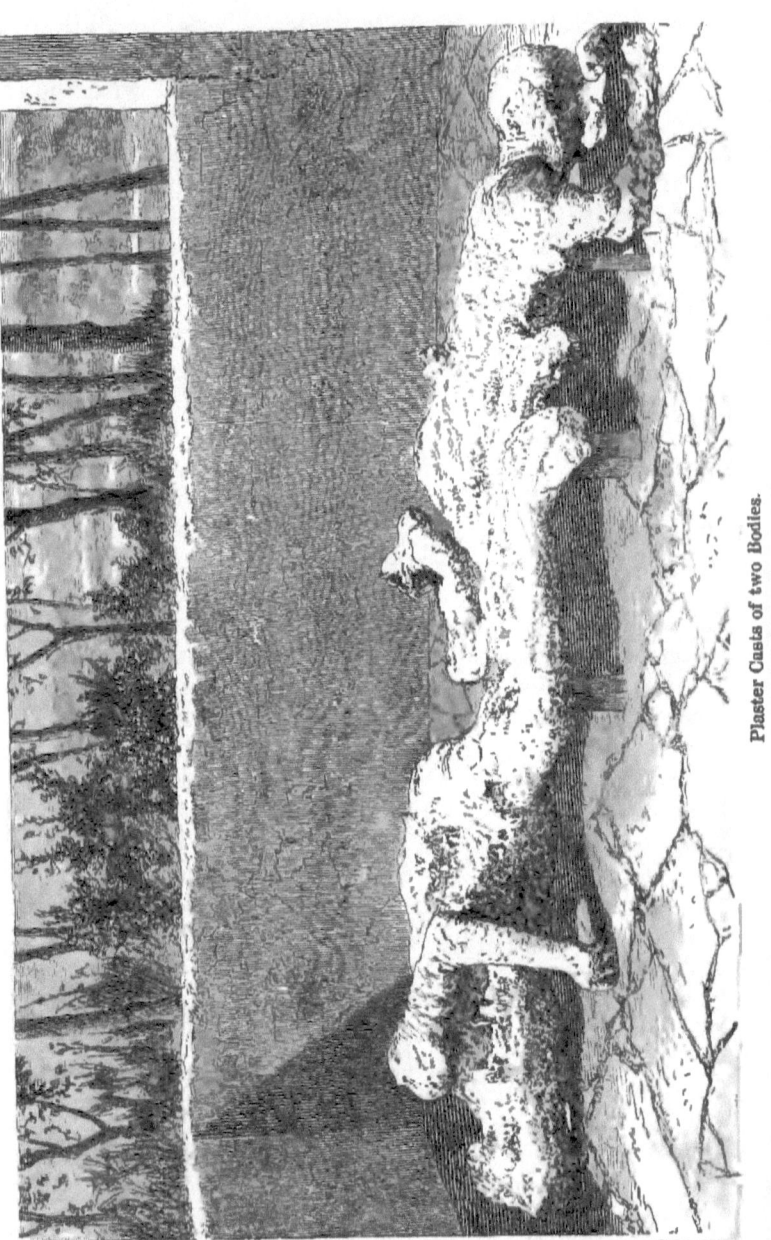

Plaster Casts of two Bodies.

as in a plaster mould; and where these objects happened to be human bodies, their decay left a cavity in which their forms were as accurately preserved and rendered as in the mould prepared for the casting of a bronze statue. Such cavities had often been observed. In some of them remnants of charred wood, accompanied with bronze or other ornaments, showed that the object inclosed had been a piece of furniture; while in others, the remains of bones and of articles of apparel evinced but too plainly that the hollow had been the living grave which had swallowed up some unfortunate human being. In a happy moment the idea occurred to Signor Fiorelli of filling up these cavities with liquid plaster, and thus obtaining a cast of the objects which had been inclosed in them. The experiment was first made in a small street leading from the Via del Balcone Pensile towards the Forum. The bodies here found were on the *lapillo* at a height of about fifteen feet from the level of the ground. The story of their discovery has been so admirably told in the article in the *Quarterly Review* before referred to,* that we shall again trespass on its pages.

"Among the first casts thus obtained were those of four human beings. They are now preserved in a room at Pompeii,† and more ghastly and painful, yet deeply interesting and touching objects, it is difficult to conceive. We have death itself moulded and cast—the very last struggle and final agony brought before us. They tell their story with a horrible dramatic truth that no sculptor could ever reach. They would have furnished a thrilling episode to the accomplished author of the 'Last Days of Pompeii.'

"These four persons had perished in a street. They had remained within the shelter of their homes until the thick black mud began to creep through every cranny and chink. Driven from their retreat, they began to flee when it was too late. The streets were already buried deep in the loose pumice-stones which had been falling for many hours in unremitting showers, and which reached almost to the windows of the first floor. These victims of the eruption were not found together, and they do not appear to have belonged to the same family or household. The most interesting of the

* No. 230, p. 382.
† In the street leading to the Gate of Herculaneum.

casts is that of two women, probably mother and daughter, lying feet to feet. They appear from their garb to have been people of poor condition. The elder seems to lie tranquilly on her side. Overcome by the noxious gases, she probably fell and died without a struggle. Her limbs are extended, and her left arm drops loosely. On one finger is still seen her coarse iron ring. Her child was a girl of fifteen; she seems, poor thing, to have struggled hard for life. Her legs are drawn up convulsively; her little hands are clenched in agony. In one she holds her veil, or a part of her dress, with which she had covered her head, burying her face in her arm, to shield herself from the falling ashes and from the foul sulphurous smoke. The form of her head is perfectly preserved. The texture of her coarse linen garments may be traced, and even the fashion of her dress, with its long sleeves reaching to her wrists; here and there it is torn, and the smooth young skin appears in the plaster like polished marble. On her tiny feet may still be seen her embroidered sandals.

"At some distance from this group lay a third woman. She appears to have been about twenty-five years of age, and to have belonged to a better class than the other two. On one of her fingers were two silver rings, and her garments were of a finer texture. Her linen head-dress, falling over her shoulders like that of a matron in a Roman statue, can still be distinguished. She had fallen on her side, overcome by the heat and gases, but a terrible struggle seems to have preceded her last agony. One arm is raised in despair; the hands are clenched convulsively; her garments are gathered up on one side, leaving exposed a limb of beautiful shape. So perfect a mould of it has been formed by the soft and yielding mud, that the cast would seem to be taken from an exquisite work of Greek art. She had fled with her little treasure, which lay scattered around her—two silver cups, a few jewels, and some dozen silver coins; nor had she, like a good housewife, forgotten her keys, after having probably locked up her stores before seeking to escape. They were found by her side.

"The fourth cast is that of a man of the people, perhaps a common soldier. He is of almost colossal size; he lies on his back, his arms extended by his side and his feet stretched out as if, finding escape impossible, he had laid himself down to meet death like a brave man. His dress consists of a short coat or jerkin and tight-fitting breeches of some coarse stuff, perhaps leather; heavy sandals, with soles studded with nails, are laced tightly round his ankles. On one finger is seen his iron ring. His features are strongly marked, the mouth open, as in death. Some of the teeth still remain, and even part of the moustache adheres to the plaster.

"The importance of Signor Fiorelli's discovery may be understood from the results we have described. It may furnish us with many curious particulars as to the dress and domestic habits of the Romans, and with many an interesting episode of the last day of Pompeii. Had it been made at an earlier period we might perhaps have possessed the perfect cast of the Diomedes, as they clung together in their last struggle, and of other victims whose remains are now mingled together in the bone-house."

We shall conclude this account with stating that the house now excavating (February, 1866) nearly opposite the new baths, in a street leading out of the Via Stabiana, and forming a continuation of those of Abundance and of Holconius, appears to be one of considerable magnificence. The pavement before the entrance is raised, and is ascended by three steps. On entering a noble atrium presents itself, having an impluvium with no fewer than sixteen columns. On the right is a handsome lararium, purporting to be erected by two freedmen of Diadumenus. We await with much interest the excavation of this house, which promises to be among the handsomest of Pompeii. The following additional particulars have been kindly supplied by the editor of Murray's 'Handbook for South Italy.' "Three human skeletons have been discovered in this house, with their gold and silver ornaments—a very handsome gold ring set with an amethyst intaglio of an Abundance, a silver ring, a gold and silver bracelet, &c. The paintings in the room opening out of the tablinum are graceful, and represent Apollo and certain Muses. Among the peculiarities of this house (besides the raised pavement) are the small porter's lodge in the prothyrum, and the four elongated windows, with bronze frames for glass, in the rooms on each side of the entrance."

Portico of the House of Diomedes, with a view of the Atrium beyond.

CHAPTER X.

SUBURBAN VILLA.

THE most interesting, and by far the most extensive of the private buildings yet discovered, is the Suburban Villa, as it is called, from its position a little way without the gates, in the Street of the Tombs, which led to, or formed part of, the suburb called Augustus Felix. Excavations were made in this part of the town in 1771, and the two or three following years, when this villa was discovered.* It is worthy of remark that the plan of this edifice is in close acccord with the descriptions of country houses given us by Vitruvius and others —a circumstance which tends strongly to confirm the belief

* See *Pomp. Ant. Hist.*, t. i. p. 257, *seq.*

VIEW OF THE VILLA OF M. ARRIUS DIOMEDES.
WHEN FIRST DISCOVERED.

already expressed, that the houses of the city are built upon the Roman system of arrangement, although the Greek taste may predominate in their decoration. We will commence by extracting the most important passages in Pliny the Younger's description of his Laurentine villa, that the reader may have some general notion of the subject, some standard with which to compare that which we are about to describe.

"My villa is large enough for convenience, though not splendid. The first apartment which presents itself is a plain, yet not mean, atrium; then comes a portico, in shape like the letter O, which surrounds a small, but pleasant area. This is an excellent retreat in bad weather, being sheltered by glazed windows,* and still more effectually by an overhanging roof. Opposite the centre of this portico is a pleasant cavædium, after which comes a handsome triclinium, which projects upon the beach, so that when the south-west wind urges the sea, the last broken waves just dash against its walls. On every side of this room are folding doors, or windows equally large, so that from the three sides there is a view, as it were, of three seas at once, while backwards the eye wanders through the apartments already described, the cavædium, portico, and atrium, to woods and distant mountains. To the left are several apartments, including a bedchamber, and room fitted up as a library, which jets out in an elliptic form, and, by its several windows, admits the sun during its whole course. These apartments I make my winter abode. The rest of this side of the house is allotted to my slaves and freedmen, yet it is for the most part neat enough to receive my friends. To the right of the triclinium is a very elegant chamber, and another, which you may call either a very large chamber (*cubiculum*), or moderate-sized eating-room (*cœnatio*), which commands a full prospect both of the sun and sea. Passing hence, through three or four other chambers, you enter the *cella frigidaria* of the baths, in which there are two basins projecting from opposite walls, abundantly large enough to swim in, if you feel inclined to do so in the first instance. Then come the anointing-room, the hypocaust, or furnace, and two

* *Specularibus.* Whether glass windows or talc windows (lapis specularis) were meant, is a controverted point. We are inclined to believe the latter, although glass windows were unquestionably in use before the date of this letter, as is proved by the excavations of Herculaneum and Pompeii.

small rooms; next the warm bath, which commands an admirable view of the sea. Not far off is the *sphæristerium*, a room devoted to in-door exercises and games, exposed to the hottest sun of the declining day. Beside it is a triclinium, where the noise of the sea is never heard but in a storm, and then faintly, looking out upon the garden and the *gestatio*, or place for taking the air in a carriage or litter, which encompasses it. The gestatio is hedged with box, and with rosemary where the box is wanting; for box grows well where it is sheltered by buildings, but withers when exposed in an open situation to the wind, and especially within reach of spray from the sea. To the inner circle of the gestatio is joined a shady walk of vines, soft and tender even to the naked feet. The garden is full of mulberries and figs, the soil being especially suited to the former. Within the circuit of the gestatio there is also a cryptoportico, for extent comparable to public buildings, having windows on one side looking to the sea, on the other to the garden. In front of it is a xystus, fragrant with violets, where the sun's heat is increased by reflection from the cryptoportico, which, at the same time, breaks the north-east wind. At either end of it is a suite of apartments, in which, in truth, I place my chief delight."* Such was one of several villas described by Pliny. The directions given by Vitruvius for building country houses are very short. "The same principles," he says, " are to be observed in country houses as in town houses, except that in the latter the atrium lies next to the door, but in pseudo-urban houses the peristyles come first, then atria surrounded by paved porticoes, looking upon courts for gymnastic exercises and walking " (*palæstras et ambulationes*).† It will appear that the distribution of the Suburban Villa was entirely in accordance with these rules.

The house is built upon the side of the hill, in such a manner that the ground falls away, not only in the line of the street, across the breadth of the house, but also from the front to the back, so that the doorway itself being elevated from five to six feet above the roadway, there is room at the back

* Plin. Ep. lib. ii. 17. We have very much shortened the original, leaving out the description of, at least, one upper floor, and other particulars which did not appear necessary to the illustration of our subject.
† Vitruvius, vi. 8.

of the house for an extensive and magnificent suite of rooms between the level of the peristyle and the surface of the earth. These two levels are represented on the same plan, being distinguished by a difference in the shading. The darker parts show the walls of the upper floor, the lighter ones indicate the distribution of the lower. A further distinction is made in the references, which are by figures to the upper floor, and by letters to the lower. There are besides subterraneous vaults and galleries not expressed in the plan.

1. Broad foot pavement raised nine inches or a foot above the carriage way, running along the whole length of the Street of Tombs. 2. Inclined planes, leading up to the porch on each side. 3. Entrance. 4. Peristyle. This arrangement corresponds exactly with the directions of Vitruvius for the building of country houses just quoted. The order of the peristyle is extremely elegant. The columns, their capitals, and entablatures, and the paintings on the walls are still in good preservation. The architectural decorations are worked in stucco; and it is observed by Mazois that both here and in other instances the artist has taken liberties, which he would not have indulged in had he been working in more valuable materials. On this ground that eminent architect hazards a conjecture that the plasterer had a distinct style of ornamenting, different from that of architects, or of the masons in their employ. The lower third of the columns, which is not fluted, is painted red. The pavement was formed of *opus Signinum*. 5. Uncovered court with an impluvium, which collected the rain water and fed a cistern, whence the common household wants were supplied. 6. Descending staircase, which led to a court and building on a lower level, appropriated to the offices, as the kitchen, bakehouse, &c., and to the use of slaves. It will be recollected that the ground slopes with a rapid descent away from the city gate. This lower story, therefore, was not under ground, though near eight feet below the level of the peristyle. It communicates with the road by a back door. From the bottom of the stair there runs a long corridor, A, somewhat indistinct in our small plan, owing to its being crossed several times by the dark lines of the upper floor, which leads down by a gentle slope to the portico surrounding the garden. This was the back stair, as we should call it, by which the servants com-

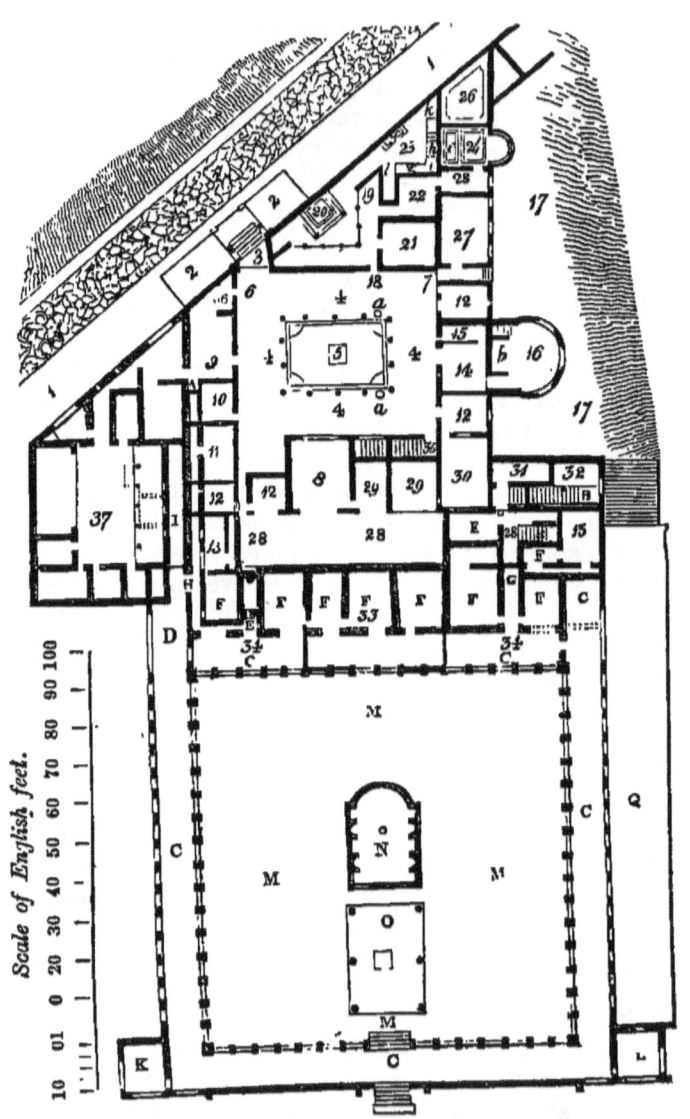

Ground-plan of the Suburban Villa of Diomedes.

municated with that part of the house. There was another staircase, B, on the opposite side of the house, for the use of the family. 7. Door and passage to the upper garden, marked 17, on the same level as the court. 8. Open hall, corresponding in position with a tablinum. Being thus placed between the court and the gallery, 28, it must have been closed with folding doors of wood, which perhaps were glazed. 9, 10, 11, 12. Various rooms containing nothing remarkable. 13. Two rooms situated in the most agreeable manner at the two ends of a long gallery, 28, and looking out upon the upper terraces of the garden, from which the eye took in the whole gulf of Naples to the point of Sorrento, and the island of Capreæ. 14. Procæton, or antechamber. 15. Lodge of the cubicular slave, or attendant upon the bedroom. 16. Bedroom, probably that of the master, or else the state-chamber. *b.* Alcove. Several rings were found here which had evidently belonged to a curtain to draw across the front of it. *c.* Hollow stand or counter of masonry, probably coated with stucco or marble, which served for a toilet-table. Several vases were found there, which must have contained perfumes or cosmetic oils. The form of this bedroom is very remarkable, and will not fail to strike the reader from its exact correspondence with the elliptic chamber or library described by Pliny in his Laurentine villa. The windows in the semicircular end are so placed that they receive the rising, noontide, and setting sun. Bull's eyes, placed above the windows, permitted them to be altogether closed without darkening the room entirely. These windows opened on a garden, where, in Mazois' time, the care of the guardian had planted roses, which almost, beguiled him into the belief that he had found the genuine produce of a Pompeian garden. This must have been a delightful room, from its ample size, elegance of ornament, and the quiet cheerful retirement of its situation. 17. Upper garden upon the level of the court.

18. Entrance to the baths, which, though originally rare in private houses had become so common, long before the destruction of Pompeii, that few wealthy persons were without them. The word *balneum* was peculiarly applied to domestic, *thermæ* to public baths. This specimen, which fortunately was almost perfect, small as it is, suffices to give a good idea of the arrangement of private baths among the Romans. 19. Portico

upon two sides of a small triangular court. There is as much skill in the disposition, as taste in the decoration, of this court, which presents a symmetrical plan, notwithstanding the irregular form of the space allotted to it. Its situation is conformable to the advice of Vitruvius; and as it could not front the west, it has been placed to the south. The columns of the portico are octagonal. At the extremity of the gallery, on the left of the entrance, there is a small furnace where was prepared some warm beverage or restorative for the use of the bathers, who were accustomed to take wine or cordials before they went away. Here a gridiron and two frying-pans were found, still blackened with smoke.* In the centre of the base, or third side of the court, is placed a bath, 20, about six feet square, lined with stucco, the edge of which is faced with marble. It was covered with a roof, the mark of which is still visible on the walls, supported by two pillars placed on the projecting angles. The holes in the walls to admit the three principal beams are so contrived that each side is lined with a single brick. Under this covering the whole wall was painted to represent water, with fish and other aquatic animals swimming about. The water was blue, and rather deep in colour: the fish were represented in the most vivid and varied tints. Some years ago this painting recovered, on being wetted, the original freshness and brilliancy of its colouring; but exposure to the weather has done its work, and now scarce a trace of it remains. In the middle of it there is a circular broken space to which a mask was formerly attached, through which a stream gushed into the basin below. Two or three steps led down to this *baptisterium*, where the cold bath was taken in the open air. This court and portico were paved in mosaic. 21. Apodyterium. 22. Frigidarium. 23. Tepidarium. These two rooms, in neither of which was there a bathing vessel, show that frequently rooms thus named were not intended for bathing, but simply to preserve two intermediate gradations of temperature, between the burning heat of the caldarium or laconicum and the open air. In fact, no trace of any contrivance for the introduction or reception of water has been found in No. 22. It was simply a cold chamber, cella frigidaria. Nor was the little chamber, 23,

* Bonucci.

large enough to receive conveniently a bathing vessel; but seats of wood were found there for the convenience of those who had quitted the bath, and who came there to undergo the discipline of the strigil, and that minute process of purification and anointing which we have before described. This room is not above twelve feet by six: the bath, therefore, could not have been calculated for the reception of more than one, or, at most, of two persons at once. Here the great question relative to the use of glass windows by the ancients was finally settled. This apartment was lighted by a window closed by a moveable frame of wood, which, though converted into charcoal, still held, when it was found, four panes of glass about six inches square. A more elaborate and curious glass window was found at a later period in the public baths.— See p. 160, Part I. 24. Caldarium. It might, however, be employed at pleasure as a tepid or cold bath, when the weather was too cold for bathing in the open air. The suspensura caldariorum, as Vitruvius calls the hollow walls and floors raised upon pillars, are in remarkably good preservation. By means of these the whole apartment was entirely enveloped in flame, and might be easily raised to a most stifling temperature. We have fully described the method of constructing these in the chapter upon the public baths, p. 170, and need not here repeat what has been said. We will however add, that Vitruvius directs a bed of clay mixed with hair to be laid between the pillars and the pavement; and some tradition of this custom may be imagined to subsist, for the potters of the country, in some cases, work up wool with their clay, a practice unknown elsewhere, as we believe, in the art of pottery. The burning vapour passed out above the ceiling, gaining no entrance into the apartment. Air and light were admitted by two windows, one higher than the other. In one of these Mazois found a fragment of glass. The bathing vessel, *e*, lined with stucco, and coated on the outside with marble, was fed by two cocks, which must have been very small, to judge from the space which they occupied. Hence hot and cold water were supplied at pleasure; and it was only to fill the vessel with boiling water, and the whole apartment would be converted into one great vapour bath. As it would have been difficult or impossible to have kept alive a lamp or torch in so dense a steam, there is near the door a circular hole, closed formerly by a glass, which served to admit the light of a lamp placed in the adjoining chamber. The hypocaust, or furnace and apparatus, 25, for heating the water, are so placed that they cannot be seen from the triangular court. They are small, but correspond with the small quantity of boiling water which they were required to furnish, *f*. Stone table. *g*. Cistern. *h*. Mouth of hypocaust. *i*. A furnace, probably for boiling water when merely a tepid bath was required, without heating the suspensura caldariorum. By the side of the hypocaust were placed the vases for hot and cold water, as described in the chapter on Baths: their pedestals were observable between the mouth of the furnace and the letter *k*. *l*. Wooden staircase, no longer in existence, which led to the apartments above. 26. Reservoir.

Such was the distribution of this bath. Some paintings and mosaics, which are ordinary enough, formed its only decorations; yet, from the little that remains, we can discover that the good taste which reigned everywhere, and the freshness of the colours, must have rendered the effect of the whole most agreeable.

27. This chamber seems to have been used as a wardrobe, where the numerous garments of the opulent masters of this dwelling were kept under presses, to give them a lustre. This conjecture is founded upon the remains of calcined stuffs, and the fragments of wardrobes and carbonised plank found in the course of excavation. 23. Great gallery, lighted by windows which looked upon the two terraces, 34, separated by the large hall, 33. This gallery furnished an agreeable promenade, when the weather did not permit the enjoyment of the external porticoes or terraces. 29, 29. These two small apartments, which were open to the gallery, and probably were closed by glass, may very well have been, one a library, the other a reading-room, since the place in which books were kept was not usually the place in which they were read: being small and confined, suitable to the comparatively small number of volumes which an ancient library generally contained, and also to the limited space within which a considerable number of rolls of papyrus might be placed. A bust, painted on the wall of one of them, confirms this supposition, for it is known that the ancients were fond of keeping the portraits of eminent men before their eyes, and

especially of placing those of literary men in their libraries. 30. The form of this hall is suitable to a triclinium, and its situation, protected from the immediate action of the sun's rays, would seem to mark it as a summer triclinium. Still the guests enjoyed the view of the country and of the sea, by means of a door opening upon the terrace. In front of the little chamber, 31, is a square opening for the staircase, which descends to the point B upon the floor below. It is to be remarked, that at the entrance of each division of the building there is a lodge for a slave. No doubt each suite of rooms had its peculiar keeper. The chamber, 10, seems to have been reserved for the keeper of the peristyle; the apartment, 15, belonged to the slave of the bedchamber, who watched the apartment of his master; a recess under the staircase, 35, was, without doubt, the place of the atriensis, or attendant on the atrium, when the hall, 8, was open, to give admission to the interior of the house; and when this hall was closed, he attended in the chamber, 12, which commanded the entrance through the passage, or fauces. Lastly, the small lodge, 31, is so placed as to keep watch over all communication between the upper floor, where is the peristyle, and the lower floor, in which the apartments of the family seem to have been chiefly situated. 32. Apartment, entirely ruined, to which it is difficult to assign a name. 33. Large cyzicene œcus, about thirty-six feet by twenty-six. All the windows of this apartment opened almost to the level of the floor, and gave a view of the garden, the terraces and trellises which ornamented them, as well as of the vast and beautiful prospect towards the sea and Vesuvius. 34. Large terraces, perhaps formerly covered with trellises, which communicate with the terraces over the gallery by which the garden is surrounded. 35. Staircase leading to the upper floor, on which may have been the gynæceum, or suite of apartments belonging to the women. So retired a situation, however, did not always suit the taste of the Roman ladies. Cornelius Nepos says that " they occupy for the most part the first floor in the front of the house." Mazois was long impressed with the idea that there must have been an upper story here, but for a long time he could not find the staircase. At last he discovered in this place marks in the plaster, which left no doubt in his mind but that it had existed here, though being of wood it disappeared with the other woodwork. He recognized the inclination and the height of the steps, and found that they were high and narrow, like those stone stairs which exist still in the same dwelling. 36. A sort of vestibule at the entrance of the building, appropriated to the offices. This lower court probably contained the kitchen. 31. Bakehouse, apartments of the inferior slaves, stables, and other accessories. These are separated from the main building by means of a mesaulon, or small internal court, to diminish the danger in case of a fire happening in the kitchen or bakehouse. There were two ways of communication from the level of the street to the level of the garden; on one side by the corridor, A, A, principally reserved for the servants, on the other by the staircase, B. C, C, C. Portico round the garden. The side beneath the house and that at the right of the plan are perfectly preserved, but it has been found necessary to support the terrace on this side by inserting a modern pillar between each of the old ones, and to build two massive piers beneath the terrace on which the great cyzicene hall is situated. This portico was elegantly ornamented. If we may judge of the whole from a part, which is given by Mazois, the interior entablature was ornamented with light mouldings and running patterns, while there was a little picture over each pillar. That in his plate represents a swan flying away with a serpent. The pillars were square, the lower part painted with flowers springing from trellises, apparently of very delicate execution. The same style of painting occurs in the court of the baths. The ceiling of the portico beneath the terrace is, in respect of its construction, one of the most curious specimens of ancient building which have reached our time. It is a plane surface of masonry, hung in the air, supported neither on the principle of the arch, nor by iron cramps, but owing its existence entirely to the adherence of the mortar by which it is cemented. It is divided into compartments by false beams (caissons) of the same construction. The whole is of remarkable solidity. D. Open hall at the end of the western portico. E. Fountain, supplied perhaps by the water of the cistern. There was formerly a well upon the terrace, 34, by which water might be drawn from the reservoir of this fountain, but it was effaced when the area of the terrace was restored. F, F, F. Different chambers, halls, triclinium, in which the remains of a carpet were found on the floor, and other rooms, to which it is difficult to assign any particular destination. They are all decorated in the most elegant and refined manner, but their paintings are hastening to decay with a rapidity which is grievous to behold. Fortunately the Academy of Naples has published a volume of details, in which the greater part of the frescos of this villa are engraved. G. Passage, leading by the staircase B to the upper floor, and by the staircase H to the subterranean galleries. There is a similar staircase, H, on the other side of the portico. These galleries form a crypt beneath the portico, lighted and aired by loopholes on the level of the ground. Amphoræ, placed in sand against the wall, are still to be seen there, and for this reason it has been conjectured that the crypt served the purposes of a cellar; but even this crypt was coarsely painted. I. Mesaulon, or court, which separates the offices from the house. K. Small room at the extremity of the garden. L. An oratory; the niche served to receive a little statue. M. Xystus, or garden. N. Piscina, with a *jet d'eau*. O. Enclosure covered with a trellis. P. Door to the country, and towards the sea. Q. This enclosure, about fifteen feet wide, appears to have been covered with a trellis, and must have been much frequented, since there is a noble flight of steps leading down to it from the upper garden. It fronted the south, and must have been a delightful winter promenade.

We have given, as a Frontispiece to this Part, a general view of this delightful abode as it now exists, taken from the surface of the ground behind the garden portico.* The parts of it need little explanation after the minute account already given. The arch to the left is the end of the open hall, D, above the portico; on each side are the terraces, 34, 34, and in the centre are the remains of the cyzicene hall. Beneath, on the level of the portico, are the several rooms marked F, probably the chief summer abode of the family, being well adapted to that purpose by their refreshing coolness. Their ceilings for the most part are semicircular vaults, richly painted, and the more valuable because few

* Some of the surrounding accessories are now altered, from the progress of the excavations.

ceilings have been found in existence. We should attempt in vain to describe the complicated subjects, the intricate and varied patterns with which the fertile fancy of the arabesque painter has clothed the walls and ceilings, without the aid of drawings, which we are unable to give; and, indeed, coloured plates would be requisite to convey an adequate notion of their effect. In the splendid work which Mr. Donaldson has published upon Pompeii, several subjects taken from these rooms will be found, some of them coloured, together with eight mosaics, some of very complicated, all of elegant design; and to this and similar works we must refer the further gratification of the reader's curiosity.*

Such was this mansion, in which no doubt the owner took pride and pleasure, to judge from the expense lavished with unsparing hand on its decoration; and if he could be supposed to have any cognizance of what is now passing on earth, his vanity might find some consolation for having been prematurely deprived of it, in the posthumous celebrity which it has obtained. But his taste and wealth have done nothing to perpetuate his name, for not a trace remains that can indicate to what person or to what family it belonged. It is indeed usually called the Villa of Marcus Arrius Diomedes, on the strength of a tomb discovered about the same period immediately opposite to it, bearing that name. No other tomb had then been discovered so near it, and on this coincidence of situation a conclusion was drawn that this must have been a family sepulchre, attached to the house, and, by consequence, that the house itself belonged to Diomedes. The conjecture at the outset rested but on a sandy foundation, which has since been entirely sapped by the discovery of numerous other tombs almost equally near. All that we know of the owner or his family may be comprised in one sentence, which, short as it is, speaks forcibly to our feelings. Their life was one of elegant luxury and enjoyment, in the midst of which death came on them by surprise, a death of singular and lingering agony.

When Vesuvius first showed signs of the coming storm the air was still, as we learn from the description of Pliny, and the smoke of the mountain rose up straight, until the

* Louis I. of Bavaria caused a perfect copy of this villa, even in its smallest details, to be erected at Aschaffenburg.—ED.

atmosphere would bear it no higher, and then spread on all sides into a canopy, suggesting to him the idea of an enormous pine tree. After this a wind sprung up from the west, which was favourable to carry Pliny from Misenum to Stabiæ, but prevented his return. The next morning probably it veered something to the north, when, in the younger Pliny's words, a cloud seemed to descend upon the earth, to cover the sea, and hide the Isle of Capreæ from his view. The ashes are said by Dion Cassius to have reached Egypt, and in fact a line drawn south-east from Vesuvius would pass very near Pompeii, and cut Egypt. It was probably at this moment that the hail of fire fell thickest at Pompeii, at daybreak on the second morning, and if any had thus long survived the stifling air and torrid earth which surrounded them, their misery probably was at this moment brought to a close. The villa of which we speak lay exactly between the city and the mountain, and must have felt the first, and, if there were degrees of misery, where all perished alike, the worst effects of this fearful visitation. Fearful is such a visitation in the present day, even to those who crowd to see an eruption of Vesuvius as they would to a picture-gallery or an opera: how much more terrible, accompanied by the certainty of impending death, to those whom neither history nor experience had familiarized with the most awful phenomenon presented by nature. At this, or possibly at an earlier moment, the love of life proved too strong for the social affections of the owner of the house. He fled, abandoning to their fate a numerous family, and a young and beautiful daughter, and bent his way, with his most precious moveables, accompanied only by a single slave, to the sea, which he never reached alive. His daughter, two children, and other members of his family and household sought protection in the subterranean vaults, which, by the help of the wine-jars already stored there, and the provisions which they brought down with them, they probably considered as sufficient refuge against an evil of which they could not guess the whole extent. It was a vain hope: the same fate awaited them all by different ways. The strong vaults and narrow openings to the day protected them, indeed, from the falling cinders; but the heat, sufficient to char wood, and volatilize the more subtle part of the ashes, could not be kept out by such means. The vital air was changed into a sulphurous vapour, charged with burning dust. In their despair, longing for the pure breath of heaven, they rushed to the door, already choked with scoriæ and ruins, and perished in agonies on which the imagination does not willingly dwell.

This the reader will probably be inclined to think might do very well for the conclusion of a romance, but why invent such sentimental stories to figure in a grave historical account? It is a remarkable instance, perhaps the strongest which has yet occurred, of the peculiar interest which the discoveries at Pompeii possess, as introducing us to the homes, nay, to the very persons of a long-forgotten age, that every circumstance of this tale can be verified by evidence little less than conclusive. Beside the garden gate, marked P, two skeletons were found; one, presumed to be the master, had in his hand the key of that gate, and near him were about a hundred gold and silver coins; the other, stretched beside some silver vases, was probably a slave charged with the transport of them. When the vaults beneath the room, D, were discovered at the foot of the staircase, H, the skeletons of eighteen adult persons, a boy, and an infant were found huddled up together, unmoved during seventeen centuries since they sank in death.* They were covered by several feet of ashes of extreme fineness, evidently slowly borne in through the vent-holes, and afterwards consolidated by damp. The substance thus formed resembles the sand used by metal founders for castings, but is yet more delicate, and took perfect impressions of everything on which it lay. Unfortunately this property was not observed until almost too late, and little was preserved except the neck and breast of a girl, which are said to display extraordinary beauty of form. So exact is the impression, that the very texture of the dress in which she was clothed is apparent, which by its extraordinary fineness evidently shows that she had not been a slave, and may be taken for the fine gauze which Seneca calls woven wind. On other fragments the impression of jewels worn on the neck and arms is distinct, and marks that several members

* See *Pomp. Ant. Hist.*, t. i. p. 268, Dec. 12, 1772. Ten other skeletons were found at various times in or near the house. See the account of the excavations in *Pomp. Ant. Hist.* (1771, March 9; 1773, Feb. 6, 13; May 29; 1774, July 30; Oct. 29; Nov. 5).—ED.

of the family here perished. The jewels themselves were found beside them, comprising, in gold, two necklaces, one set with blue stones, and four rings, containing engraved gems. Two of the skeletons belonged to children, and some of their blond hair was still existent; most of them are said to have been recognized as female. Each sex probably acted in conformity to its character, the men trusting to their own strength to escape, the women waiting with patience the issue of a danger from which their own exertions could not save them.

In the same vault bronze candelabra, and other articles, jewels, and coins were found. Amphoræ were also found ranged against the wall, in some of which the contents, dried and hardened by time, were still preserved. Archæologists, it is said, pretend to recognize in this substance the flavour of the rich strong wine for which the neighbourhood of Vesuvius is celebrated.*

Besides the interior garden within the portico, there must have been another garden extending along the southern side of the house. The passage from the peristyle, 7, the position of the elliptic chamber, 16, and the trellis work, Q, with its spacious steps, leave no doubt on this subject. It has been stated in a German periodical that traces of the ploughshare have been distinguished in the fields adjoining this villa. This is the only authority we have for supposing that the process of excavation has been extended at all beyond the house itself. The garden to the south is still, to the best of our information, uncleared, nor is it likely that it contains objects of sufficient interest to recompense the labour which would be consumed in laying it open. Our limited knowledge of ancient horticulture is not therefore likely to be increased by means of Pompeii; for such small flower-plots as are

* Sir Thomas Brown would have rejoiced in such an opportunity. "Some fine sepulcrall vessels containing liquors which time hath incrassated into jellies. For besides their lachrymatories, notable lamps, with vessels of oil, and aromaticall liquors attended noble Ossuaries. And some yet retaining a vinosity and spirit in them, which if any have tasted, they have far exceeded the palates of Antiquity. Liquors not to be computed by years of annual magistrates, but by great conjunctions, and the fatal periods of kingdoms. The draughts of consulary date were but crude unto these, and Opimian wine but in the must unto them."—Hydriotaphia, A treatise on Urne Buriall, chap. iii.

attached to houses within the town cannot contain anything worth notice beyond a fountain or a summer triclinium. We will do our best, however, to complete the reader's notion of an Italian villa, and show what might have been, since we cannot show what has been here, by borrowing Pliny's account of the garden attached to his Tuscan villa, the only account of a Roman garden which has come down to us.

"In front of the house lies a spacious hippodrome,* entirely open in the middle, by which means the eye, upon your first entrance, takes in its whole extent at one view. It is encompassed on every side with plane trees covered with ivy, so that while their heads flourish with their own green, their bodies enjoy a borrowed verdure; and thus the ivy twining round the trunk and branches, spreads from tree to tree and connects them together. Between each plane tree are placed box trees, and behind these, bay trees, which blend their shade with that of the planes. This plantation, forming a straight boundary on both sides of the hippodrome, bends at the further end into a semicircle, which, being set round and sheltered with cypresses, casts a deeper and more gloomy shade; while the inward circular walks (for there are several) enjoying an open exposure, are full of roses, and correct the coolness of the shade by the warmth of the sun. Having passed through these several winding alleys,† you enter a straight walk, which breaks out into a variety of others, divided by box edges. In one place you have a little meadow; in another, the box is cut into a thousand different forms, sometimes into letters; here expressing the name of the master, there that of the artificer; while here and there little obelisks rise, intermixed with fruit trees; when on a sudden, in the midst of this elegant regularity, you are surprised with an imitation of the negligent beauties of rural nature, in the centre of which lies a spot surrounded with a knot of dwarf plane trees.‡ Beyond this is a walk, inter-

---

* Hippodrome was, in its proper meaning, a place for horse-racing: the Greek name for a circus. Being open, it may have been used for horse, as the gestatio was used for carriage exercise; but it seems more probable that here it was merely a walk, so called from its oblong form, rounded at the end.

† Here the garden itself seems properly to begin.

‡ The plane tree was highly valued for its shade, on which account it was a favourite tree with boon companions. Virgil speaks of it as " ministrantem —— potantibus umbras."—Georg. 4. The Romans, extravagant in all their

spersed with the smooth and twining acanthus, where the trees are also cut into a variety of names and shapes. At the upper end is an alcove of white marble, shaded with vines, supported by four small columns of Carystian marble. Here is a triclinium, out of which the water, gushing through several little pipes, as if it were pressed out by the weight of the persons who repose upon it, falls into a stone cistern underneath, from whence it is received into a fine polished marble basin, so artfully contrived that it is always full without ever overflowing. When I sup here, this basin serves for a table, the larger sort of dishes being placed round the margin, while the smaller swim about in the form of little vessels and water-fowl. Corresponding to this is a fountain, which is incessantly emptying and filling; for the water, which it throws up to a great height, falling back again into it, is returned as fast as it is received, by means of two openings. Fronting the alcove stands a summer-house of exquisite marble, whose doors project and open into a green enclosure, while from its upper and lower windows also the eye is presented with a variety of different verdures. Next to this is a little private closet, which, though it seems distinct, may be laid into the same room, furnished with a couch; and notwithstanding it has windows on every side, yet it enjoys a very agreeable gloominess, by means of a spreading vine, which climbs to the top and entirely overshades it. Here you may lie and fancy yourself in a wood, with this difference only, that you are not exposed to the weather. In this place a fountain also rises, and instantly disappears. In different quarters are disposed several marble seats, which serve, as well as the summer-house, as so many reliefs after one is tired of walking. Near each seat is a little fountain, and throughout the whole hippodrome several small rills run murmuring along, wheresoever the hand of art thought proper to conduct them, watering here and there different spots of verdure, and in their progress refreshing the whole."*

---

likings, used to moisten the roots with wine, believing that it thrived best on that liquor. There was a famous one in Lycia, hollow with age, the trunk of which was eighty-one Roman feet in circumference within, which was the favourite feasting-place of a Roman proconsul, Licinius Mutianus.—Plin. xii. 1. Xerxes presented a gold cup to a plane tree in Lydia.—Herod. vii. 31.

* Plin. Epist. v. 6; Melmoth's translation.

Between this villa and the city there is another, which was excavated at different times between 1749 and 1778, and filled up again when the valuable things found in it had been removed, in conformity with the general practice at that time, to prevent the proprietors being injured by the loss of ground. Several admirable mosaics and some fine frescoes were found in it. We find mentioned the celebrated paintings of the eight female dancers; the four groups of the Centaurs; and the Funambuli, or rope-dancers, which decorated an eating-room. Hence, too, were taken the two mosaics with the name of Dioscorides of Samos inscribed upon them, one of which has been described. Both represent comic scenes, and, according to Winckelmann, deserve the preference even over the celebrated ancient Roman mosaic of the doves, which has hitherto been in such high esteem.

The general arrangement of this villa resembles that which we have just described; but it is on a still larger scale, and from the richness of the decorations evidently belonged to one of the chief persons of the place. It is usually called the Villa of Cicero, who certainly possessed a house near Pompeii, of which continual mention is made in his letters; but there is no evidence whatever to identify this as his abode. It has also been sometimes called the Baths of M. Crassus Frugi, from an inscription found in it. The front to the street is occupied by a row of shops, with an arcade before them. At the end nearest the town is a large reservoir of rain water for the use of the house. Next to it is the entrance, from which a very long passage or vestibule, with numerous apartments on each side, supposed to have been stables and other offices, led into the Corinthian atrium. Beyond and around this were numerous rooms for the use of the family, galleries and terraces commanding a view of the sea. At a lower level is a covered portico, resembling in its plan that of the Suburban Villa, and nearly of the same extent. Above the portico was formed a terrace, which still exists, and commands a fine view both of the sea and land. The court within it was a xystus, or garden. Between this portico and the street is another large court of irregular figure, containing several large basins built in masonry. The information which has been preserved concerning this house is very scanty, in consequence of the early period at which it was reinterred.

CHAPTER XI.

TOMBS.

BEFORE commencing our description of the tombs which line the way as the visitor approaches from Naples, and seem to prepare him for that funereal silence which reigns in the long-lost city, the more remarkable for its contrast with the gay and festive style of decoration which still characterizes the remains which surround him, it is our intention, as we have done in other instances, to give some general information upon the subject which we are about to treat in detail, for the benefit of those among our readers to whom the forms of Roman burial and the expressions of Roman sorrow are unfamiliar.

Great, absurdly great among the uneducated, as is the importance attached to a due performance of the rites of burial in the present day, it is as nothing compared to the interest which was felt on this subject by the Romans; and not by them only, but by other nations of antiquity, with whose manners we have nothing to do here. The Romans indeed had a good reason for this anxiety, for they believed, in common with the Greeks, that if the body remained unentombed, the soul wandered for a hundred years on the hither side of the Styx, alone and desponding, unable to gain admission to its final resting-place, whether among the happy or the miserable. If, therefore, any person perished at sea, or otherwise under such circumstances that his body could not be found, a *cenotaph*, or empty tomb, was erected by his surviving friends, which served as well for his passport over the Stygian ferry as if his body had been burnt or committed to the earth with due ceremonies. Hence it became a religious duty, not rashly to be neglected, to scatter earth over any unburied body which men chanced to see, for even so slight a sepulchre as this was held sufficient to appease the scruples of the infernal gods. The reader, if there be any readers of Latin to whom these superstitions are unfamiliar, may refer to the sixth book of the Æneid, line 325, and to a remarkable ode of Horace, the 28th of the first book, which turns entirely upon this subject. Burial, therefore, was a matter of considerable importance.

When death approached, the nearest relative hung over the dying person, endeavouring to inhale his last breath, in a fond belief that the *anima*, the living principle, departed at that moment, and by that passage from the body. Hence the phrases, *animam in primo ore tenere, spiritum excipere*, and the like. It is curious to observe how an established form of expression holds its ground. Here are we, after the lapse of eighteen hundred years, still talking of receiving a dying friend's last breath, as if we really meant what we say. After death the body was washed and anointed by persons called *pollinctores*; then laid out on a bier, the feet to the door, to typify its approaching departure, dressed in the best attire which it had formerly owned. The bier was often decked with leaves and flowers, a simple and touching tribute of affection, which is of the heart, and speaks to it, and therefore has maintained its ground in every age and region, unaffected by the constant changes in customs merely arbitrary and conventional.

In the early ages of Rome the rites of burial and burning seem to have been alike in use. Afterwards the former seems (for the matter is not very clear) to have prevailed, until towards the close of the seventh century of the city, after the death of Sylla, who is said to have been the first of the patrician Cornelii who was burnt.* Thenceforward corpses were almost universally consumed by fire until the establishment of Christianity, when the old fashion was brought up again, burning being violently opposed by the fathers of the church, probably on account of its intimate connection with Pagan associations and superstitions. Seven days, we are told, elapsed between death and the funeral; on the eighth the corpse was committed to the flames; on the ninth the ashes were deposited in the sepulchre. This probably refers only to the funerals of the great, where much splendour and extent of preparation was required, and especially those public funerals (*funera indictiva*) to which the whole people were bidden by voice of crier, the ceremony being often closed by

---

* Cic. Legg. ii. 22.

theatrical and gladiatorial exhibitions, and a sumptuous banquet. But we have no intention to narrate the pomp which accompanied the princely nobles of Rome to the tomb : it is enough for our purpose to explain the usages of private life, to which the Street of Tombs owes its origin and its interest.

In the older times funerals were celebrated at night because the rites of religion were celebrated by day; and it was pollution for the ministers, or for anything connected with worship of the deities of the upper world, even to see, much more to touch, anything connected with death. From this nightly solemnization many of the words connected with this subject are derived. Those who bore the bier were called originally *Vesperones*, thence *Vespillones*, from *Vespera*, evening; and the very term *funus* is derived by grammarians, *a funalibus*, from the rope torches coated with wax or tallow which continued to be used long after the necessity for using them ceased.* This practice, now far more than two thousand years old, is still retained in the Roman Church, with many other ceremonies borrowed from heathen rites. St. Chrysostom assures us that it is not of modern revival, and gives a beautiful reason for its being retained. "Tell me," he says, "what mean those brilliant lamps ? Do we not go forth with the dead on their way rejoicing, as with men who have fought their fight?"†

The corpse being placed upon a litter (*letica*) or bier (*sandapila*), the former being used by the wealthy, the latter by the poor, was carried out (*efferebatur*) preceded by instrumental musicians (*siticines*), and female singers (*præficæ*), who chanted the dirge (*nenia*). These hired attendants, whose noisy sorrow was as genuine as the dumb grief of our mutes, were succeeded, if the deceased were noble, or distinguished by personal exploits, by numerous couches containing the family effigies of his ancestors, each by itself, that the length of his lineage might be the more conspicuous ; by the images of such nations as he had conquered, such cities as he had taken ; by the spoils which he had won ; by the ensigns of

---

* Thus Tacitus, Plena urbis itinera, collucentes per campum Martis faces.— Ann. iii. 4.

† εἰπέ μοι—τί βούλονται αἱ λαμπάδες αἱ φαιδραὶ ; οὐκ ὡς ἀθλητὰς αὐτοὺς (τοὺς τεθνηκότας) προπέμπομεν ; Chrysost. Hom. iv. ad Herb.

the magistracies which he had filled; but if the fasces were among them these were borne reversed. Then came the slaves whom he had emancipated (and often with a view to this post-mortem magnificence, a master emancipated great numbers of them), wearing hats in token of their manumission. Behind the corpse came the nearest relations, profuse in the display of grief as far as it can be shown by weeping, howling, beating the breasts and cheeks, and tearing the hair, which was laid, as a last tribute of affection, on the breast of the deceased, to be consumed with him.* To shave the head was also a sign of mourning. It is a curious inversion of the ordinary customs of life, that the sons of the deceased mourned with the head covered, the daughters with it bare.

With this attendance the body was borne to the place of burial, being usually carried through the Forum, where, if the deceased had been a person of any eminence, a funeral oration was spoken from the rostra in his honour. The place of burial was without the city, in almost every instance. By the twelve tables it was enacted that no one should be burnt or buried within the city; and as this wholesome law fell into disuse, it was from time to time revived and enforced. The reasons for its establishment were twofold, religious and civil. To the former head belongs the reason, already assigned for a different observance, that the very sight of things connected with death brought pollution on things consecrated to the gods of the upper world. So far was this carried that the priest of Jupiter (*Flamen Dialis*) might not even enter any place where there was a tomb, or so much as hear the funeral pipes: nay, his wife, the Flaminica, might not wear shoes made of the hide of an ox which had died a natural death, because all things which had died spontaneously were of ill omen.† Besides, it was an ill omen to any one to come upon a tomb unawares. Another reason was that the public convenience might not be interrupted by private

---

* Thus Ovid, speaking of Phaeton—
————————Planxere sorores
Naiades, et sectos fratri imposuere capillos.—Met. iii
Seneca also alludes to the custom:—
Placemus umbras; capitis exuvia cape,
Laceræq: frontis accipe abscissam comam.
Phædra, Act. i. sc. 1.

† Quoniam sua morte extincta omnia funesta sunt.—Fest.

rites, since no tombs could be removed without sacrilege when once established, unless by the state, upon sufficient cause.* The civil reasons are to be sought in the unwholesome exhalations of large burying-grounds, and the danger of fire from burning funeral piles in the neighbourhood of houses. It is not meant, however, that there were no tombs within the city. Some appear to have been included by the gradual extension of the walls; others were established in those intervals when the law of the twelve tables fell, as we have said, into desuetude; nor does it appear that these were destroyed, nor their contents removed. Thus both the Claudian and the Cincian clans had sepulchres in Rome, the former under the Capitol.†

If the family were of sufficient consequence to have a patrimonial tomb the deceased was laid in it: if he had none such, and was wealthy, he usually constructed a tomb upon his property during life, or bought a piece of ground for the purpose. If possible the tomb was always placed near a road. Hence the usual form of inscription, *Siste, Viator* (Stay, Traveller), continually used in churches by those small wits who thought that nothing could be good English which was not half Latin, and forgot that in our country the traveller must have stayed already to visit the sexton, before he can possibly do so in compliance with the advice of the monument. For the poor there were public burial-grounds, called *puticuli, a puteis,* from the trenches ready dug to receive bodies. Such was the ground at the Esquiline gate, which Augustus gave Mæcenas for his gardens.‡ Public

* That it might be done under the sanction of the religious authorities, we learn from Cicero: "Statuit collegium locum publicum non potuisse privata religione obligari."—Legg. ii. 23.

† Suet. Tiber. There were tombs belonging to the clans (gentes), in which none but those of the clan, and therefore participating in the same sacred rites, could be buried. Tanta religio est sepulcrorum, ut extra sacra et gentem inferri fas negent esse.—Cic. Legg. ii. 22. [But a tomb might be under the Capitol and yet without the old Servian walls, as, for instance, the tomb of Bibulus, which may still be seen. The privilege of being buried within the walls belonged, by virtue of their office, to the Vestals, and was sometimes extended to distinguished persons.—ED.]

‡ Nunc licet Esquiliis habitare salubribus, atque
  Aggere in aprico spatiari; quo modo tristes
Albis informem spectabant ossibus humum.

Hor. Sat. i. viii. 14.

tombs were also granted by the state to eminent men; an honour in early times conferred on few.* These grants were usually made in the Campus Martius, where no one could legally be buried without a decree of the senate in his favour. It appears from the inscriptions found in the Street of Tombs at Pompeii, that much, if not the whole of the ground on which those tombs are built, was public property, the property of the corporation, as we should now say; and that the sites of many, perhaps of all, were either purchased, or granted by the decurions, or municipal senate, in gratitude for obligations received.

Sometimes the body was burnt at the place where it was to be entombed, which, when the pile and sepulchre were thus joined, was called *bustum*;† sometimes the sepulchre was at a distance from the place of burning, which was then called *ustrina*.‡ The words *bustum* and *sepulchrum*, therefore, though often loosely used as synonymous, are not in fact so, the latter being involved in, but by no means comprehending the former. The pile was ordered to be built of rough wood, unpolished by the axe. Pitch was added to quicken the flames, and cypress, the aromatic scent of which was useful to overpower the stench of the burning body. The funeral piles of great men were of immense size, and splendidly adorned; and all classes appear to have indulged their vanity in this respect to the utmost of their means, so that a small and unattended pyre is mentioned as the mark of an insignificant or friendless person. The body was placed on it in the litter or hier; the nearest relation present then opened the eyes, which it had been the duty of the same person to close immediately after death, and set fire to the wood with averted face, in testimony that he performed that office not of goodwill, but of necessity. As the combustion proceeded, various offerings were cast into the flames. The manes were believed to love blood: animals, therefore, especially those which they had loved while alive, were killed and thrown upon the pile, as horses, dogs, and doves, besides the beasts commonly

---

* Majores nostri statuas multis decreverunt, sepulcra paucis.—Cic. Philipp. ix.

† We may trace the signification of *bustum* in its derivation from *buro*, the original form of the verb *uro*, to burn, as in *comburo*.

‡ Festus.

used in sacrifice, as sheep and oxen. Human beings, especially prisoners of war, were sometimes put to death, though not in the later times of the republic. The most costly robes and arms of the deceased, especially trophies taken in warfare, were also devoted in his honour, and the blaze was fed by the costly oils and gums of the East. The body being reduced to ashes, these were then quenched with wine, and collected by the nearest relation ; after which, if the grief were real, they were again bedewed with tears; if not, wine or unguents answered the purpose equally well. The whole ceremony is described in few lines by Tibullus:—

> There, while the fire lies smouldering on the ground,
> My bones, the all of me, can then be found.
> Arrayed in mourning robes, the sorrowing pair
> Shall gather all around with pious care;
> With ruddy wine the relics sprinkle o'er,
> And snowy milk on them collected pour.
> Then with fair linen cloths the moisture dry,
> Inurned in some cold marble tomb to lie.
> With them enclose the spices, sweets, and gums,
> And all that from the rich Arabia comes,
> And what Assyria's wealthy confines send,
> And tears, sad offering, to my memory lend.—Eleg. iii. 2–17.

The ashes thus collected were then finally deposited in the urn, which was made of different materials, according to the quality of the dead; usually of clay or glass, but sometimes of marble, bronze, and even the precious metals. The ceremony thus over, the præfica gave the word, *Ilicet* (the contracted form of *Ire licet,* It is lawful to go), and the bystanders departed, having been thrice sprinkled with a branch of olive or laurel dipped in water, to purify them from the pollution which they had contracted, and repeating thrice the words, *Vale,* or *Salve,* words of frequent occurrence in monumental inscriptions, as in one of beautiful simplicity which we quote below.*

Before the urn was committed to the tomb the interval of a day frequently elapsed ; and often, after the funeral, a feast

---

* VALE . ET . SALVE . ANIMA . C. OPPIÆ . FELICISS. NOS . EO . ORDINE . QUO . NATURA . PERMISERIT . TE . SEQUEMUR . VALE . MATER . DULCISSIMA. "Farewell, most happy soul of Caia Oppia. We shall follow thee in such order as may be appointed by nature. Farewell, sweetest mother."

was held in honour of the dead, at which his urn was placed in a conspicuous situation. This portion of the subject we reserve for future discussion. Tombs were of two sorts: those which were erected for the reception of a single person, or of such persons as the builder chose to admit to a participation of it, in which case a curse was usually denounced on all who violated it by introducing the bones of others; and those again which were built as family monuments, where the freed slaves of the family, who could of course have no sepulchres of their own except by purchase, were frequently admitted. An instance of this sort occurs in the Street of Tombs, in the tomb erected by Nævoleia Tyche. Each tomb was usually encircled by a low wall or palisade; and as not only the building itself, but the plot of ground on which it stood, was consecrated, it was usual to place an inscription, stating how much ground was allotted, and consequently how far the sacred part extended. "In fronte pedes tot . in agro pedes tot."

The distinction between cenotaphs and tombs has been already explained. Cenotaphs, however, were of two sorts: those erected to persons already duly buried, which were merely honorary, and those erected to the unburied dead, which had a religious end and efficacy. This evasion of the penal laws against lying unburied was chiefly serviceable to persons shipwrecked or slain in war; but all came in for the benefit of it whose bodies could not be found or identified. When a cenotaph of the latter class was erected sacrifices were offered, the manes of the deceased were thrice invoked with a loud voice, as if to summon them to their new abode, which part of the ceremony was called $\psi\upsilon\chi\alpha\gamma\omega\gamma\grave{\iota}\alpha$, and the cenotaph was hallowed with the same privileges as if the ashes of the deceased reposed within it.*

The heir, however, had not discharged his last duty when he had laid the body of his predecessor in the tomb: there were still due solemn rites, and those of an expensive character. The Romans loved to keep alive the memory of their dead, showing therein a constancy of affection which does

---

* Statuent tumulum, et tumulo solemnia mittent
 Æternumq. locus Palinuri nomen habebit.—Æn. vi. 380.
. . . . Tumulum Rhæteo in litore iuanem
 Constitui, et magna manes ter voce vocavi.—Ib. 505.

them honour; and not only immediately after the funeral, but at stated periods from time to time, they celebrated feasts and offered sacrifices and libations to them. The month of February was especially set apart for doing honour to the manes, having obtained that distinction in virtue of being, in old times, the last month of the year. Private funeral feasts were also celebrated on the ninth day after death (*novemdialia*), and indeed at any time, except on those days which were marked as unlucky (*atri*), because some great public calamity had befallen upon them. Besides these feasts, the dead were honoured with (*inferiæ*) sacrifices, which were offered (*inferebantur*) to the manes, and with games; but the latter belong more to those splendid public funerals which we have professed not to describe. The inferiæ consisted principally of libations, for which were used water, milk, wine, but especially blood, the smell of which was thought peculiarly palatable to the ghosts. Perfumes and flowers were also thrown upon the tomb; and the inexpediency of wasting rich wines and precious oils* on a cold stone and dead body, when they might be employed in comforting the living, was a favourite subject with the *bons vivans* of the age. It was with the same design to crown it with garlands, and to honour it with libations, that Electra and Orestes met and recognized each other at their father's tomb. Roses were in especial request for this service, and lilies also:—

> Full canisters of fragrant lilies bring,
> Mixed with the purple roses of the spring;
> Let me with funeral flowers his body strow,
> This gift which parents to their children owe,
> This unavailing gift at least I may bestow.
>
> Dryden, Æn. vi. 883.

Other plants however were set apart as having a special fitness for this purpose. The Greeks used amaranthus, which, without much violence, may be translated, everlasting; and, in truth, is commonly understood to mean the flower so named. Parsley and myrtle were also funereal plants; still

---

* Thus Anacreon—

Τί δὲ δεῖ λίθον μυρίζειν;
Τί δὲ γῇ χέειν μάταια;
Ἐμὲ μᾶλλον, ὡς ἔτι ζῶ
Μυρίσον, ῥόδοις δε ....ὰ
Πυκάσον . . . . .

the rose was in early ages the favourite for this last, as for all other uses.* The Romans were so fond of it, that we find inscriptions making mention of legacies, bestowed on condition that the monument of the testator should be annually crowned with roses. They also made much use of woollen fillets (*infulæ, tæniæ*), one remarkable application of which will be noticed in the course of this chapter.

In the earliest ages of Christianity these practices were strenuously denounced as savouring of idolatry. The objectionable parts, the sacrifices and libations, once abandoned, were of course never resumed; but it is curious to see how soon the hearts of men wandered back to a simple, natural, and elegant method of testifying affection. Even so soon as the fourth century, St. Jerome and Prudentius had so far conquered their fears of Paganism, that they speak of the custom of strewing tombs with flowers, and speak of it with complacency.

The first tomb on the left, marked 1 on the following plan, which presents itself to the traveller as he approaches the Gate of Herculaneum, bears the name of Diomedes, and stands just opposite the Suburban Villa, to which it has lent a name. To modern notions there is something discordant in thus intermingling life and death, and even those who have least cause to fear the final hour, and who look with the warmest interest upon the spot where those loved ones who have gone before them are deposited, would shrink from the close association of such objects with their every-day business and pleasures. One remarkable instance of a contrary feeling in a remarkable man is well known; it is that of Nelson, who kept the coffin made, after the battle of the Nile, out of the mainmast of L'Orient, in his cabin, in full sight: but the display was not so agreeable to his friends, who never rested till they got it stowed away in the hold. In this aversion the Romans had no share. Death was to them the end of sensation and pleasure, yet, instead of regarding the emblems of it with aversion, they rather sought in them a higher relish for present enjoyment. That singular custom, bor-

---

* So Anacreon—

Εἰς ῥόδον.
Τόδε καὶ νοσοῦσιν ἀρκεῖ
Τόδε καὶ νεκροῖς ἀμύνει.

rowed from the Egyptians, is well known, by which a skeleton was not unfrequently introduced among the guests at festive parties, with the exhortation, pointed by appealing to the sapless bones, " Let us live while the power of enjoyment is ours." *

This tomb, as well as almost all which which have been found, is raised upon a platform of masonry above the level of the footway. To the extreme left is a wall, which seems to mark the limits of the family burial-place. Near it stand

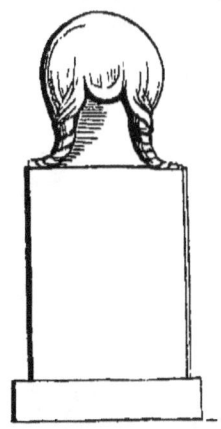

Funeral Column.

two *cippi*, or funeral columns, one erected to Arria, a daughter probably, the other to Arrius, his eldest son. These are surmounted by hemispheres, the flat side presented to the road —a form of monument not uncommon at Pompeii; and one which, when the hinder part is carved in imitation of hair, with dependent tresses, it is difficult to see without thinking of that antidote to sentiment, a barber's block. A low wall divides these monuments from the principal one; but that they all belong to one family is made evident by an inscription placed directly under this partition :—

ARRIAE · M · F · (iliæ)
DIOMEDES · L · SIBI · SVIS ·

---

* Vivamus, dum licet esse bene. The Egyptians introduced a wooden figure of a mummy, and their formula ran differently, according to Herodotus. Ἐς τοῦτον ὁρέων πῖνέ τε καὶ τέρπεο, ἔσσεαι γὰρ ἀποθανὼν τοιοῦτος. ii. 78. " Regarding this, drink and enjoy thyself, for such as this wilt thou be after death."

510   POMPEII.

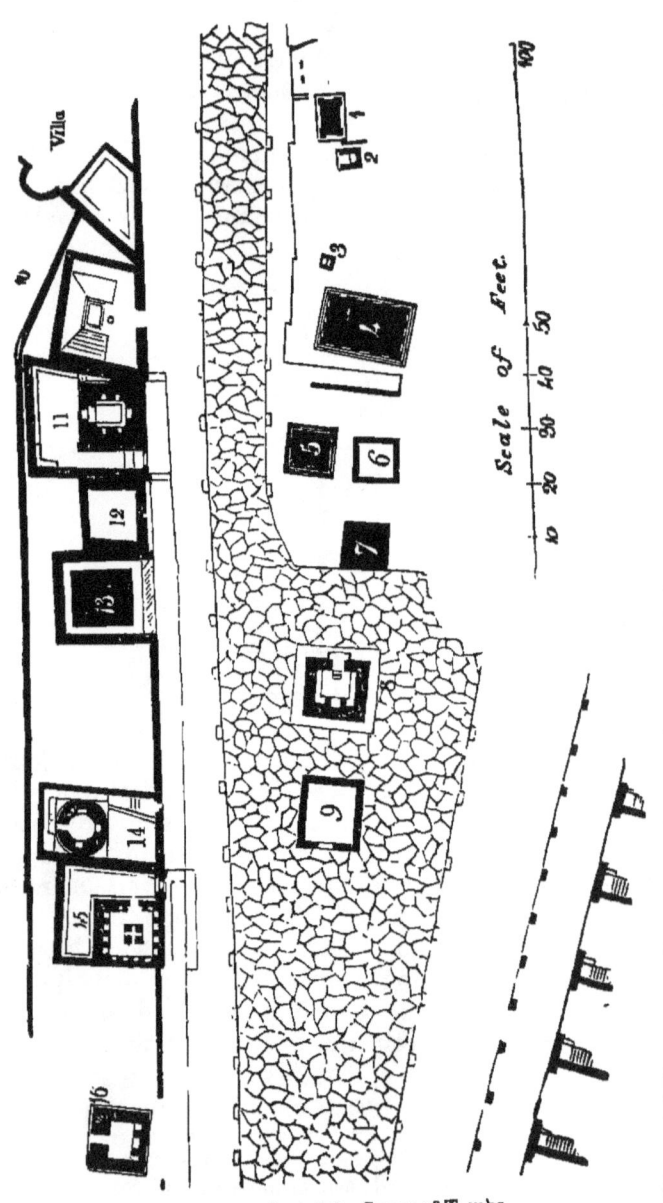

Ground-plan of the Street of Tombs

Gate of Herculaneum.

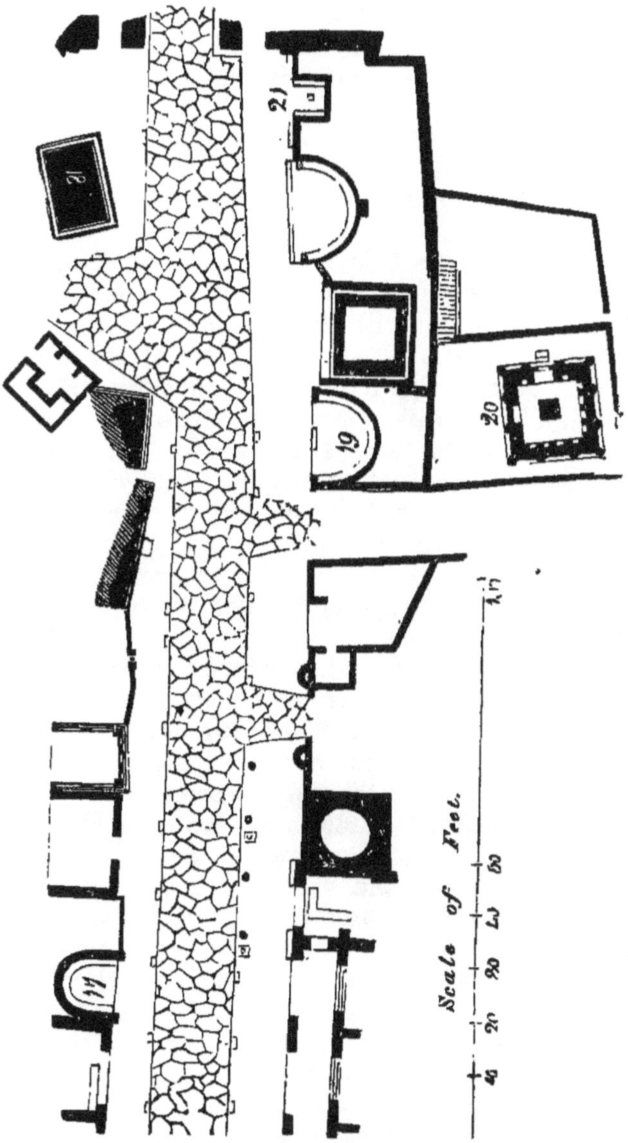

Ground-plan of the Street of Tombs.

The tomb itself is a solid building, not fitted for the reception of urns, and therefore merely erected in commemoration, like the cippi above described. The façade is about nine feet broad and twelve high, and presents two pilasters, which support a pediment. The capitals are capricious, but not inelegant. Under the pediment is the following inscription:—

M. ARRIVS · ⁚ · L · DIOMEDES
SIBI · SVIS MEMORIAE
MAGISTER · PAG · AUG · FELIC · SVBVRB.

The letter preceding the L is much defaced, and its signification not determined; it seems to have been the initial of a name. The inscription will signify that "Marcus Arrius Diomedes, freedman of . . . . . , president of the suburb of Augusta Felix, erected this building as a memorial of himself and his family." Of this suburb the Street of Tombs is supposed to have formed part. Below are fasces, the emblems of authority, which show that he was one of the chief municipal magistrates, but reversed, in conformity with the custom in cases of mourning, which we have already noticed. The building is of rough stone, covered with stucco. Beside it is a small building, 2, with a semicircular recess, apparently containing a seat.

On the same platform are two other tombs: the one, 3, striking only from its diminutive size and plainness, is evidently the humble tribute of some poor family to a departed member; the other, 4, is of considerable size and pretensions. It formed an oblong building, the sides ornamented with pilasters, which supported an entablature crowned by statues. The upper part of the tomb is now destroyed, but the fragments of the entablature and statues found about it testify plainly that such must have been the design. The side next the city is ornamented by two bas-reliefs, much broken, and the front has the remains of two medallions, which probably contained portraits of Lucius Ceius and Lucius Labeo, to whom the tomb was erected by their freedman, Menomachus.

The next tomb, marked 5 on the plan, is solid, and composed entirely of blocks of travertine; and in consequence it remains perfect, while the surrounding buildings, run up with small stones and stucco, are all of them more or less degraded. The form is simple and elegant, resembling the pedestal of a column; the base about twelve feet square, the height sixteen feet. It is decorated with a well-designed moulding and cornice, beneath which, both on the southern and western sides, is the inscription :—

M · ALLEIO · LVCCIO · LIBELLAE · PATRI · AEDILI
II · VIR · PRAEFECTO · QVINQ · ET · M · ALLEIO · LIBELLAE · F.
DECVRIONI · VIXIT · ANNIS · XVII · LOCVS · MONVMENTI
PVBLICE · DATVS · EST · ALLEIA · M · F · DECIMILLA · SACERDOS
PVBLICA · CERERIS · FACIENDVM · CVRAVIT · VIRO · ET · FILIO

"To M. Alleius Luccius Libella, the father, Ædile, Duumvir, Quinquennial Prefect, and M. Alleius Libella, his son, Decurion, who lived to the age of seventeen, was assigned the site of this monument at the public charge. Alleia Decimilla, daughter of Marcus, Public Priestess of Ceres, erected it to her husband and son."

The offices of Duumvir and Decurion corresponded in the municipal towns with those of Consul and Senator at Rome, as we have before had occasion to mention. It is remarkable that the rank of Decurion, which, according to a passage in Macrobius (*Sat.* ii. 3), was very difficult to be obtained at Pompeii, should have been enjoyed by a youth of seventeen. The same passage shows that the rank of Decurio answered to that of Senator.*

Behind this tomb the reader will observe a small sepulchral enclosure, and the commencement of another building, marked 6 and 7 on the plan. Neither presents anything worthy of notice.

The next, marked 8, placed at the junction of two roads, and called the Tomb with the Marble Door, has nothing remarkable in its exterior. It is composed of small pieces of tufa, laid sometimes horizontally, sometimes in diamonds,† the top much broken. In front is a low entrance, about four feet high, which was closed by a marble door, turning upon bronze pivots received in sockets of the same metal. It was drawn to by a ring and closed by a lock, probably of the same metal: the holes cut to receive them are still

* Cicero facilitatem Cæsaris in allegendo Senatu irrisit palam; nam cum ab hospite suo P. Mallio rogaretur ut decurionatum privigno ejus expediret, assistente frequentia dixit ; Romæ si vis habebit, Pompeiis difficile est.
† Opus reticulatum.

514 POMPEII.

to be seen. In the interior is a small chamber, lighted by a high window in the back of the tomb. Beneath the window, opposite the door, is a niche, in which an alabaster vase was found. Other vases, in glass, earth, and marble, were standing upon a ledge which runs around the chamber. The reader

Interior of the Tomb with the marble door.

will observe the *columbaria*, or little niches, so called from their resemblance to the holes of a pigeon-house, in which the urns are severally deposited.

Beyond this tomb, where the two roads separate, are the remains of a small square enclosure, 9, probably an *ustrinum* or place for burning dead bodies. Its isolated situation appears to render it peculiarly suited to this purpose. It is not uncommon to find inscriptions on monuments forbidding the application of funeral piles against them: "Ad hoc monumentum ustrinum applicare non licet."

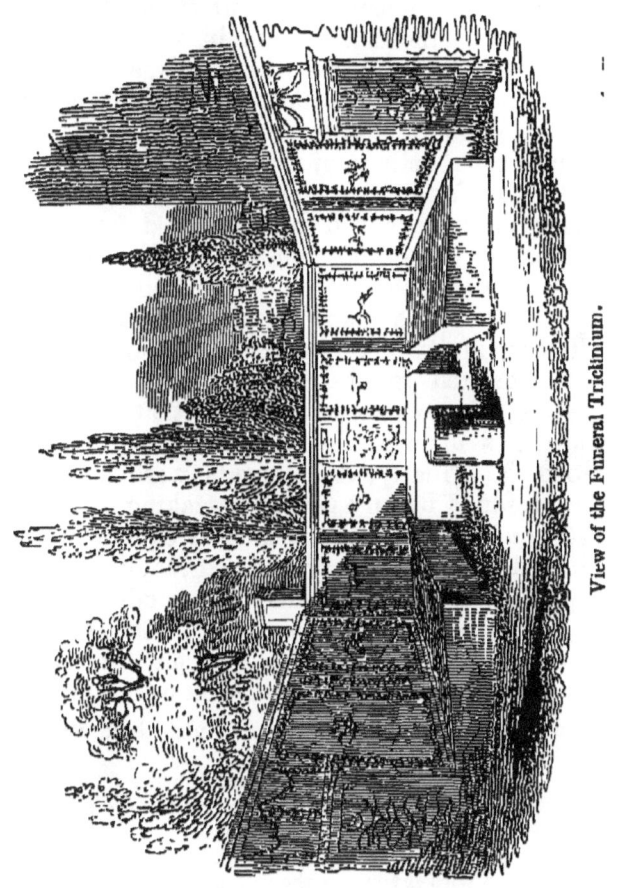

View of the Funeral Triclinium.

We will now cross to the other side of the road, where the monuments are in better preservation and more interesting. Close to the Villa of Diomedes is a small enclosure, of irregular figure, presenting to the street a plain front about twenty feet in length, stuccoed and unornamented, except by a low pediment and cornice. The door is remarkably low, not more than five feet high. Entering, we find ourselves within a chamber open to the sky, the walls cheerfully decorated with paintings of animals in the centre of compartments bordered with flowers.* Before us is a stone triclinium, with a massive pedestal in the centre to receive the table, and a round pillar in advance of it. It is a funeral triclinium, for the celebration of feasts in honour of the dead: the pillar probably supported the urn of him in whose honour the entertainments were given, after which it was deposited in the tomb. Some notice of these funeral feasts will complete our account of the honours paid to the dead.

Although a usual tribute of respect, they were not a necessary part of the funeral ceremonies, insomuch that a disappointed heir often revenged himself by defrauding the deceased of this portion of his honours.† The name given to them was *silicernium*, of which, according to a voluminous antiquary, there are as many etymologies as there are syllables. The antiquity of this practice appears from Homer; ‡ and it still existed in the fourth century, in the time of St. Augustine, who expressed wonder "that men should heap meats and wines upon tombs, as if departed spirits required fleshly food."§ Finally, those meats were burnt, lest they should be profaned by any person partaking of them, and the term *bustirapus*, tomb-snatcher, is of frequent occurrence, to denote the extreme of misery and degradation, which alone, it was supposed, could drive men to plunder these devoted banquets. Another class of funeral feasts was of a more cheerful description, and consisted of an entertainment, not only to be partaken, but to be consumed by the dearest friends

---

* These have now vanished, and the whole place is in a very dilapidated condition.

† ———— Sed cœnam funeris hæres
Negliget iratus, si rem curtaveris.—Pers. iv. 33.

‡ ———————— Eurylochus
Held fast the destined sacrifice, while I
Scooped with my sword the soil, opening a trench
Ell-wide on every side: then poured around
Libation consecrate to all the dead,
First milk with honey mixed, then luscious wine,
Then water, sprinkling last meal over all.
  * * * * *
Piercing the victims next, I turned them both
To bleed into the trench: then swarming came
From Erebus the shades of the deceased.
        Cowper, Odyss. xi. 23, *seq.*

§ De Sanctis, Serm. 15.

and relations of the deceased. Sometimes it was given at the time of the funeral, in which case the urn of the deceased appears to have been exposed to view, sometimes at the purificatory sacrifice (*novemdiale*) at the end of nine days, sometimes at later periods of annual recurrence. Legacies were sometimes left to defray the expense of an annual feast. Mention is made of Minutius Anteras, a freedman, who left an annual sum of 10,000 sesterces, about 80*l.*, to be spent in his honour. Public feasts were sometimes given by very wealthy men in honour of their relations, as did the son of Sylla in honour of his father, and Julius Cæsar in honour of his daughter. At these the whole people were entertained at an enormous expense. Certain dishes were peculiarly appropriate to the funeral meal, among which were beans, parsley, eggs, lentils, and a cake called libum, not, however, to the exclusion of meat. Even on these mournful occasions the guests came dressed in white; to appear in black seems to have been a sort of profanation. There is a remarkable charge in the Oration against Vatinius, that at a public funeral entertainment, given by Q. Arrius, he had appeared among the senators assembled in the temple of Castor in a black robe. " Who ever, at a private funeral, appeared at table in a mourning gown? who but yourself ever took a mourning gown on leaving the bath? When so many thousands were set down, when the master of the feast, Q. Arrius, was in white, you burst like an omen of evil into the temple of Castor, with Caius Fidulus, in black, and the rest of your furies."*

Bonucci calls this triclinium the sepulchral chamber of Saturninus. We have not access to his work, and cannot tell what is his authority for the assertion. Mazois gives no inscription.† It is the only erection of its kind in the Street of Tombs, and we should almost consider it as built for the general accommodation, or perhaps as matter of speculation, and let out on hire.‡

The monument which stands next is intended for the

---

* Cic. in Vatin. 13. The allusion to the bath is another proof how invariably the Romans resorted to it before the afternoon meal.

† An inscription built into the gable says that it was erected in honour of Cn. Vibrius Saturninus, of the Falernian Tribe, by his freeman Callistus. See Mommsen, *Inscrr. Regni Neap.* No. 2349.—ED.

‡ For the elevation of this and following tombs, see above, p. 429.

common burial-place of a family. It consists, as will be seen
more clearly by looking to the ground plan, No. 11, of a
square building, containing a small chamber, by the side of
which is a door giving admission to a small court surrounded

Tomb of Nævoleia Tyche.

by a high wall. The entrance to the chamber is at the back.
From the level of the outer wall rise two steps, supporting a
marble cippus richly ornamented. Its front is occupied by a
bas-relief and inscription, of which we annex a copy:—

NAEVOLEIA · I · LIB · TYCHE · SIBI · ET
C · MVNATIO · FAVSTO · AVG · ET · PAGANO
CVI · DECVRIONES · CONSENSV · POPVLI
BISELLIVM · OB · MERITA · EIVS · DECREVERVNT
HOC · MONIMENTVM · NAEVOLEIA · TYCHE · LIBERTIS · SVIS
LIBERTABVSQ · ET · C · MVNATI · FAVSTI · VIVA · FECIT

The latter is to the following purport:—"Nævoleia Tyche, freedwoman of Julia Tyche, to herself and to Caius Munatius Faustus, Augustal, and magistrate of the suburb, to whom the Decurions, with the consent of the people, have granted the honour of the bisellium for his merits. Nævoleia Tyche erected this monument in her lifetime for her freedmen and women, and for those of C. Munatius Faustus." The portrait below is probably that of Nævoleia; the bas-relief is supposed to represent the dedication of the tomb. On one side are the municipal magistrates, on the other the family of Nævoleia; in the centre is a low altar, upon which a youth is placing some offering, and by it a cippus, which is to represent the tomb. On the side next the triclinium is a curious bas-relief of a ship, which presents us with some

Bas-relief of Nævoleia Tyche.

interesting particulars concerning the naval architecture of the Romans. The ends of the vessel are remarkable. The prow is of singular shape, not clearly defined, and does not present the formidable beak of a ship of war: it is surmounted by a bust of Minerva. The poop ends in a swan or goose's neck ($\chi\eta\nu\prime\sigma\kappa\sigma$), from which there floats a flag: another flag is to be seen at the mast-head. The yard consists of two spars rudely lashed together. At the mast-head is something resembling a large block, in which ropes are fixed, which Mazois says are the halyards. In his engraving they look more like shrouds; and indeed a boy is making use of them as shrouds, and climbing up them. The crew consists of children who are furling the sail. A man sitting at the poop holds the rudder, and is said to represent Munatius. Two explanations of this sculpture are given—one literal,

Bas-relief on the Monument of Nævoleia Tyche.

that it is merely indicative of the profession of Munatius; the other allegorical, that it symbolises the arrival of the tossed ship of life in a quiet haven. The reader may choose between the two, as the gods have made him poetical or prosaic.* On the opposite side of the cippus is the bisellium, or seat of honour, granted to Munatius.

Bas-relief on the Tomb of Nævoleia Tyche.

A sort of solid bench for the reception of urns runs round the funeral chamber, and several niches are hollowed in the wall. Some lamps were found here, and many urns, three of glass, the rest of common earth. The glass urns were of large size, one of them fifteen inches in height by ten in diameter, and were protected from injury by leaden cases. They contained, when found, burnt bones, and a liquid which has been analyzed, and found to consist of mingled water, wine, and oil. In two of the urns it was of a reddish tint, in the other yellow, oily and transparent. There can be no doubt but that we have here the libations which were poured as a last tribute of friendship upon the ashes of the tenants of the tomb.

* In support of the latter opinion, Breton adduces several instances of the allegorical introduction of a ship in funeral monuments. *Pompeia*, p. 85, *seq.*

The burial-ground of Nistacidius, marked 12, offers nothing to detain us. It is surrounded by a low wall, about breast high, and contains three cippi after the manner of wig-blocks.

The next erection, 13, is of novel and commanding design. Within a court, about twenty-one feet square, a massive basement rises to the height of five feet and a half. Three steps lead up to a cippus elegantly carved. In front, within a rich border, is the inscription:—

C · CALVENTIO · QVIETO
AVGVSTALI
HVIC · OB · MVNIFICENT · DECVRIONVM
DECRETO · ET · POPVLI · CONSENSV · BISELLII
HONOR DATUS · EST ·

"To Caius Calventius Quietus, Augustal. To him, in reward of his munificence, the honour of the bisellium was granted by the decree of the Decurions, and with the consent of the people." Below is a representation of the bisellium.

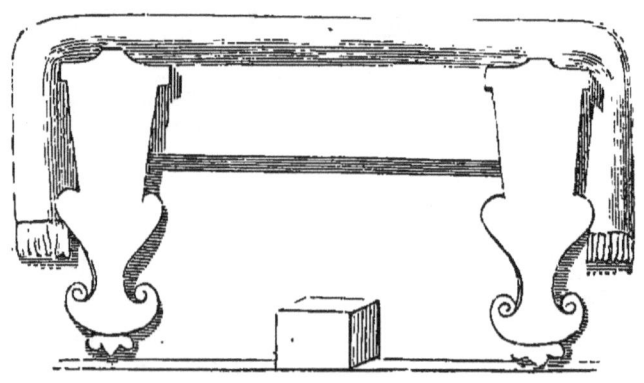

Bisellium.

It is to be remarked that all those who are mentioned in inscriptions as possessing the privilege of the bisellium bear also the title of Augustal. The learned Fabretti supposes that it was peculiar to this class of priests, but at the same time not granted to all, but only to the most distinguished of them. This distinction was purely municipal: it conferred no rank or precedence beyond the walls of the city by which it was granted; and to this perhaps it is owing, that while frequent mention of the bisellium occurs in inscriptions, Varro is the only Latin author who has spoken of it at all. The sides are ornamented with richly carved garlands of oak-leaves, bound with fillets; the mouldings and cornice are elegant in design and execution. This edifice is solid: it was therefore no place of burial, but a cenotaph, or honorary tomb, erected to Calventius Quietus. The upper part is entirely composed of marble; the basement and surrounding wall are of masonry coated with stucco. Square pinnacles, called acroteria, are placed on the wall, their sides ornamented with stucco bas-reliefs of a mythological character. One represents Theseus; another, Œdipus and the Sphinx, where the Theban hero, with an action not yet out of use, puts his finger to his forehead, as if to denote that he has there the interpretation of the riddle. The Sphinx sits on a rock, above the bodies of her victims, which are remarkable as showing some traces of the human skeleton. There is no door of access to the little area surrounding the monument, but the wall in front is scarcely four feet high; at the sides it is higher, and the back rises into a pediment which leads the eye well up to the lofty cippus, and communicates an agreeable pyramidal effect to the whole design. The extreme height from the footway is about seventeen feet.

An unoccupied space intervenes between this tomb and the next, 14, which bears no inscription. It is a round tower enclosed like those of Nævoleia and Quietus, with a wall or *septum*, ornamented with acroteria. The annexed view conveys an accurate idea of its external appearance. On the right is the tomb of Calventius Quietus, on the left that of Scaurus. Here also we find bas-reliefs upon the acroteria, one remarkable for its subject. The skeleton of a child reposes on a heap of stones: a young woman stoops over it in the act of depositing a funeral fillet. A touching explanation of this singular subject has been proposed,—that it represents the discovery of a child, who had perished in the earthquake, by the mother, who is now rendering the last service in her power. The dress of the female is still preserved in the secluded country which encircles Sora.* A narrow and steep stair leads up to the sepulchral chamber, which is vaulted

---

* Mazois, p. 46.

View of the Tomb of Scaurus, the Round Tomb, and the Tomb of Calventius Quietus.

somewhat in the shape of a bell, and painted with arabesque designs.

Immediately adjoining is the tomb of Scaurus, the bas-reliefs on which, relating to the combats of the amphitheatre, have been fully described in the first part.* In the interior of this tomb is a vaulted sepulchral chamber, the arch of which and the upper part of the monument are supported by a massive pier, pierced by four small arches, niches rather,

Bas-relief on a pinnacle of the wall enclosing the Circular Tomb.

except that they traverse its whole thickness, three of which were closed with glass and the fourth with a thick veil fastened with nails. This kind of tabernacle, contrived thus in the centre of the pier, did not contain anything when discovered, but it is probable that it was meant for

* All the figures on this tomb have now disappeared except the bas-relief over the door. Happily Mazois and Millin copied them soon after their discovery.—ED.

a lamp, from the care taken to shut up the sides with glass, leaving one aperture for the admission of air. The arches seem to have been closed, that the wind might not extinguish the lamp when the door was opened. Fourteen

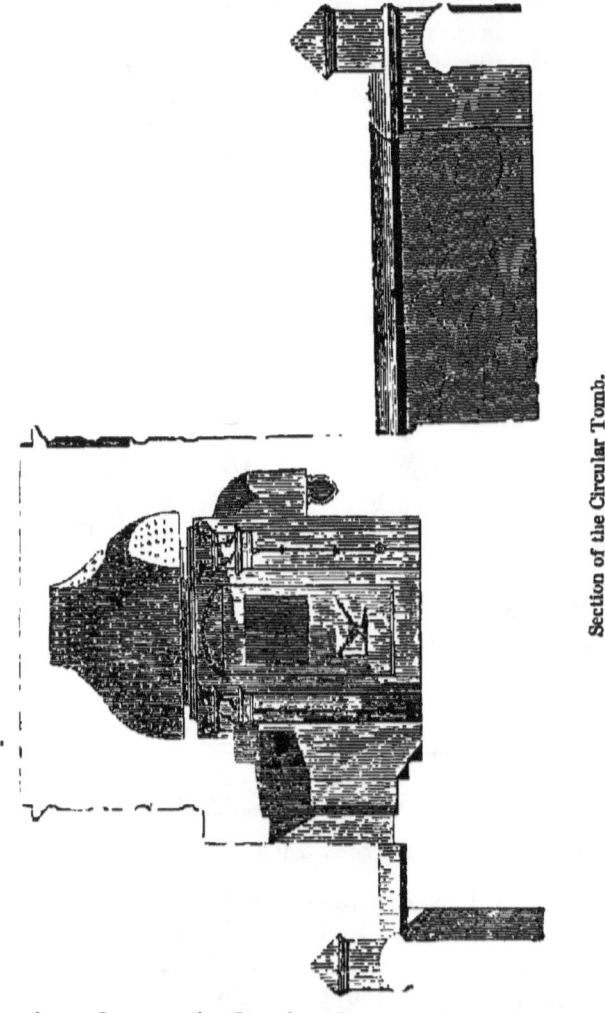

Section of the Circular Tomb.

niches pierced round the inside of the apartment were destined to receive as many cinerary urns. Daylight was admitted through a small opening at the back of the building, around which a wall is drawn, forming a small enclosure

Beyond the tomb of Scaurus is a space of eighty feet, having one unfinished tomb. Advancing towards the city we then come to one of the courts of the villa named after Cicero, and pass the row of shops which stood in front of it. On the other side of the way, opposite to the tomb of Scaurus and this

Semicircular Exedra in the Street of Tombs.

empty space, is a long row of mean shops, with courts behind them, conjectured to have been a hostelry for the peasants who resorted to Pompeii; but nothing can be more vague than this supposition. Adjoining them is another row of shops, of more pretension. The next object is a remarkable exedra, or seat,

17, in the form of a semicircle, and vaulted over. As it faces the south, and is of considerable depth, it is so contrived as in summer to afford a constant shade, and in winter to receive the full benefit of the cheering sun. It is of capricious taste, yet not inelegant; and it may be observed, as a peculiarity, that the upper pilasters spring immediately from the capitals of the lower ones. Within it was gaily, not to say gaudily, painted. The top of the vault is blue, the lower part, which is moulded in the form of a shell, is white; the walls are divided into panels by black borders relieved by golden arabesques; and the panels are red, with the figure of some animal in the centre, in imitation of life. The floor is placed at some height above the footpath; and to facilitate access there is only one small and inconvenient stepping-stone. The projecting eave is a modern addition, to preserve the building. Near this spot the skeletons of a female with an infant in her arms, and beside her of two children, their bones mingled and interlaced, showing that at the last they had sought comfort in each other's embrace, were dug up. It was a family perhaps of distinction, certainly of wealth, for among their remains two pairs of earrings, with pearl pendants of great value, were found, and three gold

Gold Ring.

rings, one of them in the form of a serpent, with its head pointing along the finger, and its body coiled around in several folds.*

Between this exedra and the gate of the city there are traced on the plan the sites of several unknown tombs, which it is not necessary to describe; only we may mention that in the little nameless tomb close to the exedra just described, and seen in the view, was found the finest glass vase that, with the exception of the Portland vase, has come down to

* The Journals of the Excavations know nothing of these skeletons. See *Pomp. Ant. Hist.*, t. i. fasc. iii. p. 74 (Dec. 14, 1811).

us from antiquity. The glass is dark blue, and is ornamented with a white opaque relief, representing bacchanal scenes in the midst of a rich foliage. Hence the tomb has been called the *Tomba del vaso di vetro blu.* The vase is now in the Museum. Just beyond is the Tomb of the Garlands.

Immediately under the walls of the town a road turned off to the left, which led to Nola, and enabled travellers who had no business in the town to avoid passing through its crowded streets. Between this road and the city gate is a square basement, 18, probably intended to support a colossal statue of bronze: at least some fragments of such a statue were found about it. Nearly opposite, but a little further from the gate, is the beginning of another road leading somewhere to the right, along the side of Cicero's villa. Here, at the angle of the wall, there was formerly a stone bracket, apparently to receive offerings of fruit, &c., by the side of which an immense serpent was painted, in the act of stooping his head, as if to partake of what was set before him. This relic was accidentally destroyed by the carts employed in removing rubbish from the excavations in the year 1813.

Between this by-road and the city gate there is a group of interesting remains, consisting of two tombs and two large uncovered semicircular seats. The first, 19, is raised upon a high step; it is about seventeen feet in diameter, and bears the following inscription, occupying the whole space above the bench, which is finished, and supported at each end by a lion's paw:—

MAMIAE · P · F · SACERDOTI · PVBLICAE · LOCVS-
SEPVLTVR · DATVS · DECVRIONVM · DECRETO·

"To Mamia, daughter of (probably) Porcius, public priestess, a place of burial is assigned by decree of the Decurions." A little in advance of this seat is an upright stone, with an inscription importing that the Decurions had granted to M. Porcius a plot of ground twenty-five feet square; and immediately behind is a tomb, 20, which, with its septum or enclosure, in fact does occupy about that space. It is upon these coincidences we imagine that P, in the inscription above given, is interpreted Porcius, and the tomb of which we have spoken is assigned to Mamia, for it bears no inscription to point out its owner. At the same time, the tomb between the

530   POMPEII.

seats occupies about the same space, and a doubt may be felt which of the two is the one meant. Be this as it may, the tomb in question is more than usually large and handsome. The septum is worked into apertures rounded at top, which give to it the appearance of a balustrade. The tomb is of masonry covered with stucco, and ornamented with engaged columns, which, from their proportions, appear to be of the

Geometrical elevation of the Tomb of Mamia restored.

Corinthian order, but the capitals are gone. Mazois has given a restoration of it, according to his notions of the characteristics of Pompeian architecture: the existing part may be distinguished by the uneven line which bounds it. Several ill-executed marble statues, now in the Royal Museum of Naples, were found in the interior, which was set round with niches: the walls were painted. In the centre is a large pedestal which probably supported the urn of the tenant.

Behind this tomb is a spot called the sepulchre of animals, because many skulls and half-burnt bones of sheep and oxen have been found there. It probably was a spot where offerings were made to the dead. An altar richly ornamented with fruit and garlands, which was dug up here, seems to confirm this opinion.

The other seat is very similar to the one described, and bore an inscription to one M. Veius. The tomb between them offers nothing worthy of notice. One building only, placed between the seat and the city gate, remains to be described. It is the niche, 21, which has been sometimes taken for a sentry-box; and an affecting story is told how the skeleton of a soldier, still grasping his lance, was found here, together with the usual accoutrements and arms; thus showing that he had died in the discharge of his duty, a victim of Roman discipline. Unfortunately, however, this story is a pure fable. The Journals of the Excavations know nothing of this soldier, although they always particularly record the discovery of skeletons, because in most cases some coins or other property were found near them.* Moreover, the place in question was no sentry-box, but a funeral monument of an Augustal named M. Cerinius Restitutus, as appeared from an inscription.†

We have now completed our circuit of that portion of Pompeii which has been restored to the light of day. To describe every building would have been useless, even in a professed guide-book. It has been our endeavour however to omit no object remarkable either for beauty or singularity; nothing to which the attention of those who have the good fortune to visit the spot ought to be directed. Occasionally we have indulged in a minuteness of detail, especially in speaking of the interior decorations of the houses, which may appear tedious: we have done so, however, from a belief that without the advantage of personal inspection, it is only by minuteness of description, and even repetition, that any sort of familiarity with the subject can be attained. In conclusion, we have to express a regret that the small size of our illustrations, and especially the want of coloured plates, prevent our doing full justice to the beauty and interest of this remarkable place.

* See Overbeck, B. i., *Anhang*, Anmerk, 4, S. 340.
† *Pomp. Ant. Hist.*, t. i. p. 152 (Aug. 13th, 1763).

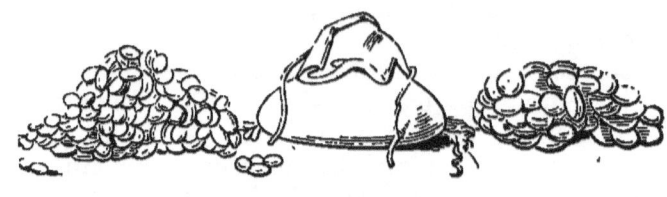

Money-bag and Coins.

CHAPTER XII.

DOMESTIC UTENSILS.

The immense number and variety of statues, lamps, urns, articles of domestic use, in metal or earthenware, &c., discovered at Herculaneum and Pompeii, have rendered the Museum at Naples an inexhaustible treasury of information relative to the private life of the ancient Italians.* To give an adequate description of the richness and variety of its contents would far exceed the whole extent of this work, much more the small space which still remains; but that space cannot be better occupied than in describing some few articles which possess an interest from the ingenuity of their construction, the beauty of their workmanship, or their power to illustrate ancient usages or ancient authors.

Writing implements are among the most important of the latter class, on account of the constant mention of them, as well as of the influence which the comparative ease or difficulty of producing copies of writing is always found to exert over society. On this head there is no want of information. The implements used are frequently mentioned, especially in familiar writings, as the letters of Cicero, and their forms have been tolerably ascertained from various fragments of ancient paintings.

It is hardly necessary to state that for manuscripts of any

* It is to be regretted, however, that there is no good catalogue, and that the objects are very difficult to find.—Ed.

DOMESTIC UTENSILS.

length, and such as were meant to be preserved, parchment or vellum, and a vegetable tissue manufactured from the rush *papyrus*, were in use. The stalk of this plant consists of a number of thin concentric coats, which being carefully detached, were pasted crossways one over the other, like the warp and woof in woven manufactures, so that the fibres ran longitudinally in each direction, and opposed in each an equal resistance to violence. The surface was then polished with a shell, or some hard smooth substance. The ink used was a simple black liquid, containing no mordant to give it durability, so that the writing was easily effaced by the application of a sponge. The length of the Greek papyri is said to vary from eight to twelve inches: the Latin often reach sixteen: the writing is in columns, placed at right angles to the length of the roll. The method of reading them will be understood from the woodcut, in which is represented one open, and, below it, another closed. To each of them is appended a sort of ticket, which served as a

Papyri and Tabulæ.

title. Hence the end of the roll, or volume (*volumen*), was called *frons*, a term of frequent recurrence in Ovid and Martial, and not always rightly understood. Hence, also, when we meet with the expression, *gemina frons*, we must understand that the volume had a ticket at each end. The open book which stands beside them is one of those which were composed of two tables or pages, and served for memorandums, letters, and other writings, not intended to be preserved. They were composed of leaves of wood or metal coated over with wax, upon which the ancients wrote with a *stylus*, or iron pen, or point rather, for it was a solid sharp-pointed instrument, some inches in length, like a lady's stiletto upon a large scale. In the middle of each leaf there appears to have been a button, called ὀμφαλὸς, *umbilicus*, intended to prevent the pages touching when closed, and obliterating the letters traced on the yielding wax. The tablets here represented would be called δίπτυχον, twofold, as consisting only of two leaves: in the next cut may be seen another sort, consisting of several leaves (πολύπτυχον), united at the back with hinges or rings. In Latin they were called *tabulæ*, or *tabellæ*, and the epithets, duplices, triplices, quintuplices, served to mark the number of the leaves.

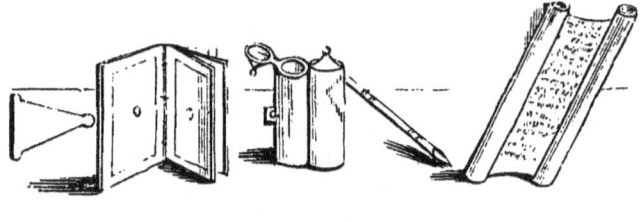

Tabulæ, Calamus, and Papyrus.

Beside them stands a double inkstand, intended probably to contain both black and red ink. The former was made either of lampblack or some other sort of charcoal, or from the cuttlefish, and was called atramentum. As it contained no mordant, and was readily obliterated by moisture, it could be used for writing upon ivory tablets; and it has been conjectured that some sorts of paper were covered with a wash, or varnish, to facilitate the discharge of the old writing, and render the paper serviceable a second time. Red ink, *miltum*, was prepared from cinnabar. The reed, cut to a point, which lies beside the inkstand, is the instrument used in writing with ink before the application of quills. It was called *calamus*, with the distinctive epithets *chartarius*, or *scriptorius*. The open papyrus explains how manuscripts were read, rolled up at each end, so as to show only the column of writing upon which the student was intent. At the other side is a purse, or bag, to hold the reed, penknife, and other writing instruments.

The next cut represents, besides a set of tablets bound up, a single one hanging from a nail. Such, probably, were those suspended at Epidaurus, containing remedies by which the sick had been cured, by the perusal of which Hippocrates is said to have profited in the compilation of his medical works. It also contains, besides a papyrus similar to those described, a hexagonal inkstand, with a ring to pass the finger through, upon which there lies an instrument resembling a reed, but the absence of the knots, or joints, marks it to be a stylus. Another of these instruments leans against the open book. These were made of every sort of material; sometimes with the precious metals, but usually of iron, and on occasion

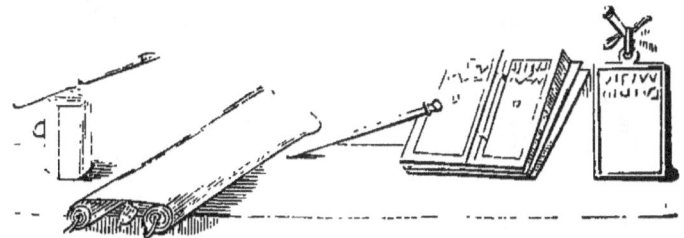

Tabulæ, Stylus, and Papyrus.

might be turned into formidable weapons. It was with his stylus that Cæsar stabbed Casca in the arm, when attacked in the senate by his murderers; and Caligula employed some person to put to death a senator with the same instruments. In the reign of Claudius women and boys were searched to ascertain whether there were styles in their *graphiariæ thecæ*, or pen-cases. Stabbing with the pen, therefore, is not merely a metaphorical expression. Tablets such as those here represented, were the *diurni*, or day-books, *breviarii rationum*,

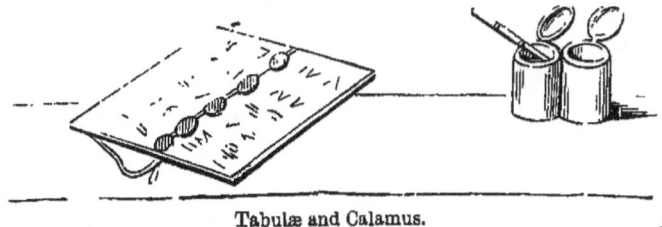

Tabulæ and Calamus.

tabulæ accepti et expensi, or account-books. When they were full, or when the writing on them was no longer useful, the wax was smoothed, and they were ready again for other service.

The cut above, besides an inkstand, represents an open book.

The thinness and yellowish colour of the leaves, which are tied together with ribbon, denote that it was made of parchment or vellum.

Below is a cylindrical box, called *scrinium* and *capsa*, or *capsula*, in which the manuscripts were placed vertically, the titles at the top. Catullus excuses himself to Manlius for not having sent him the required verses, because he had with him only one box of his books. It is evident that a great number of volumes might be comprised in this way within a

Scrinium and Capsa.

small space; and this may tend to explain the smallness of the ancient libraries—at least of the rooms which are considered to have been such. Beside the box are two tablets, which, from the money-bag and coins scattered about, had probably been used in reckoning accounts. This will bring to the student's recollection the

———— Mersam poni jubet atque
Effundi saccos nummorum *

of Horace, and the well-known lines of Juvenal—

———— Pleno cum turget sacculus ore
Crescit amor nummi quantum ipsa pecunia crescit.†

No perfect papyri, but only fragments, have been found at Pompeii. At Herculaneum, up to the year 1825, 1756 had been obtained, besides many others destroyed by the workmen, who imagined them to be mere sticks of charcoal. Most of them were found in a suburban villa, in a room of small

* Sat. ii. 3, 149. † Juv. xiv. 138.

dimensions, ranged in presses round the sides of the room, in the centre of which stood a sort of rectangular bookcase. Sir Humphry Davy, after investigating their chemical nature, arrived at the conclusion that they had not been carbonised by heat, but changed by the long action of air and moisture; and he visited Naples in hopes of rendering the resources of chemistry available towards deciphering these long-lost literary treasures. His expectations, however, were not fully crowned with success, although the partial efficacy of his methods was established; and he relinquished the pursuit at the end of six months, partly from disappointment, partly from a belief that vexatious obstacles were thrown in his way by the jealousy of the persons to whom the task of unrolling had been intrusted. About five hundred volumes have been well and neatly unrolled. It is rather remarkable that, as far as we are acquainted, no manuscript of any known standard work has been found, nor indeed any production of any of the great luminaries of the ancient world. The most celebrated person, of whom any work has been found, is Epicurus, whose treatise, *De Natura*, has been successfully unrolled. This and a few other treatises have been published. The library in which this was found appears to have been rich in treatises on the Epicurean philosophy. The only Latin work which it contained was a poem, attributed to Rabirius, on the war of Cæsar and Antony.

A curious literary monument has been found in the shape of a calendar. It is cut on a square block of marble, upon each side of which three months are registered in perpendicular columns, each headed by the proper sign of the zodiac. The information given may be classed under three heads, astronomical, agricultural, and religious. The first begins with the name of the month; then follows the number of days; then the nones, which in eight months of the year fall on the fifth day, and were thence called quintanæ—in the others on the seventh, and were therefore called septimanæ. The ides are not mentioned, because seven days always elapsed between them and the nones. The number of hours in the day and night is also given, the integral part being given by the usual numerals, the fractional by an S for semissis, the half, and by small horizontal lines for the quarters. Lastly, the sign of the zodiac in which the sun is to be found is named, and the days of the equinoxes and of the summer solstice are determined: for the winter solstice we read, *Hiemis initium*, the beginning of winter. Next the calendar proceeds to the agricultural portion, in which the farmer is reminded of the principal operations which are to be done within the month. It concludes with the religious part, in which, besides indicating the god under whose guardianship the month is placed, it notes the religious festivals which fell within it, and warns the cultivator against neglecting the worship of those deities, upon whose favour and protection the success of his labours was supposed mainly to depend.

Calendar.

No articles of ancient manufacture are more common than lamps. They are found in every variety of form and size, in clay and in metal, from the most cheap to the most costly description. A large and handsome gold lamp found at Pompeii in 1863 may be seen in the Pompeian room at the museum in Naples. We have the testimony of the celebrated antiquary, Winkelmann, to the interest of this subject. "I place among the most curious utensils found at Herculaneum, the lamps, in which the ancients sought to display elegance, and even magnificence. Lamps of every sort will be found in the museum at Portici, both in clay and bronze, but especially the latter; and as the ornaments of the ancients have generally some reference to some particular things, we often meet with rather remarkable subjects." A considerable number of these articles will be found in the British Museum, but they are chiefly of the commoner sort. All the works, however, descriptive of Herculaneum and Pompeii, present us with specimens of the richer and more remarkable class, which attract admiration both by the beauty of the workmanship and the whimsical variety of their designs. We may enumerate a few which occur in a work now before us, 'Antiquités d'Herculanum,' in which we find a Silenus, with the usual peculiarities of figure ascribed to the jolly god rather exaggerated, and an owl sitting upon his head between two huge horns, which support stands for lamps. Another represents a flower-stalk growing out of a circular plinth, with snail-shells hanging from it by small chains, which held the oil and wick; the trunk of a tree, with lamps suspended from the branches; another, a naked boy, beautifully wrought, with a lamp hanging from one hand, and an instrument for trimming it from the other, the lamp itself representing a theatrical mask. Beside him is a twisted column surmounted by the head of a Faun or Bacchanal, which has a lid in its crown, and seems intended as a reservoir of oil. The boy and pillar are both placed on a square plateau raised upon lions' claws. But beautiful as these lamps are, the light which they gave must have been weak and unsteady, and little superior to that of the old-fashioned common street lamps, with which indeed they are identical in principle. The wick was merely a few twisted threads drawn through a hole in the upper surface of the oil-vessel, and there was no glass to steady the light and prevent its varying with every breeze that blew.

Still, though the Romans had not advanced so far in art as to apply glass chimneys and hollow circular wicks to their lamps, they had experienced the inconvenience of going home at night through a city ill paved, ill watched, and ill lighted, and accordingly soon invented lanterns to meet the want. These, we learn from Martial, who has several epigrams upon this subject, were made of horn or bladder: no mention, we believe, occurs of glass being thus employed. The rich were preceded by a slave bearing their lantern. This Cicero mentions as being the habit of Catiline upon his midnight expeditions; and when M. Antony was accused of a disgrace-

540 POMPEII.

ful intrigue, his lantern-bearer was tortured to extort a confession whither he had conducted his master.* One of these machines, of considerable ingenuity and beauty of workmanship, was found in Herculaneum in 1760, and another, almost

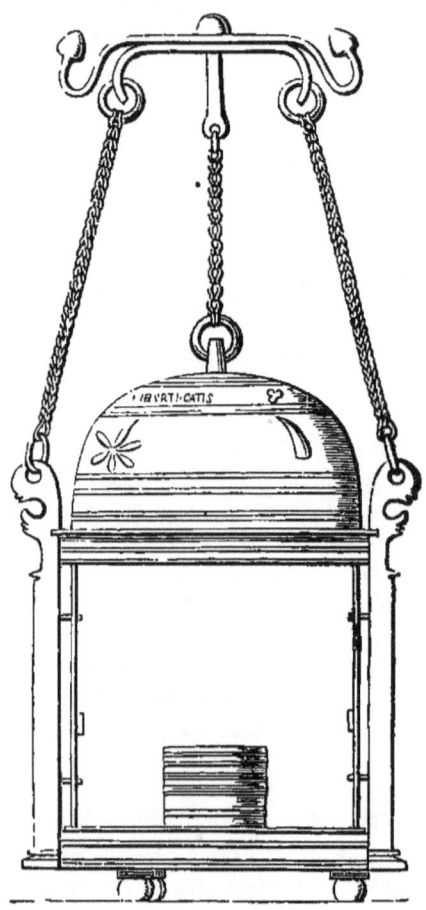

Elevation of a Bronze Lantern.

exactly the same, at Pompeii, a few years after. We give a drawing and a section of the former to explain its construction. In form it is cylindrical, with a hemispherical top, and it is made of sheet-copper, except the two main pieces, M, M,

* Val. Max. vi. 8.

which are cast. The bottom consists of a flat, circular copper plate, supported by three balls, and turned up all round the rim (*b, b*, in the section), from which rise the rectangular supports, M, M, which support the upper part of the frame, N.

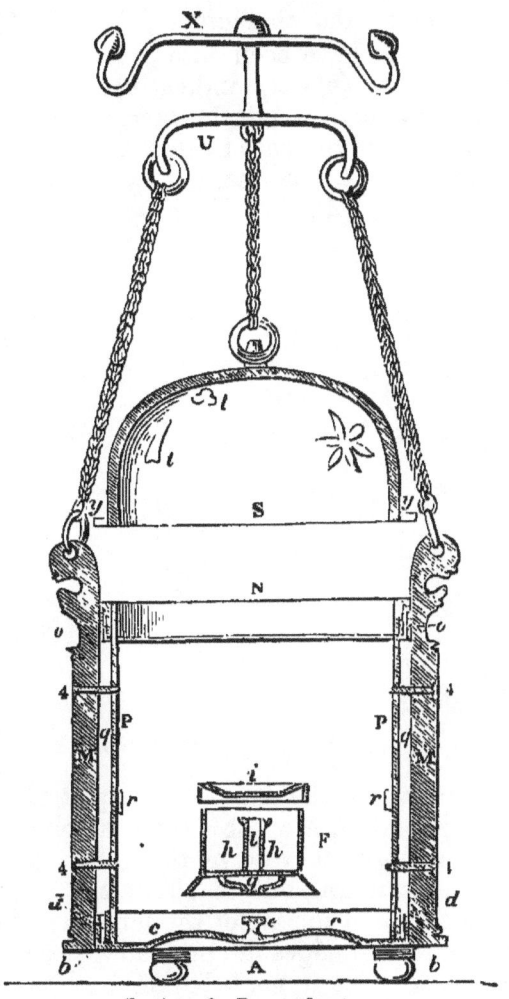

Section of a Bronze Lantern.

The top and bottom were further connected by the interior uprights, P, P, between which and M, M the laminæ of horn or glass were placed, and secured at the top and bottom by the doublings of the copper. Horn was the most common substance used to transmit the light, but bladder and other membranes were also employed. In the centre of the lantern is seen the small lamp. The cover is hemispherical, and lifts up and down: it is pierced with holes for the admission of air, and has besides the characters /IBVRTI·CATIS pricked upon it. These have been interpreted, Tiburti Cati Sum, or Tiburti Cati S. (ervus), indicating, the one that it belonged to Catus, or that it was to be carried by his slave.

A. Base. *b, b.* Rim of the base turned up. *c, c.* Interior rim, forming, with the exterior one, *b, b,* a channel, *d, d,* to receive the glass or horn side. *e.* Knob which fitted into a

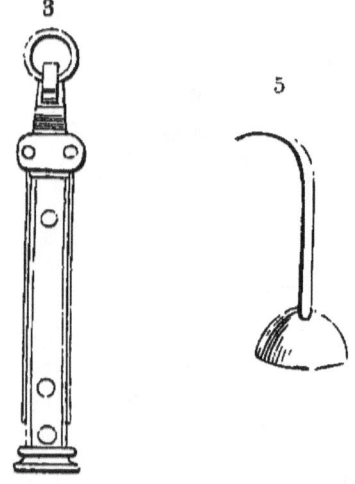

Front view of M, M.   Extinguisher.

hole, *g,* in the bottom of the lamp, to keep it steady. F. Lamp. *h, h.* Oil receiver. *i.* Moveable cover sloping inwards, and pierced in the centre to receive the wick. *l.* Tube to hold the wick, with a vertical slit to admit the oil. M, M. Supports. N. Band round the top of the lantern: it consists of a copper plate with two edges doubled down, so as to form a cavity, *ò, o,* to receive the upper edge of the glass or horn. P, P. Interior supports, connected with M, M, by pins, 4, 4, 4, 4, shown in the separate view of M. *q.* Space for the horn sides. *r, r.* Pieces of metal of uncertain use. S. Cover. *t, t, t.* Holes to let off the smoke. U. Handle. X. Another handle attached to a vertical rod which passes through U, and lifts up the cover, which receives the uprights, M, M, into two notches, and is thus kept steady. 3. View of the upright, M. 5. Extinguisher, which is a hemisphere soldered on a narrow curved tube.

One of the most elegant articles of furniture in ancient use was the candelabrum, by which we mean those tall and slender stands which served to support a lamp, but were independent of, and unconnected with it. These, in their original and simple form, were probably mere reeds or straight sticks, fixed upon a foot by peasants to raise their light to a convenient height; at least such a theory of their origin is agreeable to what we are told of the rustic manners of the early Romans, and it is in some degree countenanced by the fashion in which many of the ancient candelabra are made. Sometimes the stem is represented as throwing out buds; sometimes it is a stick, the side branches of which have been roughly lopped, leaving projections where they grew; sometimes it is in the likeness of a reed or cane, the stalk being divided into joints. Most of those which have been found in the buried cities are of bronze, some few of iron. In their general plan and appearance there is a great resemblance, though the details of the ornaments admit of infinite variety. All stand on three feet, usually griffins' or lions' claws, which support a light shaft, plain or fluted according to the fancy of the maker. The whole supports either a plinth large enough for a lamp to stand on, or a socket to receive a wax candle, which the Romans used sometimes instead of oil in lighting their rooms. Some of them have a sliding shaft, like that of a music stand, by which the light might be raised or lowered at pleasure. Of the two candelabra which fill page 544, one is of the simplest form; the other deserves notice on account of the ingenious construction by which it can be taken to pieces for the convenience of transport. The base is formed of three goat's legs, each having a ring at the end and a ring on each side. The centre piece is attached to the side pieces by rivets, 3, 4, round which these rings are allowed to turn, so that they lie either parallel when the candelabrum is taken to pieces, or may be made to stand at equal distances in the circumference of a circle, in which case the two exterior rings lap over each other, and are united by a moveable

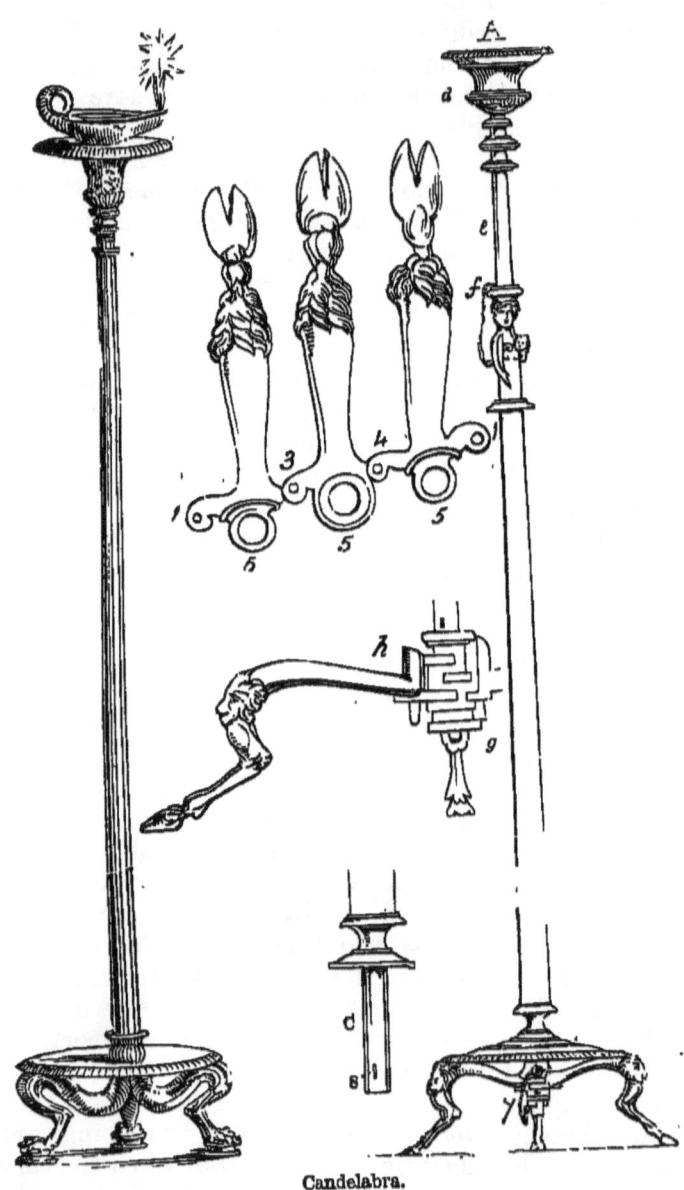

Candelabra.

CANDELABRA AND VASES.

pin. The end rings, 5, 5, 5, which are placed at different heights, as shown at *h*, will then be brought into the same vertical line, and the round pin, C, which terminates the stem, passes through them, and is secured by a pin, 7, passing through the hole, 8, which keeps the whole tight. The shaft is square and hollow, terminated by two busts placed back to back, and surmounted with a kind of capital. Within this a smaller shaft, *e*, plays up and down, and is adjusted at the desired height by a pin, *f*. The busts represent Mercury and Perseus. The richer sorts of candelabra are remarkable for the profusion of delicate ornaments which is bestowed upon them. Usually the relieved parts appear to be cast in a mould. Some are beautifully damasked or inlaid with other metals. The upper part of another candelabrum is represented in a steel plate given herewith. It is inferred, from a passage in Pliny, that the art of inlaying was carried to perfection in Ægina, while the solid parts, as the shaft and feet, were best cast at Tarentum. We give the passage in a note, which has been variously interpreted, and hardly bears out all the meaning which has been extracted from it in the above version.*

One of those elegant table lamps, by the praise of which the present discussion was introduced, is represented in the accompanying plate. Including the stand it is three feet high. On a rectangular plinth rises a rectangular pillar, crowned by a capricious capital. On the front of the pillar is a mask of a Bacchante, with fine features and long flowing hair; and on the opposite side, the head of a bull, with the Greek word Bucranion. From the extreme points of the abacus, four ornamented branches, beautifully chased, project; the lamps which now hang from them, though ancient also, are not those which belong to the stand, and were not found with it. They are nearly alike in figure, but differ in size. Three of them are ornamented with various animals, the fourth is plain. One of them has each of its ends wrought into the form of a shell. Above are two eagles in high relief, with the thunderbolt of Jupiter in their talons. Another has two bulls' heads, a third, two elephants' heads projecting from the sides. The

* Privatim Ægina candelabrorum superficiem duntaxat elaboravit, sicut Tarentum scapos. In hoc ergo commendatio officinarum est.—Hist. Nat. xxxiv. 3.

latter is suspended by two dolphins, instead of the chains generally in use, whose tails are united, and attached to a small ball and ring. The pillar is not placed in the centre, but at one end of the plinth, which is the case in almost every lamp of this description yet found. The space thus obtained may have served as a stand for the oil-vase used in trimming the lamps. The plinth is beautifully damasked, or inlaid, in imitation of a vine, the leaves of which are of silver, the stem and fruit of bright brass. On one side is an altar with wood and fire upon it; on the other a Bacchus, naked, with his thick hair plaited and bound with ivy. He rides a tiger, and has his left hand in the attitude of holding reins, which time probably has destroyed; with the right he raises a drinking-horn. The workmanship of this lamp is exquisitely delicate in all its parts.

We may here say a few words on the art of inlaying one metal with another, in which, as in all ornamental branches of the working of metals, the ancient Italians possessed great skill. In the time of Seneca, ornaments of silver were seldom seen unless their price was enhanced by being inlaid with solid gold.* The art of uniting one metal with another was called, by the general term, *ferruminare*. Inlaid work was of two sorts, in the one the inlaid work projected above the surface, and was called *emblemata*, as the art itself was called, from the Greek, *embleticé*. It is inferred, from the inspection of numerous embossed vases in the Neapolitan Museum, that this embossed work was formed, either by plating with a thin leaf of metal figures already raised upon the surface of the article, or by letting the solid figures into the substance of the vessel, and finishing them with delicate tools after they were attached. In the second sort the inlaid work was even with the surface, and was called *crusta*,† and the art was called, from the Greek, *empœsticé*.‡ This is the same as the damask work so fashionable in the armour of the fifteenth and sixteenth centuries, which is often seen beautifully inlaid with gold. It was executed by engraving the pattern upon the surface of the metal, and filling up the lines with fine plates of a different metal; the two were then united with the assistance of heat, and the whole burnished. Pliny

* Ep. 5. † Cic. vi. ver. 52. ‡ Athenæus.

has preserved a receipt for solder, which probably was used in these works. It is called santerna; and the principal ingre-

Bronze figure inlaid with embletic work.

dients are borax, nitre, and copperas, pounded with a small quantity of gold and silver in a copper mortar.

The vase which accompanies the lamp in the plate just

given was found in a house opposite to the side door of the covered portico of Eumachia. It is very elegant in shape, and is a good specimen of that which we have called embletic work. The inlaid ornaments are admirably relieved by the deep colour of the bronze. This specimen of ancient art is worthy to serve as a model to goldsmiths and chasers in metal. There are six different mouldings in it, each rich in variety of ornament. The beautiful proportions, and correspondence of the body and the foot, are also deserving of attention. Another vase in the same plate, of different form, is not perhaps less beautiful. It has three handles, one placed vertically, and two horizontally, at the sides.

We give, on p. 547, another admirable specimen of inlaid work, in a bronze figure found in Pompeii in 1824. The cuirass is inlaid with silver. The upper compartment represents Apollo encircled with rays, driving his four-horsed chariot: beneath is an allegorical figure of the earth, flanked by a bull on one side and a goat on the other. The figure is one foot eight inches in height.

Before we quit this subject we have still one candelabrum to notice, which for simplicity of design and delicacy of execution is hardly to be surpassed by any in the Neapolitan collection. The stem is formed of a liliaceous plant, divided into two branches, each of which supports a flat disc, which may represent the flower, upon which a lamp was placed. At the base is a mass of bronze which gives stability to the whole, upon which a Silenus is seated, earnestly engaged in trying to pour wine from a skin which he holds in his left hand into a cup in his right. In this figure all the distinctive marks of the companion and tutor of Bacchus are expressed with great skill; the pointed ears, the goat's tail, the shaggy skin, the flat nose, and the ample rotundity of body, leave no doubt on our minds as to the person intended to be represented. The head, especially, is admirable, both in respect of workmanship and expression.

Some remarkable tripods are figured and described in Mr. Donaldson's Pompeii, and others will be found in the works on Herculaneum. We shall only speak of one, which is peculiar in construction, being contrived to open or shut at pleasure. Each of the legs is united to the others by two braces, the lower ends of which are at liberty to play up and

DOMESTIC UTENSILS. 549

down upon rings, while at the upper ends, and at the point where they cross each other, they are only allowed to move round a pin, or hinge. The pan at top merely rests upon a ledge, and can be taken off at pleasure. It is evident from the construction, that the legs may either be pushed close together or drawn further apart, until the rings reach the

Candelabrum.

limit of their assigned range; and thus the tripod may be made to receive a larger or smaller vessel, according to the purposes for which it is wanted.

Each of the legs is topped by the sacred serpent of Egypt, bearing the lotus on its head. It was believed that this animal had the power of killing others with a look; and, as master of the life of others, it was reputed immortal and sacred

550   POMPEII.

to the gods, on whose heads it was often represented. We may presume, from this ornament, that this vessel belonged to the worship of Isis, which we know to have been extensively practised in Pompeii.

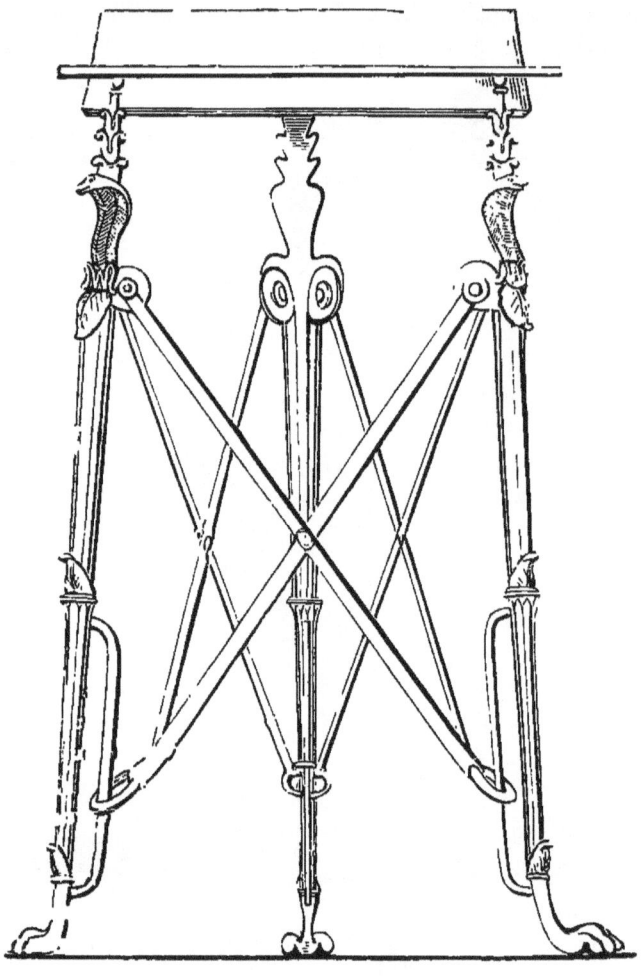

Moveable Tripod.

Another interesting class of household articles comprehends the braziers, which, in the want of that peculiarly English convenience, an open fireplace, served at once to warm the rooms, to keep dishes hot, or boil water, and perhaps to perform

DOMESTIC UTENSILS. 551

such culinary operations as required no elaborate preparation. One of these, intended merely to heat a room, we have already described in the chapter on baths; that which is here represented is on a smaller scale, being intended for private use,

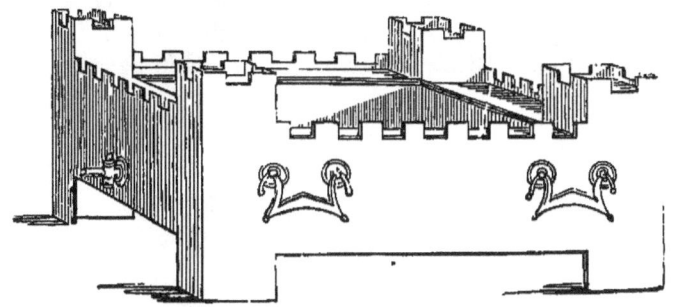

Brazier.

and has more conveniences. The sides, which are of considerable thickness, are hollow, and intended to contain water, and the four turrets at the four corners are provided with moveable lids. From one of the sides there projects a cock, to draw off the water. The centre, of course, was filled with lighted charcoal, and if a tripod or trivet were placed above it, many processes of cooking, such as boiling, stewing, or

frying, might be performed. Such a brazier as this, probably, was placed, in the winter, near the triclinium, where it would at once warm the dinner party, and minister in all its various uses to the service of the triclinium. Here is a tripod, such as might be used for the above purposes, with its pot or kettle, flanked by a frying-pan (*sartago*) on either side. The pot here figured is of the kind called *cacabus*, a cooking vessel, which is to be distinguished from *ahenum*, a caldron for boiling water.

Our next specimen is intended for the same uses, but is far more ornamental in its character. The form is new and elegant, and something modelled upon this pattern might be

Brazier.

introduced with advantage into those countries where chimneys and fireplaces are not in general use. It is fourteen inches square, exclusive of a semicircular projection, which is raised above the rim of the brazier, and made hollow to receive water. On the edge of this stand three eagles, with their heads curving downwards towards their breasts, intended probably to support a boiler. A sort of tower rises at the side of this semicircular part, which has a moveable lid, with a bust for the handle. The water was drawn off, as in the former instance, through the mask in front.

The following vase, if not equal in beauty to those already described, is curious in form and rich in ornament. The lip is elegantly finished with a double row of ovoli. The handle is elaborate and elegant. Its design seems taken from a flower-stalk, which divides at top, and falls down on each side of the vase on two cornucopiæ. Two goats recline upon the edge of the vase, looking towards each other. The junction of the lower end of the handle with the vase is richly ornamented with acanthus leaves, and a winged child among them, holding a wine-skin. The base is disproportionately small.

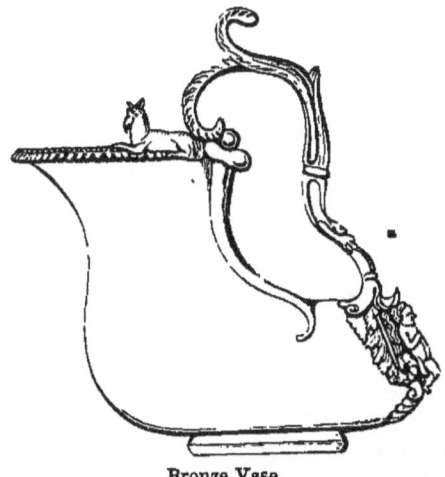

Bronze Vase.

This seems, from the ornaments, to have been a wine-vessel, and probably was used in sacrifice, as well as in domestic life.

The next groups of vessels, though nearly destitute of ornament, and probably of a very ordinary class, will serve to give us some idea of the cooking vessels of the Romans. The first four are ladles (simpula), used, among other purposes, for making libations from larger vessels. One of the most celebrated vases in the Neapolitan collection, was found with a bronze simpulum in it; and upon the vase itself there was a sacrificial painting, representing a priest in the act of pouring out a libation from a vase with the simpulum.

The other four vessels require and admit of little explanation. The first seems meant to hang over the fire, if we may judge from the eye at the top of the handle, which, with the

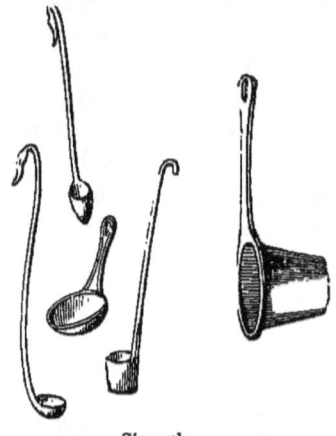

Simpula.

massive leaves and volutes below the rings, and the ovolo moulding, is not without pretensions to elegance. Fig. 2 is only remarkable for a double handle, which lies upon the

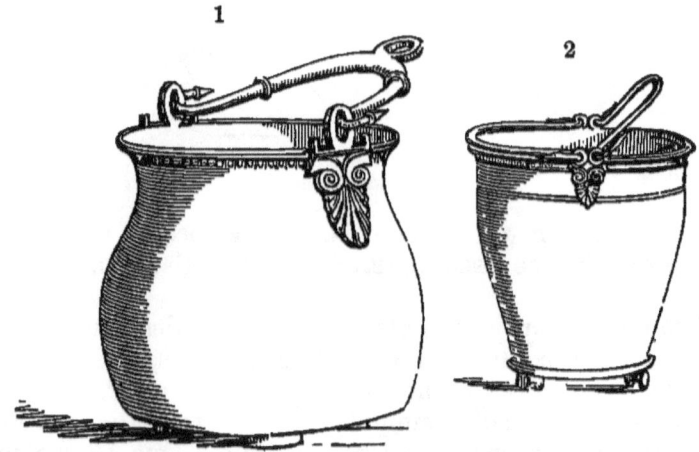

rim, and forms as it were an upper moulding. Figs. 3 and 4 are plain. Even these common vessels are not without a certain degree of elegance, both in form and workmanship.

DOMESTIC UTENSILS. 555

Great numbers of clay vases have been found, of which the following is a very beautiful specimen. The lip and base have the favourite ovolo moulding; the body has two rows of fluting separated by a transverse band, charged with leaves,

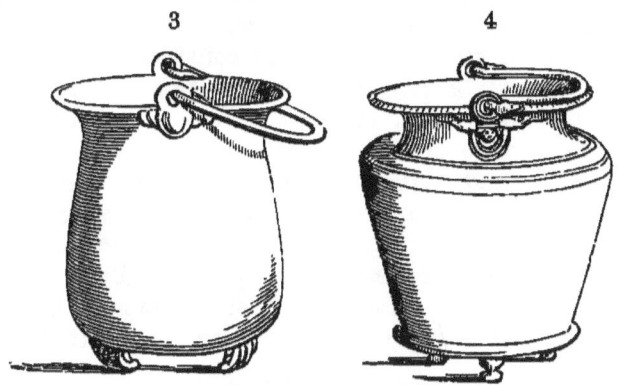

Kitchen Utensils of Bronze,

and with a swan in the centre. The neck of the vase is painted, and the same subject is given on each side. It represents a chariot, drawn by four animals at full gallop, which appear to be intermediate between tigers and panthers. A

Terra-cotta Vase.

winged genius directs them with his left hand, while with his right he goads them with a javelin. Another winged figure preceding the quadriga, with a thyrsus in his left hand, is in the act of seizing the bridle of one of the animals. The whole is painted in white on a black ground, except some few of the details, which are yellow, and the car and mantle of the genius, which are red. The handles represent knotted cords, or flexible branches interlaced, which terminate in the heads of animals. This vase is much cracked, probably in consequence of the violence of the fire.

Some drinking vessels of peculiar construction have been found, which merit a particular description. The first are of the class called ῥυτὰ, or ῥυτίδες, from ῥύω, to draw off liquid. These were in the shape of a horn, the primitive drinking-vessel, and had commonly a hole at the point, to be closed with the finger, until the drinker, raising it above his mouth, suffered the liquor to flow in a stream from the orifice, in the manner represented on p. 311. This method of drinking, which is still practised in some parts of the Mediterranean, must require great skill in order to hit the mark

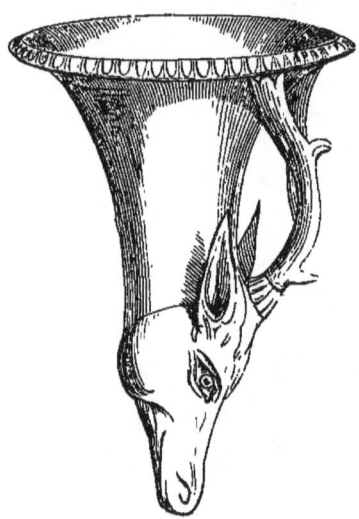

ῥυτὸν, or Drinking-cup.

exactly. Sometimes the hole at the tip was closed, and one or two handles fitted to the side, and then the base formed the mouth; and sometimes the whimsical fancy of the potter fashioned it into the head of a pig, a stag, or any other animal. One in the Neapolitan Museum has the head of an eagle with the ears of a ram. These vases are usually of clay, but cheap as is the material, it is evident by their good workmanship that they were not made by the lowest artists.

Grotesque Vases.

Above we give a group of vases of grotesque character, such as those to which Martial alludes in the epigram which we quote below.* "I am the whim of the potter, the mask of the red-haired Batavian: boys fear my face, though you laugh at it." One of them is more remarkable than the others; it represents the head of a Persian king, as we may conjecture from the upright tiara, which rises from a diadem pierced with holes, and has upon it two Persian figures, which are scarcely discernible in our engraving. The features have something of the character of a bugbear: wide, open eyes, ass's ears, a long beard, and a most tremendous pair of mustachios, ever sedulously cherished by the eastern nations. In forming these caricatures, however, the artist had a graver end in view than either amusing men or frightening boys — that of guarding the drinker while in a helpless state of intoxication from the malign influence of an evil eye or the wiles of enchantment; for among the ancients, who believed devoutly in the power of drugs and sorceries of all kinds, the salutary power of averting those evils was assigned to all such grotesque figures as we have here described.

The learned seem to have been generally mistaken on the subject of glass-making among the ancients, who appear to

* Sum figuli lusus Rufi persona Batavi :
   Quæ tu derides, hæc timet o.a puer.—Mart. xiv. 176.

558 POMPEII.

have been far more skilful than had been imagined. The vast collection of bottles, vases, glasses, and other utensils, discovered at Pompeii, is sufficient to show that the ancients were well acquainted with the art of glass-blowing.

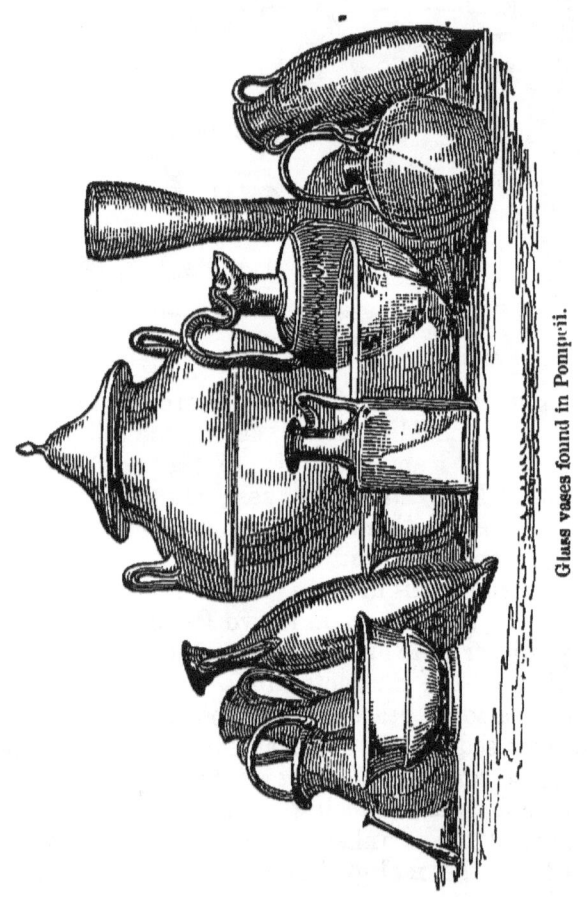

Glass vases found in Pompeii.

On the next page we have something like a wine-basket, made of clay, called ἀγγοθήκη, or ἐγγυοθήκη, by the Greeks, and *incitega* by the Romans, containing two glass vessels, of the kind called ὀξύβαφον, because, being narrow in the neck, the liquor came out drop by drop.

DOMESTIC UTENSILS.

There is no doubt but that the Romans possessed glass in sufficient plenty to apply it to purposes of household ornament. The raw material appears from Pliny's account to have undergone two fusions; the first converted it into a

Liquor-basket of clay, with Glass Vessels

rough mass called ammonitrum, which was melted again and became pure glass. We are also told of a dark coloured glass resembling obsidian, plentiful enough to be cast into solid

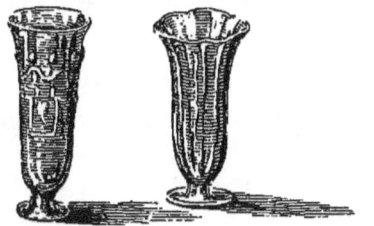

Ornamental drinking-glasses, cast in a mould.

statues. Pliny mentions having seen images of Augustus cast in this substance.* It probably was some coarse kind of glass resembling the ammonitrum, or such as that in which the scoriæ of our iron furnaces abound. Glass was worked either by blowing it with a pipe, as is now practised, by turning in a lathe, by engraving and carving it, or, as we have noticed, by casting it in a mould.† These two glasses, of

* xxxvi. 67. † Ib. 66.

elegant form, appear to have been formed in the latter way. The ancients had certainly acquired great skill in the manufacture, as appears both from the accounts which have been preserved by ancient authors, and by the specimens which still exist—among which we may notice, as pre-eminently beautiful, that torment of antiquaries, the Portland vase, preserved in the British Museum. We have already adverted to another vase of the same kind, and of almost equal beauty, found in one of the tombs near the Gate of Herculaneum. A remarkable story is told by Dion Cassius, of a man who, in the time of the Emperor Tiberius, brought a glass cup into the imperial presence and dashed it on the ground. To the wonder of the spectators, the vessel bent under the blow without breaking, and the ingenious artist immediately hammered out the bruise, and restored it whole and sound to its original form; in return for which display of his skill, Tiberius, it is said, ordered him to be immediately put to death. The story is a strange one, yet it is confirmed by Pliny, who both mentions the discovery itself, and gives a clue to the motives which may have urged the emperor to a cruelty apparently so unprovoked. He speaks of an artificer who had invented a method of making flexible glass, and adds that Tiberius banished him, lest this new fashion should injure the workers in metal,* of whose trade the manufacture of gold, silver, and other drinking-cups, and furniture for the table, formed an extensive and important branch.

The Romans were also well acquainted with the art of colouring glass, as appears, among other proofs, from the glass mosaics, of which mention has been made. Pliny speaks of a blood-red sort, called hæmatinon, from $αἷμα$, blood, of white glass, blue glass, &c. The most valuable sort however was the colourless crystal glass, for two cups of which, with handles on each side ($πτερωτὰ$), Nero gave 6000 sesterces,† about 48*l*. Under this head we may speak of the vases called *murrhina*, since one theory respecting them is, that they were made of variegated glass. Their nature however is doubtful, not so their value. Pliny speaks of 70 talents being given for one holding three sextarii, about four and a

---

* xxxvi. 67. † Ib. 67.

half pints. Titus Petronius on his death-bed defrauded the avarice of Nero, who had compelled him, by a common piece of tyranny, to appoint the crown his heir by breaking a murrhine trulla, or flat bowl, worth 300 talents. Nero himself, as became a prince, outdid all by giving 100 talents for a single capis, or drinking-cup, " a memorable circumstance, that an emperor, and father of his country, should have drank at so dear a rate."* Pliny's description of this substance runs thus:—

"It is to be noticed that we have these rich cassidoin † vessels (called in Latin murrhina) from the East, and that from places otherwise not greatly renowned, but most within the kingdom of Parthia; howheit the principal come from Carmania. The stone whereof these vessels are made is thought to be a certain humour, thickened as it were in the earth by heat. In no place are these stones found larger than small tablements of pillars or the like, and seldom were they so thick as to serve for such a drinking-cup as I have spoken of already. Resplendent are they in some sort, but it may rather be termed a gloss than a radiant and transparent clearness; but that which maketh them so much esteemed is the variety of colours, for in these stones a man shall perceive certain veins or spots, which, as they be turned about, resemble divers colours, inclining partly to purple and partly to white: he shall see them also of a third colour composed of them both, resembling the flame of fire. Thus they pass from one to another as a man holdeth them, insomuch as their purple seemeth near akin to white, and their milky white to bear as much on the purple.‡ Some esteem those cassidoin, or murrhine stones, the richest, which present as it were certain reverberations of sundry colours meeting altogether about their edges and extremities, such as we observe in rainbows; others are delighted with certain fatty spots appearing in them; and no account is made of them which show either pale or transparent in any part of them, for these be reckoned great faults and blemishes; in like manner, if there be seen in the cassidoin any spots like corns of salt or warts, for then

---

* Plin. Hist. Nat. xxxvii. 7. The capis, therefore (so called a capiendo because it had handles), must have been much smaller than the trulla.
† Chalcedony. It is thus that Holland interprets the word.
‡ Purpura candescente, aut lacte rubescente.

are they considered apt to split. Finally, the cassidoin stones are commended in some sort also for the smell that they do yield."*

On these words of Pliny a great dispute has arisen. Some think that onyx is the material described, a conjecture founded on the variety of colours which that stone presents. To this it is objected, that onyx and murrha, onyx vases and murrhine vases are alike mentioned by Latin writers, and never with any hint as to their identity; nay, there is a passage in which Heliogabalus is said to have onyx and murrhine vases in constant use.† Others, as we have said, think that they were variegated glass; others that they were the true Chinese porcelain, a conjecture in some degree strengthened by a line of Propertius:—

"Murrheaq. in Parthis pocula cocta focis."

At the same time this quotation is not so conclusive as it might have been, since Pliny speaks of murrha as "hardened in the earth by heat," and the poet may only have meant the same thing, though the expression in that case would be somewhat strained. To us, Pliny's description appears to point clearly to some opaline substance; the precious opal has never in modern times been found in masses approaching to the size necessary to make vessels such as we have spoken of. The question is not likely to be settled, and it is not improbable that the material of these murrhine vases is entirely unknown to us, as the quarries of many marbles used by the ancients have hitherto eluded our research, and the marbles themselves are only known by their recurrence among ancient buildings.

We may here notice one or two facts connected with glass, which show that the ancients were on the verge of making one or two very important discoveries in physical science. They were acquainted with the power of transparent spherical bodies to produce heat by the transmission of light, though not with the manner in which that heat was generated by the concentration of the solar rays. Pliny mentions the fact that hollow glass balls filled with water would, when held

* Holland's Pliny, xxxvii. 2 (8th edit., Valpy).
† Heliogabalus in murrhinis et onychinis minxit.—Lampridius, ap. Montfaucon, vol. v.

opposite to the sun, grow hot enough to burn any cloth they touched;* but the turn of his expression evidently leads to the conclusion that he believed the heat to become accumulated in the glass itself, not merely to be transmitted through it. Seneca speaks of similar glass balls which magnified minute objects to the view.† Nay, he had nearly stumbled on a more remarkable discovery, the composition of light, for he mentions the possibility of producing an artificial rainbow by the use of an angular glass rod.‡ At a far earlier period Aristophanes speaks of the "ὕαλος, a transparent substance used to light fires with," usually translated glass. The passage is curious, as it shows a perfect acquaintance with the use of the burning glass.

> *Strepsiades.*—You have noted
> A pretty toy, a trinket in the shops,
> Which being rightly held, produces fire
> From things combustible.
>   *Socrates.*   A burning glass
> Vulgarly called.
>   *Strep.*   You are right, 'tis so.
>   *Soc.*   Proceed.
>   *Strep.*—Put now the case—your scoundrel bailiff comes,
> Shows me his writ—I, standing thus, d'ye mark me,
> In the sun's stream, measuring my distance, guide
> My focus to a point upon his writ,
> And off it goes, in fumo ! §

---

* Plin. xxxvi. 67. Cum addita aqua vitreæ pilæ sole adversu in tantum excandescunt ut vestes exurant.

† But though he had observed the fact, he had not even approached to the cause of it, for he refers the magnifying power solely to the water, in common with all other fluids, and evidently supposes that a plane surface would magnify as well as a spherical one. "Illud adjiciam, omnia per aquam videntibus longe esse majora. Literæ quamvis minutæ et obscuræ, per vitream pilam aqua plenam majores clarioresq. cernuntur . . . . . Si poculum impleveris aqua et in id conjeceris annulum . . cum in ipso fundo jaceat annulus, facies ejus in summo aquæ redditur. Quidquid videtur per humorem, longe amplius vero est."—Quæst. Nat. i. 6.

‡ "Virgula solet fieri vitrea, stricta, seu pluribus angulis in modum clavæ torosa: hæc si ex adverso solem accepit, colorem talem qualis in arcu videri solet, reddit." He goes on to say that this is because it tries to give an image of the sun, but cannot manage it, "quia enormiter facta est," because it is irregularly made: "si apte fabricata foret, totidem redderet soles, quot habuisset infecturas," if it were fitly made it would give as many suns as it does colours.—Ib. 7.

§ Arist. Νεφ. 766, ed Brunck.

With the laws of reflection the ancients, as we know from the performances ascribed to Archimedes, were well acquainted. It is singular that being in possession of such remarkable facts connected with refraction, they should never have proceeded to investigate the laws by which it is governed.

The first object figured in the annexed block, is a glass funnel, *infundibulum;* the second is described as a wine-strainer, but the method of its use is not altogether clear. The bottom is slightly concave, and pierced with holes. It is supposed to have been used as a sort of tap, the larger part

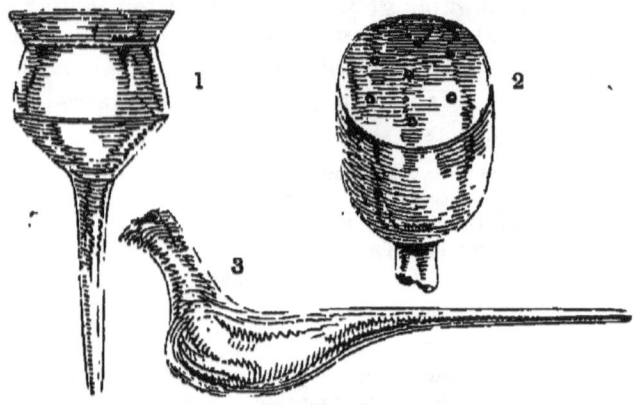

Glass Vessels.

being placed within the barrel, and the wine drawn off through the neck or spout, which is broken. Fig. 3 is a wine-taster, something on the principle of a siphon. It is hollow, and the air being exhausted by the mouth at the small end, the liquid to be tasted was drawn up into the cavity.

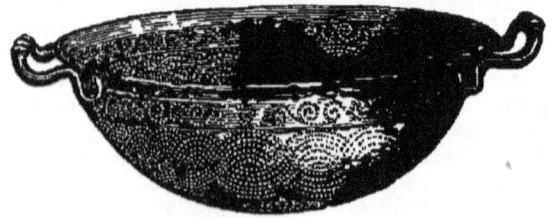

Bronze Strainer.

Another sort of strainer, of which there are several in the Neapolitan Museum, is made of bronze, pierced in elegant

and intricate patterns. The Romans used strainers filled with snow to cool their wines, and such may have been the destination of the one here represented. These were called *cola vinaria*, or *nivaria*. The poor used a linen cloth for the same purpose.*

With respect to the details of dress, the excavations, whether at Pompeii or Herculaneum, enable us to clear up no difficulties, and to add little to that which is already known on this subject. Still a short notice of the principal articles of dress, and explanation of their Latin names, may be expedient for the full understanding of some parts of our subject. The male costume will detain us a very short time. The proper Roman dress, for it would be tiresome and unprofitable to enter upon the variety of garments introduced in later times from foreign nations, consisted merely of the toga and tunica, the latter being itself an innovation on the simple and hardy habit of ancient times. It was a woollen vest, for it was late before the use of linen was introduced, reaching to the knees, and at first made without sleeves, which were considered effeminate; but as luxury crept in, not only were sleeves used, but the number of tunics was increased to three or four. The toga was an ample semicircular garment, also without sleeves. It is described as having an opening large enough to admit the head and the right arm and shoulder, which were left exposed, having a sort of lappet, or flap (lacinia), which was brought under the right arm and thrown over the left shoulder, forming the *sinus*, or bosom, the deep folds of which served as a sort of pocket. This is the common description, which, we confess, conveys no very clear notion of the construction or appearance of the dress. The left arm was entirely covered, or if exposed, it was by gathering up the lower edge of the ample garment.

The female dress consisted of one or more tunics, with an upper garment, called *stola*, which superseded the toga, originally worn by women as well as men. The stola is said to have been a more ample and ornamented sort of tunic. The tunic worn by women does not seem to have differed from that worn by men, except that it reached to the feet. Above the stola, women wore a mantle called palla or pallium.

---

* Attenuare nives norunt et lintea nostra;
Frigidior colo non salit unda tuo.—Mart. xiv.

This is said to have been thrown across the shoulders, the right end being gathered up and thrown over the left shoulder, leaving nothing but the right hand visible,* a description which does not tally with the annexed figure, taken from a statue found at Herculaneum, of a female clothed in a tunic and pallium, in which the right arm and

Draped Female Statue discovered in Herculaneum.

shoulder are uncovered. Here the pallium is short, after the Greek fashion; the ladies of Rome wore it trailing on the ground. The tunic has short sleeves which are fastened by buttons. The hair of this statue was gilt, though, since it has been exposed to the air, the lustre is gone, and nothing but a dull yellow colour remains. This singular and tasteless style of ornament may be explained by a senseless and extravagant fashion which prevailed, while blond hair was in fashion, of powdering the head with gold dust. The custom was imported from the East, where it was practised, according to Josephus, by the Jews. Several of the Roman emperors adopted it. The hair of Commodus was so brilliant, according to Herodian, partly from its natural whiteness, partly from the quantity of essences and gold dust with which

* Facciolati.

PAINTING ON THE WALLS OF THE PANTHEON.

it was loaded, that when the sun was shining on it it might have been thought that his head was on fire.

The annexed steel plate, which represents a portion of one of the walls of the Pantheon, will at once depict the female dress on a larger scale, and convey some notion of the light and airy style of architectural painting, intermixed with figures, which is one of the favourite decorations of Pompeii. It represents a priestess playing on the harp, which she strikes with both hands, using with the right the plectrum, or quill. She is clothed in a white pallium, fringed with gold, which falls in rich folds below the knees. Her under garment is a blue tunic; she has yellow shoes, a gold band confines her hair, and gold earrings and bracelets glitter on her ears and wrists. She is coming through a doorway, upon the architrave of which is a figure of Victory in a biga, lashing on her horses, which are full of animation. These figures are painted on a white ground, and produce an admirable effect.

Figure dressed in the Tunico-pallium.

Some minute speculations relative to one article in female dress have been based on a statue from Herculaneum, in which a Neapolitan antiquary thinks that he has discovered the nature and construction of that compound garment called the tunico-pallium, in which the appearance and uses of the tunic and mantle were united. It is the statue of a woman employed in buckling her dress over the right shoulder, having already fastened it on the left, in such a manner as to leave the arm bare. This dress he asserts to be the tunico-pallium, and gives the following description of it, which is stated to be the result of much study and numerous experiments, assisted by the learning of several members of the Academy of Naples.

The first and most important point is to establish that the double garment in question was composed only of one piece of cloth. This the author assumes to be four feet long and five feet six inches broad, varying in size of course with the stature of the wearer. Let this be represented by A B C D. Fold down the upper portion, one foot two

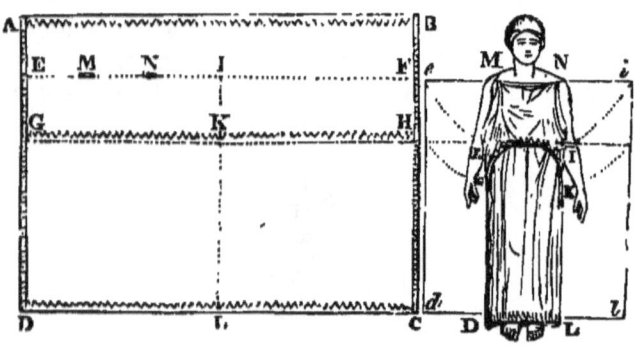

Tunico-pallium displayed.

inches deep, in the line E F, and the edge A B will coincide with G H, and E F H G will form the pallium or mantle. Join the edges E D, F C by folding the dress in the line I K L, leaving the fold E F H G on the outside; divide the top into three equal parts, and attach the back and front together by buckles placed at the points M N, and we have the tunico-pallium open at the right side.

Having described the dress, the next thing is to place it on the wearer. Let her stand in the centre of the parallelogram *e i l d*; fix a *fibula* or buckle at the point N, passing the left arm through the aperture N I, and adjusting the buckle on the left shoulder; then place the second buckle at M, on the right shoulder, passing the head through N M,

DOMESTIC UTENSILS. 569

and the right arm through the aperture M E. The corners, E G, I K, will of course fall down in the direction indicated by the dotted lines, forming a simple, but not inelegant drapery. In some figures the tunico-pallium is entirely open on the right side, E D; in others it is entirely closed from

Harp-player.

end to end, or open only for the space E G. This dress has been introduced in the ballets at the Neapolitan theatre San Carlo with very good effect.

At this place two subjects taken from paintings may be introduced, representing two different ways of playing on the harp. Each is curious, as exemplifying a method of playing which no modern nation has adopted. The first represents a female striking two harps at once, one held on her knee, the other placed beside her on a couch. The curved figure of both is remarkable, and may perhaps give a new and

Harp-player using the Plectrum.

more forcible meaning to the epithet *curva*, in the lines of Horace :—

Tu curva recines lyra
Latonam et celeris spicula Cynthiæ.—Od. iii. 28.

The Romans, in speaking of harp music, used the expres-

DOMESTIC UTENSILS.

sion "*intus et foris canere*,"* to sing within and without; and this expression is rendered more intelligible by the cut from a painting given at page 569, from which it appears that sometimes, at all events, the harp had a double row of strings, as the Welsh harp sometimes has three strings. The musician here plays with both hands, without using the plectrum, and the surrounding figures seem to be watching her with admiration.

The other subject, which is imperfect, represents a female playing with the plectrum or quill,† with which the chords were struck, instead of the fingers. This method of playing was held in early times in the highest esteem; afterwards it was superseded by the use of the fingers, a far more natural and effective instrument. Here the musician strikes with both hands at once, with the right, *intus*, or the inner row of strings, with the plectrum; with the left, *foris*. The harp is supported by a band passed round the left arm.

Numerous articles of female ornament have been found, of which we have collected a few into one block. They are drawn of the same size as the originals. The first figure is an earring, seen in front and sideways. It is a portion of a plain gold spheroid, very thick, with a metal hook at the

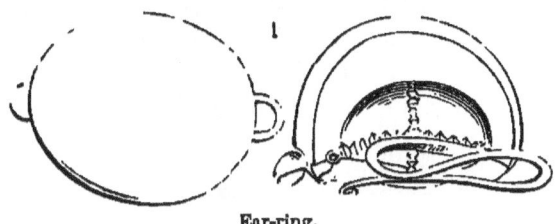

Ear-ring.

back to pass through the ear. The next is of simpler construction, having pearl pendants. Both these patterns seem to have been very common. No. 3 is a breast-pin, attached to a Bacchanalian figure, with a patera in one hand and a glass in the other. He is provided with bat's wings, and two belts, or bands of grapes, pass across his body. The bat's wings symbolize the drowsiness consequent upon hard

---

* Cic. in Var. Act. ii. lib. 1, 20.
† The mandolin is played to this day in Italy with a quill.

drinking. No. 4 is a ring, with serpents' heads. These are very common. To these we have added two combs.

We conclude with two of the most important articles of a

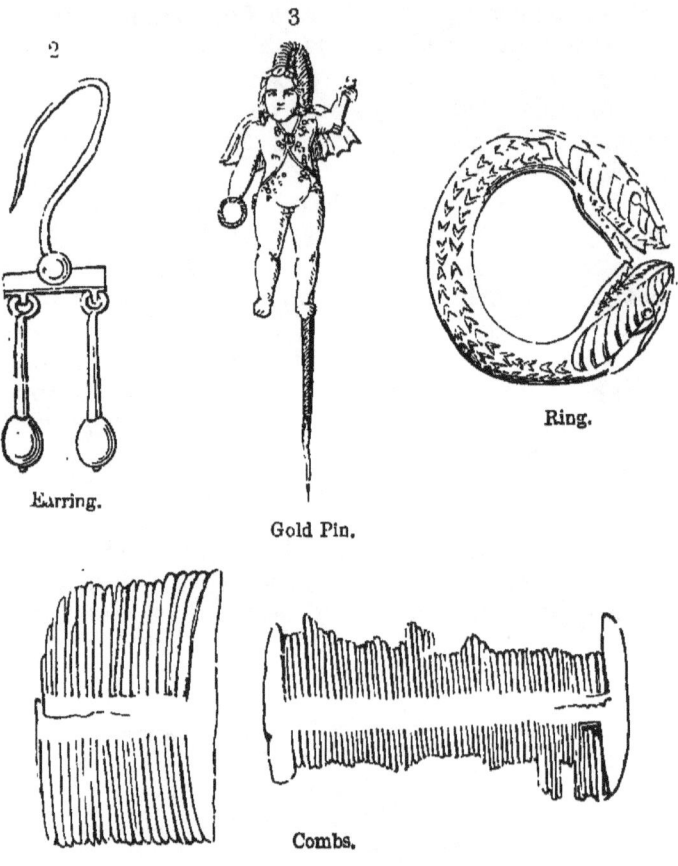

Earring.   Gold Pin.   Ring.

Combs.

lady's toilet-table—her mirrors and a box of pins. The former were made usually of steel, but sometimes of glass; the latter, we are told by Pliny, were brought from Sidon.*

* xxxvi. 36.

ITINERARY.

THE following Itinerary is chiefly intended for those who can devote only a few hours to a visit to Pompeii, and wish to see the principal objects in the speediest and most striking manner. Such visitors however must not linger on the way, and, if the time can be spared, it will be desirable to pay the buried city at least a second visit, when the principal objects may be examined more at leisure, and a few others may be added to the catalogue. The Itinerary is so contrived that the public buildings will be first visited, and then the private houses, according to the order observed in this work.

There are two ways of reaching Pompeii from Naples; either by the high road to Salerno, through Portici, Resina, Torre del Greco, and Torre Annunziata; or by the railway, which has a station within two minutes' walk of the Porta della Marina, or Sea Gate, now the principal entrance to the city. Whether the visitor enters Pompeii by this gate or by that of Herculaneum is not a matter of much importance. To those who perform the journey in a carriage both gates are equally convenient; but for the traveller by railway the Porta della Marina is much preferable, as the Gate of Herculaneum lies at a considerable distance from the station. There is another entrance at the Porta Stabiana, but this will be convenient only for those coming from the south. We have selected the Sea Gate as the point from which to commence this Itinerary because it is the most frequented; and we may add that it seems most natural to finish, rather than begin, with examining the tombs.

From this gate a narrow and rather steep street leads straight to the *Forum*. At the top of it, just before entering the Forum, on the left-hand side, is the entrance to the *Temple of Venus*. After visiting this temple, proceed into the Forum, and turning to the left, along the side wall of the temple, under which may be seen the standard measures, visit the *Public Granary* and adjoining *Prison*. These buildings occupy the remaining space on the western side of the Forum, towards the north.

From the northern boundary of the Forum the *Temple of Jupiter* is projected into its area. On the north-eastern side of the temple the Forum was entered by a *Triumphal Arch* at the top of what is called the Street of the Forum, in whic street is the temporary museum and library. Fronting the eastern side of the Temple of Jupiter stands the building called the *Pantheon,* or *Temple of Augustus.* Next to this, the remaining portion of the eastern side of the Forum is filled by public buildings in the following order towards the south —the *Senaculum*, the *Temple of Mercury*, and the *Edifice of Eumachia*, called *Chalcidicum*. The south side of the Forum is faced by three buildings called *Curiæ*, of which the middle one is supposed to have been the *Treasury*. At the south-east extremity of the Forum, adjoining the southern side of the street by which we entered it, stands the *Basilica*. These comprise all the public buildings about the Forum. In the area of the Forum will be observed several pedestals for statues. Facing the southern side of the Basilica stand the *Houses of Championnet*.

Crossing from the Basilica to the opposite, or eastern side of the Forum, we enter a street called the *Strada dell' Abbondanza*, or *dei Mercanti*. A little way down, on the right-hand side, facing the south-eastern angle of the Chalcidicum, is the house of the *Cinghiale*, or *Wild Boar*. Proceeding eastwards, the third street on the right, called Strada dei Teatri, leads down to the theatres. At the bottom of this street we enter, through a sort of Propylæum, what is called the *Triangular Forum*. Towards the extremity of it are the remains of a *Greek Temple*, called the *Temple of Hercules*, and its appurtenances. At the south-west extremity of the Forum is the *House of Joseph II.* On the eastern side is a long wall, in which there are several entrances into the *Great Theatre*. At the southern side of this theatre is the large quadrangular area called the *Quarters of the Soldiers*, or of the *Gladiators*. Adjoining the eastern side of the scene of the Great Theatre is the *Small Theatre*, or *Odeum*. This is flanked on the east by the Street of Stabiæ, leading to the *Porta Stabiana*, the remains of which may be seen. Reascending the Strada Stabiana towards the north, we find at the angle of the first street on the left, called the Street of Isis, the little *Temple of Æsculapius*. Close to it, on the left, may be seen through an aperture in the arch the aqueduct from the Sarno to Torre Annunziata. The Street of Isis brings us to the *Temple of Isis*, on the left, or south side of the street, and just beyond it to the *Curia Isiaca*, which communicates with the northern end of the Triangular Forum. Opposite the Temple of Isis is the recently excavated *House of Cornelius Rufus*, the proper entrance to which however is in the Street of Holconius. A little further on, at the angle formed by the Street of the Theatres and the Street of Holconius, is the house marked No. 4, sometimes called the *House of Holconius*, remarkable for the number and good preservation of the pictures still to be seen in it.

We now return again into the Street of Stabiæ, from which we have diverged. It is from this point that the tourist, if so inclined, should proceed to the *Amphitheatre;* but as it lies at a considerable distance, and presents nothing to distinguish it from the numerous other buildings of the same kind which may be seen in various places, the visitor, if pressed for time, will probably do best to pass it over.

Proceeding northwards along the Strada Stabiana, we find, at the angle which it makes on the north with the Street of Abundance, the more recently discovered baths, called the *Thermæ Stabianæ*.

In the little street behind the baths, called Via del Lupanare, and in the lane leading into it, called Vicoletto del Balcone Pensile, may be seen the *House with the Restored Balcony*, the *Lupanar*, and the *House of Siricus*, or *Salve Lucrum*. Opposite the last is the *caupona*, or tavern, on the outside wall of which are painted two large serpents, and the inscription—*Otiosis locus hic non est, discede morator.*

Returning into the Street of Stabiæ, and proceeding towards the north, the tourist may visit on the right-hand side the *House of Marcus Lucretius.* Hence proceeding to the point where the Street of Stabiæ is cut by the Street of Fortune, he may, if he has time, turn to the right and proceed straight to the *Gate of Nola;* but if his time is limited he will do better to turn to the left, and proceed towards the west along the Street of Fortune. Here he will see on the right, opposite the Vico Storto, the *Casa degli Scienziati.* On the left-hand side of the Street of the Augustals, adjoining the Vico Storto, is the *House of the Chace;* next to this the *House of Ariadne*, which runs back to the Street of the Augustals, on which side indeed is the principal and proper entrance. At the extremity of the Street of the Augustals, near its junction with that of Stabiæ, are the Houses of the *New Fountain*, the *Baker, and the Trident.* Returning into the Street of Fortune, the following buildings may be successively visited on its left, or southern side : the *House of the Grand Duke*, the *House of the Figured Capitals*, the *House of the Black Walls*, and at the angle made by the Street of Fortune and that of the Forum, the *Temple of Fortune.* The entrance is in the latter street. Opposite the Temple of Fortune, and occupying the whole insula which extends from the northern side of the Forum to the Strada delle Terme (a continuation of that of Fortune), are the old *Public Baths.*

We have now visited all the principal objects lying to the south of the line formed by the Street of the Baths and that of Fortune. To complete our inspection, the quadrangular mass of excavations lying to the north of that line remains to to be seen; after which, leaving the city by the Gate of Herculaneum, we shall take a survey of the suburb called Pagus Augustus Felix, and the Street of the Tombs.

We have already mentioned the House of the Scienziati. The first insula to the west of it need not detain us, but the second contains one of the most remarkable private buildings in Pompeii, the *House of the Faun.* The next insula westward is chiefly noticeable for the *House of the Anchor.* We now cross the top of the Street of Mercury, the entrance to which is spanned by a *Triumphal Arch,* on which stood an equestrian statue of Nero. The insula bounded on the east by this street contains four houses—those of the *Tragic Poet,* the *Fullonica,* or dyer's house, and those of the *Great and Little Fountain.* The next insula to the west is occupied by a single house, that of *Pansa,* which for size and magnificence may dispute the palm with that of the Faun.

Behind, and to the north of the four insula just described, lie four other insula. That which backs to the House of the Faun is chiefly remarkable for the *House of the Labyrinth.* The next, behind that in which is the House of the Anchor, contains three noticeable houses—those of *Castor and Pollux,* of the *Centaur,* and of *Meleager.* The insula behind the Fullonica has the *House of Adonis* and that of *Apollo,* close to the city walls. The insula behind the House of Pansa contains nothing very remarkable.

We will now return southwards down the street skirted on the east by the House of Pansa. At the top of this a small transverse street runs northwards into that leading to the Gate of Herculaneum. Just past their junction, on the left-hand side, stands the *House of Julius Polybius*. A little further, on the right, is the house called the *Academy of Music*, and adjoining it the *Baker's Shop and Mills*. Next comes the *House of Sallust* and the *Public Bakehouse*, which seems to form part of it. In this part of the street will also be found the room containing the casts of the four bodies found near the Street of Abundance.

At this point the street branches to the right and left. At the point of separation stands a *Public Fountain*. Taking the street on the left, we find on its left side the *House of the Female Dancers*. Just beyond, on the right, is a *Soap Shop*, and next to it the *Dogana*, or custom-house. These again are followed by the *House of the Surgeon* and that of the *Vestals*. On the other side of the street, opposite the surgeon's house, is the *House with Three Floors*, and beyond this again, close to the city gate, the *Shop of Albino*.

Before going out by the Porta Ercolanese, we may observe on the right, or eastern side, the *steps* for ascending the city walls. Outside the gate, on the left, are one or two tombs, and beyond a circular seat, or *exedra*, behind which is the *Sepulchre of Mammia*. On the right-hand side of the way, proceeding from the gate, are an *unfinished sepulchre*, then the *Tomb of Terentius*, just opposite to the exedra, and close to it, a *Sculptor's Shop*. Next come, on the same side, the *Tomb of the Garlands*. and beyond it a *public seat*, or resting-place. The remaining objects on this side of the way are a long building commonly called the *Country Inn;* before the northern end of this, the *Tomb with the Marble Door;* and beyond, the *Sepulchre of Lucius Libella* and that of the *Arrian Family*.

The other, or western side of the way, is occupied for a considerable space beyond the exedra with the frontage of a large mansion called the *Villa of Cicero*. Beyond this, facing the inn, is an *incomplete sepulchre;* then come five more tombs in the following order—that of *Scaurus*, the *Round Tomb*, the *Tomb of Calventius*, that of *Nævoleia Tyche*, and the *Triclinium*

2 P

Funebre. The visit is then closed by inspecting the *House of Diomede,* the last structure on the left-hand side of the way.

The following Synopsis of places to be visited will help to render the preceding Itinerary clearer. The figures show the pages where they are described.

	PAGE		PAGE
Baker's Shop	354	House of the Cinghiale	435
Caupona	467	—— of the Faun	392
Chalcidicum	118	—— of the Figured Capitals	443
Country Inn	527	—— of the Grand Duke	443
Custom-House	319	—— of the Labyrinth	396
Exedra and Tomb of Mammia	529	—— of the Scienziati	301
Fountain	89	—— of the Surgeon	348
Gate of Herculaneum	63	—— of the Vestals	346
Great Theatre	204	Houses of Championnet	440
Greek Temple	150	—— of the Fountains	385
House of Adonis	390	Lupanar	471
—— of Apollo	391	Pantheon, or Temple of Augustus	103
—— of Ariadne	443	Porta della Marina	67
—— of Castor and Pollux	400	Porta Stabiana	66
—— of Cornelius Rufus	453	Prison	100
—— of Diomede	480	Public Bakehouse	354
—— of Female Dancers	350	—— Granary	100
—— of Holconius, or No. 4	444	—— Seat	527
—— of Joseph II.	437	Room containing plaster casts of four bodies	477
—— of Julius Polybius	346	Round Tomb	523
—— of Meleager	421	Senaculum	110
—— of M. Lucretius	455	Sepulchres of L. Libella and of the Arrian Family	513
—— of Pansa	318		
—— of Sailust	328	Shop of Albino	344
—— of Siricus	462	Small Theatre	209
—— of Three Stories	345	Soap Shop	350
—— of Tragic Poet	366	Soldiers' Quarters	145
—— of the Anchor	399	Standard Measures	100
—— of the Balcony	473	Steps for Mounting the Wall	59
—— of the Black Walls	443	Temple of Æsculapius	138
—— of the Centaur	418	—— of Curia Isiaca	144
—— of the Chace	444		

	PAGE		PAGE
Temple of Fortune	135	The Triclinium Funebre	515
—— of Isis	139	Triangular Forum	150
—— of Jupiter	98	Triumphal Arch	100
—— of Mercury	115	Triumphal Arch	431
—— of Venus	127	Tomb of Calventius	522
The Basilica	124	—— of Nævoleia Tyche	518
The Fullonica	362	—— of Scaurus	525
The Old Public Baths	153	—— of the Garlands	529
Thermæ Stabianæ	174	—— with the Marble Door	513
The Three Curiæ	124	Villa of Cicero	529

THE END.

www.ingramcontent.com/pod-product-compliance
Lightning Source LLC
Chambersburg PA
CBHW021239240426
43673CB00057B/618